SMALL UNIT TACTICS

Please leave a review. Thanks!

Positive reviews from awesome people like you help other Soldiers to benefit from the valuable tactics in this manual. Could you take 60 seconds to share your thoughts?

Thank you in advance for helping the community!

If you liked this book, consider buying the next book, *Small Unit Raids*.

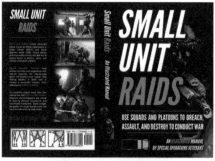

Or consider both books together, *Small Unit Tactics and Raids*.

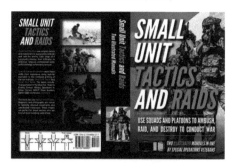

Overview Map of an Ambush Mission

Image 1: An overview map of the different locations in a mission, to be expanded on and explained throughout the manual. A mission begins with vehicle transport to the vehicle drop-off. It ends when a patrol withdraws from the ambush to either a vehicle pickup or a patrol-base. The patrol may never use the black and gold rally-points or alternate patrol-base.

You Are Joe
(Introduction: The Story of Killing Enemies)

1. The Secret Code (Definitions)   13

Individual Soldiers   13
Groups of Soldiers   15
Leadership Positions   16
Other   18

2. The Secret Ideas (Concepts)   18

Safety Procedures   18
Communications   19
Other   20

Joe Goes to the Enemy (Phase 1: Transportation to the Objective)

3. Traveling by Vehicle — 23
Loading a Truck — 23
Transport to Drop-off Site — 24
Exiting a Truck — 26
Traveling by Helicopter — 28

4. Traveling by Foot (Individual Soldiers) — 29
Moving Through Terrain to Your Advantage — 29
Going to the Prone, Taking a Knee, and Taking Off Rucks — 30

5. Traveling by Foot (Elements) — 30
Moving Through Terrain to Your Advantage — 31
Emergency Meetup Areas (En Route Rally-Points) — 32
Responsibility for Land Navigation — 33
Counting People (Chokepoints) — 35
Rear Security — 36

6. Traveling by Foot (Formations) — 36
Wedge Formation — 40
Modified-Wedge (Staggered Column) Formation — 43
Platoon Movement Formations — 44
Detecting the Enemy (SLLS) — 47
Short/Security-Halt Formation — 48
Initial Location after Exiting Vehicles (Initial Rally-Point) — 51

7. Crossing a Road or Draw (Linear Danger Area) — 52
Choosing a Crossing Location — 52
Choosing How to Cross — 53
Blast Formation — 54
Bumping/Scrolling Formation — 55
Deliberate Formation — 57
Draw Crossing Formation — 62
Actions on Detection — 62
Enemy Attack During LDA Crossing — 64

8. Crossing a Field (Open Danger Area) — 64
Directly Crossing the Area (Bounding) — 65
Going around the Area — 68

The Enemy Sees Joe (Phase 2: React-to-Enemy Contact and Medical Evacuation)

9. The Enemy Shoots at Joe (Battle Drill 2) — 71

Individual Soldiers React-to-Contact — 72
Individual Movement Techniques (IMT) — 73
Contact Element Reacts to Contact — 74
Headquarters Reacts to Contact — 76
Far Element Reacts to Contact — 79

10. Joe Returns Fire (Battle Drills 1, 3, and 4) — 80

Assaulting a Location (Battle Drill 4) — 80
Bold-flank Maneuver (Battle Drill 1) — 85
Bold-flank Variations — 92
Break-Contact (Battle Drill 3) — 93
Break-Contact Variations — 97

11. Cleaning up after Assaulting (Specialty Teams) — 99

Enemy Prisoner of War (EPW) Team — 99
Aid and Litter Team — 103
Demolition Team — 104

12. Withdrawal from Area after Assaulting — 104

13. Medical Evacuation — 106

Evacuating by Foot — 108
Evacuating by Ambulance Exchange — 110
Evacuating by Helicopter — 111

14. Fire Support — 112

Firing Artillery and Mortars (Call for Fire) — 112
Close Air Support — 114

15. Contingencies — 116

React-to-Sniper — 116
React-to-Artillery and Mortars (Indirect Fire) — 116
React-to-Mine (Improvised Explosive Device) — 118
Fixing a Split Element — 120
Reacting from a Non-Standard Formation — 120
Enemy from Multiple or Changing Locations — 121

Joe Sets His Trap (Phase 3: Occupying the Objective)

16. Creating the Long-Halt — 123

Preventing Rear Attack (Counter-Tracking) — 126
Organizing a Halt (Emplacing around a Reference Point) — 127
Grouping Soldiers (Strong-Point/Crow's Foot) — 129
360-Degree Security (Assigning Sectors-of-Fire) — 130

17. Creating the Objective Rally-Point — 133

Equipment Check (COW-T) — 133
Splitting Elements (GOTWA) — 134
Leader's Recon of the Squad ORP — 136
Surveillance and Observation Position (S&O) — 139
Actions at Long-Halt during Leader's Recon — 140
Recombining Elements (Near and Far Recognition Signals) — 141
Occupation of the Objective Rally-Point — 143

18. Creating the Ambush — 144

Leader's Recon of Release-Point, S&O, and Killzone — 146
Leader's Recon of Support and Assault — 148
Leader's Recon of Security Positions — 153
Allocating Leadership — 156
Occupation of the Release-Point — 156
Emplacement of Security and EWAC — 159
Methods of Emplacing Support and Assault — 161
Emplacement of Support — 162
Emplacement of Assault and SPARC — 163
Coordinating Sectors-of-Fire — 166
Emplacing Claymores and Final Steps — 168
Platoon Area Ambush — 170

19. Platoon Point Ambush — 171

Leader's Recon of the Platoon Formation — 172
Platoon Formation — 176
Leader's Recon of the Objective — 180
Occupation of the Objective — 181
Location of Platoon Leadership — 182

20. Contingencies — 184

Running Out of Time (Hasty Emplacement) — 184
Compromise during Emplacement — 185
Ambush at a Bend in the Road — 186
Unidirectional Ambush (T and V) — 188
Ambush for Anti-Ambush Patrols (K and X) — 190
No Radio Communications with Security — 192
Other Ambush Types — 193

Joe Attacks the Enemy (Phase 4: Actions on the Objective)

21. Squad Ambush   195
Initiating the Ambush   195
Assaulting the Objective   197
Withdrawal from the Objective   201

22. Platoon Point Ambush   202
Weapons Squad   202
Assault   203

23. Vehicle Clearing   204
One Vehicle   204
Multiple Vehicles   207

24. Contingencies   208
Dismounted Enemy Patrol   209
Enemy Stops Outside of the Killzone   209
Enemy Patrol Is Wider than the Killzone   210
Counter Ambush from Behind the Objective   211
Enemy Quick Reaction Force and Harassing Ambush   211
Assault Leader Is Combat Ineffective   214
Patrol Leader Is Combat Ineffective   214
Security Is Combat Ineffective   214
Explosive Device in the Killzone   215

Joe Goes Home
(Phase 5: Withdrawal to a Patrol-Base)

25. Patrol-Base Occupation — 217
Scouting a Good Location — 218
Leave No Trace — 218

26. Linkup — 220
Long-Halt and Signal-Site — 220
Actions of First Squad to Arrive at Signal-Site — 221
Actions of Second and Third Squads to Arrive — 224

27. Security Tasks and Priorities of Work — 226
Reconnaissance and Surveillance (R&S) — 226
Claymores — 227
Range Cards and Sector Sketch — 227
Alert Plan — 229
Withdrawal Plan — 229

28. Maintenance Tasks — 230
Weapons Maintenance — 231
Water Resupply — 232
Chow, Personal Hygiene, Snivel Gear, and Rest — 233
Planning and Briefing a FRAGO — 234

29. Hasty Patrol-Base — 235

Annexes

30. M240 Machine Gun — 237

Rate-of-Fire — 237
Firing Drills — 237
Malfunction Procedures — 239

31. AT4 Light Anti-Tank Weapon — 240

32. Communication — 242

Spare-Report — 242
PACE Communication Options — 242
Example Communication Methods — 244
Example Total PACE Plan — 244

33. Glossaries — 246

Acronyms — 246
Words — 248

34. Index — 254

35. Credits — 256

Legend

Color is the Soldier's Unit		Shape is the Soldier's Weapon	
Alpha Team	↑	M4	↑
Squad Level	↑	M249	⬆
Bravo Team	↑	M240B	⬆
Platoon Level	↑	AT4	⬆
Named position (See glossary)		⬆TL	

Throughout the manual these arrows represent Soldiers. Each arrow has a color and a shape to represent a Soldier's unit and primary weapon respectively. The direction of the arrow is the direction a Soldier is pointing. Claymores are command-detonated, and their icon is: ✖

Introduction Contents

1. The Secret Code (Definitions)   13

Individual Soldiers   13
Groups of Soldiers   15
Leadership Positions   16
Other   18

2. The Secret Ideas (Concepts)   18

Safety Procedures   18
Communications   19
Other   20

You Are Joe (Introduction: The Story of Killing Enemies)

When we understand that slide, we'll have won the war.
—U.S. General Stanley McChrystal, on an impossible chart.

Telling the story of one entire mission from start to finish, this manual teaches a simple yet complete ambush. Soldiers go from A to B to ambush and destroy the enemy. After which everyone can return home in time for hot chow.

At over 250 pages, this manual covers a lot of ground. However, every chapter only contains the essentials of small units tactics needed to succeed. (Seriously, almost every section is written in blood and exists because someone died not doing it.) That being said, the military has a language all its own. So to start, this chapter teaches common jargon and concepts.

1. The Secret Code (Definitions)

Every definition below is a common patrolling phrase that infantrymen use daily. (Did you know "weasel" means WSL and stands for Weapons Squad Leader?) While the *Ranger Handbook* uses many of these terms, it does not always provide complete explanations. For example, it describes a duty as "advises Patrol Leader in planning." That is as clear and helpful as mud on boots. Below are the most important words needed to understand small unit tactics, in the order which they need to be learned.

1.a Individual Soldiers

Rifleman – A Soldier who carries a rifle. They have no subordinates, though the battlefield can change that. Throughout the patrol, they may be given simple standing responsibilities, such as delivering accurate rifle fire on the enemy in accordance with their leader's scheme of maneuver and target precedence. Additional responsibilities may include compass checking, pace counting, and pack mule.

Point/Pointman – The first man in a movement formation. Their job is to look for enemies and traps, since they are most likely to be attacked. It is said, only half-jokingly, that the Pointman is bait. They must take care to look back to their Team Leader for directions, since the Pointman is too busy with security to do land navigation.[1]

Squad Automatic Weapon (SAW) – A light (17 lb.) machine gun. Like an M4 rifle, it is designed to be fired from standing, kneeling and prone. However, unlike the M4, the SAW Gunner cannot be accurate while kneeling or standing, and so they are prone whenever the situation allows.

Gunner – The operator of the M240 general-purpose (27.6 lb.) machine gun. They are only focused on making rounds exit the barrel.

Assistant Gunner (AG) – The most senior person on the Gun Team, and the Gun Team's Leader. They control the Gunner by physically squeezing them to fire, and by blocking their eyes to cease fire. The AG also ensures the ammo cleanly feeds to the M240 (therefore, they are positioned to the left of the gun). They are necessary because the M240 is difficult to aim and feed while simultaneously receiving orders. They do not control the gun, but they do physically control the Gunner.

Ammo Bearer (AB) – An optional third member of the Gun Team. They make the Gun Team faster by sharing their ammo load. They are responsible for changing barrels during firing (therefore, they are to the right of the gun). If the AG begins to run low on ammunition while the gun is firing, the AB retrieves more ammo from the packs.

Grenadier – A Rifleman who specializes in grenades. This position is fluid because the M203 under-barrel attachment for the M4 and M16 can transform every Rifleman into a Grenadier (albeit untrained). For this reason, any Rifleman in this manual also can be a Grenadier.[2]

Radiotelephone Operator (RTO) – A Soldier who operates and monitors radio communications, under the supervision of the Patrol Leader. This arrangement allows the Patrol Leader to devote more time to other tasks.

---

1 Applying Concepts: When might it be beneficial to have two Pointmen in the Point Team? How about a Pointman to the side?

2 Applying Concepts: Given that different weapon systems have different complexities, weights, among other characteristics, what factors should a Leader consider when assigning a Soldier a weapon? Should the strongest man get the heaviest weapon. What if the strongest man is also the best shot?

The RTO also keeps time in various situations and advises the Patrol Leader when needed. The RTO and the Patrol Leader are always together.

Forward Observer (FO) – A military observer who directs artillery and mortars onto targets. The FO stays close to either the Platoon Leader or the Weapons Squad Leader, to coordinate between the patrol and the fires.

Medic – The individual responsible for administering first aid on the battlefield. They also help make chokepoints and digs the slit trench in the patrol-base. They are always with the Platoon Sergeant.

1.b Groups of Soldiers

Unit – A group with a static and defined chain of command. The units in this manual are platoon, squad, and fire-team.

Element – Any group assigned with a task, which may include security or assault. They can be composed of Soldiers from one unit or multiple units.

Team/Fire-Team – A unit typically made up of three Soldiers and a Team Leader. It handles tasks that an individual would be unable to execute alone, such as performing a bold-flanking maneuver or resupplying water. As a Team Leader can control up to four Soldiers, a team can number between three and five Soldiers.

Gun Team (GT) – A unit controlling the M240, a crew-served weapon requiring two Soldiers: a Gunner and an Assistant Gunner. Sometimes a Gun Team also has an Ammo Bearer. Although Gun Teams can be tasked to Rifle Squads, they are native to a Weapons Squad under a Rifle Platoon.

Headquarters (HQ) – An element of a unit consisting of that unit's highest leadership, and those Soldiers directly under them. For example, Radiotelephone Operators (RTO's) are always part of Headquarters. The purpose of a Headquarters is to be an extension of the Patrol Leader. Headquarters may also contain the miscellaneous Soldiers that the Patrol Leader has direct control over, like a Gun Team and a medic in a squad.

Squad – A unit of two teams or more and a Squad Leader. In specific situations, like an area ambush, a Gun Team can be attached to a squad. A squad handles maneuvers that a team cannot, like performing an ambush.

Platoon – A unit made up of multiple squads and a Headquarters Element (e.g. a Platoon Leader, and Platoon Sergeant). In the U.S. Army, the main difference between a squad and a platoon (besides size) is that a platoon has a Weapons Squad. U.S. Army Rifle Platoons normally have three

Rifle Squads, one Weapons Squad, and a Headquarters. A U.S. Marine Corps Rifle Platoon nominally only has Rifle Squads and a Headquarters. However, the Marine's organization relies heavily on attachments and detachments. Therefore, a Marine platoon comparable to an Army platoon will attach an external Weapons Squad.

Small Unit – Either a platoon or a squad. It is ideal for performing certain mission sets like ambushes and raids. Smaller units (like teams) would be incapable, and larger units (like a brigade) would be too difficult to coordinate.

Weapons Squad – A squad that is responsible for deploying the unit's general-purpose machine guns (as opposed to a typical Rifle Squad). When a platoon separates into squads to perform squad actions, the Gun Team can split and report to the Squad Leader instead of the Weapons Squad Leader.

Support-by-Fire (SBF) – "Support" is a designated element that immediately suppresses the enemy, allowing another element to maneuver. Squads and platoons have M240s within them, and use them primarily to support the maneuvers of other parts of the unit. Therefore, "Support-by-Fire" often is synonymous with Gun Team(s). However, SAW's or entire squads can also be used. Other supports include air support and naval support.

Patrol – A group of Soldiers sent to perform a task. For example, a patrol may be a squad sent to ambush or a platoon sent to conduct reconnaissance.

1.c Leadership Positions

Team Leader (TL) – The person responsible for coordinating their Soldiers to accomplish a task that a single team member could not accomplish alone. For example, because land navigation requires more than one man to accomplish, the Team Leader delegates certain tasks to their Soldiers, like pace count, map checking, and compass checking, so that the unit can effectively work in unison. A team member and a Squad Leader rarely talk, because the Team Leader directly handles their team.

Alpha Team Leader – The leader of the Alpha Team. As this is typically the lead element, the Alpha Team Leader is primarily responsible for land navigation. They also assist the Bravo Team Leader in their accountability tasks whenever they need to be accomplished quickly.

Bravo Team Leader – The leader of the Bravo Team. As this is typically the trail element, the Bravo Team Leader is primarily responsible for accountability. They always know the count of the squad and is constantly checking the squad's equipment. They are also responsible for water resupply for their squad and any emergency medical matters.

Squad Leader (SL) – The Soldier in charge of a squad. They treat their teams like a Team Leader treats their Riflemen: i.e., they assign tasks to entire teams only. They rarely, if ever, assign tasks to individual Riflemen.

Weapons Squad Leader (WSL, pronounced "weasel") – A platoon-level position that leads all Gun Teams. They coordinate Gun Teams to maximize their fire power by "talking." (See Firing Drills, Pg. 237.) The WSL is also in charge of cleanliness and maintenance of M240s. When the Gun Teams are in a split location, the WSL controls the M240s nearest to them, while the other platoon-level leadership positions control the other M240s.

Platoon Sergeant (PSG) – The senior advisor to the Platoon Leader. They are to the platoon what the Bravo Team Leader is to the squad. They are specifically responsible for the accountability and health of all Soldiers, weapons, and equipment, and any medical evacuation. Before all movements, the PSG forms a chokepoint with the Medic for accountability (both silently count and verify each other).

Platoon Leader – The Soldier in charge of the entire patrol. During the patrol, their primary responsibility is to ensure that all the squads coordinate. They also decide which squads do what. Where there is a react-to-contact, for example, the Platoon Leader decides how many and which squads respond. They decide the tradeoff between speed and security if the patrol is behind schedule. They only assign tasks to squads. They do not talk to Team Leaders or individual Soldiers unless absolutely necessary.

Patrol Leader – The person in charge of the patrol. They may be a Platoon Leader, a Squad Leader, a Team Leader, or any other Leader.

Assistant Patrol Leader – The second in command to the Patrol Leader. They may be a Platoon Sergeant, Bravo Team Leader, or any other Leader.

1.d Other

Chain of Command – The first six in the chain of command for a platoon are Platoon Leader, Platoon Sergeant, Weapons Squad Leader, 1st Squad Leader, 2nd Squad Leader, and 3rd Squad Leader.

Battle Drill – A collective action rapidly executed without applying a deliberate decision-making process.

Ambush – A surprise attack, from a concealed position, used on a moving or temporarily halted enemy to destroy or capture them and their equipment.

Leader's Recon – A leader's reconnaissance. This is scouting performed by a small group of Leaders and Soldiers who advance to a site that the entire patrol might use. The group analyzes the location's security and utility to the patrol.

Principles of Patrolling – U.S. Army Rangers say that a patrol has five parts: Planning, Recon, Security, Control, and Common Sense. The last three principles are especially important during the patrol itself. Security means that every direction of enemy approach is guarded at all times, so the patrol is not caught off guard. Control means that there is clear communication and execution on information between every Soldier in the patrol. Common Sense can mean anything from the KISS principle ("Keep it simple stupid."), to, "Don't follow a plan if it's a bad plan."

2. The Secret Ideas (Concepts)

Certain ideas go unsaid in official military manuals, but are actually mandatory. Most Soldiers learn by trial and error (with lots of errors), but you can just read the procedures here and do them right the first time!

2.a Safety Procedures

15-Degree Offset – Firing bullets inches from friendly Soldiers is unacceptable. The U.S. military has decided that all direct shots must be offset from friendly troops by 15 degrees either vertically or horizontally.

Minimum of Two – One man is never allowed to go anywhere alone without good reason. Moreover, even within an element, security positions are filled by multiple Soldiers, and carrying casualties require rotations. If a Soldier is ever alone in a role, they must be corrected.

Noise and Light Discipline – The human ear can detect pressure 1/50,000,000 of the atmosphere, and the eye can detect a single photon. Perfect discipline is impossible, but some rules of thumb apply. Ride bolts forward to reduce noise. Do not use lights anywhere near the objective.

Pulling Security – This refers to pointing a weapon at an area and being ready and willing to fire at, or halt, anything that moves. The details vary. Are you pointing your weapon while in the prone or kneeling? How large of a sector can you fire at? If a Soldier is doing nothing else, they pull security.

Security – A term with multiple meanings specific to a patrol. Sometimes it is used to refer to the percent of Soldiers that can pull security that are actually pulling security. So for example, if the machine guns are being cleaned and Leaders are coordinating, but all other available Soldiers are pulling security, that would be 100% security. Other times, security refers to the amount of space actually secured by the patrol. In that case, 100% security at all times is impossible. (Having 360-degree coverage is possible, but people aren't robots.)

Speed is Security – There is no limit to how secure a patrol can be. However, the time needed to improve security can prolong a patrol's time in a dangerous area. For example, although a patrol crossing a dangerous area can increase security by pushing out Soldiers to provide early warning, the patrol can also increase security by not pushing out anyone and crossing the area faster. Sometimes being faster is the most secure method.

2.b Communications

Communication – The ability to pass information from one individual to another through talking, signing, etc. Effective communication requires Leaders to be in the correct positions to give orders and for Soldiers to be in the correct positions to receive orders. If formation breaks, every Soldier-Leader pair must still communicate no matter what, so they can either coordinate together or carry the other's corpse. Always establish a PACE plan for communications. (See Communication, Pg. 242.)

Dissemination – A Leader must provide relevant information. Every Soldier needs to know what is going on. For example: "This is the long-halt for to the ORP. This is our current location. (He points on a map.) Our next movement is 300 meters at 290 degrees to the ORP." Dissemination is ongoing so Leaders can be creative, like having Soldiers pass information down the line while moving.

Echoing – Every instruction that is yelled must be echoed by everyone. Echoing is not just a boost to the sound level; it affirms that the yeller correctly heard the command. If the Leader yells, "Lift-fire!" they cannot go forward without "Lift-fire!" being echoed back by every Soldier.

Verbage – Commands must be short, to the point, and agreed upon to minimize confusion. "Cease fire!" is much better than, "Halt all pulling of triggers on the line." So, "Cease fire!" is said verbatim every time.

2.c Other

Accountability – Leaders must have a correct count of their Soldiers at all times. Every time a formation stops moving, begins moving, splits, or joins, Soldiers are counted. The idea of accountability is pervasive throughout any patrol.

As If It Were Night – Many formations may seem like they contain too many small details that need to be memorized. (Creating a patrol-base is almost a choreographed dance.) However, the best ambushes are at night, so all formations must be able to be performed by brain-dead, blind-in-the-dark, no-depth-perception Soldiers.

Danger Area – An area that is dangerous based upon its terrain characteristics. Patrols need cover and concealment. A field is an open danger area because it has neither on all sides. A road is a linear danger area as it has neither in a line.

Key Terrain – When maneuvering, always move to a better position. If none is available, do not move. (Sometimes any position is a better position, like during a react-to-indirect-fire.) The U.S. Army defines key terrain as any locality, or area, the seizure or retention of which affords a marked advantage to either combatant. Applying this to small unit tactics maneuvering, key terrain can be judged by three criteria: 1) a Leader can effectively command and control their troops; 2) the position provides effective cover and concealment; and 3) there are good fields-of-fire on enemy positions.

Moving vs. Shooting – As anyone who has tried knows, shooting while moving is wildly inaccurate. Therefore, any moving element requires another separate element to provide covering fire from a stationary position. A common theme in this manual is to have one element shoot (or be prepared to shoot) while another element moves, and then alternate.

Position of Leadership – A Leader's job is to gather information and convey instructions. They must, therefore, be positioned in a formation where they can best do that. For example, during movement they are in the center of their element, so that they can move rapidly to another element that needs direction. However, during contact they may need to head to the front to quickly give orders and coordinate.

Sector-of-Fire – In any stationary position, it is important to have a Soldier on standby, ready to shoot enemies from every direction. When sectors-of-fire are not given, Soldiers get tunnel vision on the first enemy that appears, ignore everywhere else, and thereby get shot from in the rear. Because of this, Soldiers are only given responsibility for a certain area in front of their position, called a "sector-of-fire." Unless a Leader directs otherwise, Soldiers disregard firefights outside their sector. By default, a Soldier has standing instructions for a sector-of-fire from their 10 o'clock to their 2 o'clock. If a Leader has time, one of their first priorities is to assign sectors which eliminate gaps between sectors.

Small Unit Tactics – The art of organizing and employing squads and platoons of Soldiers to conduct war. These tactics prioritize moving with little-to-no footprint. This reduces the risk of compromise, and allows for disruption-operations and reconnaissance behind enemy lines.

Phase 1 Contents

3. Traveling by Vehicle　23

Loading a Truck　23
Transport to Drop-off Site　24
Exiting a Truck　26
Traveling by Helicopter　28

4. Traveling by Foot (Individual Soldiers)　29

Moving Through Terrain to Your Advantage　29
Going to the Prone, Taking a Knee, and Taking Off Rucks　30

5. Traveling by Foot (Elements)　30

Moving Through Terrain to Your Advantage　31
Emergency Meetup Areas (En Route Rally-Points)　32
Responsibility for Land Navigation　33
Counting People (Chokepoints)　35
Rear Security　36

6. Traveling by Foot (Formations)　36

Wedge Formation　40
Modified-Wedge (Staggered Column) Formation　43
Platoon Movement Formations　44
Detecting the Enemy (SLLS)　47
Short/Security-Halt Formation　48
Initial Location after Exiting Vehicles (Initial Rally-Point)　51

7. Crossing a Road or Draw (Linear Danger Area)　52

Choosing a Crossing Location　52
Choosing How to Cross　53
Blast Formation　54
Bumping/Scrolling Formation　55
Deliberate Formation　57
Draw Crossing Formation　62
Actions on Detection　62
Enemy Attack During LDA Crossing　64

8. Crossing a Field (Open Danger Area)　64

Directly Crossing the Area (Bounding)　65
Going around the Area　68

Joe Goes to the Enemy (Phase 1: Transportation to the Objective)

Appear at points which the enemy must hasten to defend; march swiftly to places where you are not expected.

— Sun Tzu, The Art of War

If you are ambushing the enemy, you are most likely in enemy territory, and everybody you meet is trying to kill you. Therefore, security is the first priority of everything. Initial movement is conducted at the platoon-level; however, squads may break off to conduct their own ambush.

3. Traveling by Vehicle

Transportation by vehicle creates a vulnerable position. Many Soldiers cannot effectively provide support from inside the vehicle. The following procedures minimize that unsafe time by allowing as many Soldiers to provide security as fast as possible in every direction.

3.a Loading a Truck[1]

Soldiers in a truck could make a mass pile, but that's probably not the safest way to travel. Securing the road is much better. Where there is an opening in the transport (or the top if there's a mounted gun), the biggest, loudest guns keep watch.

For many vehicles, like the Light Medium Tactical Vehicle (LMTV), only the back is open. The Soldiers at the very back have the machine guns at the ready with muzzles concealed. (There's no need to draw extra attention.)

---

1 Quote: Question: How many Soldiers can you fit in the back of a troop transport? Answer: At least one more. —Unknown

Image 2: A combat engineer with the 251st Engineer Co. (Sapper) pulls security with a light machine gun in an LMTV. Base Gagetown, NB, Canada, 16 Aug 2017. **He is ready to open fire at any moment.**

Behind them is the leadership that can tell the machine guns when to open fire.[1]

When loading the vehicle, the primary concern is a quick dismount. First and foremost, the patrol needs to be able to respond quickly to an attack. But moreover, a well-organized vehicle can get the patrol off the road more quickly. If the foot patrol is going to move east when leaving the vehicles, the first element in order of movement (e.g., Alpha Team) dismounts on the east side of the truck. This requires an accurate prediction of the orientation and location of the truck during planning, but avoids the entire patrol having to reorganize when dismounting. (See Image 3, Pg. 25.)

3.b Transport to Drop-off Site

Transport to the drop-off site is one of the most vulnerable times in a patrol because Soldiers cannot immediately return fire, seek cover, or identify the

---

1 **Applying Concepts:** If the Squad Leader rides in the cab, what communication methods or simple signals could they use to communicate with the back? How much preplanning will the signaling need?

Truck Formation

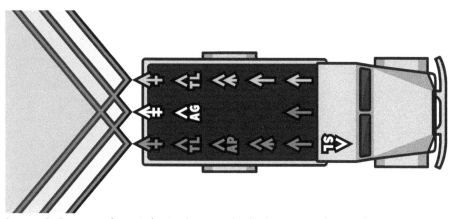

Phase 1

Image 3: Because there is limited room, the highest casualty-producing weapons (here, the machine guns) are placed in the best postion to pull security (here, the rear). This patrol intends to start foot movement to the vehicle's right, because the lead element, Alpha Team (red), will dismount to the vehicle's right side. **The highest leadership rides in the front to monitor the driver, because the patrol is ultimately their responsibility.**

enemy. Basically, the entire react-to-contact is delayed by several critical minutes. (See Individual Soldiers React-to-Contact, Pg. 72.) Therefore, fast exiting a disabled vehicle is a critical task that must be practiced and preplanned with many contingencies prepared for. Move relatively slowly, and if necessary get out of the vehicle and scout the road ahead.

To mitigate some danger, the leadership rides in the cab with the driver and actively engages in the transport. They check the driver to ensure that the correct route is followed. (Don't trust the entire mission to the driver's sense of direction.) One way that Leaders can verify the route is by locating checkpoints identified during planning. Once the Leader sees a checkpoint (e.g., an intersection or a bridge), they pass that checkpoint to the Soldiers in the rear, so everyone knows where they are. Additionally, every checkpoint has a corresponding rally-point, so that if the patrol is attacked during transport, Soldiers can move to the last rally-point. (See Emergency Meetup Areas (En Route Rally-Points), Pg. 32.)

The Leader also looks for reasons to take an alternate route (e.g., a silhouette of a Humvee, signs of IED's, etc.). Before leaving, a Leader straps

Image 4: 3rd Inf. Div. Soldiers practice dismounting an LMTV. Fort Stewart, GA, 05 March 2017. Setting security is always the priority. **The first Soldiers to dismount are the machine gunners** who secure the most likely enemy avenues of approach. Next, Leaders dismount to coordinate.

Image 5: Soldiers from 2nd Armored Bde. Combat Team, 1st Cavalry Div. dismount their Bradley Fighting Vehicle. Fort Hood, TX, 09 Feb 2019. Once all Soldiers form a **half-moon around the vehicle**, they can immediately move out away from the road.

down heavy objects so a rollover or enemy attack does not send heavy weights flying.

3.c Exiting a Truck[1]

When the truck stops, Soldiers set security as fast as possible. The largest guns exit the truck first. In the diagram, these are the M240 Gunners and Assistant Gunners, followed by the SAW Gunners and their Team Leaders. (See Image 6, Pg. 27.) **360-degree security** on drop-off with only the initial dismounts is preplanned. A common formation is to have the M240 of the lead vehicle cover the 12 o'clock; the M240 of the trail vehicle cover the 6 o'clock; and the M240 of the center vehicles cover the opposite direction of the element's foot movement (i.e., the 3 or the 9). SAW Gunners fill the gaps.

---

[1] Real World. Vehicle dismount is a very dangerous moment because it can occur under enemy fire, like an ambush. The U.S. Army has even created the specific Battle Drill 12 (Dismount a BFV and ICV) and Battle Drill 13 (Mount a BFV and ICV). Vehicle transportation requires practiced and planned dismount for the specific model of vehicle to be used.

Exiting a Truck

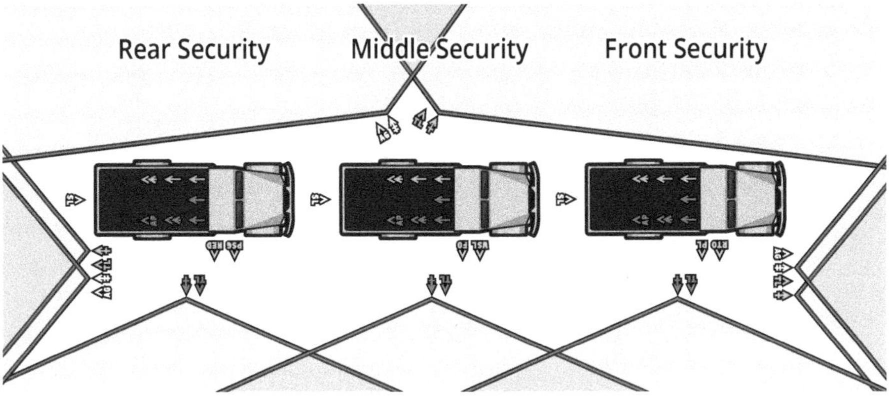

Rear Security   Middle Security   Front Security

Image 6: The first priority is always 360-degree security. First, the machine guns exit and set up a perimeter. Then the Leaders exit to coordinate and assess the location. This diagram is a snapshot at that point. Each machince gun has a Leader or AG beside them and shows an interlocking sector-of-fire. This patrol is preparing to move south, because the lead team (the red arrows) have taken the south perimeter.

Not all sectors have the same coverage. In the diagram, note that the road has more security than the side areas because the enemy are more likely to use them as avenues of approach.

Bravo Team and Alpha Team begin to exit the truck from both sides at the same time, while Headquarters helps hand out rucks. If there is equipment to offload, it is often a better idea to have it handed off the truck. It is unwise for a Soldier to jump off with a ton of weight, when their legs are potentially numb from being pressed in the truck for hours.

After the machine guns exit, **the Riflemen dismount to form a perimeter around the truck in a half-moon shape.** (See Image 5, Pg. 26.) When the Alpha and Bravo teams finish exiting, every truck is surrounded by a rough circle of Soldiers. The Alpha Team face the direction of foot movement and the Bravo Team are opposite to the direction of foot movement. Headquarters remain near the trucks, ready to move and communicate.

Once all of the Soldiers in the first vehicle's Alpha Team are in position and have their rucks on, they begin moving in the direction of travel, regardless of whether the other elements are done. (Still they must always maintain comms.) This saves time because Bravo and Headquarters will be finished by the time Alpha is the correct distance away.

Platoon leadership goes wherever they are needed. They must track when each squad leaves so they can follow in the correct position with their Gun Teams. (See Platoon Movement Formations, Pg. 44.)

The formation moves in the direction of travel until they are out of sight, sound, and small-arms fire from the road.[1] Once the formation is far enough from the vehicle drop-off site, the Squad Leader or Alpha Team Leader can call a short-halt or long-halt to get a proper azimuth of travel, and land navigation may begin.

3.d Traveling by Helicopter

The concepts behind traveling by helicopter and truck are the same, with the main difference being carrying capacity and forced exit into a field. To exit the helicopter, a Soldier drags their ruck away from the helicopter. Every ruck and Soldier must be two meters away from the helicopter to create enough room for other Soldiers to quickly exit, and for the helicopter to bounce during takeoff. Soldiers then get in the prone position in front of their rucks with interlocking sectors-of-fire around the entire helicopter.[2]

To mitigate some of the danger of landing in a field, the patrol coordinates with the air crew during planning. For example, the air crew is briefed on the patrol's initial rally-point, so both they and the patrol know where the initial movement will be to. The patrol must also coordinate the "load and bump" plan; i.e., the plan for loading and moving Soldiers among vehicles if one or more vehicles becomes incapacitated.

Once the helicopter takes off, Soldiers put on their rucks one by one while maintaining **360-degree security** and, if the infill requires multiple trips, move into the wood-line to await incoming Soldiers. Once at the initial rally-point, the patrol needs to clear the area and find cover and concealment large enough to fit all follow-on troops. The first elements must call in their precise location to avoid incoming Soldiers from committing fratricide. Soldiers waiting in the woods form a long-halt. (See Creating the Long-Halt, Pg. 123.)

---

1 Real World: If you can see the road, the road can see you. Many guerrilla enemies purchase night optical devices online.

2 **Applying Concepts:** How would exiting from a Chinook be different? (A Chinook has a rear exit.)

Image 7: MNBG-East Polish Army Soldiers quickly dismount from a UH-60 Black Hawk helicopter to provide security in the prone during a hot and cold load training exercise. Camp Novo Selo near Pristina, Kosovo, 08 Dec 2017. **Note how far the Soldiers are from the helicopter**.

4. Traveling by Foot (Individual Soldiers)

To move quietly in the wild, without getting shot, requires skill and technique. Always be aware of the ground you walk on, the terrain, your location, your teammates' locations, potential enemy locations, and a dozen other things. First and foremost, though, you must know what to do with yourself.

4.a Moving Through Terrain to Your Advantage

Good terrain provides cover and concealment in case of enemy attack. Do not ignore these positions. Instead of walking in a straight line, ping-pong between good positions (like trees or rocks) as you move forward. Vary your speed as well. When moving between two good positions speed up; once you arrive, take a moment to look around at likely enemy positions and identify your next covered position. Also look for ground traps and at teammates for signals.

While moving, it is vital to remain within sight and sound of the element's Leader. If the Leader needs to pass a "freeze" command because the patrol has just walked into a minefield, every Soldier must be available to receive it. Take this into account when choosing where to move; do not be so well concealed that your own team cannot communicate with you. Another rule of thumb is to turn around in sync with a pace count (e.g. look behind every ten paces). Soldiers and enemies give vital information from behind.

4.b Going to the Prone, Taking a Knee, and Taking Off Rucks

When halted, a Soldier by default takes a knee, and after 30 seconds goes to prone for cover and concealment. However, a Soldier may choose to stay on a knee if the situation dictates. The prone may provide more cover and concealment, but kneeling often provides a better line of sight, fields-of-fire, and threat visibility. For example, if in tall grass a Soldier in the prone cannot see anything, they kneel.

Line of sight is extremely important. A kneeling Soldier that sees an enemy from afar is often better off than a prone Soldier who lets an enemy creep up close. Either way, human eyesight is especially good at tracking movement, so being still is an effective means of concealment by itself. (See Image 8, Pg. 31.)

Whether in the prone or on a knee, security must be maintained when a Soldier takes off their ruck. Therefore, another Soldier provides security by taking a knee by the Soldier getting down. Always remove rucks deliberately without dropping them, to avoid making noise and damaging equipment. As soon as possible, a Leader assigns a sector-of-fire. (See 360-Degree Security (Assigning Sectors-of-Fire), Pg. 130.)

5. Traveling by Foot (Elements)[1]

When many Soldiers travel together, there are additional concerns that are the responsibility of the entire element. In a single movement, there may be variations in terrain, elevation, concealment, visibility, enemy capability, and

---

1   Quote: Onward we stagger, and if the tanks come, may God help the tanks. — Commander of the U.S. Army Rangers, Col. William O. Darby

Image 8: Two Soldiers from A Co., 2-23 Inf. Reg., 4th Bde. Combat Team, 2nd Inf. Div., take cover in tall grass and conduct security. Muqdadiyah, Iraq, 19 Dec 2007. **Going prone in the tall grass would obstruct all vision and lanes-of-fire.**

Image 9: A Soldier from A Co., 29th Engineer Bn., 25th Inf. Div., scans for enemies during Jungle Operations Training Center (JOTC) react-to-contact training. HI, 17 Mar 2016. This Soldier likely cannot see in the prone surrounded by vegetation.

so on. These can cover and expose, and push and pull an element apart. All of these considerations must be accounted for when considering optimal foot movement techniques.

5.a Moving Through Terrain to Your Advantage

When traveling to complete an ambush, the most pressing concerns are concealing the patrol and moving fast. The best routes are decided in planning. However, maps do not show every bump or hole in ground, so many decisions on movement must be made on the ground.

Among hills, the best area for travel is the "military crest." The military crest is the part of a hillside that starts from the low ground and continues until three vertical meters from the top of the hill. (I.e., a Soldier must not be seen from the other side of the hill.) Traveling on this hillside provides good concealment without sacrificing much high ground. During the daytime, a patrol goes as high on the military crest as possible while still being able to see all the area below it (leaving no dead space). During nighttime, a patrol moves as low as possible (but still outside of the valley bottom) so that enemies farther up the hill are silhouetted against the night sky.

When crossing roads, use a low point between two hills. The hills provide concealment from long-range surveillance and make good navigational checkpoints. Try to cross at bends in the road, where the enemy cannot see

Military Crest

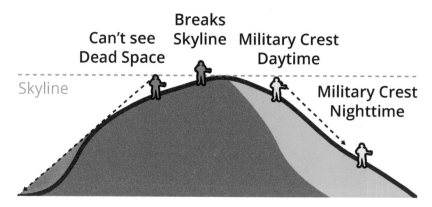

Image 10: The military crest of a terrain feature. Ideally a Soldier needs to see the entire hillside and not be silhouetted on top of the hill.

past the curve. Patrols crossing on a straight road can be seen for the entire distance of the road. When crossing draws, look for areas on maps with compressed contour lines, which indicate a steeper, shorter draw.

There are countless additional factors that a Patrol Leader must consider. Areas that are heavily wooded can provide great concealment. However, if artillery is a concern, good thick-tree coverage can become bad shrapnel. If there are dogs, local populations may know that barking indicates strangers' presence. **Whatever the case, do not navigate in straight lines without reason; use terrain to your advantage.**

5.b Emergency Meetup Areas (En Route Rally-Points)

Rally-points are locations where Soldiers meet up and wait for other Soldiers. En route rally-points (ERRP's) are locations that a patrol creates during a movement. They provide an emergency location for Soldiers to run to if they break contact with the Main Body, so they can be picked up later.

ERRPS need to be easily recognizable both day and night. Remember that stressed-out Soldiers need to find them at night. **A rally-point that is impossible to find is useless;** although dead trees often are used, forests contain many dead trees. Bigger landmarks, such as draws, are much better.[1] Though finalized on the ground, make sure to preplan some good ERRP locations. (See Image 11, Pg. 34.)

Designate ERRP's by using hand and arm signals. Every signal is made by each Soldier twice: first, to confirm receipt; and second, to relay. Signals are only relayed by the Soldier physically closest to the rally-point. This will help to identify the ERRP. To ensure that every Soldier has passed, a rally-point is only activated when the following rally-point begins to be designated.

ERRP's are also designated prior to crossing any danger area. (I.e., if an area is dangerous to move in, then a location to withdraw to is established before moving.) A near-side rally-point is established up to 300 meters before the danger area. A far-side rally-point is established up to 300 meters beyond the danger area. The far-side rally-point is also created before the danger area is crossed in case of a rear attack during crossing.

If Soldiers become separated due to enemy contact or a break-in-contact, the first to arrive at the rally-point establish a hasty defensive perimeter. As more arrive, the most senior Soldier present directs personnel, establishes security, and maintains personnel accountability. Time limits for how long to stay at an ERRP must be made during planning. Otherwise, the patrol may be halted in an area containing a large enemy force (if they caused the withdrawal to the ERRP), waiting for Soldiers who may never arrive. A common time limit for ERRP's is two hours after the first patrol member arrives.

5.c Responsibility for Land Navigation[2]

Notionally, responsibility for land navigation is assigned to the Patrol Leader; however, because all leadership has been briefed on every movement, all Leaders on the team are responsible for the patrol being on the correct route. In fact, every person in the formation should already know the planned route because it is briefed in detail during the operation order (OPORD).

---

1 Applying Concepts: Often, the best rally-points are terrain features that are hard to traverse, like draws or hills. In planning, is there a way to choose a fast route that also has the benefit of these good rally-points? Consider walking around a hill and making the hilltop a rally-point.

2 Quote: War is God's way of teaching Americans geography. —American Civil War Soldier, Ambrose Bierce

Image 11: A **good rally-point** is distinctive and large enough to be found at night. Ponds can often be heard as well. An offset can be used; e.g. 70 meters to the south-west of this pond.

Image 12: Marines with K Co., 3rd Bn., 4th Marine Reg. Big Bear Lake, CA, 7 Sep 2016. This is a **bad rally-point**. While at first it seems distinctive, forests contain a large number of dead trees.

Realistically, execution of land navigation falls on the first element in movement.[1]

Land navigation is too complicated and important for one person to handle. It includes the following tasks: looking for terrain features that match the map; keeping a pace count; staying on azimuth; watching for checkpoints and backstops; and creating ERRP's. **A good Team Leader delegates heavily.**[2]

However the Team Leader decides to delegate, there are some good guidelines. Each Rifleman holds a compass or keeps pace. The Pointman and SAW have the primary responsibility of security, and so they are never involved with land navigation. Because the Pointman is ahead of the navigation, they must constantly look back to ensure that the direction of travel has not changed on them.

---

1 **Applying Concepts:** For a squad, normally the lead element is Alpha Team, and for a platoon it is the lead Alpha Team. What happens if the order of movement changes (like during a deliberate danger area crossing), and now Bravo Team is the lead element? Either the squad needs to reorganize, or Bravo Team becomes the lead element and is responsible for land navigation.

2 **Real World:** Although many conservative experts place great importance on using analog devices like protractors and compasses, and deny relying on GPS, it is becoming increasingly clear that a dedicated GPS device is as important as a rifle on any patrol, and paper maps are going the way of the bayonet. Many GPS devices are lightweight, durable, untraceable, lead to better navigation overall, and can prevent further disaster after a split element.

In an ideal world, the route and terrain are memorized by everyone, but it is better to stop and do a map check than to get lost. Map checks distract leadership and require light at night, so they necessitate more caution than a normal stop. To verify a location, a short-halt is called. If leadership suspects that the patrol is lost, a long-halt is called. (See Short/Security-Halt Formation, Pg. 48.) (See Creating the Long-Halt, Pg. 123.)

All of the leadership moves to the center. The Patrol Leader lies in the prone and removes their rucksack to lower their profile. At night, the Patrol Leader is covered in something completely opaque as they conduct a map check under light.[1]

If for whatever reason the route has not been briefed before, or Soldiers forget the route, it must be briefed as soon as possible. Every Soldier is responsible for knowing: 1) the primary and alternative routes; 2) where they presently are on those routes; and, most importantly, 3) how to move if separated and alone.

5.d Counting People (Chokepoints)

A chokepoint is a location where a Leader counts every Soldier in the element. Chokepoints are used during every stage of a patrol, that is, every time an element begins or stops movement: for example, when withdrawing from a react-to-contact, pick up from a short-halt, etc.

The Leader directly responsible for accountability (e.g., the Bravo Team Leader or Platoon Sergeant) runs to the front of the formation. Then, they choose a tree or another Soldier, and every man in the element moves between the two. **The Leader physically touches every Soldier that passes through while maintaining a count.** If the chokepoint is formed with another Soldier, they also silently keeps a count so that both the Leader and the Soldier can compare their counts after the last man passes. (See Image 13, Pg. 36.)

If an element is moving in a formation towards a chokepoint, Soldiers wait until they are at the chokepoint to break their movement formation. They then return back to their formation position after the chokepoint. This prevents the entire formation from deforming into a file formation before and

---

Double-layering an Army-issue poncho is not enough to hide modern bright headlamps. To limit light, consider also covering the headlamp itself with semi-permeable tape.

Phase 1

Image 13: U.S. Soldiers in Bandit Tr., 1st Sq., 3rd Cavalry Reg. file through a chokepoint during a response force live-fire training. Iraq, 31 Oct 2018. Two Soldiers **count silently and check each other** at the end.

after every chokepoint. Make sure to keep an eye out for Soldiers that are unaware of (and bypass) the chokepoint.

Once a count is attained, all leadership is informed of both a number and a result: e.g., "15 Soldiers up," or "14 Soldiers missing one." Do not dismiss a count if it is above the expected number; a count must be exactly accurate with no mistakes. What to do if the count is off is discussed during planning, and is very situationally dependant. (See Image 14, Pg. 37.)

5.e Rear Security

A common theme of this manual is 360-degree security at all times. This includes foot movement. Soldiers in the back of the formation often zone out because the majority of enemy contact is at the front. However, a smart enemy will realize this and attack the rear of the formation. An effective rear element constantly scans behind itself. A good tactic is to work it into the pace count: for example, looking back every ten steps. (See Image 14, Pg. 37.)

6. Traveling by Foot (Formations)

When moving together, Soldiers need to travel as an organized unit to maximize command and control and allocate firepower. Every possible way to group four Soldiers or elements has a name. (See Image 15, Pg. 38.)

Image 14: Combat Control School students with 352nd Battlefield Airmen Training Squad, hike through overgrown woodlands. Camp Mackall, NC, 03 Aug 2016. **The Soldier in the rear looks back for rear security.**

Also, each level of organization has its own formation. So for example, a "squad-line, fire-team-box" is a line of (team-sized) box formations. All of these combinations and formations can become complicated very fast, so units heavily rely on the most common formations.

For squads and platoons, the two most common movement formations are called "wedge" and "modified-wedge" (technically, platoon-column, squad-column, fire-team-wedge). (See Image 22, Pg. 46.) Another common formation is the "file" which is used only in specific situations throughout the manual. Moving in a wedge is the default and covers most traveling situations.

Using a wedge or modified-wedge is a tradeoff between security and speed. The wedge formation is more secure against a frontal attack than a modified-wedge, because it has a broader front. The patrol can easily form that wedge into a fast, forward-facing firing line. The wedge shape also allows quick-firing lines to form against side attacks.

A modified-wedge, on the other hand, must completely deform in order to make a line at the front, while only performing equally well as a wedge when attacked from the sides. Columns in a modified-wedge are also vulnerable to machine gun fire from the front, which may shoot straight down through an entire column. The advantage of a modified-wedge is that walking in two columns is fast because almost all Soldiers are simply following the Soldier

Traveling by Foot (Formations)

Table 3-1. Primary formations.

Name/Formation/ Signal (if applicable)	Characteristics	Advantages	Disadvantages
Line Formation	- All elements arranged in a row - Majority of observation and direct fires oriented forward; minimal to the flanks - Each subordinate unit on the line must clear its own path forward - One subordinate designated as the base on which the other subordinates cue their movement	Ability to: - Generate fire superiority to the front - Clear a large area - Disperse - Transition to bounding overwatch, base of fire, or assault	- Control difficulty increases during limited visibility and in restrictive or close terrain - Difficult to designate a maneuver element - Vulnerable assailable flanks - Potentially slow - Large signature
Column/File Formation	- One lead element - Majority of observation and direct fires oriented to the flanks; minimal to the front - One route means unit only influenced by obstacles on that one route	- Easiest formation to control (as long as leader can communicate with lead element) - Ability to generate a maneuver element - Secure flanks - Speed	- Reduced ability to achieve fire superiority to the front - Clears a limited area and concentrates the unit - Transitions poorly to bounding overwatch, base of fire, and assault - Column's depth makes it a good target for close air attacks and a machine gun beaten zone
Vee Formation	- Two lead elements - Trail elements move between the two lead elements - Used when contact to the front is expected - "Reverse wedge" - Unit required to two lanes/routes forward	Ability to: - Generate fire superiority to the front - Generate a maneuver element - Secure flanks - Clear a large area - Disperse - Transition to bounding overwatch, base of fire, or assault	- Control difficulty increases during limited visibility and in restrictive or close terrain - Potentially slow
Box Formation	- Two lead elements - Trail elements follow lead elements - All-around security	See vee formation advantages	See vee formation disadvantages
Wedge Formation	- One lead element - Trail elements paired off abreast of each other on the flanks - Used when the situation is uncertain	Ability to: - Control, even during limited visibility, in restrictive terrain, or in close terrain - Transition trail elements to base of fire or assault - Secure the front and flanks - Transition the line and column	- Trail elements are required to clear their own path forward - Frequent need to transition to column in restrictive, close terrain
Diamond Formation	- Similar to the wedge formation - Fourth element follows the lead element	See wedge formation advantages	See wedge formation disadvantages
Echelon Formation (Right)	- Elements deployed diagonally left or right - Observation and fire to both the front and one flank - Each subordinate unit on the line clears its own path forward	- Ability to assign sectors that encompass both the front and flank	- Difficult to maintain proper relationship between subordinates - Vulnerable to the opposite flanks

Image 15: These are all the primary movement formations as defined by U.S. Army FM 3-21.8 The Infantry Rifle Platoon and Squad Chapter 3. In essense, every possible way to organize four Soldiers has been defined. **Although there are uses for all of the above, in reality some formations are much more useful than others.** This manual does not use the vee or echelon formations because they only have specialty uses.

Basic Movement Formations

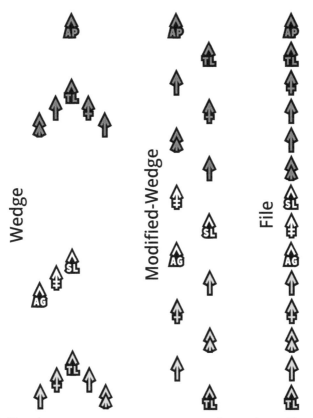

Phase 1

Image 16: The three most common movement formations. The wider, spaced-out wedge formation provides more evenly distributed security, but can be more difficult to control. The **modified-wedge is faster, but more vulnerable** to an attack from the front. The file is extremely vulnerable, and only used for short, pre-planned distance.

in front of them, instead of creating a new path through terrain. A smaller profile also means that easier terrain, like roads or river beds can be utilized.

As most enemy attacks come from the front, the wedge formation is favored for any situation where enemy contact is possible. It is most vulnerable to an attack 45 degrees from the rear, where the last wedge has a few Soldiers in a row. However, the benefits of the security to the front, and the simplicity of having every team in the same shape, outweigh that risk.

The file formation is only used when the risk of a front attack is greatly outweighed by other factors. For example, when traveling through terrain like a swamp, a distance of a few meters can split an element. Moving Soldiers to a location already occupied by friendly troops (i.e., no enemies at the front) is another.

To maintain control during movement, the Squad Leader can freely move anywhere within the Squad while the Bravo Team Leader can freely move anywhere within the Bravo Team. The Alpha Team Leader is a little different. They must always be in position to direct the Alpha Team because they are the most likely to make enemy contact.

6.a Wedge Formation

In this formation, teams are shaped like wedges and are aligned in a column. For this reason, the full name for the "wedge" is "squad-column, fire-team-wedge." However, in this manual it will be called a wedge. To create a **wedge**:

1) Place each Leader in a vertical column 20 to 40 meters apart. This will be apex of each respective wedge.

2) Place the Soldiers under each Leader 5 to 20 meters away from the Leader, at 30 to 45 degrees, with an equal number on each side. These form wedges.

3) Position a Pointman ahead of the formation to act as early warning for the entire element.

4) If enemy contact is likely, push the lead element out 50 to 100 meters ahead, as this will conceal the rear element from the enemy. Concealing the rear element is helpful in certain maneuvers, like a flank. This is called "traveling overwatch." Regular spacing is just called "traveling."

5) Place the Assistant Gunner on the left-feeding side of the M240 Gunner.

6) Balance machine guns and anti-tank weapons on opposite sides between and within teams.

Army doctrinal spacing is to space each element 20 meters apart, with the first element 50 meters from the second element. **In reality, forget specific numbers; different terrain and conditions require different spacing.** During daytime, when the enemy has reported artillery, Soldiers can each be 20 meters apart to avoid a single artillery shell from destroying multiple Soldiers. On the other hand, if a Soldier is hit, it is very difficult to find and evacuate them from 20 meters away under fire. Tighter spacing allows for faster communication and quicker maneuvering. During nighttime in a swamp, Soldiers are so close that they are almost touching each other.

Squad Wedge Formation

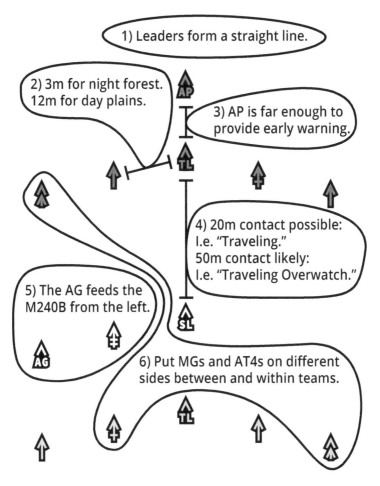

1) Leaders form a straight line.

2) 3m for night forest. 12m for day plains.

3) AP is far enough to provide early warning.

4) 20m contact possible: I.e. "Traveling." 50m contact likely: I.e. "Traveling Overwatch."

5) The AG feeds the M240B from the left.

6) Put MGs and AT4s on different sides between and within teams.

Phase 1

Image 17: Wedges take a lot of coordination and constant realignment. **Most important to a wedge is good communication.**

The Pointman of a wedge is a special security position located beyond the front of the lead element of a patrolling formation. The Pointman observes and scrutinizes their surroundings at all times and is not involved in land navigation. This position exists because the leading element of a patrol is the most likely to both receive and preempt enemy contact. Therefore, putting a single man far ahead maximizes the chances that the patrol (specifically the Pointman) will detect the enemy before the enemy detects the patrol, because a single man makes less noise than a full element.

Image 18: U.S. Army Rangers, assigned to 2nd Bn., 75th Ranger Reg., advance toward their objective in a **wedge formation** during Task Force Training. Fort Hunter Liggett, CA, 22 Jan 2014.

Image 19: Guatemalan marines react-to-contact from a wedge formation. Guatemala, 09 Mar 2016. **Why might this terrain dictate a tighter movement formation than for the Soldiers to the left?**

Similar to a Pointman, the first team in a wedge is also further out than the rest of the element.[1] Pushing the first element ahead enables the enemy to only identify the fewest Soldiers possible. The remaining unseen Soldiers in the rear can then employ a bold-flank or break-contact more effectively. (See Bold-flank Maneuver (Battle Drill 1), Pg. 85.) 50 meters is a good estimate, but the first element can be pushed farther forward if they can still easily communicate with Headquarters.

Positions within a formation are, roughly, equally distributed. If the lead team has a SAW on the right-side, then the trail squad has a SAW on the left-side, the lead team has an AT4 (anti-tank rocket launcher) on the left, and the trail has an AT4 on the right. However, if the potential threat is higher on one side, more firepower is directed to that side (i.e., a concentrated distribution).

Weapons systems can be placed at the end of a wedge to allow quicker response to enemy contact from the flank, or at the center of the wedge to allow Team Leaders more command and control. For example, an experienced SAW Gunner who can be trusted to take a good firing position on their own is placed at the edge of a wedge.

---

1 **Applying Concepts:** The Pointman and first element are usually placed further out at the front because that is where enemy contact is most likely. If enemy contact is most likely to come from the left side (for example, there might be a highway to the side), then where should the Patrol Leader place Pointmen and elements?

Image 20: Guatemalan Marines patrolling in a modified-wedge during training provided by a U.S. Marine Security Cooperation Team. Guatemala, 09 Mar 2016. If you were an enemy on the side of the road, would it cause more chaos to attack the Pointman who is alert, or **the middle, where leadership and Soldiers are more likely to be complacent?**

6.b Modified-Wedge (Staggered Column) Formation

The modified-wedge formation is used for faster movement whenever the wedge is too wide or too difficult to control. It is "modified" because the two wings of a wedge collapse into two columns. (See Image 16, Pg. 39.) Soldiers in each column stagger so that two Soldiers are never beside each other. This way, all Soldiers can fire when attacked from the side.

A narrow, modified-wedge may be necessary when:

▸ Crossing through dense vegetation.

▸ Moving at night (to increase command and control).

▸ Moving along a draw or beside a hill (using the "military crest") to remain concealed. (See Image 10, Pg. 32.) If the formation is too wide, a Soldier on the edge might be visible over the hill and give away the patrol's position.

The modified-wedge staggers Soldiers between columns to reduce the effect of attacks to the side, so only one Soldier is hit instead of two or more. An easy way to maintain staggering is to never pass and to maintain a distance from the next Soldier diagonally ahead. A bad way to maintain staggering is to follow the Soldier directly in front.

Where possible, a modified-wedge is preferred to a file formation for moving through draws because it can move double the Soldiers (two columns instead of one file); and therefore is twice as fast. The file formation in rural terrain is considered a specialty formation for specific use, like chokepoints, bramble draws, and emplacement of assault.

6.c Platoon Movement Formations

As movement formations involve more and more Soldiers, they can become complicated very fast. (See Image 21, Pg. 45.) The simplest platoon-level formations are created by taking all the squad wedges and putting them in a column. Three squads' wedges can stack one in front of the other to create a platoon-column, squad-column, fire-team-wedge (hereafter, a **platoon wedge**); or three modified-wedges can stack to form one really long platoon-modified-wedge. (See Image 22, Pg. 46.)

Consider how long a platoon formation can become. According to many standardized recommendations for wedge distances, a platoon of three squads can be extend over 300 meters. (See Wedge Formation, Pg. 40.) This can be a problem because a platoon must be out of sight of danger areas when it stops, which can be over 200 meters. So a 300-meter platoon would need 700 meters (300m plus 200m buffer before and after) to safely short-halt between two roads, which often cannot happen.[1] Length also affects the response time of platoon leadership in case of an enemy attack. Therefore, Platoon Headquarters is often split up within a platoon formation for more proximal command and control.

When stacking squads to make a platoon formation, the position and job of each squad depends on the mission and is decided in planning.

---

1 Applying Concepts: How could SOP's be altered so that a short-halt can be taken in a smaller area? When making guidelines for a particular patrol, start with what needs to happen. A wedge formation is condensed enough to expedite travel, but expanded enough to account for indirect fire. The first element is pushed ahead to provide early warning for the entire unit.

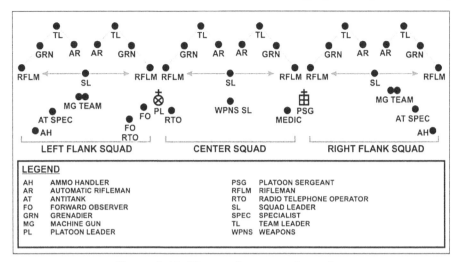

Figure 2-13. Platoon line, squads on line

Image 21: This chart is from the official U.S. Army ATP 3-21.8, April 2016. The formation is overly confusing and complicated, and is included here to show that formation construction is only limited by imagination.

For example, if the mission is a platoon point ambush, a common order of movement is to place Security Squad at the front. (See Location of Platoon Leadership, Pg. 182.) Security has less responsibility during the ambush itself, so it is tasked with the responsibility of land navigation during movement and is thereby the lead element.

For some missions (like area ambushes), the platoon needs to separate into squads who each travel to their squad-specific areas. Where all the squads have similar, separate ambushes the order of movement takes into account mission-external factors like a rotation or skillset.

When each squad travels to its area in an area ambush, they simply leave the platoon formation, and the remaining squads continue until they also part ways. There is no need to stop movement for a squad to peel off in a different direction.

When the patrol is a platoon and not a squad, the M240 Gun Teams combine to become a platoon-level asset known as the Weapons Squad. Within the formation, how the guns are positioned and allocated to leadership is mission dependent. Positioning is important enough that a platoon wedge has a second name based on where the Gun Teams are. The Platoon Wedge Formation illustration is a **"Trail, Lead, Lead"** formation because the first

45

Platoon Wedge Formation

Phase 1

Lead Squad/SQD1
(Alpha Point and
Alpha Team are
still spaced out
for early warning.)

HQ1/WPNS Squad
("Trail, Lead, Lead":
there is one Gun Team
trailing Squad 1, one
GT in front of Squad 2,
and one GT in front
of Squad 3.)

Center Squad/SQD2
(Pointmen are for
early warning.
The Center and
Trail Squad don't
have Pointmen.)

HQ2/PSG
(Splitting HQ into
2 parts is necessary
to distribute command
and control.)

Trail Squad/SQD3
(If there is 10m spacing
between men, and 50m
spacing between lead
elements, the last man
will be at least 350m
behind the Pointman.)

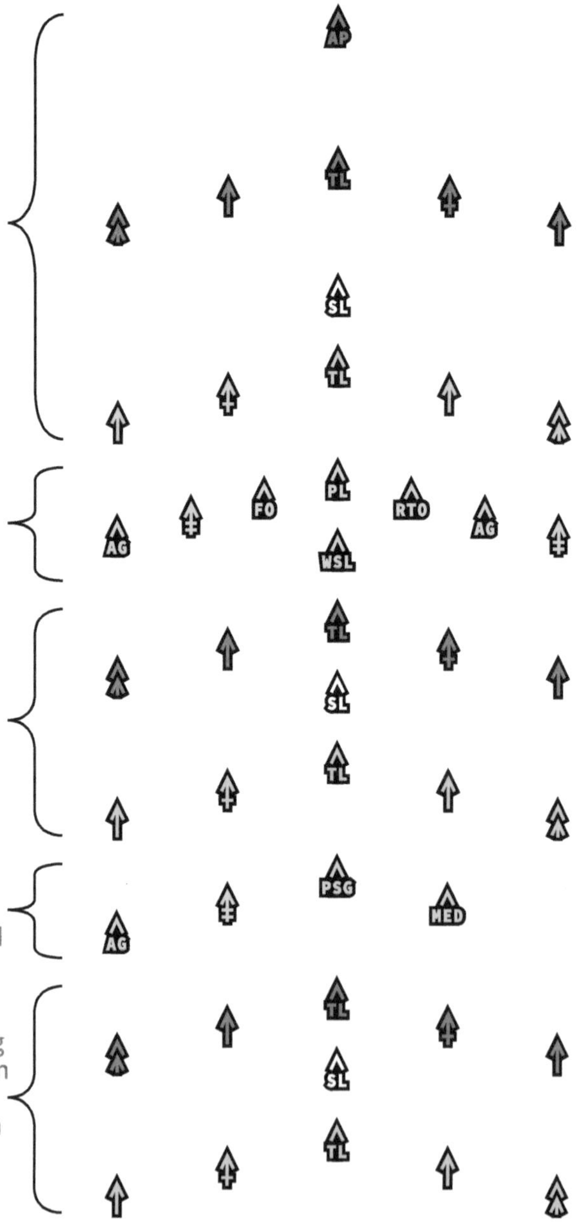

Image 22: Platoon wedge formation. **The platoon wedge is made up of three squad wedges stacked on top of each other.** The Gun Teams are separated and become part of a new squad called the Weapons Squad. Weapons Squad is controlled by platoon leadership.

Gun Team is behind (i.e., trailing) the first squad, the second Gun Team is ahead of (i.e., leading) the second squad, and the third Gun Team is ahead of the third squad.[1]

6.d Detecting the Enemy (SLLS)

An area is as dangerous as the length of time that a patrol stays there. When a patrol is moving, no area is particularly dangerous because the patrol comes and goes relatively quickly. **But when the patrol stops in one area, that area can become very dangerous.** A nearby enemy has extra time to identify, report, or attack the stationary Soldiers. Therefore, every time an element stops, the Leader signals for an SLLS detection. During **SLLS**, the element:

Stops – all movement, in complete silence.

Looks – for enemy movement or anything out of place.

Listens – to the environment. The absence of sound can also be informative.

Smells – for the 5 Fs (Food, Fuel, Fire, Feces, and Freshly turned-up soil).

When stopping, SLLS lasts for as long as the Leader deems necessary (typically three to five minutes). More dangerous situations, like when you are nearing the objective, needs a longer SLLS. Extreme silence is necessary, and creaking rucks must be silent to properly listen.

Conducting SLLS prevents the patrol from accidentally bumping into an enemy. Also, if the patrol is being tracked, there is a possibility that the enemy tracker will walk straight into the SLLS element. Once complete, confirm suspicions with general questions to other Soldiers. For example: "Did you smell anything?" instead of, "Did you smell smoke?" This avoids putting ideas in their heads.

If something suspicious is detected, it must be investigated. And if a threat is discovered, the patrol must either move or engage the enemy. The patrol cannot ignore the threat.

SLLS can be quieter by putting the patrol in the prone with a ruck on one shoulder. For a platoon, it does not take much longer to lay down, and the reduction in noise is valuable. Rocking while on a knee causes rucks to creak, and this greatly reduces the effectiveness of SLLS (especially for young troops, foreign troops, or very heavy rucks). (See Image 23, Pg. 48.)

---

1   Applying Concepts: When might other combinations be useful, like Trail, Trail, Lead, or Trail, Trail, Trail?

Phase 1

Image 23: Marines with A Co., 1st Recon Bn., 1st Marine Div. conduct SLLS during reconnaissance and surveillance training. Bellows, HI, 19 Nov 2015. These Marines sit. Compared to kneeling, this position is harder to move from if there is a threat, and has lower line of sight. But sitting reduces noise and increases comfort. **How does sitting compare to the prone? Is the size of the ruck a factor in kneeling or sitting?**

6.e Short/Security-Halt Formation[1]

A short-halt is a temporary stop of less than five minutes.[2] It is typically used for a map check. However, it can also be used to indicate a new danger, like the discovery of an unknown road ahead. **Therefore, anyone can call a short-halt.**

When the Squad Leader or higher calls a short-halt, the Alpha and Bravo Team Leaders come to them. When a Team Leader or lower calls a short-halt, they can either pull on their shirt neck to signal the Squad Leader to come to them, or a Team Leader can go directly to the Squad Leader.

When a short-halt is called, the formation compresses. (I.e., a team does not stop moving forward until it is close to the team ahead of it.) When

---

1 **Quote:** Infantry must move forward to close with the enemy. It must shoot in order to move... To halt under fire is folly. To halt under fire and not fire back is suicide. —U.S. Army Gen. George S. Patton

2 **Real World:** Leaders often underestimate how long their halts will be. If a patrol does three halts for 15 minutes, that could be 45 minutes of short-halts with Soldiers weighed down with heavy rucks. Or it could be long-halts with Soldiers resting in the prone, pulling better quality security.

Short-Halt Formation

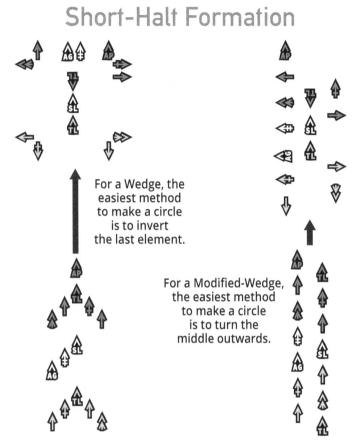

For a Wedge, the easiest method to make a circle is to invert the last element.

For a Modified-Wedge, the easiest method to make a circle is to turn the middle outwards.

Image 24: This diagram shows how each movement formation changes into a rough circle for short-halts. **Circles provide better security and an open center for Leaders to meet.** But Soldiers can't move well everywhere in a giant circle, so movement formations like wedge and modified-wedge sacrifice some security for ease of movement.

the short-halt is ceased, the formation expands. (I.e., a team does not start moving until the team ahead of it is sufficiently far away.) The metric for "close" and "far" is interlocking sectors-of-fire. For example, whereas Alpha Team may halt where they are, Bravo Team does not stop until it can achieve interlocking sectors-of-fire with the Alpha Team.

A short-halt's shape is a rough circle. To form the circle, a wedge or modified-wedge only deform a little. For a wedge, the last element in movement inverts to form a reverse wedge. The modified-wedge has all

Image 25: U.S. Army Paratroopers from 2nd Bn., 503rd Inf. Reg., 173rd Airborne Bde., **halt during a live-fire exercise** as part of Exercise Rock Knight. Pocek Range, Postonja, Slovenia, 19 Jul 2017. Presumably they are in a field, and not the more secure woodline, to make practice easier.

Soldiers in the middle pull security to the side, and Soldiers in the rear pull security to the rear. (See Image 24, Pg. 49.) (See Image 25, Pg. 50.)

During a short-halt formation, every Soldier takes a knee behind cover and concealment with rucksack on, weapon at the ready, and pulls security. (No Soldier simply takes a knee wherever they are without looking for good cover and concealment within a reasonable distance.)

At all halts the Patrol Leader immediately decides where to emplace the M240 Gun Team(s) based on the enemy's most likely avenue of approach, the enemy's most probable course of action and METT-TC analysis (Mission, Enemy, Terrain/Weather, Troops Available, Time, Civilians (i.e., anything else you can think of)). The usual answer is the 12 o'clock, because where the patrol plans on going is the greatest unknown.

When halted, the Lead Team or Lead Squad is responsible for 180-degree security ahead; and the trailing element covers 180-degree security behind. In a short-halt for larger elements, Soldiers on the side cover side security. As a wedge roughly maintains its shape, Soldiers in the center may not have

Image 26: U.S. Paratroopers, from HQ Co., 2nd Bn., 503rd Inf. Reg., 173rd Airborne Bde., **short-halt**. Grafenwoehr Training Area, Germany, 28 Jan 2017. The M240 is pointed towards the enemy's likely avenue of approach. Only the Gun Team has taken rucks off, since **belt-fed weapons cannot fire effectively when kneeling**.

sectors-of-fire. **The Team Leaders' priority is setting sectors-of-fire and ensuring their Soldiers are ready to move.**

If travel to the destination goes perfectly, then no short-halts are necessary, because a short-halt is used as a corrective tool. However, if there is limited visibility, a Leader may consider frequent short-halts to conduct SLLS.

6.f Initial Location after Exiting Vehicles (Initial Rally-Point)

The initial rally-point (IRP), as its name suggests, is the first emergency location that the platoon moves to after vehicle drop-off (VDO). It is a preplanned location and is used to orient initial movement, or as the first emergency meetup location if the patrol takes contact on infil (i.e., infiltration of enemy territory). The path from the VDO to the IRP's is typically perpendicular to the road, to move the patrol off the road as fast as possible.

The IRP is roughly chosen during planning, and is out of sight, sound, and small-arms fire from the VDO (as far or close as that may be). Always plan an alternate IRP that is in roughly the opposite direction from the primary IRP, and also a helicopter landing zone (HLZ) or ambulance exchange point (AXP) for any casualties sustained on infil.

At the IRP, the patrol consolidates and conducts SLLS to check whether it has been compromised. Headquarters performs a map check to verify that the drop-off point was as planned. The RTO calls in the spare-report for "infil complete." (See Spare-Report, Pg. 242.) From the IRP, the patrol moves out to a good long-halt position to prepare the ambush location. (See Creating the Long-Halt, Pg. 123.)

7. Crossing a Road or Draw (Linear Danger Area)[1]

A Linear Danger Area (LDA) is an area that is vulnerable to enemy observation or fire from the flanks. An LDA can have no cover, or it can have a large amount of cover. Examples of LDA's include roads, trails, rivers, and draws. Rivers and draws are LDA's because they slow the patrol to where the patrol cannot effectively respond during a crossing. (See Image 28, Pg. 53.)

A patrol almost never encounters LDA's perfectly perpendicularly. Therefore importantly, every Leader must know the orientation of the danger area they are about to cross so that they can orient their formation correctly.

7.a Choosing a Crossing Location

The location for crossing an LDA on a map is planned out beforehand. However, the patrol may come across LDA's that are unmapped or uncrossable. In these cases, the Alpha Point signals to the Patrol Leader that they need to choose a new crossing location. The Patrol Leader's decision is then signaled to and echoed throughout the formation.

When looking for a crossing point, look for a location that provides the best vantage points for security positions, and the least chance of being

---

1 **Applying Concepts:** This section focuses on how to cross a straight road. But LDA's can become complicated. How would you cross two back-to-back LDA's? How about a trench?

Image 27: Marines with K Co., 3rd Bn., 4th Marine Reg. Big Bear Lake, CA, 8 Sep 2016. This is not a "danger area" per se. However, **the lack of cover and concealment still require increased caution**.

Image 28: This danger area is NOT a linear danger area. Visibility of friendly elements is the same both on and off the road. The muddy, leafy trail also indicate this is not used as a high-speed avenue of approach.

detected by the enemy.[1] The closest location is not always the best location. Some examples of **good terrain features** that reduce enemy detection are:

► between two bends in the road (i.e., a bump in the road),

► low-lying areas,

► below the military crest of a hill, and

► areas with cover and concealment close to the LDA.

Poor terrain features to cross are at:

► road/trail intersections,

► hilltops,

► or any area that does not provide cover and concealment.

The Patrol Leader must also consider the far-side of the LDA to ensure it has adequate cover and concealment and unrestrictive terrain, so the patrol can continue movement after crossing.

7.b Choosing How to Cross

If the LDA was planned for, the crossing method is also preplanned. The Alpha Point or Alpha Team Leader can immediately act and signal for whichever plan was made, whether it be a deliberate crossing (explained below) or a clandestine crossing using either fire-team blast or scroll to the road. However, the Alpha Point of a patrol often encounters an unplanned LDA and needs further guidance on how to cross.

1 Quote: We will either find a way, or make one. —General Commander-in-Chief of the Carthaginian Army Hannibal Barca, when his generals told him it was impossible to cross the Alps by elephant.

For unplanned crossings, the Alpha Point signals their Team Leader, who initiates a short-halt. For a squad patrol, the Alpha Team Leader signals the Squad Leader, who assesses the situation and returns a signal for blast, scroll, or deliberate formation (all of which must have distinct hand and arm signals). For a platoon, the Squad Leader signals the Platoon Leader and waits for their decision.

Once the Patrol Leader is made aware of the unplanned LDA, they move to the position of the Alpha Point and views the LDA to carefully to inform their decision. However, that can take too much time: a short-halt near an unexpected LDA can be cumbersome and dangerous. Because of this, leadership often delegates the decision-making power to a subordinate Leader (e.g., the 1st Squad Leader for a platoon). When a subordinate Leader receives decision-making authorization, that does mean they cannot consult higher ups; they just do not need to.

7.c Blast Formation

A blast is a simple adjustment to the wedge formation, designed to make LDA crossings a little safer. As each team approaches the LDA in wedge formation, it straightens out from a wedge into a line. Once the line crosses the LDA, each team reverts back to a wedge shape. (See Image 29, Pg. 55.)

The logic is to have all Soldiers in a team cross at the same time. Not only does this decrease the time that Soldiers are present on the road, it also prohibits enemy fighters (who may have seen the crossing) from counting the number of Soldiers that crossed the road. While a team is on line and in the LDA, the Soldiers on either edge of the line point their weapons down the danger zone. The middle Soldiers of each element orient their weapons to the far-side as they cross.

If leadership decides to do a blast, the deciding Leader passes the hand and arm signal to everyone. The Alpha Point at the head of the formation stops in their tracks and waits for the first element to approach them until they are on line. As each wedge approaches the LDA, the wedge's Leader half-steps until their element is on line with them.

After crossing, the Alpha Point and Team Leaders must speed to the front to recreate the wedge. Similarly, the ends of the line half-step. Also, all elements must cross at a consistent speed relative to each other. Cross too

Blast Formation

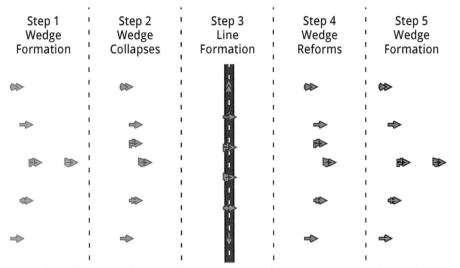

Image 29: Blasting is when an element in wedge formation crosses a linear danger area as a line without stopping movement. **Note that the two outside Soldiers are pulling security down the road when crossing.** In a formation with many wedges, each wedge blasts separately.

---

fast and an element can break contact with the element behind; too slow, and there can be a split element ahead.

7.d Bumping/Scrolling Formation

Bumping is an expedited way to cross an LDA when moving in a modified-wedge. The basic idea behind any bumping formation is to have a Soldier from each column run up to the LDA to pull security down both sides of the road. The column continues to advance and the next Soldier in the column comes up to the Soldier pulling security, and bumps or taps them. This bump indicates a change in guard; the next Soldier now pulls security; and the Soldier who was pulling security now crosses the LDA. (See Image 30, Pg. 56.)

Bumping an LDA is more secure than blasting because there is always stationary security. However, it is less secure than a deliberate crossing because the main purpose of security in bumping is to provide firepower. (See Deliberate Formation, Pg. 57.) Unlike deliberate, they cannot provide early warning because they are too close to the Main Body.

Bumping/Scrolling Formation

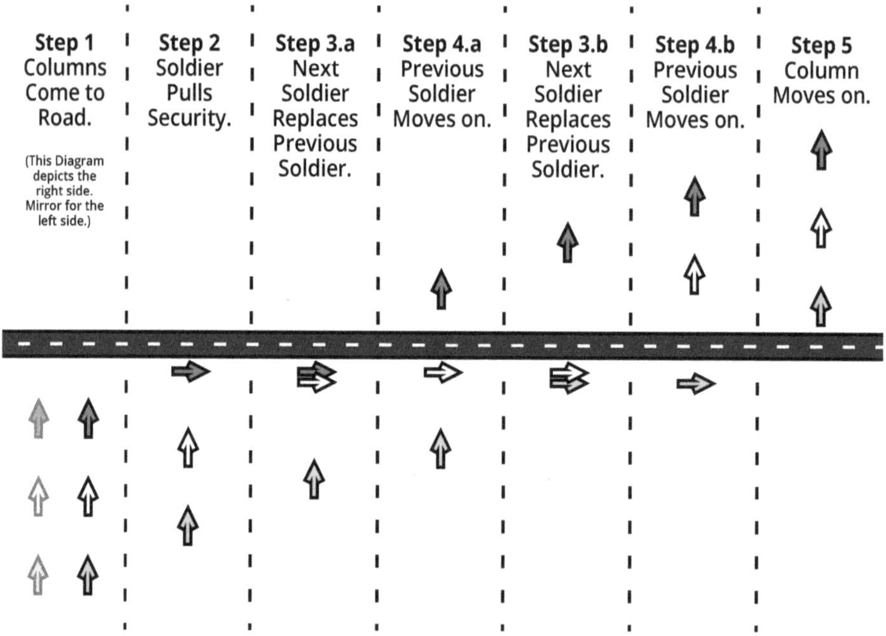

Phase 1

Step 1 Columns Come to Road.	Step 2 Soldier Pulls Security.	Step 3.a Next Soldier Replaces Previous Soldier.	Step 4.a Previous Soldier Moves on.	Step 3.b Next Soldier Replaces Previous Soldier.	Step 4.b Previous Soldier Moves on.	Step 5 Column Moves on.

(This Diagram depicts the right side. Mirror for the left side.)

Image 30: Here, one side of a modified-wedge executes a bump to cross an LDA. Notice that **there is always a Soldier pulling security down the road** while other Soldiers cross the road. Although steps 2 through 5 depict only the right column, the left column mirrors the same steps facing the opposite direction. Steps 3 and 4 repeat until every Soldier has pulled security and crossed the road. **If there is only one column,** then the first Soldier to cross turns around and points their weapon down the road in the opposite direction as they cross for security in both directions. They then stop on the far side on the road to create a second security position. Then all Soldiers bump on both the near and the far side of the road.

Bumping also can be used in a wedge formation. The leftmost and rightmost Soldiers in each wedge sprint ahead before their respective wedge nears the road. At the same time, the patrol slows down and each wedge forms a line as it crosses the LDA between the two Soldiers pulling security (just like in a blast). On both sides, the Soldier pulling security occupies that position until they are fully replaced (just like a bump), at which point they move on to the next position or movement.

Another way to use bumping when in a wedge formation is to change into a modified-wedge formation just for the LDA. Each wing of the wedge collapses inward (i.e. modifies) to form two columns (i.e. a modified-wedge). This LDA crossing is easier to coordinate, because every Soldier only coordinates with the Soldier they replace and the one replacing them, and not a line of Soldiers passing between them.

7.e Deliberate Formation

The safest and slowest method for crossing an LDA is the "deliberate" crossing.[1] Unlike blast, which has local rolling security, and bumping which has local stationary security, deliberate pushes out remote stationary security.

The purpose of pushing out security is to afford early warning of the enemy, so that the patrol has enough time to hide and take cover. If pushing out security to a nearby hill would afford ten seconds of warning, but taking cover requires more than ten seconds, then do not push out security there.

Similarly, the Security Teams cannot provide early warning if they do not have comms with the Main Body; therefore, do not push out security without a comms PACE plan. A PACE (Primary, Alternate, Contingency, Emergency) is a contingency plan in case one method fails. This prevents a mission from depending on, for example, a single radio. (See Communication, Pg. 242.)

Before and after being pushed out, Security does a comms check to make sure that an early warning can be sent. If comms cannot be made, they either need to move or return.

To improve comms, consider using Relay Teams halfway between the Main Body and Security to pass back visual signals. A Relay Team has two Soldiers, each facing opposite directions towards different elements. When a message is sent from one element, the man who see it informs their partner, who then relays that message to the other element. A binary message of "danger" and "no danger" is easy to send.

Security comes from the second team in a squad in order of movement, or the second squad from a platoon. The second team or squad provides security instead of the last element for two reasons: 1) they need to travel less to arrive at a security position; 2) Security becomes the last element when regrouping,

---

[1] A deliberate crossing can actually increase danger by keeping a patrol beside a danger area. And squads are small enough that they can cross quickly and quietly. Therefore, squads only really use a deliberate crossing for major hard roads, whereas larger elements might use a deliberate crossing more frequently. How small must a patrol be before splitting the element to recon the far side becomes impractical?

Phase 1

LDA Deliberate Crossing Part 1, Setup

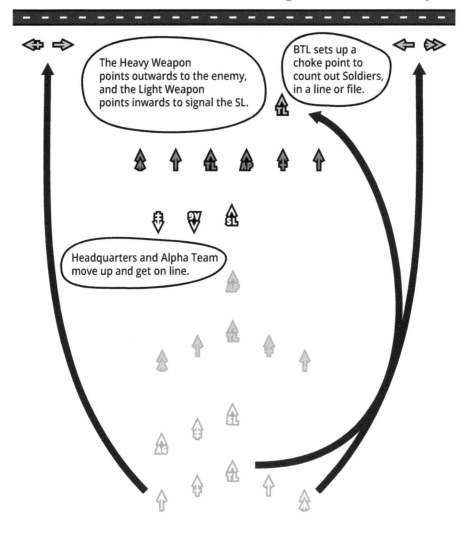

The Heavy Weapon points outwards to the enemy, and the Light Weapon points inwards to signal the SL.

BTL sets up a choke point to count out Soldiers, in a line or file.

Headquarters and Alpha Team move up and get on line.

Phase 1

Image 31: As the patrol prepares to cross an LDA, all the elements move simultaneously. The first priority is security; Bravo Team pulls security on the road. Alpha Team prepares to recon the opposite side, and Headquarters waits for Alpha Team to report on the recon. **At night Soldiers must pass through the chokepoint in a file.** They can either cross the road in a file, or reform a line just before crossing. During the day, if the chokepoint Leader can clearly identify each individual Soldier, then SOP can be to stay in a line and count each Soldier by sight.

LDA Deliberate Crossing Part 2, Recon

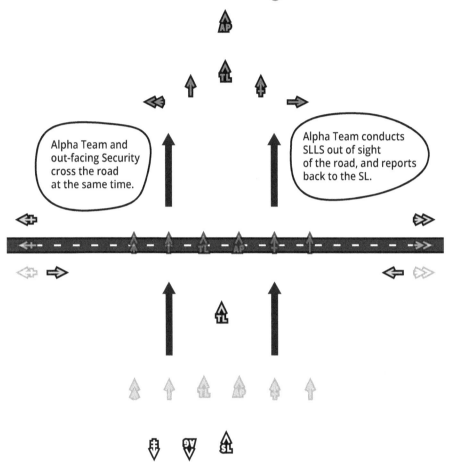

Alpha Team and out-facing Security cross the road at the same time.

Alpha Team conducts SLLS out of sight of the road, and reports back to the SL.

Phase 1

Image 32: Before the entire element crosses to the other side, **a smaller element crosses to conduct reconnaissance**. The opposite side of an LDA is an unknown, so the Main Body stays in place to enable a hasty retreat for the recon element. When recon crosses, so does out-facing Security to minimize the number of crossings.

LDA Deliberate Crossing Part 3, Cross

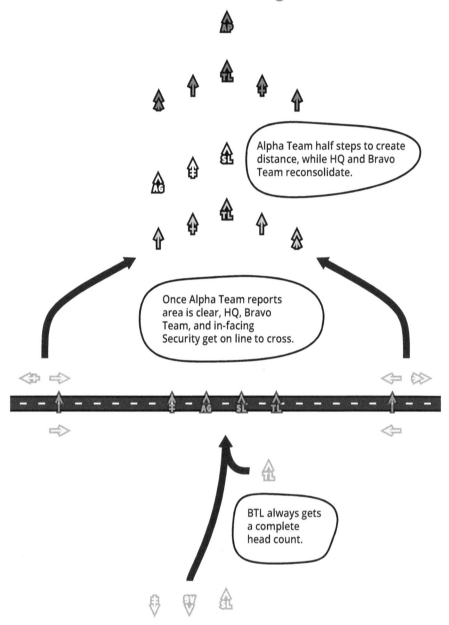

Phase 1

Alpha Team half steps to create distance, while HQ and Bravo Team reconsolidate.

Once Alpha Team reports area is clear, HQ, Bravo Team, and in-facing Security get on line to cross.

BTL always gets a complete head count.

Image 33: When the recon element declares the other side is safe, the main body may cross. To minimize the number of crossings, all the remaining Soldiers cross in one line. For a platoon, each element will cross one by one.

Image 34: Marines with 2nd Plt., FAST Company Europe (FASTEUR) conduct an LDA crossing during a patrolling exercise conducted. Naval Station Rota, Spain, 10 Nov 2016. **Soldiers are pulling security down both sides of the road.** For what reasons might the Soldiers on the side of the road be pulling security there, rather than back in the brush?

allowing them a little bit of rest after traveling. If the Patrol Leader deems it necessary, they can assign Gun Teams to each Security Team.

If the Patrol Leader decides to cross the LDA deliberately, **first the patrol conducts SLLS to determine how heavily the road is trafficked.** Then the first Team Leader or Squad Leader designates a near- and far-side rally-point. Everybody is informed of the orientation of the LDA, because crossing a curved or diagonal road is very disorienting.

The Security Teams converge on their Leader, and the Leader sends out at least two Soldiers each to right and left security positions. Once in place, each side of Security has at least one Soldier looking down the LDA, ready to shoot, with the other Soldier facing in to communicate with the Leaders. The remaining Soldiers provide rear security to the formation. Maintaining 360-degree security is very important. (See Image 31, Pg. 58.)

When Security sends the signal for "no danger," the Bravo Team Leader or Platoon Sergeant counts out the first element to cross (Alpha Team, or 1st Squad). On the Security Teams, the Soldiers facing inward also cross at the same time. Once on the far-side, the Solders face out, while the Soldiers on the near-side turn inward so they can cross with the second wave. (See Image 32, Pg. 59.)

Once on the far-side, the first element reforms into a wedge and clears the far-side. "Clearing" means to make sure an area is safe. They push out far enough so that the entire patrol can fit behind them. When far enough, the element conducts SLLS. If a Soldier detects something, the Leader sends back a signal for "danger" to the Main Body. If nothing is detected, the Leader can signal "no danger" using their PACE plan. During the night, the PACE plan is different.[1]

After "no danger" is received, the remaining Soldiers on the near-side cross. In a squad, all the remaining Soldiers (Headquarters, Bravo Team Leader, Rear Security, etc.) cross on a line. In a platoon, the number of waves is minimized. The clearing element starts half-stepping in the direction of travel until all Soldiers in the patrol reform into a wedge. Again, the Bravo Team Leader or Platoon Sergeant count all Soldiers using a chokepoint. Once every Soldier is accounted for, the LDA has been successfully crossed.[2] (See Image 33, Pg. 60.)

7.f Draw Crossing Formation

Draws crossings are very slow, and so Soldiers entering the draw at a normal speed end up in long "nut to butt" files. **Bunching is very bad** because it creates a perfect target for an enemy to come from behind and shoot every Soldier like ducks in a row. Therefore, it is important for an element to only cross a draw when the previous element has left enough space to begin crossing. (See Image 35, Pg. 63.)

While waiting to cross, the elements behind form a short-halt and face backward to provide security. On the other side, the first elements to finish crossing take a short-halt, or half-step, while they wait for the remaining elements to cross.

7.g Actions on Detection

If a potential threat is detected by Security, they alert the Main Body. Both Soldiers in the security positions have their bodies touching so they can use

---

1 Applying Concepts: To "visually clear" the far-side, means to look across the LDA and determine it is safe, instead of sending out a single element to conduct SLLS. Why would you choose to, and when might it be possible to, visually clear the far-side?

2 Applying Concepts: What kind of leapfrogging formation could be used when two LDA's are back-to-back, such that there is not enough space to reform into a wedge between the two LDA's?

Image 35: Guatemalan Army Special Forces Soldiers or "Kaibiles" lead a jungle patrol exercise for U.S. Marines. Poptun, Guatemala, 11 Sep 2010. This is a **situation where a file may be used,** because a wedge or even multiple columns may be impossible to effectively command and control. Note how close together the Soldiers are, despite having room to spread.

the tap code to communicate while remaining silent. For example, a Soldier gives one tap to their buddy if everything is okay. The other Soldier responds with one tap if everything is OK with them. A Soldier gives two taps if they see or hear something. Three taps mean that a Soldier sees or hears the enemy and the element needs to take action. In this case, Security needs to get into the prone position immediately.

Every Soldier when crossing an LDA pays attention to either the Security or a Leader who has eyes on Security. All leadership stands ready to signal that there is an unknown approaching. If danger is detected, and the leadership sees that Security has gone prone, they must make every Soldier seek immediate concealment and consider potential lines-of-fire. Lines-of-fire during LDA crossing are especially dangerous because the enemy path runs through the element.

If an enemy drives down the LDA road and stops in the middle of the patrol, the patrol cannot open fire because of friendly-fire concerns. Therefore, sectors-of-fire must be carefully chosen and distributed.

7.h Enemy Attack During LDA Crossing

If an enemy attacks during a draw crossing, the patrol defaults to a regular react-to-contact, just like any other attack. (See The Enemy Shoots at Joe (Battle Drill 2), Pg. 71.) This is true whether the enemy attacks the vanguard recon element across the road, or rear security.

However, LDA's present a special case that is different from most enemy attacks. When only part of the patrol is across the road, the enemy can drive a vehicle into the middle of the patrol, splitting it in half. If there is an enemy in the middle of the patrol, Soldiers cannot effectively fire at the enemy because it risks friendly fire against troops on the other side of the enemy. To remove the enemy from the center of the patrol, and open lanes-of-fire, **the Patrol Leader must order an element to shift left or right**. When that element moves to the side, the other element is free to fire at the enemy without hitting any friendly troops on the opposite side. From there, the patrol reacts to contact the same way as a normal attack. (See Image 36, Pg. 65.)

8. Crossing a Field (Open Danger Area)

An Open Danger Area (ODA) does not strictly refer to open fields, but rather it is an area that does not have concealment. **Whether an area lacks concealment depends on enemy capability.** If the enemy has no air assets, then overhead concealment is irrelevant. Conversely, if an enemy only has air assets, then ground concealment is irrelevant.

An ODA is different from a Linear Danger Area in that there is additional vulnerability in front of the formation. Although there are no hard distances that define "open areas," if bounding can provide significant, additional security, the danger area can be considered "open." (See Image 37, Pg. 66.)

Enemy Attack During LDA Crossing

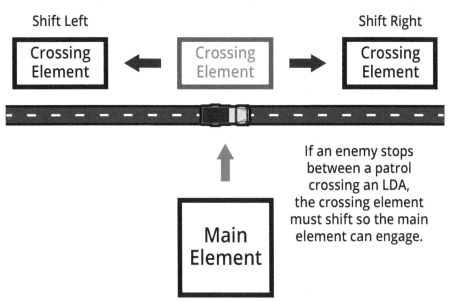

Image 36: LDA crossing with an enemy between elements. An enemy that drives into the middle of a patrol can paralyze the patrol. **If a friendly unit opens fire, it risks hitting Soldiers on the opposite side of the enemy.**

8.a Directly Crossing the Area (Bounding)

Remember: the purpose of this manual is to teach you how to conduct an ambush, not how to demonstrate a show of force. Travel is hidden and well defended. Patrols avoid crossing ODA's because, **by their very nature, they hinder a patrol's ability to hide and defend**. An ODA is only crossed is if it meets both these criteria:

1) It did not appear on the maps during planning (i.e., it was unplanned).

2) It cannot be circumvented without missing the mission deadline.

If an ODA is going to be crossed, then bounding is used. Bounding is a form of movement in which one element moves while the other remains stationary. The patrol first splits into two elements (either teams or squads). The largest weapons and leadership converge on the center to direct the formation. Then, the Patrol Leader decides whether they want to do successive bounding or alternating bounding. (See Image 40, Pg. 67.)

Image 37: U.S. Army Paratroopers with the 173rd Airborne Bde. move to the woodline after an air assault (i.e. a helicopter infil). Hohenfels, Germany, 26 Sep 2019. This is a classic **open danger area**. Note how exposed the Soldiers are.

Image 38: An Equipment Operator 2nd Class from NMCB 3 operates a road grader. Fort Hunter Liggett, CA, 09 Nov 2019. **A linear danger area through an open danger area is still an ODA.** Don't stop in a field to do an LDA crossing.

In **successive bounding**, the lead element takes a knee and pulls security, while the rear element moves forward to stop on line with (not passing) the lead element. Then, the lead element moves forward. Once both elements have moved, the rear element moves on line again, continuing the cycle.

In **alternating bounding**, again the rear element moves first. It moves past the lead element, swapping positions. The rear element becomes the new lead element, stops moving, and pulls security. The new rear element starts moving, and the process alternates, as there is always one moving and one set element.

When bounding, the M240s (the most casualty-producing weapon in a patrol) pulls security for the forwardmost element. For this reason, in alternating bounding, when the rear element passes the lead element, the Gun Team and Headquarters break off to join it (i.e., the new rear element). **Therefore, alternating bounding is not favored when there is a Gun Team,** because it is difficult for the Gun Team to switch and link in ammo twice as often as with successive bounding. Alternating is preferred when there is no Gun Team and ground must be covered quickly, like with an assault. (See Assaulting the Objective, Pg. 197.)

Bounding requires simple commands by both elements. When the bounding element starts moving they yell, "Moving!" When they stop moving, only after they are set and ready to fire, they yell, "Set!" This restarts the cycle, letting the other team bound and yell, "Moving!"

Image 39: Burkina Faso Soldiers bound during Flintlock 2017. Camp Zagre, Burkina Faso, 01 Mar 2017. The team in the background is set and supporting while the team in the foreground is bounding. **Note the bounding Leader is behind the Assault Line because the line is large.**

Bounding

Successive Bounding

The trail element and HQ get on line.
Then the lead element advances.

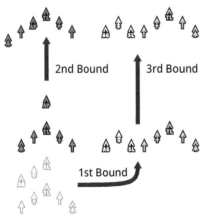

Alternating Bounding

Teams bound past each other.
HQ always bounds to the trail element.

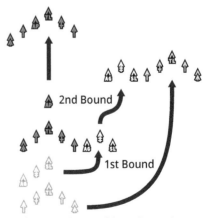

Image 40: Fire-team bounding. Note that this diagram has Soldiers bounding in a wedge formation, with the Team Leader on line. Soldiers bounding on a line with the Team Leader behind the line is also acceptable. (See Image 39, Pg. 67.)

8.b Going around the Area

There are two common methods for going around an ODA: the contour method, and the box method. (See Image 41, Pg. 69.) In the contour method, the Patrol Leader selects an identifiable point on the far-side. The patrol then moves around the border of the ODA to that identifiable point, while remaining in concealed terrain. Once at the identifiable point, the patrol moves out at normal speed on azimuth.

The box method uses four 90-degree turns to make a box around the ODA. If the Patrol Leader chooses to use the box method, they tell the Team Leader doing land navigation to turn 90 degrees to the left or right and start a second, separate pace count for the lateral movement. The patrol moves laterally until it has passed the danger area. There, the patrol returns to the original azimuth until the patrol passes the danger area again. Once past the danger area on the far-side, the patrol turns 90 degrees in the opposite direction from the first turn, left or right, and counts down the lateral pace count. When the lateral pace count reaches zero, the patrol turns 90 degrees to return to the original azimuth.

ODA Crossing

Image 41: Two methods of bypassing an ODA. The boxing method uses a compass and a map to navigate, while the contour method uses eyesight and reference points. They are both effective.

Phase 2 Contents

9. The Enemy Shoots at Joe (Battle Drill 2) — 71

Individual Soldiers React-to-Contact — 72
Individual Movement Techniques (IMT) — 73
Contact Element Reacts to Contact — 74
Headquarters Reacts to Contact — 76
Far Element Reacts to Contact — 79

10. Joe Returns Fire (Battle Drills 1, 3, and 4) — 80

Assaulting a Location (Battle Drill 4) — 80
Bold-flank Maneuver (Battle Drill 1) — 85
Bold-flank Variations — 92
Break-Contact (Battle Drill 3) — 93
Break-Contact Variations — 97

11. Cleaning up after Assaulting (Specialty Teams) — 99

Enemy Prisoner of War (EPW) Team — 99
Aid and Litter Team — 103
Demolition Team — 104

12. Withdrawal from Area after Assaulting — 104

13. Medical Evacuation — 106

Evacuating by Foot — 108
Evacuating by Ambulance Exchange — 110
Evacuating by Helicopter — 111

14. Fire Support — 112

Firing Artillery and Mortars (Call for Fire) — 112
Close Air Support — 114

15. Contingencies — 116

React-to-Sniper — 116
React-to-Artillery and Mortars (Indirect Fire) — 116
React-to-Mine (Improvised Explosive Device) — 118
Fixing a Split Element — 120
Reacting from a Non-Standard Formation — 120
Enemy from Multiple or Changing Locations — 121

The Enemy Sees Joe (Phase 2: React-to-Enemy Contact and Medical Evacuation)

If you're not shootin', you should be loadin'. If you're not loadin', you should be movin', if you're not movin', someone's gonna cut your head off and put it on a stick.

—*USMC Veteran, Clint Smith*

Moving from base to the ambush objective is filled with danger. The patrol is at its most tired and vulnerable, fatigued from hours of marching, and the enemy knows it. This section instructs what to do when the enemy attacks first.

9. The Enemy Shoots at Joe (Battle Drill 2[1])[2]

A "react-to-contact" drill demands many different actions from every element, which vary heavily depending on the situation. In fact, you can even shoot first! With all elements moving at one time to accomplish different tasks, every element must know all the tasks for quick and effective coordination.

If that was not complicated enough, contact from the enemy can come from any direction. So the actions that, for example, a squad takes are not assigned to Alpha and Bravo teams, but to the element taking contact (the

---

1   The numbering of the battle drills is from official U.S. Army doctrine. In this manual they are covered in a different order for easier explanation.

2   Quote: No plan survives first contact with the enemy. —German Field Marshal and Chief of Great General Staff, Helmuth von Moltke

Contact Element), and the element far from contact (the Far Element).[1] (Although this section uses squad-level imagery in the illustrations, all the information applies equally to platoon-level equivalents.)

9.a Individual Soldiers React-to-Contact[2]

The idea behind immediate action is to fire as many bullets at the enemy as soon and as safely as possible. **Every Soldier immediately and simultaneously finds cover, yells out the 3Ds (Direction, Distance, Description) and returns fire.** The Team Leaders stay in constant communication with every Soldier in their team.

The most important part of an ambush is to escape the ambush site as soon as possible to better positions. Do not let the enemy choose the battlefield. Good terrain has cover, concealment, and lines-of-fire; allows for easy communication; and can be as simple as a berm or ditch. However, finding good terrain can be more difficult than it might first appear. A 7.62 round can easily penetrate a thick tree, and an AK-47 can penetrate a brick wall. A smart enemy puts mines in the best cover positions, and then takes pot shots to provoke Soldiers into those mines. In a densely vegetated area there may be a lot of concealment; however, if the enemy cannot see you at all, you might not see them, meaning no lines-of-fire. Outside the engine block, regular vehicles provide no cover whatsoever. **Before patrolling, it is critical to know what constitutes good cover and concealment for the patrolled area.**

Direction, distance, and description are in order of importance. In the heat of a fight, it can be difficult to locate an enemy, so direction and distance are first. An unlocated enemy is worse than an undescribed enemy. In fact, throughout every part of this section, leadership has to make damn

---

1 **Applying Concepts:** While reading this section, imagine what orders a Squad Leader might give to a Charlie Team, if there was one. Not all squads are limited to an Alpha and Bravo Team. How could the Patrol Leader position a Charlie Team to be in reserve in case of a second enemy attack? How about stopping enemy retreat if the enemy is known for hit and run tactics?

2 **Real World:** The two most vital stress-inoculations that need practiced are when the enemy opens fire and no one wants to move, and when cover is found and no one wants to move.

Image 42: 2nd Iraqi Army Div. **Iraqi Army Soldiers take cover behind a hill** during an ambush training class taught by U.S. Army 2nd Div. Military Transition Team. Mosul, Iraq, 27 Nov 2017.

sure that their Soldiers have located what they are shooting at, or else give them something to shoot at by marking targets. Every member of the squad echoes the 3Ds to ensure the Squad Leader has the best information for their assessment of the situation.[1]

When a Leader gives instructions to fire to a Soldier, it follows a standardized fire command format for clarity. For example:[2]

Alert – Alert to grab attention and assign firing.

3Ds – Direction, distance, and description of target.

Rate-of-Fire – "Cyclic," "rapid," or "sustained."

Command – Fire command. To fire at once yell, "Fire!"

9.b Individual Movement Techniques (IMT)

When under enemy fire, it is a bad idea to run full speed toward the enemy; you become an easy target. Instead, use a three-to-five-second rush, high-crawl, or low-crawl.

---

1 **Example** 3Ds:

RFL –   "12 o'clock, 50 meters, 3 enemy small arms."

2 **Example** Fire Command:

SL –   "Saw Gunner, 12 o'clock, 50 meters, 3 enemy, Rapid, At my command."

Getting up, running, and dropping is called a "**rush**." Always rush under supporting fire from another element, and always rush from one cover to another cover. Make sure you know where you plan on rushing to!

Three to five seconds is about how long it takes an enemy to put crosshairs on a Soldier, which is why it is a good idea to drop to the ground before then. (Three to five seconds is often approximated by mentally repeating: "I'm up! They see me! I'm down!") Whether moving as an individual, or alternating rushes with another element, keep movements within that time frame. (The longer distance equivalent of a rush is a bound.) (See Directly Crossing the Area (Bounding), Pg. 65.)

In a **high-crawl**, the head is forward and the pelvis almost touches the ground. Swing your hips back and forth to move. A Soldier holds their rifle in the crux of both elbows. (See Image 44, Pg. 75.) Many people confuse a high-crawl with a low-crawl, because the hips are so low. But the defining difference is that a high-crawl still barely allows a Soldier to look forward.

A true **low-crawl** is much more uncomfortable, and has both the side of the face and pelvis touching the ground while one arm and leg are used to physically pull the body forward. Under enemy fire, crawling is only really useful for getting to better cover, because it's really slow. (However, a low profile is very useful for other operations that require a small presence, like setting in an ambush line.) (See Image 46, Pg. 75.)

9.c Contact Element Reacts to Contact[1]

Aside from their individual actions, the Contact Leader's first priority is coordinating their team and forming a line. **Soldiers not on the front line often cannot shoot at the enemy because of the risk of friendly fire.** On the line, each Soldier focuses down their own line of sight and ignores enemies already engaged to their sides. Otherwise, if all Soldiers focus fire on the first enemy to appear, then enemies that appear later from other directions will go unnoticed.

---

1 Quote: Make your attacker advance through a wall of bullets. I may get killed with my own gun, but he's gonna have to beat me to death with it, cause it's gonna be empty. —USMC Veteran, Clint Smith

Image 43: NJ Army N.G. Soldiers, C Co., 1st Bn., 114th Inf., conduct **three-to-five-second rushes**. Base McGuire-Dix-Lakehurst, NJ, 09 Apr 2018.

Image 44: A recruit with Golf Co., 2nd Recruit Training Bn., **high-crawls**. Marine Corps Camp Pendleton, CA, 30 Aug 2019.

Image 45: An A Co., 1-26 Inf., 101st Airborne Div., Soldier. Ethiopia, 26 Jun 2019. **The profile is too high to be a proper high-crawl.**

Image 46: Recruits with H Co., 2nd Recruit Training Bn., **low-crawl** during the Crucible. Marine Corps Recruit Depot Parris Island, SC, 09 Jan 2020.

The Contact Leader's second priority is to give Soldiers roughly interlocking sectors-of-fire. A good idea is to position Team Leaders slightly behind their team to be able to effectively direct their team while communicating with the Squad Leader. (See Image 48, Pg. 78.)

Soldiers can drop rucks if the rucks are inhibiting their fighting ability; however, when breaking contact is an option, the element must wait for direction from a Leader on whether to drop rucks. During a break-contact, the Contact Element retreats with their rucks, so taking them off and on wastes too much time.

9.d Headquarters Reacts to Contact[1]

Overall, during react-to-contact, Headquarters is occupied with assessing the threat and coordinating troops. First, the Patrol Leader must ensure that their Contact Leader has a good base-of-fire. Then they either confer with the Contact Leader on what is ahead, or make a decision independently of a conference. (See Image 48, Pg. 78.)

As soon as is appropriate, the Patrol Leader must make two choices and inform the entire patrol:

▶ What battle drill to use (e.g., bold-flank, peel, break-contact, assault through, etc.).

▶ What direction (left or right) to perform the battle drill.

Every Soldier in the squad echoes this command (and all other commands) to make the order louder and confirm their own understanding.

All battle drills and directions are encoded during planning. For example, a typical code word for break-contact is "red," and a code word for flank is "green." A code word for going left is "California," and a code word for right is "New York." So to signal a flank on the right, the Squad Leader would shout, "Green New York!" This prevents an enemy who knows English from understanding the plan as it is shouted across the battle.

Next, the Patrol Leader emplaces the Gun Team(s) on the side of the Contact Element that they have chosen to maneuver on. This consists of

---

1 Quote: I am more afraid of an army of 100 sheep led by a lion than an army of 100 lions led by a sheep. —French Minister of Foreign Affairs, Charles Maurice de Talleyrand

Phase 2

Image 47: U.S. Marine Corps 1st Lt. Plt. Commander assigned to C Co., 1st Bn., 3rd Marine Reg., communicates with his platoon while taking simulated fire during Korean Marine Exchange Program 17-14. North West Islands, Republic of Korea, 11 Aug 2017. **Be very, very loud!**

giving a sector-of-fire (i.e., designating a left limit, right limit, and primary direction-of-fire), a rate-of-fire,[1] and engagement criteria.

The Patrol Leader will soon leave the Gun Team(s), so they must purposefully transfer control of the team to another Leader (e.g. Contact Leader, Weapons Squad Leader, etc.). The Patrol Leader may give orders to the Gun Team(s) first and then run to the Contact Leader. Or it may be standard operating procedure (SOP) for a Team Leader to run to the Gun Team position. Whenever giving instructions to anyone, always receive a backbrief to confirm understanding. Finally, the Patrol Leader leaves to go to the Far Element.

---

[1] Rate-of-fire is critical information. If a Gun Team is carrying 2,400 rounds (160lbs.) for the mission, and a M240 fires 900 rounds per minute on a cyclic rate, then how fast will the Gun Team run out of ammunition?

React-to-Contact

Phase 2

When Patrol is Attacked

All Elements React to Contact Simultaneously

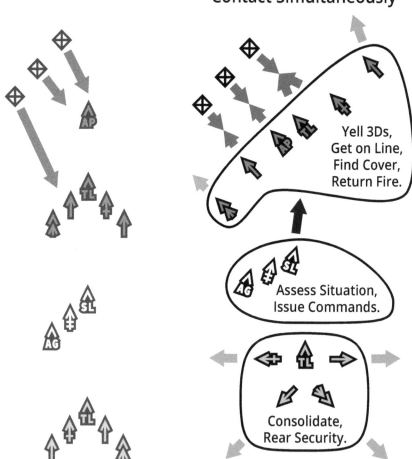

Yell 3Ds,
Get on Line,
Find Cover,
Return Fire.

Assess Situation,
Issue Commands.

Consolidate,
Rear Security.

Image 48: When a patrol is attacked, each element in a patrol has actions they must immediately react with. In short, the element in contact deals with the enemy, Headquarters assesses and controls the situation, and the element not in contact prepares to recieve instructions.

At the soonest possible time, Headquarters must send a SALUTE report to higher.[1] SALUTE's are reports on the enemy. They are distributed to other patrols, warning them of potential enemies and danger. A **SALUTE** report includes:

Size – A count of people and vehicles.

Activity – What the enemy is doing.

Location – The grid location, or else offset from key terrain.

Unit/Uniform – Features that identify the enemy.

Time– The time that the activity was seen.

Equipment – All equipment that is abnormal, military in nature, or just seems important.

From the start of enemy contact, Headquarters always considers the possibility that the enemy they see is the vanguard of a much larger force. An enemy bunker may be part of a larger defense, and an enemy cresting a hill may have a much larger force behind them. Do not overcommit.

In order to prepare for incoming reinforcements, from the beginning the RTO immediately records time. The enemy's expected reinforcement time is briefed before the patrol. A good rule of thumb is to withdraw in half that time. (See Enemy Quick Reaction Force and Harassing Ambush, Pg. 211.)

9.e Far Element Reacts to Contact

While the Contact Element is returning fire, and the Patrol Leader is emplacing the Gun Team(s), the Far Element gathers around their Leader to quickly receive instructions. Thereby, if the Patrol Leader decides to do a bold-flank, then the Far Element drops rucks around their Leader instead of randomly in the woods. Or if a break-contact is called, the Far Element keeps rucks on anyway.

---

1 **Example** SALUTE Report:

Size –	"Four PAX, dismounted."
Activity –	"Putting in IED's on Main Street."
Location –	"14WPH 8324 9183."
Unit/Uniform –	"Local militia with Al-Qaeda patches."
Time –	"Observed at 23:11 on 04 Jan 2018."
Equipment –	"Four AK-47s with possible concealed sidearms."

10. Joe Returns Fire (Battle Drills 1, 3, and 4)[1]

The first decision a Patrol Leader needs to make is to choose how to return fire. With a flank? An assault? A break-contact? **The two primary factors in deciding are the enemy's strength and distance.** An element that is too large or powerful demands a tactical retreat. For weak enemies, the second factor is distance. If the weak enemy is close, there is no time for a flank. However, an enemy that is both weak and far is best approached with a flank attack.[2] (See Image 49, Pg. 81.)

Whatever the choice, constant maneuvering Soldiers to superior positions is key. There should never be a situation where there are two stationary elements and no moving elements. The enemy certainly will be moving. Use the terrain around you to maneuver better than they do.

There should also never be two moving elements and no stationary elements. Firing while moving is very inaccurate. To suppress an enemy, fires must be accurate and frequent enough to kill or at least intimidate. A few inaccurate rounds will not suppress an engaged enemy.

10.a Assaulting a Location (Battle Drill 4)

An assault is when Soldiers get on a line and walk toward the enemy while shooting anything that moves. An assault can also use bounds. (See Directly Crossing the Area (Bounding), Pg. 65.) Assaulting is a major aspect of many drills, such as a bold-flanking maneuver where the Far Element assaults, or during an ambush where the the Assault Line assaults.

---

1 Quote: Fires without movement is a waste of ammo. Movement without fires is stupid. —Anonymous.

2 Real World: "If your attack is going too well, you're walking into an ambush." —Anonymous. If a patrol sees only two enemies firing, how likely is it that only two lone enemies decided to fire upon an entire platoon of Soldiers armed to the teeth? Using a few attackers as bait to lead the enemy into an ambush has been done for millennia.

Phase 2

React-to-Contact Decision Tree

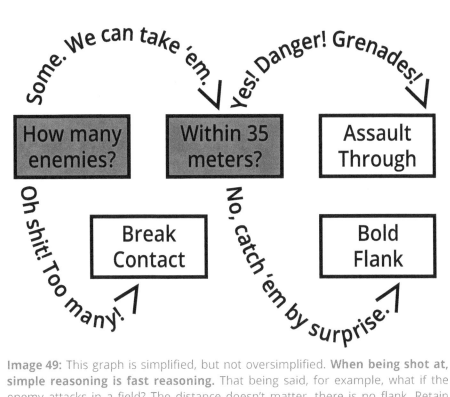

Image 49: This graph is simplified, but not oversimplified. **When being shot at, simple reasoning is fast reasoning.** That being said, for example, what if the enemy attacks in a field? The distance doesn't matter, there is no flank. Retain situational awareness.

In a near ambush (within 35 meters; i.e., hand grenade range[1]), the Contact Element assaults immediately because they are close enough that waiting for another element to flank is more dangerous than just full-on attacking. If Soldiers lack even enough time to set the machine guns, they immediately turn and fire machine guns from the hip or underarm (called "turn and burn"). (See Image 50, Pg. 82.)

---

1 Applying Concepts: 35 meters is often repeated as the distance that distinguishes a near ambush from a far ambush. This is because a standard hand grenade is limited to about 35 meters. But what if the enemy has M203 grenade launchers with 400-meter max range? Any distance is somewhat arbitrary, but a patrol needs to know when to assault or flank. What other considerations can distinguish a near and far ambush?

Image 50: A Soldier with B Co., 1st Bn., 27th Inf. Reg., 2nd Bde., Inf. Brig. Combat Team, 25th Inf. Div., lays down cover fire during a simulated near ambush. Labasa, Fiji, 1 Aug 2019. A **near ambush** is one of the few times it is appropriate to shoulder or hip fire a machine gun.

Assaults are always a line of Soldiers to maximize forward coverage, and prevent friendly fires from behind. Being "on a line" is a formation. Every Rifleman on line must know where the other Riflemen are to both coordinate movement and know the bounds of their sector-of-fire. Every Soldier has their own sector-of-fire. Do not get distracted by a firefight next to you, lest a new enemy pop out in front while you are distracted!

The pace is steady and deliberate. Do not wait to shoot; even if a target is at the end of the battlefield, the closest Rifleman must fire on the target as soon as possible. If an enemy is found, dead or alive, the closest Soldier shoots them until their face turns into mush, in the most literal sense of the word.

The Assault Leader is in the middle of their line in order to position and correct their individual Soldiers during the assault. The Assault Leader can be on the line itself, or remain slightly behind it to direct the Riflemen from behind. This depends on whether they can maintain control of their Soldiers and fire down their assault lane at the same time. (A squad with eight Soldiers probably doesn't need a Squad Leader on line.) The Assault Leader's directions may be to the line as a whole (e.g., "Pinwheel left!") or at individual Soldiers

Common Assaulting Commands

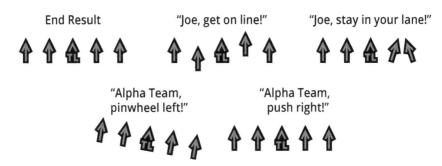

Image 51: Assaults have all Soldiers equally spaced on a line, like the top left, End Result. When Soldiers are not on one line, yell "[Names], get on line!" When Soldiers get tunnel vision and start converging, yell "[Names], stay in your lane!" To turn or shift the entire line, yell the words "[Team], pinwheel [direction]!" and "[Team], push [direction]!"

(e.g., "Jose, get on line!").[1] **People listen to specific orders and their own names better**; avoid using general commands whenever possible. (See Image 51, Pg. 83.)

Soldiers advance directly forward toward the enemy. If the Assault Leader believes there is excessive danger (such as a near ambush), they can use bounding to provide supporting fire during an advance. "**Bounding**" is when halves of an element alternate between being stationary and providing cover fire, while the other half moves. As the halves alternate, the element moves. (See Directly Crossing the Area (Bounding), Pg. 65.)

If a Rifleman's weapon malfunctions, the Soldier shouts, "Malfunction!" and drops behind the line. Soldiers on their right and left pick up their sector, or the Assault Leader can direct them to, if they do not do so automatically. When the weapon is fixed the Soldier shouts, "Back in!" and recovers their sector. Similarly, if a Soldier goes down, the first to notice yells, "Man down!" and the Soldiers cover down on that Soldiers sector.

---

1 **Example** Flanking Orders:
TL –   "Left-side bound with me."
          "Right-side bound to me."
          "Assault to the LOA."
          "Pinwheel left."
          "Get on line; stay in your lane."

Phase 2

Image 52: A Team Leader with B Co., 3rd Bn., 7th Inf. Reg., 2nd Inf. Bde., performs **BLAST**. Fort Stewart, GA, 24 Aug 2016. The Leader is checking the Soldier for blood, showing direction-of-fire, and collecting an ACE report. Being that close may seem unecessary, but imagine it were night.

When a Rifleman approaches a body, they kick the rifle away from the body in any direction, so an almost-dead enemy cannot still use it. (Do not punt kick guns like you might a Super Bowl football, as they may discharge.)

The line stops advancing at a short distance past the last dead body.[1] If there is a second Assault Line (like in a bold-flanking maneuver), the line advances a short distance past the farthest of the last dead body or the last friendly man on the other element. When the Assault Leader thinks their team has advanced far enough, they shout, "LOA! LOA! LOA!" (i.e., "limit-of-advance"). Every Soldier on the assault echoes the command, takes a knee, and pulls security.

When the Assault Element reaches its LOA, five tasks in **BLAST** happen simultaneously. (See Image 52, Pg. 84.):

Blood check/sweep – Adrenaline can make a Soldier unaware they are shot and hemorrhaging, so a Leader checks their Soldiers for bleeding.

Lights – Turn off all lights used in the assault. At the LOA, lights become targets for the enemy.

---

1 Applying Concepts: A common rule of thumb is 35 meters (hand grenade range). But what if there is a short wall at 40 meters? Surely it would be better to either get cover at the wall or see behind it. What about a wall at 25 meters, or 100 meters? What makes a good stopping point?

ACE reports – Get the status of each man's Ammo, Casualties, and Equipment. (Some Leaders prefer LACE, which includes "Liquid." Others prefer just C, and crossload later.)

SAW's face out – When EPW is called and Riflemen are pulled off the line, the SAW's must have interlocking, 180-degree security.

Tac mag reload (tactical magazine reload) – All partially-full ammo feeds (to include magazines and drums) are replaced will full feeds.

For the ACE reports, each leadership position consolidates the information of their subordinates, giving an estimate of the average full magazines, full drums, and M240 rounds (leave out partial mags or drums), a brief description of casualties, and a list of important equipment lost. All ACE reports are given to the Patrol Leader so they may redistribute resources, call for emergency resupply, and order any casualty evacuations.[1]

If there are casualties, all belt-fed weapons are re-manned, and all leadership positions are filled as soon as possible. Oftentimes, after an assault, specialty teams are called. (See Cleaning up after Assaulting (Specialty Teams), Pg. 99.)

10.b Bold-flank Maneuver (Battle Drill 1)[2]

A flanking maneuver is often used instead of a direct assault because it is safer and more psychologically damaging to the enemy. The flank occurs when the Far Element (hereafter, Flanking Element) disappears from sight and reapproachs the enemy from the side. Because the enemy is distracted by the Contact Element, the enemy is caught unguarded. An unguarded enemy is easy to scare and kill.

Flanks, however, are not always the best option, which is why there are some variations. (See Bold-flank Variations, Pg. 92.) The two main

---

1 **Example** ACE Report:

SL – "ACE reports!"

ATL – "Two drums, three mags, up, up."

AG – "800 rounds, AB got grazed on the thigh, 240 is single-shotting."

2 Quote: Battles are won by slaughter and maneuver. The greater the general, the more he contributes in maneuver, the less he demands in slaughter. —British Prime Minister during WWII, Winston Churchill

disadvantages of flanking are that flanks are harder to coordinate, and they take more time.[1] (See Image 58, Pg. 90.)

Once the Patrol Leader decides to execute a bold-flank (likely when they confer with the Contact Element Leader), they will be placing the Flanking Element out of sight. Therefore, the Patrol Leader gives the Contact Element Leader reference points for three locations and corresponding limits-of-fire:

- The location where the Flanking Element will operate, and a limit-of-fire that the Contact Element cannot fire beyond.

- The location of the Flanking Element's last cover and concealment, and a new limit-of-fire for the Contact Element on the opposite side of the killzone from the Flanking Element's approach. The new limit-of-fire is called a **"shift-fire"** limit. The Contact Element shifts their fires to the new shift-fire limit when the Contact Element sees the Flanking Element appear or shift-fire is signaled to avoid friendly fire.[2] Shift-fire maintains violence of action because the Contact Element distracts the enemy. And once the Flanking Element leaves its final cover and concealment, it fires on same area of the killzone where the Contact Element has shifted from.

- The location of the killzone, so that when the Flanking Element approaches the killzone, the Contact Element can lift-fire. **Lift-fire** is when the Contact Element ceases all firing. (See Image 58, Pg. 90.) (Both lift-fire and shift-fire are communicated with a preplanned PACE.) (See PACE Communication Options, Pg. 242.)

The reference points are also for the Patrol Leader's benefit, so that they do not become lost while flanking. In addition, the Patrol Leader still must perform the regular react-to-contact responsibilities. (See Headquarters Reacts to Contact, Pg. 76.) The Contact Leader needs to backbrief the Patrol Leader on everything they were told and disseminate the information.

---

[1] Real World: The illustrations in this section depict squads for simplicity's sake. Because Battle Drill 1 is for platoons, technically the illustrations are of Battle Drill 1A, which is the squad-size version of Battle Drill 1. Platoon-sized Battle Drill 1 is very effective and widely used. Squad-size Battle Drill 1A is much worse because of low supplies. With only a squad, how deep can Soldiers flank before a single M240 is black on ammo? How many Soldiers can a squad spare for rear security?

[2] Real World: The Flanking Element can struggle to determine if the Contact Element has successfully shifted fire. Trusting a new unit with shift-fire command can be dangerous. One American unit took a month to teach shift-fire to a foreign unit. Consider going directly to lift-fire.

Image 53: 173rd Airborne Brigade Paratroopers shift fire as smoke is employed. 21 Mar 2018. **Many methods (and reference points), like smoke, voice, whisle, and radio are all used at the same time for redundancy to communicate shift- and lift-fire.**

After giving the three reference points, the Patrol Leader personally positions the Flanking Element because it is their responsibility to coordinate elements.[1,2] (See Image 55, Pg. 89.) The Patrol Leader leads the element in a file formation to the side called for during react-to-contact. The Flanking Element must move out of the enemy's sight to surprise the enemy when the flank occurs. If the Flanking Element moves to within sight of the enemy, it

---

The perfect unit doesn't need a Leader to coordinate them, because they can act in sync without orders. Although the Patrol Leader is ultimately responsible during combat, what they actually do during react-to-contact heavily depends on a unit's training level and SOP's.

2 Applying Concepts: If the Flanking Leader is a gruff, battle-hardened Sergeant, and the Contact Leader is greenhorn, would it be better for the Patrol Leader to stay with Contact Element?

Image 54: U.S. Army Paratroopers from 54th Bde. Engineer Bn., 173rd Airborne Bde., move towards the objective during Exercise Castle Warfare. Foce Reno Training Area, Ravenna, Italy, 07 Dec 2016. When choosing which side to flank, pick the side with the best concealment, so the Flanking Element can catch the enemy by surprise. **A spotted flank is worse than no flank,** because ammunition, time, and effort are wasted.

may have to move backward and out-of-sight again before flanking to prevent the enemy from detecting the approach.[1] (See Image 54, Pg. 88.)

The Flanking Element stops positioning when it is perpendicularly aligned with the Contact Element under fire, and concealed by terrain features toward the killzone. (This is aided by the reference points the Patrol Leader decided on earlier.) The Flanking Element can face slightly away from the Contact Element; however, it is imperative that **the Flanking Element in angled no less than 90 degrees from the Contact Element** line of Soldiers. Otherwise the Flanking Element risks assaulting directly into the Contact Element. (See Image 58, Pg. 90.)

---

[1] **Applying Concepts:** How should the Patrol Leader respond if the Flanking Element takes contact from a new enemy in a new position while moving in a file to their position? What about if the Contact Element takes indirect fire (just as you would target an enemy if they flanked)? Would a third element help?

Battle Drill 1A Part 1, Flank Setup

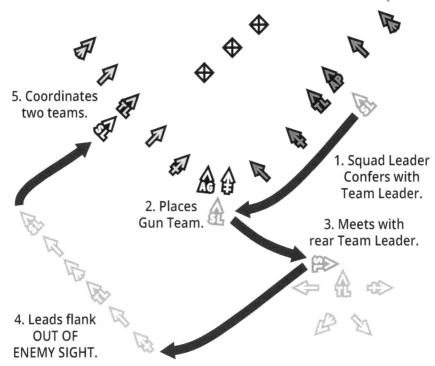

5. Coordinates
   two teams.

1. Squad Leader
   Confers with
   Team Leader.

2. Places
   Gun Team.

3. Meets with
   rear Team Leader.

4. Leads flank
   OUT OF
   ENEMY SIGHT.

Phase 2

Image 55: When the Contact Element has returned fire and attained a firing position, **the Flanking Element disappears from sight and reapproachs the enemy from the side.** This image shows a 5-step process for setting up a flank. First in steps 1 and 2, the Squad Leader stabalizes and informs the Contact Element. Then in steps 3, 4, and 5, the Squad Leader positions the Flanking Element.

Each Soldier rotates toward the killzone, turning the file formation into a line formation. The line is long enough so that every Soldier on the line has a separate, overlapping assaulting lane (rule of thumb: five to ten meters in daylight forest). After the Patrol Leader positions the Flanking Element, the Patrol Leader moves behind the Flanking Leader to supervise and coordinate the different elements.

At the last cover and concealment the flank assaults through, and, "Shift-fire!" is yelled. (See Image 53, Pg. 87.) Because of the surprise attack there is minimal danger. But if the enemy attacks the Flanking Element first, Soldiers bound to the enemy using three-to-five-second rushes. Alternately, the Flanking Leader may assault through if the enemy is close.

Image 56: U.S. and Georgian Soldiers flank. Vaziani Training Area, GA, 19 May 2015. Because the Gun Team is off to the side and positioned at an angle, it cannot see the flank as well and **is inherently less aware of lift-fire and shift-fire signals.**

Image 57: 7th Special Forces Group (Airborne) flank. Dixonville, PA, 22 Mar 2012. The flank is coming in at a little less than 90 degrees. That is okay, as long as it is never more than 90 degrees, to prevent assaulting the Contact Element.

Phase 2

Battle Drill 1A Part 2, Flank Assault

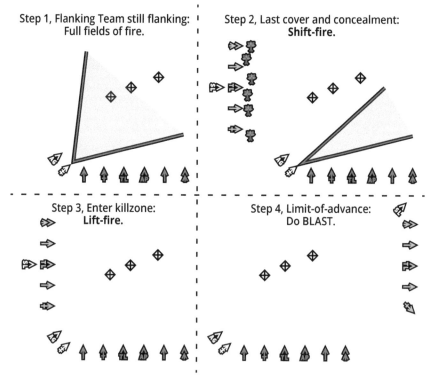

Step 1, Flanking Team still flanking: Full fields of fire.

Step 2, Last cover and concealment: **Shift-fire.**

Step 3, Enter killzone: **Lift-fire.**

Step 4, Limit-of-advance: Do BLAST.

Image 58: A critical aspect of the Flanking Element's assualt is preventing friendly fire. This is achieved through "shift-fire" and "lift-fire" commands that reduce the Contact Element's fields-of-fire. There are four steps in reducing fields-of-fire. Although this image only shows the field-of-fire for the Gun Team, all the fires shift and lift.

Battle Drill 1A Part 3, Contact Assault

Gun Team follows behind and moves to the apex.

Image 59: An assault by the Contact Element is straight-forward. The Contact Element moves across the killzone and shoots enemies and enemy bodies in front of the line. **The Gun Team follows closely behind the Contact Element to reach the apex.**

When the Flanking Element approaches the base-of-fire element's line-of-fire, "Lift-fire!" is yelled by anyone. (But specifically, the Patrol Leader yells it, since they emplaced the closest troop, the M240, and is directly responsible for coordinating the teams.) **If "shift" or "lift" is not echoed: STOP, HALT, DO NOT CONTINUE!** For a long approach or a long killzone, "Shift-fire!" can be called multiple times.

When the Flanking Element exits the killzone and passes the Contact Element, the Flanking Element shouts, "Last man!" and the Contact Element echoes. This signals the end of the killzone to the Flanking Leader, and thereby where the LOA is. (See Image 59, Pg. 91.)

When the Flanking Element reaches 35 meters (hand grenade throwing range) past the killzone or the last dead body, the Flanking Leader shouts, "LOA! LOA! LOA!" and the Contact Element assaults through the objective. The Contact Element assaults just like just like the Flanking Element did. The Gun Team(s) picks up and follows directly behind the Assault Line, moving sideways to end up at the meeting point (a.k.a., the apex) of the two teams. (See Image 59, Pg. 91.)

10.c Bold-flank Variations

The bold-flank is one of the most commonly taught battle drills in many militaries around the world. In U.S. Army doctrine, it is "Battle Drill #1." However, in reality **various issues greatly limit the usefulness of the bold-flank:**

▸ If the enemy moves, the flank might attack at a weird angle, which can ruin the coordination between elements.

▸ The Flanking Element requires concealment; without concealment, the enemy will not be surprised and the flank only delays returning fire.

▸ Leaders can easily get lost in a firefight; a flank must have great reference points for coordinating movement and fires.

▸ Flanking the correct distance takes time; M240s burn through ammo very fast, and the enemy can call artillery.

▸ The Flanking Element could be engaged while flanking, and the patrol would be engaged as a split element.

In summary, bold-flanks are useful for experienced units with good concealment, but the bold-flank is just one of many attacks that a patrol uses.

A less effective, but more foolproof tactic is the **"tactical-L."** The idea is to create the somewhat 90-degree angle between two elements (i.e., an L-shape) by directly moving to the position instead of flanking to it. An L-shape is great for attacking because the enemy receives fire from multiple directions. The Patrol Leader can order each element to get on line, and then alternate maneuvering to rotate each element until they are at a right angle from each other. Or the Patrol Leader can order an element directly to a 90-degree angle, if the terrain provides enough cover. Once the elements are at a 90-degree angle, assault through the killzone just like a bold-flank. (See Image 60, Pg. 93.)

Another variation of a bold-flank is the **"reverse-flank."** For this, the Flanking Element does a bold-flank. But it stops before entering the killzone. The Flanking Element become the new supporting element by throwing down supporting fire 90 degrees from the Contact Element. Once the Flanking Element is in a good support position, it is the Contact Element that assaults through first. Once the Contact Element reaches its LOA, the Flanking Element follows through and assaults second.

Tactical-L Formation

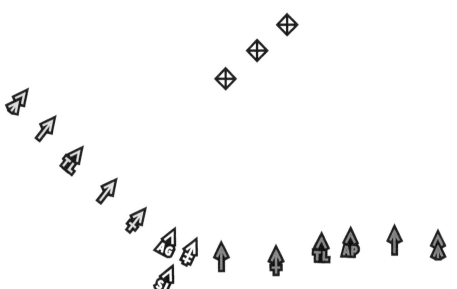

Image 60: In contrast to a bold-flank, the Maneuver Element makes no attempt to hide when flanking, and **moves into a flanking position as fast as possible.**

A reverse flank is used when the Flanking Element has easy access to a good support position, like a hill or cliff, that would be terrible for assaulting through. For example, the Patrol Leader can send a Flanking Element to lay supporting fire from a cliff face, eliminating many enemies, but leaving the Flanking Element unable to further maneuver. The attack maintains violence of action with an assault by the Contact Element instead.

10.d Break-Contact (Battle Drill 3)[1]

To choose to break contact, the Patrol Leader must believe that the contact is not worth engaging for whatever reason after assessing the situation. (See Headquarters Reacts to Contact, Pg. 76.) Maybe the enemy is too big to handle, or patrol has no time to engage. The Patrol Leader shouts the code word for break-contact, emplaces the Gun Team(s), and moves back to the element not in contact (hereafter, Suppressing Element). (See Image 61, Pg. 94.)

1 Quote: Retreat, hell! We're not retreating, we're just advancing in a different direction. —U.S. Marine Gen. Oliver P. Smith

Break-Contact Part 1, Suppression Setup

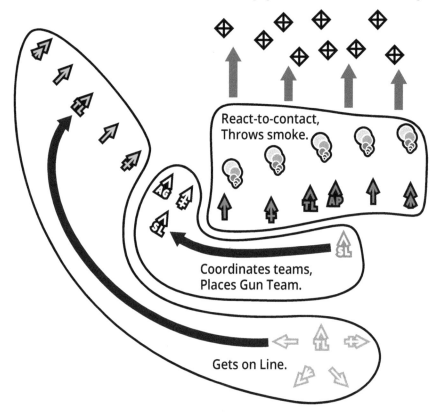

Image 61: During a break contact, all elements act simultaniously. The Contact Team (red) and Headquarters engage in a standard react-to-contact. (See Joe Returns Fire (Battle Drills 1, 3, and 4), Pg. 80.) The only difference being that the Contact Team throws a lot of smoke to mask itself. **The Non-Contact Team (blue) receives the break-contact signal and must get on line as fast as possible to provide suppressing fire.**

The Contact Element, immediately after break-contact is called, **throws smoke** to reduce enemy accuracy and vision. When using smoke, be careful to account for strong wind. Wind can blow the smoke out of the way, or even in front of the Suppressing Element, blocking their view.

When the Patrol Leader arrives at the Suppressing Element, their goal is to position the element in a line of Soldiers that can provide supporting fire for the Contact Element's retreat. The Patrol Leader can lead the element themself, or give the Suppressing Leader a direction, distance, and

Image 62: A Canadian Soldier bounds behind smoke concealment during the live-fire portion of a breaking contact and trench clearing exercise. Adazi Military Base, Latvia, 19 Apr 2016. **Note the smoke was thrown to the far left-side to account for the wind.**

reference point to move to a covered and concealed overwatch position. The overwatch position must also have good fields-of-fire that are not blocked by friendly elements.

After all elements are set and firing on the enemy, they alternate between moving back, and firing on the enemy to retreat. (See Image 63, Pg. 96.) In a break-contact, the Gun Team(s) are likely better placed near and moved with the Suppressing Element. This is because the Contact Element was caught off guard, and therefore is likely be in a bad position to fire on the enemy. In contrast, the Suppressing Element is purposefully placed by the Patrol Leader in a good overwatch.

To move back, the Patrol Leader finds a good covered and concealed reference point to retreat to, and signals the Contact Element to move to it. When the Contact Element has set into its new position, it becomes the new Suppressing Element. Breaking contact is eventually achieved by having the two elements alternate between being a supporting fire element and a maneuvering element, with the Patrol Leader coordinating movements.

Break-Contact Part 2, Bound Back

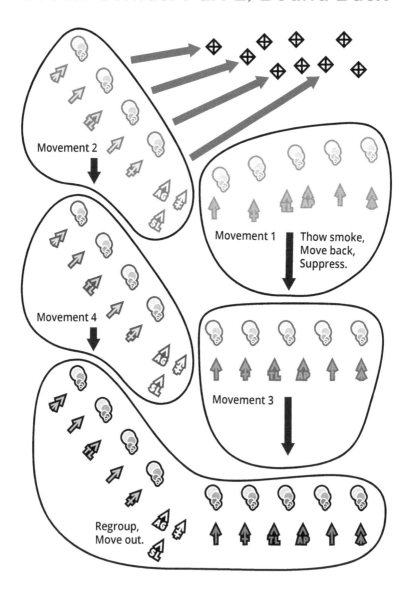

Image 63: When the Supressing Element (blue) begins firing, the Contact Element (red) can bound back to good cover and concealment (Movement 1). Once they set and fire, the Supressing Element can bound back (Movement 2). (See Directly Crossing the Area (Bounding), Pg. 65.) Bounding continues to alternate supporting fire and bounding back until the enemy no longer pursues. Then the patrol regroups and moves out.

After contact is broken, the Patrol moves 300 meters or a major terrain feature away. (Note that the Patrol Leader can break contact in any direction; not just backward.) The Patrol Leader must consider changing the direction of movement after a break-contact. Changing direction from the initial approach reduces the ability of the enemy to shoot indirect fires at the patrol. Once the Patrol Leader has moved the appropriate distance, the Patrol Leader conducts a long-halt to consolidate and reorganize.

10.e Break-Contact Variations

The most common break-contact variations are called "peels." The analogy for a peel is a small animal that is attacked, and responds by **making itself look as big as possible**. A small element, like a squad or Leader's Recon Team, rapidly fires everything (including smoke) to imply a much larger force.

As everyone fires, one or two Soldiers at the front move to the rear of the element and resume firing, while the next Soldier moves back. This way allows the element to retreat, while firing as many bullets toward the enemy as possible. This is a variation on a regular break-contact, because Soldiers retreat individually or in pairs under supporting fire, instead of as a larger element. (See Image 65, Pg. 98.)

The basic peel idea is further broken down into a "center-peel" and a "side-peel," which refer to the direction of retreat relative to the direction of the enemy. A **center-peel** is used when the enemy is straight ahead, and you peel backward. Soldiers form two columns. The two Soldiers at the front, closest to the enemy, retreat down the center of the formation to the rear of the columns. The second in line opens suppressive fire. As soon as possible, the second Soldier restarts the cycle and retreats down the center of the column, while the Soldier behind them opens suppressive fire. (See Image 64, Pg. 98.)

A **side-peel** is used to retreat sideways. One Soldier at a time moves behind the firing line from left to right, or right to left. A side-peel is restricted to retreating sideways, but it allows the entire line to fire, instead of just the front two Soldiers. (See Image 66, Pg. 99.)

There are endless tactical improvements to peels and break-contact. Consider slanting the retreat; it can give the impression of more Soldiers joining the fight. Or a Soldier in the rear can set a claymore and detonate it when they become the front.

Phase 2

Image 64: U.S. Navy combat photographers practice a center peel. Fort A.P. Hill, Virginia, 25 Oct 2004. **In the back from the left, one is starting to retreat, one is firing, and one is looking to set and fire again.**

Peels

Center-Peel   Side-Peel

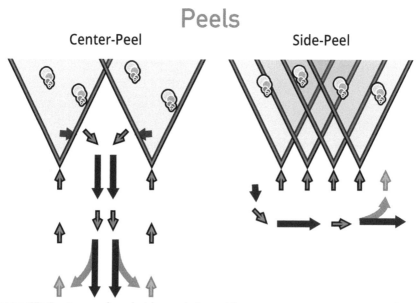

Image 65: Center-peel and side-peel. A peel is an emergency maneuver where a small force holds back a larger force. The Soldiers firing use all the bullets and smoke they can muster while the front line moves back. **The front line can either reform to fire again, or begin the retreat.**

Image 66: Able Co., 2nd Bn., 503rd Inf. Reg., 173rd Airborne Bde. Paratroopers use a side-peel during Iron Sword 2016. Pabrade, Lithuania, 29 Nov 2016. **Utilizing lots of smoke and fires implies a larger force.**

11. Cleaning up after Assaulting (Specialty Teams)

Once all Soldiers reach their LOA after assaulting, the killzone needs some cleaning up. Enemy bodies, friendly casualties, and important items all need attention. To clean up, a patrol has preassigned "Special Teams," made up of Riflemen and Leaders.

When Special Teams are pulled from the LOA, the remaining Soldiers must readjust to remove any holes in security. The SAW's on either end of the line interlock to form a 180-degree sector-of-fire; and any remaining Riflemen or SAW's cover remaining dead space.

11.a Enemy Prisoner of War (EPW) Team

Immediately after the Patrol Leader receives ACE reports (Ammo, Casualty, Equipment) from every Soldier, they yell, "EPW!" (Enemy Prisoner of War). The EPW Soldiers are predesignated roles and are

Enemy Prisoner of War Search and Clear

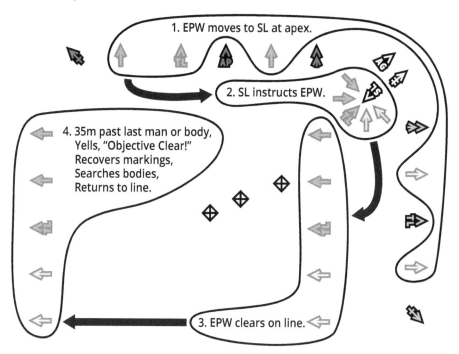

1. EPW moves to SL at apex.

2. SL instructs EPW.

4. 35m past last man or body,
Yells, "Objective Clear!"
Recovers markings,
Searches bodies,
Returns to line.

3. EPW clears on line.

Image 67: Enemy Prisoner of War Team clearing the objective. Because **the EPW team is designated during planning**, there is no confusion on who needs to report to the Squad Leader when they call for the EPW Team.

assigned to at least four Riflemen per squad during the operations order. The EPW Leader and Soldiers run to the Patrol Leader around the killzone. (Nobody can enter the killzone until it is declared clear by the EPW Team.)[1] A common assignment is to have every Rifleman and Alpha Team Leader comprise the EPW Team(s). (See Image 67, Pg. 100.)

The Patrol Leader tells the **EPW clear and search** their:

Color – Each EPW sub-Team is given a color for identification. (During search when items are called out and recorded, two Soldiers calling out the same item use their different colors for clarity; e.g. "black 1 map" and "gold 1 map.")

1 **Applying Concepts:** The idea behind this rule is that there may still be enemies that aren't dead in the killzone, and can still surprise attack a passing Soldier. In what cases might it be okay to enter the killzone before EPW clears it completely or even partially?

Clearing instructions – How the killzone is to be cleared and searched. (Usually EPW follows SOP, so this is only briefed if the killzone or situation is unusual.)

Collection instructions – What items to collect during the search and where to put them.

Clock – How long EPW has to clear and search the objective.[1]

After receiving their instructions, the EPW Team lines up along the entire killzone, with the EPW Leader in the center. Soldiers turn on their rifle lights and walk from one end of the killzone to the other to conduct **EPW clear**.

If a Soldier sees a body en route, they shout, "Body!" The line pauses or half-steps as two Soldiers clear it. The Soldier who found it first points their weapon at the body, in a direction away from the LOA's and friendly elements. Once in position, this Security Soldier does not move again.

The second Clearing Soldier works around the first. They must check under the body for weapons, while not being flagged by the Security Soldier. To perform this check, the Clearing Soldier rolls the body, so the Security Soldier can see underneath. If the Security Soldier sees a booby trap, they shout, "Grenade!" and everyone drops away.

To avoid being flagged while rolling and to prepare for booby traps, the Clearing Soldier rolls the body depending on its orientation to the Security Soldier. If the body is vertical toward the Security Soldier, the Clearing Soldier kneels beside the body and rolls it sideways toward themself. If the body is oriented horizontally, the Clearing Soldier straddles the body and picks it up. In this way, there is good line of sight for the Security Soldier to see traps. And if there is a booby trap, the body can quickly be dropped

---

1 **Example** EPW Team Instructions:

SL –   "EPW on me."

"You are black and you are gold. Begin in the center and clear to five meters past the M249. Bring all PIR to me. Place weapons and equipment on the hood of the vehicle. Weapons stacked bolt to bolt then equipment on top of those. You have three minutes."

ATL –   "Black on my Left; Gold on my Right. Start."

RFL –   "I have a body."

ATL –   "Halt."

RFL –   "Clear."

ATL –   "Continue."

"Objective clear!"

"You, search that body near the tree. You have one minute."

back on the trap. To signify that a body has been cleared, its feet and arms are crossed. The Soldiers then clear the enemy's weapon. To signify that a weapon is cleared, it is placed at the feet of the body. When the Soldiers finish clearing a body and weapon, they return to the clearing line.

Once all bodies in the killzone are clear, the EPW Team Leader yells, "Objective clear!" to the Patrol Leader. (See Vehicle Clearing, Pg. 204.) This means that Soldiers can now freely enter the killzone and **EPW search** begins.

To search bodies, the EPW Team uses their headlamps and turns off their rifle lights so that they do not flag anyone while searching. Each body needs one EPW Soldier to search it; any extra Soldiers return to their line to pull security. It is always two EPW Soldiers that clear and one that carries out the search.

When searching, a Soldier begins from the top and systematically touches, crumples, and feels for items of information and weapons as they move down the body. Although there are systematic and complete ways to search, time often does not allow for them. In a rush, prioritize body areas likely to contain important items. (Important items were specified when the Patrol Leader gave their EPW instructions.)

When an important item is found, the Soldier shouts into the assigned recorder: their EPW Team color, the item, and its quantity (e.g. "Black, one FLC"). When finished, the Soldier marks the body as searched (e.g., by pulling the enemy's shirt above their head). Once all the bodies are searched, the Soldiers bring the items to the area designated by the Patrol Leader in their EPW brief. They then return to the LOA to pull security.

During EPW clear and search, the enemies should all be dead. **If an enemy is found alive** and has survived a full assault, they can be assumed to either be injured and/or surrendered. (This assumption is why this is an "enemy prisoner of war clear," and not a "remaining enemy clear.") At this point, it is a war crime to kill the EPW, unless that enemy is an immediate threat. EPW's cannot be further injured directly or indirectly (like leaving them in the path of demolition) and the medic must eventually treat them.

If there is a live EPW, the entire mission may be in danger of failure. Securing and transporting an unwilling or injured human incapacitates multiple Soldiers. Moreover, letting an EPW free can alert additional enemies. Many attacks have multiple first passes, each by different elements, specifically to ensure all enemies are killed during the assault.

Image 68: A Paratrooper with 1st Bn., 325th Reg., 2nd Bde., 82nd Airborne Div., clears an EPW. 18 Nov 2010. The EPW is oriented horizontally to the Security Soldier, and is being picked up. **The Soldier clearing has moved to provide direct lines of sight and fire to the other Soldier.**

Image 69: A Cameroonian Soldier searches a U.S. Marine Corps Staff Sgt. Limbé, Cameroon, 20 Sep 2016. The EPW is oriented vertically and is being rolled towards the Soldier. Note the Searcher is crunching and rolling the EPW's pockets, and the boots have been removed and searched.

Regarding the mission, it is necessary to contact higher for specific instructions on a case-by-case basis. For the prisoner, standard procedure is to apply **5S&T**.

Search – prisoners immediately and thoroughly for weapons and documents.

Segregate – prisoners into groups: officers, NCO's, privates, deserters, civilians, and females. This prevents enemy organizing and issuing of orders.

Silence – prisoners to prevent any and all coordination.

Speed – (move) prisoners to their final location quickly, to maximize withdrawal of timely information.

Safeguard – prisoners as they are moved. Do not give cigarettes, food, or water until authorized by assigned interrogators.

Tag – the prisoner with time, place, and circumstances of capture. Also tag any equipment and weapons.

11.b Aid and Litter Team

If there are friendly casualties, then the Patrol Leader is informed as soon as possible. They call the Aid and Litter Team to the apex immediately after EPW to receive instructions. However, the Patrol Leader cannot release them until the EPW Team clears the killzone; otherwise, a living enemy could, for example, release a grenade. The minute that EPW yells, "Objective clear!" the Patrol Leader can send in Aid and Litter. Aid and Litter collects all casualties and brings them to the Patrol Leader. From there, the casualties are medically evacuated. (See Medical Evacuation, Pg. 106.)

11.c Demolition Team[1]

When Aid and Litter is finished, and EPW has put all the items they have found in front of the Patrol Leader, the Patrol Leader blows up all items valuable to the enemy. The purpose of the Demo Team is to deny the enemy of any weapons, vehicles, radios, and other equipment that could be used.

Because explosives are very dangerous, the demo sequence is also the withdrawal sequence. This ensures that there are no Soldiers left when the demo explodes. (See Withdrawal from Area after Assaulting, Pg. 104.) The Demo Team is comprised of the final Soldiers who stay in the killzone. The primary Demo Team for a squad is often the Squad Leader and the Assistant Gunner, or a preassigned Rifleman. The Demo Teams for a platoon could be the Alpha and Bravo Team Leaders. It is important to always have a backup Demo Team.

There is an order in which the equipment is to be blown. First, all the ammunition is placed on the ground or above an engine block. If ammunition were on top of the demo, it would spray or fire everywhere. Above the ammo, all weapons are stacked with touching receiver groups. Guns are durable, so their vital areas must be targeted. Then the charge is placed. All other equipment, like radios and Fighting Load Carrier vests (FLC's), are placed on top of the demo. Vehicles that cannot have a charge put on them are destroyed by other means.

If the patrol has spent too much time in the area, the Patrol Leader does not need to call for the Demo Team. However, they still yell out the demolition sequence to start withdrawal.

12. Withdrawal from Area after Assaulting

Once any casualties have been moved, the Patrol Leader signals for withdrawal. The Patrol Leader preps the demo themself or leads the Demo Teams, so the

---

1 Quote: Five-second fuses only last three seconds. —Unknown

Image 70: A U.S. Army explosive ordnance disposal technician with Multinational Battle Group-East, places C4 onto ordnance. Orahovac Demolition Range, 04 Apr 2016. The demo is on a time fuse so the Soldier will not be there at detonation.

Image 71: Blocks of M112 demolition charges are set on weapons. 02 Feb 2019. **After fighting the enemy, the Demo Team is responsible for destroying left over enemy weapons and vehicles to deny their reuse by the enemy later.**

withdrawal sequence is signaled with phrases for the demolition, called the "Fire in the Hole" sequence. Always echo everything!

The Patrol Leader shouts, "**Fire in the Hole 1**!" and the Bravo Team Leader or Squad Leader (or whoever is in charge of accountability) makes a chokepoint behind the killzone and shouts, "Chokepoint on me!" over and over. The first assault element withdraws first through the chokepoint. Other teams follow in file. The Accountability Leader shouts, "Assault [number counted] up!" or "Assault [number counted] missing [number missing]!"[1] Simultaneously, the Demo Team removes the safety pins on the initiators (always with gloves on).

The Patrol Leader shouts, "**Fire in the Hole 2**!" and the Gun Team(s) withdraw. The Gun Team(s) are slow and deaf, so they sound off with "Gun moving!" to indicate they heard, and run to the chokepoint. Again,

---

1 **Example** Accountability: "Assault 3 up," or "Assault 2, missing 1."

the Accountability Leader gets a count, and this time includes themself. If it is correct, they shout, "Leader and Gun Team [number counted] up!" The Accountability Leader withdraws with the second group. Simultaneously, the Demo Team pushes the pins in and turns them 90 degrees clockwise.

The Patrol Leader shouts, "**Fire in the Hole 3!**" both in person and over the radio, and the demo is ignited. Everybody remaining withdraws. If the count was incorrect at the chokepoint, do not call, "Fire in the Hole 3!" At this point, only the Patrol Leader and Demo Team are near the killzone. (Even if the Patrol Leader can do demo by themself, they can't be left alone, so the Soldier with them is just a buddy.)

Before withdrawing, the Demo Team ensures the fuse is burning (i.e., look for smoke.) After confirming ignition, the Patrol Leader shouts, "**Burning! Burning! Burning!**" and withdraws.

Once the patrol finishes withdrawing, Soldiers return to their rucks as quickly as possible to avoid any enemy reinforcements. The patrol may continue on their azimuth of movement if they do not believe they will encounter more enemies; otherwise, the patrol needs to change its route.

13. Medical Evacuation[1]

In the event of casualties, the Patrol Leader first has to decide whether the mission is still viable; i.e., do casualties require care before the mission is over? If the Patrol Leader decides that the injuries are severe enough, the casualty can be evacuated using many means of transport. If the patrol is well planned, the evacuation can meet a medical ambulance or helicopter at a preplanned location. However, if the casualty occurs during a foot movement, then some walking is required.

It is vitally important to have a PACE plan for medical evacuation! (See PACE Communication Options, Pg. 242.) A full PACE is a plan with four options at all times (i.e., Primary, Alternate, Contingency, and Emergency). A PACE guarantees multiple means of evacuation simultaneously, so that if many methods fail, another means still is usable. Otherwise, without a PACE, a Soldier's life may depend on a single point of failure.

---

1 Quote: A "sucking chest wound" is nature's way of telling you to slow down.... —Unknown

9-Line Medevac Template

This is the standard format to covey casualty and pickup information to a casevac. The left column lists brevity codes (e.g. for line 3, saying "5 A" means "5 Urgent"). A common mnemonic is,
"Low Flying Pilots Eat Tacos; Salsa Makes Nasty Nachos."

1. Location of pickup site	
2. Frequency and call sign	
3. Patient count and status	A. Urgent (2 hours) B. Priority (4 hours) C. Routine (24 hours) D. Convenience
4 Equipment required	A. None B. Hoist C. Extraction equipment D. Ventilator
5. Type of patients	L. Litter A. Ambulatory
6. Security at pickup site	N. No enemy troops P. Possible enemy E. Enemy troops X. Enemy (needs armed escort)
7. Marking of pickup site	A. Panels B. Pyro C. Smoke D. None E. Other
8. Nationality and military	A. U.S. military B. U.S. civilian C. Non U.S. military D. Non. U.S. civilian E. EPW
9 NBC contamination	N. Nuclear B. Biological C. Chemical

Phase 2

Image 72: U.S. Marines with 3rd Bn., 6th Marine Reg., 2nd Marine Div. move "wounded" role-players during a heavy Huey raid. Yuma, AZ, 09 Apr 2014. If an eight-man squad sustains three casualties, can the squad safely employ two-man carries? **The average Soldier and ruck weigh over 200lbs.**

When there is a casualty during a patrol, the leadership must call up a 9-Line Medical Request as soon as possible. If you forget the multiple-choice options, it is okay to talk like a human and, regardless, every Soldier carries a 9-Line template in their kit.

13.a Evacuating by Foot

The first priority in casualty evacuation (casevac) is finding a drop-off location. A casualty can be evacuated by moving them to a helicopter landing zone (HLZ), an ambulance exchange point (AXP), or a vehicle pickup site (VPU). Immediately after the EPW Team clears the killzone, the Platoon Leader coordinates with higher on where to drop off the casualties.

Much casevac training uses litters, but litters require lots of people to use.[1] If the enemy has just shot at the patrol and is likely to engage again,

1 **Applying Concepts:** How many Soldiers are incapacitated if a Foxtrot litter is used? How about a Talon litter? What if the casualty had been carrying a heavy ruck and other equipment?

Casualty Carry Formation

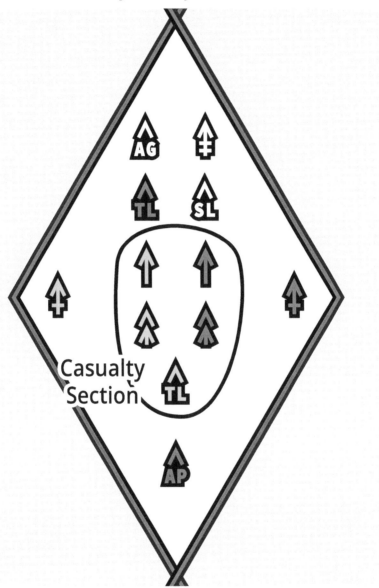

Phase 2

Image 73: This formation is also known as a "**Honeycomb**" or "Turtleshell," because it has a hard outside and a soft inside. **The basic idea behind any casualty carry formation is to have 360-degree security around casualties** and carriers because they are incapacitated. Always keep belt-fed weapons on the outside, and rotate the weapons themselves among Soldiers if necessary. Always maintain rear security.

then every man possible needs to be pulling security. At minimum, moving a casualty requires one Soldier to carry the casualty's body and one for the ruck.

Because at least two additional Soldiers are incapacitated per casualty, and casualties stay in the center of the formation, a wedge formation naturally becomes disorganized. To maintain order, the best formation is a "honeycomb." A **honeycomb formation** is very fluid and is basically defined by having a squishy inside (casualties, carriers, and switch outs) with a hard-outside shell (the SAW's and M240s). The M240 protects the most likely avenue of enemy approach, which is usually the 12 o'clock.

The casualties in the center must be tightly managed by the leadership. Soldiers who carry will fatigue at different rates and are somewhat blinded by the load, so they will constantly wander. Therefore, the Center Leader must herd the casualty carriers together for accountability, rotation, and medical monitoring of the casualties by the medic. A common strategy is to create rows and columns. First, get the casualty carriers on line so they can match each other's pace. Then, assign their replacements to stick directly behind the carriers in columns, so they are consolidated and always ready to take over.

13.b Evacuating by Ambulance Exchange

Ambulance exchanges can be dangerous because **anyone can hijack an ambulance**, so verification of the driver needs to be taken. A Leader's Recon Team verifies that the ambulance is friendly before the casualties are brought forward. (See Leader's Recon of the Squad ORP, Pg. 136.) A Leader's Recon Team consists of a Leader Team and a Surveillance and Observation (S&O) Team. The Leader Team includes the Patrol Leader and another Soldier (usually the Alpha Team Leader or the RTO), while the S&O Team has a SAW and a Rifleman.

The Patrol Leader emplaces S&O so it never loses sight of the vehicle but the vehicle cannot see S&O. S&O is also assigned a specific sector-of-fire by the Patrol Leader for safety. For example, if the sector-of-fire starts from the headlights of the vehicle and continues backwards, then Soldiers always remain in front of the headlights, so the SAW's sector-of-fire never engages them.

Image 74: USAF Pararescuemen assigned to the 82nd Expeditionary Rescue Squad, deployed in support of Combined Joint Task Force, Horn of Africa, load a HH-60G Pave Hawk helicopter as part of a casualty evacuation mission rehearsal. East Africa, 30 Nov 2018. **Helicopters require open areas and can expose troops.** How would you mitigate this?

If a generic ambulance arrives, the Patrol Leader must presume that it is hostile. To prove the ambulance is safe, the Patrol Leader and the driver can exchange prearranged challenge questions. If the ambulance cannot answer correctly, the Patrol withdraws. If the ambulance is friendly, the Leader Team returns to the Main Body and comes back to the ambulance with the casualties and their rucks.

13.c Evacuating by Helicopter

An HLZ (Helicopter Landing Zone) drop-off is straightforward because the enemy probably has not hijacked any military helicopters. The Patrol Leader may presume the helicopter is friendly and immediately hand off casualties with their rucks. Before the helicopter lands, the HLZ must have 360-degree security. A secure HLZ does not necessarily take an entire patrol; security is provided according to METT-TC.

14. Fire Support

Integrated in many infantry patrols are Soldiers whose job is to call higher for fire support. Forward Observers (FO) call for indirect fires, like mortars and artillery. Joint Terminal Attack Controllers (JTAC) direct the action of aircraft engaged in offensive operations like close air support. Naval Gunfire Spotters direct fire from ships. How these Soldiers perform their jobs is beyond the scope of this manual, but their role in combat is detailed in this section.

14.a Firing Artillery and Mortars (Call for Fire)

A Soldier who specializes in directing fires like artillery and mortars onto target is called the Forward Observer (FO). The fires may be anything from mortars to destroy the enemy, or phosphorous light shells to reveal terrain, or smoke to mask a retreat. The range and power of these weapon systems multiplies the effectiveness of an infantry patrol. (See Image 76, Pg. 113.) The resources available to an FO must be discussed during planning. An FO may also simultaneously be a JTAC for close air support or a Naval Gunfire Spotter for naval support.

FO's are necessary because troops at the fire-support base cannot see the battlefield, and they do not know the battlespace.[1] Artillery guns are rarely in line-of-sight of their target, often located miles away. The FO serves as the eyes of the guns, by sending target information and firing corrections when they observe the enemy. Usually the FO and RTO act as a team, so the FO has fast access to a radio to communicate with higher command. To quickly and properly send targets, the FO must maintain the grid coordinates of the patrol at all times.

Any mission probably includes preplanned targets. (E.g., fires can destroy roads on either side of an ambush, isolating the objective from enemy escape.)

---

1   Quote: I think carpet bombing is an absolutely tremendous idea if the enemy accommodates you by laying himself out like a carpet in the middle of the desert without any civilians or infrastructure around him. Sadly, the Islamic State has learned that that is a losing proposition and does not accommodate us in that way. —Commander of United States Central Command, David Petraeus

Image 75: Alpha Battery, Field Artillery Squadron, 2nd Cavalry Regiment, fire a M777A2 towed 155 mm howitzer. 21 Aug 2019. This artillery has a maximum firing range of 14,600 meters.

Image 76: In Djibouti, an FO with Lima Co., Bat. Landing Team 3/1, 13th Marine Expeditionary Unit, observes a strike. 12 Sep 2018. **A fire support Soldier can kill many more than a man with an M4.**

A patrol can also improvise fires against targets of opportunity (T/O). To fire on a T/O, the FO calls in using a format. One such format is **PLOT-CR:**[1]

Purpose – The goal of the indirect fire. (The FO may not be aware of higher's resources; so, PLOT-CR is a recommendation that higher may alter to achieve the purpose using a better method or resource.)

Location – The target's 8-digit grid, or its direction and distance from a preplanned location (known as, "shift from a known point"). (If friendly troops are close, make sure to announce "danger close," according to the weapon system requested.)

Observer – The Soldier(s) observing the impact of the rounds and informing higher of adjustments.

Trigger – The event that higher waits for to initiate fires.

---

1 **Example** PLOT-CR:

Purpose –	"Disrupt dismounted enemy reinforcements to the OBJ."
Location –	"17SPU 7234 4916."
Observer –	"Primary: Forward Observer; Secondary: Patrol Leader."
Trigger –	"Enemy reserve identified moving along AO Hammer."
Comms –	"Primary: FM 35000; Secondary: FM 34000."
Resources –	"4 rounds, HE/VT."

Image 77: A U.S. Air Force Senior Airman and a Tech. Sgt., 21st Special Tactics Squadron JTAC's, look on as an **A-10 Thunderbolt II** releases its munitions during a close air support training mission. Nevada Test and Training Range, 23 Sep 2011.

Communication – The method of communication between the forward unit and the unit sending indirect fire.

Resources – Planned or requested resources for each target.

14.b Close Air Support

Close Air Support (CAS) is action against enemy targets by aircraft that are both in close proximity to friendly forces and coordinated with the friendly forces' fires and maneuvers. CAS aircraft have many available munitions to provide support, including aerial bombs, glide bombs, missiles, rockets, aircraft cannons, machine guns, etc.

There are two types of CAS requests: preplanned and immediate. Preplanned air support requests are resourced with either scheduled or on-call air missions. Immediate air support requests are supported with on-call missions or by redirecting air missions that are already scheduled. CAS can be requested at any place and time friendly forces are near enemy forces.

Image 78: An **MH-60 Black Hawk** from the 160th Special Operations Aviation Regiment, provides close air support for Army Rangers from A Co., 2nd Bat., 75th Ranger Reg., conducting direct action operations during company live-fire training. Camp Roberts, CA, 31 Jan 2014.

JTAC's (Joint Terminal Attack Controllers) or FAC's (Forward Air Controllers) are Soldiers in a forward position, who direct the actions of combat aircraft engaged in CAS and other air operations. The JTAC provides the ground (or higher) commander recommendations on the use of CAS, and coordinates the CAS aircraft with ground maneuver.

To start an attack, the JTAC passes to the CAS aircraft the targeting information to be used. For each target, the JTAC and the aircraft communicate for the duration of the attack (more specific methods are beyond this manual).

After each attack, the JTAC radios the aircraft to request an "immediate re-attack" if necessary, or to move to the next target. Attacks continue until the fighters either run out of ordnance, targets, or flight time. Once the support period is over, the JTAC gives the fighters a quick "debrief" on how things went, including the number of targets destroyed and any intel to bring back to base.

15. Contingencies[1]

Enemy contact can happen in infinite ways, but there are some common scenarios to plan for.

15.a React-to-Sniper[2]

When the first Soldier goes down, or when someone hears the bullet crack nearby, yell, "Sniper!" The patrol engages in a **react-to-contact**. (See The Enemy Shoots at Joe (Battle Drill 2), Pg. 71.) I.e., all patrol members immediately seek cover, shout the 3Ds (Direction, Distance, Description), throw smoke, and begin suppressive fire. Throwing smoke to mask the patrol's location and movements is particularly important.

The difference between a react-to-sniper and a regular react-to-contact is the difficulty in knowing where enemy fire is coming from, and that snipers often lure and entrap Soldiers. Therefore, unless the sniper's location is known, the patrol breaks contact with extra smoke. Then, call in indirect fires on the sniper's general position.

15.b React-to-Artillery and Mortars (Indirect Fire)[3]

Yell, "Incoming!" when the first round is heard. All patrol members immediately go to the prone. (See Image 79, Pg. 117.) For repeating fire, Soldiers get in the prone for every single incoming. However, if it becomes clear fires are not stopping, get up and run like hell.

---

1 Quote: There are known knowns; there are things we know we know. We also know there are known unknowns; that is to say we know there are some things we do not know. But there are also unknown unknowns – the ones we don't know we don't know. —Defense Sec. Donald Rumsfeld

2 Quote: A general had barely arrived in the forward area when a sniper shot a button off his shirt. He dropped to the ground in terror, but the men stood around, unconcerned. The general yelled at a passing sergeant: "Hey, isn't somebody gonna kill that damned sniper?" The sergeant looked down and replied: "I guess not, general. We're scared if we kill him, the enemy will replace him with someone who knows how to shoot." —Unknown

3 Quote: My fellow Americans, I'm pleased to tell you today that I've signed legislation that will outlaw Russia forever. We begin bombing in five minutes. —President Ronald Reagan

Image 79: Combat Life Saver Course instructor simulates mortor fire as airmen protect simulated casualties during the obstacle course training event. Joint Base McGuire-Dix-Lakehurst, NJ, 11 Mar 2013. Can you identify who is properly hitting the ground, and **who is half-assing it?**

The Patrol Leader shouts a distance and direction to move to. Usually, the distance is one terrain feature over, out of sight of the enemy, and the direction is 90 degrees to the previous movement. This disrupts enemy adjustments that assume the patrol will stay on azimuth. **If indirect fire continues during the retreat, the enemy may be adjusting their fires to match the retreat.** In that case, Leaders must change the distance and direction, and get accountability.

Commands are echoed by everybody. When moving, all Soldiers must maintain communication with their Leader and be available to carry their Leader's body. They do not sprint ahead without regard for further instructions. They also immediately check to ensure that their buddy to the left and right also are up and moving, as this helps to ensure everyone moves out as fast as possible. If a Soldier is injured, assist them in carrying their important equipment.

When the patrol arrives at the designated direction and distance, Leaders immediately establish a security perimeter and get accountability of men, weapons, and equipment; consolidate and reorganize; and evacuate wounded.

15.c React-to-Mine (Improvised Explosive Device)[1]

Whoever finds the improvised explosive device (IED) alerts the patrol to the possible mine and its location using the 3Ds. The Patrol Leader carefully establishes security, and every Soldier scans for possible secondary IED's using **0/5/25/200-meter checks:**

0-Meter – Before every step, look at the ground underneath for possible pressure plates or wires.[2]

5-Meter – Check for anything out of place, like disturbed earth, or weird objects. Search systematically and methodically.

25-Meter – Look for larger disturbances, like large wet spots or disturbed structures.

200-Meter – The patrol must pay attention at distance for suspicious activity (like triggermen, cameramen, or snipers).

Do not immediately run to a Soldier who was just blown up, or rush to get out of there. IED's often are placed in bunches, so you may be blown by a secondary IED! As soon as possible call bomb specialists and higher command, with a 9-Line for Explosive Ordnance Disposal (EOD). (See 9-Line IED Report Template, Pg. 119.)

There are many kinds of IED's, from remote-detonated nitrate bombs, to trip-wire grenades. Globally, the kinds of IED's the enemy uses are specific to the region. It is essential to know the styles of the region so a Soldier knows what to look for. At the same time, there are standard questions that a Soldier who has been in the country asks themself. Why is this busy street quiet now? Why does no one use this trail or that field? Finally, a common tactic is to tempt Soldiers with cigarettes or dip cans attached to detonators. NEVER PICK UP ANYTHING!

---

1 Quote: Any ship can be a minesweeper... once. —Unknown

2 Real World: Be aware of minefield ambushes. Fighters mine an area with anti-personnel mines, and then shoot an RPG when vehicles roll through. This forces Soldiers to dismount the vehicle for fear of being blown up by an RPG. But then the dismounted Soldiers are blown up when they step on mines.

Image 80: 3rd Bde. Recon Team, 3rd Inf. Div. drive through trash. Outskirts of Baghdad, Iraq, 11 Aug 2005. Trash is a great way to hide IED's. Baits, like weapon magazines and energy drinks are especially attractive. **Are there safe ways to navigate areas where IED's are easy to place?**

9-Line IED Report Template

For confirmed IED's, call higher with a 9-Line for Explosive Ordnance Disposal (EOD).

1. Date-Time Group:	Date and time of discovery.
2. Reporting Activity, Location:	Unit and the grid location.
3. Contact Method:	Radio frequency, call sign, etc.
4 Type of Ordnance:	Be detailed; include: size, shape, and physical condition.
5. Nuclear, Chemical, Biological:	Be as specific as possible.
6. Resources Threatened:	Equipment, facilities, etc.
7. Impact on Mission:	Brief description of the situation, and mission impact.
8. Protective Measures:	Measures taken to protect personnel and equipment.
9. Advised Threat Priority:	Immediate, indirect, minor, none.

15.d Fixing a Split Element

An element is "split" when Soldiers in the element cannot see each other, and there is a break in all methods of communication. For example, if the emergency contact plan is a runner, and a runner is not feasible, then the element has split.

If an element splits because they advanced too fast, then the forward element must backtrack. The rear element continues to advance slowly, or stops completely and waits for the forward element to return. The rear element never sends out a search team, because that risks creating a third split element.

If a split element is lost, they must determine their location and proceed to the last designated rally-point. If the split was due to a react-to-contact, then both elements go to the last rally-point designated and wait there until the other element approaches with near and far recognition signals. The time that an element waits at the rally-point depends on planning and METT-TC. An element must never be in a position where they are separated, all comms are down to other elements and higher, they are lost, and do not know where the last rally-point was.

15.e Reacting from a Non-Standard Formation

A patrol usually engages the enemy from a small set of standard formations, like a wedge or a long-halt. However, there are times when a patrol must engage the enemy from a weird formation or no formation at all. Examples of non-standard formations include a platoon crossing a linear danger area, or a patrol engaging in a casualty-carry formation.

Whenever the patrol is engaged in any formation, the two mandates are to **maintain security and prevent fratricide**. First, any security positions that are not attacked must stay where they are. If a security position can be eliminated, and security still be maintained, then that security position was terrible to begin with.

Second, when a Leader organizes a firing line, they must ensure that there are no friendly troops in front of the line. This is an especially important step when the formation is non-standard, and there may be Soldiers in front that the Leader is not immediately aware of. Do not hesitate to maneuver every unit to achieve safe sectors-of-fire, but confirm movement!

After rushing to cover, Soldiers from different elements inevitably mix together when returning fire. When a Leader needs to form an element to maneuver with, instead of trying to reunify a team or squad, the Leader flexibly rallies Soldiers. For example, a Leader may call the EPW Team, or the five Soldiers next to them.

15.f Enemy from Multiple or Changing Locations[1]

The standard battle drill attacks specialize in killing enemies on a single, unchanging location. However, if there are enemies in multiple areas, then the patrol has to deal with every enemy location. The difficulty in attacking in multiple locations is the coordination of each element to prevent friendly fire. Multiple bold-flanking maneuvers are dangerous and are to be avoided. If each split element is given an assault-through command, they must assault outward in different directions.

If the enemy withdraws while continuing to fire on friendly forces (the most common change of location), the Patrol Leader must decide whether to pursue the enemy or break contact. Usually a good idea is to pursue for a limited distance and then break contact. Following too far can lead to many bad situations, like split elements and enemy ambushes. If the contact was unplanned, the Patrol Leader must attempt to minimize the amount of time and ammo wasted on reacting to a chance contact.

Phase 2

---

1 Quote: The enemy resembles us. Therefore, he needs to be approached not as an assembly of 'targets' to be destroyed one by one; but as a living, intelligent entity capable of acting and reacting. —Israeli military historian and theorist, Martin Van Creveld

Phase 3 Contents

16. Creating the Long-Halt   123

Preventing Rear Attack (Counter-Tracking)   126
Organizing a Halt (Emplacing around a Reference Point)   127
Grouping Soldiers (Strong-Point/Crow's Foot)   129
360-Degree Security (Assigning Sectors-of-Fire)   130

17. Creating the Objective Rally-Point   133

Equipment Check (COW-T)   133
Splitting Elements (GOTWA)   134
Leader's Recon of the Squad ORP   136
Surveillance and Observation Position (S&O)   139
Actions at Long-Halt during Leader's Recon   140
Recombining Elements (Near and Far Recognition Signals)   141
Occupation of the Objective Rally-Point   143

18. Creating the Ambush   144

Leader's Recon of Release-Point, S&O, and Killzone   146
Leader's Recon of Support and Assault   148
Leader's Recon of Security Positions   153
Allocating Leadership   156
Occupation of the Release-Point   156
Emplacement of Security and EWAC   159
Methods of Emplacing Support and Assault   161
Emplacement of Support   162
Emplacement of Assault and SPARC   163
Coordinating Sectors-of-Fire   166
Emplacing Claymores and Final Steps   168
Platoon Area Ambush   170

19. Platoon Point Ambush   171

Leader's Recon of the Platoon Formation   172
Platoon Formation   176
Leader's Recon of the Objective   180
Occupation of the Objective   181
Location of Platoon Leadership   182

20. Contingencies   184

Running Out of Time (Hasty Emplacement)   184
Compromise during Emplacement   185
Ambush at a Bend in the Road   186
Unidirectional Ambush (T and V)   188
Ambush for Anti-Ambush Patrols (K and X)   190
No Radio Communications with Security   192
Other Ambush Types   193

Joe Sets His Trap (Phase 3: Occupying the Objective)

If you find yourself in a fair fight, you didn't plan your mission properly.
—U.S. Army Col. David Hackworth

Occupying the Objective Overview

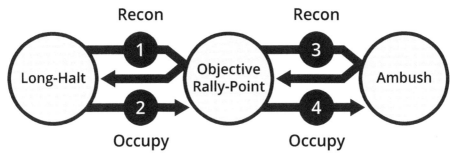

Image 81: This section instructs how to go from a long-halt to occupying an ambush while doing proper reconnaissance.

You might be wondering why this section is so damn long. Why can't you just show up to the ambush, lie down, and kill people? Well, some places are much safer for us and deadlier for the enemy, so the best locations need to be judged. During leader's recon, Soldiers are chilling in the rear for hours, so they need to be kept hidden. That rear location needs to be scouted too. The whole process is extremely time consuming, but proper recon can be the difference between killing all the enemy in the first volley and a dangerous hour-long firefight.

16. Creating the Long-Halt

After arriving in the vicinity of the ambush location, the first step is creating a long-halt. (See Image 1, Pg. 3.) (See Image 81, Pg. 123.) A long-halt is

Image 82: 352nd Battlefield Airman Training Squadron Combat Control School student scans the woods during a long-halt for his unit during a tactics field training exercise. Camp Mackall, NC, 03 Aug 2016.

much like a short-halt. (See Short/Security-Halt Formation, Pg. 48.) It can also be used when halted for more than five minutes, as it is safer but takes more time. The extra steps involved are: anti-tracking; top-down organization; taking rucks off; grouping Soldiers; and assigning, focusing, and interlocking sectors-of-fire. (See Image 83, Pg. 125.)

The long-halt in the vicinity of the ambush location is used as a place for the Main Body to wait, as Leaders scout an objective rally-point (ORP). (See Creating the Objective Rally-Point, Pg. 133.) The ORP, in turn, is a location for the Main Body to wait, as Leaders scout an ambush. (See Creating the Ambush, Pg. 144.) This pre-ORP long-halt location is roughly planned in the OPORD, and modified on the ground to account for METT-TC and counter-tracking.

The reason the ORP, a waiting location, needs its own reconnaissance is because it is located relatively close to the ambush area, and having dozens of Soldiers relatively close to a road can attract unwanted attention. Therefore,

Long-Halt Concepts

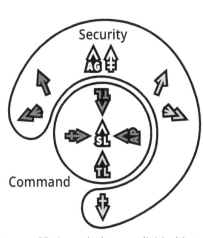

Image 83: Long-halts are divided into an **inside and outside**, or security and command positions.

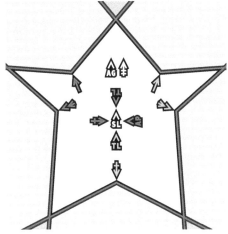

Image 84: Leadership **assigns** and confirms **360-degree** overlapping sectors-of-fire.

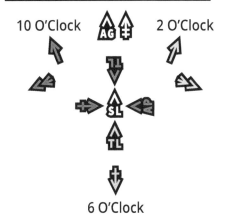

Image 85: If the direction of a threat is known, **focus security**. This is a 3-point long-halt.

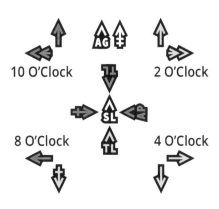

Image 86: If the direction of a threat is unknown, distribute security evenly. This is a 4-point long-halt.

Phase 3

the long-halt is a way to allow leadership to find a good ORP, where the Main Body can be stashed away for a long recon of the objective.[1]

16.a Preventing Rear Attack (Counter-Tracking)[2]

Anti-tracking techniques, like walking in streams or moving in the rain, are effective at hiding movements. However, it is unrealistic to expect that an enemy cannot track 50 grown men with heavy equipment in the woods. **If enemy tracking is suspected the best anti-tracking is a surprise ambush.**

The dogleg and fishhook put the patrol in a great position to flank and kill the enemy. They are useful whenever the patrol stops where enemy tracking is possible. To start, the Patrol Leader looks for a position to the left or right with suitable cover and concealment to completely hide an entire platoon. (Keep in mind that a platoon is really big, and can be 50 meters long when halted.) (See Image 87, Pg. 127.)

A **dogleg** is accomplished by turning the patrol roughly 90 degrees left or right, and moving into a covered and concealed location. Then the patrol secures the turning point. If an enemy unit is following, they will walk into the turning point and be flank attacked by the patrol. Without a dogleg, Soldiers would fire backward at the front of the enemy patrol instead of the side (where an attack is more effective).

In a **fishhook,** instead of making a straight right angle, the patrol makes a giant circle and points back at their original avenue of approach. Again, any enemy following the patrol will be flanked as they follow that avenue.[3] A fishhook does not leave evidence that the patrol turned, and so is harder for enemy tracking to detect. However, it take more time.

---

1 Real World: Doing a long-halt before the ORP takes time. To save time, squads can take the ORP by force (i.e. go straight from long-halt to ambush) because they are smaller elements and don't need as much hiding.

2 Quote: You're not hunting him... he's hunting you. —Trautman in First Blood regarding Rambo

3 Applying Concepts: For the dogleg or fishhook, a patrol can employ claymores. Would it be a good idea to place claymores when the patrol first passes through, or after the killzone is set?

Counter-Tracking Movements

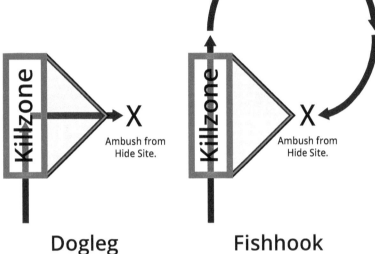

Image 87: Both the dogleg and fishhook are designed to enable an **easy flank attack** on the enemy.

16.b Organizing a Halt (Emplacing around a Reference Point)

Two refinements that a long-halt has over a short-halt include better emplacement of Soldiers and better fields-of-fire. This is because a long-halt has **top-down organization**, instead of letting Soldiers halt wherever they are at the moment. After the Patrol Leader calls a long-halt and conducts SLLS, they immediately go to the location they decide the center of the formation will be. Soldiers then form around the Patrol Leader level by level.

In a squad, Team Leaders join the Squad Leader. If there will be a leader's recon, Alpha SAW and Alpha Point go to the center too. These five Soldiers **drop their rucks** in a cross shape facing the direction of movement, which orients the rest of the patrol. (See Image 88, Pg. 128.)

A platoon does the same concept with its own leadership and formation. The Platoon Sergeant and Weapons Squad Leader drop their rucks below the

Long-Halt Command Organization

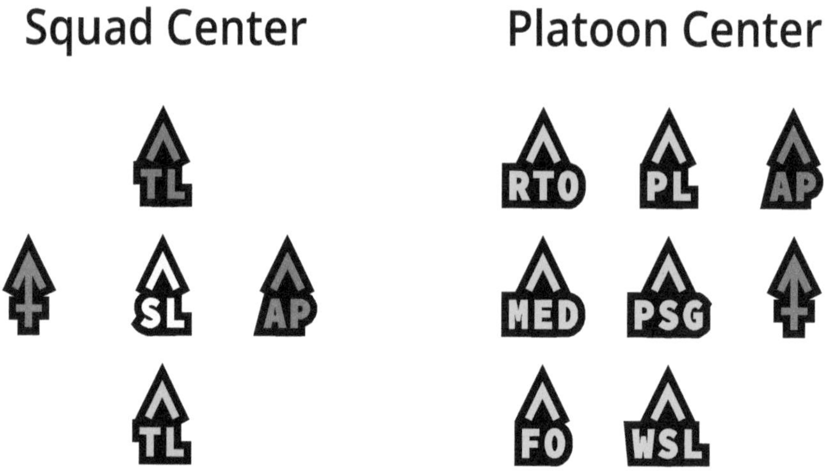

Squad Center

Platoon Center

Image 88: In a long-halt or rally-point, command is by definition the center. The patrol references the alignment and position of command to align and position itself. Here are two methods for organizing command.

Platoon Leader. Then the RTO, Medic, and FO place their rucks in another column to the right. If there will be a leader's recon, the Alpha Point and an Alpha SAW create another column to the left.

After leadership makes a center, Soldiers position themselves but do not drop their rucks yet. A position can only be finalized when a Leader assigns it. Gun Teams go to the most likely avenues of enemy approach (the 12 o'clock by default). With reference to the center, SAW's place themselves at other likely avenues of approach. Riflemen form a rough circle, to be corrected and coordinated by Team Leaders.

Leadership dropping their own rucks first is very important, so they can run to Soldiers, finalizing their positions as fast as possible. Team Leaders fill gaps, assign sectors-of-fire, and tell Soldiers to drop rucks. If a Soldier drops their ruck before they are told, the Soldier may have to put their ruck back on to move somewhere else. An exception may be machine guns, because they cannot aim and fire effectively with a ruck on.

When leadership does not create a definite reference point, the lower leadership must reposition everyone and consolidate. This is because Soldiers

Image 89: Sniper teams from the 3rd Armored Bde., 1st Armored Div., and Kuwaiti Land Forces engage a target during a joint combined arms live-fire exercise. Near Camp Buehring, Kuwait, 06 Dec 2016. **Note that Soldiers in each strong-point can silently communicate.** The two Soldiers on the right are in a typical crow's foot formation.

will have varying ideas of where the center is. In a platoon movement, repositioning like this can compromise security for over ten minutes.[1]

There are some guidelines for positioning Soldiers in a long-halt. To ease communication, Soldiers are positioned as close as possible, with appropriate cover and concealment. Soldiers are positioned in a strong-point position (next section). Each position balances manpower against threat, so a road has more Soldiers pulling security than would be the case in a swamp.

16.c Grouping Soldiers (Strong-Point/Crow's Foot)

Grouping Soldiers together is usually preferable to having Soldiers by themselves: sleepy Soldiers have a buddy to wake them up; Leaders manage fewer positions and lose fewer Soldiers (a concern in the dark); and instructions can be given twice as fast. A Soldier that sees an enemy can maintain eyes-on while their buddy alerts a Leader. Grouping Soldiers is not necessary for

---

It may seem easy to make a circle without a reference point with sunlight, but what if you are in a nighttime jungle? How about when adrenaline is rushing, or the Patrol Leader is occupied?

a five-minute short-halt, but grouping Soldiers is always good practice, and needs to be done for a long-halt.

"Strong-point" is a technique that assigns a sector-of-fire to multiple Soldiers instead of a single Soldier. Using strong-points allows a Soldier to leave their position without having a replacement Soldier stand in for them; for example, to check their ruck. A Leader can also give double sectors: each Soldier gets an individual sector and the group's sector. Then, Soldiers can themselves reallocate as needed, and cover the entire sector-of-fire if the other Soldiers in the strong-point are incapacitated.

It is common to place a strong-point in a **crow's-foot** formation. This is where two or three Soldiers lie in the prone with interlocking feet or lower legs. From above, it looks like a crow's foot. Each Soldier turns 45 to 90 degrees away from the Soldier next to them, depending on how much area the position pulls security on. (See Image 89, Pg. 129.)

The Soldiers touch legs to signal nonverbally. If one Soldier sees a potential danger, they can maintain eye contact with the target and silently tap the other Soldier's foot. The alerted Soldier can silently inform a Leader, provide backup, or perform any other task while the first Soldier never loses sight of the danger.

16.d 360-Degree Security (Assigning Sectors-of-Fire)

Sectors-of-fire are defined in the Introduction. (See The Secret Ideas (Concepts), Pg. 18.) A common error when assigning sectors is to distribute them proportionally, giving each Soldier an even slice of the surrounding area to surveil. However, that is a mistake. Soldiers are not split evenly between major road and vast desert. Instead, **sectors are focused** and allocated proportionally to the danger posed, and not the amount of area covered.

Sectors interlock at no more than 35 meters (the range of a hand grenade). The best way to assign sectors is to involve Soldiers in the process and get personal. Kneel next to, or literally lie down on, a Soldier. Then instead of quickly pointing out two trees in the forest and leaving, give the

Distribution of Sectors-of-Fire

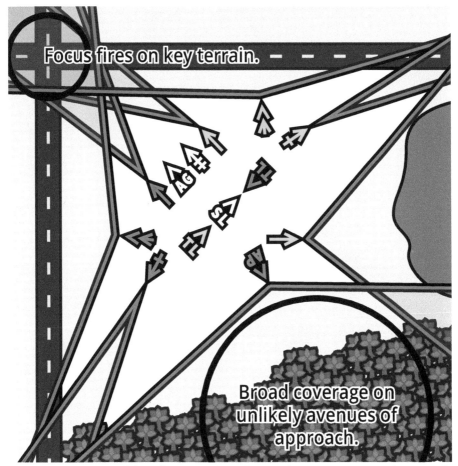

Image 90: Sectors-of-fire don't need to be, and even must not be, evenly distributed. **Areas that present more danger require more coverage.**

Soldier an azimuth and tell them to pick their own landmarks. Or give them landmarks and have the Soldier backbrief an azimuth.[1]

---

1 Example Sector Assignment:
ATL – "Take out your compass. Tell me what you see at 300 degrees."
ARR – "That tree [pointing]."
ATL – "Okay, that's your left limit. Now pick something at 50 degrees."
ARR – "That big rock."
ATL – "That's your right limit. Your PDF is that road."

131

Image 91: An NCO with 1-23 Inf., 1-2 Stryker Bde. Combat Team, gives a sector-of-fire. Yakima TC, WA, 02 Nov 2017. **The Leader is very close to his Soldier, ensuring good communication and low noise.**

Even though multiple Leaders can assign sectors at once, one Leader is ultimately responsible for completing the interlock. (See Coordinating Sectors-of-Fire, Pg. 166.) In a squad, after the Bravo Team Leader is finished with their team, they then confirm or reassign sectors to the Alpha Team to confirm there are no gaps. In a platoon, once the squads have interlocking sectors within themselves, a designated Leader ensures that there are interlocking sectors where squads meet.

While Team Leaders assign sectors to their teams, the **first priority** of squad-level leadership and higher is assigning sectors to the M240s. Gun Teams point where enemies will most likely come from, like roads or unscouted areas. M240s do not interlock with anything, because they must be able to move in and out of a position without disturbing the 360-degree coverage. For example, if the enemy attacks a flank, the Patrol Leader moves a M240 to that flank, while leaving the 360-degree security intact.[1]

A Leader emplaces the Gun Team by physically replacing the Gunner at the M240. (The Leader hands their rifle to the Gunner, so every Soldier is

1 Applying Concepts: An element that can be removed from one part of a security perimeter and placed somewhere else, while the security perimeter still retains 360-degree security, is called a "Maneuver Support Group," or MSG. MSG's are not limited to M240s and can be anything, like a pair of Riflemen or Grenadiers. Why might the Gun Team be the standard MSG?

always controlling a weapon.) The Leader then positions the M240 toward a sector-of-fire. When the Leader determines a good sector, they move the M240 to its left limit, right limit, and primary direction-of-fire (PDF) to double-check that shooting in those directions is possible. Then the Leader puts the Gunner back in position, lies on top of them, and again physically moves the gun to its limits, while describing what the M240 is pointing at so that the Assistant Gunner can overhear them. Always backbrief.

17. Creating the Objective Rally-Point[1]

The ORP is an area to stash Soldiers while Leaders scout out the ambush area. Why is there a need to scout an ambush area after looking at a map before the mission even starts? Because the ground never exactly matches the map. In heavily forested areas, loggers can come and clear-cut an area in just a day. A great, densely-wooded area on the map just became an open field. An open field is a terrible ambush location.

17.a Equipment Check (COW-T)[2]

Checks and verification are essential parts of any patrol. The ORP is a good place and time to double-check Soldiers and equipment before the ambush, as it is the last time Soldiers can freely move within the formation.

For checks to be effective, they must be performed in a systematic and predetermined manner. During a patrol, there are two primary kinds of equipment checks: **COW-T (Communications, Optics, Weapons, Tie-Downs)** and **MWE (Men, Weapons, Equipment)**, with the MWE of the M240 receiving special attention. An MWE checks every part of all equipment before the ambush. It is very dependent on the specific equipment the patrol carries. As such, it is beyond the scope of this manual.

Phase 3

---

1   Quote: In preparing for battle I have always found that plans are useless, but planning is indispensable. —Supreme Commander of the Allied Expeditionary Forces in Europe, Dwight D. Eisenhower

2   Quote: Slow is smooth, smooth is fast. —A common Army saying, which means the fastest way to complete a task is to be methodical.

COW-T is an abbreviated equipment check that is performed on every Soldier who leaves in a split element. It focuses only on communications equipment, optics like night vision, weapons, and tie-downs that secure said equipment. The first person to give a COW-T is the Patrol Leader to another Leader. Their purpose is to show the standard they want the COW-T to be at, accounting for time available and how much they trust the patrol to correct their own deficiencies. Once the Patrol Leader establishes the standard, they are backbriefed by having a COW-T performed on themself. Afterwards, all available leadership COW-Ts remaining Soldiers as quickly as possible. Unless Soldiers are experienced and can be trusted to check themselves, usually only Leaders check equipment. It is said, "Leaders check Leaders, Leaders check men."

An example COW-T is as follows. Communications means doing radio checks on every radio in the squad, and cross-loading batteries and radios as necessary. Optics is making sure that night vision devices are operational by checking both near- and far-seeing ability, and ensuring every Soldier has headlamps and spare batteries. Weapons is the Leader and Soldier exchanging and examining weapons, and examining magazines for full ammunition. Tie-downs is straightforward: it consists of following lines from where they are secured to where they end on the Soldier. Tie-down lines are also pulled down on to check they are secure.

17.b Splitting Elements (GOTWA)

To scout an ORP requires a scouting party, which splits the patrol into multiple elements. (See Leader's Recon of the Squad ORP, Pg. 136.) Whenever two elements separate, a GOTWA is always issued from the Leader of the Moving Element to the Leader of the Stationary Element. **GOTWA** means: Going to location; Others taken with; Time of emergency; What to do if late; and Actions on contact for both elements.

Where the Moving Element is going, and who is going are simple. The remaining three parts (i.e., the TWA) are a little more complicated. The time of emergency is not an estimation of how long the task will take, but rather an, "Oh Shit!" deadline, after which action must be taken. Even if the Moving Element expects to be gone for 15 minutes, the time of emergency can still be six hours ahead. The time is also never a quantity, but a clock time. (E.g., "We will return by 1500.") A duration would need to change every time a Leader re-briefs it.

The last two (i.e., WA) depend on METT-TC, but can be somewhat standardized for a patrol. A standard "what to do if late" is: "Attempt to contact me by radio every 5 minutes for a total of 30 minutes. If still unable to make contact for 30 minutes, contact higher for further instruction. And if you can't reach higher, take the entire element to come get us."[1] If the time-of-emergency passes, the what-to-do-if-late instruction must never be for the Stationary Element to wait additional time before acting. That defeats the purpose of having a time limit. And absolutely do not further split the patrol. That will lose two elements![2]

A common action-on-contact for Moving Element is to return fire and bound back to the Stationary Element. And common actions-on-contact for the Stationary Element are to fight in place, contact the Moving Element, and seek direction from higher. If either element cannot meetup, they return to the last rally-point.

After a Leader briefs a GOTWA, that Leader receives a backbrief and everyone resynchronizes watches. Right before splitting, both elements must take accountability of Soldiers who are splitting to the Moving Element (e.g., with a chokepoint).

Phase 3

---

1 Applying Concepts: If the stationary element calls higher, what would they ask for? What might higher be able to provide, if anything?

2 **Example** GOTWA:

Going to location – "We're doing a leader's recon of the ORP."

Others taken with – "The Alpha Team Leader, Alpha SAW, and Alpha Point [using Soldiers' names is advised] are coming."

Time of emergency – "It is now 1900 and we will be back by 2100."

What to do if late – "Attempt to call us by radio every five minutes for half an hour. If you cannot contact us, call higher and use the entire squad to come get us [don't split elements further]."

Actions on contact – "If we are hit, we will fight our way back to you and then withdraw together to the last en route rally-point which is 500 meters to our 6 o'clock. If we cannot come to you, we will go directly to our last en route rally-point and link up with you there. If you are hit, fight in-place and we will return to you. If you cannot hold, withdraw to our last en route rally-point and we will link up there."

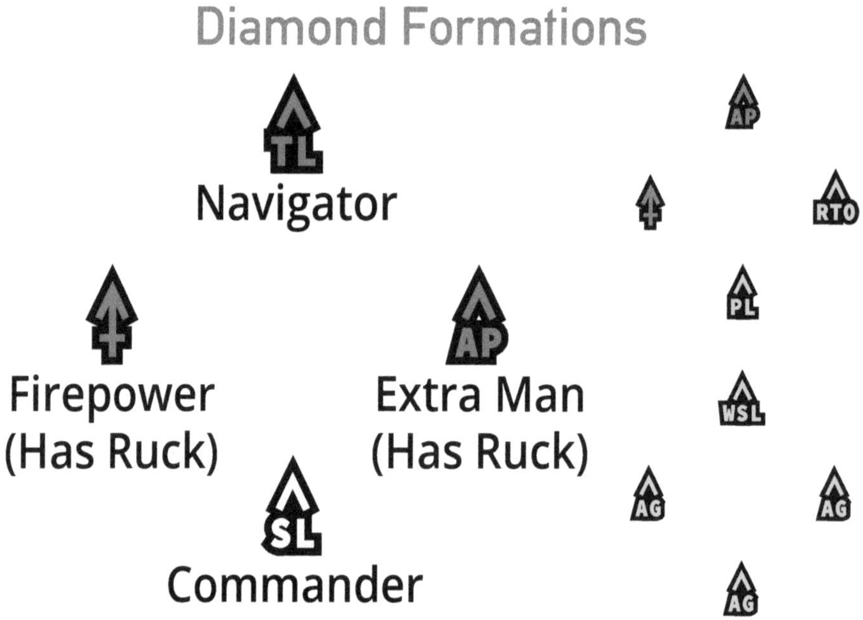

Diamond Formations

Navigator

Firepower
(Has Ruck)

Extra Man
(Has Ruck)

Commander

Image 92: Diamond formations, used for leader's reconnaissance. On the left is an example for a squad, and on the right is a platoon example.

17.c Leader's Recon of the Squad ORP

Leader's reconnaissance, or leader's recon, refers both to the action of reconnaissance and the Soldiers who do it. Leader's recon generally can be reconnaissance of anything by leadership. This section details one common way of doing leader's recon for a squad ORP.[1] Reconnaissance of the ORP is useful because a small element checking an area for the first time is less likely to be detected (and therefore safer) than the full patrol checking.

For a squad, a Leader's Recon Team is composed of two teams: the Leader Team (e.g., Squad Leader, Alpha Team Leader) and an S&O Team (e.g., Alpha Point, Alpha SAW). (See Surveillance and Observation Position (S&O),

---

[1] Real World: American forces often use a specific, standardized method of movement for detecting the enemy. The Vietcong knew the patterns, and when they heard Americans move in a big X, they went quiet. The Vietcong heard Americans trudging hundreds of meters in harsh terrain long before the Americans heard them. Can a good leader's recon be a single, long SLLS, then returning with the squad?

Image 93: U.S. Marines A Co., 1st Bn., 8th Marine Reg. in a **diamond formation**. Camp Lejeune, NC, 9 Dec 2019. Note the rear Marine is looking back for rear security.

Pg. 139.) Before setting off, all leaving Soldiers go to the center of the long-halt to get COW-Ted. If camouflage has come off, reapply it. Once ready, the Squad Leader gives a GOTWA to the highest-ranking Leader staying behind within earshot of the Leader. The Leader's Recon Team is counted out and leaves through a chokepoint.

The long-halt is 150 to 300 meters away from the prospective ORP (depending on METT-TC). For a squad, the Leader's Recon Team moves in a **diamond formation** with the Alpha Team Leader (land nav) at front and the Squad Leader (HQ) in the rear. A SAW performs best on the left because the muzzle naturally points left when carried by right-handed Soldiers. (See Image 93, Pg. 137.) (See Image 92, Pg. 136.) The diamond formation is one of the most basic movement formations, but it is often only used with very small elements like Leader's Recon Teams. (See Image 15, Pg. 38.)

Once the Leader's Recon Team reaches the tentative ORP, the Squad Leader conducts SLLS. (See Detecting the Enemy (SLLS), Pg. 47.) Then they emplace S&O for overwatch. (See Surveillance and Observation Position (S&O), Pg. 139.) A good ORP follows the acronym **COOL-E:**

C – Covered and concealed.

O – Out of sight, sound, and small-arms fire. (If the you can shoot the objective, the objective can shoot you.)

Leader's Recon, Objective Rally-Point

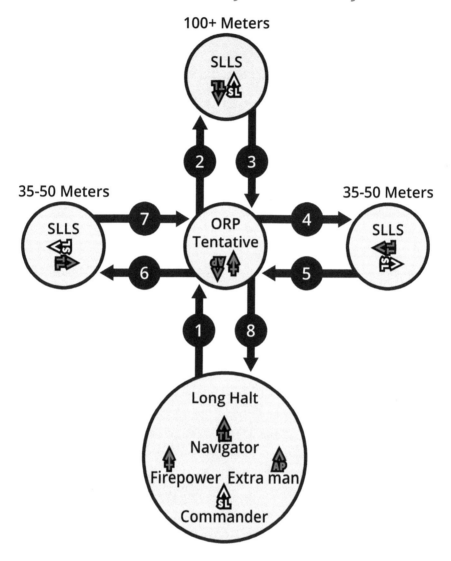

Image 94: The Leader's Recon Team (LRT) first finds a good tentative objective rally-point. Then the LRT scouts the perimeter for danger. In this example, the direction of movement contains the most unknown so has the first and longest recon. **Conduct SLLS at every leg. All distances and scouting locations are situationally dependant.**

O – Off natural lines of drift. (For example, don't go where people naturally walk, like paths to bodies of water, or next to hunting spots.)

L – Large enough to fit the entire element.

E – Easily defendable for a short time. (The patrol must be able to defend the area while a withdrawal is organized.)

Once emplaced, the Squad Leader gives S&O a GOTWA and continues recon. The Leader Team moves in and out of the S&O position to confirm that the surrounding area is safe. The Leader Team moves out 100 meters (or however far confirms relative safety), stops, and performs SLLS, then goes back to S&O in all directions.[1] (See Image 94, Pg. 138.)

Before returning to fetch the squad, the Squad Leader gives S&O a **modified GOTWA**. (A modified GOTWA only contains changes to the original, and can be given after a full GOTWA.) (See Recombining Elements (Near and Far Recognition Signals), Pg. 141.)

17.d Surveillance and Observation Position (S&O)

The Surveillance and Observation (S&O) position is a concealed, two-Soldier, overwatch position that surveils and observes an area for important information, and especially potential enemy movement. The two Soldiers are a Rifleman (to operate comms) and a SAW (firepower and security). For simplicity, the standard S&O Soldiers are the Alpha Point and Alpha SAW of the lead squad. (See Image 95, Pg. 140.)

An S&O is used for every reconnaissance (e.g., leader's recon and linkup). The purpose of the S&O is to (as best as possible) provide eyes on 100% of the target area 100% of the time until the target area is occupied by the patrol. Due to trees, micro-terrain, blinking, etc., an S&O at minimum must have eyes on 75% of the target area, 95% of the time. **Thereby, the S&O is still able to see all movements in the area.**

To achieve 360-degree surveillance, the two Soldiers face opposite directly, touching each other to enable nonverbal communication. If S&O is engaged, it will most likely be from the area observed, so the SAW faces forward to the 12 o'clock and the Rifleman faces back to the 6 o'clock. The

Phase 3

---

1 Applying Concepts: What terrain and conditions might require multiple SLLS, or a single SLLS? How much recon is necessary for METT-TC?

Rifleman must have working comms! Without comms, do not place an S&O. Finally, whenever the S&O is dropped off, it always receives a GOTWA from leadership, just like every time an element splits.

17.e Actions at Long-Halt during Leader's Recon

Back at the patrol's long-halt, while the Leader's Recon Team is gone, the remaining leadership is instructing the Main Body. They simultaneously are briefing the Main Body on the Patrol Leader's GOTWA, making sure they are awake, and refining sectors-of-fire. When the Main Body Leader gets a message of return of a returning Leader Team, they ready the Main Body to leave for the ORP. Soldiers put on rucks in pairs. One pulls security while the other puts on a ruck. They then alternate.

When the Leader Team appears, they engage in near and far recognition. (See Recombining Elements (Near and Far Recognition Signals), Pg. 141.) After the Leader Team is verified, the Main Body Leader counts them into the long-halt. The Main Body Leader stays at the front of the formation to form a chokepoint and count the patrol out of the ORP.

The Leader Team leads the entire squad to the ORP. Soldiers do not stand until they can move; this ensures Soldiers stay on a knee pulling security until the last possible moment.

17.f Recombining Elements (Near and Far Recognition Signals)[1]

360-degree "security" is meaningless if anybody can just walk up to the patrol. The patrol must secure shadows in the night before they approach, or else open fire. To verify others, patrols use prearranged recognition signals. These signals are used every time two elements meet each other (e.g., a returning Leader's Recon Team, or a returning water resupply).

Recognition signals are multilayered, usually using two layers of recognition: near and far recognition. In safe areas, a patrol could use one reliable layer, like an FM radio PACE plan. Or they could make a three-layer system in a dangerous area. (See Communication, Pg. 242.)

As the Moving Element comes to the Stationary Element, the Leader of the Stationary Element needs to be ready to receive the signals. Therefore, the patrol needs a reception plan as well. For radios, that means turning radios on, and maybe comms windows too. For visual signals, make sure someone is watching.

Far recognition signals are communications that do not identify the location of the sender or receiver. For example, using an FM radio does not give away the speakers' locations; whereas, shouting across a field does. However, if the enemy becomes capable of determining the origin of FM transmissions, FM radio ceases to be a good far recognition signal. (See Image 96, Pg. 142.)

The most common far recognition signal is FM radio. But there are infinite options. For example, drop-sites are used as far recognition in less time sensitive settings. To make a drop-site, one element can check from a distance, for example, a tree (the drop-site) every hour. Another element can put a signal (the drop) on the tree that indicates a pre-arranged message.

Near recognition signals give away the location of the sender or receiver. (See Image 97, Pg. 142.) Therefore, near recognition is dangerous

Phase 3

---

1 Quote: In waking a tiger, use a long stick. —Founding Father of the People's Republic of China, Mao Zedong

Image 96: U.S. Marine Lance Cpl. with 1st Light Armored Reconnaissance Bn., 1st Marine Div., conducts a radio check while on a recon patrol. St. Arnaud, New Zealand, 27 Oct 2017. Radios and satellite phones are common far signals.

Image 97: A U.S. Marine with Force Reconnaissance Platoon, Maritime Raid Force, 26th Marine Expeditionary Unit, adjusts night optical devices. 23 Jan 2016. **Visual and aural confirmation are common near signals.**

and requires encoding so nobody can blunder into a correct signal. Similarly, near recognition is avoided at night, when two elements need to be much too close to distinguish friend from foe using communications like sight or voice recognition. (See Image 99, Pg. 143.)

An example of recombining elements would be the following. When the Moving Element (ME) comes within sound of the Stationary Element (SE), the SE Leader orders the unknown (to them) element to halt using FM radio for far recognition. The ME halts. Then the SE Leader gives a preplanned coded order to the ME to act (e.g., "move red."). The ME acts accordingly (e.g., moves right). If the ME's actions match the coded order, then the ME is friendly and can proceed.

Another scenario could be when the ME comes into sight of the SE, the SE Leader orders the ME to halt, and the ME halts and immediately shows a halting signal for near recognition (e.g., shows a VS17 panel). The SE confirms that it received the appropriate signal and tells the ME to continue forward. Because both elements are in sight of each other, the near recognition signals can be used even if radios fail. There are infinite signals a patrol can use. (See PACE Communication Options, Pg. 242.)

Password exchanges are necessary when two elements need to join extremely quickly, like during enemy contact. A famous password combo used during D-Day in WWII was the first Soldier saying "flash," and the second Soldier responding with "thunder." Similarly, a **running password** (i.e., yelling a word when running) is useful when the ME is being actively

Image 98: Paratroopers from the 82nd Airborne Div. provide support-by-fire during a live fire exercise. Fort Bragg, NC, 28 Mar 2017. During the night they are out of sight.

Image 99: The same Soldiers as in the left image, under a flare. The dark of night can be good concealment. But how reliable is it? Even poor enemies buy night vision devices online.

pursued by an enemy and has no time to send signals. Without a password, an approaching element could be mistaken for an enemy and be shot, so make sure to use recognition signals.

17.g Occupation of the Objective Rally-Point

To occupy an ORP, the first step is to leave the long-halt. As the patrol leaves, the Bravo Team Leader or Platoon Sergeant form a chokepoint and account for all the Soldiers; sleeping Soldiers can accidentally be left behind.

When leaving the long-halt, everyone does not stand up at the same time; a Soldier only stands when they are in position to move out. Often, 360-degree security tends to fail because Soldiers are focused on the chokepoint and all face directly toward it. The Patrol Leader can even wait and call for specific elements to leave, one at a time.

There are dozens of methods for occupying an ORP, and there is no way of knowing which SOP your particular patrol will decide to use. A simple method is to occupy the ORP in the same way as the long-halt with a few small differences. The M240 is placed on its tripod (M192 lightweight ground mount). And a much more thorough check of Soldiers, weapons, and equipment is performed instead of COW-T. Team Leaders then set sectors-of-fire and question Soldiers about their duties while the Patrol Leader performs a leader's recon of the objective. The patrol sends up the spare-report for "ORP established."

Phase 3

Basic Linear Ambush Formation

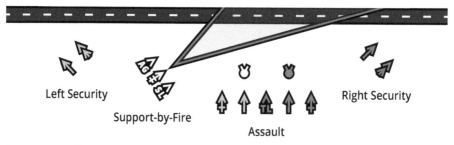

Left Security   Support-by-Fire   Assault   Right Security

Image 100: The end goal is to set a basic linear ambush. It has three locations (two security and one ambush) and six positions (each Security has a primary and a secondary position, and Assault and Support-by-Fire each have one position).

18. Creating the Ambush

Properly setting an ambush with full reconnaissance guarantees the most enemy kills with the fewest friendly casualties. The first step is to scout the actual terrain with a leader's recon, followed by emplacing and instructing Soldiers. This section gets specific, but never forget that there are infinite contingencies and scenarios, of which only a handful are listed here. Do not assume the enemy will fall for the same ambush format twice![1]

Leader's reconnaissance of the ambush site is a complicated process with a dozen each of locations and movements. To start with, leader's recon of the ambush objective area is similar to leader's recon of the ORP until the Leader's Recon Team leaves the squad. (See Leader's Recon of the Squad ORP, Pg. 136.)

Enemy contact is more likely at the objective than the ORP because the ambush objective, by its nature, is where people travel. Therefore, movement must be extremely slow and deliberate. Movement near the objective road is avoided altogether. If the Leader's Recon Team is compromised, the ambush either becomes a hasty ambush or fails altogether.

---

1 Quote: There's an old saying in Tennessee, I know it's in Texas, probably in Tennessee, that says, "Fool me once, shame on...shame on you. Fool me... you can't get fooled again." —Commander in Chief of U.S. Forces, George W. Bush

Leader's Recon of a Ambush Objective

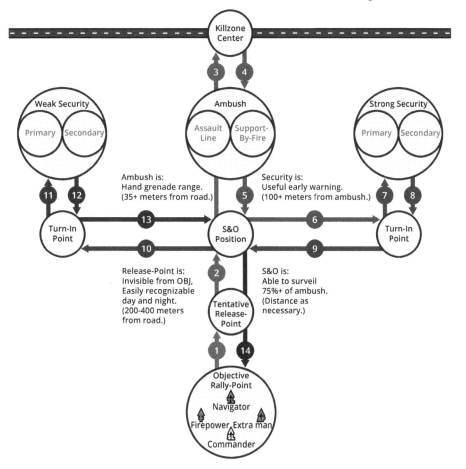

Image 101: Leader's reconnaissance of the objective (which includes the release-point, S&O position, killzone, support, assault, and security) is a complicated process with 14 different movements (shown here in numbered order) and 11 to 15 locations depending on how one counts. **This image is an comprehesive reference for the three leader's recon chapters. (See Leader's Recon of Release-Point, S&O, and Killzone, Pg. 146.) (See Leader's Recon of Support and Assault, Pg. 148.) (See Leader's Recon of Security Positions, Pg. 153.)** While reading, refer to this image for an overview of the locations, movements, and sequence of events in the order that this book presents them.

18.a Leader's Recon of Release-Point, S&O, and Killzone

To best follow along, use the diagram of leader's recon of the objective. (See Image 101, Pg. 145.) Leader's recon is useful for the ambush area, just as with the ORP, because a small element checking an area for the first time is less likely to be detected (and therefore is safer) than if the full patrol were scouting.

Before the Leader's Recon Team moves out, the Patrol Leader instructs the Main Body Leader to: check their Soldiers, check their equipment, and disseminate information. The Main Body Leader especially must ensure that each man knows the last active ERRP, in case of compromise.

While moving to the objective, the Leader's Recon Team identifies a **tentative release-point**. (It is tentative because the release-point is proposed at the start of leader's recon and confirmed at the end.) The release-point is a midway location between the ORP and the objective. It is where the patrol is stationed while the Patrol Leader takes groups of Soldiers from the patrol to position them in the ambush. While not strictly necessary, having a release-point is useful because it quickens emplacement. The ORP is relatively far from the objective; however, emplacement happens in three waves (i.e., Security, Support, and Assault), so the Patrol Leader can quickly enact emplacement by taking Soldiers from the release-point instead.

When the Patrol Leader identifies a tentative release-point, it must be:

Out of sight – but not necessarily out of sound of the objective; and,

Easily recognizable – both day and night.

Also, ideally the release-point is in a straight line between the ORP and the ambush objective to make navigation easier. That is why the release-point is tentative; if the release-point is not on a straight line, the Patrol Leader may want to choose a new one.

After a tentative release-point is identified, the Patrol Leader sets S&O into a well-covered and concealed position and gives a GOTWA. The S&O is between the tentative release-point and the objective, and must be able to surveil at least 75% of support and assault positions, though the more the better. The S&O especially need to perform overwatch for the Leader Team as it confirms the objective. (See Surveillance and Observation Position (S&O), Pg. 139.)

Image 102: Soldiers in 166th Civil Engineer Sqn., DE Air N.G., respond to an ambush. Redden State Forest, Georgetown, DE, 15 July 2017. **Note how well the ambush location applies DECAF COFFEE, and how exposed these Soldiers are.**

Image 103: A Tech. Sgt. from 166th Civil Engineer Sqn., DE Air N.G. waits to ambush a convoy during convoy operations training. Redden State Forest, Georgetown, DE, 15 July 2017. Note how well the location applies DECAF COFFEE.

When the Patrol Leader arrives at the tentative objective, they must confirm that the location is correct. The Patrol Leader and their assistant carefully walk (or crawl if necessary) close to the objective road, face opposite directions, and use their compasses. Each confirms the azimuth of the road and any terrain features as well. Even with modern maps and GPS devices, two different roads can be meters apart and easily confused if not checked.

Apart from confirming that the ambush location is correct, this is the time to evaluate whether the location is good. Once the objective is confirmed, the Patrol Leader scouts the ambush location and the security positions. The more restrictive of the two is scouted first. For example, imagine the ambush is along a mile-long road, and there are only a few good ambush spots. In that case, the killzone dictates where security positions can be located, and the ambush location is scouted first. Alternatively, perhaps the road is winding and hilly and Security could only give early warning of an oncoming enemy in a few spots. In that case, the exact ambush location depends on security positions, and security positions are scouted first. For the purpose of this manual, the ambush location is scouted first.

The Patrol Leader checks along the confirmed objective road for the ideal ambush spot. A good location can make or break an ambush, so recon takes as much time as is reasonable to look around. An ideal killzone is **DECAF COFFEE**:

DE – no DEad space between the wood line and the road (e.g., no berms, ditches, etc., that enemies could use for cover).

147

CAF – Clear lines of Assault (to walk) and Fire (to shoot) from the ambush line until the limit of the advance.

CO – COncealment (e.g., thick vegetation) and cover.

F – Flat, table-top ground surface (to allow machine guns to sweep at constant elevation, and minimize dead space).

F – Fifty meters wide.

EE – Eighteen-inch-wide Elms (i.e., trees) for claymores. (Claymore backblasts turn narrow trees into backwards shooting shrapnel.)

There are unlimited factors, including patterns of life on the road, good withdrawals routes, or expected arrival location of reinforcements. However, the perfect ambush location does not exist in imperfect real life. The best location may not meet all the requirements, and compromise is necessary. For example, maybe one location has no claymore trees, while another has bad concealment.

18.b Leader's Recon of Support and Assault

To best follow along, use the diagram of leader's recon of the objective. (See Image 101, Pg. 145.) The goal of leader's recon of support and assault is to find positions for Soldiers to most effectively ambush the enemy.

Once the Patrol Leader has found the best killzone location, they mark the killzone center as a reference point. The marker is something that the Patrol Leader can identify, but an enemy will not. For example, a large branch or a local "no trespassing" sign that is distinctive and identifiable but not unusual. The best identifiers already exist on the side of the road, like a telephone pole.

Then, the Patrol Leader backtracks and begins to find the best positions from which to attack the killzone. This section uses four weapon systems: **support-by-fire, SAW's, Riflemen, and claymores.** To ensure that no single location depends on a single weapon system, every weapon system covers 100% of the killzone, providing redundant coverage. (See Image 104, Pg. 149.)

The first weapons system to be reconned is the support position. This is because if support cannot be placed well, the killzone must be moved. Having 7.62 rounds shoot to 100% of the killzone is invaluable when ambushing vehicles. The support position is placed so the M240 will fire directly at the

Overlapping Sectors-of-Fire

100% Killzone Coverage by Support.

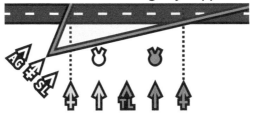

100% Killzone Coverage by SAWs.

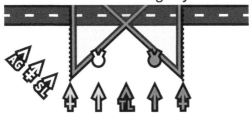

100% Killzone Coverage by Riflemen.

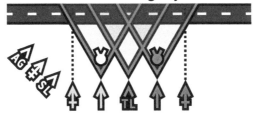

100% Killzone Coverage by Claymores.

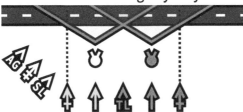

Image 104: During an ambush, redundancy is key; **no section of the killzone is deligated to a single weapon in case that weapon fails to fire.** Commonly, in order to cover every part of the killzone more than once, each weapon system completely covers 100% of the killzone. In this example, the ambush has 400% killzone coverage.

Image 105: A Gunner with A Co., 4th Bn., The Royal Regiment of Scotland, prepares to fire on insurgents 600 meters away. Nahr-e-Saraj, Afghanistan, 2 Jul 2011. **The max effective range of a M240 is 1100 meters. How far away can SBF be placed from the killzone?**

Image 106: Slovenian Soldiers perform a live-fire exercise with an FN MAG machine gun. Postonja, Slovenia, 15 Oct 2015. Distance from the killzone is their concealment. How would Support coordinate with Assault at a distance? Where should the Patrol Leader be?

front of oncoming vehicles, on the opposite side of the Assault Line. (See Image 105, Pg. 150.) So when the enemy comes, the M240 will shoot a vehicle's engine right in front of Assault. Ensure that the M240 on a tripod can cover the entire killzone from the prone. (See Image 106, Pg. 150.) The Patrol Leader gets in the prone to confirm. Mark the position well, but not so well it can be seen from the road.

To scout the assault line (SAW's and Riflemen) the Patrol Leader returns to the center of the killzone. From there, the Patrol Leader paces away from the killzone to good cover and concealment. (See Image 107, Pg. 151.) (See Image 108, Pg. 151.) However, they do not go so far that Assault cannot

Image 107: An E Co., Bn. Landing Team 2nd Bn., 1st Marines, 11th Marine Expeditionary Unit, leads a team of Malaysian Soldiers in a simulated ambush. 29 Aug 2014. **There is no cover for the Assault Line. What can the Soldiers do to mitigate this? Can they move the ambush?**

Image 108: Marines with Co. L, 3rd Bn., 25th Marine Reg., 4th Marine Div., Marine Forces Reserve. Air Ground Combat Center Twentynine Palms, CA, 14 Jun 2015. This squad has the opposite problem. **They have ample cover with no concealment. What can these Soldiers do to hide better on the Ambush Line?**

quickly assault the killzone.[1] The Assault Leader's position is here, directly behind the killzone center. For a linear ambush the Patrol Leader turns 90 degrees and walks parallel to the road, one half the Ambush Line length. This is one end of the killzone. Be precise; use a compass! (More ambush shapes are covered below.) (See Contingencies, Pg. 184.)

At each end of the Assault Line is a SAW position. SAW's are typically on the end to provide firepower against a flank attack, maintain the Assault Line's width when Riflemen perform EPW after the assault, and fire at the enemy from multiple angles.[2]

When scouting a SAW position, the Leader gets on the ground and physically looks down their rifle sights to ensure the SAW position has a good view of the killzone. Mark the spot. The Patrol Leader does the same in

---

The standard distance is 35 meters. This distance is useful because an M240 on tripod and a standard squad Assault Line fit perfectly to have 100% coverage of the killzone. Plus, claymore wires are about 35 meters long. However, imagine a perfectly flat desert with no dead space and no good concealment. How far from the killzone should the ambush line be?

One Special Forces Soldier led an ambush with foreign troops. He set himself at the center of the Assault Line as both the Assault Leader and the SAW Gunner, because the foreign troops were unfamiliar with the SAW.

Assault Line Organization

Bad - **Rigid Geometry.**

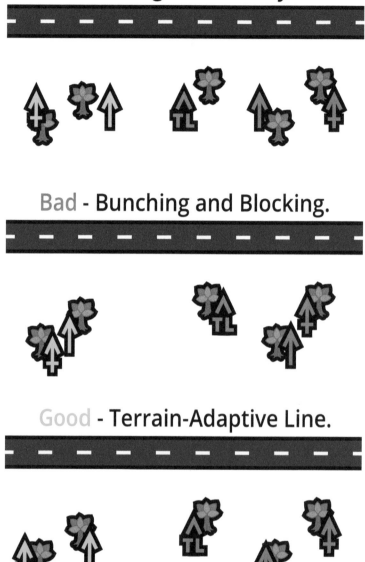

Bad - **Bunching and Blocking.**

Good - **Terrain-Adaptive Line.**

Image 109: When looking for and setting up an Assault Line, **do not use rigid distances between units.** Utilize the terrain. Soldiers can space out more when they assault the killzone.

Phase 3

reverse, to scout the SAW on the other side. The Patrol Leader can also entrust the Assistant Patrol Leader with them to scout the other SAW simultaneously.

Next, the Patrol Leader scouts for assault positions which are, roughly, evenly spaced on a line between the SAW's. The Patrol Leader looks for cover, concealment, sectors-of-fire, clear lanes of assault and fire, etc. (Use a compass to ensure perpendicular fires to the killzone!) (See Image 107, Pg. 151.) (See Image 108, Pg. 151.)

The Assault Line is terrain-adaptive, which means that placement of Soldiers does not have to be geometrically rigid. (See Image 109, Pg. 152.) So long as there are no friendly-fire concerns, and a rough line shape is maintained, Soldiers can move to better cover and concealment. If there are trees or troughs nearby, fudge the line to accommodate the better positioning. Once they have finished reconning Support and Assault, the Patrol Leader and their assistant return to the S&O position.

18.c Leader's Recon of Security Positions

To best follow along, use the diagram of leader's recon of the objective. (See Image 101, Pg. 145.) The goal of leader's recon of Security is to find positions for Soldiers to best fulfil their security roles during an ambush.

Each security position has two locations: a primary and a secondary. A primary location is occupied before the ambush initiates, and the secondary location is occupied after the ambush initiates. Each of the two locations are close in proximity and require different characteristics.

From the **primary location**, Soldiers provide early warning of oncoming traffic, and positive identification (PID) of the enemy. This normally requires visibility of at least 100 to 200 meters up the road/trail from the security position.[1] Try to place a primary position on a hill or a curved road, where the Soldiers are concealed by brush but can still see very far. Concealment is more important than cover for a primary, because if the enemy spots anyone, the whole ambush is compromised.

At the **secondary location** after initiation, Security kills anyone entering or exiting the objective. Therefore, a good secondary position has good fields-

---

[1] A vehicle moving at 40mph covers 100 meters in 5.59 seconds. Is that good early warning? Security without far vision is useless.

of-fire for all weapons.[1] Typically, this means a secondary is much closer to the road than the primary. (See Image 110 et al, Pg. 155.)

A secondary location also requires good cover. During an ambush, stray bullets from friendly and enemy fire may fire towards Security. So cover between Security and the ambush objective takes priority over cover between Security and the road. A great secondary position would be a hole on the side of the road with brush for concealment. If the secondary position has cover from Assault, then the Ambush Line can fire M4s at an enemy in the direction of Security as a last resort; for example, if the enemy flanks and gets between Assault and Security.

Though these factors are necessary to think about, there are practically unlimited factors to consider when placing Security. For example:

▸ Historical patterns for enemy movement speed.
▸ Traffic density/frequency of the objective road.
▸ Time required for emergency ambush emplacement.
▸ Difficulty in finding and evacuating Security.
▸ Lack of radios and backup plans for failed radios.
▸ Lines-of-fire and backblast areas for AT4s.
▸ How fast Soldiers can move between locations, etc.

To begin scouting security positions, the Patrol Leader starts and ends at the S&O position, where they give the S&O another modified GOTWA.[2] Then, the Patrol Leader and their assistant (together, the Leader Team) scout security positions on the side the enemy is expected to come from, called the "**strong-side**."[3] (The side that the enemy is not expected to come from is the **weak-side**.) The Leader Team walks along the road azimuth until they find a good location to turn in 90-degree towards the road. The location is a "turn-in point."

---

1 Applying Concepts: When isolating the objective, what are the benefits of giving Security a claymore versus an AT4? How do extra weapons help to isolate the objective? Why give either to Security instead of using them at the ambush?

2 **Example** Modified GOTWA:

SL –   "We're going to recon Security. We'll be back by 1730. Everything else, the same."

3 Applying Concepts: Some Soldiers advocate that an experienced Squad Leader and Alpha Team Leader can split up and recon both security positions simultaneously. What situation (if any) might warrant sending out individual Soldiers?

Image 110 et al: U.S. Army Paratroopers with 1st Sqn., 91st Cavalry Reg., 173rd Airborne Bde., provide security. Pocek Range in Slovenia, 02 Dec 2016. On the left is a **primary security location** on a hill. The berm and brush provide sufficient concealment, while the Soldier can maintain a far line of sight. On the right is a **secondary security location**. It has ample cover from all directions, and can be quickly accessed from the primary location.

The **turn-in point** is just like the release-point, easily identifiable day and night, and out of sight of the enemy. The turn-in point must be sufficiently identifiable, so that if Security has to emplace itself, the Patrol Leader can give good directions and a good description. Avoid walking diagonally straight from S&O to the security position, in order to keep Soldiers as far away from the objective road as possible.

From the turn-in point, the Leader Team turns 90 degrees and walks towards the road to find a good security position. Once at the tentative strong-side position, the Patrol Leader conducts SLLS, and recons a good primary and secondary location. After the strong-side has been reconned, the Leader Team returns to the S&O, gives another GOTWA, and recons the weak-side. If the patrol is short on time and Patrol Leader trusts Security's ability to find a good position, then Weak-Side Security can recon their own position because it is the less likely enemy avenue of approach.

After all positions have been reconned, the Patrol Leader issues a GOTWA to the S&O (who remains overwatching the objective) that the patrol will be moved to the release-point. As the Leader Team returns to the Main Body, the release-point must be finalized; the Patrol Leader either marks the tentative location as permanent or finds a better release-point. The Leader Team uses recognition signals to rejoin the Main Body.

18.d Allocating Leadership

Certain positions in an ambush require critical thinking and leadership. However, a patrol has a limited number of Leaders with various qualifications, so the Leaders need to be carefully placed to utilize their greatest potential. Typically, the highest leadership is placed with the most casualty-producing weapon, the M240. This is not only to control the weapon, but to ensure that the weapon displaces, and to position that Leader with a vantage point to watch the assault.

The Leader of Assault is more variable. In 2016 one U.S. Army school taught that the Alpha Team Leader leads. However, in 2018 they changed and taught that the Bravo Team Leader leads. This freed the Alpha Team Leader to lead Security. The tradeoff was better security, but a larger burden on the Bravo Team Leader.

18.e Occupation of the Release-Point

The release-point is the final staging location for the ambush, where Soldiers wait for Leaders to pick them up and emplace them in the ambush position. This is the place for final considerations. For example, if there are a limited number of radios, they are redistributed there (e.g., from S&O to Security). The patrol moves from the ORP to the release-point after the Leader's Recon Team returns to the Main Body. (See Leader's Recon of Release-Point, S&O, and Killzone, Pg. 146.)

At the release-point, the patrol is divided into three elements by order of emplacement: Security, Support, and Assault (SSA). Security is always emplaced first because it provides early warning of an incoming enemy; otherwise, Support and Assault would be caught off guard.

As Security is emplaced, Support and Assault pull **360-degree security** at the release-point. (Note however, that the surrounding area is relatively secure. Behind the release-point, the ORP was occupied for an entended time; and in the front, leader's recon scouted the area.)

Rucks can be left at the ORP or brought to the release-point.[1] Either way, putting rucks in three SSA columns makes withdrawal easier, as Soldiers know

---

[1] Real World: Normally, rucks would be left at the ORP; however, they are taken to the release-point for a squad point ambush in the schoolhouse so that they are not stolen.

Allocating Leadership in an Ambush

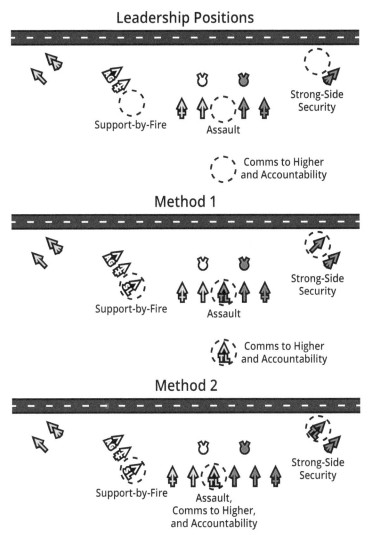

Image 111: All positions in an ambush benefit from a Leader to command and control them (or rather, someone to bark orders). The first section shows four such positions for this ambush: support-by-fire, assault, strong-side security, and comms to higher. How leadership is allocated depends on many factors. But **the two most important factors for assigning leadership are how important the position is to the ambush, and how experienced the Soldiers are** (i.e. how much leadership those Soldiers need). For example, the weak-side security position is always less important than Support-by-Fire, and so Support will always be assigned a Leader first.

Image 112: Soldiers of 1st Bn., 30th Inf. Reg., 2nd Inf. Bde. Combat Team, 3rd Infantry Division ready their rucksacks for a training mission to Senegal. Fort Stewart, Ga., 07 Jul 2016.

Ruck Plan

Security

ATL

Support-by-Fire

SL

Assault

BTL

Image 113: This is a common ruck plan for the ORP or release-point. **Leaving rucks in a planned fashion allows Soldiers to quickly withdraw with their own equipment after an ambush**. Soldiers are also organized into these same groups to pull security, so using a ruck plan quickens emplacement.

where their rucks are. (See Image 113, Pg. 158.) If rucks are consolidated at the release-point, then a plan needs to have been enacted to also consolidate the S&O's rucks, since they never come to the release-point.

18.f Emplacement of Security and EWAC

The Patrol Leader can emplace the Security for the ambush themself; or if they trust their Soldiers to emplace themselves, the Patrol Leader can describe the locations and turn-in points they have scouted and have Security emplace itself. Regardless, before they leave, the Patrol Leader briefs an EWAC plan to Security and get a backbrief.

EWAC[1] criteria are mini plans-of-action for Security:

Engagement criteria – The conditions and characteristics of the enemy with which Security will: 1) engage the enemy; 2) let the enemy pass; and/or 3) relay information to the Main Body. Security's primary purpose is PID of the enemy, and this is where Security is reminded of what to identify and what to do. (See Image 114, Pg. 160.)

Withdrawal criteria – The conditions under which Security must return to the release-point. The criteria must cover all scenarios, which often means giving a time limit.

Abort criteria – What will trigger the mission to be aborted.

Compromise criteria – What to do if Security is compromised. There are two kinds of compromise: "hard" and "soft." Hard compromise means

---

1 **Example** EWAC:

Engagement – "We will engage dismounted of 20 uniformed PAX or mounted of five light-skinned vehicles. Any element larger than this will pass. The Patrol Leader will initiate the ambush."

Withdrawal – "Withdrawal will happen: 20 minutes after first sound of engagement; two minutes after hearing the explosion; you hear 'Fire in the Hole 3'"; or 2300 at the latest.

Abort – "We will abort upon: compromise by an overwhelming force; artillery impacting on or around the objective; the arrival of an enemy reactionary force; on call from higher; or 2300 at the latest."

Compromise – "If soft compromised, attempt to PUC the individual. After PUCing or if PUCing is not possible, contact higher. If hard compromised, attempt to hide until directly engaged, and contact higher. If engaged, then fire AT4s, two magazines, pop smoke, and break-contact to the release-point."

Image 114: Serbian troops push through a simulated ambush in a convoy escort scenario during Platinum Wolf 15. South Base, Serbia, 26 Nov 2014. These Soldiers should not engage an armored vehicle with rifles. **This is a good example of why engagement criteria are necessary.**

that the enemy knows you are there (e.g., an enemy scout sees you). Soft compromise means that the enemy might know you are there (e.g., artillery fire in the distance). The line between hard and soft is often debated. Each compromise requires a different plan of action.

Once the Patrol Leader receives a brief back of EWAC from both Security Teams, the Patrol Leader gives a GOTWA to the Release-Point Leader and the S&O position that they are going to emplace Strong-Side Security. The Patrol Leader and an assistant (e.g. the original Leader Team which scouted the positions) take Strong-Side Security to their security position and conduct SLLS again. The Squad Leader emplaces Security into their primary location and points out their secondary location.

The Patrol Leader then conducts a radio check with both Security and S&O to double-check comms, and then notifies S&O and the Release-Point Leader of their return. When returning to the release-point, the Patrol Leader initiates recognition signals with the Release-Point Leader. The Patrol Leader repeats the same steps as above to emplace the Weak-Side Security.

Methods of Emplacement

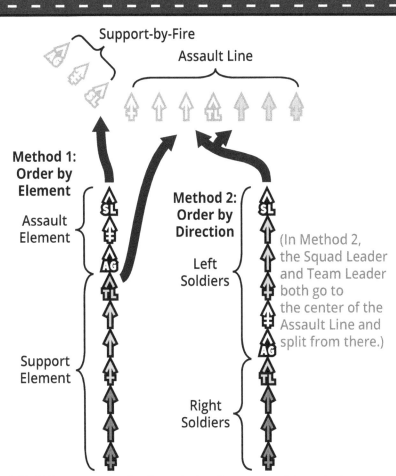

Image 115: Different methods of emplacing Support and Assault. In reality the different benefits between each method are minimal. However, a method must be chosen because **any method is better than no method**. Note the last two Soldiers in each line are the S&O, who were picked up.

18.g Methods of Emplacing Support and Assault

After Security is emplaced, the Patrol Leader must lead the Support and Assault elements from the release-point to the ambush area, while grabbing S&O on the way. There are many methods for bringing Support and Assault,

161

and two methods are listed here. Method 1 splits the Soldiers into Support and Assault, while Method 2 splits Soldiers into left and right. Both Soldiers from the Leader Team that did the leader's recon can emplace Soldiers at the same time. (See Image 115, Pg. 161.)

Method 1: the Patrol Leader emplaces Support-by-Fire first, while the Assistant Patrol Leader emplaces Assault. The benefit of this method is that it immediately allows for a hasty ambush if the enemy comes during emplacement, and emplacing one element at a time is simple. The simplicity is more important as the ambush size increases from squad size to platoon size, where the Platoon Leader has three Gun Teams and cannot overly concern themself with the Assault Line. The downside is that Assault is not fully emplaced until the Patrol Leader circles back (taking more time overall) and checks Assault's emplacement.

Method 2: both Leaders go to the center of the Assault Line and go right or left, emplacing each Soldier as they walk down the line. When Soldiers get in a file, they place themselves in the order closest to farthest from the center of the Assault Line. This way, the very next Soldier to be emplaced is directly next to the Leader who emplaces them, when they need to be emplaced. The advantage of the second method is faster emplacement, because the leadership emplaces every Soldier in their correct position the first time through (positions were premarked during leader's recon).

18.h Emplacement of Support[1]

The Patrol Leader locates the support-by-fire marking (made during leader's recon) and instructs the Assistant Gunner to quietly place down the tripod (i.e., M192 Lightweight Ground Mount). The Gunner quietly places the M240 on the tripod and locks it into position.

The Patrol Leader hands off their rifle to the Gunner and gets behind the M240 on its tripod. They adjust the elevation of the gun to attain good grazing-fire (i.e., where gunfire is about one-meter high to shoot enemy motors and hips). The sector-of-fire for the M240 covers 100% of the killzone, and the right limit is a minimum of 15 degrees off of the Assault Line. To enforce the 15-degree offset, the limit-of-fire parallel to the Assault Line is metal-to-metal

---

1 Quote: When shooting in the dark, it is a good idea to use a machine gun. —Australian television and radio comedian, Craig Reucassel

Phase 3

Image 116 et al: C Co., 1st Bn., 157th Inf. Reg., 86th Inf. Bde., CO N.G., prepare to ambush. Camp Ethan Allen, Jericho, VT, 23 Jan 2017. For this Assault Line, a small hill provides concealment, so standing would give away the position. **Crawling to to the killzone is a common technique to avoid alerting the enemy.** For this ambush crawling is necessary. If there is time, crawling can be used during every emplacement and leader's recon.

contact on the tripod. "**Metal-to-metal**" means the M240 cannot physically turn anymore on the tripod. For the opposite limit-of-fire, place some tape on the T&E to restrict the M240 from turning.

When the Patrol Leader has found the right and left limits, and set the metal-to-metal contact, they put the Gunner back into position and recover their rifle. Then, the Patrol Leader lays on the Gunner and physically moves the rifle to the left and right limits, making metal contact and describing a SPARC to the Gunner and the Assistant Gunner.

Phase 3

18.i Emplacement of Assault and SPARC

The location for each Soldier was marked in the dirt during leader's recon of the objective.[1] (If the markings are too faint, re-recon the area.) SAW's are typically on each end to provide firepower against a flank attack, maintain the Assault Line's width when Riflemen perform EPW after the assault, and fire at the enemy from multiple angles.

After the Assault Line is emplaced, the Assistant Patrol Leader stands beside the Assault Line with their compass. They check that the Assault Line is roughly on the same azimuth as the objective road. (An askew Assault Line leads to a diagonal assault to the road.) Adjusting Soldiers is as simple as giving micro-adjustments, like, "Move one meter back."

The Patrol Leader can turn one or two Soldiers to face backward, preventing an enemy counterattack from the rear. If the enemy forces have U.S. training, they probably will understand that a standard linear ambush is weak from behind, because every Soldier is facing the killzone, and weapons-noise masks enemy fires. If even one enemy makes it behind the ambush, they can pick off the entire Assault one man at a time.

Image 117: Palehorse Troop, 4th Sqn., 2nd Cavalry Reg., practices a live-fire exercise. Grafenwoehr Training Area, Germany, 24 Feb 2016. **Is this good Camouflage in SPARC?** Does the color of the pine branches match the surrounding brush? Every time this Soldier moves his head, it creates unatural plant movement. Never have camouflage stick out from the head.

Each SAW must have two full drums of ammo. One drum on the ground feeds into the SAW. The ground drum can be dug halfway into the ground to stabilize it. The other drum is attached to the SAW but does not feed. The attached drum is used when initiation stops, and the SAW Gunner needs to reload for the assault as fast as possible. Each Rifleman has two loaded magazines next to them also for quick reload.

When ready, the Patrol Leader and Assistant Patrol Leader brief SPARC's, starting with the SAW's. Ultimately, the Patrol Leader is responsible for properly emplacing and briefing Assault; however, the Patrol Leader often delegates or splits responsibility with the Assistant Patrol Leader since the Assistant leads Assault. **SPARC**'s are METT-TC,[1] but there are some general concepts to consider:

---

1 **Example** SPARC:
Sector-of-Fire – "Your sector is your 10 and 2 o'clock. Remember, Security is at your 9 and 3."
Priority of Targets – "Priority is dismounted, then the cab of the vehicle."
Assault Lane – "Your assault lane is directly forward."
Rate-of-Fire – "Fire at rapid, but go cyclic if the machine gun fire drops."
Camouflage – "Continue to camouflage yourself while I continue briefing."

Sector-of-Fire – The first priority is giving sectors-of-fire to the SAW's and M240s. (See Coordinating Sectors-of-Fire, Pg. 166.) For M4s, give a rough sector of their 10 o'clock and 2 o'clock. The Leader straddles the Rifleman's back and manually moves their rifle to its left and right limits.

Priority of Targets – Each weapon is assigned priorities of shooting among the expected targets. The priorities are determined by each weapon's capabilities. M240s are ideal for stopping enemy vehicles, so they prioritize shooting the engine block, then the vehicle's cab, and then dismounted. In platoon ambushes, each M240 from left to right targets the front, middle, and rear vehicles respectively. SAW's target the crew compartment or rear of vehicles, then the cab of the vehicle, and then any dismounted (i.e. people not in vehicles). Each SAW targets the closest vehicles first. M4s are point weapons, so they target individual dismounted Soldiers first, and then vehicles cabs. When there are no targets left, belt-fed weapons start to fire back and forth, sweeping their sector to maintain violence of action.

Assault Lane – In a linear ambush, lanes for each Soldier are straight ahead, for simplicity. The Patrol Leader briefs each Soldier on their direction. Non-linear ambushes have more complex assault lanes. (See Contingencies, Pg. 184.)

Rate-of-Fire – Rates have three designations: cyclic, rapid, and sustained. "Cyclic" means to fire an automatic weapon as fast as possible; "rapid" is slower than cyclic; and "sustained" is slower still. (See Rate-of-Fire, Pg. 237.) The rate for machine guns usually is cyclic for the first 15 seconds of the ambush. (Most enemies die in the initial fires.) Then the rate can slow to rapid for the next 15 seconds. The Leader can assign a lower rate-of-fire if the unit is low on ammunition.

M4s' rate-of-fire is sustained because their primary purpose is to attack specific targets and not necessary to create violence. To prevent all the M4s from running out of ammo simultaneously, some M4s commonly fire at rapid. Further, if machine guns are unable to fire, some M4s may move to cyclic to bring up the ambush's total rate-of-fire.

Camouflage – Soldiers must camouflage themselves, and Leaders must camouflage their Soldiers. Camouflage is outside the scope of this manual, but here are some basic guidelines. Always pull resources like brush and dirt from behind a position. Thereby, the blank spots of earth are hidden

Phase 3

Image 118 et al: A Soldier from the Japan Ground Self-Defense Force high-crawls while conducting a stalk exercise with 1st Marine Division Schools during Exercise Iron Fist 2014. Camp Pendleton, CA, 11 Feb 2014. **Note how well this Soldier blends into the environment.**

from sight. Match camouflage to the specific position, not the general area. (E.g., a giant stack of branches will seem unnatural when the nearest tree is 50 feet away.) Never stick anything above the head. Heads move and, and things on the head exaggerate that movement. Human eyes track in order, movement, outlines, and lastly color. (See Image 117, Pg. 164.) (See Image 118 et al, Pg. 166.)

18.j Coordinating Sectors-of-Fire[1]

Leadership gives each weapon system a sector-of-fire for the ambush for three reasons:

▸ To avoid friendly fire. A sector-of-fire avoids all friendly troop positions, which each Soldier may not individually remember in the heat of battle.

▸ To interlock sectors-of-fire for complete coverage. If every Soldier concentrates fires on one enemy, a second enemy may appear in an unmonitored area. Therefore, assigning Soldiers to control one area each, which together make a whole, avoids blind spots.

▸ To overlap sectors-of-fire for redundant coverage. Complete coverage never relies on a single weapon system.

To coordinate and overlap fires, standard limits-of-fire usually are employed.[2] Limits-of-fire are just like sectors-of-fire, but more specific (sectors-of-fire are each made of two limits-of-fire). (See 360-Degree Security (Assigning Sectors-of-Fire), Pg. 130.)

---

1 Quote: Cluster bombing from B-52s is very, very accurate. The bombs always hit the ground. —U.S. Air Force, Unknown

2 Applying Concepts: How might a Platoon Sergeant give coordinated fires during a react-to-contact?

Reference Points for Coordinated Fires

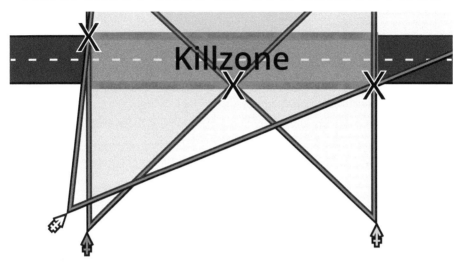

Image 119: What the sectors look like is planned during leader's recon. (See Leader's Recon of Support and Assault, Pg. 148.) (See Image 104, Pg. 149.) This image shows how to put that plan into practice. Proper coordinated fires for an M240 and two SAW's only requires three reference points. **Notice that one reference point is a back corner, while another is a front corner. Do not cross the road**; it is easy to be sighted on the road, compromising the mission.

In a linear ambush for SAW's: the left SAW's left limit is 90 degrees to the road, and its right limit is the killzone center; the right SAW's right limit is 90 degrees to the road, and its left limit is the killzone center. But again, as long as both SAW's intersect to cover 100% of the killzone, the limits-of-fire can be anywhere. (See Image 119, Pg. 167.)

Once the left and right limits of coverage are determined for the SAW's, those limits can be given directly to the M240. By using the same limits (with appropriate adjustments), it is guaranteed that there is identical, 200% killzone coverage. On the other hand, Riflemen can be given rough, broad sectors (e.g., "Your left and right limits are your 10 and 2 o'clock.") for 300% killzone coverage.

Making Soldiers remember and understand their limits-of-fire cannot be understated. Here are five examples of **enforcing limits-of-fire** (ideally use multiple methods at once):

- Lie down on the Soldier and grab and point their weapon to an identifiable feature (visible day and night). The stranger the feature, the better the memory will be.
- Walk down to the feature near the road and signal.
- Fire an infrared laser (e.g., the PEQ-15) at a limit.
- Place aiming stakes on either side of the weapon to physically limit movement to the left and right.
- Have the Soldier pull out their compass and pick their own features at an azimuth you give to them.

When choosing a marker on the near-side or far-side, on or off the road, remember to consider how angles affect the marker. If one marker on the near-side is used to designate the limit-of-fire of two weapons, each weapon will have a slightly different killzone than the other, because each uses the marker at a different angle.

Walking to the killzone and signaling is the most effective way to give sectors, but it is also the most dangerous since it makes the Leader easily seen down the road. Only go to the road if necessary and relatively secure, like in darkness with emplaced Security. And, if you do go, only make three trips to signal the left limit, center, and right limit, for both SAW's and the M240 at the same time. If going to the road, always give a GOTWA to Soldiers, so a sleepy Soldier does not wake up and start shooting you. In front of the Assault Line, only walk to and from the road, never parallel to the road traversing in front of the Assault Line. (Soldiers are intending to ambush a traversing target.)

18.k Emplacing Claymores and Final Steps[1]

Once the Assault Line is emplaced, the Patrol Leader and Assistant Patrol Leader coordinate emplacing claymores. In an ambush, the main purpose of claymores is to attack within "**dead space**." Dead space is an area with cover-from-fire that a weapon cannot hit. For example, in the killzone enemies can hide behind a berm or a large rock during initiation, so that the guns cannot target them. (A M240 can shoot through most trees, so often trees are not dead space.) If there is no dead space, claymores can be placed to shoot at the

---

1 Quote: FRONT TOWARD ENEMY —Claymore Instructions

Image 120: Sapper Co. Soldier emplaces a Claymore. East Range TC, HI, 09 Sep 2014. **This Soldier positions the claymore to attack straight ahead, while the Soldier to the right covers dead space.**

Image 121: U.S. Army Sergeant. with Iron Troop, 3rd Sqn., 2nd Cavalry Reg., arms an improvised claymore mine during a live-fire exercise with the Estonian Army. Tapa Training Area, Estonia, 15 Mar 2015.

road with interlocking sectors-of-fire.[1] A claymore's primary killing area is 50 meters in a 60-degree fan. The friendly-fire danger area for shrapnel extends to 250 meters at a 180-degree fan.

Before the claymore is emplaced, conduct a circuit test on the claymore. Test both the wire and the clacker using the M40 test set. Besides testing, you must keep the clacker (i.e., M57 firing device) off the wire and in your possession to prevent accidental firing. Plugging in the clacker is just like placing a finger on the trigger.

To install the mine, tie off the wire where the clacker eventually will be used (i.e., the locations of both the Patrol Leader and Assistant Patrol Leader). Claymore wires must be tied down to a solid object (not a machine gun leg). Unroll the wire to the installation position. Claymore wires cannot cross, because the wire from one claymore may disrupt the use of the other claymore. A good claymore location is **16, 35, 18**:

16, 35 – Between 16 and 35 meters of the firing position. (16m is the backblast area, and 35m is the wire length.)

18 – If not in dead space, put the claymore in front of at least an 18-inch tree to absorb the backblast. Any tree smaller than 18 inches becomes shrapnel when the claymore is blown, and is worse than no tree at all.

To install the mine, use the acronym **ATAR-C:**

1 Applying Concepts: If the Leader's Recon Team finds an ambush location with no dead space, should claymores be placed with Security?

Aim the mine – Push the legs one-third of the way into the ground. Pick a target at ground level about 50 meters away. Look through the rear, and aim the mine. Place a knife or pen on top of the mine for easier alignment.

Tie the mine – Secure the wire about one meter behind the mine, so the mine will not move if the wire is pulled.

Arm the mine – Screw the blasting cap into the claymore.

Re-aim the mine – Do the same as when first aiming.

Camouflage the mine – Collect brush without leaving a visible blank spot. Bury or camouflage the wire back to the firing position. If covering the line with leaves, note that a straight, defined line of leaves can look more out of place than no leaves at all.

After the Patrol Leader finishes coordinating fires and emplacing claymores, they move back to the Support-by-Fire and contacts all elements to ensure that comms are working. Then, a Leader calls the spare-report for "ambush occupied" to higher. The Patrol Leader positions themself to the right of the Gunner. Whoever holds the clackers installs claymore wire into the clacker and camouflages themselves as best as possible.

18.1 Platoon Area Ambush[1]

A platoon area ambush is composed of multiple squad point ambushes.
An area ambush is useful if multiple targets need to be ambushed, but traveling in a larger group is safer. For example, one ambush to hit a convoy and two additional ambushes to kill any reinforcements. The only unique aspects of a platoon area ambush are the splitting and combining of the platoon element. The splitting is described in the next paragraph. Recombining is complicated procedure called linkup and is described below in the patrol-base phase. (See Linkup, Pg. 220.)

There are two options for splitting the platoon element: splitting during movement and splitting during a long-halt. A movement split is when one squad seamlessly walks off to a different azimuth once the platoon moves past a preplanned location. Creating a long-halt instead, allows Leaders to recheck that the squad is splitting at the correct location. Just before a split, the Gun Team and platoon leadership assigned to the squad must also prepare to split.

---

1 Quote: The Pope! How many Divisions has he got? —Dictator of Soviet Union, Joseph Stalin, in response to being asked whether he could win favor with the Pope.

Platoon Point Ambush

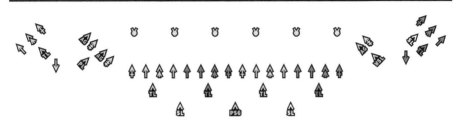

Image 122: Example of a **linear platoon point ambush**. Distances are not to scale.

19. Platoon Point Ambush

A platoon point ambush is when a platoon attacks one location as a whole. In contrast, a platoon area ambush is when a platoon breaks into different squads and attacks multiple locations at the same time. The structure and emplacement of a platoon point ambush is generally the same as for a squad point ambush. (See Creating the Long-Halt, Pg. 123.) (See Creating the Objective Rally-Point, Pg. 133.) (See Creating the Ambush, Pg. 144.)

Just like a squad point ambush, the first step is creating a long-halt. The second step is creating an ORP. A platoon is too large to use squad-sized formations, so it uses a "platoon formation." Explaining the platoon formation will be the focus of this chapter, since it is the most important difference between the previously mentioned squad point ambush and the platoon point ambush. (Other differences, like location of leadership, are discussed at the end of the chapter.)

Note: although this manual gives a detailed explanation of the platoon formation, it is not the only solution. A platoon formation is only one general-use formation for any time that a platoon stops in a dangerous area or for a long time. (This includes ORP's, patrol-bases, and even some ambushes.) It is simply easier to learn from one specific example of what works for a platoon, rather than many examples and abstract concepts.

Phase 3

171

Platoon Long-Halt

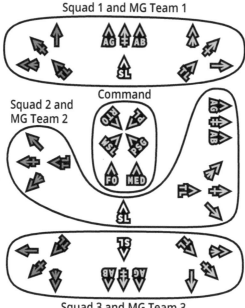

Image 123: In this example, teams in Squad 2 are split because the long-halt was made from a movement formation that had Squad 2 in the middle. There are also prominent strong-points. But as long as there is 360-degree security, any arrangement is acceptable.

19.a Leader's Recon of the Platoon Formation

Before a platoon formation is occupied, the first step is leader's recon of that location. The platoon formation is for stopping a platoon in a relatively dangerous area, and the bigger platoon has much less innate concealment than the smaller squad, so any dangers when stopped are magnified.

The first step is to halt the patrol in a platoon long-halt formation. A platoon long-halt uses the same principles as a squad long-halt. (See Creating the Long-Halt, Pg. 123.) The difference is extra layers of leadership. In a platoon long-halt, Team Leaders generally stay with their team while Squad Leader patrol the line. There are still two main areas: command and 360-degree security (here, the three squads). (See Image 123, Pg. 172.)

Leader's recon is also generally the same as with a squad, except there are more Soldiers. (See Leader's Recon of the Squad ORP, Pg. 136.) In a platoon, a Leader's Recon Team consists of eight Soldiers: a Leader Team (Patrol Leader, RTO, Weapons Squad Leader), an S&O (1st Alpha SAW, 1st Alpha Point), and all three Assistant Gunners.

The movement formation of the Leader's Recon Team can be a double diamond formation: the first diamond is composed of the Patrol Leader, RTO, 1st Alpha SAW, and 1st Alpha Point; the second diamond is the Weapons Squad Leader and the three Assistant Gunners. (See Image 92, Pg. 136.) When the Leader's Recon Team leaves, the Patrol Leader issues a GOTWA to the Main Body Leader and is counted out of the formation.

Leader's recon is performed in two steps: sweeping the formation area for danger, and then reconning the surrounding area for external threats. Once arriving at the prospective location of the platoon formation, the Leader's Recon Team **sweeps the area** in a few steps (See Image 124, Pg. 174.):

1) Leader's Recon Team arrives in double diamond formation and conducts SLLS.

2) All Soldiers get on line, except S&O and the 2nd squad Assistant Gunner. 1st squad's Assistant Gunner goes to the right end and 3rd squad's Assistant Gunner to the left end.

3) The S&O is set in an overwatch position, surveilling the entire platoon formation area. The 2nd squad's Assistant Gunner is placed at the tentative 6 o'clock position of the formation.

4) The line advances 50 meters to clear the area of traps.

After the area is swept, the area surrounding the platoon formation needs to be reconned for external threats. But first, the skeleton of the platoon formation is set. The basic shape of the platoon formation is an upside-down triangle with 35-meter sides (longer for a patrol-base to fit an area for planning). (See Image 128, Pg. 178.) To mark this triangle, the Patrol Leader sets down one of the three Assistant Gunners at each corner of the triangle as reference points.

During the initial sweep, the 2nd squad's Assistant Gunner was already placed to mark the bottom corner of the platoon formation triangle. The remaining two Assistant Gunners will be put in the other two corners next. After the three Assistant Gunners are set, they ideally will not be moved again. The Weapons Squad Leader primarily comes on the leader's recon to

Platoon Formation Sweep for Danger

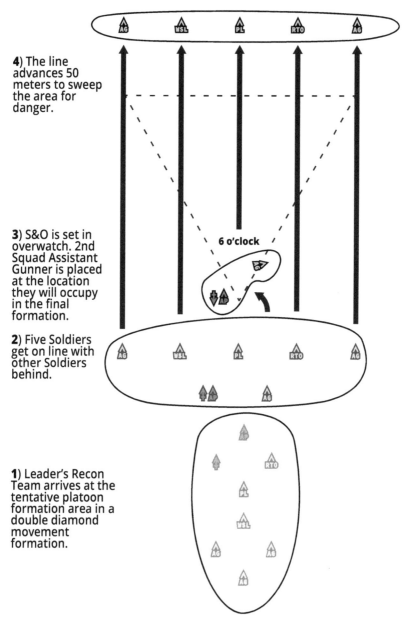

4) The line advances 50 meters to sweep the area for danger.

3) S&O is set in overwatch. 2nd Squad Assistant Gunner is placed at the location they will occupy in the final formation.

2) Five Soldiers get on line with other Soldiers behind.

1) Leader's Recon Team arrives at the tentative platoon formation area in a double diamond movement formation.

Image 124: Leader's recon of the platoon formation begins with a sweep of the area. The outline of a triangle is where the platoon formation is planned to be. To mark the bottom corner, the 2nd Squad Assistant Gunner is placed there, where they will remain in the final formation.

Platoon Formation Area Recon

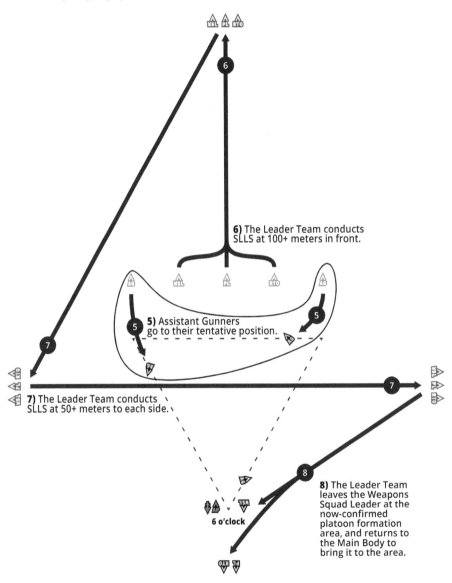

6) The Leader Team conducts SLLS at 100+ meters in front.

5) Assistant Gunners go to their tentative position.

7) The Leader Team conducts SLLS at 50+ meters to each side.

6 o'clock

8) The Leader Team leaves the Weapons Squad Leader at the now-confirmed platoon formation area, and returns to the Main Body to bring it to the area.

Phase 3

Image 125: After the sweep, the AG's are put in position as position markers. **Leader's recon finishes with a recon of the surrounding area for threats.** Every Soldier is reminded that leadership is doing SLLS, because Soldiers in the middle may forget and make noise.

supervise the Assistant Gunners once the Patrol Leader returns to the Main Body to fetch the platoon.

Once the area is swept, the next step is to **recon the surrounding area** for threats. (See Image 125, Pg. 175.)

5) From the line, the remaining two Assistant Gunners are placed in the remaining two corners of the platoon formation triangle.

6) From the line, the Leader Team goes 100 or more meters in front of formation area to conduct SLLS.

7) The Leader Team goes 50 or more meters to the left and right to conduct SLLS.

8) The Leader Team leaves the Weapons Squad Leader at the now-confirmed platoon formation area, and returns to the main body to bring it to the area. While the Leader Team is gone, the Weapons Squad Leader, Assistant Gunners, and S&O all maintain visibility of each other.

19.b Platoon Formation

In the example platoon here, there are three squads and three Gun Teams. Each squad occupies one side of the triangle. Each Gun Team occupies one corner. To occupy, first, the Platoon Sergeant creates a chokepoint at the 6 o'clock to count in Soldiers. All squads always enter (and exit) the platoon formation at the 6 o'clock. Always entering and exiting from the same, single point not only aids accountability, but prevents Soldiers on the line from shooting unknown figures in the dark. (See Image 127, Pg. 177.)

1st Squad – Goes to the right and turns left at 2 o'clock Assistant Gunner to occupy the top of the triangle. The 1st Gun Team follows the 1st Squad and occupies the 2 o'clock position.

2nd Squad – Goes right to follow directly behind the first squad and occupies the right length of the triangle. The 2nd Gun Team occupies the 6 o'clock position.

3rd Squad – Goes to the left and occupies the left-side of the triangle. The 3rd squad is led by the 3rd Gun Team instead of followed, and occupies the 10 o'clock position.

The final formation is as follows. (See Image 128, Pg. 178.) **Each line** of the triangle has only Riflemen and SAW Gunners. A line is composed of two or three crow's feet groups of Soldiers, so Soldiers always have at least one partner to switch out with. (See Grouping Soldiers (Strong-Point/

Platoon Formation Occupation

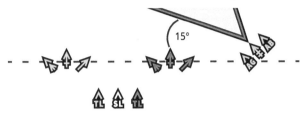

Image 126: A single arm of a platoon formation. Before entering the chokepoint, each squad creates a file in the order of which they will occupy their side. If this were 1st Squad, it would first enter with the blue Soldiers.

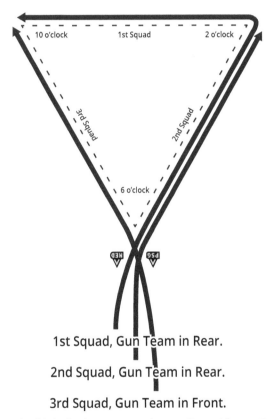

1st Squad, Gun Team in Rear.

2nd Squad, Gun Team in Rear.

3rd Squad, Gun Team in Front.

Image 127: When the Main Body comes to the confirmed formation area, it funnels into the chokepoint as a giant file or modified-wedge. Each squad enters in order. **Within their file, Soldiers are also in the order they will occupy their side of the triangle.** For example, in the top image for 1st Squad, the blue Soldiers would enter first, and the Gun Team second. However, this particular formation also demands the 3rd Squad's Gun Team enter before the 3rd Squad.

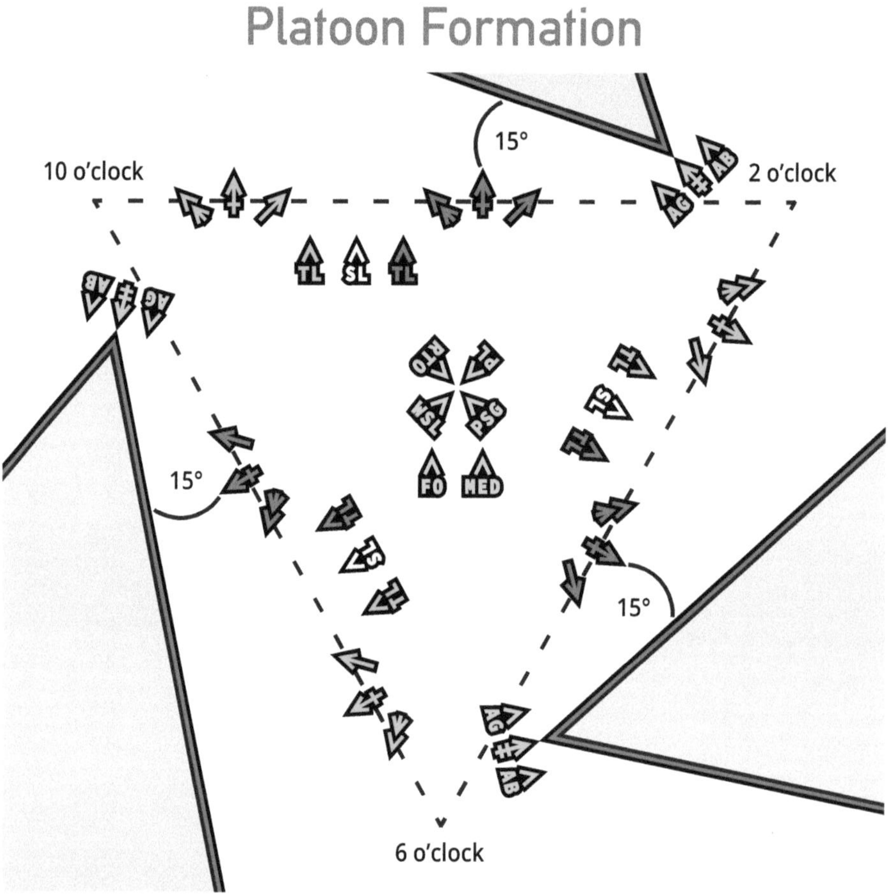

Platoon Formation

Image 128: Command is in the center, while the rest of the Soldiers defend the formation. **This is an all purpose formation for stopping as a platoon.** Although it looks complicated, note all the rotational symetry allows for easy explanation when taken apart. The sectors-of-fire for the Gun Teams are highlighted to show what a final protective line looks like. In addition to fire from each side, if an enemy gets close, a Gun Team can fire in front of the line, creating a wall of bullets.

Crow's Foot), Pg. 129.) If possible, every strong-point has a machine gun that is always manned.

Each corner of the triangle has a Gun Team. Their sector-of-fire is set to be a final protective line (FPL). An FPL is the tactic of having a left limit that shoots as close as possible in front of the line of Soldiers. The theory is that if there are too many enemies incoming, the 7.62 ammo will form a line of bullets that will rip through anything that tries to pass. (Therefore, the FPL shoots close to the ground with minimal dead space.)

Sectors-of-Fire at Corners

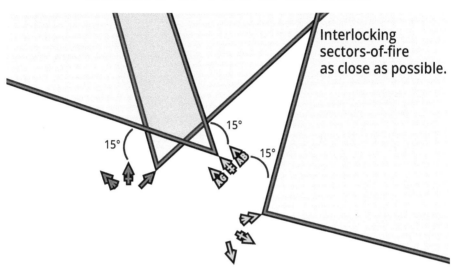

Image 129: The M240s do not count towards 360 degrees of coverage that the formation requires. Therefore it can be difficult to both get coverage and a safe 15-degree offset for all positions. **To that end, do not place the M240 as a point of the platoon formation; push them in a little.**

The difficulty of setting correct sectors-of-fire at the corners of a platoon formation deserves special mention. (See Image 129, Pg. 179.) At each corner, two squad lines must maintain a 15-degree offset from the corner Gun Team, while also intersecting for 360-degree security. At the same time, Gun Teams have their left limit 15 degrees off of a squad line to their left, and metal-to-metal contact on the tripod. (I.e., the M240 tripod won't allow the M240 to swing past the left limit.)

The inside of the formation has all the leadership. Team- and squad-level leadership is just behind the line, commanding all the Riflemen and strong-points. Platoon-level leadership is in the center of the formation coordinating the entire formation.

Finally for occupation, M240s are always manned with at least 300 rounds attached. The strong-points and Gun Teams neatly place their rucks behind them as conveniently as possible without interfering with their positions.

19.c Leader's Recon of the Objective

Leader's recon of a platoon objective is very similar to that of a squad objective, but with more people. (See Creating the Ambush, Pg. 144.) All Support and Assault leadership attend leader's recon of the objective to get a sense of the terrain they must lead on. A commonly used roster is: Platoon Leader, RTO, Weapons Squad Leader, 1st Squad Leader, 2nd Squad Leader, 1st Alpha Point, 1st Squad SAW, and all three Assistant Gunners. Before leaving, the Leader's Recon Team must be COW-Ted, issue a GOTWA, and be counted out. The movement formation to the objective is METT-TC, as long as there is an actual formation being used.

A platoon-level leader's recon follows the same guidelines as the squad-level leader's recon. (See Leader's Recon of Release-Point, S&O, and Killzone, Pg. 146.) There are more people in a platoon recon, so at the tentative release-point, the Patrol Leader and RTO leave the rest of the element as they emplace S&O and verify the ambush objective (this is to keep the footprint as small as possible). Once the ambush objective is verified, the Patrol Leader brings the rest of Leader's Recon Team at the release-point to the objective. On the objective the Leader's Recon Team chooses an ambush location according to the same procedures as with a squad-level leader's recon.

Support-by-Fire is more complicated in a platoon point ambush because there are more Gun Teams, and therefore more ways to distribute their firepower. Gun Teams and their assigned leadership may be split between three locations: left of Assault, in the middle of Assault, and to the right of the Assault. The preferred method for ambushing vehicles is to place two Gun Teams together, facing the enemy's expected avenue of approach, just like a squad ambush. This maximizes vision down the road. However, when ambushing dismounted enemies, it may be better to evenly distribute the Gun Teams to maximize line of sight behind obstacles like trees. With more M240s, each Support-by-Fire can cover 51% of the killzone instead of 100% of the killzone. (See Image 130, Pg. 181.)

To mark the Support positions during leader's recon, the Patrol Leader emplaces the Assistant Gunners at said positions. Just as with a platoon formation, occupation is sped up by using the Assistant Gunners as reference points. If there are multiple support-by-fire positions, the Patrol Leader can

Positioning Gun Teams

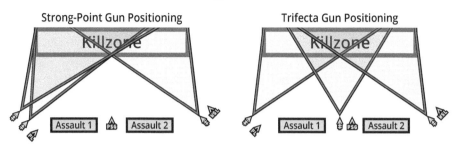

Image 130: The position of the Gun Teams largely depends on the expected target. **Stong-point** positioning is great for stopping incoming enemy vehicles, while **trifecta** positioning distributes firepower to attack foot patrols. **The position of platoon leadership very much depends on the ideal location of the platoon's most casualty-producing weapons, the M240s.** However, each Leader can still go where they are needed. Why might the Platoon Leader choose to lead Assault and not the Gun Teams?

direct the Weapons Squad Leader where they want to place Assistant Gunners to mark Gun Team locations.

While the Patrol Leader is finding and marking support-by-fire positions, the Assault Leader(s) begin(s) marking the assault positions. The Patrol Leader is responsible for verifying every position. When the leader's recon is done, all Assistant Gunners, the Weapons Squad Leader, and S&O remain on the objective, while the Patrol Leader, RTO, 1st Squad Leader, and 2nd Squad Leader return to the Main Body to begin emplacing Assault, Support, and Security.

19.d Occupation of the Objective[1]

The simplest platoon point ambush is putting two squad linear ambushes next to each other, for an approximately 100-meter-long platoon linear ambush. (See Image 122, Pg. 171.) While this section assumes that this kind of ambush will be used, the same advice applies to many other ambush types.

---

1 Applying Concepts: To be particularly aggressive in a dangerous area, a platoon can engage in a defensive ambush. A defensive ambush is an ambush that utilizes a platoon formation as an ambush formation. This ensures 360-degree security, with only one side actually ambushing. The ambush side can be plussed up with troops from the other two sides. If the defensive ambush is at an intersection of roads, two sides on the triangle can abut a road and both can prepare to ambush.

From the platoon release-point, Security is emplaced on either side of the killzone just like a squad ambush. Because the killzone size and number of Soldiers are much bigger than with a squad, the distance from Security to the ambush can be farther, and this needs to be taken into account. An entire squad can be split in two teams to handle security: one team takes strong-side and the other takes weak-side. Because a Squad Leader is in charge of Security, platoon-level Security is more able to emplace itself.

Support-by-Fire emplaces next. Each position has an Assistant Gunner already in position from leader's recon. The emplacement of the M240s themselves are the same as during a squad emplacement. (See Emplacement of Support, Pg. 162.)

The Assault Squads are led to the ambush line using the same methods as with a squad point ambush, with one notable exception. More Team Leaders and Squad Leaders are present on the Assault Line than with a squad, creating a second layer of leadership. One common SOP is to have the Assault 1 Squad Leader lead the assault after the Platoon Leader gives the cease fire or after the reengagement stops. (In this SOP, the Platoon Leader and the Assault 1 Squad Leader are equivalent to the Squad Leader and Team Leader in a squad point ambush respectively.) The Assault 2 Squad Leader advances behind their own squad, helping to direct. But mostly the Assault 2 Squad Leader waits in reserve to take over command if the Assault 1 Squad Leader is incapacitated; and the Assault 2 Squad Leader also leads special teams like the EPW Teams and Aid and Litter Teams.

A platoon point ambush has many more claymores and AT4s available. Distribution of these weapons is METT-TC. AT4s are valuable for stopping vehicles, so put them where vehicles need to be stopped. Claymores are valuable for killing dismounted troops; they are good for covering dead space on the killzone and eliminating enemies running out of the killzone. If there is time, the Patrol Leader verifies all claymore emplacements.

19.e Location of Platoon Leadership

The exact location of the platoon leadership is METT-TC dependent. That being said, the Platoon Leader and the Weapons Squad Leader are always present on the objective because the Platoon Leader is responsible for the ambush, and the Weapons Squad Leader is responsible for the Gun Teams.

Image 131: U.S. Army Paratroopers from 2nd Bn., 503rd Inf. Reg., 173rd Airborne Bde., engage a target during a blank-fire exercise as part of Exercise Rock Knight. Pocek Range, Postonja, Slovenia, 18 Jul 2017. This is a support-by-fire position with two Gun Teams. **The Soldier in the center is a Leader, coordinating both guns.** The Leader could be the Patrol Leader, the Weapons Squad Leader, or some other Leader depending on how the ambush has been planned.

However, the Platoon Sergeant can be on objective, or they can be at the Casualty Collection Point (CCP). Putting the Platoon Sergeant on objective places all the platoon leadership near the killzone, and if something goes wrong they could all be incapacitated. But keeping the Platoon Sergeant back denies the ambush the Patrol's most experienced Soldier. Placing the Platoon Sergeant on objective also allows a third Gun Position for dismounted troops to have a platoon-level leader.

Within the objective itself, the location of the platoon leadership can vary. The location of the Gun Teams plays a large part in the location of leadership, because it is important to coordinate and control the patrol's most casualty-producing weapons. (See Image 130, Pg. 181.) The Platoon Leader may stay with a support-by-fire position, or they can delegate the responsibilities to their Weapons Squad Leader and Platoon Sergeant. (See Image 131, Pg. 183.)

The Platoon Leader can also lead the assault. If the Platoon Leader stays with Support-by-Fire, they have more situational awareness over the entire ambush because a Gun Team is relatively self-sufficient. But the Platoon Leader may want to control and lead the assault since that is the most difficult part of an ambush to execute. Or, if the Platoon Sergeant is on objective, they can lead the assault because they are the most experienced Soldier in the patrol. However, often a Squad Leader leads the assault to allow the Platoon Sergeant to focus more on general supervision and medical evacuation and care.

20. Contingencies[1]

It is impossible to plan for every contingency. However, below are some of the more common scenarios that are worth planning for.

20.a Running Out of Time (Hasty Emplacement)

A mission that is running low on time to emplace can do a hasty emplacement. A hasty emplacement skips many steps of a regular emplacement to save time, but as a consequence the ambush sacrifices precision. This section describes the fastest possible emplacement from the ORP; however, there are many middle grounds and steps that can be performed or dropped depending how much time the patrol has.

Eliminate leader's recon of the objective. From the ORP, every Soldier continues until a release-point is designated by the Patrol Leader. At the release-point, SSA drop all rucks and emplace simultaneously. The Patrol Leader briefs Security on what to look for in their locations, and their EWAC criteria. Then, the Assistant Patrol Leader counts out all the teams at once. The Security Teams scout and occupy their positions while Support and Assault continue to the objective. Remember that because there was no leader's recon, conducting SLLS and moving carefully and discretely becomes even more important!

---

1 Quote: I don't underrate the value of military knowledge, but if men make war in slavish obedience to rules, they will fail. —6th Commanding Gen. of the U.S. Army, Ulysses S. Grant

Phase 3

Image 132: A U.S. Marine with Black Sea Rotational Force and a Moldovan Soldier execute a **hasty ambush**. Novo Selo Training Area, Bulgaria, 6 Aug 2017. These Soldiers did not have time to apply camouflage in accordance with SPARC, but **they are using a berm for concealment** to compensate.

As Assault approaches the objective in a file formation, it changes to a line formation, with Soldiers evenly spaced five meters apart from each other. The SAW's are at the end of either side of the line, and the Assault Leader(s) are in the middle of the line. The Patrol Leader and Gun Team(s) place themselves on the side of the ambush line opposite of the enemy's direction of approach. **The idea is to position Support and Assault while moving on the way to the objective, instead of at the objective.** Ideally, when Support and Assault arrive at 35 meters off of the killzone, every Soldier can self-emplace by dropping into the prone near cover.

20.b Compromise during Emplacement

At any time and from any direction, the patrol can be spotted and the patrol can be compromised. Contingency plans need to be prepared for many scenarios. What if a civilian sees the patrol? Often the solution is to carry a detainment kit and to hold the civilian until the conclusion of the patrol.

If the enemy approaches the patrol but does not detect anything, then emplacement halts. The Patrol Leader can either choose to let the enemy pass or do a hasty ambush. If the enemy does detect the patrol, then the ambush

Image 133: Simulated opposing forces emplace into an L-shaped ambush posture against a munitions supply truck, Exercise Beverly Herd 16-2. Osan Air Base, Republic of Korea, 24 Aug 2016. In contrast to a linear ambush where Soldiers on the ambush line can only see across the street, **note how far down the road these Soldiers can see**.

becomes a react-to-contact. (Note that a react-to-contact is complicated if the patrol is split into SSA.) **In any case, the Patrol Leader must consider asking higher for guidance if there is a risk of mission compromise.**

Security is emplaced before Support and Assault, specifically to reduce the risk of compromise. If Security can warn the main ambush, then the ambush needs to hit the ground where they are and prepare to attack from whatever positions they fall into. The Patrol Leader can decide whether the hasty positioning can support a viable attack, or whether to let the enemy pass.

However, if Security cannot provide early warning for whatever reason, not much can be done to complete the mission. An out-of-position patrol will have a hard time ambushing a fast-moving vehicle, and that vehicle will likely have seen a full patrol of Soldiers with weapons.

20.c Ambush at a Bend in the Road

An **L-shaped ambush** can be performed where the road comes to a sharp bend, creating an "L" shape. Generally, an L-shaped ambush is superior to a linear ambush because the M240 can fire straight down the road, and enemy vehicles slow down at the turn. L-shaped ambushes are uncommon only because they demand ambushing at a particular terrain feature (i.e., the bend) that may not exist. Also, because sharp bends are uncommon, one L-shaped ambush can teach the enemy to be extra cautious whenever they pass one.

Ambush at Bend in the Road (L and Z)

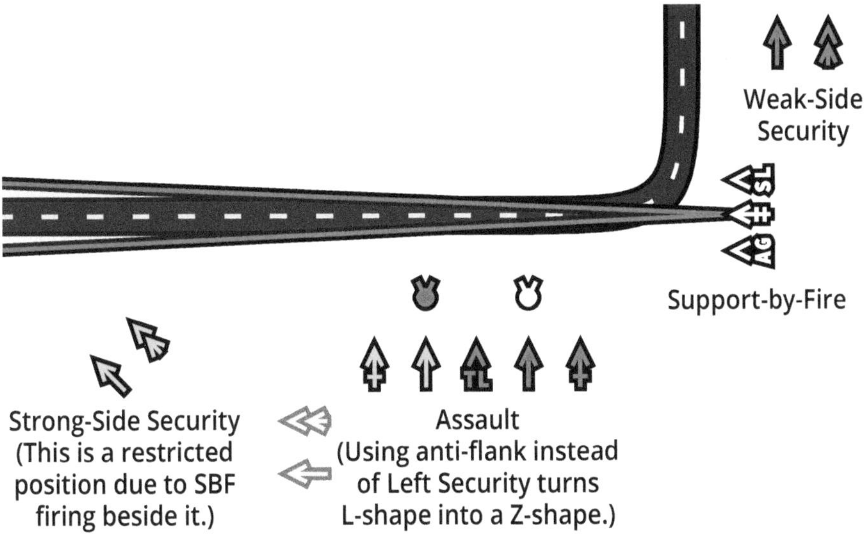

Weak-Side Security

Support-by-Fire

Strong-Side Security
(This is a restricted position due to SBF firing beside it.)

Assault
(Using anti-flank instead of Left Security turns L-shape into a Z-shape.)

Image 134: Bends in the road provide superior places for ambushes by giving Support-by-Fire more targets and stopping power. **Enemy vehicles will also naturally slow down at bends.** The main downside is that bends are limited and predictable.

The M240 is placed so that it directly faces the incoming enemy patrol. The Gun Team is then able to attain **enfilade fire** down the road directly, perpendicular to the Assault Line, instead of defilade fire at an oblique angle next to the Assault Line. The Support-by-Fire's sector-of-fire is still metal-to-metal 15 degrees off the Assault Line. Realistically, this means the near-side of the road is a firing limit. To be even more cautious, the patrol can create a **Z-shaped** ambush by changing Strong-Side Security into an anti-flank and rear-security attachment to the ambush. (See Image 134, Pg. 187.)

Because the backside of the squad is now facing two directions instead of one, and Support-by-Fire is farther from the Main Body, rear-facing security for each element becomes more important. It may be advisable to assign an extra Rifleman to the Support-by-Fire for rear security. Also, every Soldier especially needs to know the location of each Security Team, because the weak-side is diagonally in front of the Assault Line, and the strong-side is next to the M240's sector-of-fire.

Image 135: A Soldier from 1st Bn., 12th Cavalry Reg., an element of the Fort Hood-based 1st Cavalry Div., prepares to ambush a vehicle. Camp Shelby, near Hattiesburg, MS, 28 Jul 2015. **Note how advantagous bends in the road can be for enfilade fires and slowing down vehicles. Find a good position for enfilade fires when possible.**

20.d Unidirectional Ambush (T and V)

If the enemy's direction of approach is known for certain, then the ambush can focus its attention on one direction of approach, while turning its back on the opposite direction. By contrast, in a linear ambush, one reason that M240s are offset from the road is so they can easily turn and engage enemies coming from the "wrong" direction.

In a unidirectional ambush, the M240 can utilize enfilade fire by being aligned with and moving closer to the road. (See Image 135, Pg. 188.) **Enfilade fire** means that the enemy is in a line, so bullets exiting one target penetrate more targets lined up behind the first. And aiming is much faster and more accurate because targets are close together. An M240 can shoot through most materials and fire fast, so lining up enemies close together massively increases killing power.

Unidirectional Ambush (T and V)

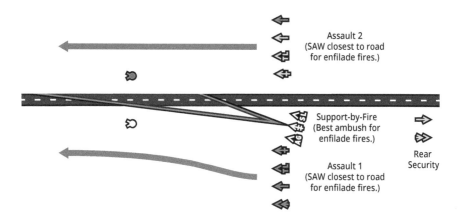

Image 136: A **T-shaped** ambush is effective for enabling enfilade fires and anti-ambush from one direction. Unidirectional ambushes are more difficult to coordinate due to the road splitting the element. They are also more dangerous because a vehicle can drive into the Assault Line. However, they provide **more effective fire because the ambush gains enfilade fires.**

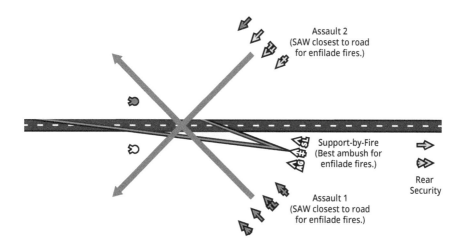

Image 137: A **V-shaped** ambush is the same as a T-shaped ambush; however, **it has two separate assaults.** Just like with a Bold Flank, Assault 1 clears the killzone first. Then Assault 2 reclears the killzone. Sweeping the killzone multiple times ensures better killzone coverage, but is much harder to coordinate.

An example of when enfilade fires are especially effective is when the enemy is traveling in convoy. Multiple vehicles in a line can protect the enemy from perpendicular fire, but are much less effective against parallel fire.

Because the ambush is pointing down the road, instead of across the road, the patrol can place a second Assault Line on the opposite side of the road. This reduces the enemy's ability to flank the patrol before the ambush, and their ability to hide on the opposite side of the road after the ambush.

However, using both sides of the road is very weak to enemies that manage to stop on the road in the middle of the Ambush Line. When that happens, the ambush cannot fire so as to avoid friendly fire. The planning for this contingency is similar to when an enemy stops in the middle of an LDA crossing. (See Enemy Attack During LDA Crossing, Pg. 64.)

20.e Ambush for Anti-Ambush Patrols (K and X)

An anti-ambush patrol is where the enemy pushes a vanguard out before the Main Body either on the road, or off the side of the road. An anti-ambush vanguard is tasked with detecting and engaging an ambush's Security elements before the enemy is ambushed.

If that vanguard detects the Security of an ambush, the enemy will engage in a react-to-contact and flank the ambush from the side. **A flank can overwhelm and outnumber a security position.** And a flank exploits a linear ambush Assault Line that is very weak, because friendly Soldiers are lined up perpendicular to the enemy flank. When shot at, bullets that miss one Soldier might hit the next; and returning fire is difficult because enemy targets are blocked by friendly Soldiers earlier in the line. (See Security Is Combat Ineffective, Pg. 214.)

To counter anti-ambush patrols, consider not placing Security at all; instead secure the Assault Line flanks. One way to do this is to place the Ambush Line diagonally relative to the road, so if the ambush is flanked from the side, many Soldiers can return fire at once without friendly fire concerns. When both sides of the Ambush Line are diagonal, the ambush is **K-shaped.** (See Image 138, Pg. 191.)

If the enemy is likely to use anti-ambush patrols, and the direction of travel is known, a **V-shaped** ambush is ideal. (See Image 137, Pg. 189.)

Anti-Ambush-Patrol Ambush (K and X)

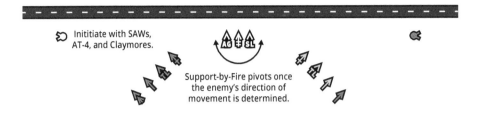

Image 138: This is a **K-shaped** ambush. **The idea behind an anti-ambush patrol is for enemies to go offroad and flank an ambush.** An anti-ambush-patrol ambush removes security positions and tilts flanks to remove that ability. Note the security positions are replaced with claymores.

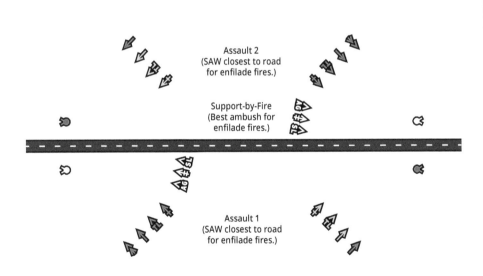

Image 139: An **X-shaped** ambush is the same as either two V-shaped ambushes or two K-shaped ambushes. It requires more Soldiers, but provides enfilade fires for an M240, and anti-ambush protections in both directions. This ambush is radically different in arrangement and utility from a regular platoon linear ambush. **It is mainly in this manual to show that ambushes are not limited to a simple linear shape, as long as the principles of patrolling are applied.**

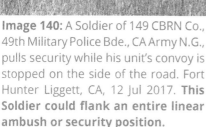

Image 140: A Soldier of 149 CBRN Co., 49th Military Police Bde., CA Army N.G., pulls security while his unit's convoy is stopped on the side of the road. Fort Hunter Liggett, CA, 12 Jul 2017. **This Soldier could flank an entire linear ambush or security position.**

Image 141: Soldiers with 1st Pt., 216th Mobile Augmentation Company, U.S. Army N.G. from Long Beach, CA, walk along side of Highway 1 sweeping for any signs of IED's. 22 Jan 2014. **Anti-IED patrols can also be anti-ambush patrols.**

It is so named because the Assault Line is shaped like a sideways "V." Two Assault Lines form each half of the sideways V. The road runs directly down the middle, so each Assault Line is at a 45-degree angle relative to the road.

By using a V-shaped ambush formation, troops that are traveling to the side of the road can still be targeted by all friendly forces in the formation. Support-by-Fire is placed next to the road for enfilade fires. Claymores face to fire parallel to the road instead of facing at the road to avoid fratricide. Because the V-shaped ambush has no Strong-Side Security, the Patrol Leader provides their own early warning by being close to the road with the Gun Team.

20.f No Radio Communications with Security

A Security Team without long-distance communication cannot give early warning and therefore cannot serve their primary purpose. If radio communications break, either some other method of communication must be substituted, or Security must be withdrawn to aid the assaulting force.

One method of long-distance communication is to use Relay Teams. **Relay Teams** are placed between two elements that can each see the Relay Team but not each other. The Relay Team relays signals between the two elements which otherwise could not contact each other. This requires an additional two Soldiers per side, and so may work for a platoon; but pulling an extra four Soldiers from a Squad may be too many. As a compromise, Weak-Side Security can be pulled and act as a Relay Team for Strong-Side Security.

Image 142: When there a valley between two hills, an ambush can employ plunging fire. The ambush uses two Supports-by-Fire to cut off any enemy escape.

20.g Other Ambush Types

The simple, linear ambush formation taught in this book is the standard taught in U.S. military schools. However, there are uncountable ways that an ambush can be planned that vary based on resources available and mission goals. How would you integrate or only use **snipers** in your ambush?

One of the most effective alternatives is to make the ambush three dimensional by **setting up on two hills and attacking a valley** between them (with a minimum 15-degee vertical offset). In cities, a patrol can even occupy multiple levels of a building. By ambushing the enemy from both sides and multiple angles, the enemy's escape by foot is eliminated.

Another common ambush is the **far ambush**. It is "far" because there is no assault; the patrol shoots at the enemy and immediately withdraws. Having no assault means that kills cannot be guaranteed or verified, but the ambush is safer because the patrol can be farther away from the killzone. Whereas a near ambush is used to destroy an enemy completely, a far ambush is used to damage and harass an enemy in order to deter, slow, instill fear, and destroy the enemy little by little.

One final example is having a **break-off element**, or third team, to perform secondary functions. A break-off element can be prepared to cut off the most common escape routes to kill any enemy Soldiers attempting to escape. Or they can be pulling security in reserve in case of enemy counterattack. Using a third element is reserved for experienced units because it increases the complexity of coordination and takes Soldiers away from the main assault.

Phase 4 Contents

21. Squad Ambush — 195

Initiating the Ambush — 195
Assaulting the Objective — 197
Withdrawal from the Objective — 201

22. Platoon Point Ambush — 202

Weapons Squad — 202
Assault — 203

23. Vehicle Clearing — 204

One Vehicle — 204
Multiple Vehicles — 207

24. Contingencies — 208

Dismounted Enemy Patrol — 209
Enemy Stops Outside of the Killzone — 209
Enemy Patrol Is Wider than the Killzone — 210
Counter Ambush from Behind the Objective — 211
Enemy Quick Reaction Force and Harassing Ambush — 211
Assault Leader Is Combat Ineffective — 214
Patrol Leader Is Combat Ineffective — 214
Security Is Combat Ineffective — 214
Explosive Device in the Killzone — 215

Joe Attacks the Enemy (Phase 4: Actions on the Objective)

Death is the solution to all problems. No man, no problem.
—*General Secretary of the Soviet Union, Joseph Stalin*

Violence of action is unrivaled speed and aggression thrown against an enemy for total dominance. It can sometimes overcome poor setup, but the best setup will never overcome weak actions. This chapter describes how to properly perform actions on the objective (for one kind of ambush), like assaulting and clearing vehicles. But most importantly, this chapter describes common contingencies for when the enemy goes off script.

21. Squad Ambush

A squad ambush (or any ambush) is composed of three distinct stages. First, the ambush is initiated, which begins when the Squad Leader opens ambush-fires on the enemy and then ceases fire. Second, Soldiers assault and secure the objective. Third, after all tasks are completed, the squad withdraws.

21.a Initiating the Ambush[1]

The Security Team radios the Squad Leader of an approaching target and communicates the following: left or right security, number of personnel, mounted or dismounted, and location.[2] The Squad Leader has their left hand on the Gunner's triceps and their right hand on the claymore clacker.

---

1 Quote: My rule is: If you meet the weakest vessel, attack. If it is a vessel equal to yours, attack. And if it is stronger than yours, also attack. —Russian Vice-Admiral, Stepan Makarov

2 Example Identification:
Security: "Left Security, four dismounted, passing security now."

Image 143: U.S. Army Paratroopers assigned to 1st Squadron, 91st Cavalry Reg., 173rd Airborne Bde., prepare to initiate an ambush. Pocek Range, Slovenia 02 Dec 2016. Before the ambush, the scene is serene and quiet.

Contact is initiated by the Squad Leader as redundantly as possible.[1] For example, squeeze the Gunner's arm to fire the M240, shout out orders, and squeeze the claymore clacker. (If the claymores cover dead space, the Squad Leader waits until the enemy has had an opportunity to occupy the dead space.) (See Image 144, Pg. 197.) If one initiator fails, use the next initiator in the PACE plan. The Assistant Gunner or RTO start calling off times and Security isolates the objective by moving from their primary to their secondary positions.

The "mad-minute" of initiation begins, during which Soldiers kill as many enemies as possible with as much firepower as possible. A machine gun's firing rate is cyclic and the M4's is rapid for 15 to 30 seconds. (See Rate-of-Fire, Pg. 237.) If the machine guns go down, the M4s pick up the rate-of-fire. Then, the firing rate switches to rapid and sustained for another 15 to 30 seconds. Even without enemies in the Soldiers' sectors-of-fire, Soldiers still fire to increase the violence and intimidate the enemy. Similarly, machine guns sweep back and forth, looking to hit enemies by chance.

When the total 30 to 60 seconds have passed, the Squad Leader shouts, **"Cease fire!"** (Every Soldier is listening for this.) After the cease fire, the squad pauses for three to five seconds to sense anything still moving. If a Soldier senses signs of life or movement, everybody must initiate again. When contact is reinitiated, a second, shorter mad-minute commences for

---

1. **Real World:** The PACE plan used for initiation varies depending on the weapons systems present, and there is often a tradeoff between reliability and maximum destruction. Very destructive open-bolt weapons like the M240 make an audible "clunk" sound when they jam and alert the enemy. Similarly, claymores may not be effective against armored vehicles. PACE plans need to be rehearsed like anything else.

Image 144: U.S. Marines with Bn. Landing Team 2/6, 26th Marine Expeditionary Unit (26th MEU), fire the M240 during a live-fire exercise in the U.S. 5th Fleet Area of Operations. 30 Nov 2015. Before an ambush, the patrol is extremely quiet. (See Image 143, Pg. 196.) **Once an ambush begins, all cover is blown.** Shout as loud as possible and utilize violence of action to confuse and disorient the enemy.

15 seconds. Again, the Squad Leader shouts, "Cease fire!" when the time has elapsed.

Immediately after a sufficient pause or a second mad-minute, the Squad Leader shouts, **"Prepare the assault!"** The Assault Leader starts the ammo reloading by responding with, "Drums!" The SAW Gunners remove their spent drums and slap in fresh drums. (They must set one out before the ambush.) Once ready, each SAW takes a knee and says "[left or right] SAW up." (See Image 145, Pg. 198.)

Once both SAW's are accounted for, or if they are taking too long, the Assault Leader shouts "Mags!" and the Riflemen reload. "Drums" and "Mags" are separate to prevent every weapon from being disabled by reloading at the same time. When finished, each Rifleman takes a knee. With every Soldier on a knee, the Assault Line is ready to enter the killzone.[1]

21.b Assaulting the Objective[2]

Assaulting the objective is very similar to an assaulting in a react-to-contact. **Assault's first and constant goal is to shoot enemies and kick away their**

Phase 4

---

1 **Example** Initiation:
SL – "Cease fire!"
  "Prepare the assault!"
ATL – "Drums! Mags!"

2 Quote: The essence of war is violence. Moderation in war is imbecility. —British Admiral, John Fisher

Ambush Initiation and Assault

Step 1, Patrol Leader signals the Assault Leader to begin. Assault Leader orders tactical reloads.

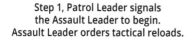

Patrol Leader:
"Prepare the assault!"

Assault Leader:
"Drums!"
"Mags!"

Step 2, Patrol Leader displaces (turns) the Gun Team to avoid flagging assault. Assault Leader centers the Assault Line on the enemy.

Assault Leader:
"Left side, bound with me!"
"Push left!"

Step 3, Assault Leader reforms the line and prepares to assault the objective.

Assault Leader:
"Right Side, bound to me!"
"Lights!"
"Assault!"

Step 4, Assault Leader assaults the objective until the limit-of-advance.

Assault Leader:
"LOA! LOA! LOA!"

Image 145: Four steps to go from initiation to a completed assault. This is the time when Soldiers focus on killing any enemies left alive. Step 3 is shown in the opposite image.

Phase 4

Image 146: U.S. Army Paratroopers from 1st Bn., 503rd Inf. Reg., 173rd Airborne Bde., approach fallen enemy role players after clearing the area during a simulated ambush. Dandolo Range, Pordenone, Italy, 18 Jan 2018. The Soldiers are assaulting from the ambush line to the limit-of-advance. **The most important part of an assault is not getting tunnel vision!** The enemies here can be seen from the ambush line, and so should have been shot dozens of times. Do not focus on corpses and lose sight of the horizon. On the way the Soldiers kick away weapons.

weapons. (See Assaulting a Location (Battle Drill 4), Pg. 80.) The Assault Leader forms their Soldiers in a line to maximize security and killing power.[1]

The second goal is to center and expand the Assault Line on the group of enemy Soldiers and corpses as a whole. By centering, the Assault Line will not miss any enemies as it assaults. The Assault Leader commands the first moving side to bound and push out by shouting, "[Left or right] side, bound with me!"[2] (See Image 145, Pg. 198.) (Before moving, Soldiers secure magazine or drums on the ground.) (See Image 146, Pg. 199.)

When the Gun Team hears the first signal to assault, they immediately **rotate the gun away from the killzone** to prevent "cook-offs" in the direction of Assault and Security. (A "cook-off" is when a barrel is so heated, that a cartridge reaches ignition temperature and spontaneously fires.)

Once the Assault Leader reaches halfway to the road or good cover, they stop. The Assault Leader then orders the remaining side to re-create the line: "[Left or right] side, bound to me!" (See Image 145, Pg. 198.) Once the Assault Line is on line and centered, the Assault Leader shouts "Lights!" and every Soldier turns on their rifle light (when dark out). Next, the Assault Leader shouts, "Assault to the near-side!" and the line assaults to the side of the road.

As Assault goes forward, the Gun Team moves to the most likely avenue of enemy approach to pull security. Usually, this means the Gun Team travels behind the Assault Line to the other side of ambush, and faces down the road where the enemy came from. Do not shoot at the Security position! The Gun Team must have a sector-of-fire that makes it impossible to aim at Security in the first place. (An example firing limit is the near-side of the road, but this only works on straight roads.)

Once Assault is on the near-side, if there are vehicles on the road, the Assault Leader orders the clearing of the vehicle. (See Vehicle Clearing, Pg. 204.) Once the vehicle is clear, or if there are no vehicles, the Assault

---

1 Real World: It must be briefed which enemies gets killed and which don't. In an ambush, usually everybody in the killzone gets killed. Also, actions speak louder than words. When a person screams, "I surrender!" that is irrelevant when reaching for a weapon or holding a hostage.

2 **Example** Positioning. For more details on positioning, see the section on assaults. (See Assaulting a Location (Battle Drill 4), Pg. 80.) (See Image 51, Pg. 83.) Leaders must be precise and scripted with commands.

Image 147: Afghan Army NCO's. Kabul, Afghanistan, 25 Oct 2010. **The time right after an ambush is one of the most vulnerable for a patrol.** If the enemy in the foreground were not dead, how much damage could they do?

Image 148: U.S. Army Soldiers from C Co., 1st Bn., 503rd Inf. Reg., 173rd Airborne Bde., stopping at the LOA. Drawsko-Pomorskie, Poland, 17 Jun 2014. The Soldiers are on high alert and take cover as if they are being actively engaged by the enemy.

Leader shouts "Assault to the far-side!" The line assaults to the far-side of the road.

Unless the Assault Leader determines a reason to stop (for example, a large berm on the side of the road that could conceal a hidden enemy or explosive), the Assault Leader shouts, "Assault to the LOA!" As the SAW's cross the road, they drop glowsticks to designate the edges of the killzone to the EPW Team. A rule of thumb for distance to the LOA is 35 meters (hand grenade range) after the road or the last dead body. However, advance until good cover and concealment is achieved. (See Image 147, Pg. 201.)

At the limit-of-advance, the Assault Leader shouts, and the Assault Line echoes, "LOA! LOA! LOA!" The Assault Leader immediately does BLAST. (See Assaulting a Location (Battle Drill 4), Pg. 80.) Then, Special Teams are sent out. (See Cleaning up after Assaulting (Specialty Teams), Pg. 99.) The only difference is that EPW collects the glowsticks on the edges of the killzone.

21.c Withdrawal from the Objective[1]

The withdrawal sequence is the same as with the react-to-contact with a few differences. (See Withdrawal from Area after Assaulting, Pg. 104.) Because a

---

1 Quote: Veni, vidi, vici. —Dictator of the Roman Republic, Julius Caesar

Team Leader may be in the rear with the rucks and a radio, the Assault Leader shouts, "Chokepoint on me!" and provides a count for the Squad Leader on the objective. One Soldier must stay behind with the Squad Leader as a battle buddy and demo helper.[1]

A Leader counts everybody again at the release-point or ORP. Security follows their EWAC criteria for withdrawal. When everybody is back at their equipment, the squad rucks up and leaves for the patrol-base. If the rucks are not organized, do not waste time; grab any ruck and sort them later. **After an ambush, the enemy will be on guard so security measures and speed must be increased.** A Leader calls up the SALUTE report and the spare report for "mission complete."

22. Platoon Point Ambush[2]

A platoon point ambush is very similar to a squad ambush (a.k.a., a squad point ambush). (See Squad Ambush, Pg. 195.) To begin, there is a preplanned initiation sequence. After initiation, the Assault Line assaults the killzone. Special teams canvas the area as needed. And finally, there is an organized withdrawal from the ambush objective area. This section focuses on how a platoon point ambush is distinct.

22.a Weapons Squad

Whereas a squad will often use the Gun Team to initiate and ambush, **a platoon will use the entire Weapons Squad.** A Weapons Squad can have three Gun Teams and a designated Weapons Squad Leader. Depending on the

---

1 **Example** Withdrawal:
SL –   "Fire in the Hole 1."
ATL –   "Chokepoint on me."
          "9 PAX. Assault up."
SL –   "Fire in the Hole 2."
AG –   "3 PAX. Gun Team up."
SL –   "Fire in the Hole 3 Burning! Burning! Burning!"

2 Quote: God is not on the side of the big battalions, but on the side of those who shoot best. —French philosopher, Voltaire; Cf. "It is said that God is always on the side of the big battalions." —French philosopher, Voltaire; See also, "A witty saying proves nothing." —French philosopher, Voltaire

ambush formation used, the Gun Teams may be placed in one, two, or three locations. Therefore, coordinating the M240s is important.

The most important coordination is for the Patrol Leader and Weapons Squad Leader to get the guns to "talk." "**Talking the guns**" means to alternate firing the guns, with one firing at all times (e.g., gun 1 fire, gun 2 fire, gun 3 fire, repeat). Talking the guns makes each gun use ammunition at a similar, moderate rate, while not allowing the enemy to hear gaps in shooting. (See Firing Drills, Pg. 237.)

After the ambush ceases fire, all Gun Teams displace and move near the road. While the Assault 1 Squad Leader is getting an ACE report from the Assault Line, the Weapons Squad Leader gets an ACE report from each Gun Team and reports them to the Patrol Leader. When the Patrol Leader calls, "Fire in the Hole 2!" the Weapons Squad Leader creates their own chokepoint and accounts for every Gun Team.

22.b Assault[1]

The platoon-level Assault Line has an extra layer of hierarchy. In a squad assault, a Team Leader controls every Soldier on the line. However, in the platoon assault, the Assault Leader (usually a Squad Leader) controls Team Leaders, and the Team Leaders control Soldiers. A Platoon Leader could even command Squad Leaders in the Assault as a third layer.

There are multiple Squad Leaders in a platoon-level ambush, but Assault only needs one Assault Leader. The extra Squad Leaders are present behind their own squad as a backup, ready to assume responsibility and echo commands. An alternate Squad Leader also leads the EPW and Aid and Litter.

For withdrawal, each Squad Leader counts their own squad only to make counting easier. They stand on different sides of the killzone, with different lights or signals, and shout that they are a chokepoint. Each Squad Leader reports their own count, including themselves, to the Platoon Leader.

During platoon withdrawal, the Platoon Leader does not do the demo themself; they coordinates the Demo Teams. The Platoon Leader looks at each demo man and says "ready," and when everybody is ready, the Platoon Leader initiates the demo sequence. (See Demolition Team, Pg. 104.)

---

1 Quote: Putting aside all the fancy words and academic doubletalk, the basic reason for having a military is to do two jobs: to kill people and to destroy. —Commander in Chief of the Strategic Air Command, Gen. Thomas Sarsfield

Image 149: A U.S. Special Operation Forces Soldier observes as Burkina Faso Soldiers clear a vehicle during Entry Control Point training, Exercise Flintlock 17. Camp Zagre, Burkina Faso, 13 Mar 2017. One Soldier opens the door, while another prepares to engage. **The Soldier engaging stands back, so a hidden enemy cannot just grab his weapon.**

23. Vehicle Clearing

Clearing vehicles is already technical before considering the number of variations in which vehicles exist in killzones. Different vehicles on different roads in different orientations all require adjustments. In fact, some units purchase the exact vehicle they plan to ambush, just to practice shooting it! Whatever the situation, in any vehicle clearing, the end state must be that all enemies are killed, and their bodies are removed from the vehicle.

23.a One Vehicle

When the Assault Line arrives at the near-side of the road, two Soldiers clear the vehicle (usually a Team Leader with a Rifleman). The remainder of Assault pulls security down their firing lanes beyond the vehicle.

If at any point the enemy opens fire from behind the vehicle, the Team Leader must decide whether the clearers drop down and return fire with the Assault Line, or if they power through to assault the covered enemy.

The two Soldiers approach the vehicle at a 45-degree angle from the front, which allows the broadest view of the interior of the car through the windshield and windows. If an enemy is visible in the windshield or windows, shoot them. (Remember, in an ambush, usually everybody is an enemy.)

Clearing a Single Vehicle

Step 1: Clear high and low, watching the cabin.

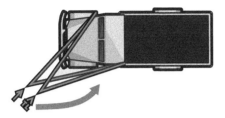

Step 2: Clear the cabin, by opening all the doors.

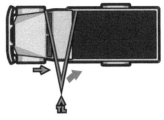

Step 3: Clear the bed or trunk, while moving.

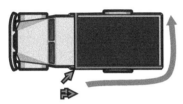

Step 4: Clear the rear side, pieing the corner.

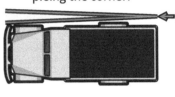

Image 150: Clearing a vehicle has a flow to it. For example **here, the Soldiers are always moving counter-clockwise around the vehicle**. This flow assists speed and completeness and needs to to be practiced.

When clearing, Soldiers need to keep a safe distance off the vehicle by remaining one to two meters away until they need to touch anything. Approaching the vehicle, one Soldier clears high (through the glass and on the roof) and the other clears low (below the vehicle). The High Soldier controls the Low Soldier's movement and so is usually a Team Leader. The Low Soldier thoroughly looks below the vehicle to the other side. If any enemies are detected (dead or alive), shoot them. (See Image 150, Pg. 205.)

Once the Low Soldier finishes clearing the underside of the vehicle, the two Soldiers clear the inside of the vehicle one door at a time. When approaching a door, one Soldier positions themself to open the door by moving to the hinged side. The other Soldier points their rifle at the door, so that when the door opens, they can immediately fire. **They also stand away from the door so an enemy in the vehicle cannot grab the Soldeir's rifle.**

Once in position, the Soldier pointing at the door shakes their muzzle up and down to signal their partner to open the door. After the door is opened,

Image 151: U.S. Army Soldiers **clear a vehicle during a simulated ambush** scenario in a convoy operations. Pocek Range, Slovenia 02 Dec 2016. The Soldier in the foreground is pulling security on a dead body. That body should be liquified. Where should he be looking for potential enemies? The three Soldiers in the foreground are bunched together in an active killzone with no cover or concealment. Where should they be? Four out of six Soldiers are staring at the vehicle. Where should security be allocated? What else is wrong with this photo?

Phase 4

the Soldier shoots all bodies (whether or not they already appear dead). The two Soldiers clear the second door in the same manner. After all the near-side doors are cleared, remove any bodies from the vehicle, and turn off the engine and lights. Finally, the Soldiers look inside the vehicle to ensure that there is nothing living there anymore. The inside of the car is clear.

The two Soldiers make their way to the rear of the vehicle. The first chance they get, they clear the trunk of the vehicle. One Soldier pulls security, while the other Soldier uses their light to see inside the back of the vehicle and to shoot threats.

The only part of the vehicle left to clear is the rear-side. As with every technique in this manual, there are multiple ways to do this. The first method is a single man rear-side clear. Both Soldiers line up shoulder to shoulder along the back of the vehicle. The Soldier far from the vehicle initiates movement by taking a step out, pulling far security, and bumping the Soldier touching the vehicle. That Soldier steps in and turns 90 degrees, looking for an enemy to shoot on the rear-side of the vehicle.

A second method is the two-man, high-low clear. For this, both Soldiers turn in 90 degrees towards the rear at the same time. The inside Soldier kneels and the outside Soldier stands. (Never stand up without looking behind you, or else you could get accidentally shot in the back of the head.) Once clear, the Soldiers yell, "Vehicle clear!" and remove anything from the rear-side doors that they could not reach on the near-side.

If a vehicle is slanted diagonally with respect to the Assault Line, it does not have a far-side. Two sides of the vehicle face the Assault Line, and the opposite sides can both be seen by the extreme ends of the Assault Line. Extreme care must be taken by Soldiers covering down on the vehicle not to flag the clearers as they work. Similarly, clearers do not pass into a friendly line-of-fire.

23.b Multiple Vehicles

If there are multiple vehicles, they must be cleared in a synchronized effort. Soldiers must be synchronized so that they clear the far-side of all vehicles at once. This is because, if there are multiple vehicles in a convoy, when a team clears the far-side of a vehicle they must point their rifle down the convoy. Any other team already clearing the far-side of a different vehicle will be flagged.

To avoid flagging, all Soldiers pause at the last corner of the vehicle and do not clear the far-side. The Leader in charge of directing all the vehicle-clearing instructs how they want the far-side to be cleared. Two methods of clearing the far-side are: first, a single team clears the entire far-side from the end of a convoy; and second, two teams simultaneously go between two vehicles, with one clearing left and one clearing right.

Because multiple vehicles must be cleared systematically, Soldiers cannot always clear from the head of the vehicle. Sometimes they must clear the vehicle starting from the rear. Clearing from the rear works the same way as clearing from the front, but in reverse. Clearing from the front often is preferred because it gives better and faster visibility into the cab.

Sometimes vehicles stop side by side on the road. In this case, a standard clear is impossible. On the far vehicle, one side of doors cannot be opened because the other vehicle is pressed against them. For this situation, Soldiers

Image 152: U.S. Paratroopers from 1st Bn., 503rd Inf. Reg., 173rd Airborne Bde., conducting ambush training with 1st Paratrooper Commando Bde. of the Greek Army, Exercise Bayonet Minotaur. Camp Redina, Greece, 18 May 2017. Clearing multiple vehicles can become complicated fast. Here there are three vehicles and four enemies visible. **Always plan for and practice for multiple vehicles.**

go between the two vehicles even if it is uncomfortable. If going between the two is impossible, then ensure everything inside the cabs is dead by using excess ammunition through windows and the windshield. The Leader also can order the Assault Line to widely split in the middle to allow carefully aimed shooting from the far-side through the gap. (Don't use this method if there is a Soldier at the release-point.)

24. Contingencies[1]

Ambushes are fast-paced, organized chaos. Further, the enemy has a mind of their own.[2] It is important to understand and internalize not just the standard drills, but also common scenarios when things go wrong. That way, when things do go wrong, you are not unprepared and do not lose your mind.

---

1 **Quote:** Be polite, be professional, but have a plan to kill everyone you meet. —USMC Gen. James Mattis

2 **Real World:** If you achieve a flawless, simple, linear ambush, will the enemy be caught off guard next time? Fool me twice, shame on me.

24.a Dismounted Enemy Patrol

A dismounted enemy patrol moves significantly slower than a mounted patrol. Patience becomes paramount. The Patrol Leader must wait to initiate until either the enemy becomes centered on the killzone or an individual is about to exit the killzone.

Dismounted Soldiers at night are harder to detect than the headlights and noise of a mounted patrol, so extra care must be taken for positive identification. To positively identify and engage, the Leader must know the rules of engagement.

24.b Enemy Stops Outside of the Killzone

One of the most essential parts of an ambush is stopping the enemy vehicle. This is a key point of the mission that is discussed in planning. (See Image 153, Pg. 210.) A U.S. Humvee can weigh more than 7,000lbs. and travel 65mph. That means a Humvee has over 10,000 times the momentum of a 7.62 round! **Fire power does not equal stopping power.** Many ambushes which initiate with shooting the enemy vehicle's engine block rely on the vehicle crashing or stopping itself.[1] If the vehicle does not stop or crash, or the initiation timing is wrong, or for any reason the enemy is outside the killzone, the patrol must be prepared to reposition and kill the enemy.

Targets outside the killzone create friendly-fire problems, where the Assault Line cannot fire without risking shooting Security or even itself. To minimize the risk of friendly fire but still reduce enemy maneuvers, the Patrol Leader must order Soldiers to engage in suppressing fire when they lack good angles to kill the enemy. The suppressing fire makes time for the ambush to reestablish itself while maintaining violence of action.

One option to create safe sectors-of-fire for an Assault Line is to have the Assault Leader order the entire line to run parallel to the road, setting down, and creating a hasty killzone in front of them. Better to have all Soldiers firing with improvised coordinated fires, than friendly fire concerns.

Phase 4

The plan for stopping enemy vehicles is dependent on terrain and resources. However, one method is to attach explosives to a tree beside the road, and blow the tree onto the road at ambush initiation.

Image 153: A Marine prepares an explosive charge for tree demolition. Motutapu Island, Tonga 25 Jul 2016. **With proper protections and precautions, a patrol can explode a tree into a road to stop a vehicle.** In urban combat, creating blocking positions is a widely used strategies because convoys are already blocked on either side by man-made structures.

If the enemy has positioned itself directly between Assault and Security, machine guns cannot fire. At the initiation of the ambush, if Security moved to their secondary covered positions, firing their M4s carefully, then firing in the direction of Security is sometimes okay. (This is why leader's recon of a secondary security position prioritizes cover from the killzone.) There is a balance between suppressing enemy fire (i.e., not getting shot yourself) and trusting Security to be in position. Regardless, the Assault must create a flank around the enemy, starting a hasty react-to-contact.

24.c Enemy Patrol Is Wider than the Killzone

If the enemy patrol is wider than the prepared killzone, then the Assault Line must expand horizontally to the width of the enemy. If the enemy is still too wide, the Assault Line can split into two Assault Lines. Or Assault can continue across the killzone, turn 90 degrees, and continue to assault parallel to the road. Or Assault can focus on one part of the enemy formation, and the Gun Team can provide suppressive fire to the remaining enemies until Assault has arrived. If the enemy is so wide that it is basically scattered, a Leader especially considers: breaking contact, repositioning Security, and reconsolidating on a larger killzone.

24.d Counter Ambush from Behind the Objective

If there are additional enemies behind the objective after an ambush, the ambush becomes a react-to-contact scenario with either another assault or a break-contact. Although the killzone may be extended farther, care must be taken not to lose control and communication between all the different elements.

24.e Enemy Quick Reaction Force and Harassing Ambush

Around the world, when an element is attacked and calls for reinforcements, those reinforcements are called Quick Reaction Forces (QRF). **QRF are prestaged units** that can literally run to a vehicle and race to the element being engaged. Their response time can be as little as five minutes, and must be briefed during planning and known by the whole patrol. The rule of thumb is to be off the objective in half the estimated enemy response time. (See Image 154, Pg. 212.)

If QRF is encountered, it is treated as a regular react-to-contact situation. A squad-size patrol likely needs to redeploy the entire Assault. But a platoon has many Soldiers to draw upon. Therefore, a Platoon Leader is much more free to grab Soldiers, while maintaining security. A common approach is for the Patrol Leader to call for the EPW Team to react to the QRF, while leaving the remaining Soldiers to secure the killzone.

A common approach for dealing with an enemy QRF is to utilize harassing ambushes. A harassing ambush is different from a regular ambush, because a harassing ambush does not fully engage. Their role is to delay and degrade the enemy QRF, giving the main ambush more time to withdraw. A harassing ambush is set up down the road from the ambush from the direction that the enemy QRF is expected to arrive from. They can be a simple as a few

Image 154: U.S. Marines stage their vehicles before conducting operations. Helmand province, Afghanistan, 24 Jun 2013. A Quick Reaction Force is prepared 24/7 to respond quickly. **Whatever the expected or reported enemy quick response time is, plan for half that amount.**

Soldiers firing into an enemy QRF, or setting off a few claymores to slow down enemy vehicles. (See Image 155, Pg. 213.)

Depending on the situation and combat environment, **harassing ambushes can even become the mission itself.** For example, if the QRF is known to be many times the size of a regular convey and fully deploys every time, the convey can be attacked to bait out the enemy QRF. Then the QRF can be engaged on favorable terms with no reinforcements left. (See Image 156, Pg. 213.)

Between a squad ambush and a harassing ambush is a team ambush. Team ambushes aim to eliminate a few high-value targets, and are often executed by long-range shooters. Team ambushes may not possess the manpower to eliminate every enemy in the killzone, and must take measures like diversions, distractions, multiple teams, or a dedicated withdrawal element to allow for a safe withdrawal. To facilitate coordination, a small command element may be inserted alongside one of the teams.

Image 155: Lithuanian National Defence Volunteer Forces (KASP) ambush an armored vehicle with anti-armor weapons. Joint Multinational Readiness Center in Hohenfels, Germany, 28 Jan 2018. **The point of this harrassing ambush is to shoot one anti-armor weapon and leave.**

Harassing Ambush

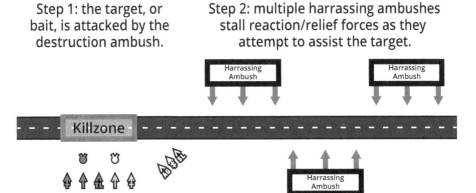

Step 1: the target, or bait, is attacked by the destruction ambush.

Step 2: multiple harrassing ambushes stall reaction/relief forces as they attempt to assist the target.

Harrassing Ambush

Harrassing Ambush

Killzone

Harrassing Ambush

Image 156: One way to counter an enemy QRF is to set harrassing ambushes on the route that QRF is predicted to take. **These ambushes do not fully engage.** Their role is to delay and degrade the enemy QRF, giving the main ambush more time to withdraw.

24.f Assault Leader Is Combat Ineffective

An Assault Leader can be ineffective because they have become a casualty, or just because they are making poor decisions. The Patrol Leader must be ready at any time to take over the Assault Line. (The assault does not stop because the Assault Leader is incapacitated.) Relieving an Assault Leader because of poor performance is a last resort. A first step is micromanaging the Assault Leader, like yelling specific orders. (E.g., "Push left!")

24.g Patrol Leader Is Combat Ineffective[1]

If the Patrol Leader has become a casualty, the assault proceeds normally. Because the Patrol Leader is responsible for calling "cease fire" and initiating the assault, **the Assault Leader needs to be aware of how much time has passed since initiation**. If no cease fire has been called after 60 seconds, it is possible that the Patrol Leader is incapacitated.

Once the assault begins, if there is no Patrol Leader, the Assault Leader inherits the Patrol Leader's responsibilities in addition to their own. The Assault Leader both receives and records ACE reports (including the Gun Team). The Assault Leader both briefs and leads the EPW Team. The Assault Leader coordinates the Aid and Litter Team, and calls the "Fire in the Hole" withdrawal sequence.

24.h Security Is Combat Ineffective

An ineffective Security is different from other casualties because **Security will be between the Main Body and the enemy**. Therefore, firing on the enemy risks friendly fire on Security. Maneuver becomes the first priority.

One half of Assault, the Patrol Leader and the Gun Team, split off to create the Suppressing Element and lay suppressive fire (just like break-contact). Special care must be used not to fire on the position that Security was in, nor where they might have retreated to. The Suppressing Element places themself in a position to fire, and bound to the release-point when necessary.

---

1 Quote: The graveyards are full of indispensable men. —French Brigadier General and Commander during WWII, Charles de Gaulle

Security Is Attacked

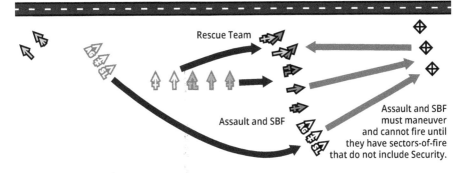

Rescue Team

Assault and SBF

Assault and SBF must maneuver and cannot fire until they have sectors-of-fire that do not include Security.

Image 157: An example of how a squad reacts when Security is attacked. **The squad cannot assist Security until it knows where Security is.** To assist Security, the squad splits into a Rescue Team and a Flanking Team to retrieve Security and flank the enemy. The extreme vulnerability of this situation highlights a few things. Security must be well hidden and always alert. Security also must follow a well-defined EWAC plan and communicate danger!

The other half of Assault becomes the Rescue Team and breaks off to the security position. Once the Rescue Team locates Security, it evacuates them to a release-point and yells, "Objective clear!" (See Image 157, Pg. 215.)

The other Security position is notified to evacuate to the release-point. Once all Soldiers are accounted for at the release-point, the patrol can withdraw.

24.i Explosive Device in the Killzone

If an active explosive device is found within the killzone area (e.g., an IED in the road, unrelated to the enemy, or a bomb on a timer in the enemy vehicle), the Patrol Leader immediately withdraws from the objective. The common codeword for immediate withdrawal is, "Landslide!" If one explosive is found, there likely are more explosives that are yet to be found. If the Patrol Leader determines that the threat is worth the risk (e.g., grenades with pins, inside the enemy vehicle, which were driven into the killzone), they can continue assaulting while avoiding that area within the killzone entirely.

Phase 4

Phase 5 Contents

25. Patrol-Base Occupation   217
Scouting a Good Location   218
Leave No Trace   218

26. Linkup   220
Long-Halt and Signal-Site   220
Actions of First Squad to Arrive at Signal-Site   221
Actions of Second and Third Squads to Arrive   224

27. Security Tasks and Priorities of Work   226
Reconnaissance and Surveillance (R&S)   226
Claymores   227
Range Cards and Sector Sketch   227
Alert Plan   229
Withdrawal Plan   229

28. Maintenance Tasks   230
Weapons Maintenance   231
Water Resupply   232
Chow, Personal Hygiene, Snivel Gear, and Rest   233
Planning and Briefing a FRAGO   234

29. Hasty Patrol-Base   235

Joe Goes Home
(Phase 5: Withdrawal
to a Patrol-Base)

I therefore determined, first, to use the greatest number of troops practicable..., [to prevent] the possibility of repose for refitting and producing necessary supplies for carrying on resistance.
—6th Commanding Gen. of the U.S. Army, Ulysses S. Grant

A patrol-base is a kind of halt used for extended tasks (of no more than 24 hours). Whereas a short-halt is for 5-minute tasks like map checks, and a long-halt is for 20-minute tasks like cross-loading ammo, a single mission can take days or more which requires an extended solution.

At some point during a long mission, Soldiers must reorganize, resupply, and sleep. However, these tasks all make a patrol vulnerable to enemy attack. Therefore, if the patrol cannot return home, the patrol establishes a patrol-base, which is the most secure formation a patrol can make.

The downside of a patrol-base is that they require lots of time to make. Because its purpose is tied to refitting a patrol, it is usually only used after an operation of some sort (like an ambush).

25. Patrol-Base Occupation[1]

The first step in creating a patrol-base is finding a good location. Because **the patrol is especially vulnerable when Soldiers are sleeping and planning**, it is very important to choose an especially good, safe location.

Phase 5

Staying in a fixed, unsupported location, in the wild, after ambushing an enemy force is a recipe for disaster. Any commander that uses a patrol-base, in the middle of the woods, for planning multiple, consecutive, hasty missions has done something horribly wrong. Patrol-bases are taught in the schoolhouse for two very good reasons: first, as a way to evaluate Soldiers at their most fatigued; and second, to teach good habits and concepts. Concepts like priorities of work, appropriate levels of security, field maintenance for weapons, and more.

And throughout the entire patrol-base process, the patrol cannot spoil that location by leaving traces of their presence.

A patrol usually uses a platoon formation to make a patrol-base. (See Platoon Formation, Pg. 176.) How the patrol gets into a platoon formation depends on whether the patrol is whole or split into multiple elements. When the patrol is one element it can use all the same platoon formation procedures described in the aforementioned platoon formation section. However, if the patrol is split into multiple elements, it must perform linkup before occupying the patrol-base and platoon formation. (See Linkup, Pg. 220.)

25.a Scouting a Good Location

Although the general location is determined during planning, a patrol cannot see ditches and bushes from a map. Therefore, whether a patrol is united or split, the first element of the patrol to arrive at the preplanned general patrol-base location must recon the area to judge the local conditions.

The criteria for an ORP location is COOL-E. (See Leader's Recon of the Squad ORP, Pg. 136.) But a patrol-base needs to be more secure, so the criteria needs an additional "NT" to make **COOLENT** because a patrol-base is occupied for longer and performs more tasks.

C – Covered and concealed position. (See Image 158, Pg. 219.)

O – Off natural lines of drift (paths people naturally follow).

O – Out of sight, sound, and small arms fire of the enemy.

L – Large enough to fit an entire element.

E – Easily defendable for a short period of time.

N – Near a source of water.

T – Tough, terrible terrain that the enemy does not care about.

COOLENT is ongoing criteria. Even after a patrol-base is occupied, if the Reconnaissance and Surveillance Teams report a close potential danger, the Platoon Leader must consider moving the element to the alternate patrol-base because of updated information.

25.b Leave No Trace

Once a patrol moves to a good location, it is essential to leave no traces behind that the patrol was there. Patrol-bases only exist in enemy territory, and the enemy can gather information from even the most mundane sources.

Image 158: U.S. Army Paratroopers from 2nd Bn., 503rd Inf. Reg., 173rd Airborne Bde., engage in Exercise Rock Knight. Pocek Range, Postonja, Slovenia, 24 Jul 2017. Choosing a good, covered and concealed location is invaluable when reconning a patrol-base. **Note how well the third Soldier on the left is concealed compared to the other two.**

A food wrapper can indicate a patrol's nationality, a shell casing can prove weaponry, and holes in the grounds can show standard operation procedures.

Throughout patrol-base tasks, and for missions in general, it is important to carry out all the waste. Burying does not work well as animals will sometimes uncover items. If holes are dug, they must be filled and vegetation left as undisturbed as possible.[1] To minimize evidence left behind if the patrol-base is attacked, Soldiers never have more than one item out of their ruck at a time, returning each item into the ruck before taking the next one out.

In the age of aerial surveillance and red-dot optics, if there's time to dig holes then there's time to move or rest.

26. Linkup[1]

Before settling in to a patrol-base, any unit that is split up must reconsolidate. A linkup is the procedure necessary after, for example, a platoon-area ambush. Within linkup, there are three locations: **the long-halt, the signal-site, and the patrol-base**. All three locations are roughly planned in the OPORD.[2]

26.a Long-Halt and Signal-Site

The long-halt is a spot to safely hide the patrol as leadership conduct reconnaissance of the signal-site and patrol-base. Each squad has a different long-halt location; they are chosen as secure locations to park a squad, one terrain feature away from the signal-site.

Each squad goes to their long-halt at a time and location that are decided during planning (e.g. after the ambush at 12UUA 8432 4079). At the long-halt, leadership prepares a Leader's Recon Team. The Leader's Recon Team consists of three smaller teams of two Soldiers each: a Leader Team, an S&O Team 1, and an S&O Team 2. (See Surveillance and Observation Position (S&O), Pg. 139.) Due to the number of split teams and units, having a robust and thorough communication PACE plan and GOTWA are vital to the linkup plan, and commo checks are frequent. (See PACE Communication Options, Pg. 242.) From the long-halt, the Leader's Recon Team departs to the signal-site.

The **signal-site** is where the Leader's Recon Teams from different element meet each other. Signal-sites are necessary as an intermediate site between long-halts and patrol-bases for two reasons.

First, joining elements together is inherently dangerous, because initial identification of enemy-versus-friendly is difficult. Meaning, if large friendly elements are allowed approach a patrol-base, then large enemy elements may

---

1 Real World: Linkup is included to illustrate that every part of a patrol can be completed in relative safety without radio comms. However, it is unclear the last time that this complicated procedure was actually used.

2 Applying Concepts: Planning for contingencies is important. The linkup plan must cover: enemy contact before, during, and after linkup; length of time to wait at the linkup site; actions in case some elements fail to linkup; and alternate linkup points and rally-points.

Image 159 et al: A disposable red light or an infrared glowstick both make good signals. **Meetup at the signal can be offset**; for example, meet 70 meters at 70 degrees from the signal.

also be able to approach a patrol-base and be mistaken for a friendly element trying to link up. Then the enemy could attack from a near position.

In the reverse, if a friendly element approaches an enemy patrol-base by accident and tries to link up, they will be easy targets. Therefore, large units must have separate locations for initial identification, and when and where they eventually join together. **Linkup is useful because it provides an alternate site for identification (i.e. the signal site).**

Second, patrol-bases by their nature are supposed to be well hidden so the enemy cannot find them. However, meetups are not be in a well-hidden area, because two joining elements will have trouble finding each other. Therefore, signal-sites are a location in a relatively well-seen area with an obvious signal. There, a few Leaders from each element can meet up and plan further movement for their respective elements.

At the signal-site, the Leader's Recon conducts SLLS (as with every stop) and drops off the S&O Team 1 in a location that is as covered and concealed as possible, while still having good vision on the signal-site.

26.b Actions of First Squad
to Arrive at Signal-Site

The first squad to arrive at the grid location (chosen during planning) picks a signal-site to place a predetermined signal, like a ribbon. (See Image 159 et al, Pg. 221.) The site ideally has poor concealment but good cover. Thereby, the signal can be well seen, but anyone can duck for cover. S&O Team 1 then monitors the signal-site, waiting for the next squad to arrive. The remaining four Soldiers in the Leader's Recon Team continue on to the tentative patrol-base ("tentative" because it was also chosen during planning). (See Image 160, Pg. 223.)

At the tentative patrol-base, the Leader's Recon Team emplaces S&O Team 2. The two remaining Soldiers conduct reconnaissance of the area, taking into account of the size of a full platoon formation and how long the platoon will be there. The distance can be 200 meters out, 500 meters, or even more. Once the Leader Team have confirmed a good patrol-base location, they return to the long-halt to bring in the squad. (See Leader's Recon of the Platoon Formation, Pg. 172.)

Once the squad arrives at the patrol-base and incorporates S&O Team 2, the squad occupies all three corners of the platoon formation where the platoons M240s eventually will go. (See Image 128, Pg. 178.) An example of the three corners can be: one has the M240, another has a SAW (the second SAW is on S&O Team 1), and the other has a surplus of Riflemen. (See Image 160, Pg. 223.) Populating only the corners creates the shape of the eventual platoon formation, and makes incorporating other squads easier. Whenever a new squad arrives, their M240 takes the position of a triangle point, and their Riflemen take their position between the points.

Once the triangle is set, the first squad pushes out a Meetup Team (e.g., the Squad Leader, Alpha Team Leader, and a Rifleman) to await the second squad's arrival. The Meetup Team takes place in a covered and concealed position where they can see the area surrounding the signal. They approach the signal when they identify another squad's Meetup Team or signal.

The Meetup Team is separate from the S&O Team 1 because they serve different purposes. The Meetup Teams physically go to the signal to talk, and so cannot remain hidden. The S&O Team provides overwatch to the meetup. If the Meetup Teams were placed with S&O, an observant enemy would be able to locate the S&O when the Meetup Team emerged to go to the signal-site, compromising the S&O position and overwatch.

There are many variations to linkup. For example, in the above method, after the first squad marks a signal-site, the Leader's Recon Team continues to the tentative patrol-base. In a different method, the Leader's Recon Team can go back to the long-halt and take the patrol-base by force, skipping the leader's recon of the patrol-base. Or, if the first squad thinks their long-halt would make a good patrol-base location, they can convert a long-halt into a patrol-base.

Linkup for the First Squad to Arrive

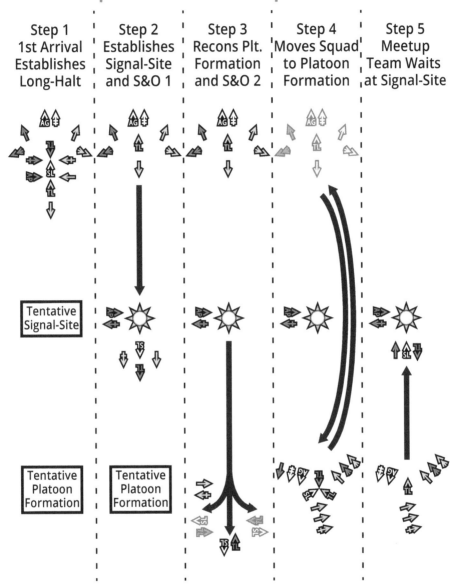

Image 160: Linkup for the first squad to arrive can be divided into **five steps and three locations.** The first location is the long-halt. The second location is the tentative signal-site, where the patrol plans on putting the signal to meet other elements. The tentative platoon formation is where the patrol plans on putting the platoon formation. Both tentative locations are tentative until they are scouted by the Leader's Recon Team.

26.c Actions of Second and Third Squads to Arrive

The next squads are the same as the first squad, until the Leader's Recon Team sees a marker already at the signal-site. The Leader's Recon Team approaches the marker and conducts the comms PACE plan for linkup with the first squad to arrive. Placing an additional marker at the signal-site is good idea, in case the first squad's Meetup Team has not returned yet from the platoon formation. So when the Meetup Team does come back, they can go directly to the signal.

Once communication is established between the first squad's Meetup Team and the next squad's Leader's Recon Team, Leaders from both squads approach the signal-site to talk. (See Recombining Elements (Near and Far Recognition Signals), Pg. 141.) During meetup, each squad's S&O positions provide overwatch in case of an enemy attack. The only topics that must be discussed are: 1) that the signal-site is secure; and 2) that the first squad has begun a patrol-base location and can lead the second squad to it.

In all, one Leader from the first squad, the second squad's Leader's Recon Team, and the second squad's S&O return to the second squad's long-halt. The first squad Leader then leads the second squad to the patrol-base location. At this point, the only Soldiers at the signal-site are the first squad's S&O and Meetup Team. Because the Meetup Team loses a member for every meetup, it is composed of one Leader for each following element, plus one additional Soldier to buddy pair the last Leader.

When the second squad approaches the patrol-base location, the first squad Squad Leader initiates far and near recognition signals. When finished, the second squad is fully integrated into the patrol-base.

The linkup for the third (or final) squad is almost identical to the linkup of the second squad. The only difference is that the signal-site must be sanitized and with all signals picked up. With all three squads in position, the patrol-base is fully occupied. The Platoon Leader may either stay in place and convert the site to a permanent patrol-base (if security permits), or move to a new location.

Linkup for the Following Squads

Step 1	Step 2	Step 3	Step 4	Step 5
Next Arrival Establishes Long-Halt	Next Arrival Prepares to Be First	Near/Far Recognition Then Meetup	Sqd.1 Guides Sqd.2 to Plt. Formation	Meetup Team Waits at Signal-Site

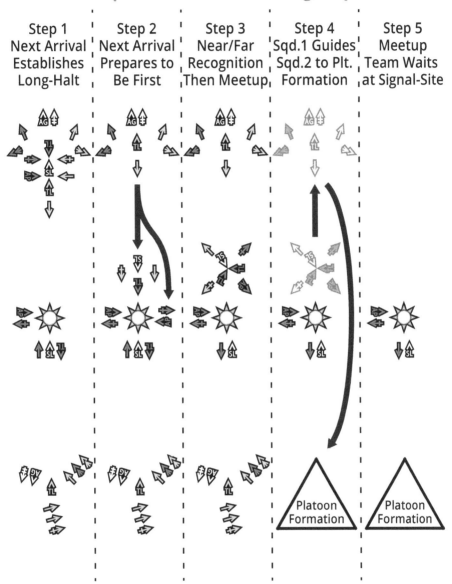

Image 161: Linkup for the second and third squads to arrive is divided into five steps and three locations, just like for the first squad. **Instead of scouting tentative locations, the second and third squad focus on meeting the first squad** to be guided to the platoon formation. Due to space limitations, the expanded platoon formation is represented by a triangle here.

27. Security Tasks and Priorities of Work[1]

After occupation, there is still a lot of work to be done in a patrol-base, and **some work is more important than other work**. Therefore, there is a standard order in which tasks must be accomplished, called the "priorities of work."[2] This section deals with the first and most important priority: security.

Security is a constant. Even after being "completed" patrol-base security must be constantly monitored and revised. The patrol-base begins with 100% security on the line (meaning all Soldiers except leadership pull security). Security can only fall below 100% once the base is secure. The base is secure once all sectors-of-fire have been assigned, coordinated, and recorded. Security also includes working communications; no talking means no coordinating which means no security. When all security tasks are done, the Patrol Leader gives a spare-report, "patrol-base occupied" to higher.

27.a Reconnaissance and Surveillance (R&S)

The R&S Team is a group of two to four Soldiers who walk out of the patrol-base and recon the surrounding area for potential danger (e.g., areas of high traffic, or fast avenues of approach). Prior to their departure, each team must have working comms and give a GOTWA. Any time anyone exits the patrol-base, security is at 100%.

The R&S Teams go out far enough to detect any danger to the patrol-base (typically 50 to 400 meters). They also confirm any water sources found on maps; water on maps sometimes is seasonal. Upon returning, R&S reports to the Platoon Sergeant. If danger is present, the Platoon Sergeant adjusts sectors-of-fire to concentrate on that area, or even relocate the patrol-base.

1   Quote: Time is everything: five minutes makes the difference between victory and defeat. —British Vice-Admiral, Horatio Nelson

2   Real World: There is a lot of grey area. For example, if a Soldier is so cold they are shaking uncontrollably, they can't really provide security. Or, what if there are four hours available, but setting up perfect security takes three? In that case, what are the tradeoffs to having more maintenance and less security?

Image 162: Paratroopers from the 173rd Airborne Bde. pull perimeter security. Juliet Drop Zone, Italy, 10 Apr 2018. A basic patrol-base is in the shape of a platoon formation. (See Platoon Formation, Pg. 176.) This picture shows a strong-point position, with command in the background. A patrol-base lasts much longer than a long-halt, and Soldiers are much more tired. **Is the prone a good position to place tired, quiet Soldiers at night for hours? What are the alternatives?**

27.b Claymores

Once all Soldiers are back from R&S with information on the potential danger, Team Leaders are briefed on where to place claymores. Claymores face the most likely avenue of approach by the enemy, which usually is in the direction of any roads. **Any time anyone exits the patrol-base, security is at 100%.** (See Emplacing Claymores and Final Steps, Pg. 168.)

Once claymores are set, their distance, location, azimuth, and sectors-of-fire must all be indicated on the sector sketch. The information must be known by the SAW position, which is given the claymore clacker and briefed on when to fire.

27.c Range Cards and Sector Sketch

A range card is a piece of paper specifically formatted to record a sector-of-fire. They are used to coordinate different weapons, quickly replace wounded Gunners, and remind Soldiers of their sector. Although the U.S. Army uses DA Form 5517, any piece of paper can work. (See Image 163, Pg. 228.)

A range card must include at a minimum: the identity of the position (e.g., 9 o'clock); the azimuth of the left-limit and right-limit; the primary direction-of-fire (PDF); any identifiable terrain (e.g., roads); and dead space within the sector. The left-limit and the right-limit define the sector-of-fire for

Range Card

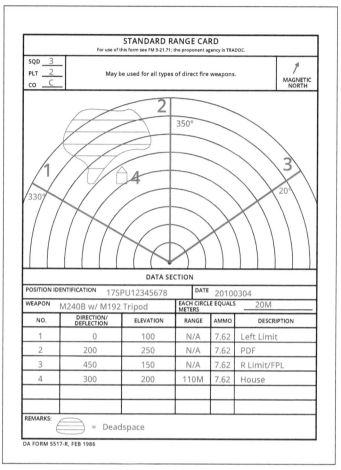

Image 163: An example of a filled range card. This is the standard U.S. Army form, but any piece of paper will do.

the weapon. The PDF is the direction that the weapon points toward and fires at by default. Range cards can be drawn for any weapon, but they must be written for weapons that are always manned, like M240s in a patrol-base, to allow for easy replacement of the Gunner.

While the range cards are being written, the Squad Leader for each squad compiles a sector sketch of their squad. A sector sketch is a single document or item that contains all of the interlocking sectors-of-fire for an element. (In the Squad Leader's case, they record the sectors for their squad leg of the patrol-base.) The sector sketch also includes the position and sector-of-fire for any claymores. When the range cards and squad sector sketches are complete, they are brought to the Platoon Sergeant so that they can draw a platoon sector sketch, which includes all sectors-of-fire for all weapons, and can verify 360-degree interlocking sectors-of-fire.

27.d Alert Plan

An alert plan is how Soldiers deal with threats and perceived threats. **It tells Soldiers when and how to call for leadership and open fire.** At a minimum, when a Soldier suspects enemy movement, they alert another Soldier sharing their position without losing sight of the threat.

An example simple alert plan is to have one man in a strong-point notify leadership. The Platoon Sergeant confirms 360-degree security. The Patrol Leader moves to the position where the disturbance was heard and makes a decision of what to do. If fired upon, Soldiers fire back.

The patrol also designates a time for "**stand-to**." For whatever reason, enemies in history have been more likely to attack during dawn and dust. Therefore, it is SOP to have 100% security at a specified time; like, one hour of stand-to starting 30 minutes prior to sunrise and sunset. (The U.S. Army is more precise, and uses "begin morning nautical twilight" and "end evening nautical twilight.")

27.e Withdrawal Plan

A withdrawal plan consists of four locations. The first location is the current patrol-base. The second and third locations are two rally-points, to where the patrol can temporarily withdraw. They are traditionally named "black" and "gold." The fourth location is the alternate patrol-base, to which the patrol continues to withdraw from a rally-point. (See Image 1, Pg. 3.)

The black and gold rally-points are used to prevent enemy tracking. If Soldiers withdrew in a straight line from the patrol-base to the alternate patrol-base, the enemy could wait and follow the withdrawal azimuth to simply attack again. By using either black or gold to change direction midway in withdrawal to the alternate patrol-base, an enemy must use more complicated tracking than following in a straight line.

There are two rally-points, but any withdrawal will only use the one that is opposite of the enemy's attack. Therefore, black and gold must be

Phase 5

in roughly opposite directions, so the patrol always has a path of retreat planned, regardless of the enemy's direction of attack. Rally-points are at least one major terrain feature away from the patrol-base.

The alternate patrol-base also is at least one terrain feature away from both rally-points and the current patrol-base. And again, the patrol-base, a rally-point, and the alternate patrol-base cannot form a straight line. Choosing an alternate patrol-base location has the same requirements as any other patrol-base. (See Scouting a Good Location, Pg. 218.)

For dissemination of the withdrawal plan, Soldiers must memorize redundant information. The more that Soldiers memorize, the quicker and therefore safer a withdrawal can be. Ideally, Soldiers know all the locations in four formats:

▸ 8-digit grids and azimuths of movement.

▸ Local terrain features on a map.

▸ Pointing to the direction of each rally-point.

▸ Moving the bezel of the left compass to the gold rally-point's azimuth ("left" and "gold" each have four letters; and moving the right bezel to the black azimuth ("right" and "black" each have five letters).

The redundancy ensures a smoother withdrawal when Soldiers are fatigued and hungry in the middle of a night. Make each point as simple to remember as possible when creating a withdrawal plan. For example, choose repeating grid numbers, or whole number azimuths, whenever possible. Although writing this information down is useful, it is very easy to lose papers in an emergency retreat. If the enemy finds the withdrawal plan, they can destroy the entire patrol with artillery.

Executing a withdrawal plan is simple. Just evacuate to the rally-point opposite of the contact, and stay in constant contact with leadership. If the patrol-base is attacked, the Platoon Leader determines whether to break contact and evacuate, or to attack and thereafter still evacuate.

28. Maintenance Tasks

Maintenance tasks in the patrol-base are very flexible. Whereas all security tasks must be completed in order, maintenance tasks must be balanced with each other. A very clean, spotless weapon is not useful in the hands of a Soldier who has been awake for 40 hours without water.

Phase 5

Image 164: U.S. Marine Corps Cpl. 3rd Bn. 4th Marines, Task Force Koa Moana 17, cleans his weapon. Vava'u Island, Tonga, 26 Jul 2017. **Presumably, this weapon was broken. Otherwise, there is no reason to disassemble a weapon in the field, and risk dropping or losing pieces.**

Image 165: Senior Airman, 823d Base Defense Squadron, loads an M240 machine gun during a mission readiness exercise. Moody Air Force Base, Georgia, 23 Oct 2017. A machine gun without ammo is deadweight. **A patrol-base without working Gun Teams is on 100% security because of how vital they are.**

28.a Weapons Maintenance[1]

During a patrol, weapons get dirty, and dirty weapons misfire. All weapons must be rubbed down, have Cleaner Lubricant Preservative (CLP) applied, and checked for internal debris. **During the day, a weapon is only minimally disassembled; during the night, it is never disassembled at all.** (See Image 164, Pg. 231.) Starting with the M240, only one can be cleaned at a time, because making all M240s nonoperational at the same time drops too much security. When an M240 is taken off the line, the patrol pulls 100% security, and a SAW from the same squad temporarily replaces the M240 position. The Weapons Squad Leader organizes the cleaning of every M240s and informs the Platoon Sergeant when they are done.

After all M240s are cleaned, the SAW's are cleaned. Again, the platoon must maintain 100% security, and only one squad can clean their SAW's at any time. Once the SAW's are clean, Soldiers can begin on their rifles. One rifle per position may be taken off the line and cleaned.

Phase 5

---

1 Quote: A slipping gear could let your M203 grenade launcher fire when you least expect it. That would make you quite unpopular in what's left of your unit. —The Preventive Maintenance Monthly

Image 166: U.S. Marine from Inf., 1st Plt., Lima Co., 3rd Bn., 1st Marine Reg. conducts a water resupply. Bridgeport, CA, 08 Sep 2014. **Note how vulnerable this position makes this Soldier.** Humans often live near clean water sources. Water resupply uses few Soldiers to avoid being sighted. How detailed should a water resupply plan be in planning?

28.b Water Resupply[1]

Water resupply is performed by a team of at least two Soldiers, with more being necessary if the water source is far. The resupply begins by collecting the patrol's canteens into bags. Empty any partially filled canteens and include them. Make sure all the canteens are marked so they can be returned to their owner. The resupply Soldiers then are counted out of the base, and tactically move to the water.

When at the resupply point, at least one Soldier needs to pull security for every Soldier filling canteens. (See Image 166, Pg. 232.) If using iodine tablets, the Soldier filling canteens never puts iodine into the canteens; the Soldier who drinks the water does that. This is to prevent a mistake where both Soldiers put in iodine, creating a double dose. Upon returning to the base, the Soldiers are counted back in.

---

1 **Quote:** They say "you can lead a horse to water, but you can't make him drink." In the Marine Corps, you can make that horse wish to hell he had. —USMC Drill Instructor, Fred Larson

Image 167: A Marine with A Co., 1st Bn., 7th Marine Reg., lays down to air out his feet after a patrol. Kahuku Training Facility, 14 Sep 2016. **Although security tasks usually take priority over maintenance tasks, a Soldier that can't shoot or move is not secure.**

28.c Chow, Personal Hygiene, Snivel Gear, and Rest[1]

A patrol-base is a group task, so **any personal time one Soldier takes is personal time another Soldier cannot have**. Therefore, a single amount of time is given to each Soldier to accomplish all personal tasks as they see fit. If the Soldier fails to accomplish any of the tasks, they must return to pulling security regardless. That being said, Team Leaders are responsible for making sure Soldiers who do not put on cold weather gear are not shaking so hard they cannot hold a weapon straight, and that Soldiers eat enough to function. (See Image 167, Pg. 233.)

Soldiers remain in complete uniform, including boots, at all times unless directed otherwise. Rucks are packed at all times, and MRE's have only one item out of the bag at all times. These minimize the time needed to pack up and evacuate if there is surprise enemy contact.

Phase 5

---

1 Quote: Coffee tastes better if the latrines are dug downstream from an encampment. —Unknown

Image 168: U.S. Marine Platoon and Squad Leaders plan a scheme of maneuver during Mountain Exercise 2014. Marine Corps Mountain Warfare Training Center, Bridgeport, CA, 09 Sep 2014. **Note how crowded and close these Soldiers are compared to the Soldiers on the right.**

Image 169: U.S. Marines assigned to the School of Infantry West, Detachment Hawaii, use a terrain model during the Advanced Infantry Course. Kahuku Training Area, HI, 20 Jul 2016. **A terrain model is great for briefing. But it takes more space, time, and planning.**

28.d Planning and Briefing a FRAGO[1]

A FRAGO (Fragmentary Order) is essentially a change of plans from higher command after receiving the original mission in the OPORD (Operations Order). When in the field, a patrol-base provides the necessary space and security for a patrol to make and brief a mission out of higher's FRAGO.

Planning a mission requires and distracts the highest leadership positions and any advisors. Therefore during the planning and briefing of a FRAGO, the patrol-base requires 100% security. Planning a FRAGO is its own process that can be found in the Ranger Handbook among other references.

Briefing a FRAGO is a four-brief process. For the first brief, all leadership except Bravo Team Leaders come to the center. The Bravo Team Leaders monitor and help their squads, while the Platoon Leader briefs their final plan to the other Leaders.

The next three briefs are the squad briefs. Each Squad Leader calls their squad to the center while the other two squads cover down on the now empty line. Because there are three briefs and time can be scarce, each squad brief has a time limit. The Weapons Squad may receive its own, fifth brief, but it will likely be briefed concurrently with the squads.

---

1 Quote: I began the revolution with 82 men. If I had to do it again, I would do it with 10 or 15 and absolute faith. It does not matter how small you are if you have faith and a plan of action. —First Secretary of the Central Committee of the Communist Party of Cuba, Fidel Castro

Image 170: 2nd Plt., Action Co., 2nd Bn., 5th Inf. Reg., with their Afghan army counterparts, resting and taking cover behind a berm. Dondokay village, Sayed Abad District, Wardak province, Afghanistan, 22 Nov 2011. **Note that two SAW positions are manned, while other Soldiers rest.**

29. Hasty Patrol-Base

Sometimes the patrol has been moving for 40 hours with hundreds of pounds of weight. Each Soldier is physically exhausted, but spending two hours creating a secure Patrol-base is impractical because the mission only has two hours to spare. In this case, the Patrol Leader must consider resting the formation in a hasty patrol-base formation.

To make the formation, the patrol splits in two lines, which go back-to-back facing outward. A platoon is large enough to make a triangle, with all Soldiers facing out. Soldiers then sit down and take off their ruck; they fall asleep in that position. Security is handled by using a sleep schedule.

At least two Soldiers must be awake at all times, facing opposite directions, while manning the machine guns. Aside from security, the primary responsibility of each Soldier is making sure their counterpart is awake. If Soldiers falling asleep is not a concern, then the patrol is not exhausted enough to need a hasty patrol-base. (See Image 170, Pg. 235.)

Annex Contents

30. M240 Machine Gun — 237
Rate-of-Fire — 237
Firing Drills — 237
Malfunction Procedures — 239

31. AT4 Light Anti-Tank Weapon — 240

32. Communication — 242
Spare-Report — 242
PACE Communication Options — 242
Example Communication Methods — 244
Example Total PACE Plan — 244

33. Glossaries — 246
Acronyms — 246
Words — 248

34. Index — 254

35. Credits — 256

Annexes

There is always one more thing you can do to increase your odds of success.
—U.S. Army Lt. Gen., Hal Moore

30. M240 Machine Gun[1]

30.a Rate-of-Fire

Ammunition equals time. Adjusting the rate-of-fire is how Leaders balance the need for ammunition later, versus the need for violence of action now.

Cyclic – 650 to 950 rounds per minute continuously; barrel change every 1 minute. Cyclic is how fast the weapon is physically capable of "cycling" (load, lock, fire, unlock, eject). Measurement of the cyclic rate does not consider operator tasks (reloading, aiming, etc.).

Rapid – 10 to 13 round bursts 2 to 3 seconds apart; barrel change occurs every 2 minutes. Rapid rate-of-fire is between cyclic and sustained.

Sustained – 6 to 9 round bursts 4 to 5 seconds apart; barrel change occurs every 10 minutes. Sustained is the rate at which the weapon can indefinitely fire without failing; and therefore, it is the actual rate at which the weapon would typically be fired in combat. Sustained accounts for operator tasks like reloading, aiming, changing barrels, cooling, etc.

30.b Firing Drills

Machine guns are complicated machines that cannot operate for more than a few minutes if handled improperly. M240s have a few drills that a Gunner and Assistant Gunner must do for optimal performance.

Barrel Change – Friction and explosive heat can literally melt a M240 barrel from firing alone. Therefore, they come with spare barrels. Barrel changes are preemptive, and are done according to the rate-of-fire. The Ammo

---

1 Quote: Whoever said the pen is mightier than the sword obviously never encountered automatic weapons. —American General of the Army, Douglas MacArthur

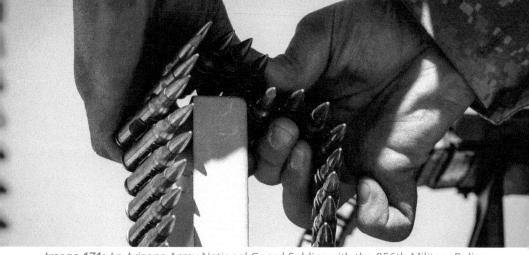

Image 171: An Arizona Army National Guard Soldier with the 856th Military Police Company from Bellemont, Arizona links two belts on ammunition together before loading it into a M240B machine gun.

Bearer or Assistant Gunner performs barrel changes, as the Gunner cannot easily reach them.

Linking and De-Linking Ammunition – "Linking" ammo means to combine two belts into one belt. Ammo is typically carried in multiple belts, which must be linked together both before and during combat. There are three ways to link and delink ammunition effectively. The first method is pushing together a link and a casing using both thumbs. This is the fastest method but also the most difficult. The second method is to use pliers to push a link and a casing together. This is the slowest but physically the easiest. A middle ground of fast and easy is to pull out a single casing on the primer end from the links, push the two empty links together, and reinsert the casing into the hole the links form.

Talking Guns – Firing a machine gun continuously is dangerous due to overheating barrels and exhausting ammunition supplies. But having no machine gun firing is also dangerous because machine guns kill enemies. Therefore, where multiple machine guns are present, they can alternate shooting: when one gun stops firing, another gun hears the halt and begins firing. It is much easier to coordinate machine guns with a designated Leader; a primary job of the Weapons Squad Leader is to "make the guns talk," or coordinate the firing of the M240s. Also, when a machine gun is not firing, that is an opportunity to change barrels or link rounds.

Image 172: U.S. Marines with Black Sea Rotational Force 18.1, execute a dead gunner drill during Exercise Platinum Lion 18. Novo Selo Training Area, Bulgaria, 03 Aug 2018. The Assistant Gunner roles the Gunner away.

30.c Malfunction Procedures

When a weapon fails, it needs to be fixed as soon as possible. A broken weapon is dead weight and worse than no weapon at all. Therefore, each weapon has a set of standard procedures that will fix most problems very fast. These instructions below are the procedures for an M240, which resolve various situations.

Dead Gunner Drill – If a Gunner dies, the Assistant Gunner must be prepared to assume control of the gun. The Assistant Gunner must push the dead body out of the way, stop the gun from firing, and roll into the gunning position. A Gunner can be removed by holding onto the body and hurling it over oneself, or by pushing the Gunner away hard by kicking their hip. If there is an Ammo Bearer, then the Assistant Gunner must roll the body, while the Ammo Bearer takes the gun. (See Image 172, Pg. 239.)

Immediate Action – First, try immediate action. Then if that does not work, try remedial action, which is a little more involved. Immediate action is essentially this: rack the charging handle, see a bullet ejected, and fire.

More specifically, immediate action is "**POPS**," which stands for Pull, Observe, Push, and Squeeze:

Pull – and lock the cocking handle to the rear while you...

Observe – the ejection port to see if a cartridge case, belt link, or round ejects. (If a round or cartridge case is not ejected, ensure that the bolt remains to the rear to prevent double feeding.)

Push – the cocking handle to its forward position, take aim on the target; and...

Squeeze – the trigger. If the weapon does not fire, take remedial action.

Remedial Action – When a stoppage occurs and immediate action has failed, the Gunner must:

1) **Point the weapon in a safe direction.**
2) Pull the cocking handle to the rear, locking the bolt. Push the cocking handle all the way forward and attempt to place the weapon on SAFE.
3) If the weapon is hot, wait five seconds.
4) Face away from the weapon and open the cover, check the feeder paws, feed tray, and tray cover, and perform the four-point safety check. Reload and continue to fire.

Runaway Firing – The weapon continues to fire after the Gunner releases the trigger. This usually is caused by the Gunner failing to pull and hold the trigger all the way to the rear. The following are immediate actions for runaway fire:

► The Gunner holds the weapon on target and fires the remaining ammunition;

► The Assistant Gunner delinks the ammo belt, so there is no more ammo to fire.

Sluggish Operation and Single Shot Firing – Thoroughly clean, lubricate, inspect, and replace worn parts. Adjust the gas regulator to maintain the rate-of-fire until there is a chance to conduct involved maintenance and disassembly.

31. AT4 Light Anti-Tank Weapon

Anti-tank weapons are very effective at destroying any kind of vehicle, and are vital to any foot patrol. However, they can also be dangerous and require practice to operate. This section shows the firing procedure for an AT4. Before

Image 173: A Soldier from 1st Bn., 4th Inf. Reg., fires a M136E1 AT4-CS light anti-tank weapon. U.S. Army's Joint Multinational Readiness Center, Hohenfels, Germany, 29 Oct 2015. This could be a **security postion** during an ambush or an linear danger area crossing.

firing, make sure the area behind the AT4 (i.e. the backblast area) is clear of people. The backblast area is 90 degrees for 100 meters.

Cradle Position – Remove the AT4 from its carrying position and cradle it in your left arm while keeping the weapon pointed toward the target.

Removing the transport safety pin – With your right hand, pull and release the transport safety pin. This pin is important to keep until firing; you must reinsert it if you do not fire the launcher.

Mounting the AT4 – Unfold and hold the shoulder stop with your right hand. Place the launcher on your right shoulder. Stabilize the AT4 by grasping the sling where it connects, with your left hand.

Opening and adjusting the sights – With the AT4 on your right shoulder, open the sights with your right hand. Press down and pull backward on the front sight cover until the front sight pops up. Then press down and forward on the rear sight cover until the rear sight pops up. The rear sight is between 2.5 and 3 inches from your eyes. Set the rear sight to the correct range for the target.

Cocking the launcher – Check the backblast area before you cock the launcher. The backblast area is 90 degrees for 100 meters. Then, unfold the cocking lever with your right hand. Place your thumb under it, and place your fingers in front of the firing mechanism. Push the cocking lever forward, rotate it downward to the right, and let it slide backward.

Firing the launcher – Pull back on the sling with your left hand to seat the shoulder stop firmly against your shoulder. To avoid a misfire, use the index and middle fingers on your right hand to hold the forward safety down and to the left while you fire.

32. Communication

Communication is a vital to any patrol. During a patrol, Soldiers will talk to their leadership. Different Leaders will talk to each other. The patrol will talk to higher command. Every time, place, method, and trigger of communication needs to be planned or accounted for before the patrol even starts.

32.a Spare-Report

A "spare" is a report to higher command that some preplanned event has been accomplished. A spare must be reported as soon as possible after the event through code phrase. The reporter is a Bravo Team Leader in a squad and the RTO in a platoon. Reporting spares is important for higher command to coordinate and assist troops on the ground. Some classic spares[1] are:

Infil Complete	– Kick Off
ORP Established	– Half Time
Ambush Occupied	– End Zone
Mission Complete	– Touchdown
In Patrol-Base	– Heaven

32.b PACE Communication Options

"PACE" (Primary, Alternate, Contingency, Emergency) plans for redundant communication are essential. Having backups ensures that mission success never rests on one radio, or one whistle. Because of the vital role of

---

[1] Real World: These football-themed spares have been used so often in war and in the schoolhouse that they should never actually be used in combat. Always refresh your code words!

Image 174: A 2-20th Special Forces Group (Airborne) Soldier demonstrates the proper use of a "**buzzsaw**" (i.e. swinging a chemlight on a string), during a live-fire training event. Camp Shelby shoothouse, 21 Jan 2019.

communication and the variety of options available, the total PACE plan always ends up complicated. **However, if Soldiers do not know the PACE, then it does not exist.**

It is important to use as many communications options as possible simultaneously. Communication options are not limited to using one after another. For example, during ambush initiation, claymores fire and the M240s fire as two separate, simultaneous indicators to start the ambush.

32.c Example Communication Methods

Kneeling/ Prone	FM Radio	Lume Tape Up/Down, Left/Right	Password Word or Number Combo	Tugline	Glowstick Present/ Absent
Hand and Arm Signals	Whistle	Satellite Phone	Smoke Grenade	Claymore	Gunshots
Runner	Voice	VR17 Panel Showing/ Hiding	Visual Identifica-tion	Phone	IR Flash Odd/Even

32.d Example Total PACE Plan

Drill	Info	Time	Primary	Alter-nate	Contin-gency	Emer-gency
Linear Danger Area Crossing	Security in Place	Day	FM Radio	VS17	Kneel/ Prone	Hand Signals
		Night	FM Radio	Lume Tape	IR Flash	Glow Stick
	Enemy Coming	Day	FM Radio	VS17	Kneel/ Prone	Relay Team
		Night	FM Radio	Lume Tape	IR Flash	Glow Stick
	Far-side Safe	Day	FM Radio	VS17	Hand Signals	Runner
		Night	FM Radio	Lume Tape	IR Flash	Glow Stick

Drill	Info	Time	Primary	Alter-nate	Contin-gency	Emer-gency
React-to-Contact	Shift-Fire	Day	SL Voice	TL Voice	Whistle	VS17
		Night	SL Voice	TL Voice	Glow Stick	Lume Tape
	Lift-Fire	Day	SL Voice	TL Voice	Whistle	VS17
		Night	SL Voice	TL Voice	Glow Stick	Lume Tape

Drill	Info	Time	Primary	Alter-nate	Contin-gency	Emer-gency
Near Recogni-tion	Friendly Return	Day	FM Radio	VS17	Hand Signals	Voice
		Night	FM Radio	Word Combo	Number Combo	Voice

Drill	Info	Time	Primary	Alter-nate	Contin-gency	Emer-gency
Ambush	Initiate	Day	Clay-more	M240	SL M4	AG M4
		Night	Clay-more	M240	SL M4	AG M4
	Cease Fire	Day	SL Voice	TL Voice	AG Voice	Runner
		Night	SL Voice	TL Voice	AG Voice	Runner

33. Glossaries

33.a Acronyms

3Ds	Direction, Distance, Description
5Fs	Food, Fuel, Fire, Feces, Freshly Turned Earth
5S&T	Search, Silence, Segregate, Safeguard, Speed, Tag
9Line	Medical Evacuation Request
A&L	Aid and Litter
A1	Assault 1
A2	Assault 2
AB	Ammo Bearer
ACE	Ammo, Casualties, Equipment
AG	Assistant Gunner
ALR	Alpha Left Rifleman
AMEX	Ambulance Exchange Point
AP	Alpha Point
APB	Alternate Patrol-Base
APL	Assistant Patrol Leader
ARR	Alpha Right Rifleman
ASAW	Alpha Squad Automatic Weapon
ASS	Assault, Support, Security
AT4	Anti-Tank Rocket Launcher
ATAR-C	Aim, Tie, Arm, Re-aim, Camouflage
ATL	Alpha Team Leader
BDE	Brigade
BFA	Blank Firing Adapter
BLAST	Blood, Lights, ACE, SAW's, Tac mag reload
BLR	Bravo Left Rifleman
BN	Battalion
BRR	Bravo Right Rifleman
BTL	Bravo Team Leader
CAS	Close Air Support
CCP	Casualty Collection Point
CCIR	Commander's Critical Information Requirements
CLP	Cleaner Lubricant Preservative
CO	Company
COOL-E	Covered and concealed, Off natural lines of drift, Out of sight sound and small arms fire, Large enough to fit the entire element, Easily defendable for a short period of time
COOLENT	COOL-E plus: Near a water source, Terrain undesirable to the enemy
COW-T	Commo, Optics, Weapons, Tie-Downs
CP	Check Point
DIV	Division
DECAF COFFEE	DEad space, Clear Assault and Fire lanes, COncealment, Fifty meters, Flat table-top surface, Eighteen-inch Elms (trees)
EOD	Explosive Ordnance Disposal
EPW	Enemy Prisoner of War
ERRP	En Route Rally-Point
EWAC	Engagement, Withdrawal, Abort, Compromise

FFIR	Friendly-Forces Information Requirements
FIST/FiST	Forward Support Team; known as FiSTers
FLC	Fighting Load Carrier Kit Vest
FO	Forward Observer
FOB	Forward Operating Base
FOOM	Formations and Order of Movement
FPL	Final Protective Line
FRAGO	Fragmentary Order
FSO	Fire Support Officer
FSS	Fire Support Specialist
GOTWA	Where Going, Others Going With, Time of Emergency, What if No Return, Actions on Contact for Both Elements
GT	Gun Team
GUN	Gunner
HLZ	Helicopter Landing Zone
HQ	Headquarters
IAW	In Accordance With
IDF	Indirect Fire
INF	Infantry
IMT	Individual Movement Techniques
IOT	In Order To
IRP	Initial Rally-Point
JTAC	Joint Terminal Attack Controllers
LACE	Liquids, Ammo, Casualties, Equipment
LDA	Linear Danger Area
LMTV	Light Medium Tactical Vehicle
LOA	Limit of Advance
LR	Leader's Reconnaissance
LP-OP	Listening Post, Outpost
LT	Leader Team
LWGM	Lightweight Ground Mount (i.e., M192)

M4	SI Carbine Rifle
M18	SI Claymore Mine
M40	SI Claymore Tester
M57	SI Firing Device
M192	SI Tripod for M240
M203	SI Grenade Launcher
M240	SI Machine Gun
M249	SI Light Machine Gun
MED	Medic
METT-TC	Mission, Enemy, Terrain/Weather, Troops Available, Time, Civilians (i.e., anything else you can think of)
MSG	Maneuver Support Group
MSS	Mission Support Site
MWE	Men, Weapons, Equipment
NGF	Naval Gunfire
NOD	Night Optical Device
OBJ	Objective
ODA	Open Danger Area
OOM	Order of Movement
ORP	Objective Rally-Point
OPORD	Operation Order
PACE	Primary, Alternate, Contingency, Emergency
PAX	Passengers/Personnel
PLT	Platoon
PB	Patrol-Base
PCC	Pre Combat Check
PCI	Pre Combat Inspection
PDF	Primary Direction-of-Fire
PEQ-15	Rifle Laser Mount
PID	Positive Identification
PIR	Priority Information Requirement
PLOT-CR	Purpose, Location, Observers, Trigger, Communications, and Rehearsal
PL	Patrol Leader
PL	Platoon Leader

POI	Point of Instruction		SL	Squad Leader
POPS	Pull, Observe, Push, Squeeze		SLLS	Stop, Look, Listen, Smell
			SOF	Sector-of-Fire
PUC	Person Under Control		SOP	Standard Operating Procedure
PSG	Platoon Sergeant			
QRF	Quick Reaction Force		SPARC	Sectors, Priority of Targets, Assault Lane, Rate-of-Fire, Camouflage
R&S	Reconnaissance and Surveillance			
REG	Regiment		SPORTS	Slap, Pull, Observe, Release, Tap, Shoot
RFL	Rifleman			
ROE	Rules of Engagement		SSA	Support, Security, Assault
RTO	Radio Transmission Operator		TA-50	Table of Allowances 50 (Army Provided Gear)
RP	Rally-Point			
RP	Release-Point		T&E	Traverse and Elevation
RPK	Soviet Light Machine Gun		TLP	Troop Leading Procedures
S&O	Surveillance and Observation		TRP	Target Reference Point
			T/O	Target of Opportunity
SAW	Squad Automatic Weapon		TTP	Tactics, Techniques, Procedures
SALUTE	Size, Activity, Location, Unit, Time, Equipment		VDO	Vehicle Drop-Off
			VPU	Vehicle Pickup
SBF	Support-by-Fire		VS17	A Neon Cloth
SEC	Security		WARNO	Warning Order
SI	Standard Issue		WSL	Weapons Squad Leader

33.b Words[1]

Ambush	A surprise attack from a concealed position on a moving or temporarily halted enemy in order to destroy or capture them and their equipment.
Area Target	Targets that present no specific aiming point to the attacker. A group of people is an area target.
Area Weapon	A weapon used to attack an area target.
Assault	A short, violent, but well-ordered attack against a location.
Assault (Element)	The unit which seizes and secures the objective and protects special teams as they complete their assigned actions on the objective.

Annexes

1 Quote: The Pentagon announced that its fight against ISIS will be called Operation Inherent Resolve. They came up with that name using Operation Random Thesaurus. —American Comedian, Jimmy Fallon

Avenue of Approach	A route of an attacking force leading to its objective or to key terrain.
Base-of-Fire	Fire placed on an enemy force or position to reduce the enemy's capability to interfere with friendly elements.
Basic Load	The quantity of ammunition required to meet combat needs until the next resupply. For M240, the standard is 900 to 1,200 rounds.
Battle Drill	A collective action rapidly executed without applying a deliberate decision-making process.
Blast	To move through a danger area in a line formation, prepared to assault.
Belt-Fed	A machine gun which uses a chain, or "belt," of ammunition. By contrast, an M4 carbine can fire on fully automatic, but uses a magazine.
Bumping/Scrolling	A technique for crossing Linear Danger Areas where one Soldier stands watch until another Soldier bumps against them.
Casevac	Emergency patient evacuation of casualties from a combat zone, excluding medevac.
Chain of Command	The succession of commanding Soldiers through which command and responsibility is transferred.
Checkpoint	A predetermined point used as a means of coordinating friendly movement.
Commander's Critical Information Requirements - A comprehensive list of information requests critical in the decision making process affecting mission success	
Comms/Commo	Abbreviation for "communications," and includes: radios, messaging, encryption, etc.
Concealment	Protection from observation or surveillance.
Coordinated Fires	A sync of weapons' fields-of-fire to ensure complete and ideal coverage of a killzone.
Cover	Protection from the fires of specific weapon systems.
Crow's Foot	A formation where Soldiers in the prone lock feet and point in different directions.
Danger Area	Any location where a patrol is vulnerable to enemy observation or fire.
Dead Space	An area within the maximum effective range of a system that cannot be covered by that system.
Defilade Fires	Fires that shoot enemies who are aligned perpendicular to the fires. Opposite of enfilade.
Direct Fire	Fire directed at a target visible to the aimer.
Dismounted	People or Soldiers not in vehicles.

Annexes

Dogleg	A 90-degree change in direction, and turn around, intended to set conditions for ambushing a tracker from the side.
Draw	A terrain feature formed by two parallel ridges or spurs with low ground in between them.
Essential Elements of Friendly Information	- Part of CCIR; information the commander wants to hide from the enemy.
Effective Range	The range at which a weapon has a 50% probability of hitting a target.
Emplacement	The purposeful and specific placement of Soldiers by command in a formation.
En Route Rally-Point	Rally-points that are determined as the patrol passes through an area suitable for a rally-point.
Enfilade Fire	Fires that shoot enemies who are aligned in a straight line to the fires. Opposite of defilade.
Exfil	Exfiltration of enemy territory.
Far Ambush	An ambush at distance used to damage and harass an enemy in order to deter, slow, instill fear, and destroy the enemy little by little.
Friendly Forces Information Requirements	- Part of CCIR; what the commander needs to know about their own forces.
Field-of-Fire	See Sector-of-Fire.
Final Protective Fire	An immediately available, preplanned barrier-of-fire designed to provide close protection to friendly positions by impeding enemy movement.
Final Protective Line	A line selected to implement final protective fire.
Fire Support	Assistance to ground forces through artillery, mortars, naval fire, and close air support.
Fishhook	A large loop around that faces the unit against their prior trail, intended to set conditions for ambushing a tracker from the side.
Formation	A group of two or more Soldiers in proximity to each other with all movements coordinated in unison.
Grazing Fire	Machine gun fire which consistently "grazes" the ground when strafing. Usually about one-meter high to shoot enemy motors and hips.
Group (Targets)	Two or more targets on which fire is desired simultaneously.
Halt	A temporary stop during a movement.
Heavy Left	M240 is on the left of the formation.
Helicopter Landing Zone	See Landing Zone.
Indirect Fire	Aiming and firing a projectile without relying on a direct line of sight between the gun and target.

Infil	Infiltration of enemy territory.
Initial Rally-Point	Where the patrol can rally if it becomes separated before departing the friendly area or before reaching the first en route rally-point.
Info. Requirements	Items of information regarding the enemy which need to be collected for the commander.
Initiation	The signal given which indicates for a larger unit to begin attacking in unison.
Killzone	The area where the enemy is predicted to move through, and will be attacked in.
Key Terrain	Any area, which when seized, retained, or controlled, affords a marked advantage to either combatant.
Landing Zone	A specified zone within a predesignated area used for landing aircraft.
Lane	A clear route through an obstacle.
Limit of Advance	An easily identified location beyond which attacking elements will not advance.
Linear Danger Area	Any location where a patrol is vulnerable to enemy observation or fire predominantly from the flanks, such as a trail, road, or stream.
Linkup	A predetermined method by which multiple elements can safely exchange recognition signals and recombine.
Leader's Recon	A reconnaissance by a subset of an element, including senior leadership, in preparation for further actions.
Long-Halt	A temporary stop during a movement longer than five minutes.
Main Body	The principal part of a tactical command or formation, excluding detached elements.
Maneuver	The movement of forces supported by fire to achieve a position of advantage from which to destroy or threaten to destroy of the enemy.
Maneuver Support Group	An element that can be removed from one part of a security perimeter and placed somewhere else while retaining 360-degree security.
Medevac	A standardized and dedicated vehicle which evacuates wounded from the battlespace, and provides en route care from medical personnel.
Metal-to-Metal	A M192 tripod only allows the M240 to turn 25 degrees left and right from center. Metal-to-metal is when the gun turns 25 degrees, hits the tripod, and physically cannot turn further.

Mission	The primary task assigned. Contains who, what, when, where, and why, but rarely how.
Mounted	Soldiers who move are moving on vehicles.
Near Ambush	An ambush at proximity used to destroy an enemy completely.
Objective (Area)	The area that includes all actions conducted and occupied positions in an ambush.
Objective Rally-Point	Staging location for occupation of the objective.
Open Danger Area	Any location where a patrol is vulnerable to enemy observation or fire from the front and flanks, such as a draw or large open area.
Overwatch	A unit that takes a position where it can observe likely enemy positions. and provide effective covering fire for friendly units.
Patrol	A patrol is a group of Soldiers sent to perform a task. For example, a patrol may be an ambush or a reconnaissance.
Phase	A specific part of an operation that is different from those that precede or follow.
Priority Information Requirements - Part of CCIR; what the commander needs to know about the enemy.	
Point Target	Targets that are well defined and small in size. An individual person is a point target.
Point Weapon	A weapon used to attack a point target.
Quick Reaction Force	A unit placed on standby in order to quickly provide reinforcement to an attacked element.
Rally-Point	A location with the primary purpose of being moved to under preplanned conditions.
Recognition Signals	Predetermined signals that two separate element both know that can be exchanged to prove identity.
Reconnaissance (Recon)	A task to obtain information about the activities or resources.
Patrol	A unit sent out to conduct a specific combat, reconnaissance, or security mission.
Priority-of-Fires	The ranking of available targets for a single weapon. Or, the ranking of different weapons (fires) for a single target.
Security (Element)	A unit that provides security at danger areas, isolates the objective, supports withdrawal, etc.
Sector/Field-of-Fire	The area that a single/group of weapons may effectively cover with fire from a given position.
Short-Halt	A temporary stop during a movement shorter than five minutes.

Strong-Side	The side of a road from which the enemy is expected to come from.
Support (Element)	A unit that provides direct and indirect fire support for another element.
Target of Opportunity	A target identified too late to be included in deliberate targeting that meets criteria specific to achieving objectives.
Task	A clearly defined, measurable activity.
Weak-Side	The side of a road from which the enemy is not expected to come.

Annexes

34. Index

3-5 second rush 73
9-line medical request 106
360-degree security 130
Abort 159
Accountability 20
Actions on the objective 195
Aid and Litter Team 103
Alert plan 229
Alpha Team Leader 16
Ambulance exchange 110
Ambush 18, 144
  K-shape 190
  L-shape 186
  Platoon area 170
  Platoon point 171, 202
  Squad 195
  T-shape 188
  V-shape 188
  X-shape 190
Ammo Bearer 14
Area ambush 170
Artillery 112
Assault 203
Assaulting a location 80, 197
Assault lanes 165
Assistant Gunner 14
AT4 light anti-tank weapon 240
Battle drill 18
  Battle drill 1 85
  Battle drill 2 71
  Battle drill 3 93
  Battle drill 4 80
Bold-flank maneuver 85
Bounding 65
Bravo Team Leader 17
Break-contact 93
Call for fire 112
Chain of command 17
Chokepoints 35
Claymores 148, 168, 227
Close air support 114
Compromise 159, 185

Cook-offs 200
COOLENT 218
Counter ambush 211
Counter-tracking 126
Crows foot 129
Cyclic 73, 164, 165, 196
Danger area 20
Dead space 31, 148, 168, 196
Demolition Team 104
Diamond formation 136
Dismount 26, 28
Dismounted enemy patrol 209
Double diamond formation 173
Element 15
Enemy Prisoner of War Team 99
Enfilade fire 188
Engagement 159
En route rally-points 32
EWAC 159
Far ambush 193
Fire-Team 15
Formation
  Platoon 44
  Staggered column 43
  Wedge 40
Forward Observer 15, 112
GOTWA 134
  Modified 139
Gunner 17
Gun Team 17
Hasty emplacement 184
Hasty patrol-base 235
Helicopter 28
High-crawl 73
Immediate action 239
Indirect fire 116
Individual movement techniques 73
Infiltration 51
Initiation of the ambush 195
JTAC 115
Land navigation 33
Leader's recon 18

Killzone 146
  Security positions 153
  Squad ORP 136
  Support and Assault 148
Limit-of-advance 84
Linear danger area 52
Long-halt 123
Low-crawl 73
M240 Machine Gun 237
Mad minute 196
Medic 15
Medical evacuation 106
Movement
  Element 30
  Formations 36
  Individual 29
Near recognition 141
Objective rally-point 133
  Leader's Recon 136
  Occupation 143
Open danger area 64
Password
  Combo 142
  Exchange 142
  Running 142
Patrol 17
Patrol-base 217
Patrol Leader 17
Peel 97
Platoon 15
Platoon formation 176
Platoon Leader 17
Platoon leadership 182
Platoon Sergeant 17
PLOT-CR 113
Pointman 14
Principles of patrolling 18
Priority of targets 165
Quick Reaction Force 211
Radiotelephone Operator 17
Rally-point
  En route 32
  Initial 51
  Objective 133
Range cards 227

Rapid 73, 165, 196
Rate-of-fire 165, 237
React-to-contact 71
Recognition
  Near 141
Recognition signals 141
Recombining elements 141
Reconnaissance and Surveillance 226
Release-point 146, 156
Remedial action 240
Reverse flank 92
Rifleman 13
Sector sketch 228
Sectors-of-fire 130, 165, 166
Security, emplacement 159
Short-halt 48
Signal-site 221
SLLS 47
Sniper fire 116
Spare-report 52, 143, 170, 202
Specialty Teams 99
Split element 118
Splitting elements 134
Squad 17
Squad automatic weapon 14
Squad Leader 17
Staggered column formation 43
Strong-point 129
Support-by-Fire 16
Surveillance and Observation 139
Team 15
Team Leader 16
Traveling 40
Traveling overwatch 40
Unit 15
Vehicle clearing 204
Verbage 23
Water resupply 232
Weapons maintenance 231
Weapons Squad 16, 202
Weapons Squad Leader 17
Wedge formation 40
Withdrawal 104, 159, 201, 229

Annexes

35. Credits

Many thanks to the government photographers who made this book possible. All illustrations and designs were drawn by the author. As a disclaimer, the appearance of U.S. Department of Defense (DoD) visual information does not imply or constitute DoD endorsement.

Front Cover Image: U.S. Army SGT Henry Villarama
Back Cover Image 1: U.S. Army SSG James Avery
Back Cover Image 2: U.S. Army 1LT Ryan DeBooy
Back Cover Image 3: U.S. Army N.G. 1LT Robert Barney
Back Cover Image 4: U.S Army SPC John Lytle
TOC Image 1: U.S. Army Timothy Gray
TOC Image 2: U.S. Marine Corps SGT Ricky Gomez
TOC Image 3: U.S. Army N.G. SGT Arturo Guzman
TOC Image 4: U.S. Marine Corps LCPL Ryan Young
Intro TOC: U.S. Marine Corps SGT Ricky Gomez
Image 1: National Parks Service Wayside Exhibit
Phase 1 TOC: U.S. Air Force SSGT Corey Hook
Image 2: U.S. Army SPC Patrik Orcutt
Image 4: U.S. Army SGT Joseph Truckley
Image 5: U.S. Army MAJ Carson Petry
Image 7: U.S. Army SSG Steven Colvin
Image 8: U.S. Army SPC Shawn M. Cassatt
Image 9: U.S. Air Force SSGT Christopher Hubenthal
Image 11: U.S. Air Force GS Heide Couch
Image 12: U.S. Marine Corps CPL Timothy Valero
Image 13: U.S. Army N.G. 1LT Leland White
Image 14: U.S. Air Force SRA Ryan Conroy
Image 18: U.S. Army SPC Steven Hitchcock
Image 19: U.S. Air Force SSGT Westin Warburton
Image 20: U.S. Air Force SSGT Westin Warburton
Image 23: U.S. Marine Corps SGT Tony Simmons
Image 25: U.S. Army VIS Paolo Bovo
Image 26: U.S. Army VIS Markus Rauchenberger
Image 27: U.S. Marine Corps CPL Timothy Valero
Image 28: U.S. Army MAJ Robert Fellingham
Image 34: U.S. Marine Corps CPT Hassett
Image 35: U.S. Marine Corps CPL Daniel Negrete
Image 37: U.S. Army SPC Ryan Lucas
Image 38: U.S. Navy MC2 Michael Lopez
Image 39: U.S. Army SGT Benjamin Northcutt
Image 41: U.S. Army Scott T. Sturkol
Phase 2 TOC: U.S. Army SGT Timothy Hamlin
Image 42: DIMOC Courtesy Photo
Image 43: U.S. Air N.G. MSGT Matt Hecht
Image 44: U.S. Air Force A1C Brennen Lege
Image 45: U.S. Marine Corps LCPL Zachary Beatty
Image 46: U.S. Marine Corps LCPL Samuel C. Fletcher
Image 47: U.S. Marine Corps CPL Aaron S. Patterson
Image 50: U.S. Army SFC Whitney Houston
Image 52: U.S. Army SPC Jose Rivera
Image 53: U.S. Army LTC John Hall
Image 54: U.S. Army VIS Elena Baladelli
Image 56: U.S. Army SGT Daniel Cole
Image 57: U.S. Army PFC Steven Young
Image 62: U.S. Army SGT Paige Behringer
Image 64: U.S. Navy CPO Johnny Bivera
Image 66: U.S. Army SSG Corinna Baltos
Image 68: U.S. Army SGT Kissta DiGrezgorio
Image 69: U.S. Marine Corps CPL Alexander Mitchell
Image 70: U.S. Army SSG Thomas Duval
Image 71: U.S. Army SSG Ray Boyington
Image 72: U.S. Marine Corps CPL David A. Perez

Image 74: U.S. Air Force SSGT Corban D. Lundborg
Image 75: U.S. Army SPC Rolyn Kropf
Image 76: U.S. Marine Corps CPL Danny Gonzalez
Image 77: U.S. Air Force TSGT Michael Holzworth
Image 78: U.S. Army SSG Teddy Wade
Image 79: U.S. Army SGT Anita VanderMolen
Image 80: U.S. Air Force TSGT Russell E. Cooley IV
Phase 3 TOC: U.S. Marine Corps CPL Cody Haas
Image 82: U.S. Air Force SRA Ryan Conroy
Image 89: U.S. Army SGT Aaron Ellerman
Image 91: U.S. Army SSG Samuel Northrup
Image 93: U.S. Marine Corps LCPL Reine Whitaker
Image 95: U.S. Army MCOE PAO Patrick A. Albright
Image 96: U.S. Marine Corps SGT Allison M. DeVries
Image 97: U.S. Marine Corps CPL Joshua W. Brown
Image 98: U.S. Army PFC Liem Huynh
Image 99: U.S. Army PFC Liem Huynh
Image 102: U.S. Air N.G. SSGT Andrew Horgan
Image 103: U.S. Air N.G. SSGT Andrew Horgan
Image 105: U.S. Marine Corps CPL Bryan Nygaard
Image 106: U.S. Army VIS Paolo Bovo
Image 107: U.S. Marine Corps SGT Melissa Wenger
Image 108: U.S. Marine Corps LCPL Ernesto Rojascorrea
Image 110 et al: U.S. Army VIS Paolo Bovo
Image 112: U.S. Army PFC Payton Wilson
Image 114: U.S. Marine Corps 1ST LT John McCombs
Image 116 et al: U.S. Air N.G. TSGT Sarah Mattison
Image 117: U.S. Army SGT William A. Tanner
Image 118 et al: U.S. Marine Corps CPL Emmanuel Ramos
Image 120: U.S. Army SSG Tramel Garrett
Image 121: U.S. Army SSG Pablo N. Piedra
Image 131: U.S. Army VIS Paolo Bovo
Image 132: U.S. Marine Corps CPL Victoria Ros
Image 133: U.S. Air Force TSGT Rasheen Douglas
Image 135: U.S. Army N.G. SSG Scott Tynes
Image 140: U.S. Army 1LT Laura Beth Beebe
Image 141: U.S. Army SFC Joy Dulen
Image 142: U.S. Army SPC Esmeralda Cervantes
Phase 4 TOC: U.S. Army SPC Steven Hitchcock
Image 143: U.S. Army VIS Davide Dalla Massara
Image 144: U.S. Marine Corps 1ST LT Johnny Henderson
Image 146: U.S. Army VIS Davide Dalla Massara
Image 147: U.S. Air Force SRA Zachary Wolf
Image 148: U.S. Army N.G. SGT Eric McDonough
Image 149: U.S. Army SGT Benjamin Northcutt
Image 151: U.S. Army VIS Davide Dalla Massara
Image 152: U.S. Army VIS Graigg Faggionato
Image 153: U.S. Marine Corps CPL William Hester
Image 154: U.S. Marine Corps CPL Alejandro Pena
Image 155: U.S. Army 1LT Benjamin Haulenbeek
Phase 5 TOC: U.S. Marine Corps CPL Christopher Mendoza
Image 158: U.S. Army VIS Paolo Bovo
Image 159 et al: U.S. Marine Corps CPL Kelly L. Street
Image 159 et al: U.S. Marine Corps LCPL Christine Phelps
Image 162: U.S. Army LTC John Hall
Image 164: U.S. Marine Corps LCPL Juan C. Bustos
Image 165: U.S. Air Force SRA Janiqua P. Robinson
Image 166: U.S. Marine Corps SGT Emmanuel Ramos
Image 167: U.S. Marine Corps LCPL Jesus Sepulveda Torres
Image 168: U.S. Marine Corps SGT Emmanuel Ramos
Image 169: U.S. Marine Corps CPL Aaron S. Patterson
Image 170: U.S. Army SPC Austin Berner
Annex TOC: U.S. Marine Corps SGT Joshua M. Jackson
Image 171: U.S. Army N.G. SSG Brian A. Barbour
Image 172: U.S. Marine Corps LCPL Angel D. Travis
Image 173: U.S. Army SGT Brian Chaney
Image 174: U.S. Air N.G. SSGT Christopher S. Muncy

SMALL
UNIT
RAIDS

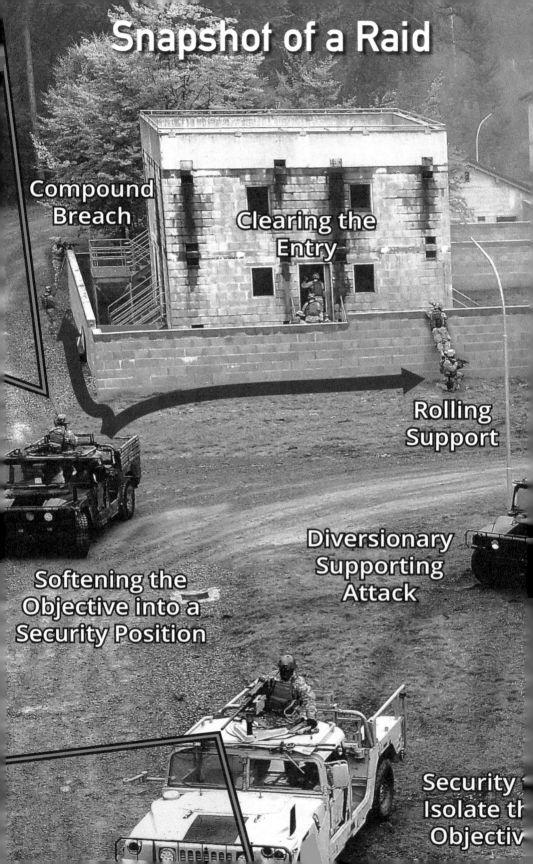

Snapshot of a Raid

Compound Breach

Clearing the Entry

Rolling Support

Diversionary Supporting Attack

Softening the Objective into a Security Position

Security Isolate th Objectiv

Enveloping

Delayed
Entry

Mechanical
Breach

You Are Joe (Introduction: You are a Raider)

1. This is a Raid

Razing and Plundering (Untargeted Actions) — 14
Assassination and Sabotage (Targeted Destruction) — 14
Acquisition and Hostage Rescue (Seizure) — 16
Strategic Effects (Information Creation) — 19
Reconnaissance-in-Force (Information Gathering) — 20

13

2. This is a Raider

Assaulter — 21
Breacher and Engineer — 22
Machine Gunner — 23
Reserve Element — 24
Equipment — 24

21

3. Support Elements

Military Working Dogs — 28
Shoulder Launched Munitions — 30
Long Range Riflemen — 32
Armored Fighting Vehicles — 33
Indirect Fire Systems — 37
Close Air Support — 41
Unmanned Aerial Vehicles — 44
Non-Combat Support — 45

27

4. Task Organization

46

Joe Invades Enemy Land (Phase 1: Infiltration of Urban Terrain)

5. Characteristics of Urban Terrain — 53

Frameworks for Attacking Vertical Terrain — 54
Tunnels and Caves — 56
Building Construction — 57
Battle and Flank Positions — 60
Urban Population Threats — 62
Traps and Improvised Explosive Devices — 65
Night and Limited Visibility Operations — 69

6. Using a Rifle in Urban Terrain — 72

Targeting — 72
Terminal Ballistics — 75
Handling a Rifle in Close-Quarters — 78
Shooting while Moving — 83
Pieing and Clearing Corners — 85

7. Moving in Urban Terrain — 88

Single, Double, and V File Formations — 91
Front Security and Navigation — 95
Rear Security — 97
Wedge and Diamond Formations — 98
Bounding and Crossing Intersections — 99
Moving between Buildings — 105
Vehicle Attachment — 107
Fighting in L Shapes — 109

8. Scheme-of-Maneuver for Infiltration — 109

Choosing and Preparing a Route — 111
Phase Lines — 113
Raid Preparation Locations — 116
Timetables — 118

9. Scheme-of-Fires — 118

Call for Fire — 123

10. Enemy Contact in Urban Terrain — 124

Medical Evacuation — 128

Joe Stages a Raid
(Phase 2: Preparation of the Environment)

11. Defining the Objective Battlespace   131
Gathering Intelligence about the Objective   132
Chunking   134
Isolation Area   136

12. Leader's Reconnaissance of the Objective   139
Splitting Elements   141
Near and Far Recognition Signals   143
Surveillance and Observation Position (S&O)   144

13. Emplacing Elements   146
Security   146
Support   148
Assault   149
Changing Roles   150
Headquarters   150

14. Final Steps   152

15. Contingencies   152
Running Out of Time   152
Compromise during Emplacement   152

Joe Secures Space (Phase 3: Securing a Foothold)

16. Attacks before Assaulting — 155

Tactical Callout — 156
Softening the Objective — 158
Enveloping and Preclearing — 159

17. Scheme-of-Maneuver for the Objective — 161

Threat Level of Spaces — 162
Footholds and Entrances — 163
Vertical Layout and Floors — 164
Horizontal Layout and Floorplan — 167
Assault Positions and Lanes — 170
Multiple Entries — 172

18. Support to Facilitate Assault's Maneuver — 173

Supporting Fires to Suppress and Divert — 176
Sectors-of-Fire and Coordinated Fires — 177
Deconflicting Support and Assault — 179

19. Outside Barrier and Compound Breach — 180

Reducing Blocking Obstacles (Walls and Gates) — 183
Reducing Entrapping Obstacles (Wire and Mines) — 187

20. Securing the Foothold — 189

21. Contingencies — 189

Weather — 190
Casualty Collection Point — 191
Quick Reaction Force — 192
Combat Ineffective Leader — 193

Joe Fights the Enemy (Phase 4: Seizing the Objective)

22. Close-Quarters Battle Basics — 195
Task Organization — 197
Synchronized Movement — 198
Verbage — 200

23. Preparation for Entry — 201
Stacking Up and Team Positions — 202
Closed Door Reconnaissance — 207
Closed Door Breaching — 208
Non-Explosive Breaching of Entryways — 210
Explosive Breaching of Entryways — 215
Grenades and Disorienting — 219
Firing Through Walls — 222
Immediate and Delayed Entry — 224

24. Seizing Rooms (Battle Drill 6) — 228
Clearing the Entry — 228
Clearing the Corner and Room — 232
Sector Sweeps and Points-of-Domination — 237
Connected Rooms and Areas — 240

25. Seizing Other Spaces — 244
Hallways — 244
Stairs and Stairwells — 252
Room Obstacles — 257
Every Space is Different — 260

26. Working and Exiting a Space — 265
Securing a Space — 265
Reporting Progress — 267
Marking a Space — 268

27. Seizing Floors and Buildings — 270
Coordinating Multiple Teams — 270
Attacking Multiple Structures — 272

28. Contingencies — 274
Noncombatants — 274
Delayed Combatants — 277
Demolition Team — 277
Failed Breach — 278
Backing Out and Reengaging — 279

Joe Goes Home
(Phase 5: Withdrawal and
Exfiltration)

29. Clear-Back and Consolidation — 281
Enemy Prisoner of War Team — 283
Aid and Litter, and Medevac — 286
Site Exploitation — 288

30. Withdrawal from the Objective — 290

31. Exfiltration — 292

Annexes

32. Realities of Combat   295

Morality and Rules-of-engagement   295
Stress and Sleep Deprivation   298
Changing Enemy Tactics   300

33. Disseminating Information   302

34. Glossaries   304

Acronyms   304
Words   306

35. Credits   312

Legends

Legend for Squads and Platoons

Color is the Soldier's Unit		Shape is the Soldier's Weapon	
Alpha Team	↑	M4	↑
Squad Level	↑	M249	⇑
Bravo Team	↑	M240B	⇕
Platoon Level	↑	AT4	⋀
Named Position (See Glossary)			⋀TL

Legend for Teams

Color is the Soldier's Position		Throughout the manual each arrow represents a Soldier. The arrow has a color and a shape to represent a Soldier's unit or team position, and primary weapon respectively.
One Man	↑	
Two Man	↑	
Three Man	↑	
Four Man	↑	

Introduction Contents

1. This is a Raid   *13*

Razing and Plundering (Untargeted Actions)   14
Assassination and Sabotage (Targeted Destruction)   14
Acquisition and Hostage Rescue (Seizure)   16
Strategic Effects (Information Creation)   19
Reconnaissance-in-Force (Information Gathering)   20

2. This is a Raider   *21*

Assaulter   21
Breacher and Engineer   22
Machine Gunner   23
Reserve Element   24
Equipment   24

3. Support Elements   *27*

Military Working Dogs   28
Shoulder Launched Munitions   30
Long Range Riflemen   32
Armored Fighting Vehicles   33
Indirect Fire Systems   37
Close Air Support   41
Unmanned Aerial Vehicles   44
Non-Combat Support   45

4. Task Organization   *46*

You Are Joe (Introduction: You are a Raider)

Osama Bin Laden is dead. Killed not by a massive troop deployment but by a commando raid carried out by a few dozen highly trained men.
—War Correspondent Richard Engel, 2011

This manual builds on simple tactics to teach effective raiding. These tactics are tried and true for a hundred years; seriously, almost every section exists because someone died from bad tactics. But simple is not easy and this manual needs to cover a lot of ground. So first and foremost, what is a raid?

1. This is a Raid[1]

A raid is an attack 1) against a stationary enemy, 2) on a location where something can't be destroyed, and 3) to achieve a purpose other than holding terrain.[2] If the enemy is not stationary, the patrol instead executes an ambush or search-and-attack. If total destruction is permissible, the patrol executes an artillery or bombing mission. And if the objective needs to be held, the patrol requires many more Soldiers and resources. (Holding ground is expensive!)

Raids can be any size and complexity. And while this manual describes raids in-depth, most raids throughout history have been basic acts. One successful, basic raid was the 1939 Christmas Raid by the Irish Republican Army (IRA), in which the IRA attacked Ireland's largest munitions dump. The entire raid essentially involved a few IRA Soldiers in civilian attire pulling guns on a few guards. The swift and simple hostage situation led to complete control of the munitions dump and the seizure of a huge quantity of weapons.

---

1 Quote: Where the Russians fought to control and hold the territory, the rebels fought to make controlling and holding the territory as unpleasant as possible—a very different mission, and one far more difficult both to grasp and to counter. —RAND Corporation Department Director Olga Oliker

2 Feature: Definitions are not absolute. For example, an attack on a tunnel system fits this definition but uses different tactics outside the scope of this book.

A raiding patrol only has one primary mission; otherwise, the patrol risks making its multiple missions compete with each other. That said, all raid forces have non-mandatory, secondary tasks and purposes like information gathering. And individual raids can be part of a larger attack with a different purpose than the raid itself. For example, a raid can be performed specifically to flush the enemy out and into an ambush, where the larger mission objective is to destroy the enemy.

1.a Razing and Plundering (Untargeted Actions)

In modern times, raids are rarely used to cause wanton destruction as opposed to artillery and carpet bombing because raids are inherently dangerous and difficult to control. But for completeness, this manual must mention that historically Soldiers stormed cities and razed them with fire.

Today, raids are used to accomplish untargeted destruction when they are the only way to do so. On April 16 and 17, 2013 in Baga, Nigeria, satellite images revealed massive destruction of civilian property wrought by a military-style raid. "I saw a group of Soldiers throw explosive devices into houses," one farmer recalled. "They would throw [the explosive] and then fire would come out of it."

1.b Assassination and Sabotage (Targeted Destruction)

Targeted destruction raids are used to destroy something specific on the objective. Targeted destruction missions often have a class of targets rather than a specific target: for example, military-aged men, fuel tanks, electric systems, or simply all of an enemy's military possessions.

Raiding is a preferred methods because Raiders can identify the target, avoid damaging the surrounding area. Raiding in secrecy also avoids letting the enemy move or defend, multiplying the damage effect. For example, if Raiders cause hidden damage to enemy vehicles, the enemy will not replace the vehicles and be ineffective at a critical moment.

Night raids to capture or kill were a military tactic employed by the United States and Afghan Special Forces during the U.S. War in Afghanistan. American generals argued that the raids were critical to success in the war. In

Image 1: Two Afghan Commandos, assigned to the 203rd Corps Commando Battalion, check documents found during a search of a suspected insurgent safehouse. Zambar Village, Sabari District, Khowst Province 27 Dec 2007. The Commandos led a combined force consisting of other Afghan National Army units, Afghan National Police, and Afghan National Border Police. The combined force was acting upon credible intelligence to search an area of known insurgent activity.

fact, despite civilian casualties, the raids were effective enough that in 2012 the Afghan government only secured the right to approve all future night raids and continued to let Americans and Afghan commandos raid together.

Sometimes the line between capture and kill is blury. The ISIS leader, Abu Ibrahim al-Hashimi al-Qurayshi, refused to surrender and killed himself in a massive explosion during a U.S. special operations helicopter raid. Marine Corps Gen. Kenneth F. McKenzie stated, "He killed himself and his immediate family without fighting, even as we attempted to call for his surrender and offered him a path to survive," noting that Abdullah was blown up during the explosion and was identified by fingerprint and DNA analyses.

A famous targeted destruction of objects, i.e. sabotage, mission was Operation Gunnerside in World War II. There, Norwegian raiders attacked a heavy-water production facility inside a dam. A raid was chosen because bombing proved ineffective. When 140 American bombers did bomb the dam, they failed to destroy the facility and stronger bombs would have obliterated the dam. So the Raiders traveled to the bottom of a gorge, crossed a half-frozen river, and climbed a five-hundred-foot-high cliff to get to the facility. There, they infiltrated, bombed, and destroyed the production facility and successfully withdrew.

Sabotage Raiders must be aware of their specific target(s) to maximize their destructive capability. For example, military artillery is difficult to quietly destroy, but thermite grenades can melt metal. Throwing thermite grenades into an artillery breech and quickly closing the breech will weld the breech shut, making the weapon impossible to load.

1.c Acquisition and Hostage Rescue (Seizure)[1]

Whereas in a targeted destruction raid, something must be damaged, in a seizure raid, **the patrol must safely extract something without damage**. Although hostage rescue is the most infamous seizure mission, the seizure can be of anything. Sometimes raiders must extract and seize information. "Sensitive site exploitation" is an entire military specialty dedicated to extracting information from objectives in order to conduct follow-on operations. (See Site Exploitation, Pg. 288.)

Whether extraction is difficult or not varies wildly, even for missions of similar scale. For example, there was a large raid at the North Cotabato Provincial Jail in Kidapawan, Philippines, in 2017. About a hundred armed men raided the jail, but the extraction was easy, as at least 158 inmates simply walked out of the jail; only seven died.

In contrast, during the Budyonnovsk hospital hostage crisis in 1995, a group of eighty to two hundred Chechen separatists raided a hospital and took 1,500 to 2,000 people hostage in order to make demands. Then Russian forces counter-raided the now-defended hospital, attempting a hostage rescue mission. The Russians failed numerous times to remove hostages without damage, and at least 140 people were killed in the process. The situation finally had to be resolved with negotiations.

---

1 Quote: In my years as the FBI's lead international kidnapping negotiator, I learned an important fundamental lesson: Hostage negotiation is often nothing more than a business transaction. —FBI Hostage Negotiator Christopher Voss

Image 2: Kurdistan Region Security Council (KRSC) in 2015 released a video and information on a joint US-Kurdish commando operation against an Islamic State (ISIS) prison south of Kirkuk. 48 Peshmerga from CTD forces and 30 U.S. Special Forces Soldiers took part in the two-hour operation. Six helicopters, three Chinooks, and three Black Hawks took part in the operation. KRSC considered the operation to be the "single most significant joint rescue operation based out of Kurdistan region conducted deep into the ISIL territory." (Continued in following image.)

Image 3: (Continued from previous image.) The prisoners were to be executed on the same day of the operation. According to the rescued prisoners, they had been told it was the last day of their life. Although the Peshmerga had led the operation, due an ensuing fight with ISIS militants, the U.S. Soldiers had to intervene. One U.S. Soldier was killed and three Peshmerga were wounded as a result. KRSC has confirmed that more than twenty of the hostages were ex-members of the Iraqi security forces about to be executed by ISIS. Near Kirkuk, Iraq, 25 Oct 2015.

1.d Strategic Effects (Information Creation)[1]

Introduction

Raids are often conducted strategically, meaning that the physical actions of the raid are far removed from the actual purpose of the raid. Strategic goals of raids often include: changing the morale of any group of people, altering enemy behavior and wasting their resources, and more.

To maximize the strategic effect, the attacking force may promote the raid after completion. In this way, strategic raids are often conducted by small units on important targets as a cheap way to create lots of news coverage.

For example, during the 1968–1970 war of attrition between Israel and Egypt, Israeli Defense Forces raided the Egyptian Naj Hamadi top-of-the-line power-transformer station and bridge, which symbolized Egypt's economic and political might. **The attack humiliated Nasser's government** by unveiling Egypt's inability to protect its prized possessions. The direct economic impact was just as important setting the conditions for peace talks.

Sometimes a raid is conducted to put a human face on war and project victory to the enemy or instill pride in supporters. For example, law-abiding citizens might feel more comfortable giving authorities the whereabouts of terrorists in their community if they feel protected because they know about multiple, successful, precision raids targeting those terrorists.

Strategically placed raids can also alter large-scale enemy plans. When Al Qaeda's core was in Pakistan, the United States conducted a few well-placed raids inside Pakistan's borders. The goals were to signal that Al Qaeda was not safe and had to move, and that U.S. forces were strong and local. This was a deception; in reality, the U.S. did not conduct full-scale terrorist clearance operations inside Pakistan.

Raids are an effective method to waste enemy resources. In 1963, Mujahideen attacked Soviet and Afghan outposts surrounding Kabul. The Mujahideen would infiltrate, stage, fire rockets to kill, and immediately withdraw, mimicking an artillery attack. The outposts were a waste because they were originally built to secure areas, but they ironically became targets of attack themselves. Further, the Mujahideen attacks tied up Soviet troops in passive security roles, denying those troops to conduct offensive maneuvers.

---

[1] Quote: Strategy without tactics is the slowest route to victory. Tactics without strategy is the noise before defeat. —Chinese General Sun Tzu

Image 4: A view of landing craft, barrage balloons, and Allied troops landing on D-Day. Normandy, France, 06 Jun 1944. To prepare for D-Day, the largest amphibious assault in history, the Allies conducted the Dieppe Raid (19 Aug 1942).

The Soviets on the other hand, wasted Mujahideen resources by interrogating potential Mujahideen and releasing them. Mujahideen networks operated utilizing very tight circles of trust. So raiding buildings to question individuals (or even imply questioning) sowed distrust within the group, as each person wondered what their companions had divulged.

1.e Reconnaissance-in-Force (Information Gathering)

Reconnaissance-in-force (RIF) is a kind of strategic raid with the primary goal of collecting information for future operations. **Actual missions are the most thorough test of allied and enemy systems.**

While typical reconnaissance forces are small to avoid detection, an RIF force requires enough force to intentionally provoke the enemy. Only then will the enemy accurately reveal its strength, deployment, preparedness, and other data. Once the data is acquired, the RIF units can fall back or, if the enemy is found to be weak enough, expand the conflict into a full engagement.

The Dieppe Raid (19 August 1942) was an RIF during World War II in which the Allies conducted an amphibious assault to remove Germans from the port of Dieppe in northern France. The tactical purpose of seizing the port was less important than the strategic purpose of gathering information about how to best conduct D-Day, the largest amphibious invasion in history.

The results of the Dieppe Raid reflected this priority. Tactically, the raid was a failure; within ten hours, 3,623 of the 6,086 men who landed had been killed, wounded, or captured. However, meta-information about amphibious landings directly influenced the success of the D-Day landings. Thanks to failures discovered in the Dieppe Raid, planners for D-Day declared that artificial harbors were crucial to facilitate ship unloading, tanks were adapted to beach terrain, a tactical air force was to be integrated with ground support, and capturing major ports at the outset was unnecessary. Churchill and Mountbatten both said the lessons learned had outweighed the costs.

2. This is a Raider[1]

A raid is a complex physical operation, and therefore it needs troops on the ground. Those troops are defined by their mission, rather than the mission being defined by the troops. That means Raiders are incredibly diverse. While this section defines the various roles that a Raider may fill, one Raider may fill multiple or blurred roles, like Breacher and Reserve.

2.a Assaulter

The simplest Raider is the Assaulter. Their job is to use a rifle and maneuver,. Assaulters are commonly tasked with neutralizing (e.g., killing, securing, or driving away) the enemy. In contrast to a simple Rifleman, they are trained to operate in close-quarters and also must be capable grenadiers. (See Close-Quarters Battle Basics, Pg. 195.) (See Grenades and Disorienting, Pg. 219.)

Assaulters must be trained to fight in close-quarters because history shows that 95% of all enemy targets are less than a hundred meters away from Soldiers, and about 90% of all targets are less than fifty meters away. In cities, the distance shrinks even more.

---

1 Quote: Combat in urban areas is primarily a small unit, infantry intensive operation. —Marine Corps Warfighting Publication 3-35.3, Military Operations on Urban Terrain (MOUT), 1998

Image 5: Assaulters from 1st Bn., 50th Inf. Reg., 198th Inf. Bde. maneuver as an Infantry Fire Team. Fort Benning, GA, 21 Aug 2020. Assaulters must be able to shoot while moving. (See Shooting while Moving, Pg. 83.)

Assaulters are required for raids because raids are precise attacks. More deadly attackers, like artillery units, are often restricted by rules of engagement in urban environments with civilian buildings, people, and communications. (See Morality and Rules-of-engagement, Pg. 295.)

2.b Breacher and Engineer

Breachers are Soldiers that break barriers. Breaching requires skill because every breach is different. Methods to perform a breach can include mechanical, thermal, ballistic, or explosive. (See Outside Barrier and Compound Breach, Pg. 180.) (See Closed Door Breaching, Pg. 208.) Breachers can request assistance from other elements, like asking a tank to shoot down a wall.

Every raid requires a Breacher or Breaching Element because every raid objective is well-presumed to have some barrier to entry. Most barriers are in front of a patrol, so Breachers typically walk at the front of any formation.

A Breacher that can handle additional tasks, like disabling explosives and clearing rubble, is a **Combat Engineer**. A seasoned Engineer directs Breachers by recognizing the intent of an enemy Engineer's obstacles, where obstacles are strongest and weakest, and whether an obstacle is even worth breaching.

For platoons and smaller units, an Assaulter can take on the role of a Breacher. Another option is to designate the Team Leaders or Machine Gunners as Breachers because Breachers, Leaders, and Gunners all fall behind Assaulters after an attack has begun, and so would be similarly placed anyway.

Larger raiding forces may include a specialized Breacher that can carry additional breaching tools and receive more specialized training. And as more Soldiers participate in a raid, a breaching plan can be broken into more steps to be handled by different elements: for example, a Support Element to suppress and obscure, an Assault Element to secure and assault, and a Breach Element to breach. (See Outside Barrier and Compound Breach, Pg. 180.)

2.c Machine Gunner

Automatic-fire weapon systems, or machine guns, can shoot hundreds of rounds per minute, making them invaluable for killing, restricting, and manipulating enemies at a distance. But machine gun systems are immobile and so **must work together with Assaulters**. For example, during the initial assault, Gunners can fire a continuous line of bullets in a certain direction or area to keep the enemy behind cover while Assaulters get into position. (See Support to Facilitate Assault's Maneuver, Pg. 173.) Gunners can continue fire at areas on an objective where Assaulters have not yet cleared as the Assaulters advance. (See Phase Lines, Pg. 113.) If these restricting lines-of-fire are connected, Gunners can create a perimeter defense that isolates an area and again restricts enemy movement. (See Isolation Area, Pg. 136.)

Assaulters do sometimes enter buildings with machine guns, usually because they are needed for some follow-on or contingency plan. Machine guns are never the first choice for room-clearing because they are heavy, unwieldy, and slow to aim.

However, if machine guns are brought inside a building, they can be used to establish hasty security and support positions. If the Assault Element has multiple machine guns, they can be combined into a Security Element that secures from the inside. (See Support to Facilitate Assault's Maneuver, Pg. 173.) More dangerously, machine guns can kill enemies by firing through walls. (See Firing Through Walls, Pg. 222.)

2.d Reserve Element

Patrols benefit from keeping a portion of highly mobile troops in reserve to **react to unpredictable changes** in an engagement. (Urban engagements are particularly unpredictable.) (See Urban Population Threats, Pg. 62.) If there is no Reserve and a problem appears, Leaders must either ignore the threat or create chaos by reorganizing Soldiers that are already engaged. Common tasks given to a Reserve include: joining Assault, securing rooms after Assaulters clear them, providing security in cleared buildings, flanking an enemy already being attacked, securing the rear, or maintaining comms.

A Reserve is not given a specific mission during planning. During movement, the Reserve **must have comms with leadership** to quickly receive orders but may be better placed close to the patrol's most likely point of enemy contact so they can immediately influence the attack.

A good default size for a Reserve is two unit-levels smaller than the patrol (e.g., for a company-sized raid, the reserve would be squad-sized). Large assets like crew-served weapons and tanks are commonly held in reserve because they are limited in number, and their best place of use is unpredictable. Engineers too are often attached to the Reserve so they can quickly deploy to remove barriers anywhere in the patrol's footprint.

If there is no specified Reserve Element, a Leader can improvise one by making a special team into an impromptu Reserve. For example in a company-sized raid, squads will normally have Demo Teams, Enemy Prisoner of War Teams, and Aid and Litter Teams. (See Support Elements, Pg. 27.) Because special team assignments are distributed among unit teams, a special team is the best way to avoid overburdening any single unit team.

2.e Equipment[1]

Raiding equipment can be divided into three categories: weapons, breaching supplies, and everything else. Weapons and breaching supplies are separate because infiltration and assaulting are the only mandatory parts of

---

1 **Quote:** Flame, napalm, shotguns, recoilless rifles, and other low-technology systems and munitions [] have proven highly effective in the urban environment.... If the United States and other nations decide to become serious about improving their ability to fight on urban terrain, they have to look closely at their existing inventories and explore the possibility of reinstating such "quaint" systems as flame-throwers. —U.S. Army Center for Army Lessons Learned

Image 6: U.S. Soldiers of 5th Bn., 20th Inf. Reg. line up to conduct a patrol through Shele Kalay, Kandahar, Afghanistan, 16 Jan 2012. The Soldiers were clearing compounds in the area, searching for Taliban Insurgents and materials used to create Improvised Explosive Devices. **They carried a lot of shit.**

raiding. One might claim that armor and medical supplies are necessary, but many successful raids have been conducted without them.

Such categories allow Leaders to prioritize Soldiers' limited weight-carrying capacity. To that end, Leaders must balance a Soldier's load with their physical exertion to reach maximum combat effectiveness. A Soldier can always carry more. However, at a certain point, the benefit of more tools is outweighed by the cost of fatigue. For example, only essential items are carried in close-quarters combat due to its fast-paced nature.[1]

The first piece of equipment to consider is the weapon. Everyone carries a pistol, either as a primary or secondary weapon. Beyond that, the ideal weaponry for a raid is determined by many factors, to include: target distance, preferred breaching, noncombatants on the objective, bullet penetration, etc. A modern military raider will have a primary and secondary firearm with various ammunition types, a knife, and an assortment of grenades. Ammo consumption is huge in urban environments, and lots must be carried. Soldiers may also carry explosives, a breaching shotgun, and less-lethal weapons. Of note, all urban combatants benefit from shoulder-launched munitions' (SLM) ability to create a large explosion at a distance, and every patrol should

While Romans carried 50-pound rucks marched 25 miles per day, modern Soldier may carry 100-pound rucks and march 12 miles. Over time, the weight to distance ratio for marching men seems to be stable at: optimal for mission success and damn any long-term consequences.

carry some. SLM's from a safe battle position can destroy a tank or bunkered position, or create a breach. (See Shoulder Launched Munitions, Pg. 30.)

Necessary breaching supplies depend on what needs to be breached. (See Building Construction, Pg. 57.) If the objective is surrounded by a compound wall, then explosives or a tank are necessary. If there is a fence, the patrol can bring a bolt cutter. There are a myriad of breaching methods and tools that must be assessed based on the raid. (See Outside Barrier and Compound Breach, Pg. 180.) (See Closed Door Breaching, Pg. 208.)

Protective equipment like helmets and bulletproof vests are not strictly necessary, but they are standard. **When choosing armor, it must be tailored to the environment.** In the heat of a jungle, using fully encasing upper-body armor could decimate a patrol with heat casualties. Soldier have often hated wearing their protection due to discomfort, but also ignorance. For example in the Vietnam War, Soldiers would sometimes not don their flak vests because bullets penetrated them. At the time it was not well-explained that flak vests were actually meant to protect against explosive fragmentation called flak (hence the name). At the time, the large majority of injuries at the time were due to this explosive fragmentation. Similarly, shooting gloves and ballistic eye protection are worn to protect a Soldier from ejected shell casings and the heat generated by their own weapon; they do not protect against bullets.

Medical equipment is not necessary, but is always a good idea. Water is "medical equipment." A dehydration level of 5% bodyweight, which can easily be reached after a full day of activity, is similar to having a 0.1 blood-alcohol level. So a Soldier who conducts an intense day-long raid without water is effectively "drunk." For injuries, Soldiers carry Individual First Aid Kits (IFAK's), which often include tourniquets, pressure dressings, and chest seals. Further, IFAK's are also important for morale. **Medical equipment lowers hesitation in battle.** To make medical supplies (and all supplies) more effective their location must be standardized. Thereby, if one Soldier becomes a casualty, another Soldier can quickly find and use the casualty's IFAK.

For other equipment, Soldiers fighting in urban areas may need: grappling hooks, ropes, snap links, collapsible pole ladders, rope ladders, poleless litters, axes, sledgehammers, pry bars, mine detectors, bulk explosives and firing devices, engineer tape or other marking devices, night- and thermal-vision devices, batteries, radios, radio jammers, cell phones, flashlights, precision targeting devices, laser range finders, and much more.

The ideal equipment is highly dependent on local conditions, and universal tools are the worst tools. A notorious failure of this principle was the U.S. Army's Universal Camouflage Pattern, which used an unassuming grey digital pattern to attempt to blend with everything. In fact, because grey is rare in nature, it blended with virtually nothing. Obviously, Siberia and Sedan require vastly different equipment. Common local conditions to consider are temperature, precipitation, humidity, wind, ice, dust, and vegetation.

When Raiders drive onto an objective, they can bring more stuff. Soldiers can bring a large medical bag or even stage a dedicated ambulance. Civilian Raiders like Police can incorporate ballistic shields into their room-clearing techniques. During particularly long raids or days, or if a medevac is brought in, Soldiers can be resupplied as they work. That said, **unused equipment is dead weight**. In Somalia, American Soldiers had highly sophisticated equipment that proved to be useless because they could not detect the power signature of the Somalis' dated, low-power walkie-talkies.

The actual mission is never the ideal time to learn how to use equipment. When training, Soldiers must use the actual equipment to be taken on the mission. For example, the first extended wearing of night-vision goggles, protective masks, or laser-protective lenses always causes stress and is terrible. But better to falter in training than on a real mission.

3. Support Elements[1]

Soldiers in a raid can be split into two groups: Assaulters and Supporters. (See Image 22, Pg. 49.) Simply put, "Support" includes everybody who is not prepared to get into a knife fight. For example, a Dog Handler may identify the location of a hostage, but the Assaulter goes and grabs the hostage. A Tanker may kill many enemies on the objective, but it is an Assaulter who physically goes to the objective and ensures every enemy is neutralized.

Support is necessary because infantry has shortcomings, like being vulnerable, that are overcome by integrating with other forces, like durable armored fighting vehicles (AFV's). There are innumerable types of support because Assaulters only specialize in assaulting. The Support Element(s) may

---

[1] Quote: At the present time, our chief difficulty is not the Germans but gasoline. If they would give me enough gas, I could go all the way to Berlin! —U.S. General George S. Patton Jr.

conduct: resupply, casualty care and evacuation, prisoner detainment, area security in cleared areas, etc. Sometimes a unit's "integration" becomes a merger; e.g., mechanized infantry provide their own AFV support. The only limit on the number of Support Elements is the number of Soldiers available.

Mission requirements dictate which supporting forces can best augment Assaulters. Therefore, there is no "standard" set of Supporters. While a single Soldier can perform an assassination, it took one of the largest manhunts in history to capture Saddam Hussein. That being said, one of the most common jobs of Support is to suppress and counter enemy fires to enable Assault to more freely maneuver. (See Support to Facilitate Assault's Maneuver, Pg. 173.)

For mission success, the proportion of Supporters and Assaulters is a trade-off between safety and speed. Having more Supporters can make a raid safe and slow. Whereas more Assaulters will make for a faster and more aggressive raid (but as always, speed is its own form of safety). Urban raids often lean toward having a large Support Element because urban terrain has many potential enemy hideouts near friendly forces. Plus psychologically, an emphasis on support and fewer frontal assaults gives Soldiers more confidence in their leadership and the raid itself.

3.a Military Working Dogs

Military working dogs (MWD's) have two capabilities that are unmatched by humans or machines, their **sense of smell and their agility**. An explosive-detection dog can smell explosives, plastic mine components, and other materials typical to booby-traps. (See Traps and Improvised Explosive Devices, Pg. 65.) Other MWD's are exceptional at detecting humans at long distances and determining whether they are threats. When clearing an objective, an MWD's sense of smell can quickly find hidden Snipers.

And a dog's agility and size allow it to apprehend enemies at high speed, where otherwise the enemy may fire rounds or escape. If an enemy is securing a doorway against Soldiers, the Soldiers can deploy an MWD to run inside and quickly attack any enemy faster than any human could (with humans quickly following). Moreover, MWD's intimidate and can cause a visceral, **psychological effect** on the enemy. (See Image 7 et al, Pg. 29.)

If an MWD is a smelling dog, they are commonly used as a Front Element to detect IED's along a route or in a building. (See Single, Double, and V File

Image 7 et al: Arko, a military working dog, attacks a U.S. Air Force Dog Handler from 386th Expeditionary Security Forces Sqn. Undisclosed Southwest Asia, 03 Jun 2014. Handlers train their dogs to be able to attack a threat on command.

Formations, Pg. 91.) An MWD Team includes an IED-detecting MWD, their handler, and a two to three-Soldier Escort Team.

MWD's carry equipment. For example, handlers determine if MWD's will be on a leash (to appease local civilians) or off a leash (to extend the dog's range up to hundreds of meters). (See Image 76, Pg. 96.) Dog radios allow the dog to hear its handler and increase range even farther. (Directing an IED-detecting MWD at a distance limits Soldiers' exposure to explosives.) And dog cameras let the handler see building layouts and enemy encounters.

MWD's are very effective, but also very specialized in doing exactly what they were trained to do. **Dogs cannot just "figure it out."** MWD's must be trained in each specific task and scent. Handlers then familiarize their dogs with that specific mission. Some things are difficult if not impossible to train, such as discerning dangerous strangers from safe strangers. For those reasons, MWD's are relatively expensive and rare, and a patrol is often better off finding a cheaper option. For example instead of using MWD's to disable enemies in room-clearing, grenades could be used.

Moreover, dogs are not infallible even after intense training. Fatigue, hunger, thirst, heat, cold, loud noise, excessive movement, bad weather, and difficult terrain, all degrade a dog's effectiveness (just like a human Soldier).

3.b Shoulder Launched Munitions

For simplicity, this manual focuses on shoulder-launched munitions' (SLM's) ability to **explode at a distance**. There are too many SLM's to discuss individual capabilities. Types include: close-combat missile SLM's, like the Spike, Javelin, and TOW, which themselves have many subtypes; and man-portable rocket SLM's like the M141, AT4, and Bazooka.[1]

Modern infantry almost always carry a few SLM's during missions because of the variety of distant, protected threats present in urban environments. Hard targets such as walls and vehicles are common. And movement distances are relatively short, so the weight of SLM's (between eight and fifty pounds) is worth carrying. In contrast, mountainous terrain may limit the number of SLM's due to fewer hard targets and longer travel distances.

SLM's are primarily used to destroy armored vehicles at a distance, but they can also destroy a Sniper hide position, a compound wall, a bunkered machine gun, etc. In an urban raid specifically, an SLM's explosion can be used to open up an entry into the objective. (See Footholds and Entrances, Pg. 163.) An M141 Bunker Defeat Munition (BDM) can allow for swift entry by penetrating double-reinforced concrete walls up to eight inches thick and triple-brick structures. For a man-sized hole, Breachers coordinate two rounds thirty centimeters apart. The impact neutralizes enemies directly behind the wall, and interior destruction may not be contained to a single room.

The utility of SLM's stems from filling the gap in power and flexibility between infantry and tanks. Tanks are very powerful, but inflexible. For example, in 1994 Grozny, Chechnya, Chechen fighters attacked tanks from ground positions with anti-armor SLM's, since the Russian tanks could not lower far enough to return fire at the ground at a close distance. In contrast, infantry are flexible but weak. SLM's maintain that flexibility but add power. SLM's can be pointed in most directions from most positions; and SLM's are also extremely easy to conceal due to their small size, making them integral to use in both ambushes and intercepting reinforcements after ambushes.

---

[1] **Real World:** Sometimes there is a choice of equipment. In Fallujah, Marines preferred the M141 over the M136 AT4 because the M136 was only effective against enemy armored vehicles, whereas the M141 were effective against many things. Marines preloaded M141's before maneuvers to provide instantaneous suppressing fire when they encountered an ambush.

Image 9: A Javelin missile fired by Marines destroys a target downrange. Balti, Moldova, 08 Dec 2012.

Image 8: Paratroopers with the 173rd (A) Bde. train with AT4 rocket launchers. Drawsko Pomorski, Poland, 29 May 2014.

Image 10: Infantry of A Co., 2nd Bn., 112th Inf. Reg., 56th Stryker Bde., 28th Inf. Div., PA Army N.G. fire AT4s. Fort Irwin, California, 15 Aug 2018.

The back-blast area is a consideration for recoilless SLM's, a type of SLM that releases gases (i.e., the back-blast) behind the firing Soldier. Although different for every weapon, the backblast area for the AT4 is a 100-meter radius quarter circle behind the weapon. There, the gases release with a force equal to the very strong force propelling the munition, and so these gases are very dangerous. **Standing in a back-blast area is dangerous.** If there is a wall behind the Soldier, the gases can even reflect and injure the firing Soldier. To compensate for back-blast indoors, Soldiers must be in positions that allow the back-blast to escape, such as between two corner windows where the round goes out one window and the back-blast escapes from the other.

SLM's represent a broad category and each specific weapon system has limitations. For example, the Javelin missile has a minimum engagement distance of 150 meters in the attack mode and 65 meters in the direct-attack mode. And its heat-seeking capability can confuse the target with the three-dimensional background, which limits its use in built-up areas. In contrast, man-portable rockets might not have distance restrictions, but they are difficult to fire on moving targets at a distance.

Image 11: A 3rd Special Forces Group (Airborne) Spotter and Sniper engage targets with the M2010 rifle. Nellis Air Force Base, NV, 27 Aug 2019.

3.c Long Range Riflemen

Riflemen who accurately shoot enemies at long distances are called Marksmen and Snipers. The effective range of a long range Rifleman depends on their skill and also their weapon system. While a Marksman may be limited to an Assaulter's rifle like the M4 with a 500-meter maximum effective range (MER), Snipers use long range rifles like the M2010 with a 200-meter MER.

The difference between the two types of Riflemen is the team they are on. A Marksman as a kind of Assaulter works in teams comprised of a variety of specialized Assaulters, like Grenadiers and Dog Handlers. In contrast, Snipers work in Sniper and Spotter Teams (SST's) that only conduct long range reconnaissance and attacks, such as area recon, assessing damage, spotting for indirect fire, isolating objectives, securing breach sites, disrupting enemy withdrawal, and counter-sniper work. Because Snipers are specialized, they carry designated long range weapon systems, side arms, additional radios, a spotting scope, camera systems, and appropriate night-vision equipment.

Long range Riflemen are valuable as stationary support or security because their **long range capability allows them to use superior distant**

cover and concealment while engaging targets. The lack of Sniper Teams was a failure point in the FBI's 1993 Waco, Texas raid which lost four special agents. The agents were engaged while too close to the compound, and were therefore pinned down by close attacks in areas with limited cover.

For planned raids, Snipers move out well in advance of the main body to remain undetected. SST's are best positioned in low-traffic areas at some distance from, and higher than, their target. Where possible, Snipers are positioned in bulletproof masonry buildings; however, if the position is too good (e.g., church steeples and rooftops), the enemy will quickly identify them. A single position may not afford adequate observation, so alternate and contingency positions are also planned. And each position must have a **planned withdrawal route** because Snipers cannot defend well against enemy attacks. For hasty attacks, the best way to employ Snipers is to give them a mission intent and let them operate on their own initiative.

Snipers are superior to armored vehicles in two ways: First, they are more difficult to detect, reducing the chance of a counter-attack. Second, Snipers attack more precisely. Where the rules-of-engagement (ROE) prohibit collateral damage, Snipers may be the most valuable tool the Leader has.

3.d Armored Fighting Vehicles[1]

Armored fighting vehicles (AFV's) have bulletproof armor, unlike light-skinned vehicles such as consumer trucks. Tanks and tther AFV's, are commonly used in urban warfare because the strengths of infantry and vehicles negate the other's weaknesses very well.

▸ **Infantry Strengths:**
  1) Excellent all-around vision and freedom to engage in all directions.
  2) Stealthy maneuverability around almost any terrain.
  3) A human presence to civilians, which aids cooperation.
▸ **Infantry Weaknesses:**
  1) Infantry weapons lack strong firepower and long range capability.
  2) Exposed light infantry forces are vulnerable to high casualty rates.

---

1 Quote: I guided the MK 19 HMMWV up onto a steep sidewalk.... [and] fired several tracers into the hotel; [the Gunner] then fired the [vehicle's] grenade launcher on automatic, hitting every single window in the building. The effects were devastating. Concrete fragments flew everywhere, and one or two Somalis fell out of the building. —U.S. Army Captain Charles P. Ferry

▸ **Armored Fighting Vehicle Strengths:**

1) Fast movement with heavier, and therefore superior, equipment.

2) Good supporting roles, like resupply, medevac, breaching, and reserve.

2) Protections against antipersonnel mines, fragments, and small arms.

4) A powerful presence to the enemy, encouraging cowardice.

▸ **Armored Fighting Vehicle Weaknesses:**

1) Poor all-around vision, with limited turret turning and firing distance.

2) Easy detection by enemies.

3) Limited maneuverability due to large size and heavy weight.

4) Every hour of use requires ten hours of maintenance.

AFV's can replace tasks otherwise done by infantry. For example, an AFV's explosive rounds can clear roadside buildings without entering.[1] AFV's can counterattack enemy Snipers or bunkers, where an infantry unit may have otherwise been forced to retreat. Tanks can become Breachers by shooting a wall with a tank round.

Moreover, AFV's enhance the maneuverability of infantry. For example, AFV's provide heavy supporting and distracting fire, removing attention from moving infantry. **AFV's can become mobile positions of cover** allowing infantry to move to new positions. A classic example of this is when a vehicle approaches a building in front of infantry, blocking all incoming small-arms fire. AFV's can destroy structures and create rubble to restrict enemy movement, or they can clear existing rubble to enhance friendly movement.

Some vehicles have onboard smoke generation systems or smoke grenade projectors that protect the tank from enemy fire and provide concealment for infantry as they either move across open areas or recover wounded. The use of smoke must be carefully coordinated with dismounted troops because of the potential fire hazard and obscured vision.

Just like Soldiers, different vehicles are ideal for different missions. In urban combat, AFV's require more protection from close attacks than in rural combat. Also, urban areas have rubble, so tracks perform better than wheels. **The lack of vehicle mobility in urban areas cannot be understated.**

---

[1] Real World: During the search and attack phase in Fallujah in 2004, Marine Corps tanks advanced through the streets while Riflemen cleared surrounding houses. When Marines encountered enemy pillboxes, Riflemen, Forward Observers, and Snipers guided the tanks forward into firing positions. The best way to guide the tank fire on target was either a M203 grenade launcher or a rifle with tracers.

Image 12: Soldiers from A Co., 2-3 Inf., 3rd Stryker Bde. run to the next Stryker during a firefight exercise. Fort Irwin, CA, 13 Aug 2011. **Vehicles are significantly larger and heavier than people.** Note how the Stryker is providing cover, while the Soldiers provide situational awareness by looking in many directions.

Image 13: U.S. and Arabian Gulf nation Special Operations Forces conduct a simulated hostage rescue mission. Kuwait, 23 March 2015. **Tanks provide great cover and concealment** for Soldiers against small arms fire. These Soldiers advanced with a double file formation. (See Single, Double, and V File Formations, Pg. 91.)

During the battles for Grozny, Chechens stationed themselves at positions high or low enough to be outside the swivel range of Russian AFV turrets. The Chechens then waited for a Russian convoy to drive into a street with buildings on both sides. They fired rocket-propelled grenades to destroy the lead and trail vehicles of the convoy, thereby trapping the Russians on all four sides between buildings and destroyed vehicles. The Chechens then picked off the Russian vehicles trapped in the middle, one by one. The Russian forces lost 20 of 26 tanks, 102 of 120 infantry fighting vehicles, and 6 of 6 anti-aircraft fighting vehicles in the first three days of fighting.

Whether infantry or vehicles are first in order of movement depends on what the most present danger is. Typically infantry lead because vehicle-targeting IEDs and shoulder-launched munitions are common. Dismounted infantry identify targets for the vehicles to engage while protecting the AFV's from traps. (See Image 74, Pg. 93.) During movement in especially dangerous areas, dismounted infantry clears corners for vehicles.

But if enemy Snipers are present, AFV's lead. When the infantry discover an enemy position or encounters resistance, the tanks immediately fire to suppress the enemy. After sufficient time passes or the patrol conducts reconnaissance, the Infantry Leader directs the patrol to continue movement.

Image 14: An Iraqi army tank moves into position to provide a show of force. Dismounted troops have better sight than tanks. Camp Taji, Iraq, 06 Jun 2015.

To integrate infantry and AFV's, a typical mix is four to five Soldiers per vehicle. The infantry's sectors-of-fire cover the vehicles' many blindspots or deadspace that exists very close to the vehicle. For further integration, **Infantry and Vehicle Leaders can create mutual range cards** to ensure 360-degree sectors-of-fire and that infantry do not enter a vehicles sector.

Soldiers can ride on the exterior of vehicles to increase the patrol's speed. The lead vehicle, however, does not carry infantry because riders restrict turret movement and are more likely to be injured or killed on initial contact. To ride, Soldiers approach the vehicle from the front to get permission from the Vehicle Leader to mount. They then mount in view of the Driver and avoid dangerous areas, like guns, lasers, ejection ports, and hot panels. Rope can be used as a field expedient railing to provide secure handholds. To increase coordination, like Leaders ride together: the Patrol Leader rides with the Vehicle Leader and the Patrol Sergeant rides with the Vehicle Sergeant.

While riding, infantry scan in all directions for enemies or obstacles. The infantry must always be prepared for sudden turret movement, so they never ride with their legs between the turret and the hull. In case of contact, Soldiers must immediately get away from the turret. Soldiers cannot fall asleep when riding; **a fall could be fatal!** Riders must always check with the Vehicle Leader for additional restrictions.

3.e Indirect Fire Systems[1]

Indirect fire support is any weapon system that **does not require line-of-sight** to engage a target. For example, indirect fire can shoot over the wall that blocks direct fire. The gamut of indirect fires runs from 60mm infantry-carried mortars to 406mm naval support guns (the ~7X larger radius allows for a ~300X larger munition by volume). However, there are commonalities in different indirect fire systems, especially as they relate to raiding.

Skirting barriers is one advantage, but the other benefit is that indirect fire systems are relatively small and cheap compared to their power because they use the ground to manage recoil. (In contrast, a recoilless M136 AT4 has a 100-meter backblast area and is more expensive.) Managed recoil allows for higher power in a smaller package.

The drawback of indirect fire is that the trajectories are long and difficult to aim. Long trajectories delay impacts; therefore, indirect fires are typically used on targets that don't move. Being difficult to aim means that at least the first round is expected to be inaccurate. Indirect fire systems employ observers (or more recently unmanned aerial vehicles) to correct inaccurate fires.

Because indirect fires are powerful and difficult to block, yet difficult to place, **they are great for destroying a stationary target**. However, imprecise destruction is rarely the purpose of a raid. At a higher level, fires can manipulate enemy movement, distract the enemy from something important, psychologically paralyze the enemy[2], or split an enemy element into parts. More doctrinal reasons include:

Prevent – and disrupt enemy maneuver through protective fires. (See Scheme-of-Fires, Pg. 118.)

Soften – the enemy position in preparation for an attack. (See Softening the Objective, Pg. 158.)

Destroy – enemy fires, positions, and observers during an attack. (See Support to Facilitate Assault's Maneuver, Pg. 173.)

---

1   Quote: Keep hammering targets and if you see a guy with an AK-47, I expect you to hose him with a .50 caliber machine gun. If firing was identified from a house, then artillery fire should be called into pancake the building because there is not a building in this city worth one of our soldiers' lives. —U.S. Army LTC Peter Newell

2   Quote: Shells would not only tear and rip the body, they tortured one's mind almost beyond the brink of sanity. After each shell I was wrung out, limp and exhausted. —E.B. Sledge's Word War II account With the Old Breed

Image 15 et al: Coalition advisors launch a 120mm mortar toward a known ISIS position (left), where it explodes (right). The Coalition fired hundreds of mortar rounds within a few days because to assist Syrian Democratic Forces to clear the Iraqi-Syrian border, 13 May 2018. **Mortars are cheap and humans are expensive.**

Distract – the enemy from an attack somewhere else. (See Supporting Fires to Suppress and Divert, Pg. 176.)

Harass – enemies to lower their morale. (See Stress and Sleep Deprivation, Pg. 298.)

In addition to the destructive power of high-explosive rounds, indirect fires also control visibility with illumination rounds that increase visibility and smoke rounds that decrease visibility. For example when the patrol is exposed during a wall breach, the patrol may fire illumination rounds to distract and illuminate the enemy, and smoke rounds to cover the breach. Specifically:

Illumination rounds allow the Patrol Leader to confirm or deny the presence of the enemy without revealing the location of friendly direct-fire weapons. Bright lights also distract the enemy away from important actions. Illumination fires are often coordinated with high-explosive fires to both expose and kill the enemy. (See Image 16, Pg. 39.)

Obscurants (smoke, white phosphorous, tear gas) are especially useful in urban combat. The Russians in 1994 Grozny, Chechnya used significant amounts of smoke and white phosphorus to mask the movement of forces. Every fourth or fifth artillery or mortar round was either smoke or white phosphorous. Obscurants can isolate a portion of the enemy force to destroy it piecemeal. And obscurants can be a signal to aircraft or other troops.

The **kinds of indirect fire support systems** include: naval gunfire, mortars, artillery, rockets, and missiles. Because indirect fire planning is varied and complex, a system-specialist helps to plan and order fires. The

Image 16: New Zealand Soldiers and U.S. Marines watch 81mm-mortar illumination rounds light the impact area. Waiouru, New Zealand, 28 Aug 2015. The visibility from illumination rounds allows efficient adjustment for **follow-on rounds**.

specialists include: Fire Support Coordinator, Naval Gunfire Spotter, Weapons Platoon Leader, Fire Support Team Leader, Artillery Forward Observer, 81mm Forward Observer, and more. Indirect fires are complicated enough to have a dedicated planning section. (See Scheme-of-Fires, Pg. 118.)

The large variety of indirect fire weapon systems and ammunition are further **affected by the environment** they are used in and require help from an expert. For example, some considerations include:

▸ Unpredictable winds and precipitation affect the accuracy of rounds.

▸ In mountain terrain, high-explosive air-bursts tend to be more effective than point-detonating rounds. Point-detonating rounds that impact rocky areas create rock shrapnel, but large rocks also protect targets from said shrapnel. Plus, peaks and steep terrain make adjustments difficult.

▸ In winter, deep snow may soften impacts, preventing detonation. And if rounds do detonate in deep snow, the snow dampens effects. Again, air-burst detonations may help improve lethality. However proximity fuses may falsely read elevation in a snowstorm causing premature detonation.

▸ Non-state armed groups may use improvised rocket-assisted munitions (IRAM's), in which an over-caliber warhead is fitted to a conventional rocket to deliver a large explosive payload. This drastically increases air resistance and reduces range and accuracy. (The accuracy of many IRAM's is the same or worse as artillery from a century ago.)

Indirect fires are not point weapons. Even the smallest U.S. mortar, the M224 60mm Lightweight Mortar, has a blast radius of 10 meters. If a mortar were perfectly dropped on an enemy (which indirect fires are not), everyone within 10 meters would be a casualty. Lethal radius is especially relevant in urban combat where there are noncombatants, and rules-of-engagement are restrictive. Further, illumination, white phosphorous, and tracer rounds can

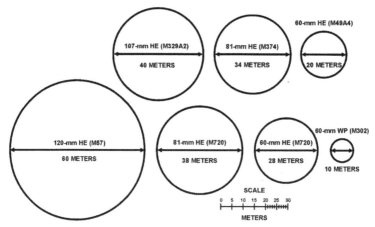

Image 17: Blast radius of various ammunition for 120mm, 81mm, and 60mm mortar systems. Adapted from U.S. Army ATP 3-21.8 2016 Figure C-10. "HE" is high-explosive, and "WP" is white phosphorus.

cause unintentional building fires. And highly penetrative rounds can pierce many walls, creating unintended damage, casualties, and fratricide.

The mortar is one of the most important indirect fire systems for raids. Mortarmen respond faster than artillery because they can quickly move with Leaders and respond to orders and corrections. Mortars have a higher angle of fire than artillery, which means less deadspace and better efficacy against trenches. And the mortar's short trajectory allows for quick fires, whereas a far-away artillery shell may take minutes to arrive.

The combined responsiveness and speed make for relatively precise repeat fires. Therefore, suppressive fires from light and medium mortars can be used to allow Assaulters to advance closer to their objective before these fires must be lifted or shifted, as compared to other fire support systems. Mortars are especially applicable for obscuring a maneuvering Assault Element or destroying a maneuvering enemy, where seconds matter.

A typical U.S. Army 60-mm mortar squad consists of a Squad Leader, a Gunner, and an Assistant Gunner, whereas an 81-mm squad has six Soldiers. Each Soldier can only carry a very limited amount of ammunition and therefore distributing, controlling, and conserving ammunition across the patrol is necessary. A key responsibility of the Mortar Section Leader is to determine a mission's ammunition requirement. A Mortar Section usually works within an area secured by Riflemen, and can be concealed between buildings, in confined areas, and on rough terrain.

3.f Close Air Support

Aircraft can support urban operations with **attack, reconnaissance, and transportation** capabilities. They can: provide flank security and direct fire support; lift single squads into position (such as a roof) or evacuate them out; or, provide retransmission capability, airborne command posts, and confirm the status of friendly forces. Even the mere presence of aircraft flying in or near an enemy position may paralyze or disorganize the enemy. Aircraft are especially effective at night, when they are harder to identify against the sky.

Fixed wing aircraft only have narrow applicability to raids because they are overly destructive. Although a mission may benefit from the destruction of a large area outside of the objective, raid objectives cannot be totally destroyed. In urban terrain, moreover, civilian considerations and minimum safe distances to the patrol limit the outside areas an aircraft can attack. Their information-related capabilities are also becoming less relevant as nations rely on other technology like cellular networks, drones, and satellites.

Rotary wing aircraft (e.g. helicopters), however, can provide more precise fires and are very easy to get on and off the objective. By being quicker than tanks to arrive and more responsive than indirect fires, rotary wing aircraft are effective in a fast-paced raid against Snipers and bunkered weapons in the upper floors. Even after Assault enters a tall building on ground level, helicopter gunships are precise enough to fire on the upper floors. Helicopters can also provide a fast infiltration and withdrawal platform.

However, rotary wing aircraft are not as destructive as ground troops. One participant in the October 1993 Mogadishu raid noted, "Air strikes are only suppressive fire...[They] did not completely destroy enemy positions or buildings. Many buildings that were struck were reoccupied by Somali guerrillas within minutes." Nor are rotary wing aircraft as durable as ground troops; they are vulnerable to weather, terrain, and anti-aircraft fire. For example, in the battle for Grozny, poor weather often kept Russian fixed-wing aircraft grounded and useless. Also, helicopter routes are limited when they fly low in urban airspace due to potential enemies on rooftops and antennas.

All aircraft also have time limits for any mission or area; a complete raid mission takes a long time and air support may not be available the entire mission. But when the patrol conducts action on the objective, the time of the air support can be preplanned, and ready to fire at the kickoff time.

Coordinating an air attack is similar to coordinating any other indirect fire. The Patrol Leader coordinates fires to the aircraft through a qualified Soldier called a Joint Terminal Attack Controller (JTAC), or a Forward Air Controller. A JTAC receives the desired effects from the Patrol Leader and recommends and directs the action of combat aircraft.

However, although ground and air personnel must make efforts to involve a JTAC in their coordination, sometimes the Patrol Leader must work without a qualified JTAC and accept the increased risk of friendly fire and civilian casualties. Aircrew must also be prepared to obtain information from untrained ground personnel to complete or enhance an attack brief.

To coordinate directly with CAS, the Patrol Leader must specifically alert their higher command that a JTAC is unavailable. This alert moves through command and prepares the aircraft crew to request additional critical information, and requires the aircrew to more rigorously verify any requests in order to minimize friendly fire and collateral damage.

Regardless of circumstance, and air-to-ground communication is ongoing. Information contained in a request for close air support in rough order of importance includes:

1) Target location and elevation.

2) Target description sufficient for identification by aircraft. (E.g.: flat rooves, pitched rooves, domed rooves, towers, or rooftop air conditioning units.)

3) Target marking by ground personnel, current and future, to include: fires (e.g. direct, tracer, flares, mortars, etc.), smoke, lasers, etc. Simple, positive identification for day and night must follow a PACE plan and be widely disseminated. Marking can also be an offset from friendly forces by direction and distance. Friendly forces then mark their position with: infrared strobes, night-vision goggle lights, smoke, signal panels, meal heaters, chemical lights, mirrors etc. Marking friendly positions is always a backup plan because it highlights friendly positions.

4) Nearest friendly locations and maneuver plans.

5) Restrictions or necessary situational awareness (e.g. presence of civilians or other friendly troops; enemy composition and disposition; location of known air defense weapons; enemy forces most recent activities; etc.).

6) Target confirmation with the ground personnel, while understanding that the ground personnel may not be trained in target confirmation.

7) Brevity terms like "abort," for unsafe situations during the attack.

Close Air Support

Image 18: A Marine Joint Terminal Attack Controller with E Co., 2nd Bn., 8th Marine Reg., runs to another position to better control air support during a six-hour firefight with Taliban insurgents. Garmsir, Helmand, Afghanistan, 13 Aug 2009.

Close Air Support Execution

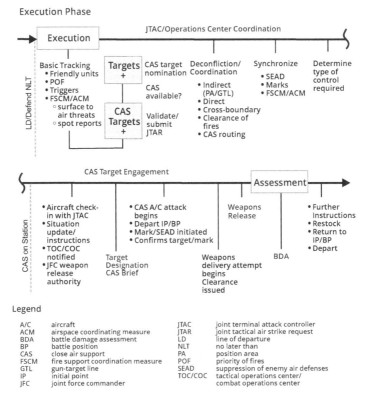

Execution Phase

Execution — JTAC/Operations Center Coordination

LD/Defend NLT

Basic Tracking
- Friendly units
- POF
- Triggers
- FSCM/ACM
  - surface to air threats
  - spot reports

Targets +

CAS Targets +

CAS target nomination

CAS available?

Validate/submit JTAR

Deconfliction/Coordination
- Indirect (PA/GTL)
- Direct
- Cross-boundary
- Clearance of fires
- CAS routing

Synchronize
- SEAD
- Marks
- FSCM/ACM

Determine type of control required

CAS Target Engagement — Assessment

CAS on Station

- Aircraft check-in with JTAC
- Situation update/instructions
- TOC/COC notified
- JFC weapon release authority

Target Designation
CAS Brief

- CAS A/C attack begins
- Depart IP/BP
- Mark/SEAD initiated
- Confirms target/mark

Weapons delivery attempt begins
Clearance issued

Weapons Release

BDA

- Further Instructions
- Restock
- Return to IP/BP
- Depart

Legend

A/C	aircraft	JTAC	joint terminal attack controller
ACM	airspace coordinating measure	JTAR	joint tactical air strike request
BDA	battle damage assessment	LD	line of departure
BP	battle position	NLT	no later than
CAS	close air support	PA	position area
FSCM	fire support coordination measure	POF	priority of fires
GTL	gun-target line	SEAD	suppression of enemy air defenses
IP	initial point	TOC/COC	tactical operations center/
JFC	joint force commander		combat operations center

Image 19: This diagram of a CAS execution timeline exemplifies the complexity of the job of a Joint Terminal Air Controller, and why calling for CAS is a dedicated job. Joint U.S. Armed Forces Publication 3-09.3, Figure V-1. CAS Execution.

Image 20: A drone (top left) can be seen moving through a simulated chemical attack against a convoy. Fort McCoy, WI, 19 Jul 2021. The drone's close-proximity GPS coordinates and video feed can be used to bracket indirect fires, acquire SALUTE reports, conduct kamikaze attacks, etc.

3.g Unmanned Aerial Vehicles

Unmanned aerial vehicles (UAV's or drones) are very relevant to today's battlefield and are used in every modern conflict. They provide unprecedented maneuverability and disposability (as compared to manned aircraft). One of the most common and effective uses of UAV's is reconnaissance. For example, Mortarmen previously had to rely on human Forward Observers (FO's) to see the impact of their rounds, and bracket in the mortars after a few volleys. To see the location of the mortar impact was difficult, because the FO's had to avoid the danger of the impact and could only observe from ground level. In contrast, **UAV's give a real-time, closeup, aerial view** of the impact, allowing Mortarmen to correctly bracket their rounds on the second shot.

All that being said, current UAV's lack an important characteristic of raids, which is discretion. Raids are used when something on the objective cannot be destroyed, and yet fires from UAV's are closer to indirect fires or close air support in that current models destroy indiscriminately. Even the models that seek human body heat to kill only determine if something is living.

When thinking about how UAV's will impact raiding in the near future, it is most helpful to consider how they will augment current tactics rather than replace them. For example, a leader's reconnaissance of the objective can be completed much faster with the help of an aerial drone. (See Leader's Reconnaissance of the Objective, Pg. 139.) And UAV's vastly increase the availability of air support. (See Close Air Support, Pg. 41.)

3.h Non-Combat Support

Almost all raids have non-combat actions to be performed. And while all these non-combat actions can be performed by Assaulters with a secondary skillset, **using a dedicated specialist with relevant skills** leads to better results. Even a single special-skill Soldier enhances an entire team when they advise non-specialized Assaulters. Namely, the act of adding non-combat support is an active decision that the skills of a Supporter are more useful to achieving the mission than the additional security that an Assaulter would provide.

The most common non-combat skills used during a raid are knowledge of, explosives, detainees, and medicine. Information gathering, personnel control, and hazard control are also relatively common. The skilled Soldiers for each knowledge domain include:

Explosives (See Outside Barrier and Compound Breach, Pg. 180.) –
Combat Engineer

Personnel control (See Noncombatants, Pg. 274.) –
Civil Affairs, Interpreters

EPW (See Enemy Prisoner of War Team, Pg. 283.) –
Military Police

Aid and litter (See Aid and Litter, and Medevac, Pg. 286.) –
Medic

Information gathering (See Site Exploitation, Pg. 288.) –
Data Collectors, Interrogators, Military Information

Hazard Control –
Hazmat

These Supporters are often attached to a patrol from a different unit for a single mission, which makes practicing together difficult to coordinate. However, it is vital to **practice as you fight**, so all raiders must be integrated into practice. But if a raid is big enough to have a few special-skill Soldiers, the Patrol Leader can put them in reserve and then forward deploy after the objective is cleared to mitigate interference. (See Reserve Element, Pg. 24.)

4. Task Organization[1]

Task organization is the determination of who needs to come on a raid, and what or who they are responsible for. Patrol composition always varies because missions are different, and different missions benefit from different raiders.

All modern militaries standardize their basic task organization. (See Image 21 et al, Pg. 47.) However, special mission units and guerrilla fighters alike have much leeway in how they organize their troops.

The act of task organizing begins by **defining the tasks**. For example, if there is the possibility of confronting tanks on the way to the objective, then the patrol must organize a task around avoiding or counterattacking tanks.

Second, after the tasks are defined, **resources must be inventoried**. Soldiers and rifles are both resources. Resources are sometimes hidden, and it is the job of Leaders to find them. For example, even if a canine units is available to support, the canine unit may not be actively advertised. Resources are inventoried after tasks are defined because a Leader can use tasks to persuade Higher Command to grant more and better resources.

Third, after tasks and resources are both well-defined, **the resources (i.e., Soldiers and equipment) must be collected and assigned tasks.** If there is a task that enemy tanks must be countered, and Soldiers have anti-armor weapons, then an assignment could be to have Soldiers with anti-armor weapons attached to every squad. Common special-assignment teams include: Aid and Litter Teams; Enemy Prisoner of War or Detainee Teams; Surveillance Teams; Breach Teams; Demolition and Engineer Teams; Site Exploitation Teams; Rope Installation Teams; Cave and Tunnel Exploitation Teams; Route Reconnaissance Teams; and Landing Zone Teams.

The goal of the Patrol Leader when assigning tasks is to create the smallest patrol that can still accomplish all the mission tasks. (A company or smaller unit typically executes raids.) A smaller raiding patrol has many

---

1 **Quote:** There is still a tendency in each separate unit... to be a one-handed puncher. By that I mean that the rifleman wants to shoot, the tanker to charge, the artilleryman to fire.... That is not the way to win battles. If the band played a piece first with the piccolo, then with the brass horn, then with the clarinet, and then with the trumpet, there would be a hell of a lot of noise but no music. To get harmony in music each instrument must support the others. To get harmony in battle, each weapon must support the other. Team play wins. —U.S. Gen. George S. Patton Jr.

Team and Squad Task Organization

TL	GRN	AR	RFLM
M4-SERIES	M203	M249	M4-SERIES
SGT	SPC	SPC	PFC

LEGEND

AR	AUTOMATIC RIFLEMAN	SGT	SERGEANT
GRN	GRENADIER	SPC	SPECIALIST
RFLM	RIFLEMAN	TL	TEAM LEADER
PFC	PRIVATE FIRST CLASS		

TL	GRN	AR	RFLM		TL	GRN	AR	RFLM
M4-SERIES	M203	M249	M4-SERIES		M4-SERIES	M203	M249	M4-SERIES
SGT	SPC	SPC	PFC		SGT	SPC	SPC	PFC

└── ALPHA TEAM ──┘   SL M4-SERIES SSG   └── BRAVO TEAM ──┘

LEGEND

AR	AUTOMATIC RIFLEMAN	SL	SQUAD LEADER
GRN	GRENADIER	SPC	SPECIALIST
RFLM	RIFLEMAN	SSG	STAFF SERGEANT
PFC	PRIVATE FIRST CLASS	TL	TEAM LEADER
SGT	SERGEANT		

GUNNER	AG	GUNNER	AG		GUNNER	AH	GUNNER	AH
M240	M4	M240	M4		JAVELIN	M4	JAVELIN	M4
SPC	PFC	SPC	PFC		M4	PFC	M4	PFC
					SPC		SPC	

└ GUN ┘ TEAM 1   └ GUN ┘ TEAM 2   SL M4-SERIES SSG   └ JAVELIN ┘ TEAM 1   └ JAVELIN ┘ TEAM 2

LEGEND

AG	ASSIST GUNNER	SGT	SERGEANT
AH	AMMO HANDLER	SL	SQUAD LEADER
RFLM	RIFLEMAN	SPC	SPECIALIST
PFC	PRIVATE FIRST CLASS	SSG	STAFF SERGEANT

Image 21 et al: Three figures (each legend is a different figure): Figure 1-2 Infantry Fire Team, Figure 1-3 Infantry Squad, and Figure 1-4 Infantry Weapons Squad from U.S. Army ATP 3-21.8 Infantry Platoon and Squad 2016.

benefits: they are more flexible, easier to control, quicker to maneuver, and harder to detect than larger forces. A smaller unit can better conceal itself in open terrain, where a larger unit would be exposed. And a smaller footprint is harder to detect and target. Fewer layers of command and smaller spans of control speed up communication. Moreover, a larger unit that successfully defends itself against an attack may ironically attract even more enemies. If enough Soldiers are available, the command should consider conducting two separate missions rather than one oversized mission.

Task assignments can be fluid, and a single task can be assigned to multiple elements. For example, every Soldier is assigned the passive task of pulling security. And multiple tasks can be assigned to a single element; an Assaulter may also execute the special task of breaching. In these fluid cases, priorities or zones must be established to ensure that different units don't compete on the same task don't hesitate, trying to decide which task is more important. At the end of it all, a patrol can still only have one primary mission above all else.

Every level of a patrol must be task organized. At the team level, the most common Clearing Teams have four Assaulters. However, a building with many open spaces may be better cleared with larger teams. Alternatively, when there are shortages of personnel, room-clearing can be conducted with two or three-man teams; although, using fewer personnel increases the risk to a team. (See Close-Quarters Battle Basics, Pg. 195.)

At the squad-level, a common task organization is to designate one squad as an Assault Squad, with any remaining squads providing security and reinforcement. (See Image 22, Pg. 49.) The Assault Squad is split between a Clearing Team and a Support team. The Clearing Team clears the room or hallway, while the Support Team provides security and prepares to reinforce the Clearing Team.

Platoons are often assigned tasks in different geographical areas, like an Assaulting Platoon on the objective, and a Security Platoon isolating the objective outside. However, if an interior is large enough, such as hangars or warehouses, two squads may need to use bounding to effectively cover the entire structure. (See Bounding and Crossing Intersections, Pg. 99.)

There is much variability, but an example Assault Platoon may organize into two Assault Squads, each with two Assault Teams, and then attach any machine guns or armored vehicles to the Support Platoon. The Support

Platoon Task Organization

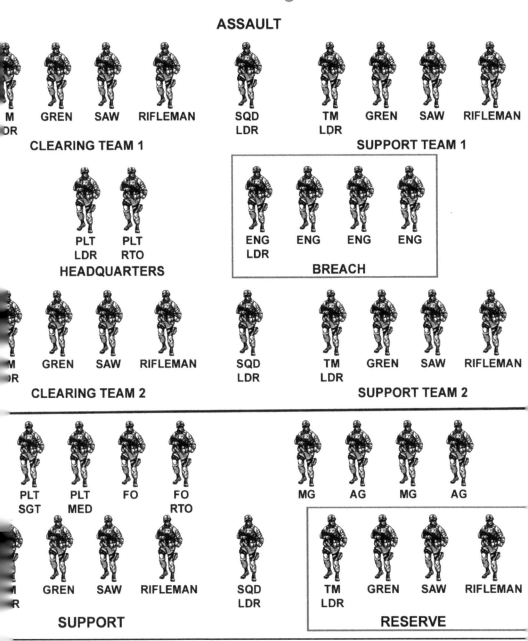

ASSAULT

M DR	GREN	SAW	RIFLEMAN

CLEARING TEAM 1

SQD LDR	TM LDR	GREN	SAW	RIFLEMAN

SUPPORT TEAM 1

PLT LDR	PLT RTO

HEADQUARTERS

ENG LDR	ENG	ENG	ENG

BREACH

M R	GREN	SAW	RIFLEMAN

CLEARING TEAM 2

SQD LDR	TM LDR	GREN	SAW	RIFLEMAN

SUPPORT TEAM 2

PLT SGT	PLT MED	FO	FO RTO

MG	AG	MG	AG

GREN	SAW	RIFLEMAN

SUPPORT

SQD LDR	TM LDR	GREN	SAW	RIFLEMAN

RESERVE

Figure 5-1. Platoon task organization

Image 22: Figure 5-1 Platoon Task Organization from U.S. Army Field Manual 3-06.11 Combined Arms Operations in Urban Terrain 2011. In this example, the platoon is made of an Assault Element (above the line) and a Support Element (below the line). Assault further has an embedded Breach Element, and Support has an embedded Reserve Element. Each Clearing Team also has a Support Team. Although this chart is a strong guideline, even the Army manual recognizes that **every mission is different**: "While the mission variables determine their size and composition, the elements should maintain unit integrity as much as possible."

Image 23: Two Romanian IAR-330 Puma helicopters provide security for a Stryker Combat Vehicle (middle) and a TR-85 Main Battle Tank (right) as they conduct operations and maneuver alongside troops from 2nd Sqn., 2nd Cav. Reg. Smardan TA, Romania, 18 April 2015. **CAS, Assaulters, and Armor operate together.**

Platoon may organize into three Support Squads, with machine guns, armored vehicles, and anti-armor weapons attached. (At the company and platoon level, combined arms patrols have always been highly successful in urban warfare.)

Fourth, Soldiers must be assigned to a chain of command according to the primary task they are responsible for. Much of this step is already done because all Soldiers already have a chain of command; and coordination can benefit from maintaining the long-term integrity of platoons, squads, and fire-teams. However specifically, the Patrol Leader must decide whether specialized Soldiers form their own unit, or are attached to other units. For example, if a platoon has three machine guns, does each Gun Team attach to a Rifle Squad, or do they combine to form a Gun Squad? Combat Engineers may be integrated into one element for better command and control. Or they may be distributed to the Assault, Support, and Reserve Elements so that the abundance of urban obstacles can be handled faster and at a lower command level. Tailoring an organization to the mission is necessary.

The Patrol Leader must also decide which patrol-level Leader controls which patrol-level element. During an infiltration, the Support Element may be controlled by the Patrol Leader, Patrol Sergeant, Weapons Squad Leader,

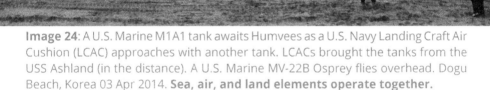

Image 24: A U.S. Marine M1A1 tank awaits Humvees as a U.S. Navy Landing Craft Air Cushion (LCAC) approaches with another tank. LCACs brought the tanks from the USS Ashland (in the distance). A U.S. Marine MV-22B Osprey flies overhead. Dogu Beach, Korea 03 Apr 2014. **Sea, air, and land elements operate together.**

Tank Platoon Leader, etc. The rule of thumb is to assign the most experienced Leaders to lead the tasks in which they are most proficient. A Patrol Sergeant with lots of medical evacuation experience should probably lead medical evacuation. A Tank Commander should probably be the Patrol Leader for a mission planned around an armored division, with armored division goals. The options for assigning a chain of command are exemplified by integrating tanks into a rifle company. The options include:

▸ Tank platoons take orders from infantry company.
▸ Tank sections take orders from infantry platoons.
▸ Tank sections are split between infantry company and platoons.
▸ Tanks individually take orders from infantry platoons.
▸ Infantry squads take orders from tank platoons.

After Soldiers are assigned tasks, resources, and chains of command, the task organization for that operational phase is finished. But **a patrol can have different task organizations for different phases of a mission.** When an Assaulting Element stops maneuvering, it can switch to become an alternate Support Element to allow the primary Support Element to then maneuver and become Assaulters. Although there are usually distinct Assault and Support Elements at any given time, which element is which can change.

Phase 1 Contents

5. Characteristics of Urban Terrain — 53

Frameworks for Attacking Vertical Terrain — 54
Tunnels and Caves — 56
Building Construction — 57
Battle and Flank Positions — 60
Urban Population Threats — 62
Traps and Improvised Explosive Devices — 65
Night and Limited Visibility Operations — 69

6. Using a Rifle in Urban Terrain — 72

Targeting — 72
Terminal Ballistics — 75
Handling a Rifle in Close-Quarters — 78
Shooting while Moving — 83
Pieing and Clearing Corners — 85

7. Moving in Urban Terrain — 88

Single, Double, and V File Formations — 91
Front Security and Navigation — 95
Rear Security — 97
Wedge and Diamond Formations — 98
Bounding and Crossing Intersections — 99
Moving between Buildings — 105
Vehicle Attachment — 107
Fighting in L Shapes — 109

8. Scheme-of-Maneuver for Infiltration — 109

Choosing and Preparing a Route — 111
Phase Lines — 113
Raid Preparation Locations — 116
Timetables — 118

9. Scheme-of-Fires — 118

Call for Fire — 123

10. Enemy Contact in Urban Terrain — 124

Medical Evacuation — 128

Joe Invades Enemy Land (Phase 1: Infiltration of Urban Terrain)

The [North Vietnamese Army] … occupied first and second-floor windows, and many of the NVA were on the roofs. Several automatic weapons raked the street from our left flank, from the tower that protected the eastern entrance to the Citadel. And I ran, and ran, and ran, and I got nowhere fast.
— *Marine Inf. Co. Cmdr. Nicholas Warr, on the Battle for Hue*

Before a raid begins, Soldiers must travel to the objective. This is no simple feat. Soldiers who move are always more vulnerable than Soldiers who hunker down because a moving Soldier's path must be free of obstacles and therefore cover. Urban movement centers around understanding and reacting to enemies in close, bunkered positions who will shoot at anything that moves.

5. Characteristics of Urban Terrain[1]

Urban terrain is distinct from other terrains, and requires urban-specific planning. First, human multistory structures are a terrain with a third, vertical dimension. (See Frameworks for Attacking Vertical Terrain, Pg. 54.) Second, urban areas are filled with different materials, (See Building Construction, Pg. 57.) and especially corners (See Pieing and Clearing Corners, Pg. 85.). Third, urban areas are cramped and filled with people, which means that Soldiers must slow down to have more situational awareness of themselves and their bullets. (See Urban Population Threats, Pg. 62.)

---

1 Quote: In one moment in time, our Service Members will be feeding and clothing displaced refugees, providing humanitarian assistance. In the next moment, they will be holding two warring tribes apart, conducting peacekeeping operations. Finally, they will be fighting a highly lethal mid-intensity battle. All on the same day, all within three city blocks. It will be what we call the three block war.
—31st Commandant of the Marine Corps General Charles Krulak

5.a Frameworks for Attacking Vertical Terrain

Human structures and defenses are three-dimensional places perfectly made for humans to exist in. They have many layers to include rooves and basements. This greater space density as compared to nature allows the enemy to sneak closer, and increases the threat of attack even if no actual attack exists.

The complexity and importance of the vertical dimension were displayed in the battle of Grozny. There, Chechnyan rebels decreased the Russian's mobility on the ground floor by boarding up and blocking first floor entrances to buildings to deny entry to the Russians. Then, the rebels increased their own mobility on higher floors and below ground by building a network of passages through the buildings, subbasements, and bunkers. Despite heavy Russian bombing and artillery, the Chechnyan rebels were always able to utilize their three-dimensional maneuver network.

Before a raid begins, a patrol must separate different parts of the mission and the urban terrain therein to create a plan for each part. This is true for: 1) the raid objective, 2) the area surrounding the objective, and also 3) all the areas surrounding the infiltration and withdrawal. For example, leadership must always consider how far the patrol will be from a flat area, like a park, that can be used as a helicopter landing zone for medical evacuation.

A few generalizing **frameworks** aid in considering each part of urban terrain. Of course, using actual city plans and building plans is ideal. But acquiring and reviewing the floor plan of every building is often impractical.

One useful framework is to separately consider five vertical layers, each of which is dominated by a different weapon and tactical system:

Airspace – air assets and anti-air assets. (See Close Air Support, Pg. 41.) (See Shoulder Launched Munitions, Pg. 30.)

Supersurface (external tops of buildings) – concealed positions for Snipers, automatic weapons, and light and medium antitank weapons. (See Long Range Riflemen, Pg. 32.) (See Machine Gunner, Pg. 23.)

Stories (interior of buildings) – intense close-quarters battle with small arms fire. (See Assaulter, Pg. 21.)

Surface (ground level) – tanks and heavy support assets. (See Armored Fighting Vehicles, Pg. 33.) (See Indirect Fire Systems, Pg. 37.)

Subsurface – harassment and traps. (See Breacher and Engineer, Pg. 22.)

Vertical-Layers Framework

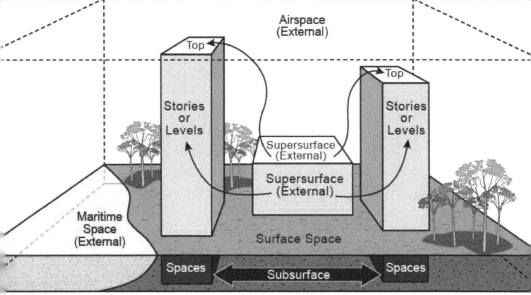

Image 25: Frameworks and categorization are an integral part of planning. For example, there are also frameworks for weather (See Weather, Pg. 190.) and for planning routes (See Choosing and Preparing a Route, Pg. 111.).

Image 26: Pictured is the boiler intake reservoir of R.G. Steel at Sparrow's Point, Baltimore, MD, 06 May 2011. On the ground, separating a battlespace into different layers is not very helpful. This framework is a useful planning and training tool only insofar as a Leader who recognizes the different spaces can better tailor their plan, and bring more specialized troops and assets to the fight.

The characteristics of each layer influences the shape and composition of a raiding patrol performing within that area. For example, a patrol traveling through areas with tall buildings must defend against more sniper fire, while a patrol that travels through an area with large subterranean structures must defend against more hit-and-run tactics.

Chechen fighters successfully applied this five-layer framework, and used completely different tactics at different levels to defeat Russian troops. Chechens fired rockets at helicopters in the air. Chechnyan Snipers situated on high-rise buildings effectively forced vehicles onto other routes through both direct fire and fear.[1] Within buildings, sometimes Chechens held the middle floors, while the Russians held the bottom floors and the roof. The Chechens would attack the ground-floor Russians, baiting a counterattack. The Russians would return fire upwards, inadvertently shooting the Russians occupying the roof. Entire battles were fought through floors, ceilings, and walls without visual contact. At the ground level, the Chechen forces ensured that there was little distance between themselves and Russian forces during ambushes, so the Russians were unable to call in artillery without attacking themselves as well. In the underground, Chechen fighters used underground sewers and water tunnels to flank the Russians and attack from below ground level.

Another framework is to consider function: crowded residential areas often have narrow streets for cars. In contrast, commercial areas are built on either side of major (at least 35-meters wide) streets to facilitate the movement of large trucks. Therefore, tanks would be easier to move in commercial areas due to wider streets. Relatedly, wider streets use different movement tactics than narrower streets. (See Moving in Urban Terrain, Pg. 100.)

5.b Tunnels and Caves

Tunnels and caves are excluded from the above frameworks because the raiding tactics in this manual are not effective at defeating tunnels and caves. Their terrain is fundamentally different. In tunnels and caves, the impenetrable "walls" surrounding tunnels and caves cannot be breached. Therefore, Raiders must use the existing entryways and Defenders know where Raiders can appear. Defenders can then barricade and focus-fire the existing

---

1 Quote: Whenever I was in the open I imagined the sights of a Sniper's rifle zeroing in on my head from some building half a mile away. —Anatol Lieven, Visiting Professor in the War Studies Department of King's College London

Image 27: A Sapper sweeps the entrance of a cave. Shomali, Uruzgan, Afghanistan, 15 Oct 2013.

Image 28: U.S. Army Soldiers explore a cave near the Pakistan border. Wardachi, Afghanistan, 13 Mar 2011.

entryways to repel anyone who attempts entry. Further, the narrow, rocky passages limit the number of fires that a patrol can attack with at one time.

In the Vietnam War, "tunnel rat" Soldiers attempted search and destroy raids into Viet Cong tunnel systems, and one in three was wounded or killed. They traveled in the pitch dark with no idea where they were going, armed with a single handgun that they didn't want to use (noise and limited ammunition), while lugging explosives on their backs. Tunnel rats could be alone or have a buddy they couldn't see five feet behind them. Using a full-size patrol would have only endangered more troops without increasing success.

5.c Building Construction[1]

Building construction and materials are critical information for planning what cover, concealment, and access are avaiable during a raid. For example, secure, 18-foot compound walls topped with barbed wire, obscure lines-of-sight from multiple directions. Against that defense, Soldiers are forced to go through instead of over.

The world contains billions of structures made from all kinds of materials that cannot be summarized in a few pages. So again, this section introduces **frameworks** to help plan. A building's characteristics fall into three important categories: construction materials, wall and roofing type, and floor plan.

In general terms, the four categories of building construction materials are wood, masonry (e.g., brick and stone), concrete, and metal. **Different materials dictate different raiding strategies.** For example, strong materials require the patrol to carry more effective breaching methods. Weak materials

---

1 Quote: Soldiers deployed to Iraq became experts in concrete during their combat tours. The most effective weapon on the modern battlefield is concrete. —Ranger Instructor Major John Spencer

require safer strategies and more coordination because bullets will penetrate the walls into other rooms. (See Terminal Ballistics, Pg. 75.) Moreover, different materials have different inherent dangers, like collapse, fire, and long-term hazardous exposure (e.g. asbestos is still globally present). Below are just a few material-specific considerations.

Wood and masonry are commonly used for residences, which are rarely built taller than four floors. Wood is flammable and prone to creating shrapnel when explosives are used. In contrast, masonry buildings offer greater load-bearing capacity, fire resistance, and bullet resistance; but they commonly have thick walls that make for narrow hallways and short ceilings.

Tall buildings use reinforced concrete in: all foundations, many support columns, walls, and rooves. Reinforced concrete is very strong, and resistant to damage. Due to its hardness and reinforcing steel bars, it is difficult to breach.

Steel or metal is a major structural material in most framed buildings. A metal framework is very difficult to penetrate, but the material between the frames is much easier to penetrate. The material between frames is often reflective, which may cause false images, for laser-based devices.

Wall and roofing types influence what weapons to take, tactics to use, and how to breach. Surfaces are first characterized by whether they are solid, framed, or both. **Solid walls** are constructed by stacking materials like stones or bricks, or with cast and precast concrete. Most solid walls are sturdy and provide good cover. Heavy walls also require strong foundations, and can therefore provide excellent cover and concealment to armored fighting vehicles. (For example, factory floors are often made to support heavy machinery.) Many solid walls are also load-bearing, and 6 to 8 inches thick, with the thickness reducing at higher levels. Thick load-bearing walls make for small rooms. So explosives like concussion grenades create stronger, more dangerous concussive waves, but movement between rooms is fast.

Framing a building is a common (because its cheap), light, and less durable method. Most common modern, tall buildings use a skeleton support frame, made of vertical and horizontal members. The holes in the frame are then covered in non-structural cladding and roofing. Knowing the material strength and support locations in a framed building is vital. Regarding explosive entry for example, warehouse doors are reinforced, and the walls may have load-bearing beams, but the areas under the windows are neither reinforced nor load-bearing.

Various Structural Materials

Image 29: U.S. Marines of 9th Eng. Bn., 3rd Marine Log. Group. Camp Hansen, Okinawa, Japan, 17 Jun 2020.

Image 30: U.S. Navy Petty Officers work with steel. FOB Tarin Kowt, Uruzgan Afghanistan, 26 Oct 2011.

Image 31: The Center for Character and Leadership Development. Colorado Springs, CO, 11 Jul 2016.

Image 32: An Iraqi soldier looks inside a mud hut, during a visit to the village of Jambur. Kirkuk, Iraq, 28 Apr 2009.

Image 33: A new navigation lock at the Tennessee Valley Authority, 21 Jul 2020.

Image 34: A wooden house at the Urban Sniper Course. Hammelburg, Germany, 04 May 2015.

Different kinds of cladding may cover a frame. Light cladding, like wooden siding, is non-structural and is relatively easily penetrated. Heavy-cladding walls are made of layers of terracotta blocks, brick, or stone veneer, and the lower floors of a heavy-cladded building can be as thick as masonry walls. In some cases, lower floors of a building may use heavy cladding, while upper floors use light cladding. Tilt-up walls are a special heavy cladding, where large precast concrete slabs are tilted up to the frame; they perform more like a solid wall for the sake of a raid.

Knowing roof structure is vital for a rooftop breach. (See Vertical Layout and Floors, Pg. 164.) Roofing material is often masonry, hale, or other rock-like materials, so a sledgehammer and pry bar can usually breach a roof. Roof slopes vary greatly from flat, to steep, multi-slope rooves. Breaching a slanted roof is often difficult because of the danger of falling off. Of course, if there is a roof access door, consider using the door.

Knowing the floor plan helps Leaders know where Soldiers are, which is vital in coordinating elements. (See Coordinating Multiple Teams, Pg. 270.) Locally, floor plans trend by building function and material. Globally, floor plans vary a lot. That being said, some generalizations can be made. Framed wooden houses are often remodeled and have unpredictable floorplans; whereas masonry and concrete buildings have permanent structural walls and so normally have similar floor plans on each floor. Public, civic, commercial, and mixed-use buildings have unique floor plans, but these plans are often publicly available. Multistory reinforced concrete buildings usually contain a centralized hallway with rows of adjacent rooms and stairways on opposite ends of the building. (See Image 281, Pg. 273.) Auditoriums, gymnasiums, large commercial stores, and factories have large windows and open interiors.

5.d Battle and Flank Positions

Battle positions are locations that have both an open section where a Soldier can observe and fire from, and a closed section that provides cover, concealment, or both against incoming enemy fire.

Effective Soldiers always fire from a battle position. And if Soldiers are firing outside of a battle position, they must stop firing and find a battle position. Similarly, Soldiers must be in a battle position as they provide security and support to an Assaulting Element. The implication is that an effective Soldier must always be near a potential battle position at all times, and an effective raid plan places Soldiers in areas where battle positions are common. **Good battle positions include**: corners, windows, loopholes, and chimneys (See Image 36, Pg. 63.) because they:

- provide a wide, deep, and elevated sector-of-fire and line-of-sight to detect and attack enemies;
- allow for firing around the side and not above (shooting over a wall or roof silhouettes and exposes a Soldier's head); and,
- avoid bright backgrounds like light-colored buildings, interior lights, or the skyline, which all silhouette a Soldier. (A lace curtain or piece of cheesecloth in front will blend a Soldier with their background.)

Soldiers can further maximize the effectiveness and concealment of their battle position with positioning (See Image 35 et al, Pg. 63.) by:

- shooting left-handed when corners open left, and right-handed when corners open right (off-handed shooting requires bracing the weapon);
- hiding as far as possible behind the corner; and,
- kneeling or going prone to reduce signature. (Humans default to scanning for people at a standing height.)

Do not stand directly in front of a window! Raiders must hide in darkness by: moving deep into the room (to hide the Soldier and muzzle flash); kneeling; turning the lights off; using a dark background; or treating the window like any other corner and staying behind the window jamb. There is a tradeoff between more concealed firing from the rear, and firing near the front for a much larger sector-of-fire.

Soldiers must avoid setting patterns where enemies can predict their battle positions. To avoid establishing a pattern of firing from existing openings, a Soldier can find or create a loophole to observe and engage targets. Loopholes are simply destructive holes in walls, made by cutting or blowing. Unlike windows, loopholes can be very small, which makes them very difficult for an enemy to detect. To further confuse an enemy, multiple decoy loopholes can be put into a wall to distract from the active loophole. Combining machine guns, buildings corners, and loopholes makes for hard-to-detect automatic fires across a wide sector-of-fire—a deadly combination.

Also if possible, Support and Security take time to prepare their fighting positions. A prepared firing position allows a Soldier to engage the enemy while reducing their exposure to return fire. Preparing a fighting position is as simple and fast as placing bricks and sandbags in front of the position, and leaving small loopholes to shoot through. For windows, glass is removed from the window to prevent injury to the shooter, and replaced with wire mesh to prevent the enemy from throwing hand grenades.

Examples of prepared positions include: barricaded windows, fortified loopholes, sandbag bunkers, and darkened rooms. Even a roof can be prepared by placing bricks around a chimney to create a barricade. Then, a few of the chimney bricks or a bit of the roof can be knocked out to create a loophole.

Although Soldiers can hastily find and improve their own battle positions, **Leaders can make battle positions more effective by coordinating them,** and must do so if time permits. (See Sectors-of-Fire and Coordinated Fires, Pg. 177.) When properly emplaced, at least one battle position can fire onto any part of the area being secured; that is, there is 360-degree coverage.

Further coordination can make every barricade and loophole look the same so that the enemy cannot identify the important ones. For example, when barricading one window, Soldiers need to barricade every window. Barricading only one window tells the enemy that that window is the location of a Soldier. Similarly, when creating a new firing hole, create many holes.

5.e Urban Population Threats

Just as urban terrain provides Soldiers with many battle positions, the enemy also has innumerable places to hide. The job of a Soldier is to neutralize these threats and, to that end, making a more rigorous definition of "threat" is useful. **Threats can be known or unknown.** A known threat can be a military age male, a bomb, or even a child (a child can shoot a gun). However, the most common threat is the unknown threat where danger is unknown and unproven. Countless locations constitute unknown threats: an open door, a window, a hallway ahead of the clearing team, under beds, within closets, or between a swung open door and a wall, etc.[1] In fact, the primary difference between urban terrain and rural terrain is a matter of scale; urban terrain has way more unknown threats.

Therefore, Soldiers in urban terrain must "**look for work**," meaning they search for threats and neutralize them. When any threat is found (known or unknown), a Soldier first secures it by aiming their rifle at the threat like a

---

1 Quote: The enemy is invisible. Ambushes out of basements, wall remnants, hidden bunkers and factory ruins produce heavy casualties among our troops.
—German General Karl Strecker on the Battle for Stalingrad

Battle Positions

Image 35 et al: Soldiers of 11th Armored Cav. Reg defend their position against Assaulters of the 3rd Cav. Reg. Fort Irwin, CA, 13 Feb 2018. This is a clean, prepared practice space. **Actual war zones are filled with rubble everywhere.** Also note, that soft skin vehicles and wooden stairs provide concealment but not cover.

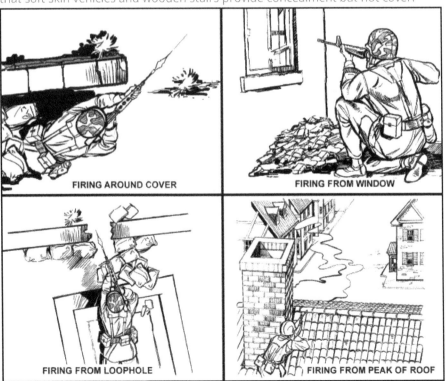

FIRING AROUND COVER

FIRING FROM WINDOW

FIRING FROM LOOPHOLE

FIRING FROM PEAK OF ROOF

Image 36: U.S. Army FM 3-21.71, Figure 6-10, 2002. Avoid going above barriers. On the roof, the Soldier avoids breaking the line of the roof by using the chimney.

Image 37: U.S. Marines 2nd Bn., 6th Marine Reg., 26th Marine Expeditionary Unit, conduct a mechanized patrol. Camp Lejeune, NC, 18 Aug 2017. Note a single shoulder-launched munition could appear from any of the dozens of windows.

pointer dog. After a Soldier has started securing a threat, the Soldier cannot simply drop security and not move, or else they become undefended against the threat they identified. **Continue to point the rifle at the threat!**

Known threats are neutralized by shooting or detaining them, but unknown threats are trickier. An unknown threat can be neutralized by gaining information. For example, the Soldier can enter the room (dangerous), or use an angled camera (resource intensive). Or the element can just leave the area.

The concept of neutralizing the unknown can be applied to the most dangerous part of a raid: known enemies in unknown locations. For example, a room with a staircase, two doors, and three windows already has six unknown areas that a cell of four Soldiers must pull security on. While the best solution is to have more Soldiers, the situation can be still made safer by neutralizing unknown threats. Security Soldiers on the outside of the building can secure windows from the outside in, neutralizing those unknown threats for the raiders inside leaving only three unknown threats: the two doors and the staircase. (See Enveloping and Preclearing, Pg. 159.)

To better coordinate coverage, Soldiers must fit into the patrol as a whole. For example, when walking, a Soldier may notice that the Soldier in front of them is pulling security on the first floor, while the Soldier to the rear is pulling rear security. To fill the gap, the Soldier pulls security on the upper floors. Using a system of self-assigned zone security (here: ground floor, upper floors, and rear security) allows threats to be systematically addressed; otherwise, Soldiers spontaneously changing zones would make coordination much more difficult. Even if an element receives enemy fire from one zone,

Image 38: Canadian Soldiers, with 3rd Bn., Princess Patricia's Canadian Light Inf. Reg. train MOUT. Pohakuloa TA, Hawaii, 25 Jul 2014. Note the two enemies hiding in the center, the four Soldiers in the back, **and the dozens of hiding positions.**

the other zones must still be secured or else the entire patrol could suffer from a flank attack. (See Fighting in L Shapes, Pg. 109.)

When traveling outside, there are almost always more threats than Soldiers, so **threat priority** becomes important. Without any prior knowledge, a Soldier is safe to assume that the overall biggest threat is an enemy with a gun. However, to better tailor priorities to a mission, threat priority is primarily based on the previous actual threats in the area. For example, during some periods in the Iraq and Afghanistan wars, IEDs caused 60% of hostile deaths in Iraq and only 25% in Afghanistan. So Patrol Leaders in each area might prioritize either security against a common IED or against suspicious men of military age. Threats change over time and must be updated, and information is key. (See Changing Enemy Tactics, Pg. 300.)

5.f Traps and Improvised Explosive Devices

Booby-traps are regulated by international law, which is irrelevant to the average man fighting for his life and his people. Booby-traps are found in every war, in every shape and size, for every purpose from maiming to killing, whether "illegal" or not. In the Iraq and Afghanistan wars, more than half of American fatalities (more than 3,500 in total) were caused by IEDs.

Defenders who make booby-traps typically exploit human nature to get attackers to trip the traps. A common tactic is to attract victims using bait. For example, trapping a flashlight is a classic tactic. First, the flashlight acts as bait, tempting the victim to pick it up. Second, a flashlight's shape can conceal items and naturally has a user-operated on/off switch. When the victim attempts to turn the flashlight on to see if it works, the resulting explosion blows their hand or arm off and possibly blinds them. Another bait could be a soda can sitting on a road. Soldiers may want to kick the can. However, the can (partially filled with sand to add weight) could rest on an M5 pressure-release firing device screwed into a buried M26 grenade. During the Vietnam War, motorcycles were rigged with explosives by the National Liberation Front and abandoned. U.S. Soldiers would attempt to ride the motorcycles and thus trigger the explosives. **DON'T PICK UP ANYTHING!**

Another way to exploit human nature is to trap obvious routes of travel; IEDs are especially common in urban warfare because Soldiers are more likely to use the obvious entrances or a predictable path. For example, enemies can attach a string between a door handle and a grenade, so opening the door pulls and explodes the grenade. Even more simply, Soldiers like to be close to walls because walls provide cover, whereas regular people walk in the middle of roads and hallways. So enemies have created targeted IEDs just by placing them along walls. **DON'T BE PREDICTABLE!** To avoid being trapped when entering buildings, breach a wall next to the door to avoid using the obvious doorway entrance. When traveling, walk where normal people walk.

Sometimes, the enemy provokes predictable reactions. In the Vietnam War, spiked holes were hidden in grassy areas behind cover, and in Iraq enemies put explosive booby-traps behind cover, like concrete barriers. When an enemy randomly fired, Soldiers instinctively sought the obvious cover, and were impaled by spikes or blown up by the explosives respectively.

In the face of all these dangers, the most effective anti-trap defense has always been the observant Soldier, who simply observes something out of the ordinary. As Soldiers become familiar with environments, they learn what looks weird. Key indicators of IEDs include: wires, cords, fuses, unusual smells, characteristics that are unusual for the area, locals avoiding an area, etc. Too many IEDs exist to cover in this manual; however, booby-trap designs tend to be **geographically isolated**. When one enemy Soldier designs one kind of trap, all nearby enemies tend to copy that design. It is important before a mission for all Soldiers to be made aware by an IED specialist of the kinds of traps and indicators found in the area. At the same time, there are standard questions that a Soldier who has been in the country should ask. Why is this busy street quiet now? Why does no one use this trail or that field?

Traps and Improvised Explosive Devices

Image 39: Members of an Afghan and coalition security force search for IED devices on a compound in Marjah district, Helmand, Afghanistan, 07 Jun 2011.

9-Line Unexploded Ordnance (UXO) Report Template

For confirmed Improvised Explosive Devices (IED's), call Higher Command using this 9-Line template for reporting Explosive Ordnance Disposal (EOD).

1. Date-Time Group:	Date and time of discovery.
2. Reporting Activity, Location:	Unit and the grid location.
3. Contact Method:	Radio frequency, call sign, etc.
4 Type of Ordnance:	Be detailed; include: size, shape, and physical condition.
5. Nuclear, Chemical, Biological:	Be as specific as possible.
6. Resources Threatened:	Equipment, facilities, etc.
7. Impact on Mission:	Brief description of the situation, and mission impact.
8. Protective Measures:	Measures taken to protect personnel and equipment.
9. Advised Threat Priority:	Immediate, indirect, minor, none.

In IED-prevalent areas, the patrol moves with IED specialists carrying wire detectors or military working dogs at the front of the movement formations. In World War II, one U.S. Soldier explained, "We had considerable success in detecting boobies by having one man precede us through the minefield holding a small stick lightly in his hand at an angle of 45 degrees with the end about 2 inches off the ground. Pressure of the trip wires against the stick warned him of eight booby-traps in one day."

That being said, it must be stated that **sometimes the IED wins**. For example, a hydraulic trigger relies on a small water bottle buried underground. The bottle is attached to a thin hose. Stepping on the bottle squeezes water through the hose, and the water pressure on the other side of the hose triggers a remote detonation. This trigger is non-metallic, non-spacious, durable, reliable, and made of cheap, common materials. There is no true counter to these IEDs. In the Afghanistan War, as enemy innovations imposed higher costs on the U.S., the IED's just got cheaper. The only tactical solution is to change and monitor routes so often that the enemy can't place enough in the first place. (See Choosing and Preparing a Route, Pg. 111.) And when the chance of IED casualties is unavoidable, Soldiers must be well dispersed so that if a booby-trap does explode, the number of casualties will be few.

The strategic solution is to talk to and befriend natives. Prisoners and civilians can be a good source of information on where and how booby-traps are employed. Plus, if they are employed to search their own buildings and neighborhoods, they are incentivized to not blow up themselves.

When a trap is found, Soldiers alert their Leader to the possible explosive and its location with a direction, distance, and description. The Leader, in turn, informs Higher to request Explosive Ordnance Disposal (EOD). (See 9-Line Unexploded Ordnance (UXO), Pg. 67.) As the Soldier observes their surrounding for other traps, they take note of the trap's physical characteristics, and the terrain features surrounding it to aid in future identification. If there is a casualty, **do not immediately run to a Soldier who was just blown up!** In fact, Soldiers cannot rush anywhere. IEDs often are placed in bunches, so they may be blown by a secondary IED. Once any Soldier detects a first trap, every Soldier systematically and methodically scans for possible secondary traps and moves away using 0/5/25/200-meter checks:

0-meter – possible pressure plates or wires on the ground before every step.

5-meter – anything out of place, like disturbed earth, or weird objects.

25-meter – larger disturbances, like large wet spots or disturbed structures.

200-meter – suspicious activity at a distance (like triggermen or Snipers).

Raiders are typically on a tight schedule and do not have the time to disarm UXO. However, if the UXO becomes an obstacle, the first step is to prevent injuries. The danger area is clearly marked at a height between the waist and head level to ensure visibility. Then if the IED must be removed, the Leader calls an EOD Team. If EOD teams are not available, the Leader receives instruction from Higher on how to proceed. An amateur should not be blowing up or dismantling booby-traps on a raid mission of their own accord.

5.g Night and Limited Visibility Operations[1]

People are less active at night, making it the perfect time for an attack. In the modern day, the Attacker's advantage is even larger due to the presence of technology that gives Attackers better vision at night than Defenders.[2] Barring a compelling reason, most raids should occur at night.

Nighttime and low visibility raids require special considerations. Compared to the daytime, Soldiers at night may move too close together, disorient easily, and slowly identify their targets. Therefore at night,

- ► everything is done at a slower pace;
- ► Leaders more frequently give instructions to and account for Soldiers;
- ► Leaders use rigid formations because it makes identification easier;
- ► Leaders brief Soldiers on clear and obvious geographic reference points (for example, distinct buildings, large boulevards, rivers, etc.);
- ► and most importantly, a patrol controls their lights and ambient lighting.

There are two broad categories of light control: addition and intensification. The most common form of **light addition** is when Soldiers attach a flashlight to the end of their firearm. Every Soldier should have one. White light from a flashlight is reliable, easy to use, fast, and allows full-color vision. Flashlights also can be used as a weapon to blind enemies at night by shining directly into their eyes. The main disadvantage of an active light source is that it can

---

1 Quote: If night raids and detentions are an unavoidable part of modern counterinsurgency warfare, then so is the resentment they breed. —War Correspondent Anand Gopal

2 Quote: Goddammit! This is a raid! I can't see! You can't see! So what? All that matters is can the fuckin' horse see! That's a raid!—Big Daddy in Django Unchained

highlight a Clearing Team's position both inside and outside of a building. However, this risk is mitigated in two ways: first by turning the light off when not in use; and second by only using the light indoors. For example, white light is appropriate to use when clearing a room for traps where high-visibility is necessary and controlled. (See Image 3, Pg. 18.)

To add brighter and safer lighting, the patrol can bring in tank-mounted and dismounted searchlights to shine on the objective. Searchlights (as well as pyrotechnics) can distract enemies and blind them and their equipment. Bright lights especially help to combat the big shadows that urban structures project.

Light reduction is also important. Muzzle flashes at night can instantly reveal a Soldier's position, and bright muzzle flashes can wash out a Soldier's night-vision. To combat this, Soldiers place suppressors on their weapons to reduce the brightness of the muzzle flashes (in addition to suppressing noise). Soldiers can also paint anything reflective, like carabiners.

More broadly, a patrol can control light by controlling electric power. In a building the patrol can target breaker boxes. And within a city, the patrol can request that higher units seek control of power stations, and thereby control background illumination. Shutting off the power to the street lights is much easier than shooting out the lights. (Although care must be taken to not disrupt critical infrastructure like hospitals.)

Light intensification devices interpret the light that is already present without adding more light to an area. They generally fall under two categories: image intensification (II) and thermal imaging (TI). An II device displays how bright an object is; e.g., a cold white rock will show brighter than a warm black cat. (See Image 43, Pg. 71.) A TI device displays how warm an object is; e.g., a cold white rock will show darker than a warm black cat. (See Image 42, Pg. 71.) Some modern devices combine both II and TI into one image.

II devices allow for the use of low-light markers like glint tape and chemlights. They shine brightly through II devices, and can be used to mark friendly units, casualties, cleared buildings and rooms, weapons positions, and individual Soldiers. (See Marking a Space, Pg. 268.)

II devices also read infrared light that is invisible to the human eye as visible light. Therefore, Soldiers can use infrared light emitters, like chemlights, patches, and lasers, to attack with daytime-level accuracy without alerting equipmentless enemies. However, because many modern enemies also have II devices, they too can now trace the infrared signal back to Soldiers.

Image 40: A nighttime U.S. Air Force KC-135 Stratotanker. Al Udeid Air Base, Qatar, 09 May 2021.

Image 41: A daytime Nebraska KC-135 Stratotanker. Pardubice Air Base, Czech Republic, 14 Sep 2020.

Image 42: A thermal image of a KC-135 Stratotanker aircraft. MacDill Air Force Base, FA, 27 Feb 2019.

Image 43: A intensified image of a 340th Expeditionary Air Refueling Sqn. KC-135 Stratotanker, 02 Sep 2017.

Another large weakness of II devices is that normal lights are disabling because the II devices intensify normal light into an unreadable, high-brightness whiteout. Thereby, enemy flares, illumination from indirect fires, and spotlights (visible light or infrared) can overwhelm II devices. Even when raiding technologically impaired enemies, burning wood can cause a whiteout. A less common problem is that II devices cannot be used in the absence of any light, like in a basement, because there is no light to intensify.

Thermal imaging devices only read infrared light generated by warm objects. They are thereby immune from being washed out by visible background light. (TI can be affected by fires, but not easily washed out.) TI especially make finding enemies easier because humans are warmer than their surroundings and so contrast sharply with the background.

However, TI is heavier, bulkier, more expensive and has less battery life than II devices. In practice, this means thermals are ideal for stationary Soldiers providing supporting fires at a distance. That being said, TI is also fooled by glass, dust clouds, and fog, since they will measure the temperature of those and not whatever is behind them. So good support has both II and TI. In close combat, TI is often given to the rear members in a stack due to their bulk. Wealthy units may use both II and TI and issue them to every Soldier.

6. Using a Rifle in Urban Terrain[1]

Urban terrain is defined by its cramped and close nature. This section details many techniques that make using a rifle more effective in that kind of terrain, whether in cramped streets or a cramped building.

6.a Targeting[2]

In urban combat where an enemy can be mere meters away, Soldiers must target vital areas that immediately incapacitate. Otherwise if an enemy remains functional, they can still move, return fire, and generally remain dangerous. Humans have three vital areas: the head, the torso, and the hips.

Shooting the brain is the only way to totally and immediately incapacitate an enemy. However, the head is a small target compared to the torso.

Shooting the larger heart and blood vessel area is easier and incapacitates via fainting by dropping blood pressure. Unlike shooting the head, however, dropping blood pressure may take several seconds to totally incapacitate, during which time the enemy can counterattack.

If the head and torso are protected, Soldiers must target the hip joint (pelvis armor is rare). Even though a broken pelvis does not kill, **a broken pelvis mechanically prohibits standing.**

Rooms may contain multiple enemies, and a Soldier must spend limited time and ammunition on each enemy. Therefore, the immediate goal is to incapacitate (not kill) each enemy as quickly as possible. A Soldier fires at least two rounds per enemy before moving to the next enemy.[3][4] To ensure a kill, Soldiers execute the failure drill: fire twice at the torso or pelvis, and then once at the head. If more than three rounds are require to incapacitate, then Soldiers shoot until incapacitation and must improve their aiming techniques.

---

1 Quote: Rules for a gunfight: 1) bring a gun; 2) preferably two guns; 3) bring all your friends who have guns. —Unknown

2 Quote: Precise marksmanship comes from the ability to afford time and money in bullets at the range. —Special Operations Forces Officer

3 Quote: Anything worth shooting is worth shooting twice. —Commander of Marine Corps Base Quantico Colonel Mike Lowe

4 Real World: This technique is variously called a "double-tap" or "controlled pair." The semantics of which technique is better and which name applies to each technique are up for debate and irrelevant.

Phase 1

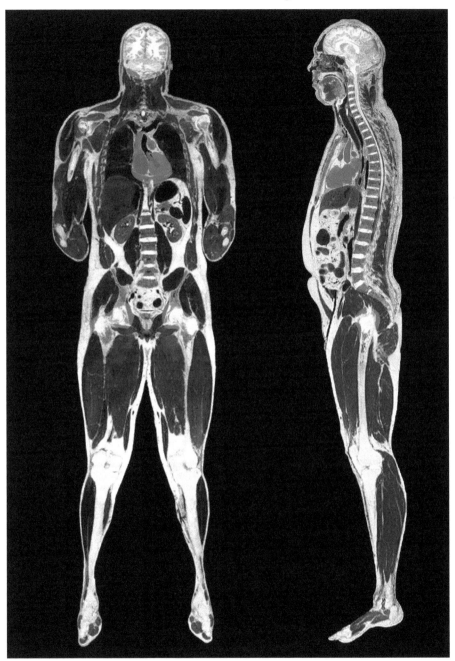

Image 44: Frontal and median adult male cross sections from the Visible Human Project 1994. Instant failure points are highlighted in blue. Namely, shooting the brain directly inhibits functioning; shooting the heart drops blood pressure, fainting the target; and shooting the femur and hips mechanically drops the target.

Holdover

A shooter aims on the **sight line.**

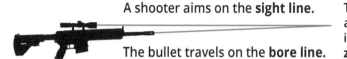

The bullet travels on the **bore line.**

The sight line and bore line intersect at the **zero point.**

On average, a sight is 4cm above a bore. And in front of the zero point, the sight line is above the bore line. Therefore, shots on near enemies must be aimed high (i.e. **holdover**) up to 4cm.

Image 45: Holdover is simple, but easy to forget. Forgetting about holdover is responsible for more hostage kills on paper targets than any other cause.

Before each round is fired, the Soldier acquires a sight picture for basic accuracy. After each round is fired, the Soldier acquires another sight picture to determine if they must fire again. (In sum: sight picture, fire, sight picture, fire, sight picture, move on.) If only one sight picture were used and it were bad, then that single sight picture would cause every shot to be bad.

Soldiers hotly debate whether accuracy beyond looking through a rifle sight is worth the effort, to which this book offers no resolution. Careful aiming has high diminishing returns in close-quarters battle (CQB) situations because engagements are close (within 15 meters) and fast (targets are exposed for only a few seconds). **Most CQB is won by whoever fires first.** (Soldiers must always fire until the enemy goes down!) So for example, controlling breathing for maximum accuracy may be unnecessary.

Specifically, there is debate on whether perfectly aligning sights to aim is worth the time because sight pictures in close-quarters are always vertically inaccurate anyway. That vertical inaccuracy comes from the vertical difference between the sight line and the bore line. The difference is called "**holdover**" because the point of aim must be held over the point of impact. (See Image 45, Pg. 74.) Holdover is difficult to calculate on the fly because it requires accurate knowledge of the distance to the target. (A worse problem is entirely forgetting holdover in the heat of battle.) Holdover is particularly relevent to CQB because each shot must incapacitate (i.e. brain, heart, or pelvis) and not just wound (i.e. whole body), so the target areas are smaller.

The U.S. Army advocates for fast firing before 15 meters, and accurate firing beyond 15 meters. (Once the first shots are fired, subsequent shots are carefully aimed.) To fast fire is to align only the front sight post with the target, turn the body to achieve a natural, hasty point of aim, and shoot. To carefully aim is to align the front sight post, rear sight aperture, and the target.

The criticism comes from people who believe that careful aiming must be used consistently to build muscle memory; and that there are too many special situations such as enemies with armor, that demand careful aiming before 15 meters anyway.

6.b Terminal Ballistics

Terminal ballistics is the study of projectiles during the time-frame when they impact and transfer energy. Close-quarters engagements by definition have Soldiers and material surfaces close to each other, which introduces two major terminal ballistic concerns: ricochets and bullet overpenetration.

Ricochets occur when a bullet reflects off of an impacted material. Reflection is when a material absorbs and then returns energy, like a trampoline. Importantly, only the energy perpendicular to the plane of impact can be absorbed or reflected. For example, when a slammed baseball hits the ground, the ground only absorbs vertical energy as the baseball continues to travel horizontally at a high speed.

Like the ground to a baseball or water to a skipping stone, typically ricocheting only returns a small portion of the perpendicular energy. Thereby when a bullet hits a wall, a small amount of perpendicular energy is reflected while all the parallel energy is retained. In layman's terms, a reflected bullet will travel along walls. When a bullet travels parallel to the wall after impact, it is called "**rabbiting**," and is common enough that Soldiers do not travel within a foot of a wall for risk of being hit by an enemy's rabbiting ricochet.

All materials deform and reflect to some extent. But against hard surfaces like metal and concrete, bullets ricochet more because the walls well-resist penetration and can interact with higher energy before fracturing. Hard surfaces also rebound faster from a deformed state, returning a higher portion of the absorbed energy to the bullet. In particular, this is why many gun ranges ban using steel-cased ammunition against steel targets and backstops.

To ricochet, neither the bullet nor the impacted material can fracture. Therefore to reduce the risk of ricochets, Soldiers can use frangible bullets that disintegrate into tiny particles on impact. Small particles are slowed more rapidly by air resistance, and are less likely to cause injury or damage to persons and objects distant from the point of impact. The downside of frangible bullet is that enemies can hide behind furniture, which the softer bullets will not penetrate.

Bullet overpenetration is also a problem in close-quarters. It occurs when a bullet goes through its intended target and still retains enough energy to be dangerous on the opposite, unseen side of the material. When many rounds are fired in the same area, overpenetration becomes more likely as initial impacts can weaken an area that a subsequent bullet can then penetrate.

Different ammunition has different penetration characteristics. The most common 5.56 rounds easily penetrate walls made of thin wood paneling, sheetrock, or plaster at any distance. The rounds may even penetrate wooden-framed buildings, single cinder-block walls, standard vehicle paneling, and common office furniture such as desks and chairs. But an 18 to 24-inch layer of books or an engine block will stop the bullet.

It is critical to know the ballistic characteristics of the ammunition and structural materials common to the area. (See Building Construction, Pg. 57.) When a patrol has identified that a structure can allow for ricochets or overpenetration, the primary mitigation is to separate cells in a building and floor as much as possible, potentially only having one cell operate per floor. A patrol can also leapfrog teams in a hallway using a strongwall technique so that all Soldiers will always fire away from each other. (See Coordinating Multiple Teams, Pg. 270.) Outside of a building, Support and Security must take cover from firefights occurring on the objective, even if enemies and Assaulters are inside buildings.

If building materials can be overpenetrated, other tactics also change. When enemies fire through walls to attack Soldiers stacked outside a room, Soldiers must use immediate entries. (See Immediate and Delayed Entry, Pg. 224.) And Soldiers can fire through walls before entry to clear rooms of enemies from the outside. (See Firing Through Walls, Pg. 222.) Materials prone to overpenetration are easily breached and so a team can make their own entrances through walls. (See Moving between Buildings, Pg. 105.)

Overpenetration is a concern not just for walls, but also floors and ceilings. During the Chechen wars, Russians would attack from both the ground floor and roof, while the Chechens held the middle floors. The Chechens would attack the ground floor unit through the ceiling and then move away. In response, the Russian ground floor units responded with uncontrolled fire through all of the ceilings, shooting Russian units still on the roof.

Bullet and Target Interaction

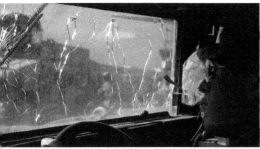

Image 47: Bullet impacts left in the windshield of a Humvee. Mosul, Iraq, 30 Apr 2007.

Image 48: A concrete wall with non-penetrating bullet holes. MCAGCC, Twentynine Palms, 11 Dec 2012.

Image 49: An M113 armored personnel carrier shot by aircraft. Bollen Range Complex, 06 Feb 2014.

Image 50: A wooden stand with bullet holes. Camp Bondsteel, Kosovo, 12 Dec 2017.

Impossible - Perfect Reflection or Perforation

Actual - Deformation and Deflection

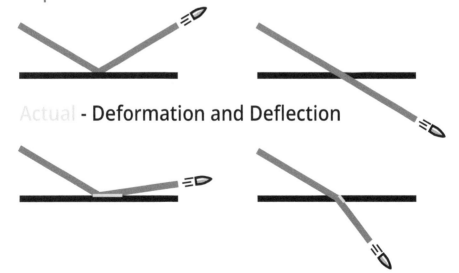

Image 46: Actual materials interact with bullets. Because materials are never perfectly smooth, consistent, or elastic, a bullet will change directions after impact. **The specific direction after impact is unpredictable**; the trajectories of post-interaction bullets form a cone pattern from the point of interaction. In the diagram, the blue is the plane of material interaction. Energy is absorbed perpendicular to the angle of the interaction. Therefore, a bullet deflected without penetration (right) stays close to the wall, and with penetration (left) it curves in.

6.c Handling a Rifle in Close-Quarters[1]

Handling a rifle properly takes a lot of practice. But first, why a rifle? Militaries use rifles and not pistols to conduct close-quarters battle for two reasons. First, military units often have to engage targets both inside buildings and outside buildings where targets can be much farther away. Second, pistols have a much sharper recoil, meaning that the first pistol shot will be accurate, but any following shots quickly lose accuracy. Thereby more bullets overall are required to incapacitate an enemy. That being said, pistols can be the superior close-quarters weapon system for interior clearing when the outside is completely secure and the smaller profile enables better maneuvering.

To properly use a firearm first requires a stable firing stance (i.e. a good body position). Feet are about shoulder-width apart and toes point towards the direction of movement. The firing-side foot is staggered to the rear of the non-firing-side foot. Knees are slightly bent and the upper body leans slightly forward. Shoulders are square and pulled back, not rolled over or slouched. The head is up and both eyes are open. (See Image 51, Pg. 79.)

There is also a proper way to hold the rifle itself. The butt of the weapon is firmly held against the shoulder. The firing-side elbow is held close against the body. (The firing-side elbow is kept in against the body to avoid hitting anything, and holding the elbow up and out is called "chicken winging.") The non-firing-hand grasps forward on the weapon and not on the magazine well. The trigger-finger stays just outside the trigger-well, and the thumb of the firing-hand stays on the selector lever. To engage a target from this position, a Soldier stabs the weapon forward and then bring the butt stock firmly against their shoulder. All bodies are different, so each Soldier adjusts to comfort.

In urban combat, a Soldier's rifle-handling technique not only maximizes killing ability, but also is a signaling system. To send distinct signals to each other, Soldiers hold their weapons in pre-determined positions, and nowhere else. **Below, three rifle positions, firing, ready, and carry, are detailed.**

---

[1] Real World. This manual required reviewing tens of thousands of military photos, and the most common question was, **why is their rifle pointed there?** Why is the rifle pointed down when entering a room? Why is every rifle pointed to the left and none to the right? The second question was, why did the Soldier stop out in the open? To be elite, a Soldier truly needs only to **master the basics.**

Image 51: A Soldier training Iraqi National Police demonstrates the correct firing stance for rifles. Rumaylah, Iraq, 07 Mar 2009.

Image 52: A Soldier of 10th Mountain Division, fires his M9 pistol in a proper pistol firing stance. Khair Kot Garrison, Paktika, Afghanistan, 02 Jun 2013.

Although a patrol may use choose to train any position before a mission, using an untrained position during a mission is incorrect.

The firing position is the horizontal position used to engage the enemy. The Soldier looks through their sights at the enemy (i.e., gets a sight picture), and imminently engages. After firing, the Soldier regains a sight picture on the target and either fires again, or moves their rifle to the ready position to look at the next target outside of their sights. (See Targeting, Pg. 72.)

A rarely used firing position is **single-armed firing**. Holding onto the grip with the firing hand, tuck the stock between the elbow and hip. This position is used for a single-man clear of a door or closet, or when directing a detainee at gunpoint. Firing using one arm is extremely inaccurate, and is reserved for enemies less than a few meters away. (See Image 57, Pg. 81.)

The ready position is employed when enemy contact is imminent and the Soldier is ready to fire. The rifle barrel is aligned with the target, so that putting a sight picture on the target only requires moving the rifle vertically

Rifle Positions

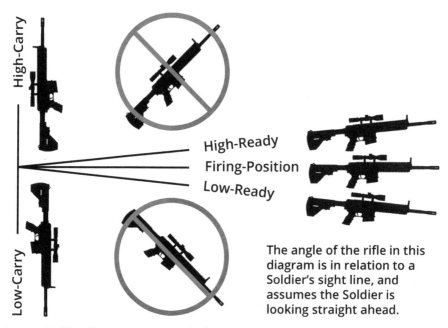

The angle of the rifle in this diagram is in relation to a Soldier's sight line, and assumes the Soldier is looking straight ahead.

Image 53: The three categories of rifle positions are the carry, ready, and firing positions. Holding a rifle in a carry position signals a lack of attack, whereas a ready or firing position signals danger and intent to attack. Therefore, holding a rifle between no-attack and attack positions at 45 degrees creates miscommunication.

up or vertically down. The modern version of the **low-ready position** is called "**depressed-muzzle**." (See Image 58, Pg. 81.) With a depressed-muzzle, the rifle is only low enough so that a Soldier sees above their optic (i.e., breaking the sight line). A depressed-muzzle balances minimizing movement to the firing position with maximizing a Soldier's ability to look around.

The depressed-muzzle is superior to the firing position for scanning an area because: looking through weapon sights causes tunnel vision; moving a rifle is slower than moving eyes; and Soldiers maintain momentum in their rifle as they scan, so when a threat does appear, shots tend to miss in the direction of rotation as the rifle continues to swing. The technical, biological reason for moving a rifle to an identified target, instead of searching with a rifle, is the "pointing quick fire phenomenon." When a person first looks at a target and then points a weapon at it, the body correctly and unconsciously aligns the weapon on the point of focus of the eyes without excess momentum.

Using a Rifle in Urban Terrain

Image 54: A U.S. Navy EOD technician reloads an M4 rifle **in their workspace at the high-carry position**. Moyock, North Carolina, 11 Jan 2018.

Image 55: The Soldiers on the left and right, from A Co., 1st Bn., 503rd Inf. Reg., 173rd (A) Bde., hold their rifles at the **high-ready position** and the **firing position** respectively. Skrunda, Latvia, 22 Jul 2020.

Image 56: A U.S. Marine holds a rifle at the **compressed-ready position**. Twentynine Palms, CA, 11 Dec 2020. All recoil is absorbed by the hands.

Image 57: A Paratrooper from 1st Bn., 325th (A) Inf. Reg., 2nd Bde., 82nd (A) Div. carries another team member. Both Soldiers use the **one-armed ready position**. Fort Bragg, NC, 24 Jun 2014.

Image 58: Paratroopers from 82nd (A) Div., stack on a door. Camp Arifjan, Kuwait, 12 Jan 2007. The first Soldier uses a **depressed-muzzle low-ready** position and the following Soldiers point down with a **low-carry position**.

Two other variations on the ready position are the high-ready and the compressed-weapon. **The high-ready position** is like the low-ready, but with a vertically elevated muzzle instead of a vertically depressed-muzzle. High-ready is used by a Number Two Man in a stack, when they must be so close to Number One Man that their muzzle goes over Number One Man's shoulder.

The compressed-weapon method (for ready or firing positions) is used to move through confined spaces more easily. To compress a weapon, a Soldier moves the buttstock off and over the shoulder, while maintaining the ability to look through the weapon sights. Care must be taken to not compress the weapon so much, that firing would recoil the optics into the Soldier's eye. All the recoil will be absorbed by the hands, so this technique is a last resort to aim a muzzle at targets in very narrow quarters. (See Image 56, Pg. 81.)

The carry positions have the barrel pointed almost straight up (high-carry) or down (low-carry). The butt of the rifle can either be in the shoulder, or tucked between the biceps and chest. A carry position is the safest and least effort position, and is recommended for use where firing is not expected, like in the middle of a hallway stack or inside a secured room.

Whether high-carry or low-carry is better is hotly contested. Some taller Soldiers say that shorter Soldiers using low-carry will point their muzzle at their head. However, other Soldiers say that objects fall better than they are lifted, and so a high-carry more easily transitions to a firing position. Most units let Team Leaders choose their preferred standard operating procedure.

Some texts recommend positions with rifles at 45-degree angles, either high or low. These positions have a few issues. First, if a Soldier is preparing to fire, they want the muzzle as close to the firing position as possible to reduce the amount of time it takes to get there. Second, pointing a rifle at 45 degrees in close-quarters can flag friendly Soldiers. Finally, pointing a rifle is a **silent signal to the group** that the Soldier senses danger. The greater the difference between carry and ready positions, the clearer that signal becomes.

A final, quasi-position is the **workspace postion**. This "position" is to keep the rifle in any orientation that allows a Soldier to continue to look forward as they reload. (See Image 54, Pg. 81.) A Soldier continues to look forward, and brings the weapon to their face and not the face to the weapon to maintain awareness of their surroundings.

Just as rifle handling signals fellow Soldiers, good handling does not signal the enemy. Soldiers avoid extending their muzzle past whatever corner they are pieing. (See Pieing and Clearing Corners, Pg. 85.) This is also called "flagging," and it allows an enemy around the corner to see or even grab the Soldier's muzzle without allowing the Soldier to see the enemy.

That being said, Israelis flag their weapons massively in comparison to Americans and claim it hasn't caused any real-world problems after decades of war. Sometimes extending a muzzle past a doorframe allows for a braced shot and better use of cover. And if an unseen enemy does attack, another Soldier on the team usually has a better angle to shoot from. If an enemy ever attempts to grab a rifle, then simply don't let go, pull back, and fire at them.

If a Soldier has a **weapon malfunction** in close-quarters, they immediately announce "gun down" and clear a path for other Soldiers to fight. If a malfunction occurs after a Soldier has committed to a doorway, they must still enter the room enough to allow following Soldiers to enter. **If an enemy is too close, a Soldier must physically tackle the enemy!** Break their nose! The Soldier's priority is to survive long enough for teammates to dominate the room. While the first Soldier is fixing their weapon, the next Soldier must advance to cover their sector. Once the weapon is fixed, they announce "gun up" and return to fight. Some texts recommend kneeling to fix a malfunction. This may aid in signaling and allow for faster maintenance; however, it obstructs movement. Further, Soldiers must wait to be directed to stand-up by the Team Leader to avoid being shot by other Soldiers; although Soldiers can continue to engage targets from the kneeling position.

6.d Shooting while Moving[1]

Moving while shooting is difficult and dangerous because shooting with the upper body and walking with the lower body is to simultaneously perform two actions. The technique is important to learn well because lives often depend on it being done correctly.

Soldiers begin with a correct firing stance. (See Handling a Rifle in Close-Quarters, Pg. 78.) Then movement is done at a walking speed to keep the rifle as level as possible, and shots are taken when both feet are on the ground to best mimic the stability of that stationary firing stance. The skills of moving toward and away from a target, and side-to-side in front of a target

---

To maintain a sight picture while both walking and experiencing recoil, it needs to be practiced extensively. An unpracticed shooter who misses is just a slow walker in the middle of a battlefield.

Image 59: U.S. Army Paratroopers from U.S. Army Dog Co., 1st Bn. (A), 503rd Inf. Reg., 173rd Infantry Bde. turn and shoot, and run stop shoot. Monte Romano TA, Italy, 17 Jan 2018.

Image 60: U.S. 7th Group Special Forces Soldiers conduct a live-fire mission. Twentynine Palms, CA, 20 Sep 2016. The casings are visible as the Soldiers fire during their assault.

Image 61: U.S. Army Paratroopers of B Co., 2nd Bn., 503rd Inf. Reg., 173rd (A) Bde. advance. Kilkis, Greece, 23 Nov 2019. **Turning toward the firing hand side is always awkward.**

Image 62: A Marine from Force Recon Plt., 31st MEU, shoots off-handedly from the left side. USS Germantown, Philippine Sea, 25 Feb 2021. **Note the crouched posture and short gait.**

are practiced as two separate drills because they require different skills. While moving toward or away from a target, the holdover (the vertical difference between the point of aim and the point of impact) will change. (See Image 45, Pg. 74.) While moving side to side, the torso twists. Moving sideways on the off-handed side is especially difficult. (See Image 61, Pg. 84.) To mitigate the difficulty, a Soldier can switch firing hands. (See Image 62, Pg. 84.)

Certain safety rules are required: 1) never point the weapon at friendlies, 2) have the safety on and fingers off the trigger, 3) do not move backwards while shooting, and 4) shoot greater than one meter off a Soldier's muzzle.

Some units teach Soldiers to situationally ignore some of these rules for faster engagement. For example, in some units, muzzle sweeping is allowed in "soft areas" like the legs with the safety on when an immediate threat is present. In some classes, the safety is always off in close environments or moving into rooms. Sometimes moving back a few steps while shooting is okay. And some people hold their finger on the trigger as they approach an entryway. (This is especially seen in slow, deliberate, delayed entries.) Safe shooting margins, like one meter off of a friendly Soldiers barrel and 15 degrees off of a Soldier are necessary and also entirely arbitrary.[1]

To some, relaxing the above safety rules may seem reckless. However, **sayings like "speed is safety" are commonplace.** A Leader must always weigh the benefit of safety against the danger of giving the enemy a tactical edge. When a Leader chooses their safety procedures, they must be few, redundant, and easy to approximate.

6.e Pieing and Clearing Corners

Another trademark of urban rifle handing is securing the ubiquitous corners that urban structures have. **A corner is the edge** between: a hard surface that covers and conceals, and open space. Doorways and windows have two vertical corners. Where two hallways meet, there is a corner. Because corners have a hard change from covered or concealed to not, an enemy behind a corner can quickly appear from behind the corner. The risk of sudden, close-quarters contact with an enemy demands systematic security on corners.

To pull security on a corner, and attack enemies as they appear, Soldiers "pie" corners. **Pieing is a technique that maximizes cover and concealment while allowing a Soldier to fire.** To pie, a Soldier identifies a corner (e.g., the corner of a building, a door frame, or a window), keeps their rifle at a depressed-muzzle, and searches for enemies in the opening. The Soldier searches and aims just past the corner to minimize the time between an enemy appearing, and acquiring a sight picture. As the Soldier moves sideways, more of the space on the opposite side of the corner is revealed until the entire open side of the corner is cleared. The technique is called "pieing" because a Soldier's rifle sector-of-fire resembles a slice of pie as they move in a semi-circle arc around the corner. (See Image 63, Pg. 86.)

Soldiers push their rifle muzzle in the direction of the pie so the muzzle is the first thing to present. Otherwise, if for example, a Soldier first presents their foot, an enemy can see and shoot that Soldier's foot without the Soldier being able to return fire. To first present the muzzle, a Soldier slightly leans in and slowly shuffles their feet side-to-side in small steps, gradually rotating

Train like you fight, because you'll fight like you train. If train by shooting paper in a shoot house, then who are you preparing to fight? How do real people act differently from paper?

Pieing and Clearing Corners

Pieing an Inside Corner	Pieing an Outside Corner	Pieing with Long Security

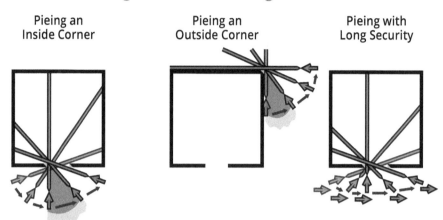

Image 63: A Soldier distances themself from the corner in order to make a larger arc and have more control over the rate of exposure (right and middle). A common mistake is to pie an opening. **Only pie corners** (highlighted in blue). When another Soldier is pulling long security (left), the pieing Soldier must move closer to the corner to make space. Note that Long Security stays behind the pieing Soldier, so that if an enemy shoots, the pieing Soldier's plates can protect both Soldiers. Both Soldiers must ensure that the first exposed thing is the pieing Soldier's muzzle.

around the corner. (See Image 206, Pg. 227.) Movement can become a little awkward because Soldiers must also face their body armor toward the corner.[1]

Soldiers must keep their rifles vertically aligned; in contrast with a cant, a sight picture that clears the edge could be paired with a bore line that fires into the wall. (See Image 64, Pg. 87.) (The rifle in this manual's cover photo is upright; the photo itself is rotated.)

When pieing, Soldiers keep their distance from the corner. Being farther away from the corner allows for more minute adjustments during the pie, thereby making the pie more precise. And also, when pieing a doorframe, distance prevents an enemy from grabbing the muzzle from the around the corner. However, sometimes there is not enough room. When one Soldier is pieing, if other Soldiers need to continue moving or pull long security, they

1 Quote: The pointman had seen a man [Osama] peeking out of the door on the right-side of the hallway about ten feet in front of him... Unlike in the movies, we didn't bound up the final few steps and rush into the room with guns blazing. We took our time...We waited at the threshold and peered inside. —Mark Owen, Team Leader on the mission which resulted in the death of Osama bin Laden.

Phase 1

Rifle Cant

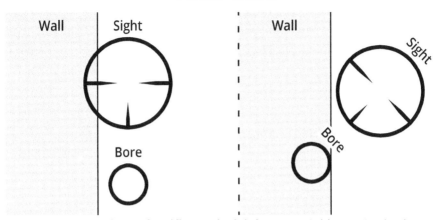

Image 64: **Always keep the rifle vertical** (left). Some Soldiers mistakenly rotate their rifle to clear their sight picture. If a rifle is canted (right), the sight can see a clear sight picture while the bore will shoot into the wall. Shoot house doorjambs are filled with pockmarks from rounds fired from canted rifles.

go behind the pieing Soldier so as to not obstruct the pieing Soldier's line-of-fire. (See Image 63, Pg. 86.) (See Synchronized Movement, Pg. 198.)

In areas with extreme danger, **the enemy may already be aiming** at a corner chest-high. (See Image 67, Pg. 88.) There, Soldiers can clear with a "prone pop." The Soldier goes prone near the corner with their weapon ready to engage. They crawl to the corner by raising their upper body onto their elbows, holding their rifle, and pushing forward with their lower body. The Soldier pushes until only their weapon and face are exposed, so they can observe and shoot from ground level. (See Image 66, Pg. 88.)

Pieing is not always the answer. Avoiding a threat altogether is safer. When passing a first floor window, a Soldier can duck below the window level on the near the side of the building. A basement window can be stepped over (basement windows are dangerous because they are commonly ignored).

Pieing is also very resource intensive when there are a lot of threats and few Soldiers. (See Urban Population Threats, Pg. 62.) In this case, individually addressing threats would slow movement down to a crawl. In a high Soldier-to-threat ratio environment (e.g., outside or in a hotel hallway), Soldiers switch from a **man-to-threat defense to a zone defense**. (See Single, Double, and V File Formations, Pg. 91.) Each Soldier in the movement is assigned to a particular zone during movement. For example, the first Soldier

Image 65: A U.S. Army Soldier from 1st Bn., 4th Inf. Reg. reveals a target as he pies. Lest, Slovakia, 08 Mar 2022.

Image 66: A U.S. Army Soldier pies on the ground to present an unexpected target. Belgium, 26 Jan 2021.

Image 67: A Canadian Soldier **moves slowly** as he prepares for a difficult pie. San Diego, CA, 21 Jun 2013.

Image 68: ANA Commandos, **pie with long security**. Behsud, Nangarhar, Afghanistan, 11 Apr 2013.

deals with threats directly ahead, while the second and third Soldiers are assigned to threats on the left and right-sides from the ground to the top floor.

Once a Soldier is done pieing, they immediately begin searching for and dominating new threats, resulting in a chain of: pieing and dominating, searching, pieing and dominating, searching, repeating.

7. Moving in Urban Terrain[1]

This section applies to all manmade structures, because manmade structures are multilayered and use straight edges and corners, whereas nature is shaped randomly. (See Frameworks for Attacking Vertical Terrain, Pg. 54.)

1. **Real World**: Mounted infiltration is not discussed because there are so many vehicles that generalizing is not useful. For example, the U.S. Army trains for vehicle infiltration by boat, plane (static-line and freefall), helicopter, car, truck, and diving.

Image 69: Marines patrol a street. Camp Lejeune, NC, 30 Sep 2015. The Marines pull security as they move; and they **stay near but not on the walls**. Leadership is in the center for command and control, but could also stay near the walls.

Dismounted Soldiers are vulnerable while moving in urban terrain because walking is slow, and urban areas have lots of people and hiding spots, making every building a potential enemy bunker. In fact, over half of casualties in urban terrain are sustained outside. Therefore, patrols follow general rules.

The first rule of movement is "**slow is smooth, and smooth is fast**." When danger presents itself, like an enemy firing, Soldiers commonly freeze or stutter. The first Soldier freezing is especially bad because they block all the following Soldiers from providing support.

Instead, Soldiers must quickly move behind cover and concealment, and then select their next covered position. While moving, they stay away from doorways and windows and move along the side of the street (not down the center) to avoid exposing themselves in open plazas and intersections. But while moving near walls (both inside and outside), Soldiers must stay 12 to 18 inches off the wall. Rubbing against walls may alert an enemy on the other side. And if the enemy engages, their ricocheting rounds often travel parallel to the wall. (See Terminal Ballistics, Pg. 75.) Finally, enemies may plant IEDs next to walls, because, normal building inhabitants never hug walls.

Complex movement, as with close-quarters battle, just starts with moving slower. Soldiers starting to learn must move slower than they are comfortable with. Adrenaline always speeds up movement faster than necessary, especially when a Soldier eagerly wants to charge into a doorway or room. (See Close-Quarters Battle Basics, Pg. 195.)

The second rule is **projection of force**. Enemies fear counterattack from Soldiers that appear strong. This is a delicate balance because civilians resent Soldiers who are unstable, disrespectful, or "evil." Fitness, equipment, and uniformity all project strength. But this is not a manual on appearance; rather this section acknowledges that perception of strength generates real safety.

Image 70: A New Zealand Army Soldier observes a simulated raid. Waiouru TA, New Zealand, 10 Sep 2018. The Soldiers are exposed and must **push to the buildings**. Urban movements prioritize cover, concealment, and speed over openness.

The third rule is to **maximize defense**; dismounted movement always emphasizes cover and concealment. Noise, light, and rank discipline are also important to avoid altering the enemy. That means that Soldiers: use minimal radio talk until contact is made (instead use hand and arm signals); avoid directional lighting, like light from a doorway of the skyline, to avoid silhouetting themselves; and avoid obvious displays of rank like saluting.[1]

During planning, routes are chosen with buildings and piles of rubble that cover and conceal troop movement. While moving, Soldiers move along walls, through buildings, or bring their own cover with armored vehicles. People on rooves can see people on the street, but not vice versa. **Always have the high ground (e.g. via air assets)!** (See Image 70, Pg. 90.)

When a patrol is attempting to avoid detection, it periodically stops, looks, listens, and smells (SLLS). This ensures that the enemy is not following the patrol or moving parallel on the unit's flank for an ambush. Rear security is especially important for SLLS. (See Rear Security, Pg. 97.)

Stops – all movement, in complete silence.

Looks – for enemy movement or anything out of place.

Listens – and attunes to the area. The absence of sound can be just as telling.

Smells – for the 5 F's (Food, Fuel, Fire, Feces, and Freshly turned-up soil).

When stopping, SLLS lasts for as long as the Leader deems necessary (typically a few minutes). More dangerous situations, like approaching the objective, need a longer SLLS. And although SLLS traditionally has demanded extreme silence in rural areas, extreme silence is often impossible in populated areas.

---

1. Real World: Stealthy movement protects Soldiers, but psychologically it can cast doubt on the legitimacy and competency of the fighting effort. Politically, secret night raids can anger the general populace and be strategically counterproductive.

Image 71: Marines with 2nd Bn. 5th Marine Reg. walk down a street during a patrol. Ramadi, Iraq, 18 Jun 2007. Note that the three Marines pictured are all looking and pulling security in **different directions**.

Once a Leader orders SLLS complete, any Soldier with suspicions only confirms with general questions. For example: "Did you smell anything?" instead of, "Did you smell smoke?" This avoids putting ideas in anyone's head. If something suspicious is detected, it must be investigated. If the patrol is okay with ignoring the result of a SLLS, it should not conduct SLLS.

And if a threat is discovered, the patrol must either move or engage the enemy. Moving is preferred because any resources used in fighting that enemy are resources that cannot be used on the mission objective. A patrol can always return later to engage discovered enemies on a followup mission.

7.a Single, Double, and V File Formations[1]

When moving together, Soldiers travel in organized formations to maximize command and control and allocate firepower. Within an urban area, single and double file are the most common formations. While the file is more vulnerable to enemy front-facing machine guns (they can fire straight through an entire file), the most common threats in a city are IEDs and open windows. A file is great for avoiding IEDs since after the first Soldier checks for IEDs, every Soldier following in a file can remain safe by stepping in the first Soldier's footprints. (See Front Security and Navigation, Pg. 95.)

The **single file** keeps teams grouped within the file. The most casualty-producing weapons of each element stay in the center of that element. This

1 Quote: Whatever comes out of these gates, we've got a better chance of survival if we work together. Do you understand? If we stay together, we survive. —Aelius Maximus Decimus Meridius, Fictional Roman General from the Movie Gladiator

Basic Movement Formations

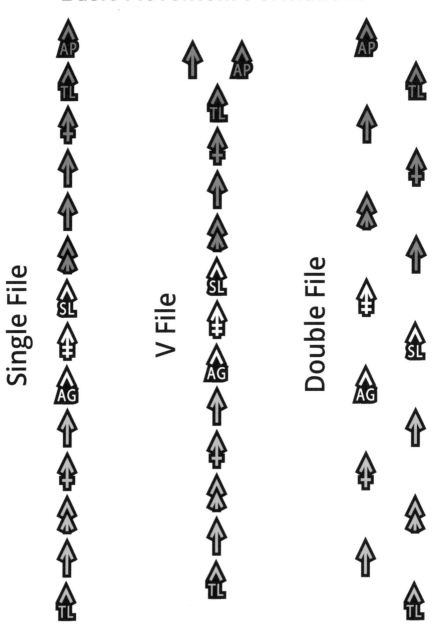

Image 72: The three most common urban movement formations are all some form of file. Files allow minesweepers to clear a path, and allow Soldiers to quickly seek cover on either side of an urban street.

Image 73: A U.S. Marine with 4th Sqd., 3rd Plt., D Co., 1st Bn., 7th Marine Reg. **leads a file with a minesweeper**. FOB Tabac, Sangin, Helmand, Afghanistan, 29 May 2012.

Image 74: Two Marines from 2nd Plt., A Co., 9th Engineer Support Bn., 2nd Marine Logistics Group, use metal detectors in a **V file**. Route Red, Shir Ghazay, Afghanistan, 01 Jan 2012.

Image 75: A Squad Leader from 1st Plt., B Co., 1st Bn., 6th Marine Reg., 24th Marine Expeditionary Unit, NATO International Security Assistance Force leads a patrol through a city in Helmand province, Afghanistan. Helmand, Afghanistan, 30 Jun 2008. The Soldiers travel in a **double file** over fresh vehicle tracks. **Walking on tracks ensures that any potential pressure-detonated explosive devices would have already been detonated.**

includes machine guns and shoulder-launched munitions. If contact is likely, then the most casualty-producing weapons move to the most likely point of enemy contact in the formation. Still, Leaders must avoid gathering every weapon in one area to maintain the patrol's defense against a second attack from another direction! (See Reserve Element, Pg. 24.)

Soldiers in a single file travel near buildings for quick cover. These Soldiers must still pull security on windows and balconies above them; but looking straight up for extended periods is difficult. Therefore, the single file is the least preferred urban formation. The single file is normally used when speed is desired, contact with the enemy is unlikely, only one side of a route has cover, passages are too narrow, or passages are so wide that splitting the patrol impacts command and control (these passages should be avoided).

The **double file** (A.K.A. the modified-wedge) comprises two files traveling on either side of a road.[1] (See Image 75, Pg. 93.) This formation allows each file the best vantage point to pull security on open windows on the opposite side of the road (i.e., Soldiers on the left side of the road scan the right side), and also for the quickest retreat into a building on the same side. (See Image 71, Pg. 91.) It is the ideal formation for urban travel with structures on both sides of a route. Headquarters (e.g., Leaders, RTO's, and Gun Teams) integrates into an element under their control on only one side of the road in order to mantain their integrity and reduce their signature.

A **V file** has two or three Pointmen and minesweepers on a line at the front of all files in the formation. Although a simple change, this formation is used to defeat the potential IED threat, where bomb detectors must create a wide path at the front of the formation. (See Image 74, Pg. 93.)

For all file types, Leaders designate sectors for Soldiers to scan. Generally, the front scans ahead, the rear scans behind, and the middle of the scans the buildings on either side of the road for threats at every vertical level. Alternating Soldiers in the middle are assigned the upper and lower levels. Specifically, buildings can conceal enemy fighters, including in doors, in windows, and on roofs. All sectors need to overlap to create full 360-degree, top-to-bottom coverage. (See Sectors-of-Fire and Coordinated Fires, Pg. 177.)

---

[1] Real World: In U.S. Army terms, a platoon-staggered-line two-squad-file would have each of the two squads in a single file next to each other. A platoon-file two-squad-modified-wedge would have the front half of two files be one squad, and the back half be the other. For brevity, all formations with two files are "double file."

To maintain control during movement, the Leaders can freely move anywhere within the formation as long as they stay close to their unit (e.g. Team Leaders remain close to their team). The Team or Squad Leader of the Front Element is a little different. They must always remain with their element because the front is the most likely to make enemy contact.

Combined-arms formations generally move vehicles in a single file convoy, with dismounted troops surrounding them. But the Armored Vehicle Leader is the subject matter expert and must be consulted on whether for example, the troops ride tanks, ride motorcycles, or walk.[1]

To some extent, **the idea of formations is being reconsidered.** Rigid formations have always been necessary to control and organize troops, but formations are time intensive to maintain and stifle movement. Nowadays, controlling troops via cell towers and trackers instead can lead to more responsive and effective combat. At the battle of Nablus in 2002, Israeli paratroopers did not clear the city block by block. The blocks were incidental to their final raid objectives. Instead, the Soldiers moved through buildings and houses, smashing mouseholes through interior walls. (See Image 91, Pg. 107.) And low-level Leaders communicated with the others without necessarily going through central command.

7.b Front Security and Navigation

The front of a patrol is in the most danger because it usually takes first contact with the enemy. The front of the patrol also leads and so navigates. Therefore, the front is filled with positions that specialize in danger response and navigation, including Minesweepers, Pointmen, and Navigators.

Minesweepers must be the first Soldiers in a movement; otherwise, a Soldier in front of them may set off a mine. Minesweepers use mine detectors in the form of dogs, wands, or robots that scan for telltale chemicals, wires, or for depressions that may hide pressure detonators. (See Image 76,

---

1 Quote: We knocked open every door, knocked down every wall, and if the road stopped in front of us, we just made a new one, driving our tanks right over sheds and making new paths through concrete buildings. There was no place for anyone to hide, the enemy thought we would use the roads and he would be able to hide among the small buildings. Again, the shock effect of seeing a M1A1 tank driving through your hiding place sent fear streaming through those who stayed to fight.
—Soldier from Avenger Company, 2nd Battalion, 63rd Armored Regiment

Image 76: Ace, an improvised explosive device detection dog, sniffs out a possible IED in front of his Handler and Pointman with E Co., 1st Light Armored Recon Bn. Helmand, Afghanistan, 27 Apr 2012. Ace and his Handler located 16 IEDs.

Pg. 96.) Military working dogs are effective at detecting chemical charges, but less effective at detecting trigger mechanisms that smell the same as the surrounding area. A wand is a handheld device that detects wires or other small devices. Wands must be carried by Soldiers, so they are more dangerous but more portable than a dedicated mine-detecting robot. Humans deploying a mine-detecting robot can use riskier detection methods, like purposefully approaching or even triggering mines. For example in Afghanistan, U.S. forces used a DOK-ING dozer, a Croatian-made minesweeper equipped with rapidly spinning chains that flail and churn to dig up or detonate buried bombs.

Minesweepers continuously clear a path. To be thorough, they are relatively slow and must mark their cleared path with chalk, chemlights, or just their own footprints. Soldiers following in a file must strictly stay within the marked path and yank back anyone who strays.

All movement formations have a **Pointman** very front of a formation. If there is a minesweeper, the Pointman becomes the second-Soldier in a formation. Pointmen are responsible for long, forward security and for pieing windows and doorways. They are also bait for attracting enemy attacks since the patrol can more effectively respond to an attack at the front or back of a formation, rather than the center where leadership is located. Pointmen cannot walk in front of minesweepers, but they must closely follow to protect them from the enemy. If there are multiple Soldiers at the point, they are all Pointmen. If there are multiple files, the Pointmen for each file walk side-by-side for mutual support. Pointmen are not responsible for navigation because they are so occupied with security.

Image 77 et al: A Soldier with C Co., 1st Bn. , 26th Inf. Reg., 1st Inf. Div. provides rear security during a dismounted patrol. Adhamiya, Iraq, 06 Apr 2007.

The Soldier immediately behind each Pointman is a **Coverman**. They are responsible for providing guidance to their respective Pointmen from the Leader of the unit. While Pointmen pull long, forward security, Covermen enhance forward security by securing the 45-degree inside angle.

Sectors-of-fire in a file are fluid. When the Pointman is pieing an opening for enemies, the Coverman covers down by pulling long, forward security. And the next Soldier in the file automatically shifts their sector-of-fire to the 45-degree inside angle. If both the Pointman and the Coverman are pieing an opening, the next Soldier pulls security to the direct front, and so on.

Navigators ensure the patrol correctly follows the preplanned route. If the patrol is using modern GPS smartphones, then a single Leader can be responsible for navigation. Although the patrol must have redundant backups; modern technology often gives a false sense of confidence, and patrols have gotten lost by dumping all navigation responsibility on one Soldier.

Maps and compasses make navigation significantly more complicated. The front of the patrol must have primary and alternate Pacemen and Compassmen to ensure the patrol is moving the correct distance on the correct azimuth. Map checks go from optional to mandatory as a slight deviation in distance or azimuth can magnify over long distances.

7.c Rear Security[1]

A common theme for all tactics is maintaining 360-degree security at all times. This includes foot movement. Soldiers in the rear often zone out because most enemies attack the front. However, a smart enemy knows this and attacks the

---

1   Quote: On patrol, always assume that you are being watched and that if being watched, you are probably being followed. —Center for Army Lessons Learned

Image 78: U.S. Marines of K Co., 3rd Bn., 1st Marine Reg., 15th Marine Expeditionary Unit, go house to house in a diamond formation. Kuwait, 28 Aug 2015.

rear. Therefore, rear Soldiers must constantly scan behind. A good tactic is to incorporate a pace count: for example, looking back every ten steps.

Indoors, the last man in a formation looks backward, pulling rear security, so the second to last man warns the rear-facing last man of a team movement by saying "last man." (If a team trains together long enough, the last man will have a sense of timing of when to move, and will no longer have to be told.)

If a Soldier believes the patrol is being followed, the Patrol Leader can order a preplanned Drop-Back Team, to go prone and cover the rear. The patrol continues on for a few hundred meters and prepares for enemy contact. The Drop-Back Team conducts SLLS for 10-15 minutes and then rejoins the Main Body. This tactic can be repeated two or three times on a normal patrol. And in dangerous areas, two Rear Soldiers can bound backwards to always have a stationary Soldier secure the rear.

7.d Wedge and Diamond Formations

A wedge formation has one Soldier at the point, with two lines of Soldiers on either side of them at a descending angle. A diamond formation has Soldiers form a diamond shape with four points. On the team level, wedges and diamonds can be useful when assaulting buildings, to provide the maximum forward facing firepower. Soldiers move 3 to 10 meters apart. The rear Soldier in a diamond formation can fire forward at an elevated angle against tall buildings. If a Soldier has a special weapon, such as a machine gun or shoulder-launched munition, the Team Leader assigns that Soldier a target and the position to best attack that target. In urban combat, wedges and diamonds are rarely used above the team level because straight walls and minesweepers provide better safety to straight formations.

Basic Bounding

Image 79: Soldiers with A Co., 3rd Bn., 172nd Inf. Reg., 86th Inf. Bde. Vermont Army N.G. bound during live-fire training. Ethan Allen Range, Jericho, VT, 16 Jul 2020.

Successive Bounding
The trail element and HQ get on line.
Then the lead element advances.

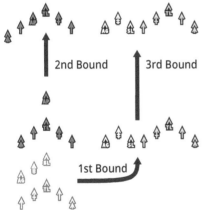

Alternating Bounding
Teams bound past each other.
HQ always bounds to the trail element.

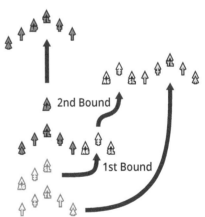

Image 80: This diagram has teams bounding in a wedge formation because contact is expected from the front. Although the Team Leader is on line in this diagram, a Team Leader staying behind Soldiers is also acceptable.

7.e Bounding and Crossing Intersections

To bound is to move and stop and move again. When multiple units bound together, the element can make forward progress by moving one element at a time, while always having at least one element stationary at all times. (See

Spikeball Bounding

Image 81: Soldiers with E Co., 20th Special Forces Group, Mississippi Army N.G. form a spikeball. Fort Richardson, Alaska, 16 Jul 2019.

Image 82: Soldiers from 2-15 Headquarters and Headquarters Service secure a corner of a building with a spikeball. Kuwait, 24 Jun 2004.

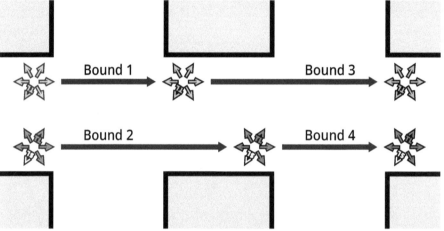

Image 83: The first bounding element covers from the far side of the road while the second bounding element covers from the near side. This is the most simple form of bounding, when surrounding danger is low and training time is short.

Image 80, Pg. 99.) A Stationary Element can provide much more effective fires than any Maneuver Element. (See Shooting while Moving, Pg. 83.) And so while bounding is slower than normal movement, it is much safer. Therefore, a patrol will bound in areas of heightened danger, like open areas.

Bounding in an urban environment can be executed in a variety of ways depending on the unit size, unit training level, and enemy threat. One way is the alternating **spikeball**. (See Image 83, Pg. 100.) It is the simplest method of bounding, and is appropriate for a large unit with low training under low threat. The patrol is split into two halves. The stationary rear half pulls security by making an impromptu spikeball, where each Soldier faces in different directions vertically and rotationally. (Their rifles are the "spikes.")

(See Image 81, Pg. 100.) To pull security in the spikeball, each Soldier in the stack looks to the Soldiers around them, assesses danger areas that are not covered, and then covers one of them. Soldiers must overlap their sectors.

The forward, maneuvering spikeball selects a forward position and a route to that position which offers the best cover and concealment. The forward element then moves to the forward position, while the rear stationary spikeball provides security and support. When the rear spikeball can no longer pull security on areas that are blocked by the forward spikeball, the forward spikeball stops and announces "set." Then the rear spikeball announces "moving," and maneuvers forward to become the new forward spikeball. The bounding cycle continues until the patrol is clear of danger.

Pass-through bounding is safer than spikeball bounding because the Stationary Element can maintain better sectors-of-fire, but it requires more time and coordination. To do pass-through bounding, the Stationary Element splits into a left half and right half, which respectively pull security on the left and right-side of the patrol's avenue of travel. Then, the Maneuver Element(s) pass through the middle of the Stationary Element. (See Image 84, Pg. 102.) Once the Maneuver Element reaches the far-side of the intersection, it sets, becomes the new Stationary Element, and covers the movement of the Rear Element (the new Maneuver Element) through the intersection.

If a patrol has three elements and conducts pass-through bounding, the Rear Element will pass through both the Lead Element and Middle Element, to permanently become the new Lead Element. Three elements moving along a city street rotate positions and assume appropriate responsibilities. This rotation is convenient because it distributes security responsibility throughout the patrol. Pulling security can quickly become tiring during urban operations.

Units with more training or fewer Soldiers can pull security more efficiently than a spikeball or pass-through formation by individually assigning responsibility to Soldiers to secure the direct front, the flank, the rear, the building on the far-side of the intersection, or even the intersection itself. (See Pieing and Clearing Corners, Pg. 85.) Extra secure bounding and individualized **double file pieing movement** exist on a spectrum because urban terrain exists on a spectrum. However, coordination is paramount when each Soldier needs to focus on areas as small as a specific window or floor.

Intersections are a special kind of open danger area where multiple paths cross. Intersections are easy locations to efficiently establish control over

Phase 1

Pass-Through Bounding

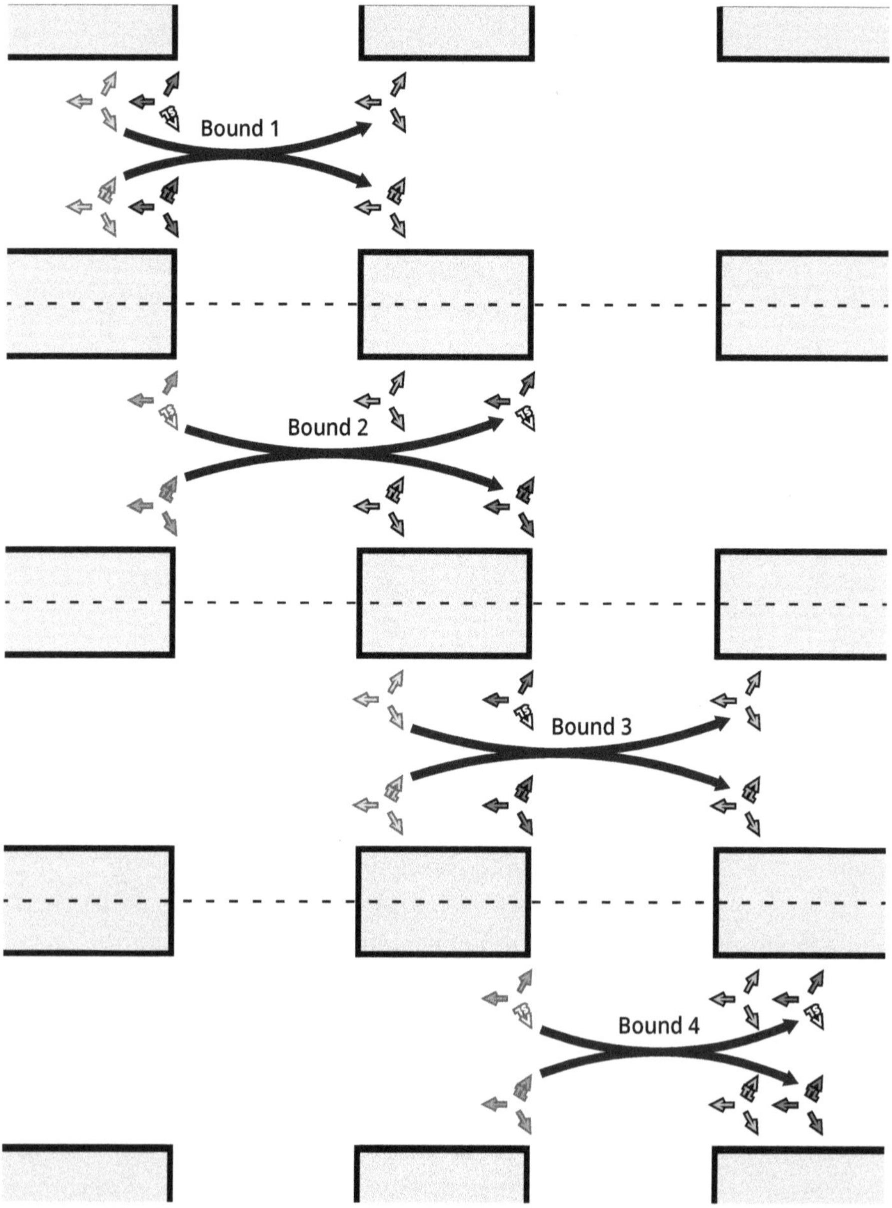

Image 84: At intersections, Bravo and Alpha Team split to the left and right so the other team can pass through their center. In pass-through bounding, the Moving Element never blocks the Stationary Element's lines-of-fire to either side.

Plugging Holes during Urban Movement

Image 85: U.S. Marines with C. Co., Bn. Landing Team 1/4, 15th Marine Expeditionary Unit run down a street for a quick reaction force training event. Al Hamra Military Airfield, United Arab Emirates, 12 Mar 2021. Soldiers plug holes on the sides of the avenue as the remaining Soldiers pass through the center.

Image 86: Norwegian soldiers of the Telemark Battalion, assess the easiest way to climb into a window. Al Asad Air Base, Iraq, 13 Jun 2020. **Security must be pulled on windows.** If a patrol deems intersections to be dangerous as they pass them, then windows are dangerous too.

Dedicated Security Element

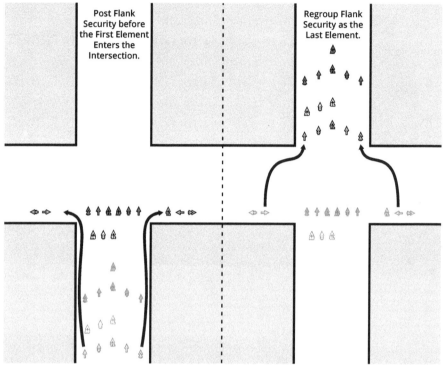

Image 87: In urban areas, posting Security far away to give early warning splits the patrol, alerts the enemy, and encourages an attack. However, a closeby stationary Security position can still provide better fires than a Maneuvering Element.

multiple routes, and so all parties want to control intersections. This likely enemy presence makes intersections some of the most dangerous areas for a patrol to be. Because they are so important, the patrol plans for intersections before the mission with satellite imagery and on-the-ground reconnaissance.

During the mission, the Pointman identifies an intersection and notifies the Patrol Leader. To cross the intersection, the patrol uses clearing corner techniques and bounding. (See Pieing and Clearing Corners, Pg. 85.) (See Bounding and Crossing Intersections, Pg. 99.) Notably, crossing an urban intersection is not at all like clearing a linear danger area in a rural area. Linear danger areas hardly exist in urban environments, almost by definition; instead, there are many **open danger areas**.

However, urban areas are littered with intersections, so a patrol cannot stop for every one. And if a patrol were to stop, intersections inherently offer the enemy many lanes of fire onto the patrol. Properly securing an intersection could be a mission unto itself. Therefore, crossing urban intersections are fluid to semi-fluid movements.

7.f Moving between Buildings

Moving on the ground is dangerous, and in openly hostile areas patrols don't cross intersections in the first place. Open areas, such as wide streets, intersections, and parks are natural killzones for enemy attackers. Instead, the patrol travels on rooves or crosses directly through walls by using explosive and mechanical force. (See Outside Barrier and Compound Breach, Pg. 180.) Artificial man-sized entries are called "**mouseholes**." (See Image 91, Pg. 107.) Bulldozers may also be used to pierce or entirely destroy buildings to provide alternate routes of advance. When a route is made through buildings, the buildings are numbered in planning to facilitate command and control.

By moving through buildings, the patrol only has to cross side-streets. During the daytime, Soldiers can use smoke grenades on either side of the side-street to **obscure themselves as they cross**. In moving to an adjacent building, Soldier keep a distance of 3 to 5 meters between themselves to limit the damage of an area-of-effect weapon. They move quickly and stay close to cover where possible. When moving from position to position, each Soldier must not mask other Soldiers' supporting fires.[1]

Doorways are avoided when entering and exiting since they are the most likely target of enemy fires. If a Soldier must use a doorway, the Soldier weighs the danger of quickly entering into a prepared defense, against the danger of staying outside. If staying outside is more dangerous, then Soldiers enter via an immediate entry. Or, if the inside is more dangerous, Soldiers enter via a delayed entry. (See Immediate and Delayed Entry, Pg. 224.)

---

1 Quote: Beginning on the eastern outskirts the [eight-inch] gun would plow a round into the side of the built up block of buildings at about ground level.... Then several more shells were fired through the first hole. Thus a tunnel would be rapidly made all the way to the next cross street. Soldiers could then rush the newly formed entrance, clear the upper floors with hand grenades and rifles and then move on to the next building to repeat the process. When a block or square, was thus completely cleared of Germans Soldiers, Skulkers, or even Snipers, the next square was treated in the same way, working forward square by square, right and left, thereby avoiding nearly all exposure in the streets. —26th Infantry Regiment Soldier in 1944

Moving Between Buildings

Image 88: Marines with 1st Bn., 5th Marine Reg. move between buildings. Camp Pendleton, CA, 17 Dec 2014. **Moving between buildings is very vulnerable.** Note how many open windows the enemy could fire from.

Image 89: Italian SOF, U.S.A.F. Special Tactics Soldiers, and Jordanian Armed Forces assault a compound. Amman, Jordan, 11 May 2017. **Movement between buildings must be fast!**

Image 90: U.S. Marines with 2nd Bn., 4th Marine Reg., 1st Marine Div. move between buildings. Camp Pendleton, CA, 22 Apr 2019. **An unseen enemy will shoot you through a tiny hole at any time!**

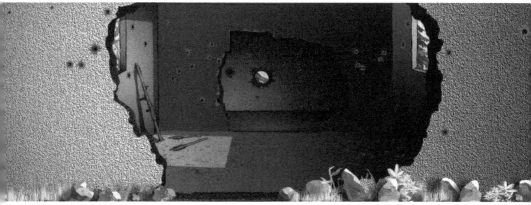

Image 91: Modification of urban infrastructure to permit ground mobility. A series of **mouseholes** can be made to create a path where hallway movement techniques may be more appropriate. (See Hallways, Pg. 244.)

Image 92: Georgian Soldiers enter a building through a mousehole. Vaziani TA, 11 Aug 2018. **The wall under windows is always non-structural.**

Image 93: Marines enter a mousehole. Camp Pendleton, CA, 17 Dec 2014. The hole could have been made by man-carried explosives, a tank, etc.

7.g Vehicle Attachment

Combined arms patrols have always been extremely effective in urban combat. (See Armored Fighting Vehicles, Pg. 33.) Combined-arms patrols have armored vehicles that provide rolling cover and concealment to dismounted Soldiers. How vehicles travel with infantry depends on the avenue of movement. If possible, vehicles travel side-by-side for mutual support. But often avenues are too narrow, and mounted or dismounted troops must provide support on both sides of a vehicle.

In general, ahead of the vehicles, infantry clear the buildings on each side to eliminate the threat of shoulder-mounter munitions to the vehicles. (See Image 74, Pg. 93.) Then the vehicular order of movement leads with the

Fighting in L Shapes

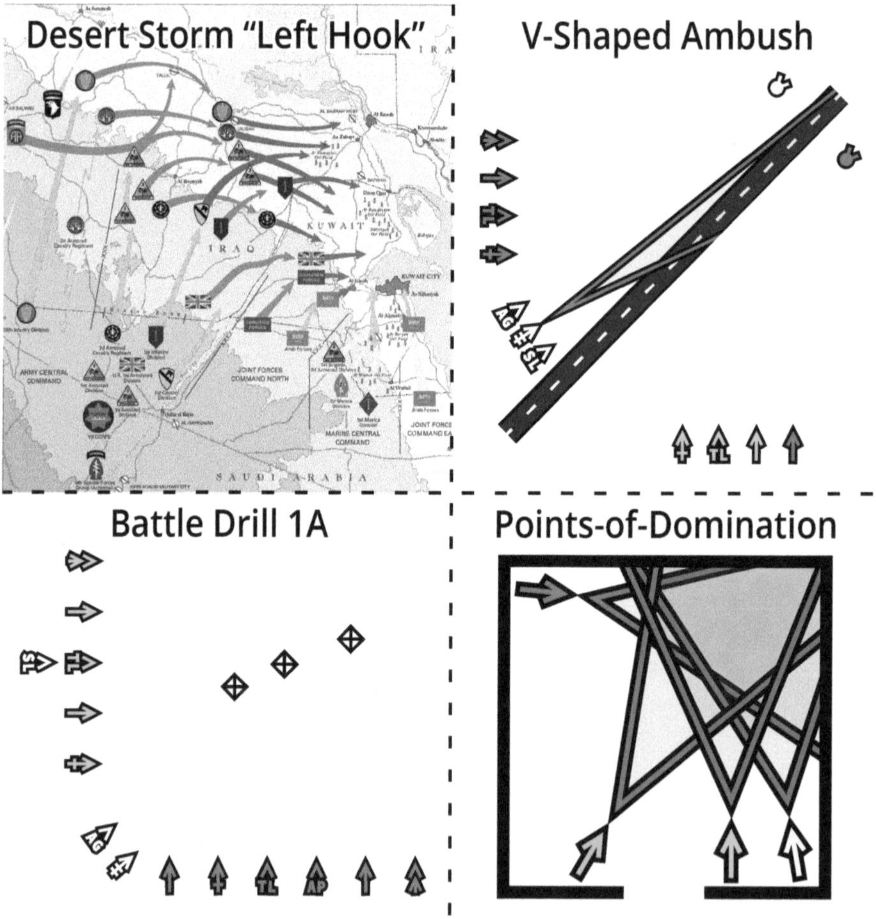

Desert Storm "Left Hook"

V-Shaped Ambush

Battle Drill 1A

Points-of-Domination

Image 94: The L (or V) shape is a vital attack formation at all levels of combat.

heaviest vehicle. Thereby if the patrol encounters enemy vehicles or positions that infantry can't defeat, the order switches and the heaviest vehicles lead.

In lightly defended areas, a mechanized platoon may proceed along the street, but send dismounted infantry forward to reconnoiter danger areas and key terrain (bridges, intersections or structural chokepoints). When needed, tanks move up to places secured by the infantry to hit suitable targets. When an area is cleared, the infantry again moves to clear the next area.

In a dangerous area (e.g., the center of a built-up area), Soldiers must dismount to allow for quick vehicle fires, and dispersion of friendly units to reduce casualties from area weapons. Still, before firing, Vehicle Leaders must have the awareness to check their surroundings to not fire on friendly Soldiers.

Vehicles have capabilities that infantry do not have, especially creating smokescreens. For example, the smoke grenade launchers on the tank provide excellent, rapidly developed local smoke clouds. However, be aware that the grenades produce burning fragments that are hazardous to infantry near the tank and that can ignite dangerous fires in urban areas. And although tank sights can see through most smoke, dismounted infantry lose visibility when enveloped in dense smoke clouds.

7.h Fighting in L Shapes

Whatever the size of the objective or counterattack, the most effective fighting position is to attack from **two perpendicular sides**. The "L" shape is shorthand for this perpendicular fighting formation. The L shape is effective because it allows for fires from two directions with neither side endangering the other. Fire from two directions is great because any barrier facing one side can likely be attacked from another side, thereby reducing deadspace. Also, humans focus on the first attack, so Soldiers can blindside enemies by opening up a second attack from a different angle.

The idea of attacking from an L shape is present at all tactical levels. Companies secure objectives using L shapes. Platoons and squads flank enemies using L shapes. Teams use points-of-domination to attack within a room. (See Clearing the Corner and Room, Pg. 232.) Whatever the situation, Soldiers should always be prepared to create a flank position and form an L.

8. Scheme-of-Maneuver for Infiltration[1]

Planning begins by looking at possible routes between the patrol's location and their objective area. After routes are chosen, Leaders assign tasks, time standards, and contingencies to every location on the route. A complete scheme enables Soldiers to know when, to where, with who, and how they are moving for the duration of movement. (See Timetables, Pg. 118.)

---

1 Quote: Get the hell off the beach! Get up and get moving! Follow me! —Colonel Audrey Newman ordered 3d Bn., 34th Inf. Reg. when pinned down on Leyte Beach.

Observation and Avenues of OAKOC

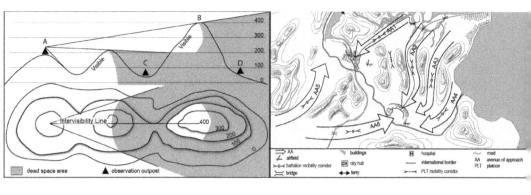

Key Terrain and Obstacles of OAKOC

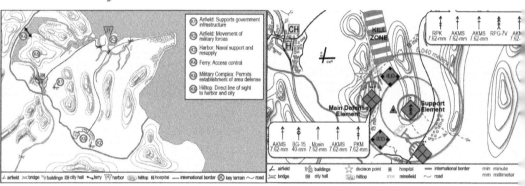

Cover and Concealment of OAKOC

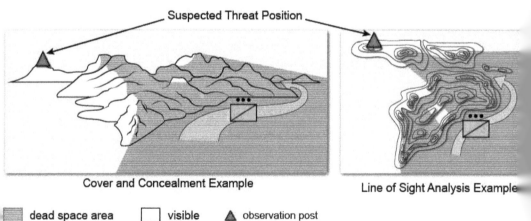

Image 95 et al: OAKOC applies to all levels of a battlefield. For example, although the top right image depicts observation and fields of fire for hills, the same principles apply to buildings within a city. (See Chunking, Pg. 134.) When each part of OAKOC is analyzed, the various components can be combined into one chart. (See Image 96, Pg. 111.) Note that here, enemy positions exemplify "obstacles," the combined chart exemplifies obstacles with "severely restricted terrain."

OAKOC Combined

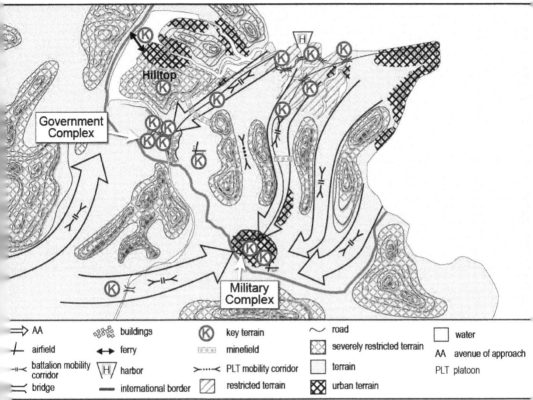

Image 96: This image has all of OAKOC combined into one image. Making a combined image can help rank which avenues of approach are the most viable when making routes. During planning, this is often the purpose of a terrain model.

8.a Choosing and Preparing a Route

There are infinite routes in theory, and routes can be complicated and large, and may comprise a kilometer-wide infiltration lane! But a patrol must only use the best routes. To compare and contrast routes, Leaders use the **OAKOC framework** to quantify the tactically relevant qualities of each route. Characterized routes are then compared and ranked. Planning for multiple routes is important; and at minimum, Leaders choose a **primary and alternate** infiltration route. Using multiple routes at the same time can split enemy forces, potentially increasing the chance of success. And any alternate infiltration route can serve as the primary exfiltration route, and vice versa.

Observation and Fields-of-Fire – The first geographical consideration is where the patrol or enemies have unobstructed lanes of observation and fields-of-fire against the opposition. The best observation and fires for shooters are from tall buildings with numerous windows. However, counter-attackers know this and will attack or avoid tall buildings.

Avenues-of-Approach – The second consideration is the quality of movement a route can provide for a patrol or enemy. Quality of movement is specific to the type of troop. Ideal avenues of approach avoid as many enemy lanes of observation and obstacles as possible, while keeping cover.

Key and Decisive Terrain – A patrol wants to control areas that give an important advantage to anyone. Whether the terrain is "key" depends on what the terrain enables, and not the terrain itself. For example, a random open field can be key terrain if it is an appropriate landing zone for medevac helicopters. Also, key terrain is only comparative; e.g. a landing zone is only key if there are no alternative landing zones. Some areas may not have any especially key terrain.

Obstacles – Obstacles require special preparations to pass them. They limit not prohibit mobility along an avenue-of-approach. Examples include: buildings, rivers, minefields, wire obstacles, enemies, etc.[1]

Cover and Concealment – The patrol and the enemy benefit from areas that offer protection from the effects of direct and indirect fire, or protection from observation. Think of larger scale things, like forests, and not trees.

After choosing the best routes, the patrol conducts route reconnaissance along all potential routes to confirm their viability. Many problems can only be seen from the ground, like enemy strongholds, enemy surveillance positions, and improvised explosive devices. If traveling with vehicles, all bridges and overpasses are checked for weight ratings and sabotage.

The patrol also plans **checkpoints**, which are locations along a route where Soldiers report their current location to Higher Command. A patrol plans multiple checkpoints along every route to allow Command to track the patrol's infiltration status. With the patrol's location, Command can link and coordinate other units' actions to the patrol's actions.

---

[1] Real World: Once a mission begins, enemies are either obstacles, chance contact, or a quick reaction force. (See Enemy Contact in Urban Terrain, Pg. 124.) (See Quick Reaction Force, Pg. 192.) However during planning, the enemy threat situation may demand more a in-depth analysis as in U.S. Army ATP 2-01.3.

During infiltration itself, information from OAKOC and checkpoints is important if a patrol changes plans. For example, the patrol can use obstacle information to avoid a break-contact directly into an enemy encampment. And to facilitate infiltration, the raiding patrol can include Soldiers whose only role is to infiltrate.[1] For example, Combat Engineers deal with actual or potential barriers. Bulldozers and tanks may be used to provide alternate avenues of approach by destroying buildings. Security Elements can be placed along a route to alert the Main Body and fight enemy reinforcements.

8.b Phase Lines

Leaders draw imaginary lines on a map for Soldiers to cross and trigger the next mission phase. That is, crossing or approaching a phase line triggers an action. For example, when Assault is crossing (or is soon to cross) a phase line codenamed "white," Assault calls out "Phase Line White!" A different element hears this trigger and, for example, ceases machine gun fire past phase line White. So when Soldiers enter the next area, machine gun fire won't hit them. Phase lines can also be used with indirect fires. (See Image 103, Pg. 122.)

Because phase lines are often used to segregate Soldiers from dangerous areas, phase lines double as **limits-of-advance**. For example, when a machine gun fires onto the opposite side of a phase line, the line limits the advance of Assault until machine gun fire has ceased and everyone is informed.

Phase lines are often the line between a Support-by-Fire position and a real **horizontal and vertical marker**, like the corner of a building. Natural lines include: streets, rivers, or floors of a building. (Wide markers are bad; is the phase line the near side or the far side?) A complicated objective with multiple buildings may have horizontal lines sectioning off different buildings and vertical lines sectioning off floors within each building. If necessary, units may use checkpoints to supplement or substitute for phase lines; although it is far less precise when a checkpoint is "crossed." Less precision is more danger.

Raid objectives often employ flanking Support-by-Fire. (See Fighting in L Shapes, Pg. 109.) Therefore, a common approach to phase lines on the objective area of a raid is to extend phase lines from Support to corners on successive buildings. Then, the fanned phase lines naturally are perpendicular

---

1 Quote: When you're doing mountain rescue, you don't take a doctorate in mountain rescue; you look for somebody who knows the terrain. It's about context. —U.K. Secretary of State for International Development and Veteran Rory Stewart

Fanned Phase Lines

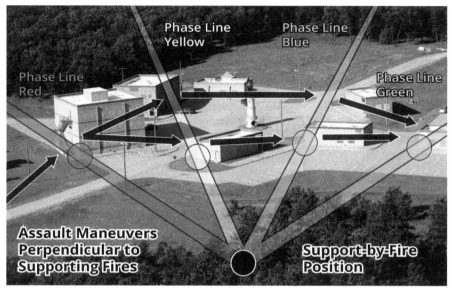

Image 97: The phase lines are fanned because the Support-by-Fire remains stationary as Assault moves through the objective. Each circle is a reference point for Support-by-Fire to use to define the line.

Vertical Phase Lines

Image 98: A Soldier prepares to provide supporting fires. Grafenwohr, Germany, 07 Mar 2010. **Phase lines are not limited to the horizontal plane.**

Terrain Model Phase Lines

Image 99: Marines brief a mission over a terrain model. Kuwait 30 Jun 2012. Each plank denotes a phase line that the patrol will cross during infil until they reach the limit-of-advance. Colored phase lines are useful shorthands for location data.

Strategic Phase Lines

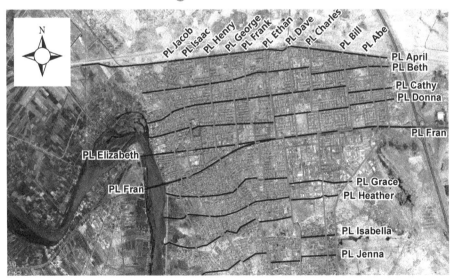

Image 100: **Phase lines are used at every operational level**. This map from the U.S. Army shows the phase lines for the Second Battle for Fallujah (not a raid). 2004.

to Assault's direction of movement. (See Image 97, Pg. 114.) Before Assault goes to a building, they must call up the corresponding phase line and order Support to shift or cease their fires.

Theoretically, a raid mission plan can have unlimited phase lines. However in practice, a plan usually only has three or fewer phase lines (delineating four or fewer sections) to make it easier for Soldiers to remember them. If more than three phase lines are needed, the raiding force may not be large enough, the raiding objective may be too large for the unit, or the raid must have delegated plenty of time to stop and coordinate. A Patrol Leader can reduce the need for phase lines by using rolling support Support-by-Fire, which travels with the Assaulters as they move through each phase line. (See Support to Facilitate Assault's Maneuver, Pg. 173.)

8.c Raid Preparation Locations[1]

The patrol may want to stop and prepare itself after arriving at the objective and before assaulting. **Preparation can increase the success of a raid** because some places are much safer for the patrol and deadlier for the enemy. A proper preparation process is very time consuming, but proper recon can be the difference between killing all the enemy in the first volley and a dangerous hour-long firefight. The full process is detailed in *Small Unit Tactics: An Illustrated Manual* because that book and this process are both more relevant to rural terrain. Many urban raids don't scout at all and move straight from infiltration to emplacement and actions-on.

The most common preparation is **leader's recon**, where Leaders separate from the Main Body to surveil and observe the objective. (See Leader's Reconnaissance of the Objective, Pg. 139.) During leader's recon of the objective, Soldiers are chilling in the rear for hours, so they must be hidden. Therefore, the rear location can be scouted too. (See Image 101, Pg. 117.)

The location where the Main Body resides as leader's recon occurs is the **objective rally-point** (ORP). To scout an ORP, the patrol stops in a pre-planned long-halt location along the infiltration route that the Patrol Leader deems relatively safe. The Patrol Leader then conducts leader's recon on the

---

1 Quote: It cannot be too often repeated that in modern war, and especially in modern naval war, the chief factor in achieving triumph is what has been done in the way of thorough preparation and training before the beginning of war. —U.S. Commander-in-Chief Theodore Roosevelt

Raid Preparation Locations

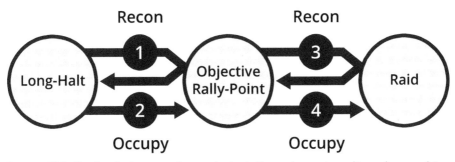

Image 101: If a leader's recon is conducted, then elements split and recombine multiple times. (See Splitting Elements, Pg. 141.) (See Near and Far Recognition Signals, Pg. 143.)

ORP location, returns to the Main Body, and occupies the ORP. After a patrol arrives at the ORP, it first establishes perimeter security and notifies Higher Command "ORP established." A good urban ORP follows the acronym **COLE:**

C – Covered and concealed.

O – Out of sight, sound, and small-arms fire. (If you can shoot the objective, the objective can shoot you.)

L – Large enough to fit the entire element.

E – Easily defendable for a short time. (The patrol must be able to defend the area while a withdrawal is organized.)

The urban ORP and the rural ORP have different requirements. Whereas a rural ORP must remain off natural lines of drift, in an urban area that is almost impossible by definition. Therefore, although an urban ORP can be done with as much effort as a rural one, the danger of staying in one location means urban ORPs are done quickly if at all.

Missions that separate elements from a Main Body have a **release-point,** which is the location from which each element is taken from the Main Body and moved to their actions-on location. (See Emplacing Elements, Pg. 146.) The ORP can double as the release-point. Or the release-point can be a new location that is scouted out; and if the points are separate, the patrol moves from the ORP to the release-point after Leader's Recon returns.

This release-point is the place for final considerations. For example, if there are a limited number of radios, they are redistributed there. The patrol also divides here into elements by order of emplacement: Security, Support, and Assault (SSA). Security is always emplaced first because it provides early warning of an incoming enemy; otherwise, Support and Assault would be caught off-guard. As Security is emplaced, Support and Assault pull 360-degree security at the release-point. Rucks can be left at the ORP or brought to the release-point. Either way, putting rucks in three SSA files makes withdrawal easier, as Soldiers know where their rucks are.

8.d Timetables[1]

Every scheme-of-maneuver (including infiltration, actions on, and exfiltration) has a timetable because making an explicit timetable helps the entire patrol to be on the same page (even if the plan is altered). Further, allocating time exposes unrealistic time requirements or unsynced elements. The plan must generously **allocate time for mistakes and contingencies**; and each contingency gets its own timetable.

A timetable includes times, locations, comms plans, and other info that helps one unit or element coordinate with another. (See Example Mission Timetable, Pg. 119.) The patrol's timetable also incorporates the enemy's timetable. The best time to conduct a raid is during an enemy change of personnel, where there is maximum chaos and distraction; or at night, where there is maximum concealment and inactivity.

9. Scheme-of-Fires

A scheme-of-fires is a plan for indirect fires from mortar, artillery, air support, etc. to support the patrol. Fires are most often used to isolate the objective area, soften the objective area, and support maneuvers under enemy fire. (See Isolation Area, Pg. 136.) (See Softening the Objective, Pg. 158.) (See Support to Facilitate Assault's Maneuver, Pg. 173.) A scheme-of-fires is often planned together with the scheme-of-maneuver to maximize coordination.

---

1 Quote: Napoleon said, "I may lose a battle, but I shall never lose a minute." Nathan Bedford Forrest told the secret of his many victories: "Get there first with the most men." General Patton said in 1943, "When the great day of battle comes remember your training and remember above all else that speed and violence of attack are the sure road to success." History's great commanders differed in many ways, but one thing they shared was a sense of the importance of speed. —United States Marine Corps MCDP 1-3 Tactics

Example Mission Timetable

EVENT	DESCRIPTION	CODE-WORD	COMMS PLAN	FROM	TO	TIME
1	BOAT LAUNCH	FORD	2	SHIP	CP1	D-1 (DTG)
2	ABORT	KATY	1/2/3			
3	CONTINUE	INDY	1/2/3			
4	ENEMY ATTACK	CHEVY	2			
5	SALUTE REPORT	ALICE	1/ 2			
6	BOATS CP1	BUICK	2	CP1	CP2	+00:30 HR
6	BOATS CP2	JEEP	2	CP2	CP3	+01:00 HR
7	BOATS CP3	GEO	2	CP3	LZ	+02:15 HR
8	SPOT REPORT	JUDY	1			
9	LANDING ZONE INSERT COMPLETED	KAY	1/2/3	LZ	ORP	+03:00 HR
10	ALT LANDING ZONE INSERT COMPLETED	GINA	1/2/1	ALT LZ	ORP	+03:15 HR
11	ORP	JEAN	1	ORP	OBJ	+04:00 HR
12	MISSION ACCOMPLISHED	BARB	1	OBJ	LZ	+04:30 HR
13	WITHDRAW	CHRIS	1/ 2	LZ	SHIP	+07:00 HR
14	EMERGENCY MEDEVAC	JOE	1/ 2			
15	EXECUTE EVASION AND ESCAPE	TOM	1/2/3			
16	EXTRACT	BILL	3/ 4			
17	SWITCH FREQ	PUNT				

Phase 1

119

Terms describing effects include suppress, neutralize, destroy, obscure, and illuminate. Terms describing the end-state of fires—i.e., disrupt, delay, limit, and divert—all essentially mean to not let an enemy formation perform a specific function. The former is combined with the latter to describe the purpose of fires, for example, destroy to disrupt, or obscure to divert.

At the most basic level, each supporting element requires only four basic instructions: a target reference, a start trigger, a stop trigger, and the desired effect. For example, a scheme-of-fires can be as simple as, "At 1400 (start trigger) Element A will fire explosive rounds (effect) between Building A's East and West sides (target reference), until and not after Element B reaches its last covered and concealed position (stop trigger)." Different units have different combinations or expansions on how this information is conveyed.

The **target reference** is at minimum a simple grid location or area description. (See Image 102, Pg. 121.) A target reference can be anything identifiable and semi-permanent (e.g., a hill, a burning vehicle, or smoke from an artillery round). To maximize visibility, references are visible in three observation modes (unaided, passive-infrared, and thermal).

Target reference points (TRP's) can be used as general reference points. For example, a patrol can use a TRP as a checkpoint and vice versa (See Choosing and Preparing a Route, Pg. 111.), or call for fire offset to a TRP.

A target reference line (TRL) can be defined as the line between two TRP's.[1] A TRL can be independent, or it can be concurrent with a phase line. (See Phase Lines, Pg. 113.) Indirect fires may use the term "restrictive fire lines" (RFL) because Assault is not expected to cross an RFL so it has no phase. Multiple TRL's or phase lines can define a target reference area.

Targets can be preplanned, creating a target list. Then the Patrol Leader can plan for on-call targets, scheduled targets, and priority targets. On-call targets have units prepared to deliver predetermined munitions to a predetermined location on call for fire. Scheduled targets are on-call targets with a predetermined time, meaning the fires are delivered without request. Priority targets have fire support units set the target data on their guns and lay on that target for a quick response to a call for fire. Priority targets are designated at the discretion of the Maneuver Leader and may be shifted or changed as the supported unit moves forward.

---

1 **Example** Target Reference Line:
Patrol Leader – "Engage between TRP's 5678 NE INT and 3579 SE INT."

Scheme-of-Fires

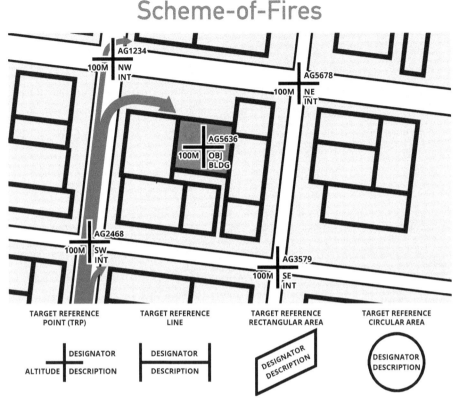

Image 102: In this example of a scheme-of-fires, the western (left) TRP's cover retreat, the eastern (right) TRP's prevent reinforcements, and the objective TRP can be used to soften the objective or to kill the occupants if the raid fails. Militaries have dedicated jobs to deal with the complex considerations of scheme-of-fires.

Targeting is the most critical point of failure. For example, an indirect fire that supports one element can easily cause casualties in geographically adjacent elements. Therefore, leadership needs to check the location of all Soldiers and noncombatants in the vicinity before calling for fire. A full fire-support plan may include: coordinated fire lines, fire support coordination lines, free-fire areas, no-fire areas, restrictive fire areas, or restrictive fire lines.

Triggers are observable events. Commonly a start trigger (e.g., engagement criteria) is a movement (e.g., two trucks arriving at a phase line), or an engagement. Each TRP can have multiple start and stop criteria. And while start triggers don't have to be exhaustive (no weapon system has to start firing), stop triggers must be exhaustive (all weapons need to stop firing at some point). Time limits are a common stop trigger, e.g., "fire for 2 minutes."

Echelonment of Fires

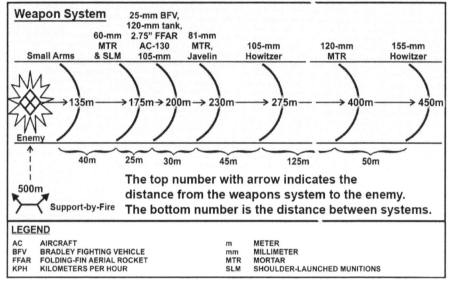

Image 103: An enemy is shown on the left, and various weapon systems to its right. The weapon systems are ordered by their 0.1% incapacitation distance to the enemy, as indicated by the numbers next to the arrows. An echelonment of fires is when successive fires engage the enemy one by one. The purpose is to maximize effects while minimizing risk. So for example, if Assaulters move from 500 meters to 300 meters from the enemy, more destructive 120mm mortars must stop firing because their 0.1% incapacitation distance is 400m. But 81mm mortars may begin to fire in their place. Adapted from U.S. Army ATP 3-21.8 2016 Figure C-1.

Leaders employ **trigger lines** to attack moving enemies. A trigger line is a reference line used to initiate and mass fires onto the target reference. Trigger lines and targets are separate lines because there is a time delay between when a commander calls for fire, and when those fires arrive on the target. Ideally, the enemy crosses the trigger line, the Leader calls for fire, and then both the enemy and the fires arrive at the reference simultaneously. The commander can designate one trigger line for all weapon systems or separate trigger lines for each weapon.

After targets and triggers, the Patrol Leader plans the intended **effect**. In fact, when the Patrol Leader requests indirect fire support, they can just request the effect and have the Indirect Fire Leader decide what weapon to use. Broadly, the effects that fire support offers are destructive power (high-explosive rounds), increased visibility (illumination rounds), and decreased visibility (obscuring rounds). (See Indirect Fire Systems, Pg. 37.)

Each weapon system has a different **risk estimate distance** (RED's), which is the distance at which a weapon creates a casualty with a certain probability (e.g. 0.1% casualty rate at 175 meters). Less powerful weapons have smaller RED's and more powerful weapons have wider RED's. (See Image 17, Pg. 40.) As Assaulters approach an objective, the patrol must switch from stronger indirect fires to less powerful fires to prevent friendly fire.

Switching to less powerful but more precise fires as Assaulters move toward the objective is called **echelonment of fires**. (See Image 103, Pg. 122.) Echelonment maintains the most powerful fires possible for as long as possible. To maintain constant fires on the targets, the next weapon system begins firing before the previous weapon system ceases or shifts. This ensures no pause between fires. Safe echelonment requires observers to confirm the Assaulter's movement past pre-planned phase lines, and the flexibility to change fires quickly and unexpectedly. (See Phase Lines, Pg. 113.)

9.a Call for Fire

Call for fire is the request from a patrol to indirect fire support with data to direct fires onto a target using a standardized fire command:

Observer identification – The element(s) ordering fires using call signs.

Warning order – Whether the mission is to adjust-fire or fire-for-effect. It also gives the method of target location: **grid** reference point; **polar** distance and direction from the observer; or **shift** from a known point.

Target location – The location data using the method in the warning order.

Target description – The target type and number, target activity, and any overhead protection; and desired effects (destroy, illuminate, etc.).

Method of engagement – Whether friendly units are danger close (within 600 meters of mortar fire). Also, the preferred ammunition; although ultimately the Fire Support chooses ammo based on the target description.

Method of control – Execution specifies when fires will be initiated. The Leader can engage immediately, delay initiation, or delegate authority to engage. By default, fires are initiated when ready.[1]

---

1 **Example** Executions: "fire"; "at my command"; "at your command."; "at phase line orange."

Phase 1

The instructions and information can be complex enough that it is the entire job of some Soldiers (like Company Fire Support Team Headquarters and Platoon Forward Observers) to acquire information about the objective and coordinate fires during planning. And then other Soldiers' primary job is to use that plan and call for fire under enemy attack (e.g., Forward Air Controllers (FACs), Naval Gunfire Spotter Teams, Joint Fires Observers).

Therefore, the most effective fires require Soldiers qualified in each weapon system to coordinate indirect fires. Certainly if a mission is supported by indirect fires then the Patrol Leader must attach qualified Soldiers to the patrol. However, a patrol doesn't always have a qualified Soldier, or the qualified Soldier may be incapacitated. Therefore, a weapons system must always be prepared to receive requests from unqualified observers. (Although any weapon may deny fires for safety reasons.) Every Soldier must carry a cheat sheet for call for fire if they must request fire support.

The Patrol Leader must also consider whether they are ordering fires (e.g. they control the fire support like mortars) or requesting fires (e.g. independently controlled fire support like artillery). Requested fires are often spread across many missions at one time and may be denied due to engagement elsewhere. Therefore, ordered fire support is always brought on a mission regardless of the availability of requested fire support.

10. Enemy Contact in Urban Terrain[1]

For a raid, **all combat on infiltration is unnecessary**. The patrol must conserve resources for the raid. Contact with the enemy is an in-depth topic covered in *Small Unit Tactics: An Illustrated Manual*. This section focuses on how enemy contact may be different in an urban environment.

First and foremost, avoid enemy contact. Use simultaneous deception operations to distract local inhabitants who are always conducting passive surveillance and reporting troop movements. Task organize a smaller unit that is harder to spot and faster to move.

---

1 Quote: Hard pressed on my right, my center is yielding. Impossible to maneuver. Situation excellent: I attack! —Marshal of France, Ferdinand Foch

Image 104: A truck destroyed by an insurgent car bomb **restricts movement** on a Diyala River bridge. Baghdad, Iraq, 14 Nov 2004. Restricting a patrol's movement is the biggest danger an enemy can create because a static patrol is vulnerable.

When an enemy attacks, Soldiers immediately return fire and seek cover. Soldiers not under direct fire provide supporting fire on known, then suspected enemy positions with individual and crew-served weapons (to include tanks and other fighting vehicles, if attached).

After the initial react-to-contact, Soldiers can either fight from inside or outside of a building. The most preferred option is to immediately conduct a hasty clearing of a structure to seek inside cover. (See Clearing the Entry, Pg. 228.) To hastily clear, Soldiers quickly scan the area and engage any threat. If no threat is present, the Soldiers establish 360-degree interior security and acquire the enemy's positions to deliver carefully aimed shots. The situation is rapidly developed and a counterattack may be ordered.

But when going inside, there is a danger that there are more enemies in the building, forcing the patrol to engage the enemy on two fronts. And entering unknown buildings may be banned due to, for example, local IED threats. The second and less preferred method is to remain outside of the building(s) and fight from the street without inside cover. This forces Soldiers to quickly seek fire superiority and whatever cover exists outside. (See Battle and Flank Positions, Pg. 60.) Going inside or not is mission dependent.

After seeking cover, Soldiers must maneuver to attack the enemy or break contact. The most important difference between rural and urban gunfights is the **ability of an Ambusher to restrict movement** and attack from any direction. For example, in 1993 U.S. forces traveling the streets of Somalia were ambushed several times. Somalis constructed roadblocks to slow the progress of the American convoy, which allowed Somali militiamen to keep pace on foot. At one point, the Somalis stopped an entire convoy by striking

Image 105: A **vehicle-borne IED** detonated 50 meters from the main gate of Mosul Airfield. Iraq, 26 Jul 2004. IED's restrict movement and alter a patrol's behavior.

one vehicle with a rocket propelled grenade. One Soldier was shot from a window behind him while taking cover and returning fire to the front. The ability of the Somali fighters to get close negated the difference in accuracy between U.S. elite forces and the Somali militia.

In Grozny, Chechen fighters would hide, only exposing themselves to attack the lead and trail vehicles of Russian convoys. With buildings to the sides, and destroyed vehicles to the front and rear, the remainder of the convoy was rendered immobile. The Chechens would then continue to destroy those remaining vehicles left stranded in the middle.

So predicting and enabling the patrol's movement after contact is mission essential. Every chokepoint on a route must be accounted for. If available, aerial support is placed on standby. A patrol must take extra Combat Engineers with multiple means of clearing thruways. Every effort must be made to allow for a **speedy withdrawal from any planned location**. If the enemy can disable multiple routes, outmatch Combat Engineers, and deny aerial support, a raid mission may not be feasible.

Once avenues of maneuver are secured, the patrol can split into a Maneuver Element and a Support Element. Or the entire patrol can maneuver together. How a patrol uses its Maneuver and Support Elements during enemy contact is determined by the characteristics of the individual raid. To give two examples, first, during the battle of the city of Fallujah, individual U.S. patrols were each clearing up to fifty buildings per day. Enemy contact was expected and so well-coordinated Supporting Elements trailed behind Maneuver Elements. Essentially, they were raiding and clearing buildings with the explicit expectation of assaulting to contact.

In contrast, in Mogadishu, U.S. forces were conducting a raid to secure high-value targets. Fast maneuver was emphasized at the expense of coordinated support. The patrol met unexpected resistance when they

126

managed to turn the entire city into a hostile force. In this react-to-contact scenario, the overwhelmed U.S. patrol tried to break contact, and used various defensive methods simultaneously, such as building a defensive perimeter and requesting evacuation and reinforcements. Frustrated ability to maneuver was perhaps this missions biggest failure.

Regardless, the Patrol Leader must identify their immediate goal during enemy contact. Even if it appears that the patrol can successfully defeat an enemy, **a patrol must not engage unless it will further the mission** in some way because an enemy-initiated battle is very risky. For example, the enemy may be trying to bait the patrol into an ambush. And because of the numerous hiding areas in a populated area, a first ambush is often bait for a second ambush. If the Maneuver Element breaks away to conduct a bold-flank counterattack, that is the perfect time for the enemy to attack the weakened Main Body and the Flank Element on two fronts.

If **breaking contact**, the Patrol Leader must position the Rear Element to have good cover and sectors-of-fire. Again, the Patrol Leader must consider that the initial attack is intended to push the patrol into an ambush. When breaking contact or withdrawing, sometimes equipment must be left behind. Sensitive equipment that is left behind is destroyed to ensure that it does not fall into enemy hands.

A correctly planned break-contact or withdrawal includes a lot of contingency planning. For example, bring two helicopters when only one is needed. If one helicopter sustains damage and needs to be left behind, the other can be destroyed. A Soldier can smash the instrument panel, the radio, and the other classified fixtures inside the cockpit. Then a Soldier can explode the avionics system, the communications gear, the engine, and the rotor head with C-4 charges under the carriage. And just to be sure, a Soldier can throw thermite grenades inside; the broken helicopter will burst into flames.

Besides assaulting and breaking contact, a third option is to take cover and **call in overwhelming indirect fires**. Due to the large resources required and disregard for collateral damage, this method is often reserved for total war. In 1982, the Israeli army was committed to a policy of disproportionate response during the Beirut siege. When enemies fired on Israelis, the Israelis responded with intense, high-caliber direct and indirect fire from tanks and artillery positioned around the city. Israeli artillery fired directly into high-rise buildings concealing Palestinian Liberation Organization Gunners and

Snipers. Floors collapsed on top of each other, and some upper floors were completely destroyed. Overwhelming indirect fires are just as psychologically impactful as physically impactful on defenders.

Because a patrol must be prepared to overcome a constrained withdrawal, unpredictable enemy attacks, and secondary ambushes, urban missions require an incredible number of troops. If a company-level patrol plans for two Security Elements, an Assault Element, and a Support Element, each element needs to be able to counterattack. And within each element, a proper counterattack requires some Soldiers to maneuver while others provide supporting fires. So the patrol can plan to successfully counterattack a force one eighth of its size.[1]

10.a Medical Evacuation

When there is a casualty, the leadership must inform higher with a 9-Line Medical Request as soon as possible. (See 9-Line Medevac Template, Pg. 129.) Everyone carries a 9-Line template, and they are very useful. But just talk like a normal person and the receiver will still understand.

Given casualties, the Patrol Leader decides whether the mission is still viable; i.e., do casualties require care before the mission is over? If the mission is more important than the casualties, then the casualties are managed by the Patrol Sergeant, and can only receive the care that the patrol has to offer.

If the Patrol Leader decides that the injuries are severe enough to inconvenience the mission, the casualty can be evacuated using many means of transport, like meeting an ambulance or helicopter at a preplanned location. However, if the casualty occurs during a foot movement, then some walking is required. Whatever the method, a medical evacuation must be treated like a full mission with step-by-step planning to include failure contingencies. (See Joe Invades Enemy Land (Phase 1: Infiltration of Urban Terrain), Pg. 53.)

It is important to have a full four-option **PACE plan—i.e., Primary, Alternate, Contingency, and Emergency**—for medical evacuation at all times! A PACE guarantees multiple means of evacuation simultaneously so that if many methods fail, another means remains available. Otherwise, without a PACE, a Soldier's life may depend on a single point of failure.

---

1 Quote: If you outnumber the opponent ten to one, then surround them; five to one, attack; two to one, divide. If you are equal, then fight if you are able. If you are fewer, then keep away if you are able. —Sun Tzu

Image 106: Medics of the 1077th Ground Ambulance Co. practice a mass casualty ground-air exchange point evacuation, Fort Irwin, CA, 23 Jun 2012.

9-Line Medevac Template

This is the standard format to covey casualty and pickup information to a casevac. The left column lists brevity codes (e.g. for line 3, saying "5 A" means "5 Urgent"). A common mnemonic is, "Low Flying Pilots Eat Tacos; Salsa Makes Nasty Nachos."

1. Location of pickup site		
2. Frequency and call sign		
3. Patient count and status	A. Urgent (2 hours) B. Priority (4 hours)	C. Routine (24 hours) D. Convenience
4 Equipment required	A. None B. Hoist	C. Extraction equipment D. Ventilator
5. Type of patients	L. Litter A. Ambulatory	
6. Security at pickup site	N. No enemy troops P. Possible enemy	E. Enemy troops X. Enemy (needs armed escort)
7. Marking of pickup site	A. Panels B. Pyro C. Smoke	D. None E. Other
8. Nationality and military	A. U.S. military B. U.S. civilian C. Non U.S. military	D. Non. U.S. civilian E. EPW
9 NBC contamination	N. Nuclear B. Biological	C. Chemical

Phase 2 Contents

11. Defining the Objective Battlespace — 131
Gathering Intelligence about the Objective — 132
Chunking — 134
Isolation Area — 136

12. Leader's Reconnaissance of the Objective — 139
Splitting Elements — 141
Near and Far Recognition Signals — 143
Surveillance and Observation Position (S&O) — 144

13. Emplacing Elements — 146
Security — 146
Support — 148
Assault — 149
Changing Roles — 150
Headquarters — 150

14. Final Steps — 152

15. Contingencies — 152
Running Out of Time — 152
Compromise during Emplacement — 152

Joe Stages a Raid (Phase 2: Preparation of the Environment)

First, we are going to cut it off, and then we are going to kill it.
—General Colin Powell, on the Iraq Army during the Gulf War, 1991

After arriving at the objective rally-point, the patrol must prepare the objective area. Security isolates the objective area, stopping the outside from getting in and the inside from getting out. Troops go to their assaulting positions. The patrol becomes ready to raid at any moment.

This section builds on the foundation of *Small Unit Tactics: An Illustrated Manual*, and focuses on new information relevant to the urban environment. Specifically, the characteristics of urban terrain apply to every part of this section. (See Frameworks for Attacking Vertical Terrain, Pg. 54.)

11. Defining the Objective Battlespace

Even if a mission has a well-defined objective structure, that is only one part of the battlespace. The objective battlespace also includes any surrounding areas that can directly affect the objective structure. In fact, to make the surrounding area safe, raiders may need to enter, clear, and secure some surrounding structures, which have their own surrounding areas.

Therefore, to systematically define a battlespace, a Raider must:

Define – what is and is not part of the battlespace. (See Gathering Intelligence about the Objective, Pg. 132.)

Chunk – the battlespace into specific tasks and areas that can be assigned to specific units. (See Chunking, Pg. 134.) (See Task Organization, Pg. 46.)

Isolate – each chunk in planning or practice to ensure that any definitions are practical and not just paper definitions. (See Isolation Area, Pg. 136.).

131

Objective Area Information Part 1

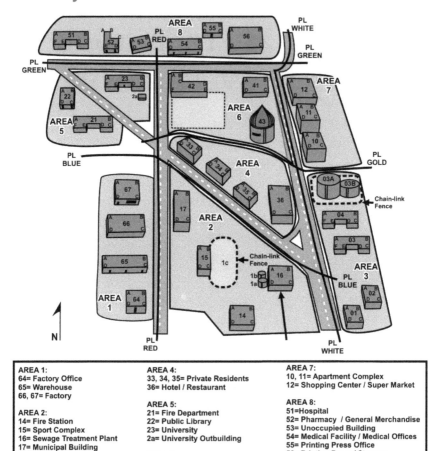

AREA 1:	AREA 4:	AREA 7:
64= Factory Office	33, 34, 35= Private Residents	10, 11= Apartment Complex
65= Warehouse	36= Hotel / Restaurant	12= Shopping Center / Super Market
66, 67= Factory		
	AREA 5:	AREA 8:
AREA 2:	21= Fire Department	51=Hospital
14= Fire Station	22= Public Library	52= Pharmacy / General Merchandise
15= Sport Complex	23= University	53= Unoccupied Building
16= Sewage Treatment Plant	2a= University Outbuilding	54= Medical Facility / Medical Offices
17= Municipal Building		55= Printing Press Office
	AREA 6:	56= Printing Press / Storage
AREA 3:	41= Post Office	
01, 02, 03, 04= Apartment Complex	42= School & Playground (chain-link fence)	
03a, 03b= Grain Storage	43= Religious Building	

Image 107: **As intelligence is gathered, it can be incorporated piecemeal.** This map shows how a town was separated into areas, and the purpose of each building was labeled with a number. When a Leader knows their area of responsibility and the functions of structures in their area, they can make more specific plans.

11.a Gathering Intelligence about the Objective

Before a raid has even begun, the patrol gathers intelligence about the objective area. At first, the patrol uses methods that don't expose Soldiers, like satellite imagery. Soldiers also question noncombatants, prisoners-of-

Objective Area Information Part 2

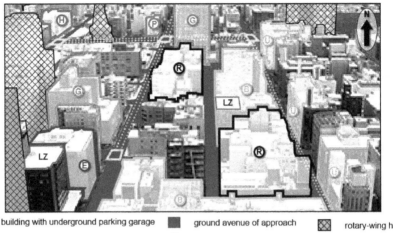

Ⓤ	building with underground parking garage	■	ground avenue of approach	▧	rotary-wing hazard
Ⓑ	business	Ⓗ	hospital		subway line
Ⓔ	embassy	Ⓟ	police		subway station
Ⓖ	government building	Ⓡ	residential	LZ	landing zone

Image 108: This city map categorizes different buildings by their relevance to a mission. For example, multiple flat surfaces are categorized as landing zones (LZ's), and streets have been recast as avenues of approach.

war, and local partners. Anyone gathering information, **always prioritizes information** that helps to make decisions. This information is the commander's critical information requirements (CCIR); further, some CCIR is prioritized against other CCIR. For example, if Higher dictates three breach points then information on other potential breach points is not a priority.

Leaders review enemy schemes-of-maneuver to generate requests for information. And they then review that information to predict future enemy schemes-of-maneuver. Requests may be for information on enemy: defensive structures, patterns of life, timetables, weapons, access points, early warning systems like dogs, signs of forced entry, location of lights and cameras, etc.

After gathering long range and second-hand information, the Patrol Leader uses the gathered information to generate additional requests for information. Then they assign those requests to Reconnaissance. Recon includes: Soldiers, aviation, radar, signals intelligence, etc. (See Surveillance and Observation Position (S&O), Pg. 144.) Drones with cameras that transmit a live feed, are especially effective at gathering information. (See Image 20, Pg. 44.) Much information like deadspace, cover, and concealment require close-range observation. And, if long range or second-hand information is relied on, then it is a good idea to validate it with close range recon.

As information is gathered, it can be compiled into a map to help understand each piece of information in the larger context. (See Image 107, Pg. 132.) Why the terrain is key and how the information relates to the raid mission can even be explicitly labeled. (See Image 108, Pg. 133.) Incorporating information also applies to infil and exfil routes. (See Choosing and Preparing a Route, Pg. 111.) For example, a local power station may be reconned because local infrastructure is important for the mission because:
1) controlling the station allows some control over background illumination;
2) shooting out the lights can permanently disrupt civilians; and
3) shutting off the power station is preferable to shooting the lights out.

11.b Chunking

Human space is fractal; rooms make buildings; buildings make blocks; blocks make zones; zones make cities. The fractal nature of space is mirrored by the fractal military unit organization (e.g., companies make battalions, etc.). Units can be mapped onto the spaces. (e.g., a battalion secures a zone and sends in companies which in turn secure blocks). (See Image 109, Pg. 135.)

Fractal unit organization mirrors fractal human spaces to standardize **span-of-control**. Large units control large spaces and small units control small spaces. When Leaders properly chunk a space, they assign to each unit a space that the unit has just enough resources to completely secure. (See Task Organization, Pg. 46.)

Chunking start with determining first the base unit (e.g., a room) and then what sized unit (e.g., a team) is required to secure that space. The typical span-of-control for a command is three to five subordinate units, and so a command should also only be in control of three to five spaces. For example, say a company is tasked to clear a building with fifty rooms. The company can assign each wing of a floor to a squad, and each whole floor to a platoon.

To ensure units do not interfere with each other, chunks are isolated by Security. For example, when a team is going from room to room, the floors are isolated at the stairwells. (See Stairs and Stairwells, Pg. 252.) The building is isolated by external Security. (See Isolation Area, Pg. 136.) And the city block can be isolated by higher-level assets. (See Scheme-of-Fires, Pg. 118.)

Phase 2

Chunking

Teams clear rooms in buildings.

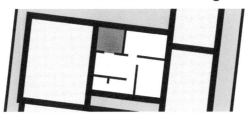

Platoons clear buildings in blocks.

Companies clear blocks in zones.

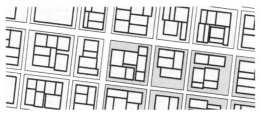

Battalions clear zones in cities.

Image 109: Begin chunking by defining the mission, like clearing a city zone. Then work down to the smallest tasks that a single Soldier can do, like clearing a room. Then work back up to the original task to figure out the number of Soldiers necessary to complete the task. This is diagram is just a rough suggestion. Companies might be limited to clearing a building, or maybe squads are tasked with room-clearing. And a Clearing Element requires equal or larger Security.

11.c Isolation Area[1]

The isolation area is an area around which Security creates a boundary, where Security **does not allow ingress or egress**. Encirclement of troops is not necessary, but encirclement of force is necessary. Because the entire battlespace must be isolated, the isolation area in effect defines the battlespace.

Without ingress or egress, outside enemies cannot enter to reinforce, and inside enemies cannot escape to fight another day. In case reinforcements overwhelm Security, the Patrol Leader must be prepared to send a Reserve Element to reinforce Security. (See Reserve Element, Pg. 24.)

Insufficient security can be disastrous. The Germans did not isolate the Soviet Red Army during the Battle of Stalingrad in 1942; so the Red Army used hidden routes to consistently infiltrate and attack previously cleared areas of the German rear. During the Iraq War in 2003, anti-coalition fighters utilized holes in walls as escape routes, converted houses into fortified bunkers, and thereby created a network of connected fortified bunkers. This network helped the anti-coalition fighters to evade and ambush coalition troops.

Encirclement takes place at every elevation, including basement tunnels and second-floor holes in walls hidden behind furniture. To isolate the objective from underground tunnels, sewers, and communications cables, basements are cleared as soon as possible, and a Security Element is placed there. The procedures for clearing a basement are the same as for any room or floor. Never follow enemies into previously unknown tunnels where defenders have a large advantage! (See Tunnels and Caves, Pg. 56.)

True isolation also requires dominating electronic transmission (e.g., power) to undermine communication, utilities, and morale. Various methods of isolation are used, like cutting all power lines to the objective. By denying communications between enemy forces and their Higher Command, the enemy's Higher may presume that forces on the objective are already defeated and abandon further reinforcement.

If there are enough troops, the Security Element is split into an **inner cordon and an outer cordon.** The outer cordon usually focuses on traffic control points and blocking positions, like checkpoints and roadblocks

---

1 Quote: The attacker won all urban battles where the defender was totally isolated.... No single factor is more important to the attacker's success than isolation of the urban area. —Marine Corps Warfighting Publication (MCWP) 3-35.3

Security Cordon

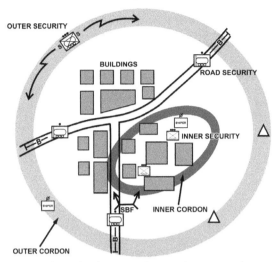

Image 110: Many plans have both a **360-degree inner cordon and outer cordon**. The inner cordon prevents enemies from exiting, and so places Soldiers to secure building exits. In contrast, outer cordons focus on avenues of approach like roads. To the top left, a Reserve Element stands ready to flex along the large outer cordon.

to block, canalize, or divert traffic. The inner cordon focuses on overwatching the objective and preventing exfiltration or repositioning of persons within the search area. (See Image 110, Pg. 137.) For both cordons, a Leader confirms clear lanes of fire and clear lanes of sight.[1]

Security can use point isolation or line isolation. **Point isolation** focuses on the end of a sectors-of-fire to secure certain focal points. For example, Soldiers can concentrate fires on entries and exits, especially vehicles ingress and egress routes. The patrol can stage shoulder-launched munitions along roads, and emplace claymore mines. Or mortar and artillery units can preset target reference points on avenues of approach. Point isolation is vulnerable to letting enemies escape, but is useful when manpower is low.

Line isolation is when multiple Security Positions connect and interlock their narrow sectors-of-fire into geometric shapes to encircle an area. (See

---

1 Quote: [The guerrillas] move in groups and withdraw perpendicular to Soldiers' forward line of troops.... Their movement is through windows of houses, down back alleys, and from roof to roof (only when obscured from Soldier overwatch positions). The routes minimize exposure in the streets. —Lessons Learned: Infantry Squad Tactics in MOUT During Operation Phantom Fury in Fallujah, Iraq

Security Formations

Image 114: In urban areas, isolation plans are made with corridors. Security positions can either be placed on (i.e., near) corners or off (i.e., regardless of) corners. On-the-corner is easier to plan for and has less risk of friendly-fire because it has only two security positions; but they are on opposite sides of the objective, and so have more difficult emplacement and communication than off-the-corner.

Image 111: U.S. Marines with C Co., BLT 1/4, 15th MEU provide security for advancing Marines. Al Hamra Military Airfield, United Arab Emirates, 12 Mar 2021.

Image 112: U.S. Marine Corps Lance Cpl. of D Co, 1st Bn., 7th Marine Reg. provides security while on patrol out of FOB Tabac, Sangin, Helmand, Afghanistan May 25, 2012.

Image 113: A Green Beret from the 7th Special Forces Group (Airborne) observes Honduran TIGRES as they secure an **avenue-of-approach** and try to identify their enemy among the many doors and windows. Eglin Air Force Base, FL, 27 Feb 2015.

Image 114, Pg. 138.) Then to prevent ingress and egress, Security attacks anyone who crosses a sector-of-fire in the surrounding shape.

To create the geometric isolation boundary, Security Positions can be placed on or off of the corners of structures. For on-the-corner, at least two guns occupy every other corner, and those guns' sectors-of-fire intersect at the remaining corners. For off-the-corner, all guns are on one side of a building. Two near firing positions secure the near sides of the structure, and two far, corner firing positions secure the far sides of the structure. Every security position has a narrow sector-of-fire that is at least 15 degrees offset to the interior of the security position to their left or right. Off-the-corner security requires more detailed lanes of fire and positioning to eliminate friendly fires, but allows for better communication between Security Elements because every element can see every other element.

Whatever method is used, Leaders must **allocate weapons appropriately**: cover mounted avenues of approach with anti-armor weapons; cover dismounted avenues of approach with automatic weapons.

Sometimes, an isolation area must be permeable due to rules-of-engagement. (See Morality and Rules-of-engagement, Pg. 295.) Also, Soldiers generally do not want to kill a person not clearly an enemy. Therefore, Security often employs less-lethal detainment methods against anyone crossing the isolation boundary. The drawback of less-lethal attacks is that enemies will be more willing to test the boundaries. For this reason, more forces are needed to isolate a less-lethal boundary. To prevent over-tasking, a Patrol Leader can task organize special teams, like Surveillance Teams, Detainment Teams, Kill Teams, etc. (See Non-Combat Support, Pg. 45.)

12. Leader's Reconnaissance of the Objective

Leader's recon is the last chance for a patrol to gather on-the-ground information before Assault enters the objective. Urban terrain can be deceptive when analyzed with second-hand information in a planning room. (E.g., a building on a map can be rubble in real life.) Therefore, leader's recon gives Leaders a personal feel for the terrain so they can make better decisions for their emplacement and raiding decisions. After leader's recon, the Patrol

Image 115: U.S. Marine Corps Cpl., a Team Leader with 1st Sqd., 3rd Plt., D. Co., 1st Bn., 7th Marine Reg. observes a village during a patrol. Sangin, Helmand, Afghanistan, 25 May 2012. A Leader gaining **on-the-ground confirmation** of information relevant to the raid plan increases the raid's chance of success.

Leader confirms, denies, or modifies the prior plan to accommodate any new information. The worse the premission intelligence was, the more leader's recon becomes necessary.

To perform leader's recon, the Patrol Leader takes a small group of Leaders and Soldiers to clandestinely observe the objective. The Leader's Recon Team (LRT) is vulnerable, and so carefully walks or crawls if necessary. Each Soldier confirms the objective with GPS or a map, and then confirms with each other. Then, the **LRT verifies**: the security, support, and assault positions, target reference points, etc., as necessary. Specifically when verifying, the LRT checks that each area has covered and concealed positions that can support each other, and lanes to facilitate maneuver. (See Battle and Flank Positions, Pg. 60.) (See Assault Positions and Lanes, Pg. 170.) (See Withdrawal from the Objective, Pg. 290.)

To maintain eyes on the objective while returning to the Main Body, the Patrol Leader can take two Soldiers on the LRT and leave them in an observation position. (See Surveillance and Observation Position (S&O), Pg. 144.)

All that being said, leader's recon is very limited in an urban setting because well-hidden enemies can attack the isolated Leaders at any time from any direction. The enemy can also observe the LRT, and vacate the objective or prepare better defensive positions. Even less intrusive techniques, like the employment of many unmanned aerial vehicles can expose the patrol's presence.

Before a leader's recon, a Leader must prioritize information that verifies or challenges information already in the plan. Most commonly, this means verifying OAKOC and enemy information. (See Choosing and Preparing a

Route, Pg. 111.) Are there unforeseen or unviable avenues of approach? Is the cover and concealment for the assault lane still there and viable? What is the SALUTE report?[1] Etc.

Therefore in an urban setting, **the patrol must create a plan that does not require leader's recon**. The plan must also be fluid and generalized to accommodate any unforeseen obstacles. Ideally, there is no gap in movement from transit to the Objective, to the placement of troops, to the start of the raid.

In this case of a raid in a rural area, the leader's recon and emplacement of troops are performed in the same manner as outlined in *Small Unit Tactics: An Illustrated Manual*.

12.a Splitting Elements

Whenever two elements separate (e.g. with leader's recon), a GOTWA is issued from the Leader of the Moving Element to the Leader of the Stationary Element. **GOTWA** means: Going to location; Others taken with; Time of emergency; What to do if late; and Actions on contact for both elements.[2]

Where the Moving Element is going, and who is going are simple. The remaining parts (i.e., the TWA) are more complicated. The time of emergency

---

1 Example SALUTE:

Size	– "Twelve riflemen."
Activity	– "Guarding and alert."
Location	– "East side of objective."
Unit	– "Unknown."
Time	– "1500."
Equipment	– "Twelve AK-47's."

2 Example GOTWA:

Going to location – "We're doing a leader's recon of the ORP."

Others taken with – "The Alpha Team Leader, Alpha SAW, and Alpha Point [using Soldiers' names is advised] are coming."

Time of emergency – "It is now 1900 and we will be back by 2100."

What to do if late – "Attempt to call us by radio every five minutes for half an hour. If you cannot contact us, call Higher and use the entire squad to come get us [don't split elements further]."

Actions on contact – "If we are hit, we will fight our way back to you and then withdraw together to the last en route rally-point which is 500 meters to our 6 o'clock. If we cannot come to you, we will go directly to our last en route rally-point and link up with you there. If you are hit, fight in-place and we will return to you. If you cannot hold, withdraw to our last en route rally-point and we will link up there."

141

Image 116: U.S. Soldiers in Bandit Tr., 1st Sq., 3rd Cavalry Reg. file through a chokepoint during a response force live-fire training. Iraq, 31 Oct 2018. Two Soldiers **count silently and check each other** at the end. Chokepoints are performed any time Soldiers move and especially when elements split.

is not a guess of the split's duration, but rather an, "Oh Shit!" deadline, after which action must be taken. Even if the Moving Element expects to be gone for 15 minutes, the time of emergency can still be six hours ahead. The time is also never a quantity, but a clock time. (E.g., "We will return by 1500.") A duration would need to change every time a Leader re-briefs it.

The last two (i.e., WA) depend on the situation and mission, but can be somewhat standardized for a patrol. A standard "what to do if late" is: "Attempt to contact me by radio every 5 minutes for a total of 30 minutes. If still unable to make contact for 30 minutes, contact Higher for further instruction. And if you can't reach Higher, take the entire element to come get us." If the time-of-emergency passes, the what-to-do-if-late instruction should never be for the Stationary Element to wait additional time before acting. That defeats the purpose of having a time limit. **Absolutely do not further split the patrol! That will lose two elements!**

A common action-on-contact for a moving element is to return fire and bound back to the Stationary Element. And common actions-on-contact for the Stationary Element is to fight in place, contact the Moving Element, and seek direction from Higher. If either element cannot meetup, they return to the last rally-point.

After a Leader briefs a GOTWA, that Leader receives a backbrief and everyone resynchronizes watches. Right before splitting, both elements must take accountability of Soldiers who are splitting to the Moving Element (e.g., with a chokepoint). (See Image 116, Pg. 142.)

Image 117: U.S. Marine Lance Cpl. with 1st Light Armored Reconnaissance Bn., 1st Marine Div. conducts a radio check while on a recon patrol. St. Arnaud, New Zealand, 27 Oct 2017. Radios and satellite phones are common far signals.

Image 118: A U.S. Marine with Force Reconnaissance Platoon, Maritime Raid Force, 26th Marine Expeditionary Unit adjusts night-optical devices. 23 Jan 2016. **Visual and aural confirmation are common near signals for day and night.**

12.b Near and Far Recognition Signals

360-degree "security" is meaningless if anybody can just walk up to the patrol. Security must positively identify shadows in the night before they approach, or else open fire. To verify others, patrols use prearranged recognition signals. These signals are used every time two elements meet each other, like with leader's recon. (See Leader's Reconnaissance of the Objective, Pg. 139.)

Recognition signals usually use two layers of recognition: near and far-recognition. In safe areas, a patrol could use one reliable layer, like an FM radio PACE plan. Or they could add a third, super far layer in a dangerous area.

Far-recognition signals are communications that do not identify the location of the sender or receiver. For example, using an FM radio does not give away the speakers' locations; whereas, shouting across a field does. However, if the enemy becomes capable of determining the origin of FM transmissions, FM radio ceases to be a good far-recognition signal.

Near-recognition signals give away the location of the sender or receiver. Therefore, near-recognition is dangerous and requires encoding so nobody can blunder into a correct signal. Similarly, near-recognition should be avoided at night, when two elements need to be much too close to distinguish friend from foe using communications like sight or voice recognition.

As the Moving Element comes to the Stationary Element, the Leader of the Stationary Element needs to be ready to receive signals; so the patrol needs a reception plan. For example, using comms windows to only allow contact during certain times, or a guard roster for a signal watch.

An example of recombining is the following. When the Moving Element (ME) comes within sound of the Stationary Element (SE), the SE Leader orders the unknown (to them) element to halt using FM radio for far-recognition. The ME halts. Then the SE Leader gives a preplanned coded order to the ME to act (e.g., "move red."). The ME acts accordingly (e.g., moves right). If the ME's actions match the coded order, then the ME is friendly and can proceed.

Another scenario could be when the ME comes into sight of the SE, the SE Leader orders the ME to halt, and the ME halts and immediately shows a signal for near-recognition (e.g., shows a VS17 panel). The SE confirms that it received the appropriate signal and tells the ME to continue forward. Because both elements are in sight of each other, the near-recognition signals can be used even if radios fail. There are infinite signals a patrol can use.

Password exchanges are necessary when two elements need to join extremely quickly, like during enemy contact. A famous password combo used during D-Day in WWII was the first Soldier saying "flash," and the second Soldier responding with "thunder." Similarly, a running password (i.e., yelling a word when running) is useful when the ME is being actively pursued by an enemy and has no time to send signals. Without a password, an approaching element could be mistaken for an enemy and be shot, so friendly element must make sure to use recognition signals

12.c Surveillance and Observation Position (S&O)[1]

The Surveillance and Observation (S&O) position is a concealed, two-Soldier, overwatch position that surveils and observes an area for information, especially movement. The two Soldiers are a Rifleman (to operate comms) and a Squad Automatic Weapon Soldier (SAW) (firepower and security).

The purpose of the S&O is to (as best as possible) provide eyes on 100% of the target area 100% of the time until the target area is occupied by the patrol. Due to buildings, micro-terrain, blinking, etc., an S&O at a minimum must have eyes on 75% of the target area, 95% of the time. Thereby, the S&O is still able to see all movements in the area.

---

1 Quote: An alert soldier is an alive soldier. —General Mark W. Clark

Image 119: Soldiers with A Co., 1st Bn., 26th Inf. Reg., 1st Inf. Div. set up a **Listening Post Observation Post** (LPOP) for surveillance and observation atop a building during a cordon and knock operation. Adhamiyah, Baghdad, 23 Aug 2007.

Image 120: Soldiers from the Tigerforce Scout Plt., 1-327th Inf. Reg., 1st Bde., 101st Airborne Div. observe and pull rooftop security during Operation Gaugamela. Hawija, Kirkuk, Iraq 20 Jul 2006.

To achieve 360-degree surveillance, the two Soldiers face opposite directions, touching each other to enable nonverbal communication. If S&O is engaged, it will most likely be from the area observed, so the SAW faces forward to the 12 o'clock and the Rifleman faces back to the 6 o'clock. The Rifleman must have working comms! Without comms, there is no point in placing an S&O. Finally, whenever the S&O is dropped off, it always receives a GOTWA from leadership, just like every time an element splits.

13. Emplacing Elements

Emplacement occurs when Soldiers move from the release-point to their starting position for the raid. (See Raid Preparation Locations, Pg. 116.) The Patrol Leader can emplace each element themself; or if they trust their Soldiers to emplace themselves, the Patrol Leader can describe the locations and route they have scouted and have the elements emplace themselves. Before elements split, they must issue a GOTWA and be counted out of the release-point by the Patrol Sergeant. (See Splitting Elements, Pg. 141.)

Elements can be emplaced simultaneously. But if they are sequentially emplaced, Security is emplaced first because raids need isolation. Support is emplaced before Assault, so they can support Assault. Assault emplaces last because they depend on Security and Support; and if they can be absent when Assault combats the enemy then they serve no purpose in the first place.

At emplacement, a Leader briefs a **SPARC** to each weapon system:

Sector-of-Fire – (See Supporting Fires to Suppress and Divert, Pg. 176.)

Priority-of-Targets – (See Support to Facilitate Assault's Maneuver, Pg. 173.)

Assault Positions and Lanes – (See Assault Positions and Lanes, Pg. 170.)
Also include shift, raise, and cease fire instructions. (See Deconflicting Support and Assault, Pg. 179.)

Rate-of-Fire – Ammunition consumption is always a large concern when attacking. The rate at which weapons fire is established beforehand to prevent a weapon system from running out of ammo during a raid.

Cover and Camouflage – While waiting for the raid to begin, Soldiers must improve their battle position. (See Battle and Flank Positions, Pg. 60.)

13.a Security

Before the raid or during leader's recon, the Patrol Leader plans for ideal security positions. (See Isolation Area, Pg. 136.) At the objective, they either emplace Security or Security emplaces itself. Although in other environments Security may move between positions during an attack, urban terrain may force Security to remain in place. (See Urban Population Threats, Pg. 62.)

The first consideration for a security position is their ability to positively identify (PID) and kill enemies. This normally requires clear lanes of sight and fire of at least 100 to 200 meters from the security position.

Phase 2

Image 121: U.S. Marines with C Co., 1st Bn., 3rd Marine Reg. practice a platoon attack. South Korea, March 17, 2016. When emplacing elements, consider how to **reduce presence**, like crawling or dismounting vehicles offset from the objective.

Second, **Security must have good cover and concealment**. Concealment is more important before a mission, because if the enemy spots anyone, the whole ambush is compromised. But cover is more important after the mission has begun. During a raid, friendly and enemy weapons from the objective may fire toward Security. So Security must have effective cover from the objective, in addition to other threatening directions.

Though these factors are necessary to think about, there are practically unlimited factors to consider when placing Security. For example:

- ► Historical patterns for enemy movement speed.[1]
- ► Traffic density/frequency of the objective road.
- ► Time required for emergency emplacement.
- ► Difficulty in finding and evacuating an incapacitated Security.
- ► Lack of radios and backup plans for failed radios.
- ► Lines-of-fire and back-blast areas for AT4s.
- ► How fast Soldiers can move between locations, etc.

After the Patrol Leader has emplaced Security, or before Security leaves to emplace themselves, the Patrol Leader briefs an EWAC plan to Security and get a backbrief. EWAC criteria are mini plans-of-action for Security:

Engagement criteria – The conditions and characteristics of the enemy that make Security: 1) engage the enemy; 2) let the enemy pass; and/or 3) relay information to the Main Body. Security's primary purpose is to stop

---

A vehicle moving at 40mph covers 100 meters in 5.59 seconds. Is that good early warning? Distance must scale to the enemy threat.

ingress and egress from the objective, and the EWAC is where Security is reminded of what to identify and what to do.

Withdrawal criteria – The conditions under which Security must return to the release-point (or withdrawal-point, if different). The criteria must cover all scenarios, which often means giving a time limit.

Abort criteria – The trigger(s) that tell Security to abort a mission.

Compromise criteria – What to do if Security is compromised. There are two kinds of compromise: "hard" and "soft." Hard compromise means that the enemy knows you are there (e.g., an enemy scout sees you). Soft compromise means that the enemy might know you are there (e.g., artillery fire in the distance). The line between hard and soft is often debated. Each compromise requires a different plan-of-action.

After the EWAC, The Patrol Leader briefs and is backbriefed GOTWA's and then conducts a radio check with Security. (See Splitting Elements, Pg. 141.) If the Patrol Leader is emplacing Security, they initiate recognition signals with the Main Body upon return. (See Near and Far Recognition Signals, Pg. 143.)

13.b Support

The Patrol Leader emplaces Support, or Support emplaces itself in a position that protects itself from both enemy and friendly troops. (See Battle and Flank Positions, Pg. 60.) Urban terrain may have 360-degrees incoming attacks.

If there is time, **Leaders verify each firing position in detail**. For example, when emplacing an M240 machine gun, the Leader instructs the Assistant Gunner to quietly place down the tripod (i.e., M192 Lightweight Ground Mount). The Gunner quietly places the M240 on the tripod and locks it into position. The Leader hands off their rifle to the Gunner as they get behind the M240 on its tripod. They confirm a good sector-of-fire, and reinforce the sector with metal-to-metal contact on the tripod. "Metal-to-metal" means the M240 cannot physically turn anymore on the tripod. For the opposite limit-of-fire, they place some tape on the T&E to restrict the M240 from turning. When the Leader has found the right and left limits and set the metal-to-metal contact, they put the Gunner back into position and recover their rifle. Then, the Leader explains the sector to the Gunner by laying on the Gunner and physically moving the rifle to the left and right limits, making metal and tape contact.

Image 122: A Danish Army Sniper aims his rifle from a hide site in an abandoned train car. Hohenfels, Germany, 30 May 2018. **Sniper Teams as Support Elements** are relatively easy to emplace, but also vulnerable, because their long standoff from the objective also place them far from the patrol.

The Support Leader **coordinates fires to ensure full coverage** of the area assigned to Support by the Patrol Leader. (See Sectors-of-Fire and Coordinated Fires, Pg. 177.) Then, the Support Leader issues a SPARC to every weapon system. (See Emplacing Elements, Pg. 146.) The A in SPARC refers to "assault lanes," and is critical information for Support, so that supporting Soldiers do not fire on Assault. (See Assault Positions and Lanes, Pg. 170.) (See Deconflicting Support and Assault, Pg. 179.)

Support must backbrief the Patrol Leader on everything they were told and disseminate the information. The Patrol Leader gets GOTWA's and then conducts a radio check with Support. If the Patrol Leader is emplacing Support, they initiate recognition signals with the Main Body upon return.

13.c Assault

Assaulters are emplaced into an assault position, which is normally the last covered and concealed location before reaching the objective. (See Battle and Flank Positions, Pg. 60.) Often, objective areas are surrounded by open areas or obstacles that allow enemies to detect and attack Assaulters. Therefore, movement near the last covered and concealed position can be the most dangerous movement for Assault. Assault must move carefully, and establish local security measures in case it is attacked out of position.

Once in position, Assault must halt if Security and Support are not also in position and prepared to execute the raid. However, if Security and Support are ready to attack, then Assault can make a continuous movement to the objective. Thereby, Assault minimizes its time in the assault position, separated from Support and Security.

13.d Changing Roles

During the course of a raid, Assaulters, Supporters, and Security Soldiers may change their role. For example, at the start of a raid, Assaulters can fire on the objective from a stationary position before they assault. In effect, they would be supporting their future action. And after the initial assault, Assaulters also can transition to become Support or Security. For example, in a building with a thick, tall compound wall, Support will be unable to fire on the inside of the compound wall. But Assaulters, after securing a foothold, can turn around and become the Support Element that controls the inside of the compound.

Assaulters can also become a Security Element by covering potential enemy routes that are better seen from inside the objective building. If this new Security Element inside the objective building sees enemy forces approaching the building, they alert the remaining Assaulters, and place a heavy volume of fire on the enemy. Security Elements inside the objective buildings can also secure: enemy mouseholes between adjacent buildings; covered routes to the building; or approaches over adjoining roofs.

The distinction between Security and Support can be blurry because many weapon systems can equally well suppress enemies on the objective, and isolate the objective. For example, a Sniper Team can support Assault by securing windows on the objective building. But Snipers can also equally and simultaneously cover roads surrounding the objective building to isolate the objective. That being said, whenever possible, Security and Support are different because the ideal emplacement location for isolating the objective area, and the ideal location for providing supporting fires are usually different.

13.e Headquarters

Headquarters is responsible for command and control. In practice, this means coordinating the movement of elements by disseminating information. For example, although Assault may know to assault, they rely on Headquarters to tell them when to assault. And when elements combine, it is Headquarters that locates and coordinates troops to prevent friendly fire.

In urban battle, there is no substitute for ground-level leadership. Fighting is likely to take place inside, and is then invisible to everyone except the men actually fighting. Further, many thick structures even block radio signals, forcing a communication blackout.

Image 123: Soldiers from 6th Inf. Reg. and 4th Inf. Div., pull security during a barrier emplacement operation. Sadr City, Baghdad, Iraq, 12 May 2008. Although lacking cover, **these Soldiers can change roles** to Assault, Support, or Security.

The success of Israeli operations in Beirut was partly due to how the Israeli Defense Force developed small-unit leadership, which long stressed **the importance of initiative and independence among junior leaders**. However, a patrol has a limited number of ground-level Leaders with various qualifications, so the Leaders must be carefully and selectively utilized.

Although the location of Headquarters is highly dependent on the specific mission and Leaders, some general guidelines can be adhered to. The Patrol Leader is placed where they can best coordinate units and prevent friendly fire, while not being attacked themself. Often that is near the Main Body Assault. The Weapons Squad Leader controls the weapons of either Support or Security. The Patrol Sergeant is positioned where they can get accountability of forces but also utilize their experience. Commonly, the casualty collection point allows the Platoon Sergeant to get accountability while still being on the objective to assist. But if Support is powerful and complex, it may require both the Weapons Squad Leader and the Platoon Leader to coordinate.

Together, every Leader must be prepared to lead Assault in an attack or a withdrawal, since they are in the most danger, require the most coordination, and the raid fails without Assault. At the same time, if all Leaders are clumped together on the objective, the entire patrol becomes vulnerable if that one location is attacked.

14. Final Steps

After the Patrol Leader confirms that all elements are emplaced and all fires are coordinated, they attach to an element and contact all elements to ensure that comms are working. A Leader calls the spare-report for "raid occupied" to Higher Command. Then the patrol marks the boundaries or points within an objective to prepare indirect fire support. (See Scheme-of-Fires, Pg. 118.)

15. Contingencies[1]

It is impossible to plan for every contingency. However, below are some of the more common scenarios that are worth planning for.

15.a Running Out of Time

A mission that is running low on time to emplace can do a hasty emplacement. A hasty emplacement skips many steps of a regular emplacement to save time, but as a consequence, the attack sacrifices precision. First, the patrol eliminates leader's recon. Second, all elements drop rucks at the release-point and emplace simultaneously. The Patrol Leader briefs Security on their EWAC criteria, and all elements give GOTWA's before departing.

The Patrol Sergeant counts out all the elements at once. The Patrol Sergeant must still have full accountability of troops. Each element at their position confirms to the Patrol Leader that they are emplaced, and what they are aiming at to ensure coordinated fires. The coordinated fires must match the fires in the planning process to ensure deconfliction between elements.

15.b Compromise during Emplacement

At any time and from any direction, the patrol can be spotted and the patrol can be compromised. Compromise during a raid emplacement with split

---

1 **Quote:** In our schools, we generally assume that the organizations are well-trained and at full strength, that subordinates are competent, that supply arrangements function, that communications work, that orders are carried out. In war, many or all of these conditions may be absent. —U.S. Army Chief of Staff George C. Marshall

Rescue Team

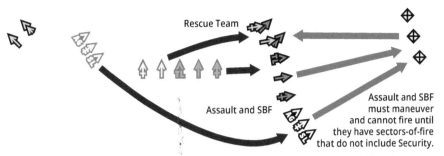

Rescue Team

Assault and SBF

Assault and SBF must maneuver and cannot fire until they have sectors-of-fire that do not include Security.

Image 124: The squad cannot assist until it knows where the split element is. A Rescue Team and a Flanking Team are used to retrieve the element and flank.

Phase 2

elements is a worst-case scenario for two reasons. First, split elements have **less manpower** available to defend against an enemy, and breaking contact with a split element is chaotic. Second, the enemy can **maneuver between** two of a patrol's elements, preventing both elements from firing (or else they might hit the element on the opposite side of the enemy). Therefore, contingency plans need to be prepared for many scenarios.

Security is emplaced before Support and Assault, specifically to reduce the risk of compromise. Security must be well hidden and always alert. And Security also must follow a well-defined EWAC plan and communicate danger. If the enemy approaches the patrol, Security can warn the other elements to conceal themselves where they are and prepare for enemy contact. The Patrol Leader or Security Leader then can choose to let the enemy pass or detain them. If the enemy attacks, then the patrol immediately performs a react-to-contact. In any case, the Patrol Leader should consider asking Higher Command for guidance if there is a risk of mission compromise.

If an attacked split-element is overwhelmed, the Patrol Leader must call on two Rescue Teams. (See Reserve Element, Pg. 24.) A raiding patrol often has Soldiers in reserve for situations just like these. The first Rescue Team splits off to suppress the enemy (just like break-contact). Special care must be used not to fire on the casualties' last known position, nor where they might have retreated to. The first Rescue Team bounds into position when necessary. The second Rescue Team moves to where the casualties are expected to be to retrieve them. All elements besides the Rescue Teams consolidate because the patrol cannot afford to engage the enemy on two fronts.

Phase 3 Contents

16. Attacks before Assaulting — 155
Tactical Callout — 156
Softening the Objective — 158
Enveloping and Preclearing — 159

17. Scheme-of-Maneuver for the Objective — 161
Threat Level of Spaces — 162
Footholds and Entrances — 163
Vertical Layout and Floors — 164
Horizontal Layout and Floorplan — 167
Assault Positions and Lanes — 170
Multiple Entries — 172

18. Support to Facilitate Assault's Maneuver — 173
Supporting Fires to Suppress and Divert — 176
Sectors-of-Fire and Coordinated Fires — 177
Deconflicting Support and Assault — 179

19. Outside Barrier and Compound Breach — 180
Reducing Blocking Obstacles (Walls and Gates) — 183
Reducing Entrapping Obstacles (Wire and Mines) — 187

20. Securing the Foothold — 189

21. Contingencies — 189
Weather — 190
Casualty Collection Point — 191
Quick Reaction Force — 192
Combat Ineffective Leader — 193

Joe Secures Space (Phase 3: Securing a Foothold)

If you get your foot in the door, kick the door in.

—*Unknown*

The golden rule of raids is to always be simple. A raid must have only one primary mission. All triggers must have multiple clear and obvious signals. Limit movement to linear directions. Enforce a strict communications plan that maximizes clear and concise communication above all else.

The raid starts when a Leader communicates that a trigger has been met. Some common triggers are: a time hack (e.g., "assault at 1400"), an enemy's attack, or on Higher's command. The first fires after a trigger are the most valuable because the enemy does not expect them. And they are important secondary triggers to elements that did not receive the primary trigger. To that end, **the second rule of raids is to always have a PACE plan.**[1]

The ultimate goal of the initial portion of a raid is to capture a foothold, which is a secure space behind the enemy's defensive perimeter. A foothold allows Soldiers to safely pass behind enemy defenses. Safe passage in turn allows for a local command, fast reinforcements, and the destruction of remaining defenses from the inside out. (See Footholds and Entrances, Pg. 163.)

16. Attacks before Assaulting

After the patrol arrives at the objective, but before Assault attempts to enter a building, the patrol can attack the objective. For example, the patrol can use external fires to force a surrender, canceling the assault entirely. If there is no surrender, Supporters use fires to soften enemy positions as much as possible

---

1 **Example** PACE Plan for Initiation of a Raid: Primary, Assault fires an AT4 and confirms via radio; Alternate, Patrol Leader fires their weapon; Contingency, Assault Leader fires their weapon; Emergency, red flare and indirect fire.

before the assault. And if fires are ineffective, Assaulters can envelope the building's outside to clear as many rooms from the outside as possible.

Finally, the patrol can always just wait for the enemy to do something stupid. The two sayings, "let the situation develop" and "take the initiative," have opposite meanings. The difference is in how an enemy acts; if the enemy is passive or even self-destructive, then Leaders may be patient on assaulting.[1]

16.a Tactical Callout[2]

A tactical callout takes place when enemies are asked to peacefully leave a building under the threat of violence. The violence is an escalation of external force; for example, if the enemy does not exit, then machine guns fire. And if the enemy still does not exit, artillery fires.

Callouts are useful if the danger of losing the element of surprise is less than the danger of entering the objective. Entering buildings in a warzone is dangerous because of booby-traps and armed resistance. And by stalling, there is strategic gain by giving the enemy the chance to surrender.

Callouts are primarily useful if the population is willing to surrender. If enemies never surrender, then either they will die from repeated attacks, in which case there was no need for a raid since total destruction was an option. Or the enemy doesn't die, and the patrol gave away the element of surprise but must raid anyway. And if the callout is prolonged, the mission becomes a siege, which is a different mission from a raid.

Callouts became commonplace in Iraq once the Iraqis realized that they could not stop U.S. Raiders. The Iraqis countered skillful close-quarters battle tactics by rigging entire buildings to explode and collapse, killing all Soldiers inside. Americans counter-countered by not entering, and conducted callouts.

American Soldiers isolated the objective to prevent enemies from fleeing. Then Soldiers conducted callouts in simple local language via microphone and

---

1 Quote: Never interrupt your enemy when he is making a mistake. —Napoleon Bonaparte

2 Quote: Whenever Russian military units proved incapable of effective urban operations, the Russians simply fell back on massive, overwhelming firepower to reduce a strongpoint. It was through the use of excessive, unrestrained firepower, and a complete lack of regard for collateral damage, that finally enabled the Russians to gain control of Grozny. —Marine Corps Warfighting Publication 3-35.3, Military Operations on Urbanized Terrain 1998

Image 125: Saddam Hussein's sons Qusay and Uday were killed in a tactical callout as they resisted coalition forces' attempt to apprehend and detain them. Soldiers of the Army's 101st Airborne Div. launched TOW missiles. Mosul, Iraq, 22 Jul 2003.

first ordered that all the women and children exit the objective. The women and children would be searched by the Iraqi Army. Then U.S. Soldiers would order the men to surrender and come out. If they opened fire, Americans would spray every window with machine gun fire. If the men fired again, U.S. forces would shoot rockets at every window. If then still the men didn't surrender and come out, the U.S. would airstrike and demolish the entire building. Tactical callouts were expensive, but they were **much safer for U.S. Forces** than entering booby-trapped buildings.

Specifically, Qusay and Uday Hussein, sons of Saddam Hussein, were killed in a 2003 operation. That morning, a Soldier called in Arabic for the people inside the house to peacefully exit. In return, the sons opened fire. Americans tried to assault the building, but backed out under more fire. Four American Soldiers were injured. Americans then fired with 50-caliber heavy machine guns, helicopter rockets, 40 mm grenades, and 10 TOW missiles. After four hours of callout and battle, Soldiers entered the house and found four bodies with no resistance. (See Image 125, Pg. 157.)

If the callout is successful, and people exit, the patrol must be wary of suicide bombers and false surrenders. And so local nationals sweep every exiting person for weapons in a designated area, and then the patrol double-checks. At this point, all exiting personnel are detainees, and unit-specific detainment procedures are used. (See Enemy Prisoner of War Team, Pg. 283.) If the goal of the raid was a person, the patrol can exfil; however, if the goal is related to the building itself then the raid may have to continue anyway.

16.b Softening the Objective

Softening is to attack and diminish an area without entering or destroying it. Raiders should always attempt to clear an objective from the outside as much as possible before engaging in a dangerous assault. The effects of preassault bombardment were illustrated during the D-Day invasion. There, the Pointe du Hoc fortification in Normandy was obliterated by eight RAF squadrons that dropped 635 tons of bombs. In contrast, bombers at nearby Omaha Beach missed their target. The casualties sustained by the assault at Omaha were 50 times that at Pointe du Hoc because Omaha Beach was not softened.

To soften an objective, a Patrol Leader orders direct and indirect fires such as mortar and artillery onto an objective before or during the initial assault. Fires can be destructive and destroy enemy positions and kill as many enemies as possible. But fires may also be nondestructive tear gas, illumination, obscuring smoke, etc. The objective can even be to "soften" strategically by restricting or encouraging enemy movement.

All firing elements, like mortars, Snipers, shoulder mounted munitions, and machine gun fire, can be coordinated in a scheme-of-fires. (See Scheme-of-Fires, Pg. 118.) For example, a common way to soften an objective is to have Snipers shoot all visible enemies simultaneously to Assault's raid initiation. When task organizing enemy threats to weapon systems, Leaders give targeting orders to the most precise level possible. For example, if there are five Soldiers and five enemies visible, then each enemy is specifically assigned to a Soldier. Thereby when the attack is initiated with surprise, the maximum number of enemies can be killed in the initial volley.

A specific modern-day example of softening is 120mm mortars destroying observation posts to cover the movement of Security as they establishes blocking positions on the enemy avenue-of-approach. Another is indirect fires distracting and killing any enemies around a breach site to protect Breachers. Breachers are very exposed because they must be stationary on the objective in front of a barrier. (See Outside Barrier and Compound Breach, Pg. 180.)

Image 126: U.S. Army Soldiers and Iraqi Army Soldiers soften an objective by destroying a possible vehicle born improvised explosive device. New Baqubah, Iraq, 02 Mar 2007. Destroying potentially dangerous or bunkered areas before Assault enters the objective **reduces the risk that Assault faces**.

Assaulting troops benefit from quickly assaulting softened areas. But that benefit must be weighed against the danger of being near the softening fires. This is why coordinating the echelonment of fires is important. (See Image 103, Pg. 122.)

16.c Enveloping and Preclearing

Enveloping is when Assaulters move around the outside of a structure, and secure as much of the inside as possible by peering in open windows and doors. For example, Soldiers can successively clear rooms as they walk around a structure clockwise or counter-clockwise. (See Image 127, Pg. 160.)

By looking in through windows, 90% of most rooms can be seen and fired on by Assaulters without ever entering a building. In fact, a patrol may be able to raid 90% of a one-story building without entering it. Thereby, Assaulters can make their later entry much safer.

Rooms cannot be marked as completely clear without a systematic internal clear. So **partial envelopments are still effective**. (See Image 128, Pg. 160.) And an envelopment can be any distance from the objective; although as

Enveloping and Preclearing

Direct Entry

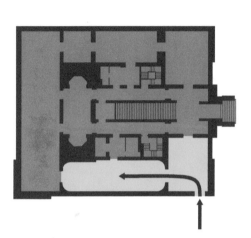

Enveloping

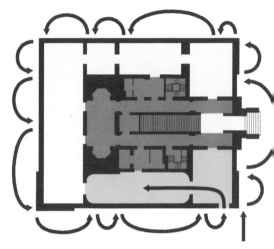

Image 127: Direct entry (left) does not preclear. Enveloping (right) preclears (yellow) through openings. Although precleared areas are safer, they are not secured areas (green) because the interior cannot be secured from the outside. **Any precleared areas must be recleared and secured upon entry.**

Image 128: U.S. SOF personnel **partially envelop** the objective buildings before assaulting during urban training. Panzer Kaserne, Stuttgart Germany, 25 Sep 2008.

Assaulters move farther, weapons become less effective, more time is needed, and more Assaulters are necessary for a complete envelopment.

Even if Assaulters cannot see into a building, enveloping allows Assaulters to assess the external structure in detail. After an on-the-ground assessment, the Assault Leader may change the pre-planned entry point. For example, the patrol may be able to use a ladder to conduct a top-down clearance.

Enveloping is useful but often unused when enemies are located outside the objective building where they can shoot Envelopers. Therefore, many urban Raiders prioritize getting into a building as fast as possible to use the building as cover from external enemy fires. (See Footholds and Entrances, Pg. 163.)

17. Scheme-of-Maneuver for the Objective

Scheme-of-maneuver (SOM) for the objective is just like SOM for infiltration, but more detailed because an objective has a denser concentration of enemies than the infiltration route. (See Scheme-of-Maneuver for Infiltration, Pg. 109.)

Specifically, a patrol gathers information about the objective, starts from the mission goal, and **backwards plans**. Assault must first secure a foothold that enables swift and secure movement. To get to the foothold, Assault must create an assault corridor, and an assaulting position. For Assault to maneuver, Support must fire on the objective to facilitate that maneuver. And Assault and Support must deconflict and coordinate their maneuver and fires. Finally, when the SOM for all Soldiers is determined, the Patrol Leader can create a scheme-of-fires to facilitate the raid. (See Scheme-of-Fires, Pg. 118.)

The following four sections are unordered because there is not a strict linear determination of what risks to take. For example, maybe the first choice is to enter from the top floor on the west side, but the foothold would require an explosive breach. So the plan is scrapped, the options are reopened, and the plan ends up being to attack from the ground floor on the east side.

Threat Level of Spaces

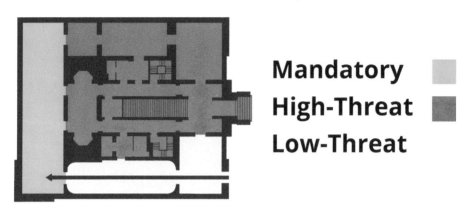

Mandatory

High-Threat

Low-Threat

Image 129: Here, the yellow area is low-threat and leads directly to the mandatory, blue area. Therefore, **the patrol need not secure the high-threat red areas** (the entrances and exits to the high-threat areas must still be secured).

17.a Threat Level of Spaces

The patrol reviews the mission to determine which locations must be secured to achieve mission success. Then much of the following analysis is determining how to secure a path to those rooms. Much of the time, the patrol secures the entire objective to eliminate as many lingering threats as possible. But equally valid to conserve resources, a patrol may cordon and isolate part of a large objective instead of securing it. (See Image 129, Pg. 162.)

Non-mandatory spaces can be divided into high-threat and low-threat. Any space with known enemies is high-threat; an empty space is low-threat; and anything in between depends on the unit. The scheme-of-maneuver secures **low-threats before high-threats**. Although every space on the objective can be high-threat; and if every space is a high-threat, the patrol may use a callout, or reconsider doing the raid. (See Tactical Callout, Pg. 156.)

Although more complex threat analysis can always be done, the purpose of analysis is not to simply know more, but to change action. For example, if a patrol is choosing not to create a foothold in a high-threat space, it matters little why that space is high-threat. Specific threat response, like to traps, is more relevant to task organization and CQB tactics than scheme-of-maneuver. (See Task Organization, Pg. 46.) After a specific threat is identified and countered in planning, the threat level of the room goes from high to low.

Image 130 et al: U.S. Marines with C Co., Bn. Landing Team 1/4, 15th Marine Expeditionary Unit climb through a window (left) to establish a foothold (right). Al Hamra Military Airfield, United Arab Emirates, 12 Mar 2021. **Compare how much safer the Soldiers are in the right image once they are inside the foothold.**

17.b Footholds and Entrances

The patrol must determine where Soldiers can enter each objective structure. Most often, the first room that Soldiers enter is the foothold. A foothold is the first secure position on the inside of an enemy's defensive perimeter from which further progress may be made. (There can also be a foothold building on an objective with multiple buildings.)

Footholds are extremely important because they allow a patrol to secure both sides of an entrance neutralizing the inherent danger of a bottleneck. Bottlenecked Soldiers are easily targeted by prepared enemies. The **primary purpose of the initial assault** of an objective is to establish a foothold behind the enemy's defensive perimeter. After a foothold is secured, the patrol possesses safe passage into and out of an enemy's defensive perimeter, effectively neutralizing it. Further, footholds have the defensive benefit of being inside. Soldiers can more safely set up a base of fire within a structure rather than out into the open. (See Image 130 et al, Pg. 163.)

Because a foothold is relatively secure, **leadership performs tasks there**, like troop accountability and a casualty collection point. And during a raid, if a more secure location is found, the patrol can move there from the foothold.

A foothold and an entrance must be chosen together at one location, because a foothold without an entrance is impossible, and an entrance without a foothold is dangerous. Sometimes the foothold and entrance location are chosen based on the best entrance. For example, entering through an unsecured, unlocked door takes no resources; whereas, entering through a concrete wall can require explosive breaching. Other times, the entrance is chosen based on the foothold; a top floor with a tactically superior foothold can require rappelling through the glass of top-floor windows.

Phase 3

17.c Vertical Layout and Floors

The Patrol Leader must decide which floor to enter on: the top, bottom, or both with simultaneous entries. **Entering a top floor is more aggressive.** Moving down stairwells, Soldiers move with more momentum, have a better view than moving up stairs, and face fewer defenses because defenders rarely consider top-down raids. Further, gravity allows grenades and explosives to be dropped on the enemy through holes in the roof or floors. For maximum violence, an Assaulter cooks a grenade and drops it through a hole in the roof, and then sprays the lower room with gunfire.

The aggression and availability of ground-level escape routes force enemies to quickly withdraw from the building, whereas a bottom-up attack corners enemies on top floors causing them to fight more fiercely. When enemies attempt to flee outside, Soldiers on rooftops with 360-degree security around the building can neutralize enemies as they attempt to escape.

The rooftop and top floor are not good footholds when there is not overwhelming force and isolation to protect a continuous inflow of Soldiers. And after the patrol makes enemy contact on the upper floors, it becomes extremely difficult for the patrol to withdraw. Casualties especially are hard to evacuate upwards. Moreover, Soldiers are vulnerable moving in exposed elevated positions. In particular, helicopters are a massive target. In Chechnya, the Russians found their helicopters highly vulnerable to rooftop Snipers and ambushes. Although Russian doctrine had long specified the capture of a building from the top-down, it became apparent in Grozny that this tactic was too expensive in terms of helicopter losses.

The largest obstacle to a top-floor entrance is getting there. Soldiers can access top floors by climbing fire escapes, drainpipes, ladders, or roofs of adjoining buildings; or they can land on the roof via helicopter. Once on the top level, Soldiers can walk through a fire door, jump through a hole in the roof, or rappel or climb through a window. Once inside, Soldiers can use stairs or just continue to break through the floor.

Climbing up a building provides quick access to the upper levels of a low building. In Grozny, the Russians found that lightweight ladders were invaluable equipment for Assaulters. Vehicle-elevated entry allows Assaulters to enter buildings from the second or third level but requires coordination with vehicles and their Security. (See Image 156, Pg. 185.)

Image 131: Greek Soldiers **fast-rope** onto a roof alongside U.S. Army Paratroopers assigned to B Co., 2nd Bn., 503rd Inf. Reg., 173rd Airborne Bde. and attack an objective. Kilkis, Greece, 23 Nov 2019.

Image 132: A U.S. Marine CPL, 31st MEU, attacks through a window while rappelling down a rappel tower. Camp Hansen, Okinawa, Japan, 14 Apr 2016. **Attacking from the roof is an effective way to raid, but requires control of the airspace.**

Image 133 et al: Multinational SOF enter a building through a second-story window. Pfullendorf, Germany, 07 Mar 2018. **Using ladders or vehicles to enter the second floor allows Assaulters to bypass a heavily defended ground floor.**

Also, helicopters can only land on buildings with a roof strong enough to carry their weight (a parking garage on the roof is a sign that it will be strong enough). If the roof is weak, Soldiers can dismount or rappel as the helicopter hovers a few feet above the roof. (See Image 131, Pg. 165.)

A **bottom-level entry** can be much easier and faster for Assault against an undefended enemy. And the Patrol Leader can switch from assaulting to an easy withdrawal; casualties can be pulled out more easily going down stairs.

But against a well-prepared enemy, a bottom-level entry is much more difficult because of enemy defenses on the ground floor. Alert and hostile enemies cover and secure ground-floor doors and windows. Against a defended enemy, Assaulters avoid windows and only use doors as a last resort. And after entry, attacking up is less safe than attacking down because the enemy has all same advantages defending from the top level that the patrol would have had attacking from the top level (listed earlier in the section).

If entry cannot be made through the top or ground floor, then Assaulters can enter a **middle floor**. Assaulters can rappel down the outside of a building with a weapon ready to fire and without silhouetting themselves in a window. Or Assaulters can climb up something. (See Image 133 et al, Pg. 166.) Middle floors are the least defended and expose Soldiers less than entering on a top floor. However, Soldiers are exposed to enemy attack from both the top and bottom floors once they enter.

17.d Horizontal Layout and Floorplan

Determining how to move on an objective starts with determining the layout of the objective and knowing where the mission objective is within that layout. If the floorplan or layout is unknown, then the patrol must guess the layout based on the building's construction. (See Building Construction, Pg. 57.) (Know that walls are guidelines to a patrol with wall breaching charges.) However, if the layout is known, then general rules about navigating a layout determine how a patrol moves within the objective.[1]

First, a patrol clears through a building by always attacking the room that **minimizes the perimeter** of the total secured area. (See Image 135, Pg. 168.) Less outer perimeter makes it easier to pull security. If the outside is secure, then the patrol must only minimize the internal border between secured and unsecured areas. (See Image 134, Pg. 168.) Maintaining the smallest secure perimeter and border between secured and unsecured areas applies to attacks of every size. (See Chunking, Pg. 134.)

In practice, this means it is safer to attack a building's corners and sides instead of charging the center. Corners and short sides typically are also the shortest distance from outside cover and concealment (thereby reducing the time that assaulters are in the open).

An exception to this occurs when supplies are unlimited and speed is essential. During a hostage rescue, for example, Assaulters may flood into the center of a building for its better access points, to clear rooms at maximum speed and get the hostage. When a raid just needs to get from point A to point B, it can focus on isolating nonessential parts of a building instead of clearing them.

Do not get lost in counter-tactics and anti-counter-tactics. It is unlikely an enemy will be able to precisely predict a scheme-of-maneuver during a live raid, even if they know the guidelines; and raiding the base of an elite enemy who is capable of timely predictions is probably a bad idea in the first place anyway.

Horizontal Layout Part 1

Securing the long side of a building makes a larger border between the secured and unsecured area.

SECURED
UNSECURED

Securing the short side of a building makes a smaller border between the secured and unsecured area.

SECURED	UNSECURED

Image 134: Attacking areas with **smaller unsecured perimeters is safer** because the emeny has a smaller perimeter to attack from. The concept of reducing ratio of border to area to the smallest size is not limited to building floorplans. It also has applicability to every kind of security.

Horizontal Layout Part 2

Schemes of maneuver aim to reduce the perimeter (whether neighborhoods or buildings), thereby reducing where the enemy can attack from.

Clearing the side does not increase the perimeter of the uncleared area at all. The green area has only four entryways.

Clearing the center first has increased the perimeter of the uncleared area by 50%! The red area has ten entryways!

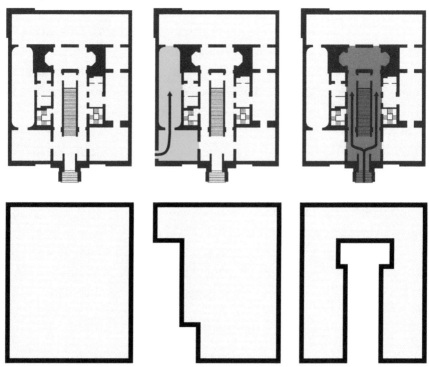

Image 135: This diagram shows two approaches to a scheme-of-maneuver: a clear from the side of a buidling (middle) and clear from the center (left). A building center is defined as any room that has **unknown openings on three sides**. If entering a center, back up, and clear rooms on one of the three sides so that the room is no longer a "center" before reentering it. (See Backing Out and Reengaging, Pg. 279.)

Horizontal Layout Part 3

Schemes of maneuver avoid a dead center because an enemy in between two elements can cause friendly fires.

Clearing from two sides reduces the risk of friendly fire by allowing each side a clear line of fire.

Clearing from three sides potentially places an enemy between two friendly elements.

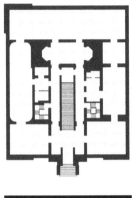
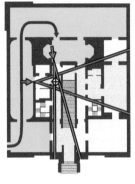
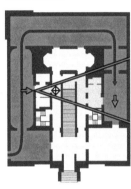

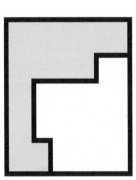

Image 136: **Never leave a center uncleared!** An uncleared center risks friendly fire. A large part of a Leader's job is tracking units to prevent friendly fire incidents caused by Soldiers in different areas being unaware of each other.

Second, the patrol must also maintain the smallest perimeter possible by **not creating a dead center** between secured areas. If two secured areas with Soldiers are opposite each other, and an enemy is between them in an unsecured area, then the Soldiers on either side must avoid shooting past the enemy and hitting each other. (See Image 136, Pg. 169.) To avoid a friendly fire incident when there are multiple Clearing Teams on one floor, the teams must coordinate heavily. (See Coordinating Multiple Teams, Pg. 270.) And the teams must secure the center between two sides before securing the third and fourth side of the objective building.

17.e Assault Positions and Lanes

An assault position is a position from which Assault assaults to the objective. **An assault position is just like any other battle position.** (See Battle and Flank Positions, Pg. 60.) Except, assault positions often offer less cover and concealment and have a shorter travel time to the next position to speed up the assault. From the release-point, Assault is emplaced into its position where it waits for the raid to start. (Note that a patrol may forgo an explicit assault position and just assault from the dropoff point for speed and simplicity.)

A string of assault positions comprises an **assault lane**; i.e. Assault may zigzag between different intermediate covered positions. If there are no battle positions, then the assault lane is a straight line. To make Assault even safer as they maneuver, the patrol enforces an artificial corridor around each assault lane. For example, Assaulters throw smoke while Support fires to the left and right of the lane, halting any enemy counterattack. (See Image 137, Pg. 171.)

Assault maneuvers to the objective as quickly as possible, and so cannot provide its own accurate fires on the enemy. (See Shooting while Moving, Pg. 83.) However, if Assault must provide its own supporting fires, it can bound to the objective. (See Bounding and Crossing Intersections, Pg. 99.)

Assault lanes can be planned at any elevation, whether that is along rooftops or underground. In peacetime, robbers have successfully used sewers to approach and raid banks. In the battle of Grozny, well-organized small groups of Chechnyan rebels (fewer than 16 at a time) moved freely using the city's sewer network, even sneaking behind Russian lines and attacking unsuspecting Soldiers from the rear. Isolating areas are so important because enemies are also free to create assault lanes. (See Isolation Area, Pg. 136.)

However, using sewers or tunnels is rare. For large units, traveling in narrow tunnels is logistically difficult; the opposing force will collapse entire underground networks in response. And for small groups, it is easier to hide in plain sight and drive up to the objective in civilian clothing. The Irish Republican Army frequently wore civilian clothing to conduct small-scale raids (despite the illegality).

Once a lane and foothold are established (See Footholds and Entrances, Pg. 163.), **the assault lane is reinforced with dedicated Security.** At least one lane must be safely maintained during the entire raid to permit resupply, medical evacuation, reinforcement, or withdrawal from the building.

Phase 3

Assault Lanes

Assault Lane is Closed   ## Assault Lane is Open

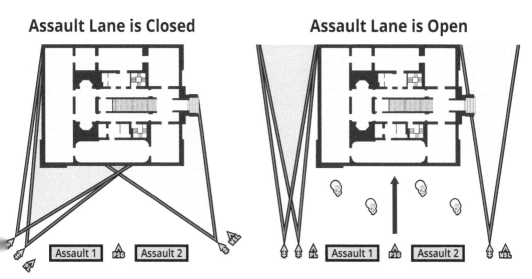

Image 137: Support attacks the objective, and then opens a lane and throws smoke.

Image 138: Soldiers of the Michigan N.G. 1st Bn., 125th Inf. Reg. run through smoke laid down to obscure their movement. 18 Sep 2017.

Image 139: Honduran TIGRES assault a building. 27 Feb 2015. **This assault in broad daylight is very dangerous without surprise or an obscurant.**

Image 140: Marines with A Co., Marine Barracks Washington, assault to a building. Marine Corps Base Quantico, VA, 11 Jul 2021. **Multiple smoke canisters** were thrown, but the smoke either did not billow or it was swept by the wind.

The movement formation along the assault lane is primarily determined by: the method of breach; Assault's intended actions at the entry point; the assault lane's width and depth; obstacles within the assault lane; and anticipated enemy resistance. For example, moving a diamond formation maximizes front security in a small element, but a file formation maximizes the speed of coordinated movement under enemy fire. Regardless of the ideal though, **any formation is better than no formation.**

17.f Multiple Entries

An advanced raiding technique is entering two locations at the same time. Two teams can enter from adjacent walls (e.g., the North face and the West face) to form an L shape, or they may enter on different floors.

Entering two locations is effective for a few reasons:

▸ Two teams create two battlefronts and clear twice as fast, which is harder to fight and barricade against.

▸ If an enemy decides to retreat from one team, they can run into the other.

▸ Violence and noise from two directions can multiply and seem to come from every direction, confusing the enemy.

In the Hypercacher kosher supermarket raid, two elements of French police **simultaneously entered** a large open space (i.e., a supermarket) from the front and left side, forming an L-shape. One team entered and pushed threats toward the other team. (See Fighting in L Shapes, Pg. 109.)

And an **offset entry** was used during the 1980 Iranian Embassy hostage-rescue raid in London, England. The Army decided that the benefits of speed and enemy-confusion outweighed the drawback of difficult coordination. On the objective, the four men of Red Team rappelled down from the roof to the top floor of the embassy. There, they broke windows, threw in grenades, and chased the grenades into the top floor. Slightly behind Red Team, Blue Team detonated explosives on a first-floor window. Red Team's bombastic, offset entry **distracted the enemy** from Blue Team's entry.

Of course, the danger of a multiple entry is difficult coordination. Multiple entries require the Assault Leader to carefully coordinate the entries. For example, if explosive breaching is used, the Assault Leader will conduct the countdown, instead of a Team Leader. Support Elements may also be timed with the simultaneous breach, in which case the Patrol Leader will conduct the countdown.

Image 141: U.S. Marines with the Maritime Raid Force, 26th MEU simultaneously clear multiple floors. Camp Lejeune, NC, 14 Jun 2017. To **maximize distraction**, the timing is offset so an enemy focused on one clear is surprised by the other.

Image 142: 5th Special Forces Group (Airborne) Soldiers, simultaneously detonate three door charges while training room-clearing. Undisclosed Location, 03 Sep 2019. To **maximize surprise**, initial contact is as simultaneous as possible.

18. Support to Facilitate Assault's Maneuver

Assault is exposed and vulnerable when assaulting because moving Soldiers cannot aim well. (See Shooting while Moving, Pg. 83.) Therefore, Support-by-Fire loudly and aggressively fires onto the objective to scare and distract the enemy, and masks the assault. Supporters attack known and unknown threats, such as enemies, doorways, windows, and adjacent buildings. Specific targets are identified and marked with tracers, M203 smoke, high-explosives, etc. And Supporters kill or detain anyone trying to exit an objective building.

Suppressive fires may be used from the start or be delayed to maintain stealth. Once suppressive fires begin, they increase and continue until they risk friendly fire on advancing Assault. (See Deconflicting Support and Assault, Pg. 179.) Fires can be offset by as little as 10 degrees during an active battle.

And Support continuously fires if the ammo supply allows. However, precise well-placed shots suppress far more effectively than a volume of fire alone.

Support and Inner Security are similar in that they both attack the objective with direct line-of-sight and do not assault the objective. (See Isolation Area, Pg. 136.) The difference is that Support furthers the assault, while Security isolates. An example of a practical difference is that Support attempts to be as distracting as possible, while Security is more subdued.

The Primary Support Element is usually positioned at a right angle to the assault and any secondary supporting fires, so that Support and Assault can create an L-shape with their fires, maximizing coverage. (See Fighting in L Shapes, Pg. 109.) (See Image 97, Pg. 114.) (See Image 150, Pg. 178.)

Every Assault benefits from having a Secondary Support on the opposite side of the Primary Support. (See Image 137, Pg. 171.) (See Image 150, Pg. 178.) The Patrol Leader may even consider having a third, Vertical Support for tall buildings. This is because Assaulters block Primary Support's fires; for example, a Support-by-Fire on the left cannot fire through Assaulters to suppress an enemy on the right. If necessary, Assaulters themselves can provide a Stationary Element by bounding to the objective. (See Bounding and Crossing Intersections, Pg. 99.)

Armored fighting vehicles, machine guns, and other direct-fire weapon systems are all useful Support-by-Fire. Other kinds of support are not as responsive or precise, but they can also assist an assault. For example, indirect fire utilizes the echelonment of fires. (See Image 103, Pg. 122.)

Based on the inherent strengths of each weapon system, the Support Leader chooses what weapons system will be Support and what their priority-of-targets will be. For example, M240 machine guns are ideal for stopping enemy vehicles, so they prioritize shooting engine blocks, then vehicle cabs, and then dismounted troops. Other examples of prioritization include:

► Riflemen engage actual enemy personnel, and not potential threats.
► Machine guns fire into probable enemy positions like streets, windows, doors, and mouseholes.
► Armored fighting vehicles and shoulder-launched munitions fire at vehicles, reinforced battle positions, breaching locations, and sniper hides.

As Assault moves through the objective, Support may maneuver between a series of static firing positions to gain better fields of fire, and to avoid being targeted by the enemy. When Support follows behind Assault or continuously

Support-by-Fire

Image 143: U.S. SOF pull overwatch **from a distance**. Kishim, Babakashan, Afghanistan, 13 Sep 2011.

Image 144: A U.S. Soldier provides support and a 50-caliber **distraction**. Iraq, 31 Dec 2018.

Image 145: U.S. Marines set **nearby** support during room-clearing procedures. Jordan, 13 May 2021.

Image 146: U.S. Marines provide **rolling support** while others assault. Okinawa, Japan, 08 Dec 2014.

Image 147: Infantrymen assigned to 2nd Bn., 35th Inf. Reg., 25th Inf. Div. fires his M4 carbine during a counterattack. Schofield Barracks, Hawaii, on Dec. 5 2017. It is a good idea to **set support in an adjacent building.**

maneuvers, it is called "**Rolling Support.**" (See Image 146, Pg. 175.) Rolling Support is especially common in enclosed areas when Assault maneuvers to a position that blocks Support's fires. Support with blocked fires is useless, and so by moving they can attain new fires and continue to contribute to the raid. If Support follows Assaulters into the objective, Support may even be able to turn around and pull security from the inside out.

After Assaulters enter the objective, if there is no more maneuver to be made nor any isolation to be done, Support often waits in place at the ready for the next phase of the operation to occur.

18.a Supporting Fires to Suppress and Divert[1]

Supporting fires are integral to raids. However, their primary purpose is often not to kill the enemy, because the enemy is bunkered and difficult to kill. Instead, **the purpose of supporting fires is often psychological.**[2] For example, An M240 machine gun firing 7.62 ammunition is loud and intimidating; and a single machine gun can fire hundreds of rounds per minute. If the Gun Team can divert the enemy's attention and get them to cower in fear, the Gun Team reduces enemy fires on Assault.

Indirect fires are even louder and even more distracting. Destructive fires can be used on a separate part of the objective, away from the Assaulters. Or illumination rounds can be fired above enemies to both reveal their position and degrade their ability to see Assaulters.

Assault often does not fire until engaged to avoid attracting attention while Support is suppressing the enemy. Once Support can no longer fire onto the objective because Assault masks fires (i.e., gets in front of the fires), Support shifts its fires away. (See Deconflicting Support and Assault, Pg. 179.)

In fact, neither Assault nor Support must fire at the start of a raid. The longer the enemy is ignorant of the patrol's presence the better. However,

---

1 Quote: To feint with one fist and strike with the other yields an advantage, but a still greater advantage lies in being able to interchange them—to convert the feint into the real blow if the opponent uncovers himself. —British Captain and Military Theorist B. H. Liddell Hart

2 Real World: The most difficult part of real battle to replicate in realistic training is fear. Fake enemies know they are immortal, and act accordingly. But real enemies being attacked don't ignore tremendous machine-gun and indirect fires.

Image 148: Soldiers with 86th Inf Bde., Maine Army N.G. establish a support-by-fire position. Jericho, Vermont, 20 Jul 2020. Machine guns are **incredibly loud**, and combined with tracer rounds can make otherwise aggressive enemies cower.

Image 149: A Paratrooper with 503rd Inf. Reg., 173rd Airborne Bde. engages with the M240B machine gun. Grafenwoehr, Germany, 20 Jul 2020. This mobile firing position can **distract enemies** with hundreds or thousands of armor piercing rounds

many patrols use explosive force to breach, alerting the enemy anyway. If a patrol is compromised, the initial attack must begin with **overwhelming force** to surprise and overwhelm the enemy.

18.b Sectors-of-Fire and Coordinated Fires

A sector-of-fire is the area within which a Soldier actively observes and fires their weapon. Attaining good sectors-of-fire is vital, and may even require the destruction of adjacent buildings blocking the view of the objective buildings.

Leaders assign and overlap sector-of-fires for each weapon system to ensure there are no gaps in coverage. To assign a sector-of-fire, a Leader gives their Soldier(s) a right limit-of-fire and a left limit-of-fire (and in 3D terrain, top and bottom limits), and instructs the Soldier(s) to secure the area between.

Each weapon system in a position can be assigned an individual sector and priority within their sector. For example, each of three M240s with overlapping sectors-of-fire is given a different priority: left, middle, and right. Or all weapon systems can be given the same sector and priorities, forming a **strongpoint**. A strongpoint is resilient because it maintains its fires even if a single weapon system is incapacitated. Every covered area of the objective area must have at least 200% coverage (i.e. coverage by two armed Soldiers or more) so that if a Soldier becomes a casualty complete coverage is not lost.

A common error when assigning sectors is to distribute them proportionally, giving each Soldier an even slice of the surrounding area to surveil. However,

Sectors-of-Fire and Coordinated Fires

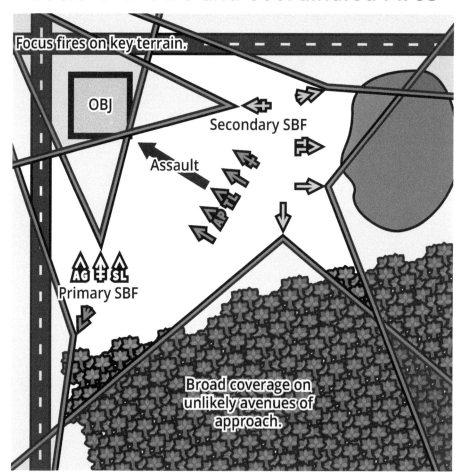

Image 150: Sectors-of-fire are focused in areas where enemy contact is expected, and are wider where enemy contact is unlikely. Assault is roughly perpendicular to Primary SBF, and Assault has support on both the right and left sides.

that is a mistake. Soldiers should not be split evenly between a golf course and a populated office building. Instead, sectors are focused and allocated **proportionally to the danger posed**, and not the amount of area covered.

During planning, the Patrol Leader begins coordinating fires by giving specific firing instructions to subordinate Leaders. For example, "Support will cover the East side of the building 22 during Assault's approach." From there, subordinate Leaders break down their assignment into smaller chunks, which they assign to individual weapons systems. For example, "Gun Team 1 covers floor 1, and Gun Team 2 covers floor 2." More important weapons systems are assigned first, in case the patrol receives enemy contact during assignment.

Making Soldiers remember and understand their limits-of-fire cannot be undervalued. Leaders assign sectors-of-fire on the ground because pre-planned battle positions and sectors-of-fire are not always viable. Here are four examples of **enforcing limits-of-fire** (ideally using multiple methods at once):

▸ Lie on a Soldier and grab and point their weapon to an identifiable feature (visible day and night). The stranger the feature, the better the recall.

▸ Have the Soldier pull out their compass and pick their own features at an azimuth given to them.

▸ Fire an infrared laser (e.g., the PEQ-15) at a limit.

▸ Place aiming stakes on either side of the weapon to physically limit weapon movement to the left and right.

The Support and Patrol Leaders are ultimately responsible for completing the interlock. So after sectors are assigned, Soldiers and Leaders must backbrief their sectors all the way up to the Support and Patrol Leader to ensure that all sectors are coordinated and there are no gaps in coverage. For example, in a squad-size Support, the Bravo Team Leader finishes assigning their own team interlocking sectors-of-fire, and then confirms or reassigns sectors to the Alpha Team to ensure 360-degree coverage.

Phase 3

18.c Deconflicting Support and Assault

Leadership must prevent Support from continuing to fire on an area or objective that Assault is entering, or risk friendly fire. Leadership controls Support by issuing the fire commands, "shift-fire," "raise-fire," and "cease-fire." Shift-fire moves fires horizontally, raise-fire (or lower-fire) moves fires vertically, and cease-fire stops fires completely. As Assault approaches Support's line-of-fire, anyone will yell "**Shift-fire!**" (or "raise" or "cease"). But specifically, the Patrol Leader also yells it, since they are directly responsible for coordinating the elements. If "shift, "raise," or "cease" is not echoed by Support: STOP, HALT, DO NOT CONTINUE!

In a raid where there are **phase lines**, Support shifts or raises fires multiple times between different sections as Assault advances. When Assault approaches or controls the area beyond a phase line, Support moves their fires to the following phase line, so they are always one phase line ahead of Assault. The first phase line is activated when Assault reaches their last cover and concealment, and can effectively fire on the objective themselves. A command could be "Shift fire to phase line red." (See Phase Lines, Pg. 113.)

Without phase lines, the patrol can still use shift and raise fire to move their fires past Assault's limit-of-advance, which becomes a restrictive fire line. These fires from Support distract and intimidate the enemy while Assault advances on the objective. If Assault approaches the limit-of-advance, Support must cease firing. Thereby, fires are always in front of Assault and there is always a large gap between Support's fires and Assault.

Before a raid, the Patrol Leader gives the Support Leader **reference points** for many locations to create a control plan for Support-by-Fire:

▸ Assault's initial location and scheme-of-maneuver on the objective. If Support is not aware of Assault's location at any time, the result can be catastrophic. Therefore, during the raid, the Assault Leader must send constant updates to Support. This is aided on an urban battlefield where terrain is easily described and identified.

▸ Every phase line on the objective, so that when Assault approaches the phase line, Support can shift-fire to the next phase line, or cease-fire if it is the final phase line. (All fire commands use a preplanned PACE.)

▸ Every last-cover-and-concealment location for Assault before each phase line on the objective. (This can be simplified via a rule such as the last cover and concealment is the first building behind a phase line.)

A common command control plan for a building raid is to first, have Support fire on the entire objective building. Then, once Assault is about to mask Support's fires on the ground floor, the Patrol Leader raises Support's fires to the upper or lower windows. When Assault enters the building, Support shifts fires to adjacent buildings to prevent enemy withdrawal or reinforcement.

19. Outside Barrier and Compound Breach

Barriers slow or stop forward movement, or alert the enemy. So, Raiders must always be prepared to breach; if barriers can't be cleared, there is no raid. This section is an overview because a full explanation would require another book.

Image 151: Soldiers assigned to 2nd Bde., 2nd Inf. Div., employ SOSRA to suppress a breaching area inside their Stryker and wait for a smoke screen to fully engulf and obsure the breaching area. NTC, Fort Irwin, CA, 12 Sep 2017.

To choose how to breach, the patrol first determines what enemy barriers are potentially present. At the most basic level, outside barriers can be broken down into two kinds: blocking (e.g., walls) and entrapping (e.g., mines). Sometimes easily destroyed barriers to visbility are also used outside. (See Closed Door Reconnaissance, Pg. 207.)

After determining potential and actual barriers, the patrol inventories their assets for specific tools that can breach the specific targets. For example, a Humvee may be able to climb over a wall, but not a dozen layers of concertina wire. In contrast, bolt cutters work great on wire but don't help climb a wall. If the barriers exceed the patrol's assets, then there cannot be a raid. For example, if the patrol has no explosives or armored vehicles, they cannot breach reinforced concrete barriers.

After determining how many breaching tools the patrol as a whole will carry, the Patrol Leader task organizes the tools to specific Soldiers. (See Task Organization, Pg. 46.) Thereby if a Soldier becomes a casualty, the breaching tools can easily be recovered to continue the mission.

Breaching may dictate how many Soldiers can conduct the raid. For example, if only one small breach can be made for a platoon-sized Assault, that means dozens of Soldiers must converge and pass through a single chokepoint. Soldiers would be vulnerable for an unacceptably long time. A safer raid uses a larger breach or multiple breach points for faster inflow. (See Multiple Entries, Pg. 172.)

To choose where to breach, the Patrol Leader uses a scheme-of-maneuver just like for the objective. (See Scheme-of-Maneuver for the Objective, Pg. 161.) Moreover, different sites have a trade-off between speed and security. Locations where breaching is unnecessary and entry is fast (e.g., an open gate) are often the most observed areas, and choosing them may compromise the patrol faster. But locations where the structure is strong but unobserved (e.g., a wall of reinforced concrete) can require extensive breaching and delay an entry by too much time.

At the breaching site with the breaching tools, Soldiers perform **SOSRA**: Suppress, Obscure, Secure, Reduce, (Proof), and Assault. (Proofing is optional so it is not in the official U.S. Army acronym.) Many units only rehearse reducing (i.e., breaching) and fail to spend time on the other parts of SOSRA; however, it is important to rehearse all parts of SOSRA.

Suppress – enemies and their fires near the breach site to allow Breachers to act. (See Support to Facilitate Assault's Maneuver, Pg. 173.)

Obscure – the breaching area to increase concealment. Usually smoke is used; however, smoke will compromise an otherwise hidden patrol. Smoke is thrown between enemy positions and the breach, or at enemy positions. But smoke is not thrown at the breach itself because intense smoke inhalation is dangerous. Do not blindly charge at an active smoke or CS tear gas grenade! Smoke grenades produce a variety of colored smoke which can be used to signal information about different breach points.

Secure – the Breachers and the breach site. At the breach site, Assaulters ensure all enemies are gone, pull security at the breach site, and check for any IEDs. In SOSRA, "secure" is somewhat redundant with "suppress" but suppressing is usually done by Support while securing is done by Assault at the breach site. A breach is not fully secured until Soldiers have secured a foothold and destroyed the enemy on the opposite side.

Reduce – (i.e., breach) the obstacle. Different obstacles require different methods. (See Reducing Blocking Obstacles (Walls and Gates), Pg. 183.) (See Reducing Entrapping Obstacles (Wire and Mines), Pg. 187.) The goal of the destruction of an obstacle is to create a lane, through which Soldiers can move. (See Assault Positions and Lanes, Pg. 170.) Creating

Image 152: Marine Recruits of 2nd Recruit Training Bn. secure and reduce a wire entrapping obstacle in preparation for an assault. Parris Island, S.C., 12 Dec 2018.

a lane and proofing it is a decisive point in a raid and is reported to the Patrol Leader. Follow-on units can improve the breach.

Every part of SOSRA needs a PACE (primary, alternate, contingency, emergency) plan, but reducing especially needs one. What if snow melts and newly wet clay stalls the breaching vehicle? What if the primary Breacher is killed? If the breaching plan fails, then the entire raid will fail.

(Proofing) – is when Breachers verify, mark, and report the boundaries of the assault lanes to guide the Assaulters. This is optional because many times Assaulters are next to the Breachers and they can talk, foregoing wasting time on proofing an obvious assault lane. And proofing some obstacles like minefields adds unnecessary risk. (See Marking a Space, Pg. 268.)

Assault – the breach. Assaulters enter the breach with a low silhouette and clear the opposite side using close-quarters battle techniques. (See Close-Quarters Battle Basics, Pg. 195.) Once the far-side is secure, broaden and improve the lane! The Clearing Team must prepare for more breaches.

19.a Reducing Blocking Obstacles (Walls and Gates)

Blocking obstacles such as thick concrete walls prevent movement. Since walls and compounds are visible from the outside, Soldiers can plan beforehand on which specific breaching tools to bring for the actual obstacles.

But before reduction, a patrol first considers **bypassing the obstacle**. Rarely do blocking obstacles form a bubble around the objective, so the easiest method to reduce a blocking obstacle is to bypass it. Going over a wall only requires a ladder, a vehicle, or even just a few Soldiers. Barbed wire on the top of the wall can be defeated by cutting it, or draping a thick carpet over it.

If going over a wall is too dangerous or slow, then the patrol can reduce a weak point—for example, ramming a gate with an armored vehicle. Even a stock sedan can bust open a chain link fence gate (although the airbags may deploy); the car only needs to breach the latch to push the gate open. Vehicles can even continue to drive straight to the objective building's entrance.[1]

Without a safer bypass or weak point, the patrol can **create a new entrance** by breaching. An effective troop entrance is at least 80 by 130 centimeters, and is away from entry points to reduce detection by the enemy. There are many ways to make a new opening: tank fire, missiles, indirect fire, explosives, or even ramming an armored vehicle into a wall.

The safest way to breach a wall is from far away. Using shoulder-launched munitions (SLM's), tank rounds, and indirect fire eliminates the danger of having Breachers stall at a wall placing a charge or cutting wire. To use SLM's requires knowledge of the material to be breached, and multiple shots must be planned. The AT4 or the Carl Gustav penetrates wooden structural walls (and may not even explode on a soft target). But they usually do not penetrate a heavy European-style stone wall and may require three to five rounds to penetrate brick walls. The M141 Bunker Defeat Munition can produce a hole in brick walls that is large enough to be a breach hole.

Sometimes the resources needed to breach from a distance are unavailable, and the patrol cannot rely on a stealth option. In that case explosives are used because they are easy to carry and can reliably create a hole in a wall. When used against non-reinforced concrete walls, 2 pounds of C4 produces a climbing hole; 5 pounds create a hole large enough for one man; 7 pounds create a hole large enough for two men side-by-side; 10 pounds can blow a vehicle-sized hole, or destroy the entirety of a weak building; and 20 pounds of C4 can penetrate a meter of concrete. Smaller amounts of C4 can be used,

---

1 **Quote:** Double-breach operations involve two sets of explosions [], which of course would mean [the enemy General would] have time to either arm himself or flee. A Tank Commander [] suggested we use one of his M1A1s and forget about the explosive charges.... The tank would roll through the gate and smash the door, and our guys could swarm around it and into the General's home in one smooth action. Naturally, we embraced this idea. —SEAL Team 6 Team Leader Ryan Zinke,

Reducing Blocking Obstacles (Walls and Gates)

Image 153: If the manpower is available, just **step on other Soldiers** to overcome a barricade.

Image 154: Barbed wire fences can be neutralized quickly with a ladder and a **heavy carpet** (or driving through it).

Image 155: Tanks can destroy most barricade in seconds. Other AFV's can also **drive through** brick and wood.

Image 156: Vehicles are great **platforms** for accessing the second floor of a building for a vertical attack.

Image 157: Blowing up reinforced concrete with explosives is very effective.

Image 158: Using excess explosives is effective. But be aware that big explosions require **big standoff**.

and a patrol can be efficient by experimenting to find the correct size for the types of walls typically found in the battle area. 5 pounds of TNT can breach a 12-inch-thick, non-reinforced, concrete wall if the explosives are laid next to the wall and are not tamped (i.e., covered and pressed with earth or water). If the explosives are tamped, about 2 pounds are sufficient.

Modern explosives are difficult to explode on purpose, and require special **detonating systems.** A detonating system sends electricity or heat to a volatile, detonating explosive. This way, the bulk explosive won't detonate on its own. And if the smaller, detonating explosive detonates on its own, it only causes limited damage. For multiple blocks of explosive chained together, a line of detonating cord is used. Detonating cord transmits a detonating wave, essentially acting as a very long blasting cap.

The detonating system includes a timing mechanism to precisely delay the initiation of the explosion. One standard system is "time fuse" cable. The gunpowder-based cable slowly burns at a constant rate and can be cut to any length to create a timer. Timing mechanisms allow personnel to light the fuse (with a specialized detonator, or just a lighter) and retire to a safe distance before detonation.[1]

After the charge is created, it needs a **mounting mechanism.** Soldiers can prepare a charge for placement in dry environments by attaching double-sided tape, and in wet environments by putting it in a bag with preparations to nail or staple the bag. Charges work best when held firmly against the target wall. When making an entry hole, the charge is placed at shoulder height.

Leaders must account for **different directional forces** exerted by different charges in placing troops near the breach. (Assault must be close enough to breach points that they can quickly enter, but not so close that flying debris injures them.) For example, a picket charge throws fragments backward 50 to 100 meters, but only throws a few sideways. 20 meters to the side of the charge, Assaulters can safely crouch with their backs turned. A picket charge is 3-foot lengths of engineer picket (V-shaped engineer stakes) with 4 to 8 pounds of C4 taped securely in place. The picket is placed upright with its open side (and the charge) against the wall, pinned in position, and then detonated. A picket charge blows about 4 by 8-foot holes in non-reinforced concrete walls (common in the developing world).

---

1 Real World: For more precise instructions on charge construction, view U.S. Army Training Manual 3-34.82 or U.S. Army Field Manual 3-34.214.

19.b Reducing Entrapping Obstacles (Wire and Mines)

Wires, mines, and even moats are obstacles that entrap rather than block. They are often more difficult for a patrol to reduce and traverse than blocking obstacles. But they don't intercept fires as a wall would.

Wire obstacles include concertina wire, barbed wire, chicken wire, etc. The most common breaching methods are mechanical and explosive. If the wire is springy, like Concertina wire, it is staked back to either side to create a middle assault lane. For a stealthy reduction, wire cutters are used to cut partway through the wire and bend the wire back and forth until it breaks. And only the lower strands are cut (leaving the top strands in place) to better hide any gaps. As a last resort, the most junior Soldier jumps on the wire, and all the other Soldiers walk on their back. (It's painful, but it works.)

Driving a vehicle through wire or mine fields is possible, but vehicles are loud so they can compromise a patrol. Between getting stuck in mud and enemy attacks, the breaching vehicle must be matched to the specific mission it is being used in. For example, a simple HMMWV (Humvee or High-Mobility Multipurpose Wheeled Vehicle) can defeat many wire obstacles. But a minefield might require a dedicated mine and explosives-clearing vehicle like the M1150 Assault Breacher Vehicle. At 12 meters long and weighing 59 tonnes, it is equipped with a mine plow and line charges.

Sometimes a mechanical breach is too slow. In Afghanistan, Mujahideen just forced explosions by: pushing captured vehicles, herding flocks of sheep, firing consecutive recoilless rifles rounds, or hurling large rocks. None of these methods were too effective, but they were effective enough.

More effective is forcing explosions with explosives. **Explosive breaching** is often the fastest and most combat-effective method. A "bangalore torpedo" is a very long rod made of sections that clears an assault lane along its length. (See Image 159, Pg. 188.) To use a bangalore, a Soldier pushes a section into the mine field, and attaches another section to the rear. Each section makes the bangalore longer and longer until it completely transverses the obstacle. As a bangalore is pushed into a minefield, it may explode random mines, causing a chain reaction back through the bangalore to the user. Therefore, when clearing mines, use a random stick as the first section in bangalore. Before a bangalore is exploded, seek cover at least 35 meters away.

Phase 3

Reducing Entrapping Obstacles (Wire and Mines)

Image 159: A **Bangalore torpedo** is an explosive charge placed within one or several connected tubes.

Image 160: Heavy cutters are very effective but **very slow**. They are a good option for a surprise attack.

Image 161: Tubes are attached at the back as the front is shoved into a mine or wire field.

Image 162: A grappling hook is an effective tool to capture and drag wire. From cover, an entire squad can pull.

Image 163: Blowing the Bangalore clears a straight path down the length of the tube for Soldiers to go down.

Image 164: Soldiers who made a path **proof (mark) it** for follow-on Soldiers. This is important for night and smoke.

Although there are premade kits, a field-expedient bangalore can be made by connecting segments of concave metal picket posts and filling the concave portion with plastic explosives. The **M1A2 Bangalore Torpedo** is intended to explode underground mines, so it is 5.4 cms in diameter. Each section is 76.2 cms long, with 2.27 kgs of B4 in the middle and 0.23 kgs of composition A3 boosters at both ends. However, a bangalore only needs to be as thick as necessary (e.g., wire will require less explosives than mines).

A modern version of the bangalore is the Antipersonnel Obstacle Breaching System (APOBS), which is lighter, faster, and has more standoff than a bangalore. Essentially, the APOBS is a rope with lots of grenades attached along its length. A Soldier sets the rope by standing 35 meters away and firing the rocket attached to the front of the rope. When the APOBS explodes, the grenades neutralize mines and sever wire, clearing a footpath for troops up to 1 meter wide by 45 meters long. The APOBS system weighs 125 pounds carried by two Soldiers, and can be deployed within 120 seconds.

The vehicle-mounted version of the APOBS is the Mine Clearing Line Charge (MICLIC). The MICLIC is a 5-inch rocket motor that projects a 350-foot explosive line charge filled with C4 across the target.

20. Securing the Foothold

Seizing and securing a foothold uses the same techniques as any other location. (See Footholds and Entrances, Pg. 163.) (See Seizing Rooms (Battle Drill 6), Pg. 228.) However, the significance of securing the foothold is that it **signals a change in the state of the raid.** Before the foothold, the patrol is focused on overcoming enemy defenses. After the foothold, the patrol is focused on their mission tasking. This change in focus demands a shift in the locations of personnel. The Patrol Leader moves to the foothold to maintain better command and control. The foothold acts as a casualty collection point for easier treatment and evacuation. Local security can replace the fires from Support, releasing Support to secure and support other areas.

21. Contingencies

Enemy contact can happen in infinite ways, but there are some common scenarios to plan for.

21.a Weather

In planning, a patrol must consider how the weather will affect the raid, and make contingency plans for sudden weather changes. Note that planning is strictly limited by how it affects the operation; for example, 72°F versus 73°F (22°C versus 23°C) does not matter. To consider the weather, use **VWCPT**:

Visibility – conditions that are low are good for ground attackers and bad for aircraft. The darkness of night (and better, a new moon) hides movement. And with night-optical devices or other detection devices, Soldiers can still see the enemy. Rarer visibility concerns include fog and storms.

Winds – above 13 kph usually make smoke operations ineffective. And as surface wind speed increases, windchill can suddenly make a cold day much colder. Therefore in windy conditions, Soldiers must carry quickly accessible warming and protective layers. Wind speed also affects the distance that sound will travel, so a clandestine raid moves upwind to the objective to maintain silence. Smoke and tear gas grenades quickly shift and disperse in wind; therefore, when using 2-chlorobenzylidene malononitrile ("CS") tear gas grenades, Soldiers must not gas themselves.

Cloud cover – reduces the effectiveness and availability of air support in all areas. However, a lack of clouds allows for solar heating which can impair infrared imaging systems like guided missiles.

Precipitation – can make some unsurfaced roads and areas impassable. The Patrol Leader must plan alternate routes that cannot be rained out, and they must incorporate extra movement time into any movement plan. Generally, precipitation above 2.5 mm per hour is considered critically relevant to tactical operations. Snow exceeding 45 cms reduces all movement speed, including tracked vehicle's. Wind, rain, and snow can all chill a Soldier and degrade their performance; so Soldiers must carry extra layers of clothing that can protect them.

Temperature – affects performance of both Soldiers and vehicles. Above the wet bulb globe temperature (WBGT) of 90°F (32°C), the U.S. Army states that Soldiers should receive 50 minutes of rest for every 10 minutes of "hard" work. Excessive movement above 90°F WBGT can result in heat casualties and death. Equipment is also very sensitive to temperature. At around 90° to 100°F (32° to 38°C), humans become invisible against the thermal background because thermal detection devices require a

Image 165: A U.S. Army Crew Chief, from the CO Army N.G., conducts preflight checks on a UH-60 Black Hawk helicopter in preparation for a blizzard response. Buckley AFB, Aurora, CO., 09 Jan 2016. Note the drop in visibility because of precipitaiton. **Weather can have drastic effects on a mission plan.**

difference in temperature or thermal contrast to "see" a target. At cold temperatures below 0°F (-18°C), a fully charged radio battery has less than half its potential power. The cooler it gets, the greater the loss of power. Both hot and cold weather can occur in desert terrain on the same day, where the day-to-night difference in temperature varies as much as 100° F (37°C).

21.b Casualty Collection Point

Outside the objective, casualties move with the patrol because the patrol is one element. However, at the objective where multiple elements are acting semi-independently, casualties are located at the casualty collection point (CCP). **Collecting casualties at one location** allows for better command and control, faster medical treatment, and more comprehensive security. In a raid, the foothold is the first CCP because it is the first location secured. Thereafter, the Patrol Leader can move the CCP if they determine a better location.

The initial and primary focus in all mass casualty incidents is always security. The Patrol must establish **360-degree security**, and remove weapons from all incoherent Soldiers. Then, the Patrol Sergeant maintains accountability and organization of all casualties and contacts Higher Command to initiate a medical evacuation. Higher either directs the patrol to hold the casualties throughout exfiltration, or they direct the patrol to move the casualties from the CCP to a medical evacuation point. When Soldiers are

Image 166: A U.S. Army Paratrooper assigned to A Co., 1st Bn., 503rd Inf. Reg., 173rd (A) Bde. receives medical aid for his simulated leg wound. Chinchilla training area, Spain, 29 Feb 2016. **Security is still a priority when operating a CCP.**

medically evacuated, the patrol retains all weapons and sensitive equipment. (See Aid and Litter, and Medevac, Pg. 286.)

After casualties have been rendered safe and accounted for, Medics and Soldiers begin triage. The most experienced Medic is responsible for organizing casualties by the severity of their wounds, and assigning Soldiers to care for the most wounded. Lightly wounded Soldiers can be assigned to care for more seriously wounded Soldiers, or secure detainees. Deceased Soldiers are separated from wounded Soldiers at all times. Seeing the dead can worsen patient outcomes.

21.c Quick Reaction Force

When an element is attacked and calls for reinforcements, those reinforcements are called Quick Reaction Forces (QRF). QRF are prestaged units that run to their vehicles and race to the element being engaged. Their response time can be as little as 5 minutes and must be briefed during planning and known by the whole patrol. The rule of thumb is to be off the objective in half the estimated enemy response time.

If the patrol encounters QRF, it is treated as a regular **react-to-contact** situation. A squad-size patrol likely needs to redeploy the entire Assault. But a platoon has many Soldiers to draw upon. Therefore, a Platoon Leader is much more free to grab Soldiers, while maintaining security. A common approach is for the Patrol Leader to call for the EPW Team to react to the QRF, while leaving the remaining Soldiers to secure the area.

A common approach for dealing with an enemy QRF is to utilize **harassing ambushes**. A harassing ambush does not fully engage, and instead delays and degrades the enemy QRF, giving the patrol more time to withdraw. A patrol sets up harassing ambushes by emplacing Security on likely avenues of approach for QRF. (See Security, Pg. 146.) The ambushes can be a simple as a few Soldiers firing into an enemy QRF, or setting off a few claymores to slow down enemy vehicles.

Depending on the situation and combat environment, harassing ambushes can even become the mission itself. For example, if the QRF is known to be many times the size of a regular convey and fully deploys every time, an objective can be attacked to bait out the enemy QRF. Then the QRF can be engaged on favorable terms with no reinforcements left. (See Strategic Effects (Information Creation), Pg. 19.)

21.d Combat Ineffective Leader[1]

Leaders are the brains of the operation, so if a Leader is ineffective then the operation is braindead. A Leader can be ineffective because they are a casualty, or just because they are a poor decisionmaker. If a Leader is ineffective due to poor decisionmaking alone, then the Patrol Leader begins with micromanagement. But if a Leader is completely incapacitated, the Patrol Leader must be ready to replace any Leader at any time, including replacing themselves.

The succession of command is part of planning, but Planners often neglect the actual, on-the-ground instructions for how a Leader will be replaced. Replacing a Leader can be complicated and must be thought out completely. For example, if the Assault Leader is killed, then how will the Support Leader physically take command of Assault? For example, the Support Leader may have to radio the Patrol Sergeant and Assaulters, move to the foothold, move to Assault with the Aid and Litter Team, and then conduct security and casualty procedures. Meanwhile, Soldiers must know what to do when their Leader is ineffective. The enemy does not stop fighting, so neither can Soldiers.

---

1 Quote: The battle is at its height. Beat my war drums. Do not announce my death. —Admiral Yi Sun-Sin

Phase 4 Contents

22. Close-Quarters Battle Basics   195
Task Organization   197
Synchronized Movement   198
Verbage   200

23. Preparation for Entry   201
Stacking Up and Team Positions   202
Closed Door Reconnaissance   207
Closed Door Breaching   208
Non-Explosive Breaching of Entryways   210
Explosive Breaching of Entryways   215
Grenades and Disorienting   219
Firing Through Walls   222
Immediate and Delayed Entry   224

24. Seizing Rooms (Battle Drill 6)   228
Clearing the Entry   228
Clearing the Corner and Room   232
Sector Sweeps and Points-of-Domination   237
Connected Rooms and Areas   240

25. Seizing Other Spaces   244
Hallways   244
Stairs and Stairwells   252
Room Obstacles   257
Every Space is Different   260

26. Working and Exiting a Space   265
Securing a Space   265
Reporting Progress   267
Marking a Space   268

27. Seizing Floors and Buildings   270
Coordinating Multiple Teams   270
Attacking Multiple Structures   272

28. Contingencies   274
Noncombatants   274
Delayed Combatants   277
Demolition Team   277
Failed Breach   278
Backing Out and Reengaging   279

Joe Fights the Enemy (Phase 4: Seizing the Objective)

There is only one tactical principle which is not subject to change. It is to use the means at hand to inflict the maximum amount of wound, death, and destruction on the enemy in the minimum amount of time.

—U.S. General George S. Patton Jr.

After a foothold is established, the raid of the entire objective can begin in earnest. Soldiers use special close-quarters battle techniques to raid every part of a building and every building on the objective.

22. Close-Quarters Battle Basics[1]

Close-Quarters Battle (CQB) is any set of tactical choreography or sequence of movements with firearms used inside confined spaces. (See Using a Rifle in Urban Terrain, Pg. 72.) Historically, this can be anything from posting a lookout at the door, to the full tactics of a modern four-man battle cell.

The three classic principles of CQB are speed, surprise, and violence-of-action. "**Speed**" is a misnomer because speed comes from practicing and becoming smooth. Almost always, new learners need to slow down at first, and only build up their speed by smoothing out their actions.[2]

Surprise is always good. Translated to tactics, Soldiers create surprise by reducing the information available to the enemy. For example, Soldiers must take cover and concealment whenever possible, so the enemy does not know where the Soldiers are. Even if the enemy is aware of Soldiers, stun grenades deny sight and hearing for a few critical seconds to achieve surprise. Soldiers

---

1 Quote: There is only one principle of war and that's this. Hit the other fellow, as quick as you can, and as hard as you can, where it hurts him the most, when he ain't looking. —British Field Marshal William Joseph Slim

2 Quote: "What is speed?" would seem to have a simple answer: speed is going fast. —US Marine Corps MCDP 1-3 Tactics

should always be asking themselves what information their actions are giving away, and how they can deny the enemy that information.

Violence-of-action is a phrase that essentially means continuity of force, and eliminating stop-and-go actions.[1] For example, if a team member has a weapon malfunction, violence-of-action is immediately pulling out the secondary weapon and continuing. Likewise, violence-of-action is fixing the primary weapon on the move in the rear, so the team doesn't have to wait. Also like speed, violence-of-action comes from practice. Just be smooth.

CQB is vital to Soldiers who continuously raid. During the Second Battle of Fallujah in 2004, 10,000 U.S. Soldiers had to clear thousands of enemies, building by building. Raiding was necessary because: mass bombing would kill lots of remaining civilians; the enemies were too numerous and hostile to negotiate with, and one of the main objectives was for the Iraqi government to demonstrate control and force over its own territory.

That being said, doing CQB incorrectly is like throwing a grenade incorrectly: both can blow up and be worse than doing nothing. As militaries train CQB, Soldiers must remember that CQB is a small part of what makes a raid successful. And, when a raid is so dangerous that CQB is necessary, then other tactics should be considered. For example, deescalation tactics and techniques (like those used by police officers) can lead to safer outcomes. (See Tactical Callout, Pg. 156.) And tactics like artillery fire can lead to more deadly results. (See Indirect Fire Systems, Pg. 37.)

Importantly, **CQB does not include hand-to-hand combat** for two primary reasons. First, the average infantry team can overpower an enemy without formal training. The chances of finding an enemy, of sufficient fitness, of sufficient size, who is willing to fight a team of American Soldiers with guns and armor, and win, are very low. Second, although martial arts are not useless, Soldiers who conduct CQB will become more effective Soldiers by further training their weapon skills, and synchrony with their team. So at best, learning martial arts is an inefficient use of professionals' time.

Phase 4

---

1. Real World: Raiders do not destroy everything; and so "violence-of-action" does not demand injuring occupants. This is important for real-world effects; for example, harming a detainee will bring far more retaliation from the populace than threats of harm to the detainee. Raiders may carry less-lethal secondary weapons like tasers and batons, and must communicate in a clear and powerful manner.

22.a Task Organization

Multiple squads are needed to clear large buildings in relative safety, with at least a Platoon Leader controlling the overall progress. A very basic task organization for a platoon of Assaulters is: one platoon per building (two squads leapfrogging floors), one squad per floor (two team clearing by leapfrogging rooms), and one team per room. (See Chunking, Pg. 134.) Additionally, platoons of Support and Security pull security on the outside, making a multi-story raid a company-sized operation. Resupply is also important. For example, the Patrol Leader must consider that on a long multi-raid mission, the patrol may use all of its grenades and need resupply.

The classic U.S. Army CQB Team is made of exactly **four Soldiers** that can rotate between positions because confined spaces make larger units unwieldy. However historically, military and paramilitary teams have used six or more Soldiers; and police and other organizations may clear with only two or three people. (See Stacking Up and Team Positions, Pg. 202.)

Larger clearing teams are favored for wide open spaces and street-like hallways. (See Bounding and Crossing Intersections, Pg. 99.) These common areas have lots of doors and unknowns that require more than four Soldiers to pull security on. Larger teams also make casualty evacuation easier; if two of four Soldiers are shot, the remaining two would be hard-pressed to provide covering fire while also pulling the casualties out. Room-clearing operations can be conducted by two and three man teams, but having a primary Soldier without an second Soldier to back them up is more dangerous and straining. Smaller clearing teams are only used when there aren't enough Soldiers.

In urban combat, Leaders cannot move by themselves. Therefore, all Leaders are attached to teams. For example in room-clearing, the Squad Leader coordinates multiple teams while attached to a team and not moving by themselves. Leaders are critical for command, and so are either the last man in the stack, or second to last so they are not pulling rear security.

Leaders are the only required specialized Assaulter position. The Team Leader decides which direction to move in, when a to secure a room after clearing, when to continue out of the room, and when to contact the Squad Leader. Because all of the Team Leader's tasks are simple, having a Team Leader is more to assign the team a single voice than to "lead" the team. In a well-practiced team, every Assaulter is capable of being a Team Leader.

Assaulters are often assigned a secondary role, like Aid and Litter Team or EPW Team. (See Clear-Back and Consolidation, Pg. 281.) (See Non-Combat Support, Pg. 45.) These roles are dispersed among the teams, so if any one team is eliminated, the entire special team is not also eliminated. Once an assault is complete and the building is secure, the Patrol Leader calls for special teams to an assembly point (often the foothold or casualty collection point) to brief them on their tasks.

22.b Synchronized Movement

Most CQB movements are sequential, meaning that One Man follows Two Man. However, some situations are more securely handled when two Soldier move together in synchronous. Four common synchronous movements are high-low, plating, back-to-back, and opposing entry.

High-low is where a High Soldier stands above a kneeling Low Soldier. This configuration allows the Low Soldier to secure an area without blocking the High Soldier's sector-of-fire. Meanwhile, the High Soldier can freely shoot 360 degrees without hitting the Low Soldier. Note that the Low Soldier must wait to be told to stand, or else risk standing into the High Soldier's sector-of-fire. And the Low Soldier is always behind the High Soldier's muzzle.

A high-low is useful in two scenarios. First, when two opposing threats are present (e.g., the left and right hallways at a T-intersection), two Soldiers face opposite directions simultaneously clear the left and right. But if a hallway is too narrow for two Soldiers to stand side-by-side, one Soldier can kneel beneath a standing Soldier. (See Hallways, Pg. 244.)

Second, high-low is useful when a known threat needs to be engaged around a corner. A high-low allows two barrels to simultaneously pie, peek, and engage a threat, instead of just one. (See Image 167, Pg. 199.) Some publications call for all corners to be cleared in a high-low configuration because two barrels are more secure than one; however, high-low is slow and not very smooth. A high-low requires two Soldiers to pause, one Soldier to crouch, and then both coordinate a push. Seconds make minutes, and having the Low Soldier do squats is unnecessary for most scenarios. Further, the second muzzle of the Low Soldier is only useful if the High Soldier is overwhelmed by multiple threats, in which case the team may be better off if it breaks contact, pulls back, and throws a grenade. In contrast, a single Soldier can quickly use a smooth pieing motion to clear a corner alone.

Close-Quarters Battle Basics

Image 167: Côte d'Ivoire Special Forces Soldier use a **high-low** formation. Near Abidjan, Côte d'Ivoire, 27 Feb 2022.

Image 168: Two Finnish Soldiers hold security down a hallway using a **high-low** formation. Helsinki, Finland 17 Jan 2014.

Image 169: A Special Forces Soldier instruct a Soldier of 1st Sqn., 75th Cav. Reg., 2nd Bde. on vehicle clearing using a **high-low** formation. Fort Campbell, 14 Aug 2019.

Image 170: Two Soldier move laterally **back-to-back** as each protects the back of the other. This technique is more effective with bulletproof vests. Chesapeake, Virginia, 15 Sep 2021.

Image 171: Coalition Soldiers **simultaneously enter** an opening to the left and right sides. Camp Price, Afghanistan on 11 Aug 2007.

Phase 4

Plating is a movement that protects one Soldier's side by using another Soldier's front plates. The most common use of plating is when two Soldiers are pieing an open doorway: one is pulling security on the door, while the other is pulling long security down the hallway. The Soldier pulling security in the door pies in a semi-circle, while facing their front plates toward the door in preparation for enemy fire. The Soldier pulling long security moves in a larger semi-circle on the outside, with their flank almost touching the other Soldier. That way, the side of the long-security Soldier is protected by the plates of the Soldier facing the door. (See Image 63, Pg. 86.)

Back-to-back is similar to plating, except both Soldiers protect each other with their front plate. If only one Soldier goes between two opposing openings, an enemy could appear from the opening to the Soldier's back and shoot the Soldier from behind. So instead two Soldiers touch their backs (i.e., go back-to-back), and move sideways together, while pulling security. (See Image 170, Pg. 199.) (See Image 225, Pg. 243.) If there are three openings (or two opposing openings in a hallway), then a third Soldier can double plate between two Soldiers, to form a three Soldier sandwich.

Opposing entry is a specific use of back-to-back when entering a room that solves the problem of One Man having their back exposed during entry. (See Clearing the Entry, Pg. 228.) Instead of One Man entering first, and Two Man entering second, both enter the room at the same time in opposing directions (hence "opposing entry"). Opposing entry is not used for every clear only because doorways typically are too narrow. (See Image 171, Pg. 199.)

22.c Verbage

When conducting precision clearing, the high volume of noise makes communications extremely difficult. However, Soldiers still must communicate what they are doing. Where possible, a patrol forgoes verbal signals completely because sounds can alert an enemy. But non-verbal communication requires a lot of practice, so brevity words and phrases are usually used to communicate common actions. Below are some common example commands:

RELOADING –	The speaker is reloading.
MAN DOWN –	A Soldier has become a casualty.
GRENADE –	An enemy grenade has been thrown.
GUN DOWN –	The speaker's gun has malfunctioned.
UP –	A Soldier is ready to continue the mission.

Image 172: U.S. Marines of MEF 21.1 coordinate room entry by using non-verbal shoulder squeezes to indicate that the entire team is prepared to enter. Fort Drum, NY, 01 Nov 2020. **Never point the rifle down when entering a room!** If the One Man here sees an enemy in the room, he can't immediately shoot them.

SHORT ROOM – The room is too small for additional Soldiers.

CLEAR – The area of operation is clear of present danger.

GO LONG – A Soldier must pull security farther into a room.

COMING OUT/IN/UP/DOWN – A Soldier is moving.

The largest difference in standard operating procedures between different units is how teams communicate. Room-clearing verbage is a great example. Some teams are fully verbal from the bottom up. For example, after an Assaulter in a room clears their portion of the room, they state "Clear." Other teams are non-verbal and top-down. For example, the Team Leader says "Status" and each Assaulter nods their rifle. If every Assaulter nods their rifle, the team moves to secure the room. (See Securing a Space, Pg. 265.)

23. Preparation for Entry[1]

An entryway (or exit) is by definition an opening in a division between two spaces. Entryways can be garage doors (See Image 178, Pg. 205.), windows (See Image 133 et al, Pg. 166.), or just a hole in the wall (See Image 155,

---

1 Quote: In traditional [urban] training, making non-standard entry points such as walls and windows, is taught. Unfortunately, Soldiers were responsible for clearing 50 to 60 structures a day. There simply was not enough time or explosive to breach the walls or barred windows. Almost all the entry points were existing doors. —U.S.M.C. Sergeant Earl J. Catagnus Jr. et al.

Pg. 185.). Moving through entryways is one of the most dangerous aspects of CQB for one reason: **prepared lines-of-fire.**[1] Defenders can prepare to fire at a narrow entry, while Attackers must return fire to a wide room. This asymmetric knowledge creates a large advantage for defenders. To deal with bottlenecks, Assaulters use a stack formation to pause the team and allow the Team Leader gives directions, coordinates actions, and conducts recon.

23.a Stacking Up and Team Positions

A stack is a formation that Soldiers use to enter a space. (The stack is so called because Soldiers stack one behind the other.) Stacking improves organization, which reduces the danger of entry; from the stack, Assaulters can: coordinate for quick room entry; ignore the existing entry completely and create an entirely new entry (i.e., a wall breach); or prepare a room by disorienting the enemy, with door explosions, grenades, or firing through walls.

How Soldiers stack varies wildly among different buildings. For example, bullet permeable walls make stacking dangerous and so Soldiers stack up far from the entrance. Buildings with many non-standard layouts require a more fluid approach. (See Building Construction, Pg. 57.) Stacks also vary based on the unit and preference. A four-man cell can all stack together on one side of a door, or can double-stack two Soldiers on either side of the door. For normal urban breaching operations, there are usually about four to six people, including the Combat Engineers and the assault force, in a single stack.

However, forming a **traditional single stack** is straightforward. Four Soldiers stand in a line and pull security in different directions. Each Soldier in a stack of four is designated by the order by which they go through the entrance, i.e., One Man, Two Man, Three Man, and Four Man. (See Image 173, Pg. 203.) The traditional stack roles are: One Man is a Rifleman securing the door; Two Man is a grenade thrower or Coverman; Three Man is the Team Leader; and Four Man is the Breacher and machine gun Gunner.

One Man's role is always the same: to pull security on the entrance. Because One Man goes through the entrance first, they benefit the most from

Phase 4

---

[1] Real World: A common name for entryways is the "fatal funnel," because attackers are funneled into a narrow area while defenders can occupy the wide room. This book avoids the funnel analogy because it doesn't fit abnormal rooms. Instead of a funnel, Assaulters overcome bottlenecks with prepared lines-of-fire.

Four-Man Stacking Formations

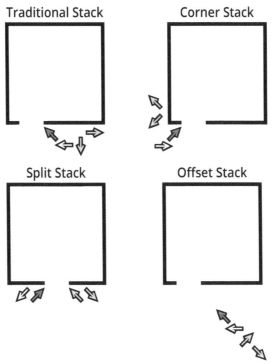

Traditional Stack   Corner Stack

Split Stack   Offset Stack

Image 173: A stack ensures that Soldiers enter in the correct order with the correct timing. Soldiers must also remain safe against enemies and explosions. In balancing different concerns, this diagram shows four common kinds of stacks for a four-man team. A traditional stack places Soldiers in order, one through four. The corner stack is a traditional stack but around a corner. The offset stack is a traditional stack but offset (used, for example, with explosive breaches. The split stack splits the stack between either side of the entry. The formations used on a mission is **highly mission dependent,** and multiple formations are often used.

Phase 4

paying attention to the entry. **Always point the muzzle at the opening!** Standoff is important here. One Man stands far enough from the opening (e.g., a few meters) so that their muzzle does not protrude in the opening and telegraph their location. (Also, be aware of lighting behind Soldiers that creates a shadow in front of the opening.) A consistent standoff also allows Soldiers to use more consistent footwork. Moreover, standoff can protect Soldiers from an enemy's indiscriminate fire through walls and doors.

Two Man throws grenades because One Man would have to drop security to throw a grenade. Soldiers can carry grenades on their backs, so

Two Man always has easy access to grenades on One Man's back. (See Image 200, Pg. 220.) Two Man can also be a Coverman and pull security to either side of One Man. This way, both men can engage any threats that present from the door, instead of just One Man. Outside of a building, Two Man pulls forward security (i.e., down the side of the building).

Three Man is the Team Leader because that position has the fewest security concerns, allowing for the greatest command and control; and also because after entering rooms, Three Man is by the door where they can communicate with other teams. Three and Four Man are far from the action, and so are responsible for support tasks. Outside of a building, Three Man is responsible for security across the street and on roofs.

Four Man is responsible for rear security. They also are the Breacher or machine gun Gunner because the Four Man has the least work to do (between security and leading combined). If breaching a door is necessary, the Breacher uses their tools (e.g., shotgun or saw), and then immediately falls to the back of the stack as One Man enters the room. If someone inside opens the door before a breach is completed, the team immediately enters the room.

Of course, the traditional stack is so specific that it is rarely used without modification. For example, where the Team Leader wants to enter rooms faster, they can be the Two Man instead. If a squad or Platoon Leader is attached, then the stack becomes five men. If Two Man is a Dog Handler, Four Man can throw grenades.

As Soldiers approach a door to stack, they can go to assigned positions or stack at random. In a unit where all Soldiers in a team have the same weapons and training, they are likely to have random positions, where Soldiers assume the role of whatever position they stacked into. However, if a Soldier is carrying an M249 automatic weapon and breaching tools, they are always Four Man. If the Team Leader ends up in the One Man position, they say "bump me," to have another Soldier move up and take their position.

Soldiers can stack loose, or stack tight. Stacking loose (an arm's length or more apart) is preferred when the enemy has access to area weapons like grenades and machine guns. In contrast, stacking tight maximizes non-verbal communication, and minimizes time delay between Soldiers entering. Without enemy threats, Soldiers group together as close as possible without tripping.

Soldiers in a stack should never touch walls for a few reasons. First, a Soldier that hits a wall may sound off their presence to enemies on the

Preparation for Entry

Image 174: A team of Afghan National Army Commandos with 3rd Co., 1st Bn. use a **traditional stack.** Behsud, Nangarhar, Afghanistan, 11 Apr 2013.

Image 175: Greek Soldiers assigned to the 71st Air Mobile Bde. with U.S. Army Paratroopers use a MWD in their **traditional stack**. Kilkis, Greece, 05 Nov 2019.

Image 176: Romanian Jandarmeria Police Officers **split stack** without rear or outside security. **Police often do not face external threats.** Bucharest, Romania, 25 Feb 2015.

Image 177: U.S. Marines with the Maritime Raid Force, 26th MEU, use a **split stack** with intense external security. **Military often face intense external threats.** Camp Lejeune, N.C., 14 Jun 2017.

Image 178: Assaulters from B Co., 1st Bn., 25th Marine Reg., raid a possible suicide vehicle bomb workshop using a **stackless entry** with a Breacher. Fallujah, Iraq, 01 Sep 2013.

Phase 4

opposite side. Many walls do not offer ballistic protection, and enemies can shoot through them. Second, when bullets are fired at walls at an angle, they tend to ricochet and continue to travel 10 to 20 cms parallel to the wall. (See Terminal Ballistics, Pg. 75.) Being on the wall places Soldiers directly along these ricochets' trajectories. Third, most people only travel in the center of a hallway, so enemies may plant IEDs on the side of hallways to kill Soldiers.

A stack does not have to be a straight file, and it can even be in-line with the door. Moreover with enough changes, a "stack" ceases to stack Soldiers at all. If Soldiers do form up but not in a line, their formation is called a "disbursed stack." Disbursed stacks allow for more specialized roles, but also require more training than a traditional linear stack. For example, there is a plan without a real stack when One and Two Man are on either side of a door, Four Man is breaching, and Three Man is a Coverman.

The most common disbursed stack is the **split stack**, where Soldiers prepare to enter on either side of an entry. (See Image 176, Pg. 205.) Split stacks allow Soldiers to view both near sides of the next room immediately before entry. (See Immediate and Delayed Entry, Pg. 224.) A single stack can transform into a split stack if One Man and Two Man pie the entry to the opposite side. But pieing moves Soldiers in front of the entry, which may alert the enemy. So alternatively, Soldiers can move directly to a split stack.

When a unit becomes so skilled that stacks are second nature, they can start performing stackless entries. With **stackless entry,** Soldiers know their role but do not have a set formation. (See Image 178, Pg. 205.) Stackless entries are faster; but they are more complicated because the Clearing Team must be able to enter from many different positions. Without a stack, the team informs a designated One Man that they are ready to follow, and then they follow. Stackless entries are limited in closed door environments, where Assaulters must pause behind a door anyway. But the technique can be used for hostage rescue because the safety of the hostage makes speed paramount.

Before entering a room, Soldiers non-verbally communicate that they are ready to enter by giving a squeeze on the bicep, hard enough it can't be accidental. The Last Man gives the first squeeze, and each Soldier signals the Soldier in front of them. (If a tap method is used, an inadvertent bump may be misunderstood as a tap.) Once the One Man receives a squeeze they can move as soon as they are ready. In a split stack, the One and Two Men nod muzzles. And in a stackless entry, Soldiers may give verbal confirmation.

Image 179: An SF Chemical Reconnaissance Detachment (CRD) Soldier recons air quality for safe entry before a breach. Dugway Proving Grounds, UT, 05 Feb 2019.

23.b Closed Door Reconnaissance

If an entry is closed, then the patrol must breach it. And before breaching, **the patrol can gain valuable information about the opposite side** through recon such as human or chemical presence. With information about occupants, the patrol can improve their breach by choosing a better breach location and type, planning grenade throw locations, preparing to shoot at certain areas, etc. Information yielded by the recon is relayed to the entire stack using non-verbal signals to maintain concealment. The danger of recon is that if the enemy senses the patrol, they may immediately attack. Never linger!

The most effective recon tools today are special cameras that fit below a door. Because it takes hands to use, the One Man and Two Man pull security while the Three or Four Man operate the camera. Using these handheld devices, a team can view the entire contents of a room from behind a closed door. The team can also preclear a room with a periscope or mirror. Cutting-edge recon uses through-the-wall, radar-signal systems that detect the presence and location of people in a closed space without alerting anyone.

Even if the team doesn't have extra equipment, they can **listen for noise** that indicates movement inside the room. Moreover, if the enemy is already aware of the patrol's presence, then yelling orders into a room before entry is also a valuable reconnaissance tool. Responses to the orders can reveal the number of respondents, their mental state, gender, and age. While angry men may warrant a grenade, distressed children require a different response.

Finally, Leaders should always consider using subterfuge or other scams to gain information and access to the target building. Human intelligence methods eliminate many of the risks of breaching. For example, a person familiar to the residents of a house can request entry, and when the door opens then Raiders can simply force their way past anyone in the doorway. This method requires extensive preparation, as a familiar person who can provide access would not usually be provided by aggressive Raiders.

23.c Closed Door Breaching

After stacking and recon, the Breacher begins the breach. The most common breach is using the doorknob. Not everything closed is locked! That being said, using handles and entering doorways generally is risky. Defenders may have booby-trapped the door or prepared lines-of-fire toward the door. Moreover, turning a knob may alert the enemy to the patrol's presence.

Therefore, breaching is common while raiding. Breaches are categorized into four methods: mechanical, power tool, ballistic, or explosive. The breaching methods complement each other and are summarized below.

	Mechanical	Power Tools	Ballistic	Explosive
Speed	Slow	Slow	Fast	Fast
Weight	Heavy	Heavy	Light	Light
Ease of Use	Easy Use	Easy Use	Hard Use	Hard Use
Scope of Use	Wide Use	Wide Use	Narrow Use	Narrow Use
Reusability	Reusable	Consumable	Consumable	Consumable
Reliability	Reliable	Less Reliable	Reliable	Less Reliable

Image 180: Different breaching methods have different benefits and drawbacks.

When breaching, multiple backups must be planned in a PACE. If one method of breaching is not working then the Breacher must quickly transition to a different type. Standing in front of a door and beating it with a sledgehammer for 10 minutes is unacceptable.

The first consideration for breaching is placing the patrol. Stacks usually stay close to the breach point because being close allows for faster entry. However, an explosive or thermal breach (for example, on reinforced concrete) requires a large standoff in proportion to their power. And when the patrol also wants to destroy everything behind the breach, the Breachers can use shoulder-launched munition or a tank. (See Shoulder Launched Munitions, Pg. 30.) (See Armored Fighting Vehicles, Pg. 33.)

After a distance-breach, Soldiers move while using all available cover and concealment, smoke, suppressive fire, and diversionary measures to occupy the enemy's attention. **Situational awareness must be maintained!** For example, if a team takes cover behind a corner to execute an explosive breach, they must resecure the entry's hallway. Teams can often become solely focused on an entry and drop security. If the breach is outdoors, the patrol can apply the fundamentals of SOSRA to entryway breaching; however, suppress, obscure, and proof rarely apply indoors making the acronym less useful there. (See Outside Barrier and Compound Breach, Pg. 180.)

Task organizations for breaching are innumerable. Ideally, a separate Breach Element exists, but otherwise the Soldiers in the rear of the stack are the Breach Team. Regardless, One Man is never the Breacher because they pull security. Soldiers have died as One Man because they attempted to split their attention between breaching and pulling security on the breach point.

An example task organization for explosive breaching has the Two and Three Men be the Breach Team and set the pace of the breach. Two Man carries and places the demolition charge. Three Man carries a fabricated blast shield. One Man secures the breach point. Four Man is the Team Leader, providing direction and rear security. After Two Man places the explosive charge, all Soldiers fall behind Three Man's blast shield. After the breaching charge explodes, Three Man becomes One Man.

With premission reconnaissance, breaching information (i.e., the stack location, breaching method, and task organization) is briefed in the premission brief, or during the mission in a hasty brief. A breaching brief is a minute-by-minute scheme-of-maneuver for breaching:

Who – carries what charges and tools to where.

What – target type (such as the door or window) is being breached. Any breaching limitations. (E.g., excessive explosive destruction.) Any hazards, like fragmentation, dense smoke, fiberglass dust, or grease.

When – the breach occurs and signals for imminent breaching. A detailed order of operations for charges. Delays between breaching and entry. Coordination with other units. For example, leadership uses the countdown, "5, 4, 3, 2 (Snipers Fire), 1 (Breach Executed)."

Where – the target is located in relation to the position and surrounding area. The patrol's minimum standoff.

Alternate – plan(s) if the breach fails. Alternate Soldier(s) if the Breacher becomes a casualty. Abort and withdrawal criteria.

Phase 4

23.d Non-Explosive Breaching of Entryways

Mechanical breaching is the safest, simplest, and most reliable method, and every Soldier can do it. If a unit must clear dozens of structures every day, the same door ram can breach all of them. Therefore, a patrol always incorporates mechanical breaching into the breach PACE plan (even if the mechanical breach is just kicking a door open, it must still be practiced).

The biggest danger of mechanical breaching is that being in front of a breach point for extended periods is very dangerous. The enemy will become aware of the team and may attack them. **Once the door is breached, consider throwing a grenade.** (See Grenades and Disorienting, Pg. 219.)

To ensure the fastest and smoothest entry possible on an unlocked, closed door, the One Man stacks on the side of the closed door that will provide first sight into the room, while the Number Two Man goes on the opposite side. If a door opens inward, One Man stacks on the hinge side. (See Image 182, Pg. 211.) The Number Two Man opens the door, pushing it inside the room, and the One Man gains immediate sight into the room. If the door opens outward, the team lines up on the doorknob side. (See Image 181, Pg. 211.) If two Soldiers end up on opposite sides of a door, the way the door opens determines who is One Man and who is Two Man. If possible, the team moves from a covered or concealed position already in their entry order.

Mechanical breaching tools include, sledgehammers, picket pounders (as makeshift rams), halligan bars, bolt cutters, etc. Each tool application can be summarized as: bludgeon the weak point (hammers and rams), or apply leverage around weak points (halligan bars and bolt cutters). An advantage of mechanical tools is how intuitive and safe their basic use is. That being said, every tool has a more specific and effective method of use depending on the structures and tools. Once a patrol has identified its actual targets and actual tools, Soldiers can review the tools' own instructions, or learn from firefighting manuals. **Firefighters are experts in mechanical breaching**.

Mechanical breaching also includes lock picking. Picking requires time, a trained operator, and knowledge of the lock to be picked. But lock picking is near silent and does not damage the lock or door. Using specialized lock cylinder tools (i.e., A-tool, K-tool), an entire lock can be quickly dismantled without removing it from the door, and then reassembled and relocked.

Mechanical Breaching

Image 181: **Consider the handle!** Although this is dangerous if shaking a handle alerts enemies.

Image 182: Kicking doors while **turned around** prevents Soldiers from falling down (a real problem).

Image 183: Mechanically breaching any door is possible if the Breacher can carry the **extra weight**.

Image 184: Even a tool as simple as a hooligan bar (used by firefighters) requires **practice and research**.

Image 185: If the door opens from the ground, a Soldier may **lie down** to secure the opening at once.

Image 186: Attack doors at the **places of attachment such as the hinges**, and not the center (as seen here).

If no better forceful breaching method is available, a Soldier can resort to kicking the door open. Kick a door with the back facing to the door, kicking backward (i.e., a "mule kick"). (See Image 182, Pg. 211.) Soldiers who mule kick are less likely to injure themselves or fall down into the door. Kicking is the least preferred since it is difficult and tiring for the Soldier, and it won't work at all on a sturdy door that opens outward. Further, kicking open a door rarely works the first time, giving any enemies in the room ample warning.

Power tools are a valuable breaching asset because they are much safer than ballistics and explosives, while offering much more strength and precision than unpowered mechanical tools. Power tools are a broad category and include gas tools, electric tools, hydraulic tools, and plasma tools.

Despite their benefits, power tools have limited application for a few reasons. First, their extra power can be in excess of what a mission actually needs. Often, a sledgehammer works fine. Second, because they are not 100% reliable, a non-powered tool (like a sledgehammer) must always be carried as a backup anyway. Finally, a patrol can only carry a limited amount of power source. Therefore, power tools are reserved for known or limited breach points, rather than the other methods which can be used more generally.

Gas and electric-powered tools are often used for cutting. Gas tools have exceptional power, but are heavy. A 16-inch gas-powered cordless cut-off saw weighs less than 30 pounds and can cut through rebar-reinforced concrete. If their power is excessive, an electric tool can be used instead. A 9-Inch electric cordless cut-off saw weighs less than 20 pounds and can cut through wooden walls easily.

Hydraulic tools utilize an electric pump to reliably generate an incredibly high force over a small distance. This is very useful for separating doors from frames, cutting rebar, lifting vehicles, etc. Unlike explosives, or a saw, hydraulic systems can be used in a quick, controlled, and sometimes silent manner, allowing the tactical operators to stay relatively hidden. They are also generally more durable than cutting tools.

A plasma cutter is essential when attacking a large steel barrier. For a land war, that may be rare, but police raids or raids onto ships do use plasma cutters. A portable thermal cutter combined with a portable 4000W generator can precisely and quickly cut through a wall of 12mm plate steel.

Ballistic breaching is forcing a door to open by shooting rounds at, and breaking, the door bolt or hinges. Ballistic breaches are easy, fast, and

Power-Tool and Ballistic Breaching

Image 187: Breaching is a team effort because the Breacher is completely occupied by breaching.

Image 188: To conduct a ballistic breach, use a 45-degree angle and look away to be safe from ricochets.

Image 189: Power tools are great but loud. Using a chainsaw in a house will surely alert everyone.

Image 190: The gun is held 45 degrees up to reduce overpenetration and 45 degrees in to destroy the frame.

Image 191: Know the target that needs to be breached. A plasma cutter can cut anything, but they are heavy.

Image 192: Because space is limited and the target is two inches away, it is acceptable to hold a shotgun like this .

Ballistic Doorway Breaching Targets

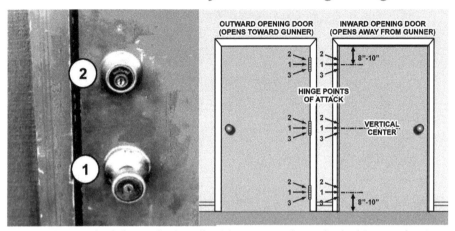

Image 193: On the left are the handle-side targets; shoot the locking mechanism. On the right are the hinge-side targets; aim shots at the estimated hinge location.

effective. Much like power tools, the two drawbacks are less than 100% effectiveness and high resource consumption.

The optimal ballistic system for breaching doors is a shotgun with a special 12-gauge projectile (a "breaching round") designed to break the door and then dissipate. (The rounds contain powdered metal which cannot penetrate eyepro after ricocheting.)

Other weapon systems can also be used. A 12-gauge shotgun loaded with buckshot or slugs quickly breaches most standard doors. Even 9mm or 5.56 rounds can breach doors. However, bullets and shot are likely to overpenetrate after breaching, potentially injuring noncombatants or the other side of the door. (This is also a concern when using breaching rounds, albeit less so.) And ricochets are always a concern. (See Terminal Ballistics, Pg. 75.)

To breach with a shotgun, a Soldier places the muzzle toward the space between the knob and the door jamb, targeting the door bolt. (Shooting the doorknob itself can bend the locking mechanism into the doorframe, preventing entry.) And to reduce the risks of overpenetration and ricochets, the Soldier tightly holds their muzzle against the door and fires up or down at the doorknob and hinges at a 45-degree angle. To blow out the doorframe, the shotgun is angled 45 degrees toward the inside. (See Image 193, Pg. 214.)

Once the Clearing Team is ready, the Breacher fires. The first shot gives away the team's presence and position, but one shot doesn't always completely

Phase 4

disable a door even if the door appears defeated. Therefore, the Breacher always fires two quick shots in the same location, ensuring the second shot is aimed as carefully as the first. If the lock is not defeated by the second shot, the Breacher fires again. Immediately after firing, the Breacher kicks the door in or pulls it out. The Breacher then points the shotgun barrel up and turns away from the doorway to signal that the breach is complete.

When the doorknob cannot be breached (e.g., a deadbolt is present), a Breacher can shoot the hinges instead. Hinges are often hidden, and so targeting the hinges is more difficult. Generally, hinges are 20 to 25 cms from the top and bottom of the door; the center hinge is generally in the center, one meter from the top. Each of the middle, top, and bottom hinges (in that order) gets two or three rounds each, or nine shotgun rounds for a single door.

Similar in use to a shotgun is a **thermite cutter**. A handheld thermite breaching tool is a chemical-based tool that weighs less than two pounds, that can safely and reliably melt through any door lock in one second. A single-use thermite cutting charge weighs a pound, which is heavier than a shotgun shell; but thermite charges are stronger and more reliable.

23.e Explosive Breaching of Entryways[1]

Explosive breaching reliably provides a fast entry. The Breaching Team quickly attaches a charge to the breach point with tape, nails, or staples anywhere on a wall. Then the Breacher explodes the charge and an opening appears. Breaching a wall instead of a door can distract, confuse the enemy inside, and bypass static defenses on the door like emplaced guns or booby-traps.

The danger of explosive breaching is that, even when performed properly and precisely, explosions inevitably create dangers such as fragmentation, toxic gases, fire, and blast pressures. These dangers especially place the occupants of a building in danger, which can be good or bad depending on the mission. Also, many walls contain hidden gas lines and electrical cords. Because of the danger to the patrol, explosive entry is never the first choice.

Phase 4

---

1   Quote: Police breaching techniques generally involve removing a door by its hinges or knocking it open with a battering ram. Military breaching techniques are more aggressive: they don't just try to get by the door, they use it as a weapon.
—Fictional Spy Michael Westen

To construct explosive breaches, Engineers require math equations and information (e.g., material, location, construction, etc.) that is specific to the barrier(s) being breached. That information fills books. Anyone with access to military-grade explosives can find details in official manuals.

That being said, broadly charges can largely be divided into two groups, cutting charges and pushing charges. After deciding whether pushing or cutting is more optimal, a Breacher must choose the kind of charge that weighs the least while still achieving the goal (because the less a single charge weighs, the more charges that can be carried).

Cutting charges are used to instantly cut through things like door latches and walls. The most basic cutting charge is constructed from detonation cord (i.e., "det cord"), so called because it can detonate other, attached explosives. However, det cord is a powerful cutting device by itself; it is a thin, flexible plastic tube usually filled with pentaerythritol tetranitrate (i.e., PETN or pentrite). PETN explodes at a rate of approximately 6400m/s, so det cord appears to explode instantaneously. (See Image 198, Pg. 217.) Det cord may be carried in a bent or an unbent, preformed configuration. Bent det cord is easier to carry, but must be used within a few days to prevent shape memory.

A det cord charge is simply lengths of det cord tightly taped together, and then attached to whatever needs to be cut. A det cord linear charge slices through whatever it is attached to, for example cutting through hinges or door bolts. Det cord linear charges are compact when rolled, allowing for easy transport of many charges. The charge is versatile in what it can cut, and the charge is forgiving as to exact placement while still achieving desired results. For a thick door, consider multiple charges.

Oval det cord charges are good at cutting ovals, are emplaced quickly, and produce minimal fragmentation. (See Moving between Buildings, Pg. 105.) Using det cord to cut an oval shape into a wall is efficient because the center of the oval is not exploded, but falls when it is cut out by the surrounding explosion. A 4-wrap oval det cord charge will cut an oval into plywood, sheet rock, light plaster walls, and wooden or metal doors; a shingled roof requires 6 wraps, while a triple brick wall requires 8 wraps, and so on. A man-sized oval charge can easily be constructed on cardboard or a tarp for easy placement (wood and metal backing create fragmentation). (See Image 195, Pg. 217.)

A small det cord oval charge is called a "donut charge." The donut charge can open a solid wood or metal door by looping the charge around a doorknob

Explosive Breaching

Image 194: A **water charge** creates a blast that makes a door a projectile. It can use normal saline bags.

Image 195: Every patrol should carry **man-sized charges** to make impromptu wall charges.

Image 196: A **strip charge** is very effective at pushing the strip through anything (in this case, the lock).

Image 197: To enter the structure as fast as possible after the explosion, the Marines **use an offset stack**.

Image 198: Explosives usually use an **explosive line** as a trigger. This limits offset from the breach.

Image 199: A destructive explosion **releases shrapnel**. So the Marines stack around the corner for cover.

to cut it out of the door. To improve the effectiveness, a donut charge includes a 5-wrap uli knot on the side of the bolt, that provides extra force to push out the bolt. The only disadvantage of the donut charge is its limited application.

For thick materials, like concrete up to 20 cms, C4 blocks can be attached to either a det cord linear charge, two linear charges in a cross shape, or an oval charge. These are called **"mousehole" charges**, because the circular holes that C4 makes in thick walls resemble the holes that mice make. (See Image 91, Pg. 107.) The addition of C4 makes the charge heavier to transport, more dangerous to the breacher, and it will not cut rebar or other reinforcement. (Plan for secondary breach assets, such as rebar cutting weapon attachments or a tank.) However, anyone on the other side of a breach charge with multiple blocks of C4 will be nonfunctional.

A **pushing charge** which uses an explosive to push and deform materials is sometimes more appropriate than a cutting explosion. For example, a linear det cord charge effectively cuts wooden doors, but may not be able to cut a metal door. In contrast, an explosive push at the center of a metal door, can deform it enough to pull the door's bolts out. Also, a pushing force that deforms metal results in less fragmentation compared to cutting or exploding.

One way to transform the cutting force of det cord into a pushing force is to use duct tape to sandwich det cord between two 1000ml saline IV bags. When exploded, the breaching-side saline bag pushes against the breach point with high-velocity water. The non-breaching-side saline bag is a tamp for the explosion to push against. The second bag also reduces back-blast, meaning a **water charge** can be used in relatively close proximity to friendly personnel. (See Image 194, Pg. 217.)

A more complex water charge is the water-slider charge, which has multiple small water charges chained together on one long piece of det cord. The water-slider charge can defeat the locking mechanism of wooden or metal doors. Each small water charge can slide along the det cord to attack hinges with different spacing. The water-slider charge's pushing force limits the collateral damage on the opposite side of the door, whereas a cutting force or ballistic entry may cause more fragmentation.

A **rubber-strip charge** is essentially det cord duct taped to the back of thick, 1-inch by 18-inch rubber strip. Plastics like truck mud flap or polystyrene cutting board can also be used. A rubber-strip charge can defeat the locking mechanism of wooden or metal doors and windows by pushing a nonexplosive medium (rubber) through the target, like a linear det cord charge with less fragmentation. The charge is placed between the doorknob and the doorjamb to blow through the bolt. (The doorjamb can protect from the blast.) (See Image 196, Pg. 217.)

A strip charge can be used on the bottom of a heavy window as well. Glass is brittle and a pushing force may more effectively shatter the glass than a cutting force. The charge pushes the strip into the bottom of the window or frame, removing support. Then the window falls down under its own weight.

23.f Grenades and Disorienting

Combat in urban areas often requires extensive use of hand grenades because they effectively disorient and kill enemies without precise aiming. In World War II, it was common for a battalion fighting in a city to use over 500 fragmentation grenades each day. In room-clearing, Soldiers throw hand grenades into a room before they enter to disable and disorient enemies inside and make the room safer. (Disorienting the enemy is an important tactic at all levels. (See Supporting Fires to Suppress and Divert, Pg. 176.))

That being said, grenades are not standard issue for room-clearing in the U.S. Army because of the danger of friendly fire. In a closed space, throwing a grenade incorrectly can kill the entire Clearing Team. Further, throw too many grenades, and the enemy will learn that the grenades are a warning that the room is about to be cleared. (See Changing Enemy Tactics, Pg. 300.)

Interior use hand grenades come in four general types: stun, tear gas, concussion, and fragmentation. The **stun hand grenade** is a flash-bang distraction device, which produces a brilliant flash and a loud bang to momentarily surprise and distract an enemy force. The stun grenade is often used for close-range work and non-lethality; for example, when clearing rooms with thin walls or when noncombatants are present in rooms. It has a low risk of friendly injury. **Tear gas grenades** are used very similarly; they also disorient the enemy. The problem is that they disorient everyone without gas masks in a closed space for a long time.

The **concussion grenade** causes injury or death to people in a room by creating a wave of overpressure from its explosion. They are very effective against enemies in bunkers, buildings, and underground passages. In open areas, they are ineffective because of minimal overpressure and fragmentation. (Although, there is a secondary fragmentation hazard though from rocks,

Phase 4

Image 200: Marines throw flash bangs. Camp Pendleton, CA. 07 Jan 2014. The thrower exposes himself to attain the **largest target (i.e., opening) and easiest throw** possible.

Image 201: An Italian Soldier throws a flash bang. Germany, 12 Mar 2018. The thrower stabilizes himself with One Man's shoulder, because **missing could be catastrophic.**

gravel, wood splinters, glass, etc.) Some concussive grenades can be used for makeshift demolitions, light blasting, and interior wall breaching.

The **fragmentation grenade** produces substantial overpressure when used inside like a concussive grenade. But additionally, the grenade produces shrapnel which is extremely dangerous for everyone in the area. The fragments cannot penetrate a single layer of sandbags, a cinder block, or a brick building; but they can perforate wood, sheetrock, and tin buildings. If the walls of a building are weak, consider using stun or concussion grenades instead.[1]

The measure of a fragmentation or concussion grenade is the "effective casualty radius," meaning the circle around the point of detonation where a minimum of 50% of the personnel exposed in that area become casualties. For example, the M67 high explosive grenade has a 15-meter effective casualty radius. The casualty radius depends a lot upon the type of grenade.

Aside from hand grenades, there are also **grenade launchers**, like the M203. The M203 grenade launcher is the best method for throwing a grenade beyond 14 to 38 meters, as the rounds are designed to not explode before that distance (minimum distance depends on the round). Before 14 meters, the hand grenade is superior because it can be rolled, bounced, or ricocheted into areas that cannot be reached by grenade launchers.

---

1   Quote: My company conducted a raid in Mogadishu to capture an enemy mortar tube. We entered the building by first clearing a hallway with a fragmentation grenade. The resulting explosion made the building almost impossible to clear due to poor visibility and obstructions from the collapsed roof. The mortar cache was never found in the rubble and the extra time needed to clear the building resulted in us receiving RPG and small arms fire from enemy reinforcements. —Captain Drew R. Meyerowich

Image 202 et al: Iraqi Counter Terrorism Service students prepare to enter a building after throwing a flash bang. Near Baghdad, Iraq, 02 Oct 2019. Notice that in the first photo, the Right Soldier is looking at the grenade and not at the opening where an enemy could appear. And in the second photo the Left Soldier only has one hand on his weapon, and is unprepared to engage. **Do not drop security!**

When choosing grenades, it is vital to not choose grenades that are too powerful for the building or mission. For example, fragmentation grenades detonated on the floor may not only throw fragments laterally but also send fragments and spall downward to lower floors. Fragmentation grenades should only be used on strongly resisting enemies, whereas stun grenades are preferred in all other cases due to less fratricide potential.

That being said, less-lethal options are not non-lethal. Stun and tear gas grenades use fast chemical reactions for quick dispersion and so present a **fire hazard**. During the 1980 SAS Iranian Embassy Siege, stun and tear gas grenades were simultaneously deployed. The stun grenades set the window curtains on fire, which in turn set an Assaulter's gas mask on fire. The Soldier was forced to remove his mask and assault directly into his own tear gas.

To use grenades once the Team Leader orders a room entry, the Two Man shows a grenade to the One Man. The One Man verifies the grenade with their peripheral vision and nods if they approve. This step not only notifies the One Man of the imminent throw but also serves as a check that Two Man chose the correct grenade. If the grenade is wrong, **do not put the pin back in!** Throw it in a safe direction. (Reinserting a pin is possible, but putting pins in pin holes during active combat is a recipe for exploding grenades.)

A voice alert can precede the throw, but the element of surprise may be lost. Shout "BANG OUT" for a stun grenade or "FRAG OUT" for a fragmentation grenade. Only shout "GRENADE" if an enemy grenade is seen. On the signal to go, or immediately after the grenade detonates, Soldiers begin their entry.

There are multiple ways to throw hand grenades. A Soldier can chuck the grenade so hard that it bounces and skips across the room, making it difficult for the enemy to pick up and throw back. Or the Soldier can hold the live grenade for two seconds before throwing it, thereby hastening the explosion when the grenade is thrown (called "cooking off"). Cooking off a grenade works because grenades have timed fuses for throw distances longer than a few meters into a room. That being said, cooking grenades is rarely recommended because it leaves no room for error.

When throwing a grenade, it is important to recognize barriers to the explosion, including: common office furniture, mattresses, doors, and bookshelves. Because enemies can hide behind barriers, a room should never be considered safe just because one or two grenades have detonated inside. How grenades bounce is also important. Grenades tend to bounce off of hard targets and break through glass. But if the grenade strikes at a sharp angle or the glass is thick, the grenade could deflect somewhere useless.

In most situations, throwing a grenade up a staircase (or up in general) is not recommended. If a grenade is thrown too strongly or the staircase is too steep, the grenade can roll back down the staircase. Therefore, if a grenade is thrown upward, it is thrown underhand to reduce the risk of it bouncing back and rolling down the stairs. Also, stairways can have varied construction and may be structurally damaged by a grenade. In fact, being able to throw grenades down is a primary reason to conduct a top-down assault. (See Vertical Layout and Floors, Pg. 164.)

23.g Firing Through Walls[1]

Before a room clear, Soldiers can fire through walls to kill enemies. Whereas fragmentation grenades are used in buildings where walls are bulletproof, shooting through walls is only used in buildings where walls are bullet-permeable and non-load-bearing because of ricochets. (There is no good solution for walls that are bullet-permeable in some places but not others.)

Like fragmentation grenades, shooting through walls is indiscriminate, and the technique is reserved for attacks where it is acceptable to kill everyone. (Note, the enemy can fire through walls, even if the patrol chooses not to.) If multiple rooms are side by side (like in a hallway), then assume the

---

[1] Real World: Sprayed fire was often ineffective fire in Iraq and Afghanistan. During the Second Battle of Fallujah, an Infantryman attempted to clear a house in the Jolan District on his own. Upon entering one room, he sprayed about five hundred rounds from his light machine gun toward a barricaded insurgent. Despite the close range and hundreds of rounds, the Infantryman did not hit anyone.

Firing Through Walls

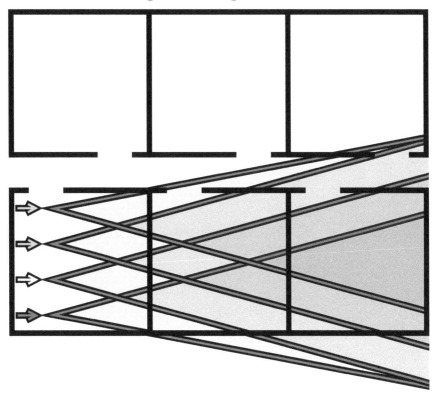

Image 203: This diagram shows sectors-of-fire for Soliders who fire through walls. Firing through walls can preclear rooms. But it is a dangerous technique because bullets will ricochet and deflect in many directions. **Ammo consumption** is also a major also concern because mass fires are not very effective.

bullets will penetrate every room. Shooting through many rooms parallel to a hallway can be an effective room-preparation technique. For example, if there are enemies in a position bunkered toward the door, then attacking their flank through the wall is a viable method. (See Fighting in L Shapes, Pg. 109.)

When firing, a Soldier must traverse the entire width of the room and not focus on a single spot. They stop traversing at least one meter off of other Soldiers' muzzles. Vertically, shooting at waist level misses enemies in the prone, but shooting at the feet is more likely to miss entirely. Machine guns are used where possible because firing through walls quickly consumes ammunition. Therefore, the patrol must plan for a larger ammunition consumption and more frequent resupply if they plan on firing through walls.

23.h Immediate and Delayed Entry[1]

Immediate entry (a.k.a. dynamic entry) is when Assaulters enter a room as fast as they can after stacking and breaching. Near-constant motion or physical movement is beneficial in some raids. During hostage rescue, a fast raid denies the enemy time to execute or threaten to execute the hostage. And in structures where the enemy can fire through walls and doors, standing behind walls and doors is more dangerous than simply entering the room.

Immediate entry can be further split into loud and stealth entries. A **loud immediate entry** reaches maximum speed and violence and is aggressive from start to finish. Commands are verbal and yelled. Assaulters lead by fire, shooting two rounds in every closed door and blacked-out window. Fragmentation and stun grenades are used. The Raiders' movement is swift and overwhelming for the enemy inside. A loud, immediate entry may be useful for a hostage rescue where every second is essential.

Stealth clearing is slower than loud clearing but does less to alert the enemy of the Raiders' location. During a **stealth immediate entry**, Soldiers quietly breach, move slowly, speak only in whispers, and listen for any movement within the house. During night clearing, night-vision goggles and infrared lights are used instead of surefire flashlights. A stealth immediate entry is useful for a structure with thin non-protecting walls where an alerted enemy can blindly fire through walls or throw grenades into hallways.

When deciding how to raid, Leaders can combine some elements of noise and stealth to, for example, loudly enter a room and then stealthily prepare to enter another. Constantly changing the level of stealth can disrupt the enemy's ability to properly create counter-tactics.

However, immediate entry causes three problems for Assaulters. First, every breach and entry is susceptible to booby-traps; and an immediate entry does not allow for an entryway check, potentially running the team into a trap. With a delayed entry, Soldiers may observe and sweep an entryway for hidden traps and explosives. While one Soldier checks for traps, another Soldier pulls security. The thoroughness of a sweep depends on how prevalent traps are in the area, and can be as simple as deliberately and physically checking a doorframe. (See Closed Door Reconnaissance, Pg. 207.)

---

1 **Quote:** My first rule is not to get shot. That starts with not putting myself in the most vulnerable position... not putting myself within the room. —Unknown

Image 204: Soldiers from the 1st Inf. Div. clear houses. Fallujah, Iraq, 12 Nov 2004. They do an **immediate entry** because the window would expose any stack. They use flashlights to avoid being surprised by the inside as they rush in.

Second, enemies within rooms know where Assaulters will enter (i.e., entryways), whereas Assaulters do not know where the enemy is in a large room. Therefore, the enemy's shots will be more accurate since they are scanning a smaller target (the doorway) than the Assaulters (the entire room). Delaying entry allows Soldiers to scan rooms from the outside, identifying enemy positions within a room.[1]

Third, humans instinctively hug cover and shuffle step when they suddenly receive enemy fire. Even the best-trained humans don't move under fire like rolling invincible tanks, and the idea of a smooth flow into a room while receiving fire is largely theoretical. Therefore, enemy fire on the entrance will halt the entry, defeating the purpose of immediate entry.

One way to mitigate the dangers of immediate entry is to use military working dogs as the first Soldier to enter. (See Military Working Dogs, Pg. 28.) Dogs are fearsome and distracting, but are low to the ground and so enemy shots are more likely to miss them. Also, Soldiers are less likely to freeze under fire when they follow another Soldier (i.e., the dog) into a room.

Another way to mitigate the shortcomings of immediate entry is to instead use **delayed entry** (a.k.a. limited-incursion or limited-penetration). Delayed entry is when a Soldier moves from an undetected position outside of a room to another location that is still outside of the room. In this way, Soldiers can address threats more methodically, cover and conceal themselves with the doorframe, and preclear from the outside with two muzzles.

Phase 4

This information asymmetry is what others call a "fatal funnel." But information asymmetry is a more useful framework because changing information solves the problem. For example, recon with a camera, create a new entrance, disorient with flash-bangs, or acquire more information through delayed entry.

To preclear a room from the outside, One Man begins by leaning toward the wall to pie the far-side of the doorframe, attempting to see the corner of the room and shooting any enemies they see. This is called "**diminishing returns**" because as a Soldier leans into a wall, they may never quite be able to see the inside corner of a room. (See Image 205, Pg. 227.)

Then, One Man returns to their original stacked position and pies in a semi-circle around the near-side doorframe. (See Pieing and Clearing Corners, Pg. 85.) While pieing, Soldiers do not move their gun barrels beyond the doorframe because then the enemy would know the location and orientation of the shooter. To maintain distance, one can imagine a one-meter square on the ground touching the entryway; Soldiers do not enter that square.

As One Man pies, Two Man replaces One Man's original position and pulls security into the room to increase the number of guns in the fight. In a narrow hallway, Two Man may need to crouch. (See Synchronized Movement, Pg. 198.) **If enemy contact is made at any point, return fire, seek cover, and throw a grenade.** (See Grenades and Disorienting, Pg. 219.)

Once One Man completely pies their semi-circle, both One and Two Man lean against the wall to attempt to see the near-side corners of the room (i.e. diminishing returns again), and then they return to entry positions. At this point, without entering, the Clearing Team has cleared all of the room that is visible from the outside. One and Two Man prepare to enter the room. Immediately before entering, they can again do one last check by quickly leaning toward the entry. (See Image 206, Pg. 227.)

However delayed entry, like immediate entry, has drawbacks. Slowing pieing can alert an enemy. If the walls are permeable, the enemy can barricade and shoot Soldiers through walls. And if enemies begin to fire through the doorway, Soldiers are unable to enter the room and leave the dangerous hallway. In contrast, immediate entry avoids alerting the enemy and may allow Soldiers to exit dangerous hallways (i.e., enter a room) before a battle even begins. **In sum, delayed entry is preferred when Soldiers can stay outside of a room, and immediate entry is preferred when they cannot.**

Immediate entry and delayed entry are not mutually exclusive within one mission. Soldiers can default to delayed entry but change to immediate entry when they cannot stay in the hallway. Further, the patrol must prepare for a jumpy Soldier to mistakenly initiate an immediate entry, and a scared Soldier to mistakenly do a delayed entry, when opposite approach is appropriate.

Delayed Entry

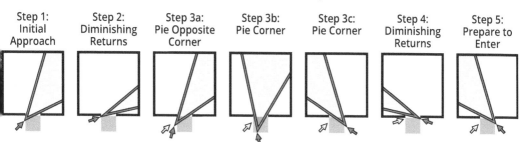

Step 1: Initial Approach

Step 2: Diminishing Returns

Step 3a: Pie Opposite Corner

Step 3b: Pie Corner

Step 3c: Pie Corner

Step 4: Diminishing Returns

Step 5: Prepare to Enter

Step 6 (optional): Lean in to Double Check

Combined Sectors for Steps 1-5

Image 205: For safety, stay away from the entry by at least the width of the entry. (Represented by the blue square.) After diminishing returns on one side, pieing, and diminishing returns on the other side, almost all of the room is cleared before entering (see the combined sectors box).

Image 206: Mexican Sailors clear a doorway while participating in a mechanized assault. Camp Pendleton, 18 Jul 2016. After a delayed entry, but before the One Man makes his center-step, One and Two Man can lean in from opposite sides of the door jamb to peek the entry for one last chance at engaging with multiple guns. (Step 6 above) This is useful when One Man delays entry after pieing.

Whatever the SOP, it needs to be drilled into Soldiers because entering a new space is always the most dangerous and frantic part of any military operation.

24. Seizing Rooms (Battle Drill 6)

After a room has been breached and prepared, Soldiers seize the room. Entering a room that contains an armed enemy is up there with crossing a minefield as one of the most dangerous things that a Soldier can do. For that reason, very specific techniques have been developed to mitigate the danger. (The only way to eliminate the danger is to not enter the room.[1])

There are a variety of room entry techniques. However, each variation can be broken into three steps: clear the entry and immediate area; choose and clear a corner; clear the room. The actions of each Soldier in the stack are also standardized: One Man clears the blind corner; Two Man then clears the opposite corner; Three and Four Man follow to engage threats directly ahead.

24.a Clearing the Entry

Clearing the entry begins with deciding who clears; i.e., who is One Man. When only one Soldier is on the door, there is no question. But when two Soldiers stack on opposite sides of an open entry, One Man is whoever pied the entryway or has seen more of the room. Or at a closed door, One Man is whoever will have first line-of-sight when a door is opened. In case of confusion, whichever Soldier first says "on you" (i.e., "You are the One Man."), or "on me" (i.e., "I am the One Man.") decides the order of entry. The Two Man then allows for entry by pointing their rifle vertically up or down to signal One Man to enter, and not flag One Man as they enter. One Man pulls security on the door until they receive a vertical rifle signal.

One Man begins entry by "**center-stepping**," moving directly in front of the entryway. They square their hips to the entrance. The rifle's muzzle is still outside of the room by less than a meter, ready to engage any threats. The

---

[1] Real World: Room-clearing techniques, such as U.S. Army Battle Drill 6, are very popular to train for a few reasons. It's fun. It's personal, and one of the only man-to-man battles remaining today. It earns facilities and funding for a unit. But in reality, clean techniques are marginally safer than sloppy techniques; both are dangerous. Properly training room-clearing techniques takes a hell of a lot of time that could be spent on basics like weapon handling, IED identification, or grenade throwing.

Clearing the Entry

Image 207: Before entering, One Man **center-steps** the entry, shooting any enemies and backing out if needed.

Image 208: The very **first thing** that an enemy in the corner should see is an entering Soldier's muzzle.

Image 209: This Soldier (left) did not **dig his corner (to the right)**, and so is vulnerable to enemies in the corner.

Image 210: Two Man **fights to enter** behind One Man as fast as possible to cover One Man's rear.

Image 211: Like One Man, Two Man also digs his corner and both Soldiers **protect each other's backsides**.

Image 212: Entering a corner-fed room uses the same principles as entering from a center-fed room.

Soldier takes a good look into the entire room, scanning for any threats. (See Image 207, Pg. 229.) The brief center-step gives Soldiers one last chance to detect and engage immediate and obvious threats before entering, or to halt entering entirely when the threat is too high. (See Image 221, Pg. 238.) Doing a center-step is a continuous motion from the entry position to the entryway. This needs to be timed to be as fast as possible to the degree that there is specific footwork; as the Soldier turns from the stack to the door, they plant their outside foot as they rotate their hips and walk through the entry.

One of the reasons that immediate entry is often unsuccessful is because some versions omit the center-step. Hypothetically in those versions of immediate entry, if an enemy was standing in the direct center of the room, an entering Soldier would ignore them to clear their corner as fast as possible. Ignoring an enemy goes against all of human nature; if One Man is engaged in the entryway, they will freeze in the entryway. That being said, some units use grenades to disable obvious central threats instead of using a center-step.

Two Man is prepared to follow One Man. In a split stack, Two Man can either be the Soldier opposite One Man ("cross entry") or the Soldier Behind One Man ("stack entry"). Stack entry is faster and simpler. But if the Soldier behind One Man is pulling long security, they are instead the last Soldier to enter. Entering priority can be as complicated as a unit wants to make it.

If the One Man continues to enter the room after their center-step snapshot, they choose to go toward the right or left corner.[1] One Man travels to the corner with the **largest perceived threat**.[2] Usually "threat" means the corner not cleared during delayed entry; but it could also be the corner of the room where enemy presence is suspected, or just a suspicious pile of trash.

If threats are equal, the default direction of entry depends on the clearing formation. (See Clearing the Corner and Room, Pg. 232.) If the Clearing Team uses a strongwall or shallow horseshoe formations, the One Man leads

---

[1] Real World: Going left or right in a center-fed room can be described as a "cross" (i.e., One Man crosses to the opposite side corner), or a "hook" (i.e., One Man does a u-turn around the doorjamb and hooks the same side corner). Importantly, crossing and hooking not prescriptive; they are descriptive. That is, Soldiers do not choose to hook, which is a movement technique; they choose to address the threat on in the same-side corner using a hook. And if the threat changes, use a cross.

[2] Quote: In tactics, the most important thing is not whether you go left or right, but why you go left or right. — United States Marine Corps General Alfred M. Gray Jr.

the team to whichever wall is longer so the team can spread out. And if using points-of-domination formation, the One Man goes to a near-wall corner.

Another entry-clearing technique is to take the **path of least resistance**. When using a doorway as the point of entry, the path of least resistance is determined initially based on the way the door opens. If the door opens inward then One Man moves away from the hinges. (See Image 182, Pg. 211.) If the door opens outward, then One Man moves toward the hinged side. (See Image 181, Pg. 211.) When threats are equal, taking the path of least resistance makes sense; but it makes little sense for a Soldier to take the path of least resistance if they can address a greater threat on one side or the other. Always take the path to the largest perceived threat first.

A third alternate technique is for One Man to always go in one direction; e.g., One Man always goes left. This system is incredibly simple to teach, yet is also dangerous because half the time the Soldier ignores the bigger threat.

Once One Man enters, they **get out of the doorway** as soon as possible! The gap between when One Man and Two Man enter is the time that One Man has their back exposed. So, Two Man follows behind One Man as closely as possible. (See Image 210, Pg. 229.) Sometimes as Two Man enters, they are so close to One Man that they place their rifle over One Man's shoulder, and drop from high ready to depressed-muzzle. (See Image 55, Pg. 81.)

For entry techniques where One and Two Man enter to opposite sides, One Man **obviously directs their rifle and hips** as they enter to whichever corner they are pursuing. This nonverbally telegraphs their direction of travel to Two Man, who then goes in opposite direction. In fact, if the entry is wide enough, One and Two Man simultaneously enter with a back-to-back entry. (See Image 171, Pg. 199.) For a simultaneous entry, One Man and Two Man nod muzzles, instead of Two Man vertically pointing their rifle. Then One and Two Man both center-step together and each hook to their near corners.

If Soldiers enter one after the other, Three Man follows One Man, and Four Man follows Two Man. (E.g., One Man left, Two Man right, Three Man left, Four Man right.) (See Image 213, Pg. 233.) Three and Four Man stop only one meter from the entry so they can balance staying close to the entry while not silhouetting themselves in the entryway. The primary role of Three and Four Man is as backups to One and Two Man. If One Man goes down or becomes preoccupied, Three Man pushes past them and becomes the new One Man (same for Two Man and Four Man). Therefore, Three and Four Man very rarely shoot anything, because One and Two Man will have already engaged all threats. And if the room is very small, (e.g., a closet or bathroom), One or Two Man say "short room," and Three and Four Man do not enter at all.

If a team has more than four Soldiers, they alternate sides in the same way. And if squeezing extra bodies into a small room would overcrowd and create confusion, the Team Leader and SOP determine which Soldiers do not enter. Soldiers that stay outside pull security.

If a team has fewer than four Soldiers, they still use the same techniques as a four-man clear using the same positions. The danger of a small team is that there is inherently a lack of backup Soldiers. For example, in a three-man room clear, Two Man has no backup. If Two Man goes down without a Four Man, One and Three Man will have their backs exposed and also go down.

24.b Clearing the Corner and Room

After a Soldier enters the room, they clear their corner. Clearing a corner is as simple as looking to the corner with the rifle at the depressed-muzzle. However, clearing the corner is such a vital step that it has a name: "**digging**" the corner. After clearing the entry, Soldiers push their rifles forward and back into the correct shoulder position as if they were digging with a shovel. Soldiers have historically moved so fast, they forget to take clearing the corner seriously, and so the step must be highlighted.

Soldiers clear the rest of the room using three basic formations: strongwall, shallow horseshoe, and points-of-domination. Each technique differs in how far Soldiers walk into the room (i.e. penetration). Strongwall has Soldiers on a single wall for command and control (minimal penetration); shallow horseshoe advances the Soldiers on either side one to two meters (medium penetration); and points-of-domination places Soldier at opposite corner to maximize angles-of-fire (maximum penetration). (See Image 213, Pg. 233.) Free-flow is a fourth, advanced technique that as the name suggests allows Soldiers to adjust their penetration as needed (variable penetration).

Strongwall is easy to implement: all Soldiers end up on the same wall, i.e., the strongwall. In a center-fed room (i.e., a room with an entry in the center of a wall), One Man and Two Man enter and stop at their first corner; Three and Four Man enter and stop one meter off of the door. In a corner-fed room (i.e., a room with an entry in a corner), all Soldiers follow One Man. Soldiers must spread out from each other to evenly spread their forward-facing

Phase 4

Room-Clearing Techniques

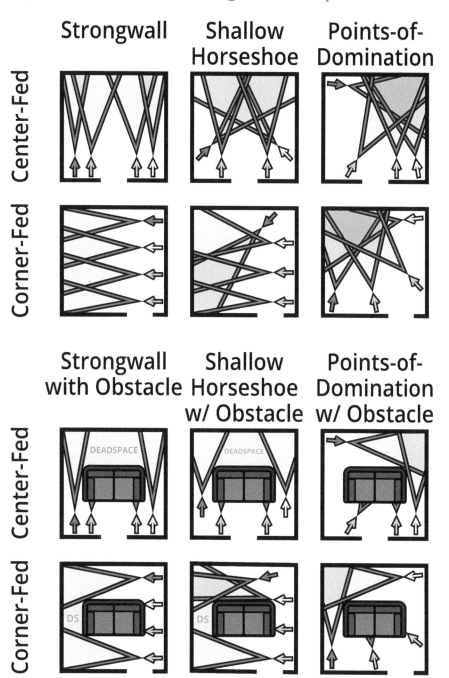

Image 213: Broadly, there are three room-clearing techniques. Strongwall keeps Soldiers on one wall, shallow horseshoe pushes One and Two Man a bit forward to increase their angle-of-fire, and points-of-domination pushes one Soldier to a far corner to create an **L-shaped attack**. In a barren room, points-of-domination is overly complicated. However, the advantage of pushing a Soldier deep in the room becomes more obvious when obstacles are present. Obstacles also show why the One Man in a strongwall must still **clear to the far wall** after initial entry.

Strongwall and Shallow Horseshoe

Image 214: Iraqi Security Forces clear a room using a **strongwall** formation. FOB Marez, Mosul, Iraq, 01 Sep 2006.

Image 215: Soldiers of 37th Inf Bde. clear a room using a **strongwall** formation. Camp Shelby, 15 Nov 2011.

Image 216: Navy, Marine Corps, and Air Force Members perform live-fire close-quarters battle room-clearing. Azusa, California, 18 May 2016. Here, only two Soldiers fit at the front. However, **the entire team enters** if they can fit because Three and Four Man take over for One and Two Man if they are incapacitated.

Image 217: U.S. Army Soldiers with 3rd Sqn., 2d Cav. Reg. clear a room in a **shallow horseshoe** formation. Grafenwoehr TA, Germany, 22 Aug 2019. Using points-of-domination on this irregular room shape would be difficult.

Points-of-Domination

Image 218: Philippine National Police and U.S. Coast Guardsmen clear a room with **points-of-domination**. Puerto Princesa, Palawan, Philippines, 30 May 2022. One and Two Man quickly sweep their sectors and prepare to shoot as they move to their opposite corners.

Image 219: U.S. Marines with L Co., 3rd Bn. 2nd Marines, and Republic of Korea (ROK) Marines use points-of-domination. Pohang, South Korea, October 20, 2016. Three and Four Man are entering. Every Soldier should be entering much closer together to get guns in the fight as fast as possible.

Image 220: U.S. Marines with Force Reconnaissance Company, III Marine Expeditionary Force, conduct room-clearing drills. Camp Hansen, Okinawa, Japan, June 15, 2021. **Once all Soldiers are in a room using points-of-domination, they form an L shape.** (See Fighting in L Shapes, Pg. 109.)

sectors-of-fire. (A room with a door one meter off the wall is still corner-fed.) **Shallow horseshoe** is the same as strongwall, but with some additional movement at the end. With shallow horseshoe, any Soldier who reaches a corner continues one or two meters into a room for better angles-of-fire.

The problem with every Soldier being on one wall, is that no Soldier can clear the deadspace behind obstacles within the room. To clear deadspace, One and Two Man can cheat up a little from their corners (i.e., a "shallow horseshoe formation"). But an enemy can still be hiding behind a couch deep in a room. Therefore, after the strongwall or horseshoe is complete, Soldiers still need to advance deeper into the room to clear behind obstacles. Because this two-step process of entering, and then clearing is easy to teach and implement, units with high turnover and low training time favor strongwall.

Points-of-domination (POD) turns this two-step process into a one-step process, and sends one Soldier deeper into the room right after entry. To achieve POD in a center-fed room, One Man moves past the first corner and advances to the next corner. In a corner-fed room, One and Two Man both advance to their first corners. In POD, One and Two Man always end up diagonally opposed to each other, with Soldiers in an L shape. (See Fighting in L Shapes, Pg. 109.) Three and Four Man enter and stop one meter off of the door. (See Image 213, Pg. 233.)

Points-of-domination is so named because Soldiers occupy points during entry that are capable of dominating the entire room. Thereby, the Soldier can achieve an angle-of-fire behind obstacles, preventing an adversary from hiding behind an obstacle and attacking the team. POD is typically favored by experienced units because the advantage of gaining multiple angles-of-fire as soon as possible outweighs the disadvantage of more complex movement.

The **"free-flow"** approach allows One and Two Man to adjust their penetration, and balances strongwall and POD techniques. Free-flow can be superior to POD because sometimes sending a Soldier deeper into the room can be dangerous, despite gaining an advantageous angle-of-fire. For example, sending Soldiers deep can overexpose them to open doors and windows. (See Image 262, Pg. 261.) Because free-flow has on-the-spot decision making, the SOP is very unit-dependent. Adopting and developing "free-flow" always comes after a unit has mastered strongwall and POD.

Regardless of the room-clearing technique, Soldiers must not move to the room center to shoot. Moving to the center leaves the Soldier vulnerable from all sides, and the Soldier blocks any other Soldiers from firing on the threat.

Shooting while moving is difficult but vital to room-clearing. (See Shooting while Moving, Pg. 83.) With adrenaline pumping, a recently trained One Man often moves too quickly when room-clearing, which causes jerky movement and fires, and prevents Two Man from smoothly following in time to protect One Man's back. For these reasons, Soldiers must be slow and avoid being jerky. Further, Soldiers must be prepared to engage from centimeters away, and be able to shoot an enemy that is also moving themself!

24.c Sector Sweeps and Points-of-Domination

A sector-of-fire is an area in which a Soldier is prepared to fire their weapon. When a Soldier moves, their sectors move with them, and Soldiers sweep their focus across an area (i.e. their sector-of-fire) as they move and engage threats as they see them. Changing the focus of attention while moving is difficult. (See Shooting while Moving, Pg. 83.)

"Sweeping" a sector means to move the eyes and not the muzzle. Sweeping with an entire rifle can lead to swinging too far and shooting to the opposite side of a target. And eyes sweep faster than rifles, so swinging a rifle rather than just looking, is slower to identify threats. To make sweeping easier and to better coordinate coverage, each Soldier has a scheme-of-maneuver.

Every unit uses their own SOP, and in fact sweeps aren't very useful for strongwall where everyone's sector-of-fire is straight ahead. So this section focuses on one example scheme-of-maneuver for points-of-domination. This example uses a "primary sector sweep" and "secondary sector sweep." Between One through Four Man positions, center-fed and corner-fed rooms, and going left or right, every Soldier learns sixteen different ways to conduct their primary and secondary sweep. And although each sweep follows a simple pattern, shooters must develop muscle memory to be fast and precise.

One and Two Man have the same sweeping pattern, but mirrored because they enter in opposite directions. To conduct the first sweep, a Soldier first clears the near-side corner as a starting point. Then they rotate the head and eyes toward the far wall, looking for and engaging threats. The

POD Sector Sweeps One and Two Man

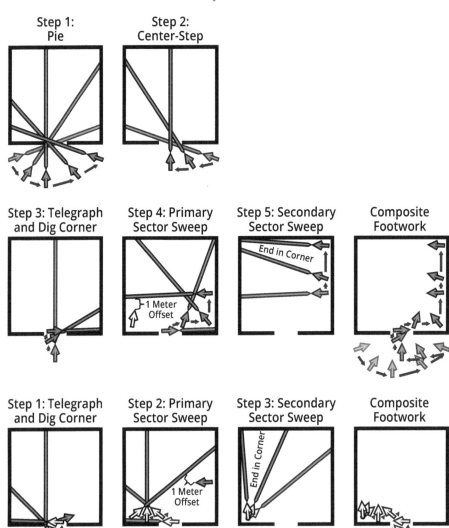

Image 221: In the top two rows of this diagram, One Man pies, center-steps, hooks to dig the corner, changes rotation to conduct their primary sector, and changes rotation again to conduct their secondary sector. If a target is in the center of the room, One Man engages them when pieing, center-stepping, primary sweeping and secondary sweeping. Every Soldier alway engages with at least two bullets, so One Man **shoots eight times** and Two Man shoots six times!

POD Sector Sweeps Three and Four Man

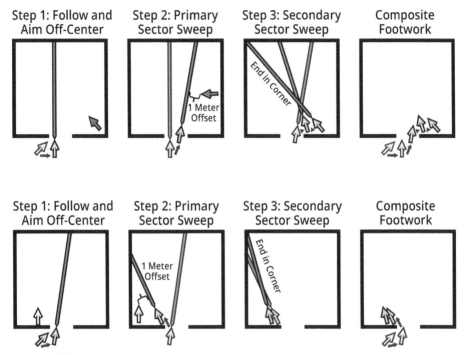

Image 222: Although each step is derived from a pattern (e.g., dig corner, primary sector, and secondary sector), in reality it is necessary to separately practice each position and step because **muscle memory** is the driver behind smoothness and thereby speed. This is also true for different room compositions and obstacles.

Soldier stops rotating one meter off of the opposite Soldier's barrel. This arc from the near-side corner to one-meter-off is the **primary sector**.[1] Then they switch directions and rotate until the far-side corner is encountered. The arc from one-meter-off to this corner is the **secondary sector**. One and Two Man end movement in diagonally opposed corners, and so will have the same corner in front of them. There is no third sweep, and in fact sweeping the rifle incorrectly is bad because it falsely signals a threat presence to the rest of the team. (See Image 221, Pg. 238.)

Three and Four Man also use primary and secondary sectors, but with different reference points. As Three and Four Man enter, their starting point is

---

Sometimes it's a meter off of the Soldier, and sometimes it's off of their barrel. But no one is carrying a yardstick anyway. Do whichever feels safer.

Phase 4

the point directly opposite of where they entered. So, for a corner-fed room, it is the opposite corner; and for a center-fed room, it is a point on the opposite wall. (Beginning from a little behind the starting point ensures both Three and Four Man sweep the starting point itself.) They then sweep for threats until one meter off of the Man they are following. The arc from the starting point to one-meter-off is the **primary sector**. Then they switch directions and rotate until the far-side corner is encountered. The arc from one-meter-off to this corner is the **secondary sector**. After Three and Four Man clear their sectors, the Soldier who can most easily pull rear security on the entryway toward the direction of movement does so. (See Image 222, Pg. 239.)

If any threat or obstacle is encountered during a Soldier's sweep, (e.g., furniture; noncombatants; deadspace behind a door; an opening to another space; a Soldier is disabled due to an injury; or weapon's malfunction) then that Soldier engages the issue. If the threat is neutralized, the sweep is continued. But if the threat requires additional attention, then the Soldier stays on the threat. If One or Two Man become distracted, then immediately, Three or Four Man take over One or Two Man's sectors and movement. Replacing One and Two Man is the primary job of Three and Four Man.

24.d Connected Rooms and Areas

Every unknown and unsecured opening in a room is a threat because an enemy can appear in the opening and fire.[1] Therefore, rooms with many unsecured openings are filled with threats and are avoided at first. Instead, the patrol clears the surrounding structures and rooms so that fewer of the openings in the original room lead to uncleared areas. This is essentially enveloping but within a structure. (See Enveloping and Preclearing, Pg. 159.)

If a Soldier does enter a room with unsecured openings, they begin their primary sector sweep as normal. But once the Soldier comes to an unsecured opening during their sweep, they stop sweeping and **"own" that threat**. That means that the Soldier clears the seen area (i.e. the opening), continues pieing, and maintains security on the opening without revealing himself to the opposite side. Unlike with a known enemy, for which the Soldier shoots and continues to sweep, an unsecured opening (i.e., an empty space where

---

[1] Real World: Note that "unsecured" is a vague concept. Enemies can always blindly fire through thin walls or draped windows. And they can accurately aim through a fist-sized hole in a wall.

Image 223: A U.S. Soldier from C Co., 1st Bn., 1st Special Forces Group (right) and an Iraq SOF Commando (left) clear an L-shaped room. 03 Dec 2008. The Left Soldier has temporarily stopped advancing on his side because the Right Soldier has better angles-of-fire. The Right Soldier continues to sweep all the way to the back. Assume the Left Soldier is One Man, meaning that he stopped short. The Right Soldier continues to the opposite corner to complete points-of-domination.

an enemy may potentially appear) cannot neutralized with shooting. Because the soldier cannot neutralize the threat, they cannot continue to sweep.

A Clearing Team can easily secure a room with **one unsecured opening**, since the opening interrupts the primary sectors of both One and Two Man. One Man, Two Man, or both pull security on the opening while the remaining Soldiers secure and mark the room. Then the Clearing Team can collapse on the unsecured opening. (See Image 224, Pg. 242.)

Two unsecured openings are also manageable, since one interrupts the primary sector of One Man, and the other of Two Man. To pie both openings on both sides, Three and Four Man do a back-to-back synchronized movement to the area between the openings. Thereby, while One and Two Man secure each opening from one direction, Three and Four Man pie and secure each opening from the other direction. (See Image 225, Pg. 243.)

Three or more unsecured openings cannot be secured with a standard SOP, besides clearing with more than four Soldiers. To clear the room with four Soldiers, the team has to change their room-clearing method to strongwall or back out and envelope. (See Clearing the Corner and Room, Pg. 232.)

If the unsecured opening is close to the room's initial entryway, then a Soldiers must still fit between the opening and entryway. Finally, Three and Four Man must be prepared to move to a different part of the room if there is no space behind One or Two Man.

Clearing Rooms with One Extra Opening

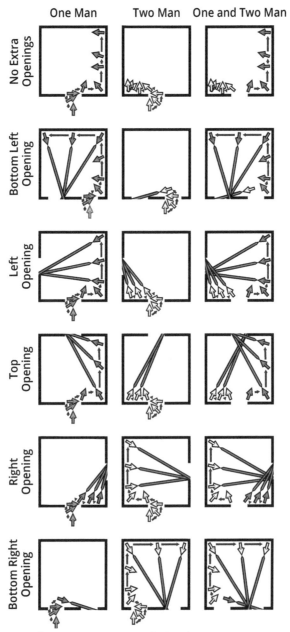

Image 224: One and Two Men interrupt their primary sector sweep to own a threat (indicated with red line-of-sight). Because One and Two Man sweep in opposite directions, they always **pie to opposite sides of the door**, maximizing coverage.

Clearing Two Extra Openings

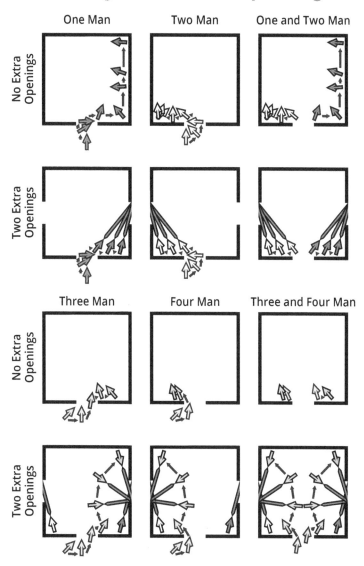

Image 225: If there are two threats, then both One and Two Man interrupt their primary sector sweeps to own a threat. Then the far side is cleared by Three and Four Man. This is exactly why clearing with fewer than four Soldiers is dangerous. Note that Three and Four Man use **synchronized movement** to cover each other's back to the opposite-side doorway. (See Synchronized Movement, Pg. 198.)

25. Seizing Other Spaces

Buildings contain many different kinds of spaces besides the standard room, such as hallways, stairs, closets, etc. Rooms are used to introduce all spaces because most enemies will be in rooms. But patrols must prepare for all spaces.

25.a Hallways

A hallway is a room designed to facilitate movement between spaces. For this reason, hallways are dangerous because enemies have many angles-of-fire into the hallway from its numerous entrances. **Teams spend the least amount of time in hallways as possible.** If fact, hallways are so dangerous that a team may choose to avoid hallways entirely and go through walls; and if a problem arises, such as an injured Soldier, the Clearing Team may enter a room and deal with the problem there instead of in the hallway.

Hallway movement formations are defined by the number of Soldiers in the front line: single file, double file, or triple file (i.e. "rolling T").[1] (See Image 226, Pg. 245.) There is no four-file formation because Four Man always pulls rear security, and looks backward every few steps. Any automatic weapon systems provide rear security because large weapons are unwieldy indoors.

A **single file** is used in hallways so narrow that only one Soldier can comfortably be at the front. Trying to fit two Soldiers in full kit side-by-side in a narrow hallway limits the Soldiers' ability to actively engage; and rubbing against walls may alert an enemy on the other side of that wall. Further, enemy ricochets can travel parallel up to a foot away from a wall. It is a bad idea to force a double file for the sake of having a double file.

The sectors-of-fire for single file are simple. One Man takes the direction of movement until they encounter a threat. Then, One Man owns that threat, and Two Man takes the direction of movement. A single file has no good answer to a four-way intersection or opposing doors in narrow hallways because there are unsecured areas in three directions, but space for Soldiers is limited. To compensate, the One and Two Men pull security left and right, while Three Man looks past them and pushes forward. (See Image 235, Pg. 248.)

1 Real World: Some texts recommend a "diamond" or "serpentine" formation where two Soldiers stand side-by-side behind one front Soldier. But two barrels at the front are better than one.

Hallway Movement Formations

Single File Double File   Triple File

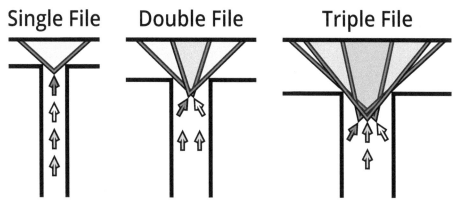

Image 226: Hallway movement formations are defined by the number of Soldiers at the **front line**. In double and triple file, the Left and Right Soldiers secure the opposite side corner to have a better angle-of-fire; this is **cross-coverage**.

Double and triple files use "cross-coverage," which means that they do not pull security on their own wall of the hallway, but on the opposite wall of the hallway. Thereby, the Soldiers have better vision and angles-of-fire around corners. Whichever Soldier sees a threat first takes the threat, while the other Soldier(s) maintain front security. (See Image 226, Pg. 245.)

When an entire squad travels a hallway, the frontmost team clears alone. Because hallway clearing requires tight teamwork, adding additional Soldiers may be detrimental as they disrupt a team's practiced flow. However, this is not a rule, and a unit may use one team to secure a large intersection while a following team passes through. (See Image 84, Pg. 102.)

Securing an intersection begins with a Soldier verbally identifying the intersection's characteristics. For example, if a Soldier sees a dead-end, they state "dead-end"; if they see a room on the left, they state "room left"; and if they see a four-way intersection, they say "four-way." Hallway intersections (and hallway openings generally) have eight variations of offshoots: none (dead-end); one (straightway, left turn, right turn); two (T intersection, hallway/room left, hallway/room right); and three (four-way intersection).

Once a Team Leader decides to enter a hallway or intersection (from a room, from a T intersection, etc.), they dictate the direction of movement by ordering "take left," "take right," or "take straight." Or to be clearer, the Team Leader can say "Hold [opposite direction], push [direction of travel]."

Phase 4

T Intersection Movement Part 1

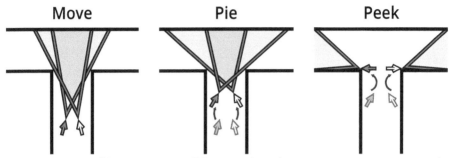

Move	Pie	Peek

Image 227: As Soldiers move to a T intersection, they use cross-coverage to gain better angles-of-fire. They then **switch from the opposite to the near corner**, and pie and peek the near corner.

Image 228: Soldiers of 709th Bn., 18th Military Police Bde., move in a **triple file with cross-coverage**. Vaziani Training Area, Georgia 15 Sep 2020.

Image 229: Korean and U.S. Marines in a high-low formation after **peeking**. HI, 22 Jul 2014. The central Soldier is has their back is exposed.

The specific method of entering a hallway or intersection is called the "**pie, peek, push.**" (See Pieing and Clearing Corners, Pg. 85.) (The reason why Soldiers cannot "pie, peek, push" into rooms is that doorways are typically too narrow.) Left and Right Soldiers in a double or triple file (or two Soldiers in a high-low formation) pie corners as they approach them.

Also, to make clearing safer but slower, the Two Man can use **grenades** while the One Man pulls security. Two Man throws a grenade where threat(s) are suspected and then after, One Man proceeds in the direction of movement. (Soldiers still secure and prepare to enter the grenaded space if necessary.)

After pieing and grenades, all Front Soldiers nod their rifles (a small up-down movement) to indicate that they are ready to peek and push their side.

T Intersection Movement Part 2

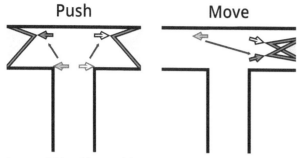

Push   ## Move

Image 230: After Soldiers have established that a hallway does not contain an enemy or other danger, they push to the **far side of the hallway** to create space for any following Soldiers. Finally, Soldiers consolidate to move.

Image 231: U.S. Marines of 3rd Marine Reg. push into the intersection. HI, 22 Jul 2014. Two Soldiers **push** either side because space allows.

Image 232: U.S. Marines with 1st Plt., Force Recon Co., III MEF have **pushed** into an intersection. Camp Hansen, Okinawa, Japan, 29 June 2020.

(Because they pied the opposite side, and peek the same side, each Soldier rotates 180 degrees.) Soldiers simultaneously rotate and peek at the near-side corner. And if the intersection has uneven corners, the Soldier on the side with the closer corner peeks first. **Peeking** means to take a quick peek into the next area which gives the Soldier a "snapshot" or "picture" of an area. Peeking is used because hallways have too much deadspace far away on the near-side wall that diminishing returns cannot see. (See Image 205, Pg. 227.) After peeking, a Soldier is prepared to, or does, immediately withdraw back from danger. There is no point in peeking if Soldiers never withdraw!

If no threat is found when peeking, Soldiers **push** (i.e. move) into the hallway they peeked. They move one step to make room for any following

Four-Way Intersection Movement Part 1

Image 233: U.S. Army Soldiers, with 2d Sqn., 2nd Cav. Reg., conduct training with German Army Soldiers. Grafenwoehr Training Area, Germany, 01 Aug 2013. The Soldiers **move** in a double file formation. The Front Soldiers use a depressed-muzzle rifle position with cross-coverage, while the Rear Soldiers use a low-carry rifle position. When they arrive at the four-way intersection, the Soldiers **dip their rifles** to signal they are both ready to peek the corner.

Move, Pie, Peek, Push, Move in a Four-Way Intersectoin

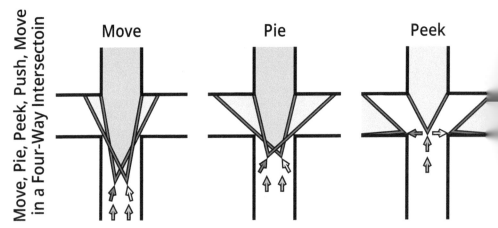

| Move | Pie | Peek |

Image 234: Moving into a four-way intersection is largely the same as moving into a three-way intersection. (See Image 227, Pg. 246.). This illustration shows the first three steps, **move, pie, and peak.** When the Front Soldiers move to the four-way intersection with cross-coverage (See Image 233, Pg. 248.), they come to the corner and pie it. (See Image 63, Pg. 86.) (See Image 227, Pg. 246.). During the peek, Three Man steps between One and Two Man to maintain long security to the front (See Image 235, Pg. 248.).

Image 235: Coast Guardsmen assigned to Law Enforcement Detachment 408, conduct close-quarters combat (CQB) drills aboard the USS Billings (LCS 15). Caribbean Sea, 07 Feb 2022. **Three Man pulls long security between One and Two Man as soon as possible.** Sometimes there is a momentary drop in security as One and Two Men peek. This complex movement pattern is a good example of why practice is so vital for smooth and secure movement.

Four-Way Intersection Movement Part 2

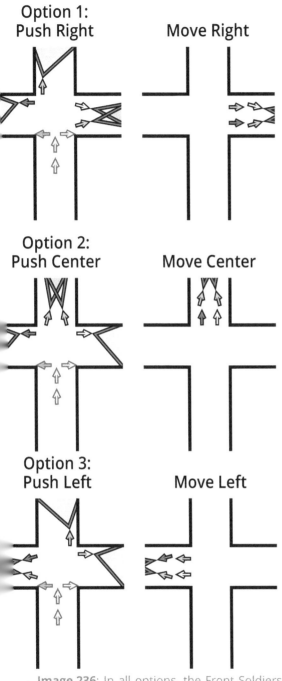

Option 1:
Push Right

Move Right

Option 2:
Push Center

Move Center

Option 3:
Push Left

Move Left

Image 237: When moving right, the Right-Side Soldiers push right. All additional Soldiers follow behind.

Image 238: When moving center, the Rear Soldiers push center. Here, the Side Soldiers did not push enough and are blocking.

Image 236: In all options, the Front Soldiers (red and yellow) push left and right to the far-side. If the Clearing Team is moving right, then the Rear-Right Soldier pushes right, and if moving left the Rear-Left Soldier pushes left. Otherwise, the Rear Soldiers pushes forward. After all Soldiers have pushed, the team consolidates in the hallway of movement.

Image 239: When moving left, the Left-Side Soldiers push left. Even if the center does not exactly align, the **same principles apply.**

Soldiers passing them. (See Image 232, Pg. 247.) One and Two Man enter the intersection in the order of movement and opposite the order of movement respectively. Then One and Two Man push to the opposite wall to free space for Three and Four Man to follow. (See Image 230, Pg. 247.) Someone says "last man" to collect Two Man. The team reforms and moves out.

To push from a double or triple file, the Right Soldier hooks into the right hallway (if there is one), and the Left Soldier hooks into the left hallway (if there is one). A Rear Soldier (double file) or the Center Soldier (triple file) continues straight. If there is no right, left, or straight direction, then the Soldier goes in the direction of movement. (See Image 234, Pg. 248.)

At this point, up to **three directions have security from three Soldiers**: two Soldiers have pushed left and right, and one Soldier maintains long security. Finally, any remaining Soldiers pulling security continue in the direction of movement with the Soldier securing that direction. The whole team continues in the direction of movement. Note that to use this SOP, every Soldier must be able to perform every position because Soldiers rotate positions depending on which direction is taken. (See Image 236, Pg. 249.)

If a patrol comes to a three-way intersection where one direction is forward and the other is either left or right (like a room attached to a hallway), the team uses the same technique as a four-way intersection; however, the Soldier on the opposite side continues pulling forward security.

To pass open doorways in a hallway, the closest Soldier pulls security on the opening from within the hallway as the remaining Soldiers pass behind them. (See Image 285, Pg. 282.) Passing two opposing doorways in a hallway is one of the worst possible scenarios in CQB. Although, it is a form of a four-way intersection, Soldiers often cannot pie, peek, push because they cannot enter the room without doing a full room clear. Therefore, the hallway becomes very crowded with simultaneous security requirements in three directions.

To solve the problem, two opposing openings require the two frontmost Soldiers to pull security on each door as the remaining Soldiers pass between them. This is similar to the simultaneous room-clearing technique. (See Image 225, Pg. 243.) To not drop forward security, the rear Soldier can pull security over a shoulder, which itself is unsafe. **So practice until transitions are so fast and smooth that the team never drops forward security!** As the last Soldier passes, they say "last man" to recover Soldiers pulling securing.

Phase 4

Hallway Communication

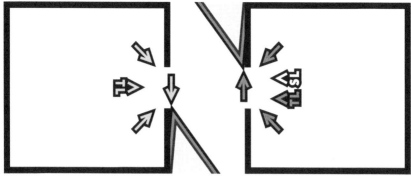

Image 240: Soldiers take cover behind doorjambs when communicating and pulling security in hallways. (See Image 241, Pg. 251.)

Image 241: Norwegian Soldiers secure a hallway. Al Asad Air Base, Iraq, 13 June 2020. Both Soldiers use the doorframe as cover. The Soldier on the right could switch to a **left-handed shooting position** to take more cover.

To enter a room from a hallway, Soldiers form a stack. (See Stacking Up and Team Positions, Pg. 202.) In fact, a single file essentially is a stack. The closest Soldier to the entry pulls security on the opening and becomes One Man. To enter the left room of two opposing rooms, the Left Soldier pies the left opening and is the One Man; and vice versa for the right side.

To enter a room across a T intersection, One and Two Man enter the hallway using the same pie, peek, push method. Three and Four Man follow behind to stack on the entry to the room. Three and Four Man become the new One and Two Man. This is a dangerous situation, and speed is security.

25.b Stairs and Stairwells

Stairwells are different from rooms and hallways because they have a vertical dimension to maneuver in. The configurations of stairs are immeasurable, and each kind is optimally cleared in different ways. Never assume one stairwell will be identical to another, even if blueprints indicate they are. Stairs can be:

▸ Narrow vs wide.

▸ Risers vs no risers.

▸ Going up vs down.

▸ Straight vs switchback.

▸ Landing window vs wall.

▸ Direct entrance vs landing.

▸ Gap between stairs vs no gap.

▸ Space under stairs accessible vs not.

▸ Above landing can see down vs cannot.

▸ Attic entrance on side of room vs center hatch.

▸ Outside vs in a room vs enclosed in a dedicated stairwell.

That being said, the **principles of clearing remain the same.** (See Seizing Rooms (Battle Drill 6), Pg. 228.) To begin clearing a staircase, Soldiers first clear the area around the staircase. (See Clearing the Entry, Pg. 228.) The only difference with a regular room is that Soldiers must avoid penetrating too far, exposing themselves to the upper or lower landings (i.e., using a strongwall technique is often appropriate). (See Image 250, Pg. 256.)

After entry and sweeping the immediate area, Soldiers secure threats (e.g., doors and windows, deadspace behind the staircase the top of stairs, the bottom of stairs, etc.) (See Connected Rooms and Areas, Pg. 240.) (See Image 243, Pg. 254.) Soldiers continue to pull security on these areas until they are cleared. **Only then does a team begin to clear the stairs.** If there are multiple teams, only one team each clears upstairs and downstairs. Multiple teams on stairs overcrowd and don't allow for a hasty break-contact.

The two Soldiers closest to the stairway become One and Two Man. To go upstairs, One and Two Man slowly walk up side-by-side. Three Man follows and backs up One Man. Four Man follows and backs up Two Man and covers rear. If the stairs are straight, both One and Two Man point their weapons at the doorway (i.e., the threat) in front of them. If the stairs switch back, however, there are two threats: the switchback landing and the upper landing.

Clearing Switchback Stairs

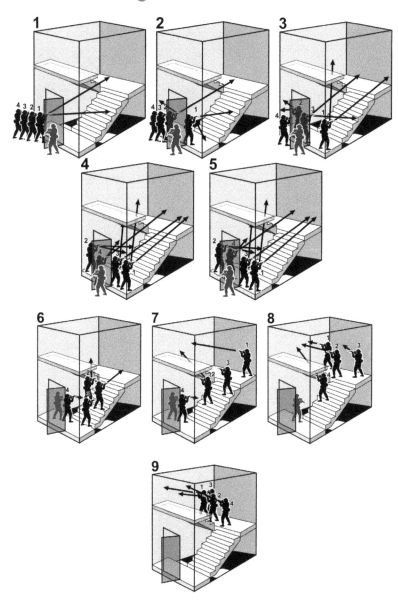

Image 242: **Switchback stairs** are an especially important kind of stairs to practice because they are common in commercial and public buildings, and because the above landing requires a Soldier to rotate on the staircase. (See Image 249, Pg. 256.) In these U.S. Army illustrations, Soldiers are shown clearing staris. Note how they **acquire as many lines of sight and fire as possible** before advancing.

Phase 4

Clearing Stairs and Stairwells Part 1

Image 243: Staircases and stairwells often have **many smalls spaces** and corners to clear.

Image 244: The more rifles that can be placed on openings and unknown threats the better.

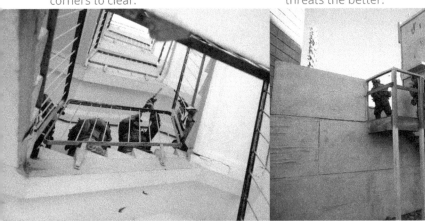

Image 245: If there is **space between** stairs, consider posting a Soldier to secure the shaft at the bottom.

Image 246: Stairs that are outside require security to the outside direction.

Image 247: Check behind the stairs for an enemy hiding. This is a common non-standard space.

Image 248: Some stairs do not have risers, and an enemy could shoot from **space behind the staircase**.

Therefore, clearing **switchback stairs** requires One and Two Man to perform a synchronized clear of both threat areas. Before getting on the stairs, One and Two Man line up, with One Man on the inside and Two Man on the wall side. (On a narrow staircase, One and Two Man may have to ascend and descend back to back, with Two Man acting as the Inside Soldier.) The Inside Soldier pulls security on the upper switchback stairs between the switchback and upper landing, while Outside Soldier secures the switchback landing. Being on the outside gives a better angle-of-fire. (See Image 251, Pg. 256.)

As the pair approaches the stairs, the Inside Soldier rotates their body while moving forward to pull security on higher and higher stairs as they appear. (See Image 242, Pg. 253.) When the pair is at the threshold of where the upper landing can be seen, the Inside Soldier has fully rotated 180 degrees, and is facing backwards. Then when crossing the threshold, the first thing that can be seen from the upper landing is the Inside Soldier's muzzle pointed directly up, ready to shoot a threat on the upper landing. All the while, Two Man continues to clear the switchback landing. (See Image 249, Pg. 256.)

After crossing the threshold, One Man continues to walk backward up the stairs next to Two Man. This can lead to very awkward walking and is done very slowly. **Not a normal walking pace!** (Be aware, slow movement can lead to bunching up, which is bad.) All Soldiers pie as much area as possible before stepping up. Essentially, because stairs are a three-dimensional structure with changing directions of movement, unknown areas can quickly appear in different locations as a Soldier moves through the space. When the two Soldiers reach the switchback landing, Two Man circles around behind One Man to remain on the outside. (See Image 252, Pg. 256.) The upper landing is cleared like a room. (See Clearing the Corner and Room, Pg. 232.)

For many stairwells, there is a central gap (the "shaft") in the staircase, where enemies from many stories above can see Soldiers. (See Image 245, Pg. 254.) It is the duty of all Soldiers, but especially Three Man, to secure this central gap. (See Image 244, Pg. 254.) And at the switchback landing, Four Man covers the landing's windows or door.

Descending stairs uses the same procedures but in reverse. Going down stairs is safer than going up because: gravity assists grenades thrown downwards; it is easier to aim rifles down than up; and a higher floor can always see the entire landing of the floor below.

Phase 4

Clearing Stairs and Stairwells Part 2

Image 249: With **switchback** stairs, clear by rotating and first exposing a rifle muzzle to the above landing.

Image 250: **Move slowly** in areas where the layout quickly exposes new areas. Especially monitor the above.

Image 251: The Outside Soldier moves ahead of the Inside Soldier because he has a **better angle** to pie.

Image 252: At the upper landing, the Outside Soldier secures the entry and the Inside Soldier clears the corner.

Image 253: These Marines used a **high-low formation** to pie, peek, push the turn.

Image 254: Descending stairs is as tactical as ascending. Note the Soldier on the left pulling **down security**.

Once a landing is clear and secure, the Clearing Team can:

▸ Wait in place for other elements to pass through.

▸ Post door security and continue clearing the stairs.

▸ Establish a foothold on the floor and continue clearing the stairs.

▸ Post stair security and clear the whole adjacent floor.

Regardless, stairwell landings are critical points of transit that the patrol must keep secured. Some patrols even go as far as leaving a pair of Soldiers on every landing in a stairwell, both to secure the landings and to serve as an emergency communication line. Other patrols rely on forward squads up the stairs and on each floor to block reentry. So clearing a multistory building easily becomes a platoon-level task.

Stairs are a terrible place to have a firefight. Confined concrete stairwells will create ricochet problems and deafening sounds when firing rounds. Wooden stairs often creak when stepped on. (Try walking along the sides of the stairs with slow foot pressure.) And some stairwell doors lock in one direction, and only open from the outside. (Before any door closes, make sure that it can be opened again.) Because stairs are so idiosyncratic, it is best to avoid a firefight in stairs altogether. Consider avoidance methods like cutting all the lights, or releasing tear gas.

25.c Room Obstacles[1]

An obstacle is anything within in a room that hinders movement or sight. For example, a car in a garage, a couch in the middle of a room, a noncombatant, or deadspace behind a door. Obstacles often provide locations for enemies to hide, so Soldiers must immediately pull security on the obstacles and deadspace. And in a dangerous environment, Soldiers immediately shoot obstacles like tables or couches to kill potential enemies on the other side. **Obstacles are also prime locations to hide traps; always be aware of traps!**

An example of the disconnect between training and real spaces with obstacles is the 2015 Hypercache Supermarket raid in Paris, France during which a terrorist killed people and held hostages. The supermarket was full of long rows of bullet-permeable store shelving, which was unfamiliar terrain for the officers. The obstacles in the room could have led to a friendly fire incident when the terrorist, hidden by shelving, rushed between the police elements. To properly train Soldier for the real world, trainers must put obstacles in their training rooms!

Clearing Room Obstacles

Bed   Sofa   Non-Closing Door

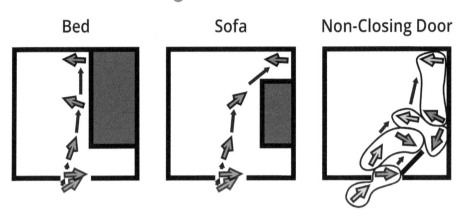

Image 255: Three levels of attention can given to an obstacle: 1) For the bed, One Man cleared under the bed from outside the room; so they treat the bed as already cleared and continue as if the room were just a smaller room. 2) For the Sofa, the behind cannot be cleared from the outside, but the One Man continues to the far corner since the deadspace is on the opposite side of the room. 3) For the non-closing door, the One Man stops short to clear the near corner, and Three Man takes over the One Man position as One Man. All that being said, hesitation is bad and **clearing at all is more important that perfectly adapting a formula**.

Center-room obstacles, like couches, create deadspace in the middle of a room. To clear that deadspace, Soldiers use the points-of-domination (POD) technique. In fact, points-of-domination (POD) is only more useful than strongwall if a room has obstacles! In a barren room, the technique is just overcomplicated for no reason. (See Clearing the Corner and Room, Pg. 232.)

Obstacles alongside a wall in a Soldier's room-clearing path prevent the One or Two Man from clearing their initial corner. They can be a dresser, a half-open door, a noncombatant, a bed, etc. Upon entering a room, if the One or Two Man is blocked on their wall of travel (e.g. by a non-closing door), the Soldier switches focus to clear the obstacle. Three or Four Man speed up to do a simultaneous back-to-back clear. Three or Four Man take over One or Two Man's Sector and clear forward, while One or Two Man clear backward into the obstacle's deadspace. (See Image 255, Pg. 258.) One or Two Man clear the wall obstacle's deadspace by pieing around the obstacle.

The most common wall obstacle is a door which is not closed enough to touch the wall. An enemy could hide behind them. The potential for deadspace

Various Room Obstacles

Image 256: Obstacles always present a **ricochet hazard**. Always be aware of what you are shooting at.

Image 257: Obstacles in a hallway can **restrict movement** and hide traps. Consider alternate routes.

Image 258: **People** are also obstacles and the Soldier becomes occupied by handling them.

Image 259: Obstacles **restrict sight** or movement. The Right Soldier stopped, but should clear behind.

Image 260: The most common obstacle is an **unshut door**. Note that the space behind can fit a man.

Image 261: If there are too many obstacles with a large threat, **use grenades**.

there is why Soldiers always force doors against walls on initial entry. (Soldiers must force doors with a foot and not the body to ensure no gear gets caught.) If there is an enemy behind, the Soldier must change combat tactics, because the enemy is close enough to stab the Soldier. Either fire through the door, or otherwise violently move the enemy to a more favorable position.

If an **obstacle is a noncombatant** standing next to the near-side wall, the blocked Soldier maintains positive control over the noncombatant, or forces the noncombatant into the center of the room so that the entire team can pull security on them. "Positive control" means using a non-firing hand to push the noncombatant at an arm's length, while being ready to fire if the noncombatant becomes an enemy. When using the non-firing hand to action something, the firing hand is still holding the rifle in the single-armed firing position, ready to fire. (See Image 57, Pg. 81.)

The worst obstacle is a bed, which completely blocks off moving into sections of a room, and can deny a team from achieving points-of-domination. Plus, the underside of a bed is the perfect place to hide unseen, and needs to be checked immediately after a Soldier identifies a bed. Even during the pieing of a room from the outside, a Soldier crouches to see under a bed.

Obstacles in hallways are also important. If Soldiers must get through an obstacle, they can bypass it by going over, or even breaching it. If there is furniture and rubble outside a room entrance, a team can stand on it and gain a height advantage. This allows the Soldier to unpredictably peek inside the room or engage. A team can even bring its own step ladder if enemies are known to expect Soldiers at eye level.

25.d Every Space is Different

All spaces are different. Supermarkets have lots of shelving. Many hotel rooms have glass shower walls. Airports have large areas surrounded by windows. A hoarder's residence can look normal on the outside, but be filled with so many items every room is just a narrow corridor.

It is impossible to train for all these weird and unusual spaces individually, which is why Soldiers must always apply the basics. (See Close-Quarters Battle Basics, Pg. 195.) Soldiers must avoid silhouetting themselves in doors and windows. They must always be checking for booby-traps everywhere. (See Traps and Improvised Explosive Devices, Pg. 65.) And Soldiers must never forget rear security and accountability. (See Rear Security, Pg. 97.)

Phase 4

Clearing Irregular Rooms Part 1

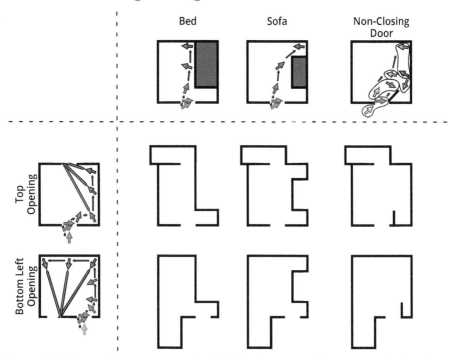

Image 262: Irregular rooms come in infinite shapes, and so are a pain to clear, even with a four-man team. **The best method is to combine the techniques of multiple openings and obstacles.** In this illustration, a Soldier can imagine a complex room (bottom right) as a combination of a room with extra openings (bottom left) (See Image 224, Pg. 242.) and a room with interior obstacles (top right) (See Image 255, Pg. 258.). Of course, copious use of grenades is a good idea.

Phase 4

After the basics are applied, almost all the techniques for normal spaces can be applied to abnormal spaces. In fact, one useful way of framing an irregular room is to consider it a normal room filled with obstacles and connections. (See Image 262, Pg. 261.)

One example of applying normal principles to an abnormal space is the U.S. Army's **Battle Drill 5**, "Knock Out Bunkers." The only deviation from normal room-clearing is that the defeat occurs outside the bunker. From the Army, "Buddy team #2 moves to a blind spot near the bunker.... [The] Soldier cooks off a grenade (two seconds, maximum), announces, 'FRAG OUT,' and throws it through an aperture. After the grenade detonates, the Soldier covering the exit enters first and the team clears the bunker."

Clearing Irregular Rooms Part 2

Image 263: Try to find another way to clear **small areas** where moving a weapon becomes difficult.

Image 264: Use flash bangs when children are directly in the center of the room. **Children can still shoot**.

Image 265: There is not a safe way to enter a room like this without grenades. It is **essentially a bunker**.

Image 266: If many areas need to be secured, either use more Soldiers or first **clear the surrounding area**.

Image 267: Raiding a **guard outpost** is near impossible. Use a tactical callout or a shoulder launched munition.

Image 268: **Curved walls** and paths require extra patience to clear because the layout is unpredictable.

Clearing Irregular Rooms Part 3

Image 269: **Ships** contain unique architecture. If a raid is on a ship, the practice also needs to be on a ship.

Image 270: When clearing into a small opening, consider switching to a **handgun** for greater maneuverability.

Image 271: Humans don't look up! A single enemy in the **rafters** can kill a dozen Soldiers and vice versa.

Image 272: Difficult terrain requires **slower movement**. A single sprained ankle can jeopardize an entire mission.

Image 273: A sudden change in **elevation** doesn't change much. First pull security while crouching.

Image 274: **Small rooms** or areas like this can be precleared with a flash bang grenade.

Clearing Irregular Rooms Part 4

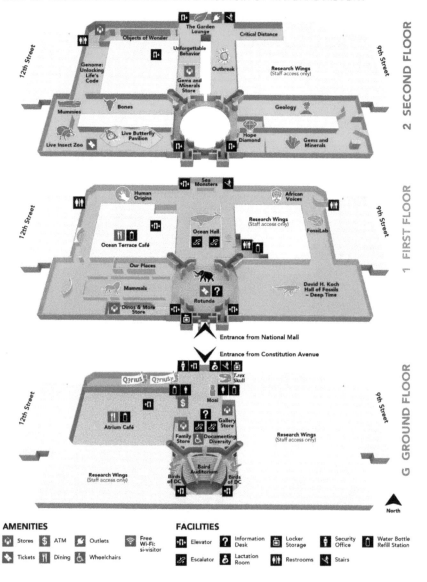

MAP OF THE SMITHSONIAN NATIONAL MUSEUM OF NATURAL HISTORY

Image 275: Irregular rooms are especially common in **public buildings**. This building is a great example where most rooms are irregular. Take a moment to think about how to raid an auditorium, and how difficult it would be.

More generally, the CQB tactics in this book can be applied to any space with a near wall if a strongwall formation is used. One and Two Man clear left and right, while Three and Four Man clear forward. (See Image 213, Pg. 233.) **And always pie every corner!**

The oddest CQB scenario is for attics and basements, where the stairs end directly into the center of the floor or ceiling. The enemy could be in any direction. Situations like this demand a mirror or camera to see into the room, grenades, and an extremely slow and careful entry. Every step up or down a ladder requires a 360-degree clear of any visible area. Soldiers step carefully; dynamic entry on stairs into the center of a room is asking to trip and fall. And step slowly; if the One Man moves too fast, they leave the stack behind.

The exception to applying indoor close-quarters battle (CQB) tactics, is when it is **more appropriate to use outdoor military operations in urban terrain (MOUT) tactics**. (See Moving in Urban Terrain, Pg. 88.) Indoor spaces are usually small and enclosed, but "small" and "enclosed" are relative terms with lots of grey area. That grey area is important because, within large open spaces, a patrol must choose to use indoor CQB tactics or outdoor MOUT tactics. For example, an auditorium or a sports stadium is technically a building, but using CQB inside it would be a mistake. (Specifically, CQB shooting techniques are very inaccurate beyond short distances.) Industrial, commercial, and religious buildings have all sorts of large rooms and open areas where a patrol may be better off using outdoor MOUT tactics.

26. Working and Exiting a Space

After seizing a space, the Clearing Team secures the space, reports the seizure, and marks the space as seized. The entire procedure is quick and follows a preplanned SOP. Exiting a space is simple: after securing, reporting, and marking, Soldiers stack on the next entry to seize the next space. When exiting, the team can leave a Soldier in the room to maintain security because once the team exits the space, security drops; an enemy can reenter.

26.a Securing a Space

Once all obvious threats in a space are neutralized, the space is searched for hidden threats. This procedure is called (securing) **"dead, room, living."** To start the search, an experienced team can all nod their rifles, or a Team Leader

Phase 4

Image 276: Bulgarian Forces of 61st Mech. Bde. Karlovo capture an enemy. Novo Selo, Bulgaria, 17 Sep 2009. The "living" in "dead, room, living" refers to securing the already neutralized living. The room is not clear yet, so **securing has not started.**

Image 277: U.S. Marines with B Co., 1st Bn., 6th Marine Reg., 2nd Marine Div. detain an enemy. Camp Shelby, MS, 16 Nov 2020. It always takes at least **two Soldiers to detain** an enemy. Other enemies can be secured by a third Soldier while they wait.

can verbally order "dead, room, living." (Generally, speaking is minimized to reduce confusion and to prevent enemies from discerning what is going on.)[1]

Securing the dead consists of verifying death. With one Soldier pulling security, another moves all weapons away from the enemy corpse and taps each body's eye with their rifle muzzle to ensure the enemy corpse is truly dead. If alive, the enemy must be secured so they can't pose a threat.

Securing the room focuses on searching for traps and weapons that can pose a threat. (In contrast, room searches for other purposes are called site exploitation.) (See Site Exploitation, Pg. 288.) Room searches, like all searches, are systematic. But the thoroughness of a search depends on the time available. Where a thorough search covers the ceiling and floor, a briefer search may only cover more obvious locations, or search the living first. If an explosive threat is found in a room, Soldiers back away and DO NOT TOUCH IT! Soldiers contact the Patrol Leader who can order the Demo Team to: disable the explosive, call Higher, abort the mission, or continue the mission. If the Patrol Leader continues, they must always consider that where there is one trap, there are likely many more. (See Demolition Team, Pg. 277.)

Securing the living is last because presumably if they are still alive then they didn't and don't present enough of a threat to kill (i.e. the living that are an obvious threat are killed during the room clear). Soldiers focus their searches on removing weapons and giving clear and concise instructions to

---

1. Real World: Some texts recommend kneeling to signal that a room is clear. But in general, kneeling inhibits mobility and also going from kneeling to standing can be mistaken as a threat, inciting friendly fire.

Image 278: Anti-Tank Missilemen Marines with Weapons Co., 1st Bn., 3rd Marine Reg. secure a room. Central TA, Okinawa, Japan, 20 Aug 2014. Once the room is secured, Soldiers **stack on the next entryway** to continue on.

ensure orderly compliance. During the search, the detainee can be standing, kneeling, or handcuffed in the prone. The circumstances dictate the position of the living. However, all living are controlled by two Soldiers, where at least one Soldier is pulling security on the living at all times. (See Enemy Prisoner of War Team, Pg. 283.)

26.b Reporting Progress

Each Soldier's priority after securing the room is to ensure they remain combat ready, and report to a Leader if they are not. Specifically, each Soldier always does a blood sweep on themselves and a tactical magazine reload on their weapon system. A **blood sweep** is a visual or tactile inspection for blood, which is done because adrenaline can make a Soldier unaware that they are shot and hemorrhaging. A **tac mag reload** is when a Soldier replaces their partially full ammo feeds (to include magazines and drums) with full feeds. Room-clearing has a fast tempo, so Leaders do not pause to remind Soldiers.

Soldiers report any issues they have in the **ACE report format**: i.e., the status of their Ammo, Casualties, and Equipment. If a Leader cannot fix the issue on the spot (for example by cross-loading ammunition between the team), they consolidate ACE reports from every Soldier, and report to their own Leader: an estimate of the average full magazines, full drums, and M240 rounds (leave out partial mags or drums); a brief description of casualties; and a list of important equipment lost. All ACE reports (self-initiated and requested) are passed to the Patrol Leader so they may redistribute resources, call for emergency resupply, or order any casualty evacuations.

Team Leaders are also tasked with reporting their team's **battle position** as they travel. The Patrol Leader is located with a Headquarters away from the front line, and so needs constant updates on the location of all their teams and elements to best coordinate the patrol. Further, if an entire team is incapacitated at once, the Patrol Leader must know that team's rough location to retrieve the casualties. (See Aid and Litter, and Medevac, Pg. 286.)

As the team kills enemies, they must track **how many enemies** they kill and encounter in each room or area. Many times, the Patrol Leader will have intelligence regarding the exact number of enemies on location, and the Patrol Leader adds up the teams' reports to match that number. If the teams encounter fewer enemies than the intelligence reported, the Patrol Leader knows that enemies are likely still hiding on the objective.

The Patrol Leader constantly reports to Higher Command about the raid. The reporting standards depend on the mission. However, the purpose of reporting is for Higher to grant resources and make changes. The Patrol Leader may not know what resources Higher has. For example, if the Patrol Leader reports casualties, Higher can send medevacs without a specific request.

26.c Marking a Space

Soldiers mark spaces to indicate to the rest of the patrol that a space has been searched and secured. After a room is marked, the Team Leader informs their Leader. The purpose of marking during a raid is not to declare a space to be safe but to ensure that the Clearing Teams are clearing systematically and do not skip or reclear a space. Follow-on forces especially read markings.

A **marking system** can use a single mark to indicate secure or not secure; or a system can include more markings, for example, to declare that a room has weapons and is a priority for site exploitation. Special rooms, like the casualty collection point or a dangerous off-limit area, can get special markings.

The kind of marking used depends on the resources available and who is reading the marks. If the reader is outside the building, rooms can be marked with spray paint or bed sheets hung out of windows. Flares, strobes, and signaling mirrors may be effective as well.

Image 279: A Machine Gunner with 2nd Bn., 1st Marine Reg. is rolling support that has moved into position after the start of the raid to suppress the enemy as his squad clears other buildings. (See Support to Facilitate Assault's Maneuver, Pg. 173.) Camp Pendleton, CA, 06 Aug 2015. Although this particular SOP is unknown, **Green usually means go**; and this chemlight would signal the room is safe, which prevents both friendly fires and wasting time by reclearing a room.

On the inside of buildings, chalk, spray paint, and tape (regular, glow, or thermal) are all easy; but they may be invisible at night, always visible at night, permanent, or bulky. And so chemlights are commonly used. Chemlights do not reveal a signature until activated. A variety of chemical lights are available (infrared, high intensity, multiple colors). Activated chemlights can be seen in a variety of conditions (light, dark, smoke, etc.). If Soldiers have night-optical devices (NOD's), then infrared chemlights can be used to further reduce signature. And if Soldiers are using thermal devices, then two 9-volt batteries can be connected to form a heat source for 45 minutes.

Markers can be combined to make a better product. The envelope can also be written on. When chemlights, batteries, tape, and a weighted rope are combined, the product is called a wolf tail. This marker can be seen with night-vision or thermal devices, and can be attached with either the tape or by draping the weighted rope. Markers can also be brought to eye level by using a packing-list envelope (clear on one side and adhesive on the other).

Markings require some variety over time. When the same marking is used by many units for many months, the enemy can confuse Soldiers by premarking all rooms in a building with the same marking.

Phase 4

27. Seizing Floors and Buildings

Rooms exist in diverse structures, from skyscrapers to compounds. Navigating a series of rooms requires additional tactics on top of navigating just a single room. To navigate, the patrol follows the planned scheme-of-maneuver (SOM). (See Scheme-of-Maneuver for the Objective, Pg. 161.) However, sometimes plans fail. An impromptu SOM follows all the same principles as a preplanned SOM, with coordination being the most important part.

27.a Coordinating Multiple Teams

Although a single team may know how to attack a single room, multiple teams attacking multiple rooms is a different skillset. In fact, command, control, and coordination, of teams is the primary job of leadership.

A Leader must first understand the battlespace to affect the battlespace. Specifically, the Patrol Leader learns about the floorplan and building plan of the objective structures. (See Frameworks for Attacking Vertical Terrain, Pg. 54.) Often, the internal blueprints of a building are not known before the raid or are incorrect, and Raiders must improvise. Teams communicate their movement between rooms as they secure structures so that leadership can build a mental layout of the objective building(s). Thereby, leadership can communicate where to go or not go, and where to shoot or not shoot.

Leaders prioritize tasks by directing resources. Although resources are allocated before a raid, a battle may change priorities. (In fact, this is the reason Reserve Elements exist.) (See Reserve Element, Pg. 24.) For example, if a Clearing Team discovers unknown noncombatants or obstacles, they relay the new information to the Patrol Leader. Then, any Leader in the chain decides what the best response is (or even if any response is warranted). For example, the Team Leader can request reinforcements. Or the Patrol Leader can call for a break-contact. The skill is in determining what is not the priority in order to best direct resources elsewhere because resources are always limited.[1]

Third, Leaders prevent mistakes. The most important mistake to prevent is friendly fire, which is always a risk when two teams operate in

---

1 **Applying Concepts:** Prioritizing is a skill that most Leaders only train passively. To actively practice prioritization, review raids for the smallest decisions. Why was Reserve sent there? Why was retrieval of casualties delayed or expedited?

Image 280: U.S. Marines with Crisis Response Africa and Portuguese Marines clear a building. Troia, Portugal, 25 Feb 2019. Although technically mere meters from each other, **their focus is completely separated.**

close proximity. Friendly fire is a concern because teams and external support can all be working with completely separate areas of focus. (See Image 280, Pg. 271.) Thereby, it is the job of the Leader to make the different elements aware of each other at all times. (However, when two teams simultaneously clear within sight of each other, their awareness is not completely separated.)

One aforementioned deconfliction technique is phase lines. For example, the Patrol Leader can receive information that a team has taken the stairwell to the second floor (i.e. crossed a phase line), and thereby order Support to cease firing onto the second floor. (See Phase Lines, Pg. 113.) Another universal deconfliction technique is to only **move one element at a time**. (See Bounding and Crossing Intersections, Pg. 99.)

One specific deconfliction method for squads clearing a floor is called "**leapfrogging**." (See Image 281, Pg. 273.) In leapfrogging a hallway with two teams, one team clears the right-side rooms, and the other team clears the left-side rooms. Only one team at a time moves between rooms. The Stationary Team provides overwatch, covering fire, or security for the other team. For example, first, the Right-Side Team clears a room. Then it waits for the Left-Side Team to clear a room. Then the Left-Side Team waits for the Right-Side Team to clear another room. Having only one team in the hallway prevents the enemy from attacking the entire squad by blindly spraying bullets down the hallway. But the Squad Leader still keeps teams close to communicate and protect each other. (See Image 240, Pg. 251.) Teams use near-recognition signals (e.g., yelling "Eagle," or non-verbal signals like lights and lasers) to combine after separation. (See Near and Far Recognition Signals, Pg. 143.)

In wide hallways, having an entire squad disabled by spraying is less of a concern, and the squad can speed up a clear by **flooding**, meaning that each team clears rooms on either side as fast as possible. Flooding uses a third team that stays in the hallway to facilitate communication and pull hallway security as other teams clear rooms. (See Image 281, Pg. 273.)

When multiple teams clear a floorplan without hallways, coordination is driven by planning, moving slower, and using cardinal directions. For example, if two teams enter a floor, one from the North and another from the East, they both know that firing to the eastern or northern side of the floor risks fratricide. Team Leaders direct movement and fires to the Southwest corner of the floor, and are in constant communication with the Squad Leader.

When **multiple teams stack on a single room**, any teams behind the first one can wait behind cover within running distance of the door. Once the first team secures the foothold, additional teams flow in from their position. Or if teams are entering a room through different directions, the teams can employ coordinated diversion. For example, while one team jiggles the doorknob to distract the enemy, the actual Clearing Team enters through a second door.

27.b Attacking Multiple Structures

A raid may require attacking multiple structures on the objective. The first structure raided is the **foothold structure**, much like a building has a foothold space. The foothold structure follows the same rules as the foothold space; e.g., a corner building and easy to access. (See Footholds and Entrances, Pg. 163.) (See Chunking, Pg. 134.) And moving between buildings follows the same rules as moving through a layout; e.g., sides first and secure large areas with small perimeters. (See Horizontal Layout and Floorplan, Pg. 167.)

To attack the next structure, Soldiers exit their current building and move to the next building. Leadership chooses the next building before exiting to minimize the time outside. Generally the next building is whichever allows the patrol to continue a linear progression across the battlefield from the current building. The linear progression is punctuated by **phase lines**, so Support can continue to shift supporting fires to buildings that have not been cleared yet to support the maneuvering Assault Element. (See Image 97, Pg. 114.)

Soldiers who need to exit a structure inform the Patrol Leader that they are exiting, so that they aren't engaged with friendly fire. The Patrol Leader then gives those Soldiers permission to exit.

Phase 4

Leapfrogging and Flooding

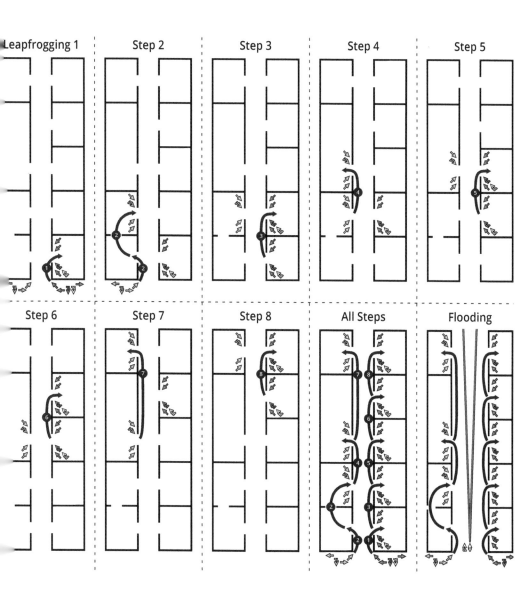

Image 281: In the diagrams above, a Left Team and Right Team clear a structure full of rooms using the leapfrogging method. **Leapfrogging is a form of bounding** where Soldiers only clear rooms until they are slightly ahead of the team on the opposite side. Advancing too far ahead risks an enemy appearing between the teams. Because both teams are actively clearing, the Stationary Team can only provide limited support to the Maneuvering Team. Therefore leapfrogging is primarily used for deconfliction of movement instead of mutual support. If there is a wide hallway and enough Soldiers, then the Raiders can employ flooding. **Flooding** clears each side of the hallway as fast as possible. A third team secures the hallway as a rolling Support Element, and facilitates communication.

Before exiting, Soldiers mark the structure to indicate that the structure has been cleared. As Soldiers exit, they move as quickly and low as possible. Slow movement can be exploited by an enemy Sniper. Preselect destinations, be speedy, have a low silhouette, and employ covering fires. Although formations (e.g. a file) may help, do not correct formations while outside. Moving to another building generally uses the same techniques as entering the first one. (See Moving between Buildings, Pg. 105.) After a building is cleared, it becomes a great location to post Support and Security Elements. And if there are enough Soldiers, the patrol posts a Guard Element by each entrance and the roof to prevent the enemy from reoccupying the structure.

28. Contingencies

It is impossible to plan for every contingency. However, below are some of the more common scenarios that are worth planning for.

28.a Noncombatants[1]

Soldiers will encounter noncombatants in urban areas. Noncombatants are people in the area of operations who are non-threatening and include refugees, local inhabitants, foreign civilians, personnel from non-governmental organizations, journalists, chaplains, medical personnel, prisoners of war, casualties, and more. All Soldiers must be briefed on how Higher Command wants them to deal with noncombatants, or else Soldiers must take the liberty to decide themselves.[2] (See Morality and Rules-of-engagement, Pg. 295.) A military that attacks noncombatants may win battles, but it will lose wars.

First, the patrol must be able to **identify noncombatants**. In some cases identification is easy, such as with uniformed foreign aid workers. But in other cases, the enemy purposefully masquerades as noncombatants—a problem that has plagued armies forever. For example, during the battle of Grozny, Russians resorted to searching people for: "military" equipment in pockets; the smell of gunpowder and gun oil; singed hair (from weapon firing); burn

---

1 Quote: Anyone still present five minutes into a gunfight is a participant. —U.S. Army Master Sergeant Paul Howe.

2 Real World: Historically, many Soldiers receive these orders as guidelines, since Soldiers rarely face consequences for war crimes when they have quietly informed their chain of command. But having guidelines is better than not having guidelines.

Image 282: 34th Combat Aviation Brigade UH-60 Black Hawks insert a multinational response force to simultaneously raid **multiple structures** during a simulated hostage rescue mission. Kuwait, 23 Mar 2015.

marks on forearms (from hot cartridges); shoulder bruising (from weapon firing); fibers from ammunition packaging; etc. Using subjective indicators was crude, and unreliable; and unfortunately subjective indicators were the most effective method available to the Russians. Raiders should not rely on subjective indicators because they lead to too many false positives.

However **objective indicators** are vital to quickly distinguishing between combatants and noncombatants. Objective indicators are briefed in the rules-of-engagement. (See Morality and Rules-of-engagement, Pg. 295.) For example, "is the person on the objective with a gun," or "is the person wearing an enemy uniform?" But again, the patrol must decide whether it will err on the side of too much or too little. If "military-age male" is an indicator, then almost half the human population would be considered combatants.

Once noncombatants are identified, Soldiers must be ready to fire at everyone and/or issue clear and concise gestures and commands. Soldiers take a dangerous pause when confronted with a potential enemy to detect direct indicators. Again, Leaders must give **objective triggers** such as, "if a potential enemy steps toward you, you have permission to shoot them." Vague guidance, like "shoot if threatened," either creates hesitation or excessive aggression. To a Soldier in a firefight, everything unknown feels

threatening! Patrols task organize Enemy Prisoner of War Teams partly to control noncombatants. (See Enemy Prisoner of War Team, Pg. 283.)

Communication is a valuable method of control; words usually lead to better results than force. To that end, Soldiers can learn basic commands and phrases in the local language (or carry written phases and translations), and speak loudly, clearly and slowly while using gestures. Simple phrases include: "Halt."; "Your Name?"; "Permitted."; "Yes."; "No."; "Stand."; "Walk."; "Sit."; "You will be searched."; "Toilet?"; "Medical Aid."; "Do not talk."; and "Water."

Do not antagonize people more than necessary. For example, using spray paint to mark rooms is effective, but leaves the owners with paint all over their houses. Culturally educate Soldiers; a common example is to only allow female Soldiers to search other females. Religion is usually considered especially sensitive. Do recognize that noncombatants may want to cooperate but be unable to in the moment because they: e.g., may not speak English, may be scared and hiding (especially children), or may be dazed from a breach.

If force is necessary, start small. A traditional patrol carries the most lethal weapons possible; however, less-lethal weapons can incapacitate without making martyrs or irreversible mistakes. If Soldiers attack a father, his son will become far more radicalized if the father is dead rather than just sore. As an example, a patrol can start a room clear with less-lethal weapons (e.g., stun grenades) and still move up to lethal weapons (e.g., frag grenades).

Antagonizing the local population is unlikely to affect the current mission. But a pattern of offensive behavior, intentional or not, will negatively affect followup missions. Due to the sheer number of people, working against a local population can be worse than failing a mission. To this end, combat Leaders use Civil Affairs, Psychological Operations, Military Police, Chaplains, and Civilian Leaders where possible. During a raiding mission, non-combat Soldiers can be staged behind the battlefield to take charge of noncombatants.[1]

28.b Delayed Combatants

Sometimes a Raider just doesn't know whether a detainee is hostile. To prevent hostility in the first place, Soldiers must always be easily understood and powerful. For example, the most important part of maintaining control is clear and concise orders with clear and concise consequences. (See Verbage, Pg. 200.) For example, police say "hands behind your head" with hands on a gun pointed in a safe direction.

To prepare for hostility, Soldiers control any potential enemy at the **farthest possible range**. The idea is distance creates time for a teammate to join and help. If a Soldier must take physical control of a potential enemy, they still attempt to keep the detainee at arm's length.

If a former non-combatant becomes combative or comes too close, again, the Soldier first creates distance. The Soldier can aggressively push the enemy away, spin, or redirect the enemy to regain projectile weapon range. Direct the enemy toward the center of the room if possible to allow other Soldiers good lines-of-fire. If distance cannot be created, a Soldier uses their secondary weapon (e.g. a handgun), which is specifically carried for situations like this.

28.c Demolition Team

During combat a certain percentage of all munitions always fail to function properly. And numerous Soldiers and civilians have been killed or injured during every major conflict or operation as a direct result of handling or mishandling explosives. Therefore, only qualified Soldiers on the Demo Team can deal with unexploded ordinance (UXO), explosive breaches, or explosives in general. (See Traps and Improvised Explosive Devices, Pg. 65.)

The first reaction of the Demo Team to UXO is to mark it and leave it. Do not move anything on or near a UXO, because while modern explosives do not spontaneously explode, they can be very sensitive. If moving or destroying the

Phase 4

---

1 Footnote: Respect costs you nothing. —Army Proverb

Image 284: A simulated IED explodes as the 11th Armored Cavalry Regiment enters a bunker. Fort Irwin, CA, 06 Sep 2012. This image simultaneous demostrates the importance of having **dedicated explosive experts**, such as a Demo Team, and when **it is important to have a plan for backing out and reengaging later.**

UXO is vital to the mission, the Demo Team attempts to contact a specialist in that specific UXO. Finally, the Demo Team attempts to use their training to handle the UXO as a last resort. When reporting UXO to higher, use the UXO Spot Report. (See 9-Line Unexploded Ordnance (UXO), Pg. 67.)

28.d Failed Breach

A mission cannot occur without a breach. Therefore, not only are there primary, alternate, contingency, and emergency breaching methods, but there are separate **PACE's for breaching** locations and breaching times. If the primary breach fails and the PACE's for method, time, and place also fail, then the patrol must abort the mission. A failed breach is a failed mission.

The breaching PACE's must consider that failing a breach likely reveals the patrol's presence. Sometimes a breach fails because the Breachers are compromised or attacked. Obviously, the patrol must react-to-contact (See Enemy Contact in Urban Terrain, Pg. 124.) or withdraw (See Withdrawal from the Objective, Pg. 290.). But after engaging the enemy, the patrol may switch from a quiet mechanical breaching method into an explosive breach.

Another important consideration is unforeseen traps. It is common in defended areas to come across booby-traps, and a Breacher will likely be the first one to encounter traps at the front line of a breach. Alternate breaching methods may need to be more resilient to the presence of IED's. For example, an alternate method may be to blow cover and shoot a shoulder-launched munition. Also, if the Breach Team goes down due to an explosion, someone alternative must be able to detect and navigate any remaining explosives.

The patrol must have a plan for if a Breacher becomes a casualty before the breach is even attempted. The Patrol Leader must designate who will take over the breaching and who carries the breach tools and explosives. (A Breacher's kit is standardized and known, so that if they go down, then the designated replacement can recover charges without a search.)

28.e Backing Out and Reengaging[1]

Before entering a room, Soldiers center-step the entryway to get a snapshot of the dangers in the room. (See Clearing the Entry, Pg. 228.) If in their snapshot, a Soldier determines that entering the room is a bad idea, they must **back out and cease entry**. For example, if the Soldier sees a barricaded, belt-fed weapon, there is no reason to charge into the room. (Backing out of a room when there are already casualties in the room must also be planned for, and introduces a whole new layer of complexity.)

If the Soldier does decide to abort the entry, the patrol needs a plan for reengaging. Commonly, Soldiers restack and throw a bunch of grenades in the room. The patrol can also leave that entrance to find a different entrance to the same room. A team can also try to navigate the building to find the wall that is closest to the enemy in the room and breach that wall with explosives. Thereby, the wall charge explodes into enemies on the opposite side.

Or the patrol can abort all room-clearing, exit the building and conduct a tactical callout.[2] (See Tactical Callout, Pg. 156.) If the building has outside windows, Soldiers can envelope the building to clear it from the outside. (See Enveloping and Preclearing, Pg. 159.) However, being outside may also be dangerous. If all else fails, then patrol can withdraw completely. It is ill-advised to bite the bullet and force entry into a room with a well-barricaded, grenade-proof enemy.[3] Sometimes an aerial bombardment is more appropriate.

Phase 4

---

1 Quote: There are only two tactics a real warrior needs! Frontal assault, and death by frontal assault! —Fictional Video Game Character Barras Lehr; Cf. He who fights and runs away, may live to fight another day. —Ancient Proverb

2 In the Battle for Fallujah, rather than clearing houses with insurgents by fighting room to room, which had led to numerous casualties, Marines and Soldiers would back out of houses once they had made hostile contact and use whatever means they had to level the houses and kill everyone inside.

3 Applying Concepts: What does a "no fail mission" really mean when dead men cannot succeed?

Phase 5 Contents

29. Clear-Back and Consolidation — 281

Enemy Prisoner of War Team — 283
Aid and Litter, and Medevac — 286
Site Exploitation — 288

30. Withdrawal from the Objective — 290

31. Exfiltration — 292

Joe Goes Home (Phase 5: Withdrawal and Exfiltration)

Nothing is so devastating as to pounce upon the enemy in the dark, smite him hip and thigh, and vanish silently into the night.
                                        —British Major General Orde Wingate

Withdrawal (i.e. getting off the objective) begins after the objective is secured with the **consolidating and accounting** of all Soldiers and equipment. After everything is accounted for, the patrol completes any secondary mission taskings. Once the Patrol Leader is ready to leave the objective, they oversees a sequenced withdrawal. And finally, the patrol exfiltrates (i.e. travels back to base). Soldiers in the final stages of a raid are fatigued and more likely to make mistakes. Therefore, withdrawal and exfiltration are always preplanned, sequential processes complete with extra plans for any contingenies.

The difficulty of withdrawal and exfiltration is directly tied to the purpose of the raid. A withdrawal for a hostage rescue mission requires more planning than a withdrawal for a sabotage mission. For example, in the early night of January 30th, 1945 at Cabanatuan, Philippines, 121 U.S. Rangers and 250 Filipino guerrillas and porters sought to liberate prisoners of war. The patrol raided a large camp and in half an hour the patrol rescued 513 sickly prisoners. The exfiltration movement was 40 kms with an estimated 2,000 Japanese Soldiers pressing down. However because the patrol had planned to transport non-ambulatory casualties, the raid force came with 51 carts which enabled the raid force to reach friendly lines by the following morning.

Phase 5

29. Clear-Back and Consolidation

After an objective is cleared, teams are scattered. The teams assume hasty defensive positions to immediately gain security as they wait for further instructions. The Patrol Leader (or another designated Leader) gives an order and a time hack for teams to consolidate to prepare for Special Teams to

Image 285: U.S. Marines with 1st Plt., Force Recon Co., III Marine Expeditionary Force, clear back after finishing a raid. The Soldier on the right **plugs the hole** as the remainder of the team continues. Camp Hansen, Okinawa, Japan, 29 Jun 2020.

act, counterattack, or withdraw. Then, all Soldiers not pulling mandatory security, and sometimes just all Soldiers, consolidate.

Consolidating requires a **clear-back**, where Soldiers reclear all rooms on the way to the consolidation point, which is typically on the Patrol Leader. (Spaces not on the way to the consolidation point are not recleared.) A proper clear-back is conducted with the same tactical intensity and momentum as the initial clearing process. For example, Soldiers still maintain control of noncombatants, EPW's, casualties, etc. Upon reclearing rooms that were already marked, mark them again to indicate a reclear. For example, if the initial clear has chemlites in doorways, the reclear-marking can be a chemlite kicked to the center of the room or adding a different color.

To expedite a clear-back, Soldiers can do a **hasty clear-back**. The One Man does not fully enter a room to clear it, but instead just stands behind or in the doorway as the rest of the team travels behind One Man. A hasty clear-back is only possible when all rooms have been already been cleared once, and the safety of speedier movement outweighs the danger of hastily clearing.

When Outer Security consolidates, they "collapse." (See Isolation Area, Pg. 136.) **Collapsed Security can create a new, smaller isolation area** or entirely collapse and set up 360-degree security at the consolidation point. Collapsing conserves resources and increase responsiveness, so it can be done at any time. Regardless, 360-degree security always needs to be maintained.

At the consolidation point, the Patrol Leader briefs and receives backbriefs on the current situation. Then, the patrol leadership reorganizes Assault for follow-on tasks. The Support and Reserve Elements can push replacements, ammunition, and supplies to Assault or join Assault.

Once Special Teams (e.g., EPW Teams and Aid and Litter Teams) are organized and ready, the Patrol Leader briefs the Special Teams on exactly what to do. This reinforces the premission brief and highlights any changes. Then the Patrol Leader sends out the Special Teams. On a large objective, the patrol can fully or partially consolidate after each task.

29.a Enemy Prisoner of War Team

Enemy Prisoner of War (EPW) Teams control enemy detainees and enemy dead after Clearing Teams have secured them. EPW Teams reconfirm death, search bodies, and control all detainees until the patrol exfiltrates. EPW roles are given to Soldiers before the mission; a common assignment for a platoon-sized EPW Team is to have a Squad Leader lead as many Riflemen as possible. To aid Raiders, support-role Soldiers like Civil Affairs can be integrated into EPW Teams. The EPW Team can also become a Site Exploitation Team after dealing with EPW responsibilities. (See Site Exploitation, Pg. 288.)

EPW begins its job at the consolidation point when the Patrol Leader briefs them. The Patrol Leader tells the EPW Team their[1]:

Color – Each EPW sub-Team is given a color identifier. (During search when items are called out and recorded, two Soldiers calling out the same item use their different colors for clarity; e.g., "black 1 map" and "gold 1 map.")

Clearing instructions – How the objective is to be cleared and searched. (Usually, EPW follows SOP, so this is briefed if the situation is unusual.)

Collection instructions – What items to collect and where to put them.

Clock – How long EPW has to clear and search the objective.

After receiving their instructions, the EPW Team Leader sends their sub-Teams to search and clear systematicly.

The enemy dead first must be **confirmed dead**. If the dead are to be left where they are, Soldiers muzzle thump the eye of every suspected corpse. However, if the dead are to be searched, and therefore moved around, a

---

1 **Example** EPW Team Instructions:
Patrol Leader – "EPW on me."
> "You are black and you are gold. Begin in the center and clear to five meters past the M249. Bring all PIR to me. Place weapons and equipment on the hood of the vehicle. Weapons stacked bolt to bolt then equipment on top of those. You have 3 minutes.
EPW Team Leader – "Black on my Left; Gold on my Right. Start."

Image 286: British Royal Marines with 43 Commando Fleet Protection Group evacuate a simulated detainee. Chesapeake, Virginia, 21 Sep 2021. **Maintain physical control.**

Image 287: Personnel of 36th Combat Aviation Bde., Air Guard, and 1-19th SF Group move simulated detainees with bag masks and zip-tied hands. Camp McGregor, NM, 24 Jun 2012.

Clearing Soldier and a Security Soldier must check the dead for booby-traps. To signify that a body has been cleared, its feet and arms are crossed. The Soldiers then clear the enemy's weapon. To signify that a weapon is cleared, it is placed at the feet of the body. Soldiers can then safely search the body.

When searching an alive or dead enemy, a Soldier begins from the top and systematically touches, crumples, and feels for items of information and weapons as they move down the body. Although there are systematic and complete ways to search, time often does not allow for them. In a rush, Soldiers **prioritize body areas likely to contain important items**. (Important items were specified when the by Patrol Leader during consolidation or before the patrol.) When the Soldier finishes searching anything, they mark it; for example, they "mark" a searched person by segregating them, and a searched body by pulling the dead enemy's shirt above the head. Once searching is complete, Soldiers bring any items to the consolidation point designated in the EPW brief. There, the Patrol Leader assigns the Soldiers to other tasks.

Detaining enemy prisoners of war (EPW's) is a foregone conclusion since any enemy who refuses detainment can be forced at gunpoint. But shooting is not the default, and Soldiers must employ escalating force to obtain compliance: for example, first threatening in the native language that some type of force, lethal or nonlethal, will be used after a specific amount of time.

EPW's can often feel cornered and lash out, which means the Patrol Leader must have a plan and give very specific instructions to their Soldiers to improve relations between the patrol and its detainees. By having relatively good relations with EPW's, a Soldier can better extract good information from detained persons. This information can then impart tactical value if the patrol processes, accurately documents, and evacuates detainees and material to the rear quickly. Oftentimes this information is important at a higher level, and so Higher Command may dictate EPW instructions and safeguarding[1]

On the other hand, Soldiers know that a live EPW can jeopardize an entire mission. Securing and transporting an unwilling or injured human incapacitates multiple Soldiers. Moreover, letting an EPW free can alert additional enemies. Many attacks have multiple first passes, each by different elements, to specifically ensure that all enemies are killed during the assault.

When detaining an EPW, demeanor is important. Soliders must only ever be violent as a reaction. A calm and powerful demeanor makes detainees calm and submissive. A good detainment protocol is **5S&T**:

Search – prisoners immediately and thoroughly for weapons and documents. Never search alone; always have one Soldier pull security while another searches. Have the detainee raise their arms and conduct a visual inspection. Test suspicious occupants for explosives and metals such as concealed weapons or other devices. Pat down the person being searched, starting from the head and moving systematically to the individual's feet. Conduct tactical questioning during the search regarding information of tactical significance. Handcuff everyone!

Segregate – prisoners into groups: officers, NCO's, privates, deserters, civilians, and females. This inhibits coordination and command structure. While searching and segregating, have designated dirty and clean rooms as well as a tactical questioning area. Extra precautions must be taken when guarding groups; being in groups can give individuals the confidence to overwhelm guards at their slightest distraction. Consider using a marking system to separate military-aged males from women and children.

Silence – prisoners to prevent any and all coordination.

Speed – (quickly move) prisoners to their final location to maximize withdrawal of timely information. During the raid, use a covered and concealed location away from the immediate combat area. Clearing Teams hand off EPW's to the EPW Team. The EPW Team hands off detainees to the Patrol Sergeant and Support. And the Patrol Sergeant releases EPW's while the patrol is exiting the objective, or hands off EPW's to higher-level command for further processing. If EPW's are retained, Patrols send them back on vehicles already heading toward the rear.

---

1   Quote: I don't get intelligence off a satellite. Iraqis tell me who the enemy is.
—U.S. Major General James Mattis

Safeguard – prisoners from harm, and Soldiers from detainees for the duration of detainment. Do not give cigarettes, food, or water until authorized by assigned interrogators. All available personnel can safeguard, to include the walking, wounded, or Soldiers moving to the rear for reassignment. The patrol must also give necessary medical treatment.

Tag – the prisoner with time, place, and circumstances of capture. Also tag any equipment and weapons.

29.b Aid and Litter, and Medevac[1]

If there are friendly casualties, then the Patrol Leader is informed as soon as possible. The Patrol calls the Aid and Litter Team (A&L) to collect the casualties. A&L can only go to locations that are already secured, or else risk becoming casualties themselves.

A&L brings the casualties to the casualty collection point (CCP). (See Casualty Collection Point, Pg. 191.) Unless the patient is about to die, care is never done in place because enemy attackers may only be meters from the casualty. The CCP is a secure location with a Leader and a Medic. Often it is the original foothold. (See Footholds and Entrances, Pg. 163.) From the CCP, the casualties are fully accounted for and medically evacuated.

After casualties are collected, the Patrol Leader decides whether the mission is still viable; i.e., do casualties require care before the mission is over? If the Patrol Leader decides that the injuries are severe enough, the casualty can be evacuated using many means of transport. If the patrol is well planned, the evacuation can meet a medical ambulance or helicopter at a preplanned location. However, if the casualty occurs during a foot movement, then some walking is required. (See Medical Evacuation, Pg. 128.)

It is vital to have a **PACE plan** (i.e., Primary, Alternate, Contingency, and Emergency) for medical evacuation! A PACE guarantees multiple means of

---

1   Quote: We had a Marine that was wounded early in the battle [for Fallujah]. He got shot in the leg. They medevaced him up to the railroad station. . . . They put him on the table and took his uniform off and were treating his leg. When they took his jacket off, they found he had a bullet wound in his arm. They asked when that happened. He said "It happened a couple of days ago, but I wanted to stick with my buddies." After the battle was essentially over, we got 75 additional wounded reports. These were 75 Marines who after the battle reported their wounds.
—United States Marine Corps Lieutenant General Richard Nitonski

Image 288: Marines with F Co., 2ndBn., 1st Marine Reg. carry a simulated casualty. The casualty is aiding in his own carry. Twentynine Palms, CA, 31 Aug 2015.

Image 289: Soldiers from 4th Bn., 23rd Inf. Reg., 5th Stryker Bde. carry a wounded Stryker Soldier on a litter to be medically evacuated after rolling over an anti-armor mine. Zabul, Afghanistan. The 82nd Combat Aviation Brigade Medevac Team was able to respond to the evacuation of the Soldier within 15 minutes of the incident. The Soldier suffered minor injuries to his back. Note how many things these Soldiers are carrying in comparison to the simulated casualty above. **Actual casualties take a large amount of resources and significantly reduce security.**

evacuation simultaneously, so that if one method fails, another is still usable. Otherwise without a PACE, a Soldier's life depends on a single point of failure.

When there is a casualty during a patrol, the leadership must call up a 9-Line Medical Request as soon as possible. Although multiple-choice options are available, it is okay to talk like a human and, regardless, every Soldier should carry a 9-Line template. (See 9-Line Medevac Template, Pg. 129.)

29.c Site Exploitation

After an objective is secure but before withdrawal, Soldiers can exploit (i.e., identify, collect, protect, and evaluate) sites for resources (e.g., documents, material, and personnel) to provide: intelligence for future operations, answers for information requirements, and provide evidence to keep detainees in prison.[1] The exploited resources can vary widely, from DNA collected from prisoners to collecting hard drives for review of potential future enemy plans.

Commander's Critical Information Requirements (CCIR) for the search are briefed by the Patrol Leader before the mission. For example, does the Site Exploitation Team (SET) prioritize hide-sites for weapons or hide-sites for paper documents? Given unlimited time, SET's search buildings, yards, underground, and even underwater; but regardless, SET's prioritize sites that are likely to contain CCIR.

Site exploitation is methodical and systematic to be efficient. Soldiers take photos and videos to establish the condition of the house before and after the search, and they document all sensitive material or equipment found in the house. SET's report everything they find because if it finds something unusual the new information can change the scheme of the search. Before removing material, ensure that the date, time, location, possessor, and the reason for the confiscation are all recorded.

All locations and objects are booby-trapped until an inspection proves otherwise. One technique to ensure safety is to make a resident detainee open and enter unknown locations and containers. Detainees from the objective are more knowledgeable of booby-traps and motivated to not set them off. This is especially relevant for the inspection of suspicious vehicles.

With enough Soldiers, a SET is organized into more specialized teams, such as a Search Team, a Detainee Team, a Recording Team, etc. A Search Team consists of one Soldier who searches and one Soldier who pulls security; all teams require security. SET's should be specifically prepared to handle female personnel with a female searcher and to handle hazardous materials

---

1 Quote: When we entered Somalia in December 1992, we had a one-line database on the military forces there. Our attempt to use standard collection means and strategies was only partially successful because these conventional means could not deliver the kind of specific information we wanted. There were no Somali motorized rifle or tank divisions, no air defense system, no navy, and no air force. — Defense Intelligence Agency Officer Jeffery B. White

Image 290: An Intelligence Analyst Marine, HQ Co., 3rd Bn., 5th Marine Reg. marks enemy weapons during tactical sight exploitation training. Camp Pendleton, CA, 11 Sep 2013.

Image 291: In a search for IED cells, Coalition Forces and 2nd Afghan Commandos fingerprint detainees. East of Khost City, Afghanistan, 31 Aug 2009.

like biohazards and toxic elements. If interrogating detainees is planned, then bring an interpreter and a qualified interrogator; bad "interrogation" can be worse than no interrogation.[1]

SET's use many tools. All Search Element Soldiers may carry biometrics tools, breaching tools, video recording devices, markings and signals, and a standardized labeling convention. Recording equipment is the most vital; if a video is taken, then transporting the recorded materials may be redundant. SET's also bring mine detectors to locate metal objects underground or underwater and military working dogs to locate hidden people or objects.

Finally, **mutual respect with local people is a powerful military tool**. There is no point in neutralizing enemies on the objective, only to make more enemies in the aftermath. Searchers must make every effort to leave the house in the same condition from when the search began. And it is a good idea to bring a local police officer. The SET must be briefed on and follow the limits of search authority and any ROE. (See Morality and Rules-of-engagement, Pg. 295.) For example, body searches of female detainees by male Soldiers can greatly anger neutral civilians and turn them toward the enemy; and may even be banned by Higher Command. Moreover, searching non-hostile religious institutions, and historical, cultural, or governmental sites is also often restricted. The idea behind restrictions is that, at some point, the cost of angering local citizens outweighs the benefit of a site exploitation.

Phase 5

---

1 Quote: When we have incurred the risk of a battle, we should know how to profit by the victory, and not merely content ourselves, according to custom, with possession of the field. —Marshal General of France Maurice de Saxe

30. Withdrawal from the Objective

Withdrawal is the act of moving off of the objective area. It can occur at any time, due to mission abortion or mission completion. But a planned withdrawal begins after an objective is declared secure and Special Teams have completed their taskings. The urgency of withdrawal is influenced by the time it takes to attack and assault the objective, enemy reactions, the time needed to care for and evacuate casualties, and the mode of transportation. The patrol effort does not leave anything of intelligence value.

The Patrol Leader **withdraws the patrol in stages**, withdrawing Assault, Support, and Security in that order. As Assault withdraws, Support protects them. As Support withdraws, Security protects them. Security is withdrawn last because they repel enemy reinforcements. When withdrawing, each Element Leader accounts for their own element so in case of a split element, each element can independently move. If there are casualties, the Patrol Sergeant must ensure that those casualties have the highest priority evacuation.

Demolition is an important part of withdrawal. (See Demolition Team, Pg. 277.) For example, when a patrol's equipment (e.g., a helicopter) cannot be withdrawn, the Demo Team destroys it. They also destroy enemy equipment as thoroughly as possible so it cannot be used by different enemies. There is an specific arrangement in which consolidated equipment is blown. First, all ammunition is placed on the ground, or above an enemy engine block. (If ammo is placed above the demo, it will spray everywhere.) Above the ammo, all weapons are stacked with touching receiver groups. Guns are durable, so their vital areas are targeted. Then the charge is placed. All other equipment, like radios and combat vests, are placed atop the demo. Vehicles that cannot have a charge on their engine block are destroyed by other means.

Withdrawal and any significant explosions by the patrol are synchronized, because the explosions are safer once Soldiers are off the objective. Soldiers consolidate that equipment or valuable items in one spot (typically in front of the Patrol Leader) during the clear-back or site exploitation. (See Clear-Back and Consolidation, Pg. 281.)(See Site Exploitation, Pg. 288.) Then the Patrol Leader gives verbal orders that simultaneously signal withdrawal actions and demolition actions. (Even if there is no demolition on a particular mission, the same verbal orders are given to adhere to an SOP.)

The Patrol Leader shouts, **"Fire in the Hole 1!"** in person and on the radio, and the Assault Leader makes a chokepoint and shouts, "Chokepoint on me!" over and over. Always echo everything! Assault, casualties, and detainees withdraw through the chokepoint. The Assault Leader counts themself and tells the Patrol Sergeant, "Assault [number counted] up!" or "Assault [number counted] missing [number missing]!" Simultaneously, the Demo Team removes the safeties on their charges.

The Patrol Leader shouts, "Fire in the Hole 2!" and Support withdraws in the same way to the Support Leader. Heavy weapon systems operators are slow and deaf, so they sound off with "Gun moving!" to indicate they heard, and run to the chokepoint. Simultaneously, the Demo Team makes final preparations on their charges, so that all that is left is a squeeze or pull.

The Patrol Leader shouts, "Fire in the Hole 3!" and the demo is ignited. Security and everybody else remaining withdraws, without going through the objective. If any personnel or sensitive item count was incorrect, do not call, "Fire in the Hole 3!" At this point, only the Patrol Leader and Demo Team are near the objective. (Nobody can be left alone, so a buddy must always stay.)

Before withdrawing, the Demo Team confirms a visual indication of ignition. Then, the Patrol Leader shouts, "Burning! Burning! Burning!" and withdraws. As the patrol withdraws from the objective, it can lay mines and traps on its path to delay and destroy any enemy pursuers.

Sometimes a mission is aborted, and the withdrawal needs to occur immediately. In this case, demolition is foregone, but the sequence remains the same. All Assaulters need to be accounted for before Support can withdraw. And all Supporters are accounted for before Security can withdraw. The withdrawal sequence can be chaotic, and early withdrawal must be practiced!

Phase 5

31. Exfiltration

Exfiltration (exfil) is when a patrol moves from the objective area back to base. It is almost identical to infiltration, but in reverse. (See Scheme-of-Maneuver for Infiltration, Pg. 109.) The most important difference is that after attacking, **the patrol is compromised and vulnerable to attack.** An attacked enemy will counterattack or attempt to otherwise intercept the raid force. Meanwhile, the raid force may now have casualties, evacuees, and captured personnel or equipment that further complicates exfil.

In fact, the security demands of exfiltration have led to some outsized Security Elements. During the Soviet-Afghan War, the Mujahideen placed heavy security on the routes into and out of the objective areas, which sometimes consisted of up to 80 percent of their troops. That large Security Element was divided between: isolating the objective to intercept quick reaction forces; surveilling Soviet security posts to ensure the patrol was not revealed or ambushed; and general security along the infil and exfil routes.

The route used for exfil must be different from the infil route. Typically two routes, a primary and alternate route, are planned for infiltration; and when one is actually used to infil, the other is used for exfil. (See Choosing and Preparing a Route, Pg. 111.) If the patrol places Soldiers along the exfil route to secure it before the raid, those Soldiers must also have a withdrawal plan.

The patrol must be prepared to fight while moving, and break-contact from anywhere. (See Image 294, Pg. 293.) If a patrol has enough forces to defend against a pursuing enemy, they defend and counterattack before breaking contact. However, if all else fails, and an element of the raiding force is closely pursued by the enemy, then that element must attempt to break contact away from the remainder of the patrol. In urban terrain, smaller elements can break contact more easily.

Although breaking up may be considered unacceptable by many modern armies, those armies have rarely been faced with an enemy of overwhelming power in urban terrain. Guerrilla fighters often split up into small groups or even individuals to evade close pursuit by the enemy. Dispersed withdrawal has the added advantage of not providing a lucrative target to enemy air and fire support elements. In fact, guerrilla-style units may be burdened by moving with a large element, and plan to split into smaller elements for every exfil.

Image 293: Special Forces Soldiers with 3rd Special Group (Airborne) signal a UH-60 Black Hawk Helicopter for exfiltration. Near Hurlburt Field, FL, 15 Aug 2019. They spin a chemlight on a string to make a highly visible "**buzzsaw**" (the red circle).

Image 294: Air Force Special Tactics Operators exfiltrate off the target as explosives go off around their convoy during a scenario part of a training exercise. Fort Knox, KY, 31 Jan 2020. **The convoy must move!**

Annex Contents

32. Realities of Combat   295

Morality and Rules-of-engagement   295
Stress and Sleep Deprivation   298
Changing Enemy Tactics   300

33. Disseminating Information   302

34. Glossaries   304

Acronyms   304
Words   306

35. Credits   312

Annexes

The truth is that the jungle is neutral. It provides any amount of fresh water, and unlimited cover for friend as well as foe...The jungle itself is neutral.
—*British Army Officer Frederick Chapman, in Malaya.*

32. Realities of Combat

Soldiers are not robots. Research has determined that only three out of ten Soldiers fire their weapons when confronted by an enemy during room cleaning operations. If the realities of combat are ignored, then units begin to practice tactics that don't work in reality. Or worse, Soldiers will have no plan for real world scenarios. For example, sometimes a Soldier must choose between killing children and saving their friends. These uncomfortable scenarios are defining features of war and cannot be ignored.

32.a Morality and Rules-of-engagement[1]

History has shown many times that preventing immoral, vicious attacks is important because of the **negative long-term effects** of those acts. (Militaries are not overly concerned with morality for morality's sake.) For example, in 1993 American and Pakistani forces opened fire on a crowd of Somali Soldiers, women, and children after United Nations peacekeeping troops came under attack. As many as 100 Somalis may have been killed in the fighting, and some appeared to be women and children. It didn't matter whether the killings were justified to Americans. Killing women and children to disperse crowds radicalized many Somalis, and created even more enemies than would have existed in the first place. Three weeks later the battle of Mogadishu occurred (the "Black Hawk Down" incident), where thousands of Somalis were mobilized against invading American forces resulting in almost 100 American casualties.

---

1 Quote: Will Turner: You didn't beat me. You ignored the rules-of-engagement. In a fair fight, I'd kill you. Jack Sparrow: That's not much incentive for me to fight fair, then, is it? —Exchange from Pirates of the Caribbean: The Curse of the Black Pearl

Annexes

Image 295: A Judge Advocate teaches Rules-of-engagement to Transition Teams who aid the Iraqi military and police. Camp Taji, Iraq, 13 Apr 2006. **Rules-of-engagement go through a game of telephone before reaching the operator.**

To reduce future negative consequences, nations impose rules-of-engagement (ROE) to restrict Soldiers on what they may or may not do. Before every raid, the ROE must be briefed. And typically, the ROE is followed by Soldiers, because Soldiers follow orders. One example of an ROE is, "Treat all civilians and their property with respect and dignity. Do not seize civilian property, including vehicles, unless you have the permission of a company-level commander and you give a receipt to the property's owner."

However regardless of what some commander declares ROE to be, a Soldier no longer cares about abstract future consequences when they have just witnessed an enemy kill their best friend. Armies by their very nature do not attract sympathetic men who greatly care about future consequences. Ground troops usually care about immediate danger and crushing the enemy as violently as possible. Going to war further radicalizes Soldiers to be more aggressive and unforgiving. Moreover, this unforgiving nature and radicalization of Soldiers is in some ways necessary for war. It is very difficult to train a Soldier to be emotionally connected to their fellow Soldiers, neutral toward civilians, and also unhesitating but moral about killing enemies. And it is impossible to field these paradoxical Soldiers in large numbers.

In fact, preying on fragile morality has always been a war tactic. In the battle of Grozny, Chechen forces hanged upside-down Russian wounded and dead in front of their positions. Russian troops then had to shoot through the corpses of their dead comrades to engage the Chechens. Russian prisoners were decapitated and at night their heads were placed on stakes beside roads

Image 296: A Squad Leader Sergeant with 8th Marine Reg. looks back for a casevac during a six-hour firefight with insurgents. Garınsir District, Helmand, Afghanistan, 13 Aug 2009. **His concern is casualty evacuation and not rules-of-engagement.**

leading into the city, over which Russian reinforcements had to travel. Both Russian and Chechen dead were routinely booby-trapped.[1] A Russian Leader telling a Russian Soldier to be "moral" to enemy Chechens, or follow rules-of-engagement, can even backfire and breed mistrust against leadership.

In Iraq, one U.S. Soldier recounted how the enemy halted convoys to ambush Soldiers. "[The enemy] would send little kids out in the middle of the road, so that the convoys would stop and not hit [the kids]. Well, it worked a couple of times. And then it came down the chain of command that 'you don't stop for anything, even including little kids,' which is really sad. But it was our lives or theirs, and I guess a few little kids got mowed over."

Insofar as a raid is concerned, **a Leader must be aware of the reality** beyond out-of-touch ROE. Will a Soldier go violently rogue? Will they refuse or hesitate to kill? If so, what will the Leader do with that Soldier? To be clear, the most common answer is nothing. It is incredibly rare for an infantry Soldier to be punished for a war crime when they sincerely inform their chain of command. A Soldier similarly must also answer hypothetical questions before the raid even begins. Will I shoot kids? Will I shoot through my buddy's dead body? What will my reaction be to a mid-mission fratricide? Questions of morality are often ignored or briefed by Higher Command in the most boring way possible because these questions are uncomfortable to talk about. But they are vital to answer before going on a mission to kill.

1 Quote: Distinct tactical advantages accrue to the side with less concern for the safety of the civilian population. —U.S. Army Field Manual 3-06.11 Appendix H

Annexes

32.b Stress and Sleep Deprivation[1]

Stressed Soldiers are less combat effective. For example, The U.S. Centers for Disease Control and Prevention says, "Being awake for at least 24 hours is equal to having a blood alcohol content of 0.10%. This is higher than the legal limit (0.08% BAC) in all states." Leaders would never take drunken Soldiers on a mission, but they will take sleep-deprived Soldiers. And although sleep deprivation (SD) during one important mission can be a tactically sound sacrifice to increase mission success, the military has extended the experience of SD to the culture itself, pervading missions and training.

The culture of sleep deprivation starts in schools like Ranger School, where Soldiers are deprived of sleep in order to stress them as they learn. This is justified with the idea of "practice drills under realistic conditions." However, the side effect is that Soldiers who graduate begin to think that it is appropriate to be sleep deprived during a raid because those were the conditions in which they learned. In fact, many Soldiers in the military are proud of their ability to go without sleep and view sleep as a necessary evil.

To be clear, both acute and chronic sleep deprivation will biologically degrade a Soldier's ability to perform a mission. And while this seems uncontroversial, the issue is Leaders' may not acknowledge how much sleep loss is "deprivation." The research paper, *Alhola, P., & Polo-Kantola, P. (2007). Sleep deprivation: Impact on cognitive performance. Neuropsychiatric disease and treatment, 3(5), 553–567,* has this to say:

"The need for sleep varies considerably between individuals. The average sleep length is between 7 and 8.5 h per day.... In addition, sleep is essential for cognitive performance, especially memory consolidation. Sleep loss... can lead to a rise of blood pressure and an increase in cortisol secretion.... People who are exposed to sleep loss usually experience a decline in cognitive performance and changes in mood....

"The decrease in attention and working memory due to SD is well established. Vigilance is especially impaired, but a decline is also observed

---

1 Quote: We must be ruthlessly opportunistic, actively seeking out signs of weakness, against which we will direct all available combat power. And when the decisive opportunity arrives, we must exploit it fully and aggressively, committing every ounce of combat power we can muster and pushing ourselves to the limits of exhaustion. —U.S. Marine Corps FMFM 1 Warfighting 1989

Image 297: U.S. Soldiers of 1st Sqn., 40th Cav. Reg. in their hasty fighting position after a night patrol in the mountains. Sar Howza, Paktika, Afghanistan, 04 Sep 2009.

in several other attentional tasks. These include measures of auditory and visuospatial attention, serial addition and subtraction tasks, and different reaction time tasks....

"Sleep deprivation impairs visuomotor performance... It is believed that visual tasks would be especially vulnerable to sleep loss... [R]easoning ability seems to be maintained during short-term SD. However, [one study] repeated the cognitive test every 2 h and found deterioration after as little as 16 h of SD. In the studies with zero-results, cognitive tests were carried out in the morning ... [t]herefore, the different results may reflect the effect of circadian rhythm on alertness and cognitive performance. ...

"**[SD] increases rigid thinking, perseveration errors, and difficulties in utilizing new information in complex tasks requiring innovative decision-making. Deterioration in decision-making also appears as more variable performance and applied strategies, as well as more risky behavior**....

"The adverse effects of total SD shown in experimental designs have also been confirmed in real-life settings, mainly among health care workers, professional drivers and military personnel. Performance of residents in routine practice and repetitive tasks requiring vigilance becomes more error-prone when wakefulness is prolonged. However, in new situations or emergencies, the residents seem to be able to mobilize additional energy sources to compensate for the effects of tiredness. More recent meta-analysis shows that SD of less than 30h causes a significant decrease in both the clinical and overall performance of both residents and non-physicians....

"Chronic partial sleep restriction[:]... In the 3 hour [of sleep per night] group, both speed and accuracy... deteriorated almost linearly as the sleep restriction continued. In this group, performance was clearly the worst. In the 5 and 7 hour groups, performance speed deteriorated after the first two restriction nights, but then remained stable (though impaired) during the rest of the sleep restriction from the third night onward. Impairment was greater in the 5 than 7 hour group....

"The effects of sleep restriction have also been addressed by drive simulation studies, which are interesting and practical designs. Just one night of restricted sleep (4 hour) increased right edge-line crossings in a motorway drive simulation of 90 minutes.... One sleep-restricted night did not increase the probability of a crash, but after five nights of partial SD, the quantity of accidents increased....

" [I] n the long run, people tend to get used to experiencing sleepiness and thus may not even recognize being chronically sleep deprived....

"[One study] suggested that some people are more vulnerable to the effects of sleep loss than others, which could probably explain the lack of significant results in some group comparisons...."

If all else fails, Leaders must be prepared to remove Soldiers from their rolls, or rethink their operation. During the fighting in Grozny, 72% of the attacking Russian Soldiers demonstrated some kind of psychological disorder symptoms such as insomnia, lack of motivation, high anxiety, emotional stress, fatigue, and hypochondria. More than anything, this was proof of terrible tactics and strategy by the Leaders of an attacking army.

32.c Changing Enemy Tactics[1]

Enemies are human and will learn, counter, and overcome any military action as they observe the same patterns over and over again. In real life, Russia's overuse of powerful Russian indirect and aerial firepower against Chechens

Annexes

---

1 Quote: Professional Soldiers are predictable but the world is full of amateurs. —Unknown

Image 298: A 5th Special Forces Group (A) Soldier and his Military Working Dog scan for threats during a night-training exercise. United States, 02 Mar 2018. Standard issue night-vision devices can see invisible infrared light, making night raids much more effective. However, in the past twenty years, this capability has become widely purchasable by civilians online, meaning **tactics had to evolve**.

was eventually countered by "hugging" the Russian unit. Chechens would get so close to the Russian forces that indirect fires would hit everyone.

In Iraq, once enemy troops realized that they could not stop the CQB tactics of U.S. Forces, they began rigging entire buildings to explode and collapse, killing everybody inside regardless. Realizing that their CQB had been countered, Americans countered in response. U.S. Forces took to police tactics, and conducted callouts. (See Tactical Callout, Pg. 156.) They would get on a microphone and order everyone inside to come out. If the inhabitants didn't surrender and come out, the U.S. would order an airstrike and destroy the entire building.

Not just actions and tactics, but every part of a raid must be periodically changed. When markers are used for extended periods, the enemy may be able to capture or manufacture and use these marking devices to their advantage. Even how missions are scheduled can be exploited. Conducting every mission during the night encourages the enemy to post more guards at night; so, the raiding force may want to conduct some raids at night and some in daylight

When considering how an enemy may exploit a pattern, Soldiers must acknowledge that even if they are bound by rules-of-engagement, the enemy is not. It is against international treaties to wear the enemy's uniform during military engagements. To name one of many armed rebel groups, the Democratic Forces for the Liberation of Rwanda in the eastern Democratic Republic of Congo, purposely wear civilian attire on their raids because they noticed the pattern of government forces not killing civilians.

Image 299: U.S. Army Soldiers assigned to the 2nd Cavalry Reg. and French Army Soldiers conduct an after action review (AAR) immediately after training. Hohenfels Training Area, Germany, 15 APR 2021. AAR's can be extremely informal.

33. Disseminating Information

Troops need to be trained with the lessons learned from prior missions.[1] However there is a broad spectrum of opinions on what information needs to be disseminated to who.

On the end of too much dissemination, moron reporter Geraldo Rivera was kicked out of Iraq in 2003 for drawing a map in the dirt that disclosed the location of the 101st Airborne Division relative to Baghdad. He gave away present and future troop positions on live television to millions of viewers.

Contrast this with the security measures of a Mujahideen Commander, Shabuddin, whose own men didn't even know the plan! Shabuddin said on his 1983 raid on the Kabul Metropolitan Bus Transportation Authority, "I assembled 120 Mujahideen for the raid at our base at Yakhdara. We had 16 RPG-7s, three mortars, three 82mm recoilless rifles and numerous small arms.... To preserve mission security, only my subcommanders and I knew the plan." The Mujahideen were not renowned for their combat effectiveness.

This manual does not resolve the debate, but it does offer a method.

Annexes

Image 300: Army Reserve Soldiers from Task Force 76 conduct an after action review (AAR). Camp Williams, Utah, 02 May 2021. More formal AAR's require lots of preparation, and are **part of mission planning from the beginning.**

The U.S. Army suggests using an After Action Review (AAR) to disseminate information about completed missions. An AAR has four phases:
1) Review what was supposed to occur according to the mission plan.
2) Review what actually occured in chronological order.
3) Determine what was right or wrong with what occured.
4) Determine how the task will be done similarly or differently in the future. This is an effective method of review. Further, the U.S. Army in *Field Manual 7-0, Training* says, "[r]ecording the results of training is critical for leaders to project future training requirements based on unit personnel turbulence. Training requirements are catalogued in leader books and battle rosters to ensure these training gaps are filled as expeditiously as possible."

How exactly an AAR is performed step-by-step is outside the scope of this manual because it is not a raid specific task; every mission or project must have an after action review. But a good resource for leading an after action review is a manual titled *How to Conduct an After Action Review*, created by the National Police Foundation and funded and hosted by the U.S. Department of Justice. Because after action reviews are so vital, many more resources can be found on the internet. Whatever resources a Leader uses to disseminate mission information, they must not form an impromptu huddle and ask Soldiers what they think. **Always have a detailed plan, and execute it!**

Annexes

34. Glossaries

34.a Acronyms

(A)	Airborne
5S&T	Search, Silence, Segregate, Safeguard, Speed, Tag
9 Line	Medical Evacuation Request
AAR	After Action Review
A&L	Aid and Litter
ACE	Ammo, Casualties, Equipment
AG	Assistant Gunner
AFV	Armored Fighting Vehicle
AP	Alpha Point
APOBS	Antipersonnel Obstacle Breaching System
ASS	Assault, Support, Security
AT4	Anti-Armor Rocket Launcher
BDE	Brigade
BDM	Bunker Defeat Munition
BLT	Battalion Landing Team
BFV	Bradley Fighting Vehicle
BN	Battalion
C4	C4 is a name of an explosive and not an acronym.
CAS	Close Air Support
CCP	Casualty Collection Point
CCIR	Commander's Critical Information Requirements
CO	Company
COLE	Covered and concealed; Out of sight, sound, and small-arms fire; Large enough to fit the entire element; Easily defendable for a short time.
CQB	Close-Quarters Battle
CQC	Close-Quarters Combat (synonym for CQB)
CP	Check Point
CS	2-Chlorobenzylidene Malononitrile Gas (Tear Gas)
DIV	Division
DTG	Date Time Group
EOD	Explosive Ordnance Disposal
EPW	Enemy Prisoner of War
EWAC	Engagement, Withdrawal, Abort, Compromise
FFIR	Friendly-Forces Information Requirements
FIST/FiST	Forward Support Team; known as FiSTers
FAC	Forward Air Controller
FM	Field Manual
FO	Forward Observer
FOB	Forward Operating Base
FPL	Final Protective Line
FRAGO	Fragmentary Order
FSO	Fire Support Officer
FSS	Fire Support Specialist
GOTWA	Where Going; Others Going With; Time of Emergency; What if No Return; Actions on Contact for Both Elements
GT	Gun Team
HE	High Explosive
HLZ	Helicopter Landing Zone
HMMWV	(Humvee) High-Mobility Multipurpose Wheeled Vehicle
HQ	Headquarters
IED	Improvised Explosive Device
IDF	Indirect Fire
IFAK	Individual First Aid Kit

II	Image Intensification		MOUT	Military Operations in Urban Terrain
INF	Infantry		MSG	Maneuver Support Group
INT	Intersection		MSS	Mission Support Site
IR	Infrared		MWD	Military Working Dog
IRAM	Improvised Rocket-Assisted Munitions		NCO	Non-Commissioned Officer
JTAC	Joint Terminal Attack Controllers		N.G.	National Guard
			NGF	Naval Gunfire
LAW	Light Anti-Tank Weapon		NOD	Night-Optical Device
LDA	Linear Danger Area		OACOK	Observation and Fields of Fire; Avenues of Approach; Key and Decisive Terrain; Obstacles; Cover and Concealment
LMTV	Light Medium Tactical Vehicle			
LOA	Limit-of-Advance			
LPOP	Listening Post Observation Post			
LR	Leader's Reconnaissance		OBJ	Objective
LT	Leader Team		ODA	Open Danger Area
LZ	Landing Zone		ORP	Objective Rally-Point
M1	Abrams Tank		OPORD	Operation Order
M1A2	Bangalore Explosive		PACE	Primary, Alternate, Contingency, Emergency
M4	Standard Issue Rifle		PL	Phase Line
M68	Standard Issue Close Combat Optic		PLT	Platoon
			PDF	Primary Direction of Fire
M72	Light Anti-Armor Weapon		PEQ-15	Rifle Laser Mount
M141	Bunker Defeat Munition		PETN	Pentaerythritol Tetranitrate Explosive
M192	Standard Issue Lightweight Ground Mount		PID	Positive Identification
			PIR	Priority Information Requirement
M203	Standard Issue Grenade Launcher		PL	Patrol Leader
M240	Standard Issue Machine Gun		PL	Platoon Leader
			POD	Points-of-Domination
M249	Standard Issue Light Machine Gun		POW	Prisoner of War
			PSG	Platoon Sergeant
M1150	Assault Breacher Vehicle		QRF	Quick Reaction Force
MED	Medic		R&S	Reconnaissance and Surveillance
MEF	Marine Expeditionary Force			
MER	Maximum Effective Range		REG	Regiment
METT-TC	Mission, Enemy, Terrain/Weather, Troops Available, Time, Civilians (i.e., anything else you can think of)		RFL	Rifleman
			RIF	Reconnaissance-in-Force
			ROE	Rules-of-Engagement
			RPG	Rocket Propelled Grenade
MEU	Marine Expeditionary Unit		RTO	Radio Transmission Operator
MICLIC	Mine Clearing Line Charge			
			RP	Rally-Point

RP	Release-Point
RPK	Soviet Light Machine Gun
S&O	Surveillance and Observation
SAW	Squad Automatic Weapon
SALUTE	Size, Activity, Location, Unit, Time, Equipment
SBF	Support-by-Fire
SD	Sleep Deprivation
SET	Site Exploitation Team
SI	Standard Issue
SL	Squad Leader
SLLS	Stop, Look, Listen, Smell
SLM	Shoulder-Launched Munition
SMAW	Shoulder-Launched Multipurpose Assault Weapon
SOF	Scheme-of-Fires
SOF	Sector-of-Fire
SOF	Special Operations Forces
SOM	Scheme-of-Maneuver
SOP	Standard Operating Procedure
SOSRA	Suppress, Obscure, Secure, Reduce, (Proof), Assault
SPARC	Sectors, Priority-of-Targets, Assault Lane, Rate-of-Fire, Camouflage

SSA	Support, Security, Assault
SSE	Sensitive Site Exploitation
SST	Sniper and Spotter Team
SUT	Small Unit Tactics
TA	Training Area
TI	Thermal Imaging
TLP	Troop Leading Procedures
TM	Training Manual
TNT	Trinitrotoluene
TRL	Target Reference Line
TRP	Target Reference Point
TOW	Tube-Launched, Optically-Tracked, Wire-Guided Missile
TTP	Tactics, Techniques, Procedures
U.S.A.F.	U.S. Air Force
U.S.M.C.	U.S. Marine Corps
UXO	Unexploded Ordnance
VDO	Vehicle Drop-Off
VPU	Vehicle Pickup
VS17	A Neon Cloth
WARNO	Warning Order
WBGT	Wet Bulb Globe Temperature
WSL	Weapons Squad Leader
WVCPT	Visibility, Wind, Cloud cover, Precipitation, and Temperature

34.b Words

Ambush	A surprise attack from a concealed position on a moving or temporarily halted enemy in order to destroy or capture them and their equipment.
Area Target	Targets that present no specific aiming point to the attacker. A group of people is an area target.
Area Weapon	A weapon used to attack an area target.
Assault	A short, violent, but well-ordered attack.
Assault (Element)	The unit which seizes and secures the objective and protects special teams as they complete their assigned actions on the objective.
Assistant Gunner	The most senior person on the Gun Team, and the Gun Team's Leader. They control the Gunner

Annexes

Avenue-of-Approach	A route of an attacking force leading to its objective or to key terrain.
Back Blast Area	The area behind an SLM where the projectile blasts exhaust with dangerous force.
Base-of-Fire	Fire placed on an enemy force or position to reduce the enemy's capability to interfere with friendly elements.
Basic Load	The quantity of ammunition required to meet combat needs until the next resupply. For M240, the standard is 900 to 1,200 rounds.
Battle Drill	A collective action rapidly executed without applying a deliberate decision-making process.
Beer Can Grip	Holding the front of the rifle with fingers and thumb on opposing sides (like holding a can of beer).
Breach	The action of penetrating a barrier, and the opening created through said penetration.
Bounding	The collective movement of two or more elements, where at least one element is stationary at all times.
Casevac	Emergency patient evacuation of casualties from a combat zone, excluding medevac.
Center-Fed Room	A room with an entry in the center of a wall.
Chain of Command	The succession of commanding Soldiers through which command and responsibility is transferred.
Checkpoint	A predetermined point used as a means of coordinating friendly movement.
Chicken Winging	Elevating the elbow on the firing arm when using a rifle.
Combat Arms	Troops that employ weapons to conduct direct tactical ground combat, such as infantry, armor, and artillery.
Combined Arms	The integration of different combat arms to achieve mutually complementary effects.
Commander's Critical Information Requirements – A comprehensive list of information requests critical in the decision making process affecting mission success	
Comms/Commo	Abbreviation for "communications," and includes: radios, messaging, encryption, etc.
Concealment	Protection from observation or surveillance.
Coordinated Fires	A sync of weapons' fields of fire to ensure complete and ideal coverage of a killzone.
Corner-Fed Room	A room with an entry in a corner.
Cover	Protection from the fires of specific weapon systems.
Danger Area	Any location where a patrol is vulnerable to enemy observation or fire based on its terrain characteristics.
Deadspace	An area within the maximum effective range of a system that cannot be covered by that system.

Annexes

Defilade Fires	Fires that shoot enemies who are aligned perpendicular to the fires. Opposite of enfilade.
Dig a Corner	To dig a corner means to physically point a muzzle at a corner of a space with intent (like punching a shovel into the ground).
Direct Fire	Aiming and firing a projectile with direct line-of-sight to the target.
Dismounted	People or Soldiers not in vehicles.
Element	Any group assigned with a task, which may include security or assault. They can be composed of Soldiers from one unit or multiple units.
Essential Elements of Friendly Information – Part of CCIR; information the commander wants to hide from the enemy.	
Effective Range	The range at which a weapon has a 50% probability of hitting a target.
Emplacement	The purposeful and specific placement of Soldiers by command in a formation.
Enfilade Fire	Fires that shoot enemies who are aligned in a straight line to the fires. Opposite of defilade.
Exfil	Exfiltration of enemy territory.
Friendly Forces Information Requirements - Part of CCIR; what the commander needs to know about their own forces.	
Fire Support	Assistance to ground forces through artillery, mortars, naval fire, and close air support.
Fire(s)	A fire is a traveling projectile (e.g., a bullet). Fires, plural, are multiple projectile attacks from multiple weapons, the same weapon over time, or both.
Formation	A group of two or more Soldiers in proximity to each other with all movements coordinated in unison.
Forward Observer	A Soldier observes the battlefield and directs indirect fires onto targets.
Group (Targets)	Two or more targets on which fire is desired simultaneously.
Gun Team	A unit controlling the M240, a crew-served weapon requiring at least two men: a Gunner and an Assistant Gunner.
Gunner	The operator of the M240 general-purpose (27.6 lb.) machine gun.
Halt	A temporary stop during a movement.
Headquarters	An element of a unit consisting of that unit's highest leadership, and those Soldiers directly under them.
Helicopter Landing Zone	See Landing Zone.
Indirect Fire	Aiming and firing a projectile without relying on a direct line-of-sight between the gun and target.
Infil	Infiltration of enemy territory.

Initial Rally-Point	Where the patrol can rally if it becomes separated before departing the friendly area or before reaching the first en route rally-point.
Killzone	The area where the enemy is predicted to move through, and will be attacked in.
Kit	Set of equipment.
Key Terrain	Any area, which when seized, retained, or controlled, affords a marked advantage to either combatant.
Landing Zone	A specified zone within a predesignated area used for landing aircraft.
Lane	A clear route through an obstacle.
Leader's Recon	A leader's reconnaissance. This is scouting performed by a small group of Leaders and Soldiers who advance to a site that the entire patrol might use.
Leapfrogging	A form of bounding where the stationary element can only provide limited support to the maneuvering element. Primarily used for deconfliction of movement instead of mutual support.
Limit-of-Advance	An easily identified location beyond which attacking elements will not advance.
Linear Danger Area	Any location where a patrol is vulnerable to enemy observation or fire predominantly from the flanks, such as a trail, road, or stream.
Leader's Recon	A reconnaissance by a subset of an element, including senior leadership, in preparation for further actions.
Marksman	A long range rifleman that is integrated into a mixed-specialty team.
Main Body	The principal part of a tactical command or formation, excluding detached elements.
Maneuver	The movement of forces supported by fire to achieve a position of advantage from which to destroy or threaten to destroy of the enemy.
Medevac	A standardized and dedicated vehicle which evacuates wounded from the battlespace, and provides en route care from medical personnel.
Metal-to-Metal	A M192 tripod only allows the M240 to turn 25 degrees left and right from center. Metal-to-metal is when the gun turns 25 degrees, hits the tripod, and physically cannot turn further.
Mission	The primary task assigned. Contains who, what, when, where, and why, but rarely how.
Mounted	Soldiers who move are moving on vehicles.
Mouse Hole	A rough, man-sized entryway made through force.
Military Working Dog	A dog who is a Soldier with rank, trained to use canine abilities to accomplish tasks.

Annexes

Objective (Area)	The area that includes all actions conducted and occupied positions in an ambush.
Objective Rally-Point	Staging location for occupation of the objective.
Open Danger Area	Any location where a patrol is vulnerable to enemy observation or fire from the front and flanks, such as a draw or large open area.
Overwatch	A unit that takes a position where it can observe likely enemy positions and provide effective covering fire for friendly units.
Patrol	A patrol is a group of Soldiers sent to perform a task. For example, a patrol may be an ambush or a reconnaissance.
Phase	A specific part of an operation that is different from those that precede or follow.
Pieing	Rotating around a corner while pointing a weapon at the open side of that corner in order to slowly reveal and secure the opposite side of the corner.
Priority Information Requirements – Part of CCIR; what the commander needs to know about the enemy.	
Point Target	Targets that are well defined and small in size. An individual person is a point target.
Point Weapon	A weapon used to attack a point target.
Points-of-Domination	A room-clearing technique where Soldiers end the clear in an L-shaped formation.
Pointman	The first man in a movement formation. Their job is to look for enemies and traps, since they are the most likely to be attacked.
Pull Security	To actively secure an area with a sector-of-fire by facing and pointing a rifle in that direction.
Quick Reaction Force	A unit placed on standby in order to quickly provide reinforcement to an attacked element.
Raid	A raid is an attack against a stationary enemy where something at the objective can't be destroyed, for a specific purpose other than seizing and holding the terrain.
Rally-Point	A location with the primary purpose of being moved to under preplanned conditions.
Recognition Signals	Predetermined signals that two separate element both know that can be exchanged to prove identity.
Reconnaissance (Recon)	A task to obtain information about the activities or resources.
Reconnaissance-in-Force	An mission conducted to test the enemy's response to that mission.
Rifleman	A Soldier who carries a rifle. They have no subordinates, though the battlefield can change that.

Patrol	A group of Soldiers sent to conduct a specific combat, reconnaissance, or security mission.
Platoon	A unit made up of multiple squads and a headquarters element (e.g. a Platoon Leader, and Platoon Sergeant).
Priority-of-Fires	The ranking of available targets for a single weapon. Or, the ranking of different weapons (fires) for a single target.
Sabotage	Destruction or obstruction done in order to hinder efforts.
Security (Element)	A unit that provides security at danger areas, isolates the objective, supports withdrawal, etc.
Security (Task)	The act of maintaining vision and weapons presence on an area.
Sector/(Field)-of-Fire	The area that a single/group of weapons may effectively cover with fire from a given position.
Sensitive Site Exploitation	Collecting information, material, and persons from a designated location and analyzing them to answer information requirements, facilitate subsequent operations, or support criminal prosecution.
Small Unit	Either a platoon or a squad.
Small Unit Tactics	Basic battlefield tactics used by squads and platoons.
Sniper	A long range rifleman that works in teams which specialize only in long range reconnaissance and attacks.
Squad	A unit of two teams or more and a Squad Leader.
Squirter	An enemy who attempts to breach the inner cordon and escape the objective.
Stack	A formation in front of an opening that the formation plans to enter.
Strongwall	A room-clearing technique where Soldiers all end the clear on the same wall (i.e. the "strongwall").
Support (Element)	A unit that provides direct and indirect fire support for another element.
Task	A clearly defined, measurable activity.
Team/Fire-Team	A unit typically made up of three Soldiers and a Team Leader.
Unit	A group with a static and defined chain of command. The units in this manual are company, platoon, squad, and fire-team.
Urban Terrain	Areas with structures where the majority of terrain is manmade or man-maintained.
Verbage	Concise and precise language.
Weapons Squad	A squad that is responsible for deploying the unit's general-purpose machine guns (as opposed to a typical Rifle Squad).

Annexes

35. Credits

Many thanks to the government photographers who made this book possible. All illustrations and designs were drawn by the author unless listed below. As a disclaimer, the appearance of U.S. Department of Defense (DoD) visual information does not imply or constitute DoD endorsement.

Front Cover Image: U.S. Army SPC Justin Young
Back Cover Image 1: U.S.M.C. SGT Emmanuel Ramos
Back Cover Image 2: U.S. Army SSG Iman Broady-Chin
Back Cover Image 3: U.S.M.C. CPL Carl King
Back Cover Image 4: U.S.M.C. CPL Carl King
TOC Image 1: U.S. Air Force TSGT Jerry Morrison
TOC Image 2: U.S. Air Force TSGT Jerry Morrison
TOC Image 3: U.S.M.C. CPL Jacob Yost
TOC Image 4: U.S. Army SSG John Mark
TOC Image 5: U.S. Army CPT Thomas Cieslak
Intro TOC: U.S. Air Force SRA Ryan Brooks
Image 1: U.S. Army SSG Marie Schult
Image 2: Kurdistan Region Security Council
Image 3: Kurdistan Region Security Council
Image 4: Department of Defense Katie Lange
Image 5: U.S. Army Patrick A. Albright
Image 6: U.S. Army SPC Kristina Truluck
Image 7 et al: U.S. Air Force SSG Jeremy Bowcock
Image 8: U.S. Army SPC Marilyn Spencer
Image 9: U.S.M.C. LCPL Ryan Young
Image 10: U.S.A.N.G. SGT Shane Smith
Image 11: U.S. Army SGT Steven Lewis
Image 12: U.S. Army SPC Ryan Hallock
Image 13: U.S. Army MAJ Tiffany Collins
Image 14: U.S. Army SGT Charles M. Bailey
Image 15 et al: U.S. Army SSG Timothy R. Koster
Image 16: U.S.M.C. CPL Isaac Ibarra
Image 17: U.S. Army ATP 3-21.8 2016
Image 18: U.S.M.C 1LT Kurt Stahl
Image 19: Joint U.S. Armed Forces Pub. 3-09.3 2019
Image 20: U.S. Army SGT William A. Parsons
Image 21 et al: U.S. Army ATP 3-21.8 2016
Image 22: U.S. Army ATP 3-21.8 2016
Image 23: U.S. Army SGT William A. Tanner
Image 24: U.S.M.C. CPT Caleb Eames
Image 25: U.S. Army ATP 2-01.3 2019
Image 26: U.S. Coast Guard PO2 Brandyn Hill
Image 27: A.D.F. CPL Chris Moore
Image 28: U.S. Army SSG Ryan Matson
Image 29: U.S.M.C. CPL Ryan Harvey
Image 30: U.S. Air Force TSGT Kevin Williams
Phase 1 TOC: U.S.M.C. CPL Victoria Decker
Image 31: U.S. Air Force Carole Chiles Fuller
Image 32: U.S. Army SGT Olgiati, Gustavo
Image 33: U.S.A.C.E. Leon Roberts
Image 34: U.S. Army SPC Dee Crawford
Image 35 et al: U.S. Army SGT David Edge
Image 37: U.S.M.C. LCPL Tojyea G. Matally
Image 38: U.S.M.C. LCPL Wesle
Image 39: U.S. Army PFC Franko DaRe
Image 40: U.S. Air Force SRA Brennen Lege
Image 41: Department of Defense Courtesy Photo
Image 42: Department of Defense Courtesy Photo
Image 43: U.S. Air Force SSG Trevor T. McBride
Image 47: U.S. Air Force SSG Vanessa Valentine
Image 48: USMC LCPL D. J. Wu
Image 49: U.S. Air Force SSG Greg L. Davis

Image 50: U.S. Army SSG Nicholas Farina
Image 51: U.S. Army MSG Mark Woelzlein
Image 52: U.S. Army SPC Chenee Brooks
Image 54: U.S. Navy PO2 Charles Oki
Image 55: U.S. Army CPT Ryan Jernegan
Image 56: U.S.M.C. LCPL Joshua Sechser
Image 57: U.S. Army SGT Eliverto V. Larios
Image 58: US Army SGT Mike Pryor
Image 59: U.S. Army Elena Baladelli
Image 60: U.S. Air Force TSGT Efren Lopez
Image 61: U.S. Army SPC Ryan Lucas
Image 62: U.S.M.C. CPL Brandon Salas
Image 65: U.S. Army SSG Jose H. Rodriguez
Image 66: U.S. Army Pierre-Etienne Courtejoie
Image 67: U.S.M.C. SGT Jacob H. Harrer
Image 68: U.S. Army SSG Kaily Brown
Image 69: U.S.M.C. LCPL Jason Jimenez
Image 70: U.S.M.C. LCPL Harrison Rakhshani
Image 71: U.S.M.C. SGT Timothy Stephens
Image 73: U.S.M.C. PFC Jason Morrison
Image 74: U.S.M.C. CPL Meredith Brown
Image 75: U.S.M.C. CPL Randall A. Clinton
Image 76: U.S.M.C. SGT Alfred V. Lopez
Image 77 et al: U.S. Army SGT Jeffrey Alexander
Image 78: U.S.M.C. SGT Emmanuel Ramos
Image 79: U.S.A.N.G. 2LT Nathan Rivard
Image 81: U.S.A.N.G. SGT Shawn Keeton
Image 82: Department of Defense Courtesy Photo
Image 85: U.S.M.C. CPL Patrick Crosley
Image 86: U.S. Army SPC Derek Mustard
Image 88: U.S.M.C. LCPL Garrett White
Image 89: U.S. Air Force SRA Ryan Conroy
Image 90: U.S.M.C. CPL Audrey M. C. Rampton
Image 91: U.S. Army ATP 2-01.3 2019
Image 92: U.S.A.N.G. SSG R. J. Lannom Jr
Image 93: U.S.M.C. LCPL Garrett White
Image 95 et al: U.S. Army ATP 2-01.3 2019
Image 96: U.S. Army ATP 2-01.3 2019
Image 97: U.S. Army Scott T. Sturkol
Image 98: U.S. Army SPC Michael Alexander
Image 99: U.S.M.C. 2LT Joshua W. Larson
Image 100: RAND Corporation, Reimagining the Character of Urban Operations for the U.S. Army, 2017
Image 103: U.S. Army ATP 3-21.8 2016
Image 104: U.S. Army SPC Jan Critchfield
Image 105: U.S. Army SPC Blair Larson
Image 106: Department of Defense Courtesy Photo
Phase 2 TOC: U.S.M.C. LCPL Colton Garrett
Image 107: U.S. Army ATTP 3-06.11 (FM 3-06.11) 2011
Image 108: U.S. Army ATP 2-01.3 2019
Image 110: U.S. Army ATTP 3-06.11 (FM 3-06.11) 2011
Image 111: U.S.M.C. CPL Patrick Crosley
Image 112: U.S.M.C. LCPL Jason Morrison
Image 113: U.S. Army CPT Thomas Cieslak
Image 115: U.S.M.C. PFC Jason Morrison
Image 116: U.S. Army N.G. 1LT Leland White
Image 117: U.S. Marine Corps SGT Allison M. DeVries
Image 118: U.S. Marine Corps CPL Joshua W. Brown
Image 119: U.S. Army SSG Michael Pryor
Image 120: U.S. Army SPC Linsay Burnett
Image 121: U.S.M.C. LCPL Sean M. Evans
Image 122: U.S. Army SGT Karen Sampson
Image 123: U.S. Army LTC Steve Stover
Phase 3 TOC: U.S. Army SGT Henry Villarama
Image 125: U.S. Army SPC Robert Woodward
Image 126: U.S. Air Force SSGT Stacy L. Pearsall
Image 128: USAF MSGT Kevin J. Gruenwald
Image 130 et al: U.S.M.C. CPL Patrick Crosley
Image 131: U.S. Army SPC Ryan Lucas
Image 132: U.S.M.C. Lance CPL Carl King Jr.

Image 133 et al: U.S Army 1LT Benjamin Haulenbeek
Image 138: Michigan Army N.G. MAJ Charles Calio
Image 139: U.S. Army CPT Thomas Cieslak
Image 140: U.S.M.C. LCPL Allen Sanders
Image 141: U.S.M.C. LCPL Alexis C. Schneider
Image 142: U.S. Army SSG Justin Moeller
Image 143: U.S. Army PFC Devon Popielarczyk
Image 144: U.S. Army 2LT Jamie Douglas
Image 145: U.S.M.C. CPL Jacob Yost
Image 146: U.S.M.C. LCPL Richard Currier
Image 147: U.S. Army SSG Armando R. Limon
Image 148: U.S. Army N.G. 2LT Nathan Rivard
Image 149: U.S. Army SGT John Yountz
Image 151: U.S. Army SPC JD Sacharok
Image 152: U.S.M.C. LCPL Shane T. Manson
Image 153: U.S. Airforce A1C Matthew Plew
Image 154: U.S.M.C. LCPL Alvin Pujols
Image 155: U.S. Army SPC John Crosby
Image 156: U.S. Army 1LT Lynn Chui
Image 157: US Army SPC Mike Pryor
Image 158: U.S. Army MAJ Carson Petry
Image 159: U.S.M.C. SGT Hector de Jesus
Image 160: U.S.M.C. LCPL Jesus Sepulveda Torres
Image 161: U.S.M.C. SGT Hector de Jesus
Image 162: U.S.M.C. CPL Danny Gonzalez
Image 163: U.S.M.C. SGT Hector de Jesus
Image 164: U.S. Army 1LT Ellen Brabo
Image 165: U.S.A.N.G. SPC Ashley Low
Image 166: U.S. Army SSG Opal Vaughn
Phase 4 TOC: U.S.M.C. SGT Audrey Rampton
Image 167: U.S. Army SSG Andrea Salgado Rivera
Image 168: U.S.M.C. 2LT Danielle Phillips
Image 169: U.S. Army SSG Iman Broady-Chin
Image 170: U.S.M.C. LCPL Angel Alvarado
Image 171: U.S. Army SPC David Gunn
Image 172: U.S.M.C. LCPL Scott Jenkins
Image 174: U.S. Army SSG Kaily Brown
Image 175: U.S. Army SPC Ryan Lucas
Image 176: U.S.M.C. SGT Esdras Ruano
Image 177: U.S.M.C. LCPL Alexis C. Schneider
Image 178: U.S.M.C. CPL Brian Reimers
Image 179: U.S. Army SSG Iman Broady-Chin
Image 181: U.S. Air N.G. SRA Joseph Morgan
Image 182: U.S.M.C. LCPL Ujian Gosun
Image 183: U.S.M.C. LCPL Seth Starr
Image 184: U.S. Army SPC Jordan Buck
Image 185: U.S.M.C. CPL Brian Reimers
Image 186: U.S. Army SGT Richard Jones
Image 187: U.S. Air Force SRA Sahara Fales
Image 188: U.S. Army SSG Armando Limon
Image 189: U.S.M.C. CPL Miguel Rosales
Image 190: U.S.M.C. LCPL Jered T. Stone
Image 191: U.S. Army SPC Jordan Buck
Image 192: U.S. Army SSG Armando Limon
Image 193: U.S. Army ATTP 3-06.11 (FM 3-06.11) 2011
Image 194: U.S. Army PFC Rachel Christensen
Image 195: U.S. Army SGT Richard Daniels Jr.
Image 196: U.S.M.C. CPL Eric Tso
Image 197: U.S.M.C. LCPL Isaiah Gomez
Image 198: U.S. Army SFC Jorden Weir
Image 199: U.S.M.C. LCPL Matthew Teutsch
Image 200: U.S.M.C. LCPL Joshua Murray
Image 201: U.S. Army 1LT Benjamin Haulenbeek
Image 202 et al: U.S. Army SSG Rory Featherston
Image 204: U.S. Army SGT Kimberly Snow
Image 206: U.S.M.C. CPL Skyler E. Treverrow
Image 207: U.S.M.C. CPL William Chockey
Image 208: U.S. Army SPC Yolanda Moreno Leon
Image 209: U.S. Army SPC Mitchell Murphy
Image 210: U.S.M.C. LCPL Manuel Alvarado
Image 211: U.S.M.C. CPL William Chockey
Image 212: U.S.M.C. SSGT Bobby J. Yarbrough
Image 214: U.S. Army SPC Yolanda Moreno Leon
Image 215: U.S. Army SGT Kimberly Lamb
Image 216: U.S. Navy MC1 John Callahan

Image 217: U.S. Army CPT Ellen C. Brabo
Image 218: U.S. Army SFC Jared N. Gehmann
Image 219: U.S.M.C. LCPL Natalie Greenwood
Image 220: U.S.M.C. LCPL Cameron Darrough
Image 223: U.S. Navy PO3 Thomas L. Rosprim
Image 228: U.S. Army SPC Isaiah Matthews
Image 229: U.S.M.C. LCPL Wesley Timm
Image 231: U.S.M.C. LCPL Wesley Timm
Image 232: U.S.M.C. LCPL Francesca Landis
Image 233: U.S. Army VIS Markus Rauchenberger
Image 235: U.S. Navy MC3 Aaron Lau
Image 237: U.S. Army VIS Markus Rauchenberger
Image 238: U.S. Air Force SRA John Linzmeier
Image 239: Idaho Army N.G. Thomas Alvarez
Image 241: U.S. Army SPC Derek MustardImage 242: U.S. Army ATTP 3-06.11 (FM 3-06.11) 2011
Image 243: U.S. Navy PO1 Lynn Friant
Image 244: U.S.M.C. CPL Emily Dorumsgaard
Image 245: U.S. Army SFC Silas Toney
Image 246: U.S. Army SPC Austin Riel
Image 247: U.S.M.C. SGT Kealii De Los Santos
Image 248: U.S.M.C. LCPL Garrett White
Image 249: U.S.M.C. LCPL Ujian Gosun
Image 250: U.S. Army SSG Jose H. Rodriguez
Image 251: Idaho Army N.G. Thomas Alvarez
Image 252: Idaho Army N.G. Thomas Alvarez
Image 253: U.S. Navy PO2 Michael Lindsey
Image 254: U.S. Army MAJ Randall Stillinger
Image 256: U.S. Air Force SSGT Greg C. Biondo
Image 257: U.S. Army SPC Reyna, Jessica
Image 258: U.S. Army 1LT Benjamin Haulenbeek
Image 259: U.S. Army Reynaldo Ramon
Image 260: U.S.M.C. LCPL Jack Chen
Image 261: U.S.M.C. CPL Brian Reimers
Image 263: U.S. Army PFC Franko DaRe
Image 264: U.S. Army SPC Freire, Matthew
Image 265: U.S.M.C. LCPL Michael Petersheim
Image 266: U.S. Navy PO1 Lynn Friant
Image 267: U.S. Army SSG Malcolm McClendon
Image 268: U.S. Army PFC Devon Popielarczyk
Image 269: U.S. Marine CPL Isaac Cantrell
Image 270: U.S. Army SPC Bryan A. Randolph
Image 271: U.S.M.C. SGT Tia Nagle
Image 272: U.S. Navy MC2 Jacob L. Dillon
Image 273: U.S. Army SGT Michael J. MacLeod
Image 274: U.S.M.C CPL Brian Reimers
Image 276: U.S. Army SPC Sophia R. Lopez
Image 277: U.S.M.C. LCPL Jacqueline Parsons
Image 278: U.S.M.C. LCPL Devon Tindle
Image 279: U.S.M.C. LCPL Alvin Pujols
Image 280: U.S.M.C. SGT Katelyn Hunter
Image 282: U.S. Army MAJ Tiffany Collins
Phase 5 TOC: U.S. Air Force SRA Christopher Griffin
Image 283: U.S. Army SGT Fred Minnick
Image 284: U.S. Army SGT Anthony Lecours
Image 285: U.S.M.C. LCPL Francesca Landis
Image 286: U.S.M.C. SGT Kealii De Los Santos
Image 287: U.S. Army MAJ Randall Stillinger
Image 288: U.S.M.C. SGT Hector de Jesus
Image 289: U.S. Navy CPO Brain Naranjo
Image 290: U.S.M.C CPL James Gulliver
Image 291: U.S. Army SPC Freire, Matthew
Annex TOC: U.S.M.C. SSG Victor Mancilla
Image 292: U.S. Army SFC Osvaldo Sanchez
Image 293: U.S. Army SPC Peter Seidler
Image 294: U.S. Air Force SSGT Rose Gudex
Image 295: U.S. Army SSG Monika Comeaux
Image 296: U.S. Army 1LT Kurt Stah
Image 297: U.S. Army SSG Andrew Smith
Image 298: U.S. Army SSG Iman Broady-Chin
Image 299: U.S. Army SGT Amanda Fry
Image 300: U.S. Army SFC Brent Powell

Annexes

313

Credits

Please leave a review. Thanks!

Positive reviews from awesome people like you help other Soldiers to benefit from the valuable tactics in this manual. Could you take 60 seconds to share your thoughts?

Thank you in advance for helping the community!

If you liked this book, consider buying, *Small Unit Tactics*.

Or consider both books together, *Small Unit Tactics and Raids*.

CPSIA information can be obtained
at www.ICGtesting.com
Printed in the USA
BVHW010740120623
665686BV00036B/1493